BY ALISON WEIR

NONFICTION
ENGLAND'S MEDIEVAL QUEENS
Queens of the Age of Chivalry
Queens of the Crusades
Queens of the Conquest

The Lost Tudor Princess: The Life of Lady Margaret Douglas
Elizabeth of York: A Tudor Queen and Her World
Mary Boleyn: The Mistress of Kings
The Lady in the Tower: The Fall of Anne Boleyn
Mistress of the Monarchy: The Life of Katherine Swynford,
Duchess of Lancaster
Queen Isabella: Treachery, Adultery, and Murder in Medieval England
Mary Queen of Scots and the Murder of Lord Darnley
Henry VIII: The King and His Court
Eleanor of Aquitaine: A Life
The Life of Elizabeth I
The Children of Henry VIII
The Wars of the Roses
The Princes in the Tower
The Six Wives of Henry VIII

FICTION
SIX TUDOR QUEENS
Katherine Parr, The Sixth Wife
Katheryn Howard, The Scandalous Queen
Anna of Kleve, The Princess in the Portrait
Jane Seymour, The Haunted Queen
Anne Boleyn, A King's Obsession
Katherine of Aragon, The True Queen

The Last White Rose
The Marriage Game
A Dangerous Inheritance
Captive Queen
The Lady Elizabeth
Innocent Traitor

Queens of the Age of Chivalry

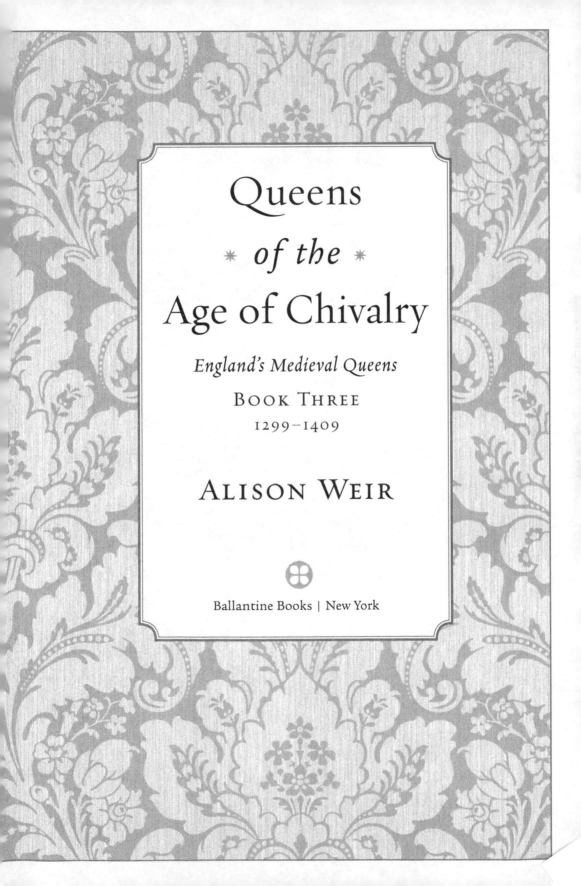

Queens

* *of the* *

Age of Chivalry

England's Medieval Queens

BOOK THREE

1299–1409

ALISON WEIR

Ballantine Books | New York

Published in the United States by Ballantine Books, an imprint of
Random House, a division of Penguin Random House LLC, New York.

BALLANTINE is a registered trademark and the colophon is a trademark
of Penguin Random House LLC.

Originally published in hardcover in Great Britain by Jonathan Cape,
a division of Penguin Random House Ltd., London, in 2022.

LIBRARY OF CONGRESS CATALOGING-IN-PUBLICATION DATA

Names: Weir, Alison, author.
Title: Queens of the age of chivalry, 1299–1409 / Alison Weir.
Description: New York: Ballantine Books, [2022] | Series:
England's medieval queens; Book three | Includes
bibliographical references.
Identifiers: LCCN 2022038992 (print) |
LCCN 2022038993 (ebook) | ISBN 9781101966723 (hardcover)
| ISBN 9781101966730 (ebook)
Subjects: LCSH: Queens—England—Biography. | Great
Britain—History—Plantagenets, 1154–1399—Biography. |
Isabella, Queen, consort of Edward II, King of England,
1292–1358. | Margaret, Queen, consort of Edward I, King of
England, 1279?–1318. | Philippa, Queen, consort of Edward III,
King of England, –1369. | Anne, Queen, consort of Richard II,
King of England, 1366–1394. | Isabella, of Valois, Queen,
consort of Richard II, King of England. | Plantagenet, House of.
Classification: LCC DA28.2 .W449 2022 (print) | LCC DA28.2
(ebook) | DDC 941.03092/2 [B]—dc23/eng/20220822
LC record available at https://lccn.loc.gov/2022038992
LC ebook record available at https://lccn.loc.gov/2022038993

Printed in Canada on acid-free paper

randomhousebooks.com

2 4 6 8 9 7 5 3 1

First Edition

Book design by Virginia Norey
Title and part title art: Andrea Izzotti/stock.adobe.com

*This book is dedicated to
the cherished memory of two great ladies,
Elizabeth Weir
and
Eileen Latchford*

Contents

Part Three: Philippa of Hainault, Queen of Edward III

Part Four: Anne of Bohemia, First Queen of Richard II

Part Five: Isabella of Valois, Second Queen of Richard II

England, Scotland, and Wales

France and the Low Countries

The Plantagenets,
1299-1399

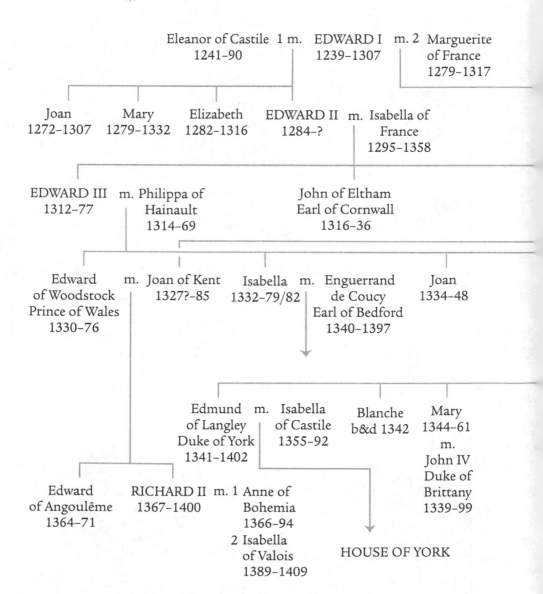

Eleanor of Castile 1 m. EDWARD I m. 2 Marguerite
1241–90   1239–1307   of France
                                1279–1317

Joan   Mary   Elizabeth   EDWARD II m. Isabella of
1272–1307   1279–1332   1282–1316   1284–?   France
                                  1295–1358

EDWARD III m. Philippa of   John of Eltham
1312–77   Hainault   Earl of Cornwall
          1314–69   1316–36

Edward   m. Joan of Kent   Isabella m. Enguerrand   Joan
of Woodstock   1327?–85   1332–79/82   de Coucy   1334–48
Prince of Wales   Earl of Bedford
1330–76   1340–1397

Edmund m. Isabella   Blanche   Mary
of Langley   of Castile   b&d 1342   1344–61
Duke of York   1355–92   m.
1341–1402   John IV
                                        Duke of

Edward   RICHARD II m. 1 Anne of   Brittany
of Angoulême   1367–1400   Bohemia   1339–99
1364–71   1366–94
                      2 Isabella
                       of Valois   HOUSE OF YORK
                       1389–1409

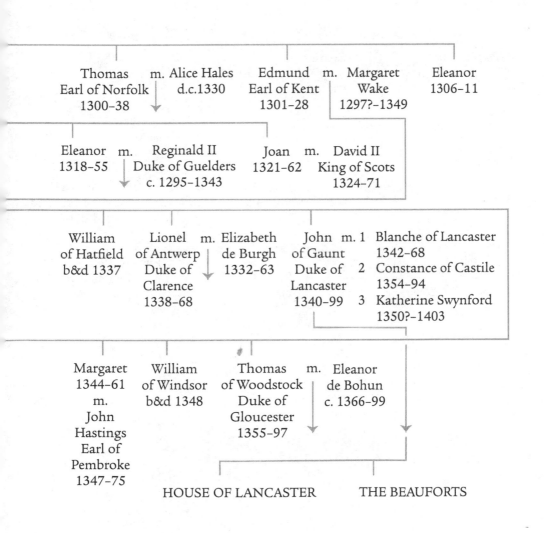

Thomas m. Alice Hales Edmund m. Margaret Eleanor
Earl of Norfolk d.c.1330 Earl of Kent Wake 1306–11
1300–38 1301–28 1297?–1349

Eleanor m. Reginald II Joan m. David II
1318–55 Duke of Guelders 1321–62 King of Scots
c. 1295–1343 1324–71

William Lionel m. Elizabeth John m. 1 Blanche of Lancaster
of Hatfield of Antwerp de Burgh of Gaunt 1342–68
b&d 1337 Duke of 1332–63 Duke of 2 Constance of Castile
Clarence Lancaster 1354–94
1338–68 1340–99 3 Katherine Swynford
1350?–1403

Margaret William Thomas m. Eleanor
1344–61 of Windsor of Woodstock de Bohun
m. b&d 1348 Duke of c. 1366–99
John Gloucester
Hastings 1355–97
Earl of
Pembroke
1347–75

HOUSE OF LANCASTER   THE BEAUFORTS

French Royal Connections

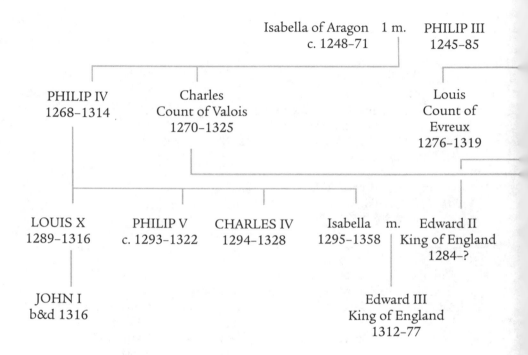

Isabella of Aragon   1 m.   PHILIP III
c. 1248–71   1245–85

PHILIP IV   Charles   Louis
1268–1314   Count of Valois   Count of
               1270–1325   Evreux
                                             1276–1319

LOUIS X   PHILIP V   CHARLES IV   Isabella   m.   Edward II
1289–1316   c. 1293–1322   1294–1328   1295–1358   King of England
                                                       1284–?

JOHN I   Edward III
b&d 1316   King of England
                                               1312–77

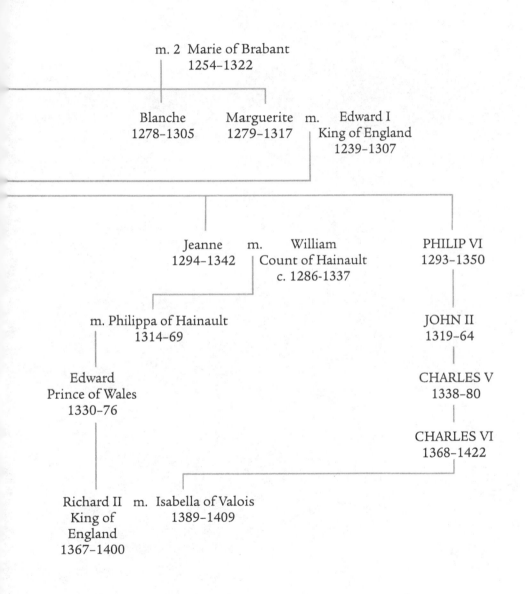

m. 2 Marie of Brabant
1254–1322

Blanche   Marguerite m.   Edward I
1278–1305   1279–1317   King of England
                                   1239–1307

Jeanne   m.   William   PHILIP VI
1294–1342   Count of Hainault   1293–1350
                  c. 1286-1337

m. Philippa of Hainault   JOHN II
        1314–69   1319–64

Edward   CHARLES V
Prince of Wales   1338–80
1330–76
                                       CHARLES VI
                                       1368–1422

Richard II m. Isabella of Valois
King of   1389–1409
England
1367–1400

The House of Lancaster

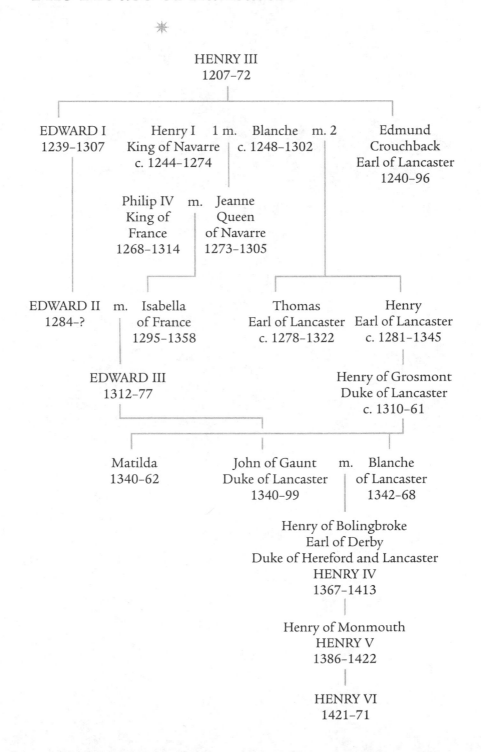

HENRY III
1207–72

EDWARD I
1239–1307

Henry I   1 m.   Blanche   m. 2
King of Navarre   c. 1248–1302
c. 1244–1274

Edmund
Crouchback
Earl of Lancaster
1240–96

Philip IV   m.   Jeanne
King of   Queen
France   of Navarre
1268–1314   1273–1305

EDWARD II   m.   Isabella
1284–?   of France
1295–1358

Thomas
Earl of Lancaster
c. 1278–1322

Henry
Earl of Lancaster
c. 1281–1345

EDWARD III
1312–77

Henry of Grosmont
Duke of Lancaster
c. 1310–61

Matilda
1340–62

John of Gaunt   m.   Blanche
Duke of Lancaster   of Lancaster
1340–99   1342–68

Henry of Bolingbroke
Earl of Derby
Duke of Hereford and Lancaster
HENRY IV
1367–1413

Henry of Monmouth
HENRY V
1386–1422

HENRY VI
1421–71

List of Illustrations

✳

Introduction

✳

THIS BOOK TELLS THE STORIES OF THE LIVES OF ENGLAND'S fourteenth-century queen consorts and covers the Plantagenet period, 1299 to 1399. It is a chronicle of the history of England through the perspective of five queens, starting with Marguerite of France, who became Edward I's second wife in 1299 and was more of a political animal than she has usually been credited as. Isabella of France was the subject of a biography I published in 2005, and I still believe that she did not deserve her reputation as "the She-Wolf of France." Philippa of Hainault was one of England's most loved queens, and she and her husband, Edward III, presided over a court that epitomized the Age of Chivalry. Anne of Bohemia was one of the most cosmopolitan princesses ever to grace the English consort's throne, and Richard II loved her to the point of obsession. After her tragic early death, he married the six-year-old Isabella of Valois, who, for all her youth, later proved to be feisty and determined when adversity struck. We follow her through her return to France and her second marriage.

This was an age that witnessed high drama: the toppling of two kings, the Hundred Years War, the Black Death, and the Peasants' Revolt. It was the height of the Age of Chivalry, an epoch dominated by the social, religious, and moral code of knighthood that prized noble deeds, feats of arms, courage, honor, kindness (in theory) toward the weaker members of society, and the game and play of courtly love between aristocratic men and women. It was also a period when feudalism was breaking down, a process accelerated by the Black Death and its subsequent shortage of manpower. England saw a burgeoning nationalism and the rise and prosperity of the merchant classes.

The sources for the fourteenth century are plentiful and include the colorful, detailed chronicles of Froissart and others, which illuminate that long-gone age and underpin this book. There are various translations of Latin and French sources into English; some of those undertaken in the Victorian age utilize the prim, flowery language of that time. As this book is intended for a general readership, I have kept references to a minimum and restricted them to original sources. Limitations on the word count do not permit me to list all the secondary sources in the references, so I wish warmly to acknowledge my indebtedness to the modern historians of the period and the recent biographers of these queens, especially (in alphabetical order) Richard Barber, Lisa Benz St. John, F. D. Blackley, Elizabeth Brown, Helen Castor, Steven J. Corvi, Paul Doherty, Anna M. Duch, Christina Earenfight, Christen L. Geaman, D. A. Harding, Lisa Hilton, Mary McGrigor, Ian Mortimer, Elizabeth Norton, Mark Ormrod, Michael Packe, Michael Prestwich, Nigel Saul, Alfred Thomas, Louise Tingle, and Kathryn Warner, whose wonderful collective scholarship and insights have been invaluable. Their works, and the many other excellent books I consulted, are listed in the bibliography.

Where sums of money are quoted in the text, I have entered the equivalent value today in brackets. For this, the National Archives' online currency converter has been helpful.

I am truly grateful for the tremendous support and creative input of my commissioning editors, Bea Hemming at Jonathan Cape in London and Susanna Porter at Ballantine in New York, for commissioning this series of books; and my editorial director, Anthony Whittome. Warm thanks are due also to the publishing teams at Penguin Random House in London and New York. Very special thanks, as ever, go to my agent, Julian Alexander, and my husband, Rankin, for their unfailing support.

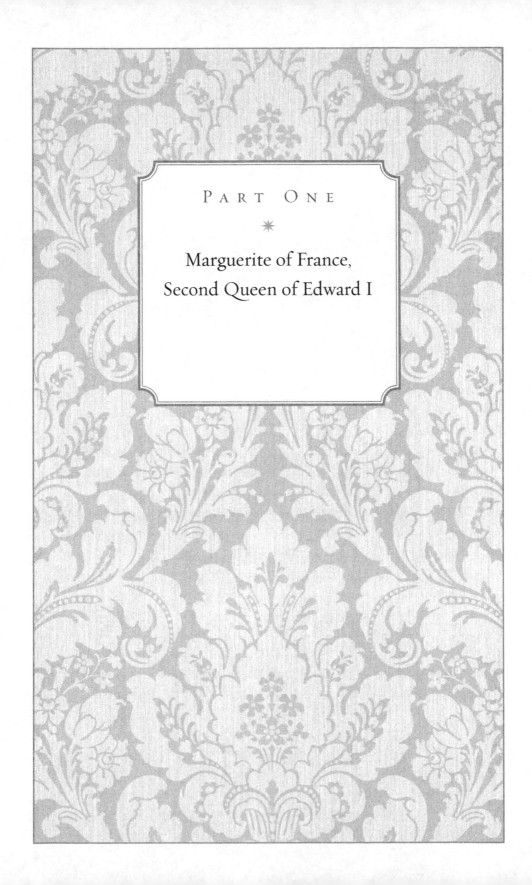

PART ONE

✳

Marguerite of France,
Second Queen of Edward I

I

"When Love Buds
Between Great Princes"

✳

IN SEPTEMBER 1299, THE PRINCESS MARGUERITE OF FRANCE
found herself on a ship crossing the English Channel, with the white
cliffs of Dover drawing ever nearer as she sailed to England to marry its
King, Edward I. He was sixty and she was twenty, and probably in awe of
his fearsome reputation. Her body was to seal a peace between England
and France.

Her crossing was apparently smooth. Her half-brother, King Philip IV
of France—known as "Philip the Fair" because of his good looks—had
provided her with a retinue befitting a queen. The dukes of Burgundy
and Brittany headed an impressive, elegantly dressed train of nobles and
"people of knowledge."[1] Among Marguerite's female attendants were
seven French ladies, and two English ones sent by King Edward to wait
on his bride and teach her English customs.

When her ship docked at Dover, Marguerite was received "with great
ceremony"[2] and news of her coming was sent to the King, who had temporarily ceased fighting the Scots to attend his wedding and was awaiting her twenty miles away in Canterbury, where lavish preparations for
the welcome of the royal parties had been put in place. As Edward gave
thanks for Marguerite's safe landing, she settled into the chambers prepared for her in the twelfth-century Great Tower in Dover Castle, where
she spent the night behind walls twenty feet thick. The next day, she set
out for Canterbury.

* * *

Edward I had been a widower for nearly nine years. His adored wife, Eleanor of Castile, a formidable and grasping woman, had died in 1290. In her memory, he had erected twelve beautiful crosses along the route taken by her funeral procession from Lincolnshire to Westminster Abbey, where she now lay buried in a magnificent tomb. "The impiety of death, which spares no man, has stricken our heart with vehement sorrow and turned the harp of our house into mourning," Edward had written of "our Queen of good memory, whom in life we dearly cherished, and whom, in death, we cannot cease to love."[3] But now, driven by political imperatives, he was contemplating marrying a second time.

Edward I was one of England's greatest medieval kings. "In build, he was handsome and of impressive stature, towering head and shoulders above the average." His body, well preserved when his tomb was opened in 1774, was six foot two inches tall. "His brow was broad and the rest of his face regular," apart from "a drooping of the left eyelid."[4] Neither this nor a slight stammer or lisp detracted from his awe-inspiring majesty. He was formidable: autocratic, forceful, fierce-tempered, fearless, and full of boundless vigor. A born leader and a talented and dynamic ruler, he was magisterial and statesmanlike, yet unscrupulous, ruthless, cruel, and occasionally violent.

Under Edward I, the prestige and authority of the English Crown reached its medieval zenith. In every respect, he personified contemporary ideals of kingship. A distinguished warrior, he had inflicted a devastating conquest upon Wales, and had since spent years relentlessly trying to conquer Scotland, his ultimate aim being the unification of Britain under his rule. He had streamlined the administration of his kingdom, enforced the royal prerogative, implemented far-reaching legal reforms that won him the epithet "the English Justinian," and promoted parliamentary government. He understood the need to curb the power of the great feudal lords and, by sheer force of character and judicious marriage alliances, he kept them firmly under control.

Edward's great adversary was Philip IV of France, the most powerful ruler in Christendom. From 1296, Philip had been at war with both England and Flanders.

The conflict was the result of a long-standing feud over England's possessions in France. In the twelfth century, through the marriage of

Henry II to Eleanor, Duchess of Aquitaine, the empire of the Plantagenets, the ruling dynasty Henry had founded in 1154, had extended from the Scottish border to the Pyrenees and encompassed roughly the western third of France, while the French royal demesne had been limited to the regions around Paris. By 1204, Henry's son, King John, Edward I's grandfather, had lost most of the English Continental territories, including Normandy, to the ambitious Philip II "Augustus" of France, and there were further French encroachments under John's son Henry III, as successive French monarchs sought to broaden their domain. By the time of Edward I, all that remained of England's lands in France were the prosperous wine-producing duchy of Gascony (the southern part of the duchy of Aquitaine) and the counties of Ponthieu and Montreuil, which had come to the English Crown through the marriage of Edward I and Eleanor of Castile in 1254.

In 1296, vigorously pursuing his predecessors' expansionist policy, Philip IV had seized Gascony. Edward was determined to get it back, while Philip wanted to drive a wedge between him and the people of Flanders, who had united against the French Crown. By 1298, the two kings were engaged in secret peace negotiations. That spring, Pope Boniface VIII wrote to Edward, urging him to marry Philip's eldest half-sister, eighteen-year-old Blanche, as a means of ending the war. The match appealed to Edward, who sent envoys to Paris to find out if she was beautiful and had a good figure. When told that no fairer creature could be found in the whole world, he offered for her. But after his brother, Edmund "Crouchback," Earl of Lancaster, arrived in France to conclude negotiations, he discovered that Blanche was already betrothed to Rudolph, Duke of Austria. Edward was angered by the deception, but Philip IV substituted her younger sister, "the Lady Marguerite, in whose least finger there is more goodness and beauty, whoever looks at her, than in the fair Idoine, whom Amadus loved,"[5] Idoine being the princess won by the knight in an English rhyming romance *Sir Amadas*. Edward may have met Marguerite in 1286 when she was seven and he and Queen Eleanor enjoyed a lengthy stay in Paris.

Boniface now suggested a double marriage alliance between France and England: Edward I was to marry Marguerite, while his son and heir, Edward of Caernarfon, Prince of Wales (later Edward II), would wed Philip's daughter Isabella, then two years old. Once this peace had been sealed, Gascony was to be returned to King Edward. The plan was approved by both sides and the English Parliament. For Philip, it conjured up the tantalizing prospect of French influence being extended into England and his grandson eventually occupying the English throne. For Edward, it promised two brilliant marriages and the return of Gascony. Marguerite would be the first French princess ever to become queen of England, and the first English consort in 150 years not to hail from southern France or the Iberian peninsula.

Marguerite and Isabella had been born into the most illustrious royal house in Christendom. In the early fourteenth century, France was the wealthiest and most heavily populated kingdom in Europe: it had an estimated twenty-one million inhabitants, compared to four and a half million in England, and eighty thousand of them lived in Paris, twice the population of London. French society was essentially feudal, and the royal domain now covered more than half of modern France; the rest was made up of vassal feudatories.

The Capetian dynasty had ruled France since 987, the crown having passed unfailingly from father to son. The imperial blood of the great Emperor Charlemagne ran in its veins. It had gained its reputation largely through the successes of its thirteenth-century kings, and the canonization in 1297 of Marguerite's grandfather, Louis IX, one of the greatest of medieval monarchs.

Isabella and Marguerite must have grown up with a strong sense of their importance. They would have been raised to believe in the sanctity of the royal line of Capet and its superiority over all other ruling dynasties. They would also have learned that royal and aristocratic marriages could bring about changes in the ownership of feudal territories, which sometimes led to kings and lords owning lands far from their own domains.

Edward I's mother, Alienor of Provence, had been the sister of Marguerite of Provence, the wife of St. Louis. The family ties between the two royal houses had led to the signing of the Treaty of Paris of 1259, which had brought peace between England and France. These new marriages would preserve those ties.

Marguerite had been born in 1279 (she was "of the age of twenty years"[6] at her marriage in 1299), probably in Paris. She was the youngest child of Philip III "the Hardy" and his second wife, Marie of Brabant, a cultivated beauty who came from a northern European feudal duchy that had emerged after the fall of Charlemagne's empire and along with Flanders, Luxembourg, Hainault, and other states comprised what became known as the Low Countries, which were often at odds with neighbouring France. Consequently, Marie was resented at the French court for her forceful character and her interference in politics. Rumor had it that she had poisoned her stepson Louis in 1276 and intended to destroy her husband's other sons by his first marriage, so that her own son, Louis, Count of Evreux, could rule France. The truth of the matter cannot be proved, but she was a good, protective mother to her own children.

Philip III was a mild, moderate ruler who briefly carried on the work of the sainted Louis. Marguerite was six when he died of dysentery in September 1285, aged forty, and her half-brother, Philip IV, who was eleven years her senior, succeeded to the throne. Tall and strongly built, he possessed a cold, calculating intelligence, a stern capacity for business, and a ruthless character. He further enhanced the prestige of the French monarchy by extending the royal domain, founding the Estates General (which evolved from his Paris Parlement), and centralizing the royal administration. Yet there was an ascetic side to his nature: beneath his costly velvets and furs was concealed a hair shirt, to mortify the flesh, and he regularly whipped himself with monastic discipline on the orders of his confessor. Those who met him found his fixed stare, his long silences, and his mysterious manner disconcerting. "He is neither a man, nor a beast, but a statue," commented one bishop.[7]

As a ruler, Philip was authoritarian, despotic, efficient, and feared by his subjects. He was a resolute defender of the royal prerogative and obsessed with the acquisition of wealth. Being perennially short of money, he resorted to drastic measures to get it. He dispossessed the Jews in his realm of vast sums, confiscated much of the property of the Lombard bankers, taxed the Church heavily, sold peerages to commoners, and, notoriously, debased the coinage several times. His daughter Isabella inherited his obsession with money, and his avarice.

In 1284, Philip had made a brilliant marriage with Jeanne, Queen of Navarre, who had succeeded in infancy to the throne of that northern

Iberian kingdom. The acquisition of Navarre and Jeanne's counties of Champagne and Brie further strengthened Philip's power. It was a love match, on her part at least, for the couple had been brought up together at the château of Vincennes, after Jeanne's mother had seen fit to place her fatherless daughter under the protection of the King of France.

Jeanne was no beauty. Plump and plain, she was a dignified, pious, and intelligent woman, eminently capable of managing her domains, although she tactfully adopted her husband's French reforms as her administrative model. Twice, and with great vigor, she successfully defended her territories, notably against the combined might of the Spanish kingdoms of Aragon and Castile.

Philip and Jeanne had seven children. Four lived beyond childhood: the heir, Louis, born in 1289, Philip, born around 1292-3, Charles, probably born in 1294, and Isabella, the sixth child. As the only surviving daughter, she was much favored by her father. According to the chroniclers Guillaume de Nangis and Thomas Walsingham, she was twelve years old at the time of her marriage in January 1308, which suggests that she was born in 1295. Twelve was the canonical age for marriage and, in June 1298, the Pope stipulated that she should marry Prince Edward as soon as she reached that age. In the same document, he described her as being "under seven years," while the Treaty of Montreuil (June 1299) provided for her betrothal and marriage to take place when she reached the respective canonical ages of seven and twelve. Therefore, she must have reached seven before May 1303, and twelve before January 1308.

France at that time was at the hub of European culture, and Paris the intellectual center of Christendom. Philip was a generous patron of the arts, and Jeanne set a high cultural standard at court. In her retinue she kept minstrels and trouvères, who provided sophisticated musical entertainment. In Paris, in 1304, she founded the College of Navarre (also known as the Hôtel de la Reine Jeanne) as a cultural center for the city's flourishing university. Her mother's career seems to have impressed itself upon Isabella, who may consciously have emulated her example.

Marguerite and Isabella spent their childhoods in the royal palaces of Paris, at the Louvre, then a moated château built in the twelfth century, and the Palais de la Cité, which was rebuilt by Philip IV; the Palais de Justice now occupies the site. Very little is known of the girls' early years.

Isabella evidently became attached to her nurse, Théophania de Saint-Pierre, Dame de Bringuencourt, who was to accompany her to England, remain with her for many years, and, in time, care for her children. The princesses would have become familiar with the formalities and ceremonial of royal life and been taught the courtesies. Great importance was attached to table manners and clean fingernails.

Marguerite and Isabella grew up in an age in which society regarded women as inferior beings. "We should look on the female role as a deformity, though one which occurs in the ordinary course of nature," stated a thirteenth-century edition of Aristotle's *Generation of Animals*. "Woman is the confusion of man, an insatiable beast, a continuous anxiety, an incessant warfare, a daily ruin, a house of tempest and a hindrance to devotion," fulminated Vincent de Beauvais. In 1140, the canon lawyer Gratian had asserted that "women should be subject to their men. The natural order for mankind is that women should serve men and children their parents, for it is just that the lesser serve the greater."

In a world that regarded chastity as the ideal state, women were seen as the wayward descendants of Eve, who had led Man to destruction in Eden by tempting him to eat the forbidden fruit. This view was endorsed by the Church and by society. In law, women were regarded as infants, and had few legal rights. They were viewed as assets in the marriage market, chattels in property deals and alliances, or prizes in the game of courtly love, and their roles were narrowly defined.

The education of princesses would have been structured to increase their desirability in the royal marriage market and equip them to be the ornaments of courts. The Church encouraged female education to foster devoutness and piety. Marguerite and Isabella would have learned from infancy to say their prayers; they would have been taught stories of the saints and to observe the holy days, of which there were about 150 a year. They would have been made aware of the joys of heaven, the horrors of hell, the seven cardinal virtues, and the seven deadly sins.

Some high-born ladies were taught to read and write, but they were the fortunate few. In the thirteenth century, Philip of Navarre thought that women "should not learn to read or write unless they are going to be nuns, as much harm has come from such knowledge. For men will dare to send letters near them containing indecent requests in the form of songs or rhymes or tales, which they would never dare convey by message or word of mouth. And the Devil could soon lead her on to read the letters or"—even worse—"answer them."

There is no evidence that Marguerite was literate, but Isabella was certainly taught to read; her love of books—usually history or romances—remained with her throughout her life. She may have learned some Latin and, later, a little English. Possibly she was taught music. This was the dawning of a great age in French music, the age of the *ars nova* of notation and polyphony, which became increasingly secular and was exemplified by masters such as Philippe de Vitry and Guillaume de Machaut. The popular tunes of the girls' youth would have been those for dances known as *ductias* and *estampies*, which were played on harps, lyres, and citterns.

In an age in which lineage and inheritance were paramount, women, especially queens, were expected to be beyond moral reproach. Queens were meant to follow the virtuous examples of the Virgin Mary, who was revered for her intercessions, and the Biblical Queen Esther, who proved a wise counselor and supplicant to her husband.

Because they were descended from Eve, who had committed the original sin, and were thus more likely to give in to temptation than men, women had carefully to guard their reputations. There was much comment on the frailty of the female sex. "Wheresoever beauty shows upon the face, there lurks much filth beneath the skin."[8] A wife's infidelity imperiled her husband's lineage. If he caught her in adultery, he had the legal right to kill her.

There were, of course, women who circumvented the conventions. Many ran farms or businesses or administered estates. Some practiced as physicians. Queens, by virtue of their exalted marital status, could exercise political authority and the power of patronage. Marguerite and Isabella would have been brought up to know exactly what was required of them as daughters and wives, and Isabella had before her the example of her mother, who was a queen in her own right.

On May 15, 1299, King Edward appointed Henry de Lacy, Earl of Lincoln, to negotiate the double marriage treaty, and plans were set in hand for the proxy betrothals. Three days later, Lincoln, Amadeus, Count of Savoy, and Guy de Beauchamp, Earl of Warwick, departed for France.

Edward had privately instructed the Count to find out as much as he could about Marguerite's personal attributes, including the size of her foot and the width of her waist. The Count reported back that she was "a fair and marvellously virtuous lady," pious, charitable, and "good withouten lack"—"the flower of France."[9] Queen Jeanne and Marguerite's mother, the Dowager Queen Marie, were actively involved in the diplomatic negotiations for the marriages.

The Treaty of Montreuil, which enshrined the marriage alliances, was drawn up on June 19, ratified by Edward I and the Prince of Wales on July 4, and expanded by the Treaty of Chartres on August 3. Under its terms, Marguerite was to have the dowry of £15,000 ($14.3 million) left her by her father, while Philip was to give Isabella a dowry of £18,000 ($17.2 million). Any sons Marguerite bore Edward were to receive 10,000 marks ($6.4 million) each on the King's death. When Marguerite became queen of England, she was to have in dower all the lands formerly held by Eleanor of Castile, which amounted to £4,500 ($4.3 million) a year, as well as Eleanor's counties of Ponthieu and Montreuil. A queen's dower lands had hitherto provided her with an income in the event of her outliving her husband, but Marguerite would be given control of them during her husband's lifetime. They were to pass to Isabella when she, in turn, became queen. This settlement set the pattern for the dowers of future English queens for more than a century. (Frequently, however, their heavy and sometimes extravagant expenditure exceeded their income.)

If Edward I defaulted on the treaties, he would forfeit Gascony; if Philip defaulted, he would pay Edward a fine of £100,000 ($96 million). The treaty was concluded amicably. Edward's subjects were gratified that the war over Gascony was at an end, and Marguerite came to England on a tide of goodwill. "Through her, the kingdoms receive a more complete peace. When love buds between great princes, it drives away bitter sobs from their subjects."[10]

2

"An Abundance of Splendour"

✳

A S MARGUERITE RODE TO CANTERBURY, SHE GOT HER FIRST
good look at the land of which she would soon be queen. England
was prosperous and largely rural, with an economy based on farming,
wool, and overseas trade. Foreigners waxed lyrical about its beauty, its
lush green pastures and rolling hills, its pretty stone or timbered dwell-
ings, towering castles and moated manor houses.

Society was still predominantly feudal and agrarian, yet the towns and
cities were growing fast thanks to trade and mercantile enterprise. London, with its seven gates and its hundred churches, was by far the biggest
city, with a population of about 40,000. York, the virtual capital of the
north, had a population of 7,500 at most. Towns were where prosperous
burgesses lived and guilds of craftsmen controlled trade, but they were
often crowded and dirty, with buildings and people crammed into narrow streets within walls that prevented expansion.

In the 233 years since the Norman Conquest of 1066, Normans and
English had learned to live together, although Norman French was still
the language of the court and the aristocracy, and Middle English the
language of the commons. English would replace French as the official
language of the law courts in 1362 and of Parliament in 1363. By the
beginning of the fourteenth century, Parliament was well established
and incorporated both lords and commons. It was not a permanent institution and could only be summoned by order of the King. The Church
wielded enormous authority within the state, being the largest landowner after the Crown.

England, as Marguerite would soon have seen, was predominantly a land of great forests, green fields, quiet villages, and many beautiful churches.

The bells were ringing out when she arrived at Canterbury, where the Archbishop's palace had been made ready for the King and his new Queen and tents had been erected for their retinues. Marguerite was presented to her future husband, who evidently liked what he saw. If the stone heads of her on the Alard tomb in St. Thomas's Church at Winchelsea and in Malmesbury Abbey are likenesses, then she was beautiful, with wide-set eyes and long, fashionably curled locks. Unmarried girls, and queens on ceremonial occasions, wore their hair loose in symbolic emulation of the Virgin Mary. On her first "uprising" as a married woman, Marguerite would be obliged to cover her hair and wear a triangular-shaped linen or silk headdress comprising a chin barbe, veil, and wimple, which was padded at the sides with ramshorn and exposed the hair only at the temples. Her statue on the south side of Lincoln Cathedral also shows her with loose hair beneath her coronet and veil, although the head is a nineteenth-century replacement. What this twenty-year-old girl made of her sixty-year-old bridegroom is not recorded, but that she pleased him is not in doubt.

The wedding took place in Canterbury Cathedral on September 8, with Archbishop Winchelsey officiating and "an abundance of splendour."[1] The bride wore a crown. The fifteen-year-old Prince of Wales was present with many English nobles and Spanish princes. A score of minstrels and vielle players from all over Christendom had been hired to play during the ceremony. Afterward, at the church door, as was customary, the King granted his bride her dower.

There followed two or three days of celebratory feasts, jousts, and sports, after which the dukes of Burgundy and Brittany returned to France, well satisfied and laden with gifts. Edward had funded the feasting from loans given him by the Frescobaldi bankers of Florence, and had spent extravagantly on 245 pieces of gold and silver plate and jewels purchased in Paris for himself and his new Queen.

On September 10, he made a brief visit to Chartham, then the newlyweds resumed their honeymoon in Canterbury and spent a further week at Leeds Castle, which stood on two connected islands on a beautiful lake and had been the property of Edward's first wife. Eleanor's stone gloriette, or pavilion, which enclosed a courtyard garden with a fountain, stood on the smaller island, and Edward later built a second castle on the larger island for Marguerite. The chambers and bathroom she used initially were in the gloriette, which must have been imbued with memories of Eleanor. Edward next took her to Winchester, where she was warmly welcomed, and another tournament was staged in honor of her marriage. Henry III had extended the defenses of Winchester Castle and converted its royal lodgings into a palatial residence with a magnificent great hall that now housed the so-called Round Table of King Arthur, which had in fact been commissioned by Edward I.

From the twelfth century onward, the English royal family had reverenced the memory of Arthur, who had come to embody all the idealized valor and virtues of the ideal medieval monarch. He featured large in aristocratic literature and the mythology of the English monarchy. The supposed remains of Arthur and his Queen, Guinevere, had been discovered at Glastonbury Abbey—the Isle of Avalon in the Arthurian legends—in 1191, and Edward I and Eleanor of Castile had been present when their tomb was opened in 1278.

On October 12, the King took Marguerite to London. Four miles outside its gates, she was received by 600 citizens, all wearing liveries of red and white with the symbols of their guilds embroidered on their sleeves. They conducted her to the Tower of London. The keep of this mighty fortress—known as the White Tower since 1240, when Henry III had had it whitewashed—had been built by William the Conqueror in the late eleventh century to stand sentinel over London. Richard I had encircled the bailey with a vast curtain wall bisected by towers, and Henry III had built more towers and, between the keep and the river, constructed a palace with a great aisled hall; but the most recent and impressive improvements were those made by Edward I, who had created a moat and built massive concentric defenses, including a water gate (now known as Traitor's Gate) and new royal apartments above it in St. Thomas's Tower.

The Tower housed the King's treasure, the Great Wardrobe (a repository for royal furniture, jewels, clothes, and food), the state archives, the largest of the royal mints, and the greatest arsenal of weapons in the kingdom. It also contained a menagerie created by Henry III in 1235 to house the many animals that were given to monarchs as gifts. At various times this had held lions, bears, leopards, and even an elephant. In Edward I's time, the Tower had not gained its later notoriety as a state prison, although a few prominent persons had been held prisoner there.

Edward and Marguerite stayed in the sumptuous state apartments, which lay at the west end of the great hall. They were brilliantly decorated in bright colors with gold stars, painted angels, heraldic emblems, and Purbeck marble fittings, with hooded fireplaces and large Gothic windows in the main chambers. The walls of the Queen's chamber were wainscoted, whitewashed and painted with roses and *trompe l'oeil* imagery that looked like cut stonework. Edward had refurbished for Marguerite the apartments created for his mother, Alienor of Provence.

London had suffered an outbreak of smallpox in the summer, and, from Carlisle, on June 28, Edward had written to the citizens that, since "our beloved companion the Queen will in a short time come to the Tower of London and remain there for a certain time, we, fearing the dangers which our consort and her attendant nobles may incur from the infection and corruption of the air by access of petitioners from the City and other places near the Tower, command you to proclaim publicly in the City that none shall presume to approach that spot on pain of heavy forfeiture, lest the person of the Queen be endangered by the contagion being brought from the infected air of the City."[2] Mercifully, the epidemic had since abated.

On October 13, Marguerite made her ceremonial entry into the City, escorted by Edward's cousins, the counts of Savoy and Brittany, the Lord Mayor and aldermen of London and 300 burgesses, who conducted her through streets hung with cloth of gold and packed with cheering crowds, along Cheapside, where two conduits ran with red wine, and finally to Westminster.

There were then about twenty-five royal castles and palaces in England, but Westminster had been the chief residence of English kings since the Saxon King and saint, Edward the Confessor, had built a palace by the River Thames around 1050. In 1097, William II had erected a massive great hall abutting it; measuring 240 by 67 feet, Westminster Hall was probably the largest and grandest hall in Europe. Between 1154 and 1189, Henry II had rebuilt the palace itself, extending the site to incorporate Old Palace Yard, a new hall with white walls, a chapel dedicated to St. Stephen, and a great chamber. He had also instituted a sophisticated system of water supply, with fountains and conduits.

In the thirteenth century, Henry III had spent a fortune creating luxurious, brilliantly decorated apartments that set a new standard for royal residences; he had rebuilt the old great chamber as the famous Painted Chamber, so called because of its vast murals depicting events in the life of his favorite saint, Edward the Confessor, and warlike scenes from the Bible. This room, with its great Gothic windows, glazed tiled floor, and private oratory, served as the King's bedchamber, and was dominated by a large state bed with a gilded and painted carved wooden canopy and green curtains. Edward I had begun the rebuilding of St. Stephen's Chapel, intending that it should rival the Sainte-Chapelle in Paris, the private chapel of the kings of France and the greatest architectural masterpiece of its time, which Marguerite would have known well.

The Palace of Westminster was not only a royal residence, but the administrative hub of the kingdom. It housed the Treasury, the Exchequer, and the chief law courts. The palace site now occupied several acres along the north bank of the River Thames. To the east lay Westminster Abbey, which had also been founded by Edward the Confessor, but had been rebuilt by Henry III as a fittingly splendid setting for the Confessor's shrine and a mausoleum for himself and his descendants.

By the fourteenth century, the English court was expanding in size and expenditure. Several hundred people resided there at any given time. The court was a social as well as an administrative and political center and had its own elaborate code of courtesy and etiquette. Its language at this time was Norman French, a bastardized version of the tongue spoken by the Conqueror and his companions; Latin was the traditional language of the government and the royal secretariats, although English, long the tongue of the lower classes, was gaining in general usage.

Medieval courts were essentially nomadic; state business and the need to have houses cleaned and freshened after large numbers of people had been staying for some time meant that the royal households were kept constantly on the move. Edward II, for example, lodged at more than 4,000 places in England during his twenty-year reign. When royalty traveled, most movable goods, even the furniture, went with them, stacked onto carts and covered with waxed canvas to keep the rain out. Smaller items were packed in saddlebags carried by sumpter horses. Boys rode as outriders beside the baggage train to keep it safe from robbers.

When Marguerite traveled—she too was to cover great distances in her married life—she either rode a palfrey or sat in a *charette*. *Charettes*, also known as "chairs" or "chariots," were essentially elaborately decorated wagons pulled by two chargers, with room for the Queen and her ladies. These conveyances were unsprung, which was why they were well upholstered and liberally provided with cushions to buffer passengers from the jolts. Marguerite's had cushions of dimity, a sheer cotton fabric, with cloth-of-gold covers. Isabella of France would have similar cushions, and the ceiling of her chariot was lined with silk. Tucked away into the vehicle would be two small barrels bound with iron, one containing wine, the other water to dilute it.

Travel could be arduous. No decent roads had been built since Roman times, and those that did exist were rarely well kept. Bad weather might make them impassable, and it was easy to get lost in remote areas, for there were few milestones, so guides were needed in some places. An average day's journey on horseback could cover between twenty and thirty miles. Medieval kings and queens, despite their large retinues and baggage trains, often traveled long distances at a good pace. Sometimes it made more sense to go by river, with baggage being transported by barge. During her frequent journeying, Marguerite or her almoner would distribute money to the poor, usually 2s. ($95) a day.

Harbingers would ride ahead to warn the keeper of a manor or castle that the royal party was on its way, often precipitating a frenzy of repairing and cleaning. When the servants arrived, they would unpack everything and put it in its place. If the royal personage needed to make an overnight stop, they would sometimes lodge in inns or abbey guesthouses, while their retinue might be housed in tents or wooden huts, or might even have to sleep out in the open.

Kings and queens lived lavishly, thanks in part to Henry III's great program of improvements in the middle years of the previous century. Castles were still being used primarily for defense, but palaces and manor houses were being built with only minimal fortifications, and there is evidence of a new accent on domestic architecture, comfort, and privacy, novel luxuries in an age of communal living.

The life of a medieval household centered upon the hall, where retainers and servants lived, ate, and slept. The halls in royal residences usually had two aisles of stone pillars extending along their length, as at the castles of Winchester and Oakham. The ceilings were lofty, usually dwarfing the two-story blocks of apartments at each end. Most were built in what the Victorians would call the Decorated style, following a trend set by Henry III when he began rebuilding Westminster Abbey in 1245 and embellished the older Early English style with fluid lines, floral ornament, and the novel double curved, or ogee, arch.

At the top end of the hall was a dais where the King and Queen held court, seated on carved chairs beneath a canopy of estate. They also dined here. At the opposite end of the hall, there was usually a decorated screen with arched doorways set into it and, above, a galleried area where minstrels might play. Beyond the doors was the screens passage, which led to the kitchens and service area. Halls were usually heated by a fire on a central hearth, the smoke escaping through a louver in the roof. Some royal halls abutted courtyards, around which other ranges of lodgings might have been built. For some time, the wealthier had been building chamber blocks, which were suites of private rooms adjoining the hall.

Until the thirteenth century, English queens had lived in chambers in the King's household. Separate lodgings for a queen consort were first built for Alienor of Provence in the middle of the thirteenth century. She and her successor, Eleanor of Castile, had imported southern European tastes and set new standards in comfort and style. Since then, queens had been allocated spacious suites of rooms in each royal residence. They usually comprised a chamber, a bedchamber, a chapel, and a wardrobe.

The Queen's chamber often featured a great hooded fireplace of stone or marble. Smaller rooms were heated by charcoal braziers. No fires were lit after Easter Sunday, when the hearths were cleared and adorned with floral displays. Beside the fireplace was set a heavy wooden chair, resembling a bishop's throne, for the King or Queen. Settles, stools, or benches were provided for their attendants, and other furnishings comprised tables and chests. Cushions afforded greater comfort. Windows with painted mullions, transoms, sculptural moldings, and linen curtains were usually built into deep embrasures with upholstered window seats. Large oriel windows had been introduced in many royal houses during the previous century to make rooms lighter. Glass, a luxury available only to the rich, featured prominently in royal palaces. Lesser rooms or service quarters had wooden shutters, or glass panels above the shutters.

What would strike us most today about these royal apartments was their vibrant color schemes and sumptuous decor. The walls were often brightly painted with murals, chivalric emblems, or decorative borders and were normally hung with tapestries or hangings of silk, wool, damask, or extremely costly and rare velvet from Florence. The floors were laid with tiles that were often embossed with heraldic designs. It was customary for floors to be strewn with herb-scented rushes or laid with rush mats, but Turkey carpets, which were expensively imported from Italy, had been introduced by Eleanor of Castile in the thirteenth century and used extensively by her as floor coverings; carpets were more often laid over tables or utilized as wall hangings to preserve them.

Eleanor had also embellished her apartments with jeweled plate, Venetian glass, and Damascus metalwork, which must have still been in evidence when Marguerite became queen. Rooms were lit with oil lamps and candles in decorative sconces or torches in iron cressets on the walls. Candles might also be fixed on spikes on a metal hoop that could be hoisted to the ceiling by means of a pulley.

The Queen's bedchamber was dominated by her canopied bed with its opulent hangings. Similar carved canopies can be seen on fourteenth-century tombs. Beds were fitted with a rope-mesh base that supported a feather mattress; Marguerite's feather bed was covered with dimity. Pillows were stuffed with feathers and made of dyed fustian, and the Queen's beds were made up with two scarlet covers. At least two of her damsels slept in her bedchamber on truckle or pallet beds that were stored beneath her own during the daytime.

Clothes for the Queen's immediate use hung from "perches" (poles) on the wall, but the rest would be kept in her wardrobe. Here, her clothes were stored in chests, presses, or cases of rawhide. When Isabella of France traveled, it took between three and six carts to transport her wardrobe.

Each of the principal chambers had its own privy, or garderobe, built into the wall. There was no effective system of flushing, so an open chute discharged waste into the moat below. Rags were used as toilet paper. Sometimes clothes were hung in garderobes (hence the name), because it was believed that the ammonia in urine kept moths away.

Standards of hygiene had improved in the thirteenth century. Bathing had become fashionable when Eleanor of Castile popularized the practice. Queens and aristocratic ladies now bathed fairly regularly in water scented with flowers or sweet herbs. They wore linen garments and sat on sponges in wooden tubs that were lined with linen sheets and covered with circular linen canopies. Royal children usually had baths on the eves of the great festivals of Easter, Whit Sunday, and Christmas. Judging by the amount of bathing items in her trousseau, Isabella of France had high standards of hygiene.

At most residences, the Queen had her own private gardens, many of them created for Alienor of Provence and Eleanor of Castile. They boasted lawns, fishponds, herb beds, fruit trees, vines, aviaries, fountains, arbors, and water features, and were flanked by covered paths, pleached alleys, cloisters, or iron trellises. Outdoor areas, stairways, and courtyards were lit at night by lanterns.

Hardly any of these queenly lodgings survive today, and where they do exist, all trace of their decoration or contents has long disappeared; to obtain an idea of what they might have looked like, one can visit the reconstructed royal apartments in the Tower of London or the Queen's apartments at Leeds Castle.

Each royal residence had a service area, with kitchens and scullery, a buttery (where drinks were stored), a pantry (where bread was kept), a ewery, and a saucery. In castles, the kitchens were often built in the bailey because of the risk of fire; in manor houses, they were frequently in a block at the opposite end of the hall to the chambers. Food for the King and Queen was prepared in separate kitchens by their own personal cooks.

Not everyone ate breakfast, and if they did, they took it very early. Dinner, the main meal of the day, was served between nine and ten in the morning; a lighter repast, or supper, was served around five o'clock. Trestle tables were set up in the hall and spread with linen cloths. A fanfare of trumpets heralded the arrival of the King and Queen, who would take their places on the dais. Important guests would sit with them, above or below the salt cellar, according to their degree; the salt was always placed in front of the most important person present, and only he or she could use it; there were smaller salt cellars for everyone else. Edward I gave Marguerite of France a silver salt in the shape of a ship.

The rest of the household ate at long trestle tables set at right angles to the dais. Before the meal started, pages would enter with basins, ewers, and napkins for the washing of hands. A Latin grace was said by one of the household chaplains and there was another grace after the meal.

Then the nef, a gold model of a ship studded with jewels, which contained precious spices for flavoring the food, was brought in with much ceremony and set before the King and Queen. The royal couple were served by squires on bended knee, who also carved the meats. The King and Queen ate from gold and silver plates, using beautifully crafted knives and spoons; forks were still rare. They drank from cups and goblets of precious metal, or from mazers, covered cups that were often used for drinking toasts. Table manners were refined: men and women often shared chargers and cups, and it was up to the man to help his lady to the finest morsels.

Several different dishes were served at each course, the choicer ones being reserved for the high table. Much of the food served was highly flavored or smothered in sauces. There was a lot of game, meat, and fish, but few vegetables. The devout abstained from meat during Lent. Bread was served at every meal; it was the staple of everyone's diet, but a refined variety was offered to the King and Queen and their guests in the form of white manchet rolls, wrapped in napkins. Much care was taken with appearance and presentation; the Flemish chronicler Jean le Bel, who visited England in 1327, was deeply impressed by the standard of the food at court.

A variety of sweet dishes and fruits comprised the dessert course. Sugar was very expensive, but had been used in the royal kitchens since the thirteenth century; most people still used honey as a sweetener.

The wine served at the royal table was usually imported from Gascony, France, or the Rhine, and had to be drunk young; ale was the drink of the masses. Water was consumed, but was probably boiled first. Hippocras, or spiced wine, was sometimes served at the end of a meal or feast.

A disastrous fire in 1298 had rendered the Queen's apartments at Westminster uninhabitable, so Edward arranged for Marguerite to use York

Place, the Archbishop of York's palace, as her London residence. Dating from the twelfth century, York Place stood by the river between Westminster and the Eleanor Cross at Charing.

Marguerite now assumed the trappings and privileges of queenship. Her function was primarily to reflect the magnificence of her husband. She was admirably to fulfill all expectations, being faithful, loving, pious, and merciful, and it was hoped that she would be fruitful. The King had only one surviving son and wanted more heirs.

Her new great seal was made of silver and her privy seal of gold. Supplied by a London goldsmith, they were the first English royal seals to bear a queen's arms with her husband's, displaying the three lions of England and the lilies of France. These arms can also be seen in the altar window in St. Mary's Church at Froyle, Hampshire. Marguerite would never have a coronation, for Edward's resources were reserved for the war with Scotland. The Queen's personal expenditure (her chamber expenses) on clothes, jewels, gifts, and alms was funded by the Exchequer.

Many members of Eleanor of Castile's household were reappointed to Marguerite's. She was assigned three ladies of the chamber and four noble damsels. Two, Agnes de la Croise and Mathilde de Val, were French and had come to England with her. She had her own minstrel, Guy of the Psaltery, who received a stipend of 28s. ($1,339) and the use of three horses when he accompanied her on her travels. In 1302, she persuaded the King to grant him houses in London. While in her service, her young doctor, John of Gaddesden, would write *Rosa Medicinae,* a Latin treatise that became so famous that Geoffrey Chaucer would use him as the model for the physician in *The Canterbury Tales.*

Marguerite enjoyed a game of chess; she owned a casket in which she kept sets of jasper and crystal with figures bound with silver (one of which had probably been owned by Edward's first wife), and a set of "tables" (backgammon) made of nutmeg with metal stems, with matching playing pieces.

She did not lack for company. Those of Edward I's surviving children who were living in England were more or less her contemporaries: the Prince of Wales, who was fifteen, and his sisters, Joan of Acre, Countess of Gloucester, aged twenty-seven; Mary, a nun at Amesbury Abbey, Wiltshire, who was the same age as Marguerite; and Elizabeth of Rhuddlan,

Dowager Countess of Holland, aged seventeen. These lively young women and their brother provided congenial company for their stepmother.

There are few clues to Marguerite's character in her surviving letters, which deal with petty disputes and routine business, although when writing to the Chancellor, she sent him her true love, which argues a warm nature. Other evidence suggests that she was gentle, peace-loving, and mature beyond her years. It is unlikely that Edward was quite as close and devoted to her as he had been to Eleanor of Castile—Marguerite was forty years his junior—but their marriage proved happy and successful, and he was reported to be in a fervor of love after they married. A devoted and obedient wife who came to love and respect her husband, Marguerite learned that while he was terrible to those who displeased him, he could be gentle to those who were humble and dutiful. Having been raised by parents who had enjoyed a long and happy marriage, Edward had proved a good and adoring husband to Eleanor of Castile and ensured that she had every fine thing in life. Now he embraced marital happiness again, equally successfully. One chronicler stated that he doted on his new Queen.

3

"Like a Falcon Before the Wind"

✳

MARGUERITE SOON LEARNED THAT HER MARRIAGE, LIKE THAT of Eleanor of Castile, was to be one of long journeys and frequent separations. In the autumn of 1299, Edward, bent on the utter subjugation of Scotland, prepared for another offensive against that kingdom. Since 1290, when he had been asked to arbitrate among thirteen claimants to its vacant throne, he had cherished ambitions to annex Scotland to the English Crown. By 1296, he had overrun the northern part of the kingdom, captured Berwick, and overthrown John Balliol, whom he had chosen as king. Continually frustrated by the resilience and tenacity of the Scots under the leadership of the doughty William Wallace, he had remained firm, even obsessive, in his resolve. In 1298, he had defeated Wallace at the Battle of Falkirk. Now he was determined to make a final push and conquer all Scotland. During his marriage to Marguerite, he would spend half his time there.

Marguerite traveled north with Edward to the royal manor of Langley (near St. Albans), where Edward of Caernarfon, the Prince of Wales, was then residing. Langley had once belonged to Eleanor of Castile. It was situated on a gentle rise on the banks of the River Gade and surrounded by parkland. Fruit trees and vines grew in the gardens, and the manor house, which was built round three courtyards, boasted the very latest in interior decoration and had extensive suites of private apartments, with fireplaces in the royal bedchambers. The great hall was embellished with fifty-four painted shields and a mural in brilliant gold and vermilion depicting knights riding to a tournament. There was also a built-in organ. The Queen's rooms overlooked the Great Court; she had a great chamber, a middle chamber, and a cloister, all paved, and even a bathroom, which had been installed for Eleanor. It was at Langley that Marguerite bade the King farewell when he departed for Scotland on November 3. His "fervour of love" had resulted in a child conceived immediately after their marriage, to his great joy.

At Langley, Marguerite spent three weeks getting to know her stepson and his sister Mary, a very worldly nun who left her convent at will to visit her family. Fruit, nuts, and sugar were bought for the Queen's sojourn.

Edward of Caernarfon, the future Edward II, was the only survivor of the four sons of Edward I and Eleanor of Castile. When he had been born at Caernarfon Castle on April 25, 1284, just after his father's conquest of Wales, his older brother Alfonso was heir to the English throne. Alfonso had died of a fever the following August, and four-month-old Edward had become the heir apparent. A later legend had it that Edward I had presented his newborn son on a shield to the Welsh as their prince, having promised them a native-born ruler who spoke no English, but young Edward was not created Prince of Wales until February 1301, and the story was first recorded in 1584, by John Stow, the Elizabethan antiquarian.

Edward had spent most of his early years at Langley, which became his favorite residence. Queen Eleanor died when he was six, and his father was a terrifying and remote authoritarian figure. His parents had been away in Gascony for three years of his short life and must have seemed like strangers to the five-year-old when they returned. The boy was probably closer to his nurse, Alice Leygrave, who was to remain in his service for twenty-five years.

Edward I could show affection to his parents, his siblings, and his wives, but his children learned not to provoke his rage. Hundreds of his letters to his heir survive, bristling with hectoring advice or stern reproofs. Small wonder that the Prince grew fond of his sympathetic young stepmother.

In December, the two of them stayed at St. Albans Abbey, where Marguerite won the praise of the monks for her grace and piety, her rich gifts, the alms she distributed, and her request to join the monastic confraternity, which comprised those who had made substantial donations.

Entrance to a confraternity was believed to confer spiritual benefits. She would have been received with great ceremony and her name would have been entered in the book of benefactors. But it was felt that she stayed too long and had too large a train with her, which the community was expected to feed and accommodate.

While Edward spent a gloomy Christmas at Berwick, Marguerite and her stepson made good cheer at Windsor Castle, forging a bond of friendship. Marguerite was to exert much influence in private, smoothing relations between the King and his children. To Prince Edward, for whom she acted as a buffer in his fraught relations with his disapproving and terrifying sire, she became a "very dear lady."[1]

Windsor Castle was the largest royal stronghold in England; it was said that there was no finer castle in the whole of Europe. Raised by William the Conqueror in the late eleventh century, it had been enlarged and rebuilt by successive kings and was now a mighty fortress surrounded by massive stone walls. There were two baileys within its precincts: the Lower Ward, in which stood the great hall erected by Henry I; and the Upper Ward, where stood the palace known as the King's House, which contained sumptuous royal apartments and chapels, as well as a lesser hall and the royal kitchen. The Upper Ward commanded fine views of the surrounding countryside.

As at Westminster, the royal apartments had been extensively refurbished and improved during the thirteenth century by Henry III. The Queen's lodgings were on the first floor and overlooked the herb garden in the cloistered nursery court. They featured an oriel window, a turret, marble pillars, stained-glass windows, ceilings of traceried wood, and tiled floors. Archaeological evidence shows that the stonework in the windows was painted vermilion, red, ochre, and black. In Marguerite's chamber, a wall painting depicted the Wise and Foolish Virgins, while the wainscot was painted green with gold stars. Her private chapel was built in the two-storied collegiate style, her pew being on the upper gallery while her household worshipped below in the nave.

In the Lower Ward, there was a chapel dedicated to St. Edward the Confessor, founded by Henry III in 1240. It had a timber vault painted to look like stone, and six columns of Purbeck marble; the west doors, with their splendid iron scrollwork, still survive in St. George's Chapel, which stands on the site.

* * *

By the end of January 1300, Edward had joined his wife and son at Windsor. Soon afterward, the three of them made a pilgrimage to the shrine of St. Thomas Becket at Canterbury, where Edward offered four gold florins ($384) "for the foetus currently in the Queen's belly,"[2] while the Prince also gave money to the saint for her safe delivery. The King made other offerings at St. Augustine's Abbey. Easter was observed at St. Albans with great magnificence.

Marguerite now began to extend her patronage and make intercessions to her husband. These two great privileges of queens enabled them to influence events and enhance their reputations, and allowed kings to show the humane side of monarchy without losing face or authority.

She was a great peacemaker. There are fifty-six instances of her successfully interceding with the King on behalf of others. Often, her requests for pardons, gifts, and protections were granted "solely on the intercession of our dearest consort" or "at the instance of Marguerite, the King's consort."[3] There is no hint in the sources of rapacity; unlike Eleanor, Edward's first wife, Marguerite was seen to be charitable, merciful, and generous. In 1301, she was instrumental in persuading Philip IV to sign the Treaty of Bruges, which secured the release of Edward's son-in-law, Henry III, Count of Bar, who had been imprisoned in 1297 for supporting the English in the war over Gascony.

The Exchequer Rolls record many instances of her pleading that debts to "her dear lord the King might have their time extended or be excused." At her request, Edward pardoned several outlaws and at least nine murderers, one of whom had killed his own brother. She would also invoke the names of her sons in her pleas, to soften Edward's heart.

After Easter, the King left St. Albans to launch a new offensive against the Scots. "Queen Marguerite, by command of her lord the King," also "proceeded towards the North; she was advanced in pregnancy."[4] Prince Edward went with them. In April, they visited the shrine at St. Edmundsbury, and on May 5, they made a pilgrimage to that of Our Lady at Walsingham, Norfolk, where Marguerite offered a clasp of gold; then they rode through Lincolnshire and crossed the River Humber into Yorkshire.

Edward camped at Selby, planning to march on to Scotland after Marguerite's child was born. He had arranged for her to be confined at the Archbishop of York's castle at Cawood, ten miles south of York, after which she would follow him in easy stages.

Having lodged on the way at Pontefract Castle, Marguerite began making her way north toward Cawood. On June 1, she reached Brotherton, a village on the banks of the River Wharfe, where her retinue paused to go hunting in Wharfedale. Although at full term, Marguerite (who loved riding and hunting and who sent horses to her stepson, Prince Edward) was following the chase when she went into labor and was taken to a house near the church, the site of which can still be seen today. It was a difficult delivery and, in fear of death, she cried out to St. Thomas Becket to succor her. Seemingly miraculously, she was safely delivered of a son, who would become the ancestor of the Howard dukes of Norfolk.

Edward was ten miles away at Selby when he heard the news. Delighted, he rewarded the messenger and "prepared quickly to visit the lady, like a falcon before the wind,"[5] having ordered two fine cradles. One bore the royal arms and was upholstered with thirteen ells of fine scarlet cloth, the other with the same quantity of blue cloth; both had covers of fur and sheets of fine Rheims linen. For the nursery, the King had ordered some striped hangings and others of gold embroidered with heraldic emblems. Because Marguerite was convinced that St. Thomas had saved her life, he named the child after the murdered Archbishop, and sent offerings to the shrines of his name saints, Becket's at Canterbury and St. Thomas Cantilupe's at Hereford. Thomas was reportedly a patriotic infant, refusing the milk of his French nurse and only taking that of an Englishwoman called Mabille. Engaging her, a worried Marguerite had a doctor test her milk.

Once the Queen had been installed at Cawood with her baby, Edward visited her, sailing along the River Ouse from Selby. The castle was a luxurious residence, but nothing remains today from Marguerite's time, the fabric dating only from the fifteenth century. It was customary for women to undergo a service of purification and thanksgiving known as a churching forty days after giving birth, because the Feast of the Purification of the Virgin Mary at Candlemas was celebrated on February 2, forty days after the birth of Jesus. Once Marguerite had been churched, the King resumed his journey to Scotland, having ordered Archbishop Winchelsey to attend her while she "waited at Cawood, much at her ease."[6] The Archbishop, however, was determined to brave the Scots (and his master's temper), and followed the King north.

On August 14, Edward granted Marguerite Leeds Castle and its manor "for the expenses of herself and of Thomas, the King's son, and their household."[7] From then on, Leeds Castle formed part of the dower of several queens of England and became known as the "ladies' castle."

In September, Marguerite received a visit from the King's daughter, Elizabeth, Countess of Holland, who accompanied her and the baby north toward Carlisle to meet up with Edward. On September 18, they joined him at the abbey of Holmcultram in Cumberland (modern Cumbria). From there, the royal party traveled south to Northampton, where they spent Christmas.

On May 13, Edward granted Marguerite the marriage of his ten-year-old grandson, Gilbert de Clare, heir to the earldom of Gloucester and son of his daughter, Joan of Acre. The wardships and marriages of heirs below the age of majority were a lucrative form of income for queens, for they could use the profits from the estates, and Marguerite was to hold several, the annual income from them amounting to 6,000 marks ($4 million).

On September 27 Joan was ordered to "deliver to Marguerite, Queen Consort, on her demand, Gilbert, son and heir of Gilbert de Clare, as it is the King's will that he shall stay in the Queen Consort's custody until further order. This order and present letter shall be her warrant."[8] Marguerite informed Edward that she had had to send two men to Joan to take charge of Gilbert, which suggests that Joan was reluctant to give him up to her young stepmother. The King's intention was not to deprive his daughter of her son, but to ensure that young Gilbert received the most advantageous education, passing through the ranks from page to esquire and then to knight, making important connections and learning the arts of courtesy and warfare. Marguerite was a kind guardian and made sure that mother and son had opportunities to be together. In 1304, Edward decreed that if Gilbert married without Marguerite's consent, she would get the fine due to the King.

When, at the beginning of June 1301, Edward returned to Scotland, Marguerite was pregnant again, and she took up residence at Woodstock Palace for her confinement, with her stepdaughters Elizabeth and the nun Mary for company. Woodstock stood in Wychwood Forest and had been a royal retreat and hunting box since before the Conquest, but the present house, with its aisled hall, had been built by Henry I in the early twelfth century. The stone wall surrounding the hunting park extended for seven miles; within its precincts was a royal menagerie that housed lions, lynxes, leopards, and porcupines. Henry III had remodeled the royal apartments in the thirteenth century and Marguerite's chambers overlooked a garden with a maple tree by a pool. She could take the air in open cloisters, or walk to the spring at nearby Everswell, where there was a garden with a hundred pear trees. In 1301, chambers were built at Woodstock for Thomas's laundress and the Queen's apothecary.

At Woodstock, on August 5, Marguerite gave birth to a second son, Edmund, named in honor of the martyred Saxon saint. The King gave a reward to the messenger who brought him news of the birth, and ordered the Mayor and townsfolk of Oxford to contribute £200 ($172,000) for the expenses of the Queen's household during her sojourn, but her purveyors were so rapacious, demanding goods at the lowest prices, that merchants tended to make themselves scarce when they learned that she was staying in the vicinity.

Marguerite's sons were assigned a household of between fifty and seventy attendants, which cost the King £1,300 ($1,117,370) annually and included wet-nurses, maids, laundresses, and Perrette, Edmund's rocker. These women remained in service for six years until the boys were assigned governors, and were given gifts of money by the Queen in 1305.

In 1301, the King appointed a chaplain for the princes, and in 1302 gave stern orders that they were to sit still and make their offerings during High Mass in Canterbury Cathedral, deputing the keeper of their wardrobe to report to him afterward on their behavior. At Easter, the boys gave raiment, shoes, and money to the poor, and Marguerite taught them to remember the Franciscans in their almsgiving.

Their daily life was not all duty. They played chess and tables, rode their palfreys, and enjoyed music played by the minstrels hired by their mother to entertain them. Their toy drum was apparently banged so often that it had to be repaired. Their mother gave them an iron cage for their pet birds.

Marguerite had to endure separations from Thomas and Edmund, but she showed constant interest in their welfare, asking to be assured that they were keeping to the healthy diet she had decreed, which included meat, fish, spices, and plenty of vegetables. They were allowed sweet treats such as almonds, dates, figs, and sugar sticks. They were clad in mantles and tabards of silk or wool, and in winter wore buskins, beaver-skin hats, and robes lined with fur. When Thomas caught small-pox, John of Gaddesden cured him, it was claimed, by wrapping him in scarlet cloth in a room also hung with scarlet.

In September 1301, attended by Joan of Acre, the nun Mary, and young Gilbert de Clare, Marguerite undertook a pilgrimage to Hereford, offering at churches and shrines on the way and giving thanks for her safe delivery of a healthy child. Marguerite and Mary seem to have become close. In 1302, they would jointly persuade the King to grant custody of the parks of Restormel and Penlyn to Mary's steward.

In November 1301, Marguerite bade farewell to her stepdaughters and accompanied Edward's army on its march through the Tweed Valley, Selkirk Forest, and Clydesdale, finally reaching the castle of Linlithgow, where they spent Christmas. During their stay, Edward demonstrated his trust in his wife's political acumen. A truce was to be agreed with the Scots, but he was not sure whether he had granted the Earl of Lincoln or the Treasurer, Walter Langton (whom Marguerite called "the King's right eye"),[9] the authorization to negotiate it. He instructed them to ask the Queen to scrutinize the letters of authority for the truce and advise both men of any amendments that needed to be made.

The royal couple remained at Linlithgow until February 19, 1302, when they returned to England. That month, Marguerite made a short visit to France, for which she purchased twelve pairs of robes. One outfit consisted of a three-piece robe of green velvet trimmed with fur, two surcoats, and a mantle. She may have sailed in the King's ship, *The Margaret of Westminster*, which was named after her.

Charitable as she was, Marguerite was now incurring criticism for her extravagance and for getting into debt. She splashed out freely on clothes and jewels, having been given only a few of the pieces once owned by Eleanor of Castile; the rest had been sold. By 1302, she owed the Balliardi of Lucca £1,000 ($859,000) for fabrics, and various creditors £3,000 ($2,577,000). Her debts to merchants had mounted up alarmingly. In August, so that she could settle them, Edward ordered the Lord Treasurer to give her wardships and marriages worth £4,000 ($3,436,000), and in February 1303, he increased her dower to £5,000 ($4,295,000). Yet she still managed to overspend, for in 1305, he would give her another 1,000 marks ($636,700) to pay her creditors. He seems, however, to have regarded her excesses with indulgence. That year, he expressed his indebtedness to a London citizen who had bought jewels worth £132.6s.8d. ($127,000) on Marguerite's behalf.

Just after Easter 1302, Edward and Marguerite had a lucky escape while they were staying in Winchester Castle. A chimney caught fire and they woke to find flames blocking their exit. Fortunately, they "managed to escape through an outside door of whose existence they had not previously been aware."[10] The royal apartments were gutted, and the King and Queen were obliged to move to Wolvesey Palace, the seat of the bishops, near Winchester Cathedral. In July, they were at Windsor, where they were joined by their sons, who had arrived with fifteen carts carrying their chapel furniture and wardrobe stuff.

In July, war broke out again between the French and the Flemings, and the latter begged Edward for aid. Over fifty years later, in his *Scalacronica,* Sir Thomas Gray asserted that the King wrote to the citizens of Ghent, informing them that he had bribed some French lords to betray Philip's whereabouts to them so that they could capture him. But he did not send the letter. Instead, he left it on Marguerite's bed for her to read, enabling her to send a warning to her half-brother and persuade him to abandon the sieges of Douai and Lille. French historians have accused her of falsifying this information so as to distract him from his purpose, for it lost him those towns and forced him to withdraw from the war in early October. But the tale may be a fabrication, born of English distrust of the French.

That July, Marguerite's mother, Queen Marie, and her brother, Louis, Count of Evreux, visited Westminster. Prince Edward had been deputed to meet them on arrival and "keep them company," striking up a friendship with Evreux.

On November 14, Marguerite was present with Edward when his daughter Elizabeth married Humphrey de Bohun (pronounced Boon), Earl of Hereford and Essex, at Westminster Abbey. Elizabeth wore a rich coronet that may have belonged to Marguerite's sister Blanche, in which case it was almost certainly the Queen's wedding gift to her stepdaughter. One of Elizabeth's eleven children would be called Margaret; Marguerite was probably her godmother.

At Christmas, the King and Queen were guests of Prince Edward at Langley. He entertained them lavishly for a week and had his pipe organ repaired when they visited again the following February, knowing how much they both loved music.

Prince Edward's gift to his stepmother at New Year 1303 was a gold ring set with a large ruby. In February, King Edward ordered a goldsmith, Thomas de Frowick, to make a rich crown for Marguerite to wear for the feast of St. John the Baptist in June; it cost £440 ($422,000), but the King was tardy in paying for it, which caused Frowick to suffer a great loss.

4

"All Men Died to Me"

✳

EDWARD HAD CONTINUED TO PRESS FOR THE IMMEDIATE RES-toration of Gascony, but Philip would not agree to this until after the Prince of Wales had fulfilled his promise to marry Isabella, who was still too young to live with him as his wife. By April 1303, Edward I was making martial noises and beginning to look elsewhere for a bride for his son. Not wanting a war on two fronts, Philip agreed to restore Gascony without further delay, wanting it to be inherited by his grandchildren, the heirs of Edward and Isabella. The Treaty of Paris, which officially restored the duchy, was signed on May 20, 1303, and, that same day, Isabella and Edward of Caernarvon were betrothed in Paris. The bride was seven years old, the absent groom nineteen.

The auguries were not good. The Prince had tried to emulate his magnificent sire and live up to his expectations. He had attended council meetings, fought ably in Scotland, and carried out ceremonial duties. But he had now come under the influence of a young man whose name would soon become infamous.

Piers Gaveston was the son of a leading Gascon baron who had fought for Edward I in France and Wales. In 1300, after he had served in two campaigns in Scotland and impressed the King with his courtly manners, he had been placed in the Prince of Wales's household as one of his squires. Before long he had become "the most intimate and highly favoured member"[1] of it.

Piers was then a handsome boy of sixteen, about the same age as Edward. He was graceful, active, intelligent, and skilled in arms, with boundless self-confidence. He was also ambitious, indiscreet, greedy, extravagant, and arrogant: his pride, it was said, would have been intolerable even in a king's son. He was a witty companion, but his tongue could be barbed and he showed little respect for those of higher rank.

The attraction between Edward and Piers was instantaneous. "When the King's son saw him, he fell so much in love that he entered upon an enduring compact with him and chose to knit an indissoluble bond of affection with him, before all other mortals."[2] It was not unusual, among a military aristocracy, for young men to swear blood brotherhood, but Edward was to refer constantly to Piers—or "Perrot" as he called him—as "my brother," because of his excessive love for him, which "surpassed the love of women."[3]

"I do not remember to have heard that one man so loved another," wrote the royal clerk who was the author of the *Vita Edwardi Secundi*. The friendship drew much adverse comment. Edward loved Gaveston "beyond measure,"[4] and Gaveston returned that love "inordinately."[5] The chronicler of Lanercost openly accused them of having improper relations; Robert of Reading called it an "illicit and sinful union" and charged Edward with desiring "wicked and forbidden sex," while the *Chronicle of Meaux* baldly stated that he "particularly delighted in the vice of sodomy." Ranulph Higden asserted that Edward always put Gaveston first and could not bear to be separated from him.

In the climate of the times, these were serious concerns. A homosexual king might fail to father heirs to ensure the succession—and he was flouting contemporary sensibilities and taboos. In the fourteenth century, homosexuality was viewed as a grave sin against nature and the divinely appointed order of the universe. Those caught often faced secular punishment and excommunication by the Church, because it was regarded as a form of heresy.

Yet both Edward and Gaveston married and fathered children. Edward acknowledged a bastard son, Adam, who was probably born before his accession, proving that he chose to have sex with a woman. He was said to have been "given to the company of harlots"[6] in youth. Probably he and Gaveston were bisexual.

Marguerite must have been aware of this friendship, for she was close to the Prince. We do not know if she worried about what would happen when he married her niece, Isabella, but it may have come to trouble her, because a queen's influence could easily be undermined by that of a royal favorite.

In 1303, Edward I again commandeered the use of York Place for himself and Marguerite, since the royal apartments at Westminster were still in need of repair. He ordered that major building works be carried out at York Place, creating a separate lodging for Marguerite, which consisted of a hall, a privy chamber, a little chamber, a chamber for her damsel, and a wardrobe.

In the spring of 1303, the King returned north to resume the war with Scotland. He sent for Marguerite to join him at Roxburgh, where he was mustering his forces, and she began her journey up from Cawood Castle, where she had been awaiting his summons. With her she took her two boys, her stepdaughters Elizabeth, Countess of Hereford, and Joan of Acre, Countess of Gloucester, and Joan's husband, Ralph, Lord Monthermer. But the border country was dangerous, Elizabeth was about to give birth, and Marguerite dared not risk capture by adherents of the Scottish resistance fighter William Wallace, so she returned south with her companions. On June 6, they reached Tynemouth Priory, for which Marguerite would later secure the privilege of an annual fair. From there, they kept in touch with Edward by letter. During their stay, Elizabeth bore the daughter she named for the Queen. Marguerite was still at Tynemouth at the beginning of August because Edward was concerned about a wave of crimes committed after dark by lawless vagabonds in Newcastle and had ordered an inquiry, "reflecting that it may go from bad to worse and desiring that the peace be firmly observed while he is in Scotland, especially in this town and in the parts adjacent, lest terror or danger arise to Marguerite, Queen of England, dwelling there."[7]

For safety, Marguerite retreated to York. Her sons and the infant Margaret de Bohun were sent south to Windsor for safety. When the Queen and her stepdaughters finally followed the King north in November, she faced further danger from the raiding parties sent across the border by Wallace and John Comyn, Lord of Badenoch, but managed to evade them and made her way safely to Dunfermline, Scotland's ancient royal capital, where she and Edward spent Christmas in the abbey that housed the relics of St. Margaret, Queen of Scots. Their accommodation was large enough to accommodate three kings and their trains.

By then, they would have learned of Philip IV's quarrel with the Pope. From 1294, notwithstanding his title "the Most Christian King," Philip had wrangled with the violent and intransigent Boniface VIII over the extent to which the pontiff should wield power over French affairs. When, in September 1303, he sent men to kidnap Boniface, they roughly dragged the Pontiff from his throne, slapped his face and held him prisoner for three days of ill treatment, for which Philip was promptly excommunicated. Even more shocking, later that month Boniface died as a result of the attack. Fortunately, the election of a compliant elderly Frenchman, Clement V, in 1305 would pave the way for a reconciliation and, in 1309, under pressure from Philip, Clement would move the seat of the Papacy from Rome to Avignon in southern France, where it was to remain for nearly seventy years, in thrall to the kings of France. This exile was described by some contemporaries as "the Babylonian Captivity," comparing it to the Biblical exile of the Jews to Babylon.

Marguerite and her stepdaughters remained at Dunfermline until Edward laid siege to Stirling in April 1304, when she joined him. The siege lasted for twelve weeks and to enable her and other ladies to watch it, he had an oriel window installed in the house in the town where she lodged. On June 21, he made substantial grants of properties and rights to her. Elizabeth left for England just before Stirling fell on July 24. After Wallace was captured on August 5, the King began a triumphal march south. On September 8, he and Marguerite were at Tynemouth Priory and, on December 6, they stayed at the royal manor of Burstwick, Yorkshire. Christmas was kept at Lincoln amid great splendor.

On the King's return south early in 1305, great festivities were held at Westminster to celebrate the victory at Stirling and the capture of Wallace. On February 24, Edward paid £134 ($111,000) to a London goldsmith for jewels and plate for Marguerite. In the spring, he would increase her dower to £5,500 ($4.6 million).

Marguerite's sister Blanche died in March. She was just twenty-seven, but may have suffered complications from a miscarriage. Edward deputed the Queen's confessor to break the news to her as kindly as he could; if it affected her deeply, he was to remind her that since Blanche had married Rudolph of Austria, she had effectively been dead to her for a long time. The King also asked the Archbishop of Canterbury to offer up special prayers for Blanche's soul and to comfort Marguerite, "for she was the dear sister of his beloved consort." Ten-year-old Isabella also suffered a bereavement when, in April, her mother died, aged only thirty-two. Philip IV's grief at Queen Jeanne's passing was evident as he followed her funeral cortège to the abbey of Saint-Denis, near Paris. Jeanne was succeeded as sovereign of Navarre by her eldest son, Louis. After her death, Philip remained faithful to her memory and never remarried.

With Queen Jeanne's steadying influence removed, the French court lost much of its gravitas. Marguerite, Jeanne, and Blanche of Burgundy, the wives of the King's sons Louis, Philip, and Charles, now emerged as the leaders of fashionable society, but they were flighty girls, intent only on pleasure. Soon, the court was plunged into a hectic round of fêtes, dancing, and novel diversions, and moralists professed themselves shocked at the new fashions promoted by these princesses, who had set a trend for daringly slit skirts.

By June 1305, it had become clear to the old King that Gaveston was a bad influence on his son, who had abandoned the Scottish campaign to go jousting in France, and then—the final straw—he and Gaveston, abetted by a gang of youths, had trespassed on the estates of Walter Langton, the King's Treasurer, pulling down fences and scattering the deer and other game. When Bishop Langton complained to the King, the Prince "uttered coarse and bitter words to him"[8] and was sent in disgrace to Windsor Castle with just one servant in attendance. Edward was so angry that he forbade his son to come within thirty miles of his presence for nearly six months and cut off his household supplies. He also banned him from seeing Gaveston.

The Prince knew that Marguerite was his friend and that she had the ear of his father. He had written often with requests for her to intercede on behalf of those he wished to reward—eight survive from 1305 alone. Now he begged for her help in bringing Gaveston back. Marguerite may have had doubts about the suitability of their friendship, but she did intercede for the Prince. By August, she and Anthony Bek, Bishop of Durham, had persuaded the King to restore his household. "Our lord the King has now allowed most of the gentlemen of our chamber to resume their accustomed dwelling with us, and we know well that this was done at your request, for which we are dearly grateful to you, as you know," her stepson wrote to her.

That month, Marguerite hosted a great tournament to celebrate—somewhat prematurely—the conquest of Scotland and presided over it wearing her rich crown. The Prince had not ceased to urge her to bring about Gaveston's restoration. On August 4, he asked his sister Elizabeth to press Marguerite to intercede with the King on his behalf. Days later, he sent the Queen a heartfelt plea in much the same words, begging her to "pray our dear lord and father that he will grant unto us two valets besides those we have, that is to say, Gilbert de Clare and Piers Gaveston. For truly, my lady, if we had these two besides the others, we should be much comforted and eased of the anguish we have endured and still suffer by the ordinance of our said lord and father. My lady, will you please take this business to heart and pursue it in the most gracious manner you may, so dearly as you love us?"[9]

But the Prince knew that he had to make his peace with the King first, for Edward had vowed that he would not allow his son to enter his presence until he had apologized to Langton. Marguerite persuaded the Prince to do as his father wished and, on October 13, the feast of St. Edward the Confessor, she witnessed their reconciliation at Westminster, in which she had played no small part. It may have been thanks to her continuing intercessions that Gaveston was back at court by the following Whitsun.

In 1305, Marguerite also interceded on behalf of the Mayor and leading citizens of Winchester, who incurred the King's wrath when a valuable Gascon hostage escaped from the castle. Summoned to face Edward at Westminster, they were committed to the Tower and fined heavily, while the Sheriff of Hampshire was ordered to seize the city of Winchester and declare its liberties void. A deputation of the citizens appealed to the Queen, showing her a charter granting her the right to receive all fines levied on them. Recalling how warmly the people of Winchester had welcomed her when she first arrived in England, she braved Edward's temper, showing him the charter and begging him to grant her both the Mayor and the fine. It took her a while to persuade him, but in the end, Edward remitted half the fine, freed the prisoners, and restored the city's privileges.

In the months following Queen Jeanne's death, Pope Clement had been urging Edward I to expedite plans for his son's marriage to Isabella. On October 15, the Prince of Wales authorized English envoys to conclude the contract. There was talk of a proxy wedding at Lyon, to coincide with the new Pope's coronation there, and Philip empowered Isabella to appoint her proxies. Clement issued the necessary dispensation for the marriage on November 27. Yet there is no record of the proxy marriage ever taking place. The evidence suggests that it was prevented by further disputes over Gascony.

By December, Marguerite knew that she had conceived a third time. Edward was proud of her, and of their sons. During his frequent absences, he corresponded with them all; his letters reveal that he fussed over them and fretted about their health. In 1305, in response to the Queen's physician's request to bleed her (a practice meant to balance the four humors of the body and so prevent illness), Edward insisted that it be done promptly, and wrote to Marguerite ordering her to comply. When she contracted measles that year, he warned her doctor that, "by God's thigh,"[10] he would suffer if she were not properly looked after. He also demanded that he be kept informed, without delay, of her progress.

The King and Queen spent Christmas at the royal hunting lodge at Kingston Lacy in Dorset, which stood to the north of the present stately home; its walls lie beneath the park and were uncovered in 1990 when a tree blew over in a storm. On December 28, Edward sent a hopeful offering to the shrine of St. Richard of Chichester on behalf of his son, "Sir Richard," as yet unborn.

Early in 1306, Marguerite took up residence at Wolvesey Palace near Winchester Cathedral, the royal lodgings in the castle being still uninhabitable after the fire. New chambers had been built for her in the palace, with a painted throne studded with gilt and silver nails, and an enclosed turfed garden with a water channel running through it was created. Edward joined her with his daughters Elizabeth and Mary, and his nieces Eleanor of Bar and Eleanor de Clare.

* * *

Robert le Brus, known as the Bruce, was one of the most accomplished of military tacticians and the grandson of one of the thirteen claimants to the Scottish throne. Having fought his countrymen under Edward's banner, he defected to the Scots in 1306. While Edward and Marguerite were at Winchester, they learned that he had been crowned king of Scots on March 27. Edward's wrath was boundless. He would have punished the goldsmith who "had committed the heavy transgression and malediction of making the coronel of gold that crowned the King's rebel and enemy," but pardoned him "solely at the intercession of our dearest consort, Marguerite, Queen of England."[11]

Robert the Bruce himself was another matter. Edward declared him a traitor, dispatched an army, and drove him into hiding. Thereafter, the war dragged on bitterly and expensively, as the English tried to root him out. But Bruce was a canny and intrepid strategist, and there was no end to the conflict in sight.

Marguerite's child was born on May 4 at Winchester. Contrary to Edward's hopes, it was a girl, but he wrote to ask for a description of his new daughter and it was agreed that she would be given the name of his first wife (although she was sometimes called Margaret by the chroniclers). Four days after Eleanor's birth, Edward began negotiating her marriage to four-year-old Robert, the youngest brother of Hugh V, Duke of Burgundy. A chamber was created for her in the new royal lodgings at York Place, where Marguerite took up residence when she returned to Westminster. Later, Eleanor joined her brothers' household.

Marguerite was still in childbed at Whitsun 1306 when Prince Edward and over 260 other young men, including Piers Gaveston, Hugh le Despenser the Younger, and Roger Mortimer, who were all to play fateful roles in his life, were knighted in a magnificent ceremony at Westminster. But she was present when the King celebrated his sixty-seventh birthday on June 18, sitting at the foot of his throne at Westminster. He was soon to depart with the Prince for Scotland and moved to Winchester after the festivities. On June 23, the Prince traveled there to bid the Queen farewell. The next day, the court celebrated the feast of St. John the Baptist, for which Edward gave Marguerite a circlet of gold.

In 1306, wishing to assist Marguerite's charitable works, of which he had heard glowing reports, Pope Clement V awarded her £4,000 ($3.4 million) from tithes collected in England, for the relief of the Holy Land. That year, Marguerite, who was devoted to the Franciscan order, gave land and 2,000 marks ($1.27 million) for the rebuilding of the church of the Grey Friars at Newgate in London, founded by her husband's late brother, Edmund Crouchback, Earl of Lancaster; here, the heart of Alienor of Provence, Edward's grandmother, had been interred in 1291. To enhance its prestigious status as a royal mausoleum, Marguerite wanted to see the church rebuilt in the style of the great church of the Cordeliers (Franciscans) that her grandfather, St. Louis IX, had founded in Paris around 1250 and in which Isabella's mother, Jeanne of Navarre, had been laid to rest. It is no coincidence that there was a chapel dedicated to St. Louis at Newgate. An English mason, Walter of Hereford, was employed to design and build what turned out to be an architectural triumph, second only to St. Paul's Cathedral in size, which became the most fashionable church in London up to the Reformation. Marguerite also gave land to the Carmelite friars of Kingston upon Hull, and persuaded Edward to grant a weekly market to St. Helen's Priory in London, to be held at their manor of Brentford, Middlesex.

In late June 1306, Marguerite and her sons were lodging at Northampton Castle with the nun Mary. The Prince joined them there.

It is possible that Marguerite visited her family in France that year; on October 18, the King paid out for jewels and other items "for the passage of the Lady Queen beyond the seas."[12] However, there is no other reference to this trip, so it may never have got past the planning stage. Late that summer, escorted by John, Lord Hastings, Marguerite traveled north to join Edward, who had set off in September to continue his onslaught on Scotland. By now, every major fortress in that kingdom was in his hands and victory was in sight. He was enraged, therefore, when twenty-two of the Prince's friends deserted, and ordered that they be hunted down.

At the end of September, Edward suffered an attack of dysentery and had to return to England, where Marguerite joined him. When they arrived at Lanercost Priory in Cumberland on October 1, he was very sick and infirm. After four days, he recovered sufficiently to visit Carlisle, but his health was declining daily, so the couple returned to Lanercost, where they "dwelt with the monks" until the following March.[13] For their comfort, glass windows were fitted in their lodgings.

Despite pleading with her husband, Marguerite failed to save the life of John of Strathbogie, Earl of Atholl, who had abandoned his allegiance to Edward and taken part in Bruce's coronation. It was his misfortune to have been captured in June at the Battle of Methven. The King was bent on his suffering a traitor's death, but Marguerite at least persuaded him to commute the sentence. On November 7, Atholl was hanged from a high gallows in London, after which his head was spiked on London Bridge and his body burned.

Isabella MacDuff, Countess of Buchan, who had crowned Robert the Bruce, had been captured by Edward along with other royal ladies. His vengeance was harsh. He decreed that the Countess be incarcerated in a turret of Berwick Castle in "a cage of stout lattice work of timber, barred and strengthened with iron," which was sometimes to be "hung up out of doors in the open air at Berwick, that both in life and after her death, she may be a spectacle and eternal reproach to travellers."[14] Bruce's sister Mary was imprisoned in a similar cage at the castle of Roxburgh. Both women endured their punishment for four years. There is no record of Marguerite interceding for them.

The twenty-two knights who had deserted had now been rounded up. When, in January 1307, the King ordered that they be deprived of their lands and property, Marguerite prevailed on him to pardon sixteen of them and seems to have persuaded him not to proceed against the rest.

But the Prince again offended his father, asking him to give Piers either the royal earldom of Cornwall, or the counties of Ponthieu and Montreuil, which he himself had inherited from his mother. The King, who was planning to give Cornwall to Edmund, his youngest son, erupted in rage, grabbing his son by the hair and dragging him around the room, shouting, "You baseborn whoreson! Would you give away lands, you, who never gained any?"[15]

His fury betrayed his concern about his son's "inordinate affection"[16] for Gaveston. On February 26, 1307, he banished Piers to Gascony, "on account of the undue intimacy which the Lord Edward had adopted towards him, publicly calling him his brother."[17] In the meantime, the

Prince was not to go near his friend and was commanded never to bestow on him any lands or titles. Before Gaveston left, he and the Prince were made to swear on the Blessed Sacrament and Edward I's holiest relics not to disobey the King's commands.

On March 1, the King and Queen left Lanercost for Carlisle. Clement V had sent Cardinal Peter the Spaniard to England to negotiate the final arrangements for the marriage of the Prince of Wales and Isabella, and expressed the hope that peace between England and France was imminent. Cardinal Peter was received by Edward I on March 12 at Carlisle, where, on the 16th, the King gave his formal consent to the union. When Parliament met at Easter at Carlisle, the marriage was unanimously approved and preparations for it were immediately put in hand.

In May, defying his father, a miserable Prince Edward accompanied Gaveston to Dover, where he lavished gifts on him and watched him sail away. Piers went to Ponthieu, apparently with the King's blessing, and the Prince announced his intention of visiting him there, but his father forbade it. Young Edward was supposed to sail from Dover to France to marry Isabella; he waited there nine days for the order to embark, but it never came. Instead, he was summoned to Scotland to assist his father in a new campaign. But the King was a sick, bedridden man, suffering from dysentery and possibly cancer of the rectum. Despite this, he insisted on going on campaign in Scotland. When he left Carlisle on July 3, Marguerite returned to Lanercost Priory with Prince Edward.

The King was so weak that he could cover only two miles a day. On the night of July 6, he camped on the marshes at Burgh by Sands. He knew he was dying; already, he had made his son swear to "be kind to his little brothers and, above all, treat with respect and tenderness his mother, Queen Marguerite." He had also commanded him to marry Isabella, and never, "on pain of his irrevocable malediction,"[18] to recall Gaveston, and he charged the earls of Lincoln and Warwick, and his cousin Aymer de Valence, to block Piers's return. According to the chronicler Jean Froissart, writing many decades later, he instructed his son to have the flesh boiled from his bones so that they could be carried at the head of a conquering army into Scotland.

The next morning, the King breathed his last as his servants were raising him to partake of some food, and the Prince of Wales succeeded him as King Edward II.

Marguerite was informed of the King's death by a letter sent on July 8. Grief-stricken, she stayed on at Lanercost and, at some stage, commissioned her chaplain, John of London, to write a long panegyric recording the noble deeds of her husband. Entitled *"Commendatio lamentabilis in transitum magni Regis Edwardi Quarti,"* it was dedicated to herself and began: "The noble and generous matron, Marguerite, by the grace of God Queen of England, invites all men to hear these pages. This is the lamentable commemoration of Marguerite the Queen. Hear, ye isles, and attend, my peoples, for is any sorrow like unto my sorrow? Though my head wears a crown, joy is distant from me and I listen no more to the sound of my cithara and organs. I mourn incessantly and am weary of my existence. Let all mankind hear the voice of my tribulation, for my desolation on our Earth is complete. At the foot of Edward's monument, with my little sons, I weep and call upon him. When Edward died, all men died to me."[19]

There can be little doubt that Marguerite had loved Edward. She never remarried, but devoted herself to her children. Eleanor died, aged five, in late August 1311 at Amesbury Abbey. Edward II generously paid £113 ($93,000) for the expenses of her burial at Beaulieu Abbey, Hampshire, where her ten-foot ledger stone survives today, with an indent where its lost brass once rested. He had also, the previous year, assigned the estates of the late Earl of Norfolk, who had died childless, for the maintenance of his half-brothers, Thomas and Edmund.

For all her extravagance, Marguerite had been a dutiful consort in the traditional mold, a devoted helpmeet to the King, a good stepmother to his heir, and a peacemaker. Her public influence was negligible, yet she had won the love of a formidable man old enough to be her grandfather, and she had been able at times to mitigate his harshness. It was only after his death that she was stirred to venture into politics in a way the old King could never have envisaged.

Edward I left his son a kingdom nearly bankrupted by a war that looked to be unwinnable, with a great portion of his future revenues mortgaged to Italian bankers. Edward II also inherited a nobility that had chafed and grown resentful under the iron fist of the Crown and was determined to regain its lost influence and privileges. Nevertheless, the new

King's accession was the occasion of great rejoicing, for he was young and charming and had the common touch and the immense goodwill of his people. It was said that "God has bestowed every gift on him, and made him equal to, or indeed more excellent, than other kings."[20] But Robert the Bruce had his measure, and drily stated that he feared dead Edward's bones more than his living heir's sword.

"What high hopes he had raised as Prince of Wales!" related Edward's biographer, but "all hopes vanished when the Prince became King."[21] Edward II's first act was to recall Piers Gaveston, on whom he bestowed the royal earldom of Cornwall, which brought with it the vast income of £4,000 ($3.4 million) a year and had previously been held only by members of the royal family. No commoner had ever been raised so high at a stroke. Most barons were appalled, "as much because Piers was an alien of Gascon birth, as through envy."[22] Marguerite had more reason than most to be angry, because her late husband had earmarked the earldom for their son Edmund.

Edward had begun his reign on a tide of public approval, but he recklessly threw that away through his irresponsible promotion of Gaveston, whom he looked upon almost as a co-ruler; he allowed himself to be ruled by his advice while despising the counsel of the magnates, and gave him thousands of pounds from his already depleted Treasury. It was Gaveston, not the chief barons, who controlled the network of royal patronage, which was one of the chief causes of their wrath and envy. It seemed to them that there were now two kings in England, "one in name and the other in reality." Piers's arrogance was intolerable to the barons and a prime cause of hatred and rancor. If he had "from the outset borne himself prudently and humbly towards the magnates, none of them would ever have opposed him."[23] But "the more virulently people attacked Gaveston, the more keenly the King loved him."

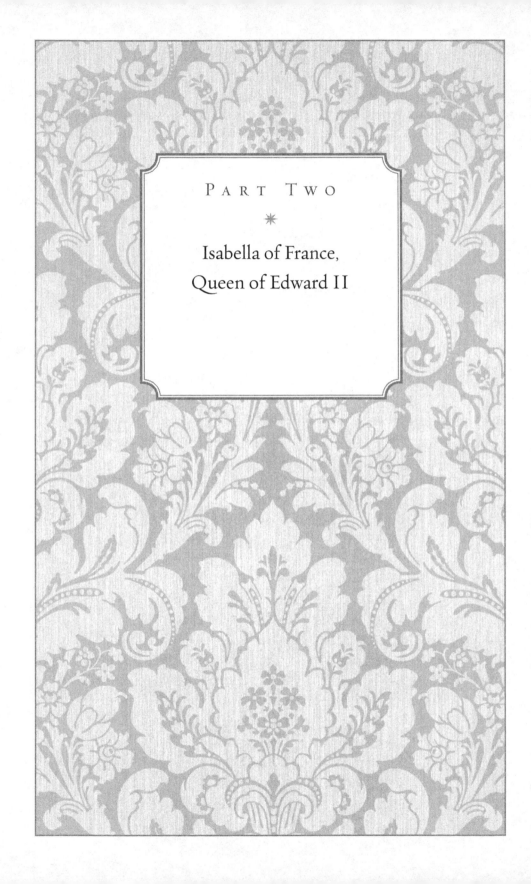

PART TWO

*

Isabella of France,
Queen of Edward II

I

"The Most Wretched of Wives"

*

SOON AFTER HIS ACCESSION, EDWARD DISPATCHED ENVOYS TO France to conclude negotiations for his marriage. They waxed lyrical on Isabella's beauty. But Gaveston was now entrenched at court. The King "did him great reverence and worshipped him" almost as if he were a god, but he was "reviled far and wide."[1]

Late in August, King Philip ordered his half-brother Louis, Count of Evreux, to treat with Edward's envoys. In October, Parliament voted funds for the coming royal wedding and the coronation that was to follow.

Edward II had immediately abandoned the war with Scotland and ignored his father's dying request. On October 27, after a slow progress south, Edward I's body was buried in Westminster Abbey, where the inscription *Malleus Scotorum* ("the Hammer of the Scots") was later inscribed on his plain marble tomb. In October, Edward paid out £53.6s.8d. ($44,095) for the expenses of Marguerite's children and, in December, he would defray for £100 ($82,500) her expenses from the time of Edward I's death to his burial. Marguerite was still at Lanercost on December 23, mourning the late King, whom she called, in a letter to her stepson, "your most noble father, our husband, may God have mercy on him."[2] She returned south soon afterward.

To bring Gaveston into the royal circle, the King bestowed on him the hand of his niece, Margaret de Clare, the daughter of Joan of Acre, who had recently died. The wedding took place on November 1 at Berkhamsted Castle, which was owned by Queen Marguerite (who presumably made no protest, even if she did resent Edward disparaging the royal family). The King spent most of that month at Langley with the newly-weds. He gave orders to commence preparations for his own marriage, and for the restoration of the royal lodgings and gardens at Westminster. *The Margaret of Westminster* was commissioned to bring the new Queen to England; Edward had it repainted and refitted, and himself designed wardrobes and butteries to be fitted inside it. At the instance of the Pope, Philip had agreed to the wedding taking place at Boulogne. He had a well-known devotion to Our Lady of Boulogne, and the location would be convenient for the English.

Edward planned to leave for France after Christmas. To the barons' indignation, he appointed Gaveston Keeper of the Realm, which provoked outraged comments from the chroniclers, and must have upset Queen Marguerite, who could reasonably have expected one of her sons to be nominally appointed to the office.

Edward and Piers spent Christmas together. Neither can have relished the prospect of the King's marriage. Gaveston had every reason to resent Isabella and what she stood for. He would probably have seen her as a threat to his ascendancy over the King. His family had been driven from Gascony during the French occupation. The evidence suggests that he did his best to stir up trouble between Edward and Philip in a last-ditch attempt to make Edward abandon his treaty with the French, urging that Philip would not rest until he had finally conquered Gascony. But there were others on Edward's council who greatly feared the consequences if their master reneged on his obligations and, for once, they prevailed over the favorite.

We do not know how much Isabella already knew of her future husband's relationship with Gaveston. It may have been common gossip at the French court. But preparations for her marriage were now complete. In her trousseau, she had gorgeous gowns, some of gold, silver, baudekin, velvet, and shot taffeta; six were of green cloth of Douai, six beautifully marbled, and six of rose scarlet. They would have had tight-fitting bodices and sleeves, and circular skirts with trains. Isabella had seventy-two coifs in her trousseau, many costly furs, two gold crowns ornamented with gems, gold and silver cups, golden spoons, fifty silver porringers, and twenty-four silver-gilt dishes. She was provided with 419 yards of linen for her bath, body linen for chemises and hose, and tapestries blazoned with gold-embroidered lozenges framing the arms and heraldic emblems of England, France, and Navarre for her chamber.

Early in the morning of Monday, January 22, 1308, Edward II sailed from Dover with Queen Marguerite and a great retinue, arriving in Boulogne on the evening of the 24th. Philip IV was waiting to greet him and present his bride.

Isabella was then an enchanting twelve-year-old who would grow into "a most elegant lady and a very beautiful woman."[3] It was conventional for chroniclers to describe queens and high-born ladies as fair, yet their praise for her looks is unanimously enthusiastic, suggesting that she was a great beauty. Edward himself may have given her the nickname "Isabeau the Fair,"[4] while Froissart called her "one of the fairest ladies in the world."

Isabella and her brother Charles (also nicknamed "the Fair") probably took after their father in looks. Yet there is no precise description of Isabella, not even a mention of the color of her hair. Contemporary ideals of beauty favored plump blond women, and several extant representations of her suggest that she conformed to this type. Some are merely images of a queen, others possible attempts at an accurate portrayal. Most manuscript illustrations representing Isabella date from the fifteenth century and are imaginative depictions, while the few pictures in contemporary manuscripts are in no sense portraits. She also appears on her seal in the conventional image of a queen, her figure standing between two shields.

A corbel head of a woman in a crown and wimple in Beverley Minster, Yorkshire, is said to portray Isabella, and bears a striking resemblance to the stone head of her on the Oxenbridge tomb in Winchelsea Church, Sussex, which dates from c.1320. Both depict a woman with a plump face, arched brows, and curly hair, and may be attempts at likenesses. Isabella traveled widely in England, and the men who sculpted these heads might have seen her. The heads also appear to bear a familial resemblance to the tomb effigies of Isabella's father and two eldest brothers at Saint-Denis, which are near-contemporary. By this period, there was a trend toward realism in funerary effigies, although most were idealized images.

A corbel head and a roof boss in Bristol Cathedral and a boss in the quire of Exeter Cathedral, both said to be Isabella, are probably generic images of a queen. Three stone heads in Fyfield Church, Berkshire, dating from *c.*1308, are said to represent Isabella, Edward II, and the ship's master who had brought them from France, while carved heads in the gatehouse of Caldicot Castle and in Butterwick Church perhaps represent a crowned Isabella. A painted fourteenth-century roof boss in Malmesbury Abbey, also said to be her, shows an older woman with cadaverous features.

A representation of Isabella showing her crowned, with curly hair escaping from her wimple, is in the Psalter of Queen Isabella (now in the Bavarian State Library in Munich), which was probably commissioned by her. She is shown wearing a long gown belted under the bust and a cloak with an embroidered hem; in her hand is a shield bearing the royal *fleurs-de-lis* of France.

If Isabella was lovely, her bridegroom was everything a young girl could dream of. Edward II was about six feet tall, "a handsome man of outstanding strength."[5] "God had endowed him with every gift."[6] Even hostile chroniclers praised his good looks. He had shoulder-length curly fair hair, with a mustache and beard. He was well spoken—his mother tongue was Norman French—and articulate. He dressed elegantly, even lavishly. He must have made a good impression on his young bride.

For centuries, English kings had held land in France, for which they were obliged to pay homage to French monarchs as their feudal overlords. They often did so reluctantly, not wishing to bend the knee to England's traditional enemy, but failure to do so could lead to war. Soon after his arrival in Boulogne, Edward swore fealty to Philip IV for his Continental fiefdoms, and Philip handed over Isabella's dowry, which had been appropriated from the confiscated wealth of the Knights Templar, whose order had been brutally suppressed in France the previous year. On her marriage, Isabella was supposed to receive the lands customarily assigned to the queens of England, but these were still in the possession of Marguerite of France, so Edward undertook to dower her from his lands in France and assign her other estates in England. To mark the marriage, Philip gave Edward and Isabella costly gifts of jewelry, rings, chains, and fine warhorses.

On Thursday, January 25, 1308, Edward and Isabella were married in the cathedral of Our Lady of Boulogne. The bride was a rainbow of color in a costly gown and overtunic of blue and gold, and a red mantle lined with yellow sindon (heavy satin or linen), which she was to preserve for the rest of her life. On her head was one of the crowns given her by her father. Edward was resplendent in a satin gardcorp (a sleeved cyclas, or long tabard) and a cloak embroidered with jewels, while Philip IV's robe was rose-colored.

The importance of the marriage was underlined by the magnificence of the ceremony and the presence of so many royal guests: the kings of Navarre, Sicily, and the Romans, Queen Marguerite and her mother, the French Dowager Queen, Marie of Brabant, and Elizabeth of Tyrol, Queen of the Romans. For Marguerite, this was a happy family reunion. Her wedding gift to her niece was probably the silver gilt casket bearing their arms and those of their husbands in quatrefoils, which is now in the British Museum.

After the ceremony, Edward and Isabella retired to the lodgings appointed for them near the cathedral. Given the tender age of the bride and the fact that she did not become pregnant for another four years, it is unlikely that the marriage was consummated that night. There is no record of a bedding ceremony.

Eight days of celebrations, feasts, and tournaments followed the nuptials. Philip struck a discordant note when he presented Edward with a list of grievances concerning Gascony and warned him never to think of having his marriage annulled, because Gascony had only been restored to him because of his union with Isabella and the children that would be born to them.

The festivities came to an end on February 2. The next day, accompanied by Isabella's uncles, Charles, Count of Valois, and Louis, Count of Evreux, Edward and his new Queen said their farewells and traveled along the coast to Wissant, where they took ship and "returned joyfully"[7] to England.

Gaveston was waiting to greet them when their ship docked at Dover on February 7. Impulsively, Edward ran to him and fell into his arms, "giving him kisses and repeated embraces" and calling him "brother,"[8] while Isabella and her kinsmen looked on, greatly offended by this public display of affection for a commoner.

Gaveston had brought the chief ladies of the Queen's newly established household to Dover to attend her on her progress to Westminster. Among them were Elizabeth, Countess of Hereford, the King's sister; Joan de Genville, the wife of Roger Mortimer, a leading marcher baron; and Isabella de Beaumont, Lady de Vesci, who was to become as favored by the Queen as she already was by the King, who was related to her through his mother.

Edward and Isabella spent two nights at Dover, then traveled to Eltham Palace, where they were to stay until their state entry into London for their coronation. Eltham Palace lay six miles southeast of London and was originally a fortified manor built by the Clare family. In 1295, it had been acquired by Anthony Bek, Bishop of Durham, who rebuilt it. His house had turrets, a tower, a timber drawbridge, and a moat surrounded by a stone wall. The great hall was tiled, and there was a wine cellar. The Bishop also created a hunting park to the south of the palace. Isabella, like her aunt, loved the chase, and Eltham became one of her favorite residences.

She was dismayed to discover that the income promised by her husband was showing no signs of materializing, for there was no money in the Treasury. Indignantly she wrote to her father complaining that she was expected to live in great poverty. Philip demanded that Edward state in writing exactly what financial provision he intended to make for his wife and any children of the marriage. Edward replied that he had already drawn up such a statement for Isabella, but that his advisers had counseled him not to put his seal to a copy for Philip in case it laid him open to further obligations in respect of their children if Isabella predeceased him.

Then Isabella noticed Gaveston—"whose passion for finery was insatiable"[9]—wearing the jewels and rings her father had given the King and some of the jewelery she had brought from France as part of her dowry. Again she wrote to Philip, expressing her fury at Piers's avarice and the favor shown to him by her husband. She was, she declared, "the most wretched of wives."[10]

She had allies, for her kinsmen and the barons were now determined to resolve the problem of Gaveston. They warned the King that unless Piers was banished, they would not take part in the coronation ceremony, which was tantamount to refusing him their oaths of allegiance. It took so long for Edward to win them round with fulsome promises that the crowning had to be postponed until February 25.

The King and Queen were magnificently received in London when they entered in state on February 19. The Lord Mayor, the aldermen, and the London guildsmen, all wearing new liveries, rode out to meet them and ceremoniously surrender the keys to the City. The four-mile-long procession moved slowly through streets gaily decorated with banners and pennants and thronged with thousands of people, who cheered their young Queen enthusiastically. Pageants were enacted in temporary castles of canvas or fairy bowers decked with artificial flowers, while free wine flowed in the City's conduits.

On February 24, after spending five nights in the Tower, Edward and Isabella rode in procession through the City of London to the Palace of Westminster. Throughout the autumn and winter, working by candlelight through the hours of darkness, masons had been cutting and dressing stone and marble, and craftsmen and workmen had shaped timbers, forged metalwork, painted walls, and glazed windows. The King himself had supervised the work, but it was still not finished by the time of Isabella's arrival, and would not be until the following summer, by which time the cost of the repairs and refurbishments amounted to some £5,000 ($4 million).

The restored palace was as impressive and comfortable as Henry III had intended, and its gardens were delightful, with newly turfed lawns, paved paths, pear and cherry trees, trellises, vines, and restocked fishponds. There was a "Queen's pool," and the aviary established by Eleanor of Castile. Inside the palace, the King had built two new chambers: that attached to the Painted Chamber was to serve as his bedroom, and the other was added to the restored Queen's apartments.

The coronation of Edward II and Isabella of France took place on February 25, 1308, the feast of St. Matthias the Apostle. The ceremony was conducted by Henry Woodlock, Bishop of Winchester, because Archbishop Winchelsey, having quarrelled with Edward I, had not yet returned from exile. For the first time, the wives of peers were invited, in honor of the Queen. Gaveston had been given the responsibility of planning the coronation and accorded himself a central role in it, which many were to hold against him for a long time to come.

The King and Queen went in stately procession from Westminster Hall to the Abbey, walking along a timber pathway laid with blue cloth strewn with herbs and flowers, with the Barons of the Cinque Ports holding an embroidered canopy above their heads. The crowds were so dense that they almost had to fight their way to the Abbey and enter by a back door. In advance of the King had come the chief magnates, bearing the regalia, but all heads turned when Gaveston appeared "so decked out that he more resembled the god Mars than an ordinary mortal."[11] Many were outraged to see him wearing pearl-encrusted silk robes of imperial purple, a color reserved for the King himself, whose own finery was somewhat eclipsed by that of his favorite. Gaveston also managed to upstage the other earls, who were wearing the traditional cloth of gold, the richest fabric normally permitted to those of their rank; "he transcended them all"[12] and they were bristling with jealousy.

Isabella's kinsmen and numerous French nobles and knights were guests at the coronation. They too were appalled by the prominence accorded to Gaveston. The greatest outrage was occasioned by Gaveston's "soiled hands"[13] carrying the sacred crown of St. Edward the Confessor into the Abbey, a privilege that should have been bestowed on the highest noble in the land. It was seen as a deliberate affront, never to be forgotten or forgiven. One earl was so furious that only consideration for the sensitivities of the Queen and the sanctity of the Abbey prevented him from coming to blows with Gaveston in the church itself.

Edward II took his coronation oath, was anointed with holy oil on the head, hands, and breast, and then ascended to a high wooden platform on which was set the gilded and painted wooden coronation chair commissioned by Edward I in 1297 to house the Stone of Scone, on which the Kings of Scotland had long been crowned, and which had been seized by the English in 1296. Edward seated himself in this chair (which has been used at every coronation since) and the crown was placed on his head. After the peers had paid homage to the enthroned King, it was Isabella's turn. The consort's crown was an open circlet surmounted by eight motifs interspersed with trefoils and set with many precious stones.

Gaveston's ineptitude gave rise to several mishaps. He had crammed so many guests into the Abbey that a wall behind the altar collapsed, killing a knight. Even at the moment of crowning, there was little elbow room for the King and the officiating bishops because the crowds were inadequately marshaled.

After the disorganized ceremonies belatedly ended at 3 p.m., the King and Queen led the vast congregation to a huge temporary timber hall that had been erected by the river for the coronation banquet. The King's throne was at one end, beneath an arch, and in the center there was a fountain spouting red and white wine and pimento, a drink spiced with ginger. But what drew comment were the tapestries, which were woven, not with the arms of the King and Queen, but with those of Edward and Gaveston. It looked like a calculated insult to Isabella and her French relations, and Valois and Evreux were incensed.

The food was not ready, although there were forty ovens and an abundance of provisions of every kind, and when it did arrive, it was inedible. The King had chosen to sit next to Gaveston rather than the Queen, and the lords could barely contain their fury. "As a result, rumours circulated that the King was more in love with this artful and malevolent man than with his bride, that truly elegant lady, who is a most beautiful woman."[14] Her uncles were so angry that they returned to France in disgust as soon as the coronation celebrations were over, declaring that their niece was insulted because the King preferred the couch of Gaveston to hers.

Isabella soon discovered that her husband did not conform to contemporary expectations of what a king should be. He didn't behave like a monarch, wasn't interested in ruling England, and cared nothing for his royal duties. He was content to share his power with Gaveston and use the advantages of his office to enrich his friend and enjoy himself. He was finding it impossible to impose his will on his barons and was rapidly forfeiting their respect.

For a monarch, he had the oddest tastes. Traditionally, medieval kings were war leaders, and their interests reflected this. They enjoyed hunting, tournaments, and planning military campaigns. Edward II loved hunting and horse racing, and did not lack courage, but he hated tournaments, and never went to war unless necessity drove him to it, which exasperated his martially minded barons beyond measure.

They were horrified at their monarch's choice of leisure activities. He dug ditches on his estates, thatched roofs, trimmed hedges, plastered walls, worked in metal, shoed horses, drove carts, rowed, swam—even in

February—and indulged in "other trivial occupations unworthy of a king's son."[15] His manner with the common people was affable and familiar—too familiar, in the opinion of his barons, who were mortified to see him consorting with grooms, carters, ditchers, mechanics, oarsmen, sailors, and villeins. And they could only deplore his friendships with artists, buffoons, jesters, singers, choristers, actors, and jongleurs. Edward loved plays and was a great patron of writers and players, but the barons despised such interests as being vulgar and disreputable.

The King was literate and wrote poetry. He understood Latin and was a copious letter writer. He collected exquisitely produced books of French romances and legends; the royal library at the Tower of London contained 340 manuscripts. He had a passion for music and employed a group of Genoese musicians to entertain him on their trumpets, horns, harp, and drum. He owned a Welsh instrument called a crwth, an early type of violin.

Kings were expected to look the part and, with his handsome face and strong physique, Edward certainly did. He was elegant and showy as a peacock in his dress, spending a fortune on clothes and jewelery. He was "splendid in living," but inclined to "vanities and frivolities."[16] Given that he had inherited huge debts from his father, his tastes were extravagant.

Edward enjoyed practical jokes and horseplay. He once paid a royal painter, Jack of St. Albans, "for having danced on a table before the King and made him laugh beyond measure."[17] Another man was rewarded for falling off his horse in a comic manner. Edward employed several fools and was not above indulging in mock fights with them; once he had to pay compensation to a jester called Robert, whom he had accidentally injured during some boisterous game in the water. His wardrobe accounts show that he lost large sums at vulgar games of chance such as dice, chuck-farthing, heads or tails, and pitch and toss.

In company, he was congenial, a good conversationalist, articulate and witty. He loved good food and wines, but often over-imbibed and became garrulous or quarrelsome. He could be wayward, difficult, petulant, vindictive and cruel when provoked, and "savage,"[18] even with members of his household. Passion, anger, and resentment could smolder in him for years, and provoke outbursts of the famous Plantagenet temper. He lacked judgment. He was lazy by nature, loving to lie abed late in the mornings. However, once his affection was given, he could be unswerv-ingly loyal, and he would prove a good and loving father to his children.

The King was genuinely pious, and had a special devotion to St. Thomas Becket, which Isabella came to share. Both made frequent pil-grimages to the murdered saint's shrine at Canterbury. Edward attended Mass often, spent a great deal of time with his chaplains, and was gener-ous in his almsgiving.

The tragedy was that he had the potential to be a great king. "If only he had given to arms the labour that he expended on rustic pursuits, he would have raised England aloft, and his name would have resounded through the land." His good qualities, however, were insufficient to com-mand the respect of his people. His faults, especially his indiscriminate promotion of unsuitable favorites, looked set to damage the institution of monarchy itself. In short, few kings of England have attracted as much criticism from their contemporaries as Edward II.

Edward's marriage made no difference to his relationship with Gaveston. It exposed the strength of his "excessive and irrational"[19] love for him, which fueled the jealousy not only of the magnates, but of the neglected little Queen. Robert of Reading scathingly condemned the "mad folly of the King of England, who was so overcome with his own wickedness and desire for sinful, forbidden sex that he banished his royal wife from his side and rejected her sweet embraces."

Isabella was resentful of Gaveston's influence over the King and his being given precedence before her. She told her father that Piers had caused "all her troubles, by alienating King Edward's affection from her, and leading him into improper company," and that her husband was "an entire stranger to my bed."[20] But there was nothing she could do about it. The King could hardly be blamed for preferring the company of a man of his own age above that of a mere child. But many of the barons were incensed that Isabella was being slighted.

There was never an open rift between her and Gaveston. Wisely, she refrained from voicing any protest that could prejudice her chances of establishing a good relationship with her husband; we know this because in 1325, Edward declared that he had only ever rebuked her once in pri-vate, and that was for being too proud. But Isabella had good cause for complaint. With Gaveston's star in the ascendant, she stood little chance of exercising any political influence as Queen. For now, she was too young to do so. She played a very insignificant part in the King's life during these early years and was in no position to counteract the favorite's supremacy. She was effectively alone in a strange country and a court seething with tensions and hostility.

2

"Mortal Enemies"

✳

BY NOW, ISABELLA WAS BECOMING BETTER ACQUAINTED WITH England's leading barons, most of whom were related to her or the King. Foremost among them were the Earl of Lincoln and his son-in-law, Thomas, Earl of Lancaster, the King's cousin and Isabella's uncle, the son of her maternal grandmother, Blanche of Artois, and Edmund Crouch-back, Earl of Lancaster. Historians have made much of Lancaster's sup-posed sympathy for his niece, but there is very little evidence to show that he was especially supportive of her.

Thomas of Lancaster had married Lincoln's daughter, Alice de Lacy, a great heiress who stood to inherit rich lands and earldoms on her fa-ther's death. Thomas was already earl of Lancaster, Leicester, and Derby, and the wealthiest landowner in England after the King. Well connected and blue-blooded, he had every reason to expect to be Edward's chief adviser; but Edward's reliance on Gaveston had incurred his undying jealousy.

Humphrey de Bohun, Earl of Hereford and Essex, had married Eliza-beth, the King's sister. He was prickly and quick-tempered, but also intel-ligent, with a sense of humor. His early friendship with Edward II had been soured by Edward's excessive favoring of Gaveston, and he was now reluctantly siding with the opposition.

Guy de Beauchamp, Earl of Warwick, was one of Gaveston's fiercest opponents. A cultured, literate man, he had served with great distinction in Scotland under Edward I. "In prudence and counsel" he was "without parallel,"[1] and his fellow magnates often sought his advice before taking any action. He could be ruthless and arrogant, but the author of the *Vita Edwardi Secundi* lauded him as a hero.

The most honorable and able of the magnates was the moderate Aymer de Valence, Earl of Pembroke, the King's cousin. Pembroke had been one of Edward I's most trusted captains and was a skilled diplomat who was respected for his honesty and integrity. He deplored Edward II's reliance on Gaveston because it threatened to undermine the prestige of the monarchy. Given his loyalty to the Crown, Pembroke was sometimes to find himself embroiled in a conflict of loyalties.

Immediately after the coronation, "almost all the barons rose against Piers Gaveston, binding themselves by a mutual oath never to cease from what they had begun until Piers left England."[2] When Parliament met at Westminster in April, the magnates came armed and accused him of accroaching the powers of the Crown, demanding his banishment. Only Lancaster and Hugh le Despenser sided with the King, who announced that he was deferring discussion of the barons' demands until after Easter.

Despenser, who was in his late forties and married to Warwick's daughter, "was one of the most distinguished men of his day, both in judgement and in probity."[3] He had been one of Edward I's most faithful and able servants and was to prove as loyal to Edward II. He was an efficient administrator, a capable politician, and a trusted diplomat with a genial manner. He was the only baron Edward could really trust, and he was friendly toward Gaveston, which earned him the King's undying affection and the implacable enmity of the other magnates. They complained that he was greedy and had accumulated large estates through underhand means and brute force. In 1306, Edward I had agreed to the marriage of Despenser's son, Hugh the Younger, to his granddaughter, Eleanor de Clare, whose sister Margaret had married Piers Gaveston.

After the royal wedding, Queen Marguerite remained in Paris until after Easter, which fell on April 14, 1308. She had not attended the coronation. She had ceased making intercessions and from early 1308, she virtually disappears from the records, suggesting that she was not at court after her return and that her influence had declined. It seems unlikely that a queen who had been so proactive and got on so well with her stepson should voluntarily have stepped into the shadows.

Her absence from court was probably the result of her antipathy toward Gaveston. It is likely that she fell out with Edward over the favorite, and that this led to the King—perhaps spurred on by Gaveston— sending her away, a theory supported by a report in an anonymous French newsletter of May 1308[4] that Marguerite had sent the huge sum of £40,000 ($33.1 million) to Lincoln and Pembroke to finance their campaign to oust Gaveston from his lands in England.

If Marguerite had ever felt sympathy for Edward and Gaveston, that was clearly now in the past. She must have resented the slighting of her niece and the implied insult to the French royal house and, indeed, herself. The strength of her anger toward Piers is evident from the amount of money she invested in getting rid of him. Even before the newsletter turned up at court, Edward had redistributed the keeperships of some of her castles to men he could trust, suggesting that he no longer trusted her and was undermining her power to oppose him. (In December 1308, her castles were returned to her control, by which time Edward had evidently come to believe that she was no longer a threat to him.)

Marguerite's brother King Philip, who, according to the newsletter saw Gaveston as an enemy, sent a large supply of wine to the earls. It is likely that Marguerite had written to Philip of her concerns about Gaveston's influence and its effects on herself and her niece. She certainly wrote to Archbishop Winchelsey, reminding him that, in her presence at St. Albans, the King had specifically entrusted Isabella and her business to him. This was the only time Marguerite ventured into politics and it cannot but have caused bad feeling between her and Edward. She had conspired against him with a foreign power and his own nobles—it could have been seen as treason. There is no record of her exercising any influence again, and her visits to court were rare. However, Isabella's household book shows that she and Marguerite kept up a correspondence.

Marguerite seems to have retired with her daughter Eleanor to Marlborough Castle. All that remains today is its mound within the grounds of Marlborough College, but in the fourteenth century, it was a major royal residence. Built soon after the Norman Conquest to afford the

Norman kings good hunting in nearby Savernake Forest, it had been converted into a luxurious palace by Henry III, who bestowed it on Alienor of Provence in 1273; it would be assigned to succeeding queens as a dower house until it fell into disuse in the 1370s. It was eventually demolished in the seventeenth century. Here, Marguerite enjoyed use of two chapels, a hall, a keep, and luxurious apartments, all protected by two barbicans, a stout curtain wall, two bridges, and a gatehouse.

Yet she did not have her sons with her. After Edward II's accession, her name is not mentioned in their household accounts. They were then seven and six, old enough to be sent to a great household to serve as pages and learn the knightly accomplishments essential to their rank.

At Easter 1308, Edward took Isabella and Gaveston to Windsor. The situation between him and his barons was now grave. That spring, it was reported that the Queen, the earls, the Pope, the cardinals, and the King of France were likely to hinder anything that concerned Piers. All thought it advisable that Isabella be kept informed of Gaveston's misdeeds so that, prompted by hatred for him, she could send secret reports to her father, the Pope, the cardinals, and Charles of Valois. Edward spent most of April summoning men and fortifying castles. One man who offered his support was Roger Mortimer, who joined him at Windsor.

Mortimer, who was to play such a fateful role in Isabella's life, was the most powerful member of a fiercely independent group of barons known as Marcher lords. Their lands bestrode the Welsh border and their remit was to keep the peace in that region. Mortimer had been born around 1287. In 1304, he had succeeded his father as lord of Wigmore, where his family had been established since 1074, the first Roger Mortimer having been a companion of the Conqueror. Edward I had made Roger a ward of Piers Gaveston, but the young man had quickly bought his independence.

Despite his youth—he was twenty-one in 1308—Mortimer was one of the outstanding military leaders of the period, tough, energetic, and decisive. Like many barons, he was arrogant, grasping, and ambitious, but he was also an excellent political strategist and a faithful servant of the Crown who was respected by his peers. Clever, cultured, and literate, he took a keen interest in the legends of King Arthur and the Mortimers' supposed descent from Brutus the Trojan, the mythical British King, after whom, according to twelfth-century chroniclers, Britain was named, and who was said to have founded London as a second Troy and been the first king to hold a Round Table in the Arthurian manner. Roger had refined tastes, enjoyed tournaments, wore rich clothes, and transformed his castles at Wigmore and Ludlow into luxurious palaces.

His wife, Joan de Genville, had brought him Ludlow and lands in Ireland and Gascony. They had twelve children and Mortimer frequently took her with him on his travels, which suggests that theirs was a companionable relationship.

Mortimer was to spend most of the early years of Edward II's reign helping to govern Ireland, serving in Scotland and Gascony, and ruling efficiently—and ruthlessly—on the Marches and in Wales, where he and his uncle, the violent and lecherous Roger Mortimer of Chirk, wielded power like independent princes.

Mortimer had been present at the royal wedding in Boulogne. He was on good terms with the Queen, who corresponded with him occasionally and, in 1311, helped him obtain the release of the Chamberlain of North Wales, who had been imprisoned on a false charge. When Edward sent Mortimer to Ireland in the autumn of 1308, he deprived himself of a valuable ally.

By the spring of 1308, the Queen's antagonism toward Gaveston was well known. In May, incensed at the reports of Evreux and Valois, Philip IV sent envoys to England to let it be known that, unless Gaveston left the kingdom, he would "pursue as his mortal enemies" all who supported him. At the behest of her father and brothers, Isabella covertly offered her support to Gaveston's enemies. It has been claimed that she was one of the leaders of the baronial opposition, but her youth makes this implausible. More likely, the barons were happy to exploit her plight for their own purposes.

Wanting to establish a channel of communication between himself and his daughter, Philip sent a clerk, Ralph de Rosseleti, to guard Isabella's Privy Seal and control her correspondence. Rosseleti probably operated as a spy, keeping his master informed about her situation. Philip was angry because she had no money. He had had to raise money through taxation for her wedding and dowry, which had prompted many complaints and angry refusals on the part of his subjects. Now Edward had reduced her to penury, having failed to provide her with a dower or even small sums for her daily expenses. She was entirely dependent on him and obliged to live in his household, without a separate establishment of her own. He had given her no presents or shown her any mark of favor, apart from granting three pardons to criminals at her instance; yet he had not ceased to shower Gaveston with lands, gifts, and grants. Philip was determined to resolve the situation by uniting all Gaveston's opponents in one cohesive party. A monk of Westminster observed at this time that whatever concerned Gaveston, "the Queen, the earls, the Pope and the King of France would wish to impede it."[5]

Edward had troubles enough without further antagonizing his formidable father-in-law. On May 14, he assigned "his dearest consort" the counties of Ponthieu and Montreuil in dower.[6] Philip was partly mollified. Four days later, Edward capitulated to Parliament's demands and agreed to strip Gaveston of his title and banish him from his realm by Midsummer Day. Archbishop Winchelsey warned that Piers would be excommunicated if he stayed in England one hour too long.

Edward, Isabella, and Gaveston were at Langley together on June 4, when the King, in defiance of his submission to Parliament, granted Piers castles, manors, and lands in Gascony, and appointed him lieutenant of Ireland, to the barons' chagrin. With devastating naivety, he wrote in vain to King Philip, begging him to ask his magnates to bring about a concord over Gaveston. He also urged the Pope to annul Winchelsey's threat to excommunicate him.

Isabella remained at Langley when Edward left for Bristol with Piers to see him off on a ship bound for Dublin. On the day he sailed, June 25, the King took his earldom of Cornwall into his own hands until such time as he should return. During his time in Ireland, Gaveston proved an efficient deputy. But Edward was bereft and miserable, and badgered his barons to agree to Piers's return, trying to bend them to his will with gifts and promises.

On July 14, Isabella left Edward at Windsor and made a short pilgrimage to the shrine of Becket at Canterbury. She was probably at Northampton when Parliament met there on August 4. By then, Edward was enjoying better relations with his barons and, later that month, Isabella entertained some of them at a great feast at Westminster. By September, Edward was reconciled to most of his leading nobles. With Gaveston out of the way, he was treating Isabella with greater respect and allowing her to take her rightful place as queen of England. She now appeared constantly at her husband's side and traveled everywhere with him. She also began to exercise the patronage that was her queenly prerogative. Edward made lavish grants of money and manors to her and gave her the right to appoint priests and clerks to benefices.

They spent Christmas together at Windsor with great solemnity. At the beginning of March 1309, Isabella dined with Richmond, Gloucester, and other royalist earls at Westminster. In March and April, to sweeten her and her father in preparation for Gaveston's recall, Edward assigned her further grants and privileges and immediate payment of all the queengold—the tenth due to her on voluntary fines paid to the King— that had accrued since her marriage.

That spring, Edward took Berkhamsted Castle and three manors from Queen Marguerite and gave them to Piers, which—in the light of later events—probably infuriated her. In March, the King wrote to the Pope informing him that the barons were now ready to agree to Gaveston's return because he had promised certain administrative reforms in return. But he was deluding himself. When Parliament met at Westminster on April 27, it refused his request outright. But the King bided his time. When, in June, he received a Papal bull quashing Archbishop Winchelsey's threat of excommunication and paving the way for Gaveston's sentence of banishment to be lifted, he had the satisfaction of reading it aloud before a tight-lipped Winchelsey, who knew he had been bested.

The King summoned Gaveston home. "Rejoicing at his return," he met him at Chester on June 27, "very thankfully receiving him with honour as his brother" as Piers arrived "exulting and in state."[7] In July, at a Parliament at Stamford, most peers grudgingly gave their formal assent to Gaveston's homecoming. "None of the barons now dared to raise a finger against Piers. Their ranks wavered and their party, divided against itself, broke up."[8] Edward restored the earldom of Cornwall to Gaveston and wrote to thank the Pope for his assistance.

The uneasy peace between Edward and his barons did not last. Rashly, he allowed Gaveston once more to control the flow of royal patronage. Piers did not bother to hide his contempt for those who had opposed

him, or his triumph at the victory he had scored over them, and "his behaviour was worse than before."[9] He provoked the barons by openly calling them "degrading names." The portly Lincoln was "Burstbelly,"
Lancaster was the "Churl," the "Old Hog," "the Player," or "the Fiddler,"
and Warwick was the "Black Dog of Arden." "Does he call me a dog?"
raged Warwick. "Let him take care lest I bite!"[10] Even Isabella was not
exempt from Gaveston's sarcasm, which incensed the barons, even the
moderate Pembroke. They accused him of appropriating the revenues of
the kingdom to such an extent that the King could not meet the charges
of his court and the Queen lost revenues, provoking her once more to
complain to her father.

By October, baronial hostility to Gaveston was again simmering dangerously and, for safety, the King took Piers and Isabella to York, where
they lodged in the Franciscan friary, which had spacious apartments for
visitors and gardens that stretched as far as the outworks that encircled
nearby Clifford's Tower. Edward summoned Parliament to meet in York
on October 18, but Lancaster, Hereford, Warwick, and others refused to
attend because of Gaveston's presence at the King's side.

Edward, Isabella, and Gaveston left York on November 17 and spent
Christmas at Langley with Queen Marguerite. Presumably a truce had
been called, possibly on Isabella's account. But the fourteen-year-old
Queen seems to have been largely ignored, while her husband and
Gaveston spent their time "fully making up for their earlier absence by
their long-wished-for daily sessions of intimate conversation."[11]

She could not have been blamed for feeling angry and hurt.

When Parliament met in February 1310, its mood was ugly. The barons appeared in arms, prompting a fearful Edward to send Gaveston
back north for safety. He was in a weak position and knew it. Parliament's condemnation of his rule was shattering. He was accused of corruption and extortion, heeding evil counsel, losing Scotland, and
dismembering the Crown without the lords' assent, this last being a direct reference to Gaveston, whom the barons described as "their chief
enemy, who was lurking in the King's chamber."[12]

There was worse to come: on March 16, the barons demanded that
Edward agree to the appointment of a controlling committee comprised
of twenty-one "Lords Ordainers," whose brief would be to draw up ordi-

nances for the reform of abuses within the government and the royal household; their real agenda, however—of which Edward was aware—was to place restraints on him, undermining the royal prerogative. He protested strongly, but the barons held firm, telling him that unless he cooperated, "they would no longer hold him as their King, nor keep the fealty they had sworn to him, since he himself would not keep the oath which he had sworn at his coronation."[13] He had no choice but to capitulate.

The names of the Ordainers were announced the next day. Foremost among the hardliners were Lancaster, Warwick, and Archbishop Winchelsey, yet the moderate Pembroke, Lincoln, and Gilbert de Clare, Earl of Gloucester, were also appointed. That same day, Queen Marguerite's dower properties were returned to her. Edward desperately strove to reassert his authority and, to placate the barons, announced his intention of leading a campaign against the Scots. His other motive for going north was to establish his court away from London.

In July, Gaveston rode north to prepare for the Scottish campaign. The Queen left London at the beginning of August. Having appointed Lincoln Keeper of the Realm, Edward followed in September and was reunited with Gaveston at Berwick, whence the English army marched into Scotland. The campaign proved a humiliating failure, for Robert the Bruce had laid waste the Scottish Lowlands. Faced with starvation, the English were forced to retreat.

Edward stayed at Berwick with Isabella and Gaveston until the following July. Heading the list of Isabella's four ladies in attendance was eighteen-year-old Eleanor de Clare, the wife of Hugh le Despenser the Younger. She was the Queen's principal lady-in-waiting and a great favorite with Edward. Among those serving alongside her were Isabella de Vesci, her brother Henry de Beaumont, and his wife, Alice Comyn. The ladies received no wages, but were entitled to allowances for ceremonial winter and summer robes. Since most of them had families and feudal responsibilities, they attended the Queen in shifts. They did not just wait on their mistress, but attended to business matters for her, and four had pages to assist them in their duties. Isabella was also attended by at least nine unmarried damsels, among whom were her and Edward's former nurses, Théophania de Saint-Pierre and Alice Leygrave.

After Christmas, Gaveston surrendered to Isabella the rich wardship of Thomas Wake, heir to the barony of Liddell. He was now constantly in her company and needed her goodwill.

On Lincoln's death in February 1311, Lancaster inherited the earldoms of Lincoln and Salisbury, making him the richest and most powerful of the magnates. His arrogance was such that, when he went north to pay homage to the King for them, he forced Edward to cross the River Tweed to come to him, rather than cross it himself, as courtesy demanded, and then pointedly ignored Gaveston. He now emerged as the natural leader of the Ordainers, by virtue of his birth and wealth. He saw himself as a political reformer like Simon de Montfort, who had established Parliament in the previous century; he aimed to save the kingdom from misgovernment and control the King. He would prove a dangerous enemy.

By the summer, the Ordainers had drawn up their proposed reforms and required the King's presence in the capital. Reluctantly, on June 16, Edward summoned Parliament to London. At the end of July, he left Berwick, having appointed Gaveston his lieutenant in Scotland. But Piers was unable to make any inroads there and, having provoked a series of savage Scottish raids into northern England, he withdrew to Bamburgh Castle in Northumberland.

On August 3, the Lords Ordainers sent a list of forty-one ordinances to the King. To his dismay, he saw that they were determined to limit his power: he was not allowed to grant land, go to war, or even leave the realm without the consent of the barons in Parliament. His bankers, the Frescobaldi, were banished—and ruined—and his financial privileges curtailed. The list of prohibitions was long. This was shocking enough, but Edward was far more distressed by Ordinance 20, which demanded that Gaveston be permanently exiled as a public enemy of the King and his subjects. Desperately he tried to bargain with the Ordainers, offering to agree to all their provisions on condition that his "brother Piers" was allowed to remain with him. But the barons were implacable. "Coaxing them with flattery" and "hurling threats" had no effect.[14]

Isabella had followed Edward south, joining him in London around August 21. Her household book shows that, during her journey, she dictated letter after letter to several people, including the Bishop of Durham and the Keeper of the King's Wardrobe. This correspondence was to continue when she returned to court. Her letters are lost, but it might be inferred that she was trying to win support for Edward.

She brought in her train a Scottish orphan boy, "little Thomeline," for she had been "moved by piety of heart by his miseries." In London, she gave him "sustenance and clothing"[15] and found him a home with the wife of one of her French musicians; she also provided for his keep and small necessities and had him cured of sores on his head. Her care for him reveals an innate kindness, and perhaps a frustrated longing for a child of her own, which can only have fueled her unhappiness.

Isabella had been brought up to regard kings as virtual autocrats. She cannot have been pleased to learn that her husband's royal prerogatives had been usurped by his barons, and must have had mixed feelings as she watched him agonizing over approving the ordinance that demanded Piers's banishment. Yet he had no choice. The alternative was civil war, and he was in no position to win. Given Marguerite's concerns about Gaveston, Isabella perhaps confided her anxieties in a letter she wrote to the Dowager Queen, then at Devizes Castle in Wiltshire, on September 4.

The Ordinances were publicly proclaimed on September 27 in St. Paul's Churchyard in London, and Archbishop Winchelsey threatened to excommunicate anyone who dared to violate them. Three days later, Edward agreed to them all, without exception. On October 8, determined to spend as much time as possible with Piers before their parting, he issued a safe conduct and summoned him. They had only until All Saints' Day, November 1, when Piers was to leave England forever. In accordance with the Ordinances, the King was forced to strip him of the earldom of Cornwall. Defiantly, he placed it in the hands of Piers's cousin, Bernard de Calhau.

On October 9, Isabella left London to go on another pilgrimage to Becket's shrine, running up a huge sum in expenses. From Canterbury, she sent a messenger to France with letters for her brother Charles and other lords and ladies. When she arrived at Eltham on October 19, she dispatched a letter to John de Warenne, Earl of Surrey, "with great haste."[16] Possibly she was again building bridges on the King's behalf. Her household book lists many more letters sent during the weeks prior to Christmas; several were concerned only with domestic issues, but, given the names of some of the recipients, others are likely to have been prompted by the political situation.

Edward had sent envoys to ask King Philip for support against the Ordainers, and it was to sweeten him and "comfort"[17] Isabella that he joined her at Eltham before October 29 and granted her two manors and Eltham itself, Bishop Bek having died and bequeathed it to the King. Over the coming years, Isabella would make various improvements. In 1315, the royal apartments were refurbished; they contained two halls, chapels for the King and Queen, and a bath house. From the windows, she could see the spire of St. Paul's Cathedral. The extended palace was built round three courtyards and stood in a hunting park. Isabella had a new stone wall with fifty-six buttresses erected around the moat, but the work was shoddy and the wall had to be rebuilt, while the three masons responsible were briefly imprisoned. The foundations of this wall still survive on the northwest side of the Great Court.

On October 29, perhaps in gratitude for Edward's generosity, or at his instance, Isabella wrote to her receiver in Ponthieu "for the affairs of the Earl of Cornwall,"[18] which suggests that she had agreed to shelter Piers in her domains or was willing to transfer funds to him through her officers there. The continuing favor shown by Edward to Isabella now bore fruit, for Philip agreed to issue Gaveston a safe conduct through France, should he need it; he was probably all too eager to get him as far away from England as possible. Their frequent exchanges of messengers show that the Queen was keeping her father closely informed of events in England and receiving advice from him.

On November 3, Gaveston left England under guard. The next day, Parliament met at Westminster and the Ordinances were promulgated. The Queen was present when her friends Henry de Beaumont, Isabella de Vesci, and several officers of the King's household and her own were dismissed from court, the Beaumonts having been censured for giving evil counsel to the King. Isabella may have expressed her anger at their dismissal in letters she sent that month to her father, her three brothers, Evreux, Valois, and other magnates.

Gaveston secretly returned to England at the end of November. Hearing rumors that he had been sighted in various places, or was hiding in the royal apartments at Westminster, the barons made the King instigate a search for him. On December 18, having again begged Philip for support, Edward retreated to Windsor, complaining bitterly that the Ordainers were treating him like an idiot. Isabella, already in residence, was a witness to his fury. Her household book records that, on December 26, she paid the clerks of the King's Chancery to make her a copy of the Ordinances for her own use; she was perhaps looking for ways to circumvent them.

By December 21, the King and Queen had returned to Westminster for Christmas. That day, Isabella wrote to Marguerite, who was keeping Yuletide at Berkhamsted.

Gaveston had remained in hiding, but, by Christmas, he had joined the King and Queen at Westminster, making no secret of his presence. Isabella was "greatly moved"[19] to see him back.

Edward and Isabella may have consummated their marriage that Christmas. Married couples, especially royal ones, often waited until the bride had begun menstruating, for it was recognized that pregnancy and childbirth were more hazardous for adolescent girls, and no one wanted to risk a death in childbed where a marriage alliance was at stake. Edward may have been content anyway to wait until Isabella was sixteen. The births of her children were to occur at four-, two-, and three-year intervals, which suggests that he did not visit her bed regularly. It is possible that he chose to mollify her by timing the consummation of their marriage to coincide with Piers's unauthorized return, in order to win her support and that of her father, and also reassure them that Gaveston was no threat to her position. Indeed, the consummation of her marriage may well have contributed to the improvement in her relations with Gaveston. Thrown into his company as she often was, she had perhaps come to find him an amusing companion, and not as menacing as she had earlier feared.

3

"Not the Least Pity"

✳

O N DECEMBER 30, THE KING TOOK CONTROL OF THE GREAT
Seal of England, which was normally held by the Lord Chancellor
or Lord Keeper and used to authenticate documents of the highest importance, signifying royal approval. Edward had resolved to reassert his
authority, build up his own party, and escape from bondage.

Isabella stood with him. In January 1312, demonstrating that she
was not to be dictated to, she sent New Year's gifts of wild boar meat to
Lancaster and Hereford, and to Isabella de Vesci, who received Brie
cheese as well. Isabella also gave various choice foodstuffs as New Year's
gifts to Gaveston's wife, who was pregnant, again suggesting that she
had thawed toward Piers or was making an effort to please her troubled
husband.

The King had decided that he would be better able to assert his authority and protect Gaveston if he moved the seat of government to York.
Leaving Isabella behind, he and Piers left London on January 7. Then he
conceived a scheme to seek a safe refuge for Piers in Scotland, even asking his arch-enemy, Robert the Bruce, to give him sanctuary. Bruce refused, saying, "If the King of England will not keep faith with his own
people, how then will he keep faith with me?" "Thus was the King's hope
shattered."[1]

Edward and Gaveston reached York by January 18. The King returned
Gaveston's forfeited estates and sent orders to London that public proc-
lamation be made at the Guildhall that his "good and loyal"[2] Piers
Gaveston had now returned at the royal command, having been exiled

contrary to the laws of England. He also restored the confiscated property of Isabella de Vesci and Henry de Beaumont. On January 27, he announced that only the Ordinances that were not prejudicial to his prerogative should be observed. Then he began preparing for the civil war that seemed inevitable.

Isabella had arrived in York by February 24, in time to be present with the King at the christening of Gaveston's newborn daughter Joan in the Franciscan friary. In March, Edward was able to impart to King Philip the happy news that Isabella was "in good health and will (God propitious) be fruitful."[3] Isabella sent letters, probably announcing her pregnancy, to Queen Marguerite, the Countess of Pembroke, and Edward's sister, the nun Mary.

It was not an auspicious time to be expecting an heir to the throne. Gaveston's recall by the King had been tantamount to a declaration of war, and by March, the barons had taken up arms. Lancaster, Warwick, Pembroke, and the earls of Arundel and Hereford all swore to kill Piers if they laid hands on him. That month, the lords assembled at St. Paul's to witness a wrathful Archbishop Winchelsey strike Piers with anathema for having contravened the Ordinances. Meanwhile, Isabella was writing numerous letters, some to the chief Ordainers. Given that she would soon earn a reputation as a peacemaker, she was probably trying to mediate with the opposition.

On March 17, Gaveston was at Scarborough Castle, surveying the fortifications. Soon afterward, Edward granted it to him, to hold against all comers. In York, at Easter, the King and Queen observed a tradition established by Edward I. In the morning, Alice Leygrave, Edward's old nurse, and the Queen's damsels burst in on him as he lay in bed, dragged him out of it and made him their prisoner, forcing him to pay a ransom before they would release him to join the Queen in bed, this being the first day on which sex was permitted after the Lenten fast. Amidst much laughter, Edward paid them a generous sum. The fact that this interlude took place at all shows that the household knew that the royal marriage had been consummated.

But Lancaster and his private army were now closing in on York. On April 5, having summoned troops from Gascony, Edward fled north with Gaveston to Newcastle, abandoning his pregnant Queen. His first priority was to protect Gaveston, and he may have reasoned that Isabella had little to fear from her uncle of Lancaster, although he must have known that she would be a valuable hostage.

She knew it too. She departed from York in such a hurry that she left her wardrobe behind. She stayed four nights in Thirsk, perhaps needing to rest on account of her pregnancy, and arrived at Newcastle before April 22. Only then did she send for her belongings. Because Gaveston was ill and possibly infectious, Edward sent her to Tynemouth Priory for safety, knowing that she could escape by sea if necessary. Perched upon a clifftop overlooking the North Sea, the priory dated from the seventh century, but its fabric was Norman. Nearby stood one of the largest castles in England, both castle and priory being surrounded by a curtain wall. Yet, fortified though it was, Tynemouth was highly vulnerable to Scottish raids or attack from the sea—the priory had once been destroyed by Viking invaders—so Isabella was by no means safe there. On April 27, she wrote to her father and various French lords, doubtless to tell them of her plight.

On May 4, having taken York, Lancaster's army surprised Edward and Gaveston at Newcastle, whence they just managed to escape, leaving behind their baggage, clothes, jewels, and horses. Lancaster occupied Newcastle and seized Gaveston's wife and baby and all his goods, among which were precious ornaments given to Edward by Isabella. While he was making an inventory of them, Edward and Piers had sailed down the River Tyne to Tynemouth. There, on May 10, fearing that Lancaster would lay siege to the castle and priory, they decided to flee. "Though the pregnant Queen, with many tears" had begged Edward "to stay with her, he had not the least pity for her, but, taking Piers, sailed to Scarborough."[4] There, he left Gaveston to hold the castle and made for York, hoping to raise an army.

For the second time, Isabella had been abandoned. Lancaster sent her a secret message, reassuring her that the barons intended her no harm and that their sole object was to secure the person of the favorite. He said he would not visit her, "lest he should awaken the King's anger against her,"[5] but he would not rest until Gaveston had been driven from the King's society. It is unlikely that Isabella received the message, since she fled from Tynemouth soon after Edward and Gaveston had sailed away, leaving most of her possessions at South Shields so that she could make speedier progress; they were not retrieved for several weeks. She made her way south to York, where she rejoined the King on May 16.

The Lords Ordainers' army, under the command of Pembroke, had laid siege to Scarborough, ignoring the King's commands to desist. Unable to hold out due to lack of provisions, Gaveston surrendered to Pembroke on May 19, on very generous terms. He was to be held under house arrest at his own castle of Wallingford until he could give Parliament an account of his actions. If Parliament had not decided his fate by August 1, or he disputed its verdict, he would be free to return to Scarborough; in the meantime, his men could hold the castle for him. Pembroke himself swore on the Gospels, on pain of forfeiture of his estates, to keep his prisoner safe until August 1.

Piers was taken to York, where he had a brief meeting with the King, and then escorted south toward Wallingford. On June 9, he was brought to Deddington, Oxfordshire, where Pembroke arranged for him to lodge in the rectory. As Pembroke's wife was staying nearby, he rode off to spend the night with her, leaving his prisoner—as he thought—safely under guard.

Warwick, however, had learned of Gaveston's whereabouts. Early in the morning of June 10, he surrounded the rectory with soldiers and had him dragged out, half dressed, and taken under guard to Warwick Castle. Barefoot, stripped of his belt of knighthood, and deafened by blaring trumpets, he was compelled to walk through Deddington, running the gauntlet of a jeering, taunting mob. Only outside the town was he allowed to mount a mule, a sorry steed for one who had been such a great earl and the King's beloved.

At Warwick, Gaveston was thrown into a dungeon and bound with chains. The King was distraught when he heard and dashed off frantic letters to Philip IV and the Pope, beseeching them to intervene with the barons, and even offering them joint possession of Gascony if they could save Gaveston's life.

Isabella knew nothing of these events. She had left York for Selby, Beverley (the roof boss in the cathedral may commemorate her visit), and Burstwick, where Edward joined her.

When Lancaster, Hereford, Arundel, and other magnates arrived at Warwick, they debated with Warwick what to do with Gaveston. Everyone agreed that he should be put to death, and that the proceedings should be cloaked with a semblance of legality. Warwick did not want to be implicated in the killing of Gaveston, so Lancaster, "being of higher birth and more powerful than the rest, took upon himself the full peril of the business."

"While he lives, there will be no safe place in the realm of England, as many proofs have hitherto shown us," he declared.[6] There was a travesty of a trial in the presence of two hastily summoned royal justices. Gaveston was not allowed to speak in his own defense. It was Lancaster, presiding over the hearing, who ordered his execution. Pembroke, who had given his oath to keep Gaveston safe and stood to lose his estates if he broke it, tried in vain to persuade the other Ordainers to release him.

At three o'clock on the morning of June 19, Gaveston was dragged from his dungeon and handed over by Warwick to Lancaster, who told him that he was to be beheaded as befitted a nobleman. Piers threw himself to his knees and begged for mercy, but he was hastened off to Blacklow Hill, a mile or so north of Warwick, just beyond the boundary of Warwick's estates and on Lancaster's land, because Warwick wished to dissociate himself from what was to happen and stayed behind in his castle. Crowds had gathered to watch the hated favorite pass, blowing horns and shouting for joy to see him brought so low. At Blacklow Hill, he was handed over to two of Lancaster's men, who dragged him up the hill, ignoring his pleas for mercy. One pierced him through the heart with his sword, and the other cut off his head and brought it to Lancaster.

When they brought the news of Gaveston's death to the King, he burst out, "By God's soul, he acted like a fool! If he had taken my advice, he would never have fallen into the hands of the earls." When this "flippant utterance became public, it moved many to derision." But the author of the *Vita Edwardi Secundi* was "certain the King grieved for Piers as a father grieves for his son. For the greater the love, the greater the sorrow."[7] And to grief was added deadly rage, as Edward vowed to destroy those who had killed Gaveston and avenge his murder. His "mortal and perpetual hatred"[8] for them and his need for vengeance were to dominate his life for years to come.

Gaveston's assassination split the barons' party, removing the threat of civil war. It brought an angry Pembroke, still smarting at that broken oath, over to the King, and the younger Despenser and others with him. It led to the emergence of the elder Despenser, whom Lancaster loathed, as leader of the court party that supported Edward. There were many who rejoiced in the fall of the favorite—"the death of one man had never before been acceptable to so many"[9]—but others felt strongly that the Lords Ordainers had acted unlawfully. Consequently, there was considerable sympathy for the King. Edward was now in a stronger position than he had been since his accession.

Isabella returned to York. Finding that Edward had hastened south the day before, she wrote to him. She stayed in York until the end of July, when he sent an escort to conduct her to Westminster. He was then taking counsel of his loyal advisers as to what action he should take against Gaveston's murderers. Pembroke and Surrey were urging him to declare outright war on these "traitors,"[10] and for a time it appeared that Edward was preparing for a military confrontation. He put his defenses in order and asked King Philip and Pope Clement V for help. But Parliament wanted peace. When Lancaster, Warwick, and Hereford marched on London in arms, intent on facing down the King, they were forbidden to enter the City. While Lancaster was determined to force Edward to observe the Ordinances, Edward wanted him and Warwick tried and executed. Only the mediation of Gloucester averted a military confrontation.

Isabella returned to London on September 9. Her father, spurred on by news of the murder of the favorite, letters from Queen Marguerite, and a visit from a smarting Pembroke, responded to Edward's request by sending Louis of Evreux to England with a team of lawyers to help bring about a peace between the King and his barons, and the Pope sent legates to assist. Evreux had arrived by September 15, when he dined with Isabella. She played her part in the negotiations, supporting Gloucester, the legates, and the bishops in their efforts to bring about a reconciliation, but feelings ran high on both sides and the parleying went on for weeks.

When Isabella was seven months pregnant, she retired to Windsor to await the birth of her child. There she was joined by Queen Marguerite, who stayed to be present at the birth. The King visited them in the middle of September, probably bringing Evreux with him. He granted Isabella permission to make a will, in which she made provision for the founding of a hospital for the poor, for the salvation of her soul and Edward's.

At 5:40 a.m. on the morning of St. Brice's Day, November 13, 1312, she gave birth to a strong, handsome son, attended by King Philip's own physician, Henri de Mondeville, and a husband-and-wife team of midwives, John and Isabel Launge, who were paid £24 ($19,850). The King was so delighted to have a son that he bestowed £20 ($16,500) and a life pension of £80 ($66,300) on the Queen's squire who brought him the joyful news, and promptly created Queen Marguerite's son Thomas earl of Norfolk.

Hours later, it being traditional for the Queen to announce the birth of an heir, a triumphant Isabella had the glad tidings proclaimed in London:

> Isabella, by the grace of God, Queen of England, Lady of Ireland and Duchess of Aquitaine, to our well-beloved the Mayor and aldermen and the commonalty of London, greeting. Forasmuch as we believe that you would willingly hear good tidings of us, we do make known to you that our Lord, of His grace, has delivered us of a son, on the 13th day of November, with safety to ourselves, and to the child. May our Lord preserve you.
>
> Given at Windsor, on the day above-named.[11]

Isabella, Evreux, and the French lords in his train wanted the heir to be called after St. Louis or King Philip, but Edward and the nobles would not allow it and insisted that he be named after the sainted Confessor and his father and grandfather, a decision that greatly pleased the King's subjects. London erupted in celebration; the Mayor and aldermen led the dancing in the streets, and tuns of free wine were provided so that the citizens could drink to the health of the royal mother and child. The festivities continued day and night for a week.

On November 17, Prince Edward was baptized with much pomp in Henry III's chapel, in the presence of an august company that included Queen Marguerite. Cardinal Arnaud Novelli, one of the Papal legates, officiated, and the child had no fewer than seven godfathers: Evreux, the earls of Richmond and Pembroke, the archbishop of Poitiers, the bishops of Worcester and Bath and Wells, and Hugh le Despenser the Elder. On November 24, the proud father created his son earl of Chester, a title he had himself borne before his accession, and which is still borne by the Prince of Wales today.

"To some extent" the birth of the Prince "soothed the King's grief for Piers's death."[12] It boosted public support for Edward and put a stop, for the time being, to Lancaster's scheming to undermine royal authority. On December 20, thanks to the continuing efforts of Evreux and the Papal legates, the King and the magnates agreed to a peace; Gaveston's killers were humbly to beg the King's pardon and return to him all Piers's treasure, which they had seized at Newcastle; in return, he was to grant them a free pardon. This must have been galling to Edward, who wanted to wreak a bloody vengeance on those who had murdered his favorite. Nevertheless, it was proclaimed that the King and the lords were now at peace. "And so the dispute died down, but neither party had obtained what it had sought."[13]

Immediately after the Queen's churching at Isleworth on December 24, she and the King went to Windsor for Christmas. Beneath the surface gaiety, tensions and enmity simmered. By January 1313, cracks were appearing in the fragile façade of friendship, as Lancaster and Warwick published a list of twenty objections to the peace, and Lancaster declared that he would not hand over Gaveston's treasure unless the King acknowledged that Piers was a common felon and undertook to maintain the Ordinances. This led to further wrangles, with Hereford acting as a go-between and Edward vehemently refusing to accede to Lancaster's demands.

Late in January, the King and Queen returned to London, leaving the Prince in the care of his nurse, Margaret Chandler. Young Edward spent his infancy at Bisham Priory, where Isabella visited him in May 1313 and Queen Marguerite in June 1314.

On February 4, a pageant was staged in London in the Queen's honour by the Fishmongers' Guild. "They caused a boat to be fitted out in the guise of a great ship, with all manner of tackle that belongs to a ship; and it sailed through Cheap[side] as far as Westminster, where the fishmongers came, well mounted and costumed very richly, and presented the ship to the Queen." The guild members were wearing a livery of linen shot with gold and embroidered with the arms of England and France; the Mayor, aldermen, and guildsmen wore their ceremonial robes. After the pageant, members of the Fishmongers' Company escorted Isabella to Eltham Palace, the procession being preceded by the model ship "with mast and sail erect."[14] The Queen then made another pilgrimage to Canterbury, to give thanks to St. Thomas for her safe delivery of a son.

4

"A Special Kind of Love"

✳

As MOTHER OF THE HEIR TO THE THRONE, ISABELLA'S POSI-
tion was now secure, and her influence with the King considerably
greater. At seventeen, she was blossoming into a beautiful and charming
woman. Always conscious of her status as a princess of France, she was to
be diligent in promoting friendly relations between the two kingdoms.

She was proud, ambitious, materialistic, acquisitive, and jealous of her
dignity and the privileges of her high status. She was also tenacious, resolute, strong-willed, intelligent, and wise. She could be kind and thoughtful, and was extremely generous to her household staff. She was active
and often successful in exercising patronage, especially in the bestowal of
grants and honors and the preferment of her servants. Her intercessions
on behalf of others were frequent—seventy-nine in all—and she obtained
for herself lands, castles, manors, towns, honors, boroughs, wardships,
knights fees, sheriffdoms, and fines.

Isabella was healthy, energetic, and forever on the move, her household in tow. Her four known children survived into adulthood, in an age
in which approximately one third of children died in childhood and the
average age of life expectancy for a man was thirty-five; for women it was
less, given that many perished in childbed.

Edward had generously provided Isabella with a magnificent household of about 180 persons. She had a chaplain, a physician, and two
apothecaries. Her almoner dispensed charity on her behalf daily and on
feast days. The most important servants were the senior officers: the
Queen's steward and her wardrobe keeper (or treasurer), who were re-

sponsible for running her household and supervising her expenditure. They were assisted by the comptroller and the cofferer. These four officers formed the core of the Queen's council, which dealt with the administration of her household and estates. The Queen's wardrobe, which was based in a building known as the Tower Royal (or La Reole) by St. Paul's Cathedral, supplied them with ink, parchment for her household books and memoranda, a checkerboard for reckoning, and a pair of scales for weighing silver.

The Queen's household was divided into several departments, or offices: the hall, chamber, pantry, buttery, kitchen, scullery, ewery, napery, and saucery, and the Marshalsea, which was responsible for her chargers and palfreys. A smith ensured that her horses were properly shod. When she traveled, she was afforded the services of six carters, thirty-nine grooms and harbingers (who rode ahead to commandeer accommodation, if necessary, and ensure that all was in readiness for the Queen's arrival), twenty-five palfreymen, twenty-two sumptermen to load baggage, porters, outriders of the Queen's carts, and three keepers of the hackneys.

Isabella's kitchen staff was headed by three cooks for her household and one who prepared food exclusively for her. Drinks and bread were provided by her butler and pantler, and a clerk of the spicery, waferer, saucerer, and various scullions assisted the cooks.

The Queen also employed two sergeants-at-arms, an usher and a marshal of her hall, pages, five messengers, two watchmen, ten clerks to whom she dictated her correspondence (for queens in this period did not write their own letters), and a chandler who provided wax for candles and seals. She had a fool called Michael, a courier of the wardrobe, and several laundresses and washerwomen. For her protection, she was assigned several household knights and twenty-eight squires.

Isabella's receiver collected the revenues from her lands and other assets. Many officials administered her estates: stewards, bailiffs, castellans, and the keepers of her manors and forests. Like the King, she enjoyed the right of purveyance—the right to buy a wide selection of goods below market price, a practice not popular with merchants or with local people who had to pay higher prices, and easily open to abuse.

Edward provided well for Isabella. His wardrobe was responsible for her household finances, and he himself supplied the jewels, cloths of gold, and Turkey carpets she gave as gifts and offerings. The only gift she paid for herself during her marriage was a gold nugget she offered at the shrine of Becket. She lived in luxury and wanted for nothing in a material sense. The King allowed her to overspend by up to £10,000 ($6.2 million) each year. With her vast landed assets scattered throughout north Wales and seventeen English counties, and her generous income, she was as great a feudal magnate as any of the earls.

Isabella had strong cultural interests. She shared with Edward a love of music, kept an organist called Jean, and paid for one of her watchmen to go to London to receive musical training. Together, she and Edward spent vast sums on musical entertainment. She was interested in art and possessed three panels of Lombard work, which were presumably sculptured reliefs, as well as ten Italian paintings.

She was an avid reader. Throughout her life, she collected exquisitely illuminated manuscripts in the latest taste. Her library, which numbered thirty books when she died, included manuscripts of the Arthurian legends, reflecting her fascination with the chivalric myths of King Arthur; one was bound in white leather. She owned a copy of *The Brut* chronicle and a royal genealogy. Edward gave her Vegetius's *De Re Militari,* which Eleanor of Castile had commissioned for Edward I. Between 1322 and 1341, Isabella would acquire eight histories and romances, among them tales of the Trojan War, Charlemagne, Tristan and Yseult, and Aimeri of Narbonne. She also borrowed many books (among them a history of Normandy) from the royal library at the Tower of London.

Three missals, two books of hours, a breviary, a book of homilies, two graduals, a martyrology, and an ordinal (service book) testify to her piety. The heraldic emblems in the Isabella Psalter, dating from 1303–8, show that it belonged to her and was perhaps made as a wedding gift. It has also been credibly suggested that the so-called Queen Mary's Psalter, a vividly illuminated English manuscript produced around 1310–20, was Isabella's too; it contains many prominent illustrations of Biblical queens and noblewomen. We know, again from heraldic evidence, that Isabella had a French Apocalypse, or Book of Revelation, which was perhaps given to her by her father, and she may have been the owner of two beautifully illuminated psalters that are now in the Bayerische Staatsbibliothek in Munich.

She treasured several sacred relics. For the Easter service of Tenebrae, the clerk of the Queen's chapel acquired a large wooden figure of Judas to hold the twelve Paschal candles that would be snuffed out, one by one, to symbolize the disciples abandoning Jesus. Among the chapel furnishings were two alabaster statues, one of the Virgin and another, broken, of St. Stephen. There were cushions and kneelers embroidered with monkeys and butterflies, a dorsal of worsted painted with a Nativity scene, and a painted wall hanging showing the Apocalypse. Isabella gave gifts of clothing and jewelery to various churches, and, in January 1312, sent some cloth to a hermit who lived in Windsor Forest, so that he could make himself a chasuble. In Canterbury Cathedral, she donated a great window depicting St. Thomas Becket, which was destroyed in the seventeenth century. She visited the shrine of Our Lady of Walsingham, which was especially popular with mothers-to-be and those desiring a child. Like many queens before her, she was patroness of the Royal Hospital of St. Katharine by the Tower of London, which had been founded in the twelfth century by Matilda of Scotland, wife of Henry I.

The royal couple were great patrons of the Dominican Order, but Isabella, like Queen Marguerite, had a special affection for the Franciscans, who, through their emotive preaching, were inspiring the laity to practice personal devotional rituals and attracting the interest of many influential people. Inspired by the life and teachings of St. Francis of Assisi, the friars were forbidden to own property, and had to earn their living by work or begging. All Isabella's confessors were Franciscans, and she was a great benefactor of the Franciscan houses at Bishop's (King's) Lynn, Coventry, and Newgate. In 1344, she gave land in Coventry to the Guild of St. Mary for the founding of the Guild's chapel in the collegiate church dedicated to St. John the Baptist. The magnificent Guildhall, begun in her lifetime, still stands today.

Isabella liked to dress fashionably and introduced French styles of costume that were so widely copied that her influence on fashion could still be detected in the middle of the fourteenth century. She popularized the sideless surcoat, which was worn over the gown (or kirtle) and trimmed with fur. She favored the pelicon, a voluminous fur-lined mantle with slits in front for the arms, wearing hers with a great cowled hood falling over her shoulders, as depicted in a manuscript illustration of her in the Bodleian Library, Oxford. This same picture shows her wearing a crown and a diaphanous gauze veil over netted cauls, without the chin barbe shown in other representations of her. Isabella and her ladies also set a trend for gowns of a lower cut than had been seen for centuries. Details of her clothes appear in her wardrobe accounts, which survive for the period 1314–15. Her tailor, John de Falaise, employed no fewer than sixty workmen for making, maintaining, beating, cleaning, and repairing her clothes. In 1311–12, he supplied fifteen robes, thirty pairs of stockings, thirty-six pairs of shoes, three cloaks, another cloak of linsey woolsey (a blend of wool and linen imported from Florence), six hoods, six bodices, a pelicon of triple sindon, and a tunic of Luccan silk. He also made the hangings for the Queen's chapel and scarlet ones for her bed.

The Queen's two goldsmiths supplied her with jewelry, melted down her old plate and refashioned it anew, and carried out repairs. When not in use, her plate, rich robes, and other valuables were locked up in great leather strongboxes and coffers bound with iron and kept in her wardrobe.

Each notable occasion was marked by the purchase of a new chaplet of gold, one being set with rubies, sapphires, emeralds, diamonds, and pearls. When Isabella attended the wedding of one of her damsels, she wore a new golden circlet and a girdle of silk studded with silver and encrusted with 300 rubies and 1,800 pearls. On the Feast of the Purification of the Virgin Mary in 1312, she appeared in a beautiful cloak adorned with fifty gold knots (decorative bows or loops). Five hundred silver-gilt knots were attached to other garments made for her.

Entries in her household book show that Isabella's favorite dishes were oysters, pigeons, venison, pickerels (small pike), and pottage (a thick soup or stew) with beans; she particularly enjoyed cheese and fruit. Some was imported for the royal table by Italian merchants, who also supplied oriental spices, while one William of Writtle delivered to her pears, cherries, and apples. Isabella enjoyed sweetmeats, which were made by her apothecary, who also bought cloves for flavoring and medicinal use, and mixed cordials for the Queen. The household book reveals that she and her retinue drank gallons of wine. She drank water too, owning two silver water pitchers.

Three times a year, at Easter, Whitsuntide, and Christmas, the King held court and gave a great feast, at which he and the Queen wore their crowns, a custom dating from Norman times. There was much revelry after these feasts, with games, theatricals, and disguisings. At other times, the court was entertained by minstrels, jesters, acrobats, and tumblers, while gambling was rife. Isabella enjoyed games of chess, draughts, or "tables" (backgammon) with her ladies. She owned two sets of crystal and jasper chessmen, perhaps those that had belonged to Eleanor of Castile and Marguerite of France. She also regularly partnered Edward for gambling and games of chance. They shared an enthusiasm for hunting and hawking. Isabella owned eight greyhounds and several falcons and hawks. Most of the royal residences had their own hunting parks or were situated in or near the royal forests, which were specifically reserved for the King.

Isabella could never be accounted a major political figure in the years prior to 1325, but her surviving household books reveal that she worked indefatigably behind the scenes, writing an endless stream of letters on both domestic and political issues, many of them to influential people.

For the rest of the time, she lived the traditional life of a medieval queen, gracing state and ceremonial occasions, managing her household, estates, and financial interests, dispensing charity and making benefactions. Above all, she supported her husband. Even though he had done much to forfeit her love and respect, she was exemplary in her devotion, and for this, and her many other evident qualities, she earned the respect and love of the barons and people.

Relations between Edward and Isabella improved after Gaveston's death. No longer did she have to compete for her husband's attentions or endure the humiliation of other people's pity. Nor did she have to suffer a favorite usurping her position. For some years to come, there is no record of any discord between the King and Queen.

Edward appreciated Isabella's good judgment and loyalty. He was happy for her to mediate in political affairs from time to time, especially after it became clear that this was generally beneficial to him. When they were apart, husband and wife corresponded frequently, although Edward's letters were sent under his secret seal, so few survive. If they were not lovers in the truest sense, they had at last achieved an amicable partnership with shared mutual interests and were supportive of each other. To all appearances, theirs was a successful royal marriage.

* * *

When Parliament met in March 1313, some barons declined to attend, furious that the King was still refusing to see Gaveston's execution as lawful punishment for a felon. Yet Edward could count on at least one loyal supporter. Roger Mortimer was at Westminster at this time, having returned from service in Ireland and Gascony.

Philip IV, delighted with the birth of his grandson, had no intention of supporting the English barons any further; from now on, his relations with his son-in-law would be far more cordial. In the spring, he invited Isabella and Edward to Paris for the ceremonial knighting of her brothers. The magnates were concerned about the King leaving England at this critical juncture, with Scottish raids continuing and the issues with Lancaster still unresolved, but in May, their party was weakened by the death of that inflexible adversary of the King, Archbishop Winchelsey. Edward was hoping to replace him with someone more loyal and accommodating.

He and Isabella sailed from Dover on May 23, 1313, with a splendid retinue of 220 persons, leaving Gloucester as Keeper of the Realm. Edward had spent nearly £1,000 ($827,400) on clothes and jewels for the trip. Isabella had a new portable altar for the celebration of Mass during her journey. The royal couple traveled south to Gascony, where they were received with great honor as they passed through the duchy, and then rode north to Paris, arriving on June 1 at the abbey of Saint-Germain-des-Prés, to the west of the city, where apartments had been prepared for them. The next day, they entered the city in state.

On Pentecost Sunday, in a magnificent ceremony, Isabella's three brothers, Louis, Philip, and Charles, were knighted by King Philip. The event was marked by weeks of pageants and feasts, with the two kings and Louis of Evreux acting as hosts; Edward's wine bill for the visit came to £4,468.19s.4d. ($3.7 million). A morality play was staged, entitled *The Glory of the Blessed and the Torments of the Damned*, and Philip's minstrel Hurel played for the guests. Edward rewarded him with 40s. ($1,600). Isabella's brothers staged a satirical puppet show, after which she gave silk purses that she herself had embroidered to her sisters-in-law, Marguerite, Jeanne, and Blanche of Burgundy. On June 9, there was a great parade of—it seemed—all the citizens of Paris, watched by the royal party.

The visit gave the two monarchs an opportunity to discuss business. Edward found Philip most accommodating over Gascony and open-handed when it came to lending money. The fact that Isabella was now the mother of the heir to England and no longer had a rival had much to do with this, and Philip was also keen to underline the diplomatic and dynastic importance of her marriage; she was mentioned in every document detailing his concessions to her husband, and he gave her many gifts. Edward too was lavish in his giving—his present bill came to £3,016.13s.8d. ($2.4 million).

On June 6, both monarchs declared their intention of going on a crusade to free the Holy Land from the Turks, and solemnly took the Cross from the Papal legate. In his sudden enthusiasm for the venture, Edward persuaded Isabella to join them, but, on June 7, having clearly achieved a new intimacy, they overslept after their "night-time dalliances"[1] and missed the ceremony for the ladies who were taking the Cross. Isabella eventually received it on June 13 at Pontoise, yet she was unenthusiastic about fulfilling her vow and agreed to go on crusade only on condition that she do so in company with Edward, probably realizing that he would never make the effort.

At Pontoise, Edward was aroused from sleep when fire swept through their silken pavilion, destroying all their possessions. He got Isabella out, barely escaping with their lives, then, "completely naked," rushed back to save others. According to the contemporary French chronicler Geoffrey de Paris, "Edward had rescued Isabella above all else because he loved her with a special kind of love, which can be called 'courtly love.' Love made him do it."[2]

The term "courtly love" (*amour courtois*) was rarely used in the Middle Ages. From the nineteenth century it has been widely deployed to describe the game and play of love in the Age of Chivalry. The courtly lover existed to serve his chosen lady, who was (theoretically, and in the highest ideals of chivalry) unattainable. Initially he worshipped her from afar, vowing eternal fidelity. If he proved his love with passionate devotion or deeds of chivalry, she might allow him to be her servant, and become his mistress, in the sense of having mastery over him. The object of courtly desire was often married and of higher rank, and such relationships were expected to be chaste, although it was argued that courtly chastity extended to sleeping naked together, but not having sex. Needless to say, consummation was the lover's ultimate reward in many cases, one that called for secrecy and subterfuge. Most scholars held that it was not possible to experience love within marriage, so in Edward's case, the chronicler was probably using the term "courtly love" to describe married love, rather than courtly love as the age understood it.

Escaping from the fire, Isabella suffered burns to her hand and arm. Her apothecary used various remedies to treat them, including green wax, resin, hempseed oil, quicksilver, verdigris, formalin, rose leaves, and plasters, none of which were particularly effective.

After saying farewell to Philip on July 5, the King and Queen traveled back to Wissant. They docked at Dover on July 15, then rode to Westminster. There, to celebrate their return home, they gave a feast, which was attended by some knights of the French court who had accompanied them back to England. Isabella was disconcerted to see, hanging from the belts of two Norman brothers, Philip and Gautier d'Aulnay, the purses she had given her sisters-in-law, Marguerite and Blanche. She is said to have confided her concerns to her father, but she cannot have done so immediately since nothing was done about the matter until the following May. She may have reasoned that the purses could have been given as favors in the game of courtly love. And the knights were wearing them openly.

Shortly afterward, Isabella's apothecary twice supplied her with pennyroyal, which had long been used to stimulate menstruation, as an abortifacient, or to expel a dead fetus. Possibly she had suffered a miscarriage. But pennyroyal was also believed to have many benefits, and was used as a remedy for headaches, dizziness, insect bites, menstrual and joint pain, hysteria, and flatulence, so she could have been suffering from any of these complaints.

In Scotland, Robert the Bruce had been scoring success after success. By the summer, Stirling was the only important Scottish castle left in English hands, and Bruce's men had been laying siege to it since October 1312. Fearing that King Edward would not bestir himself to come to Stirling's defense, the castle's governor reached an agreement with Bruce's brother Edward that if the English had not relieved Stirling by June 24, 1314, he would surrender it to the Scots.

There was much murmuring at the King's failure to counteract the advances made by Bruce and put a stop to the savage raids that were terrorizing the north. "Our King has now reigned six full years, and has till now achieved nothing praiseworthy," observed his biographer, "except that he has married royally and has thereby raised up for himself a handsome son and heir to the throne."[3]

In July, Isabella was at Bisham Priory with little Edward, probably staying in the former preceptory of the Knights Templar. In August, she moved to the Benedictine abbey at Chertsey, renowned for its hospitality to royalty. There, she wrote an affectionate letter to Edward about her affairs in Ponthieu, addressing him as "my very dear and dread lord."[4] The letter shows that she had her finger on the pulse of affairs, was able to prioritize matters of urgency, and could use her political judgment shrewdly and to her husband's advantage. There is also a suggestion that, for all her humble courtesy, she was accustomed privately to giving Edward advice, and it appears that he had come to rely on it. We might infer that she was a stronger and more forceful character than he.

Isabella returned to London in September, when the barons appealed to the King to remit his rancor toward them. "He did not immediately yield, but dragged out the business as usual."[5] During the Parliament that met on September 23, Evreux, Gloucester, and representatives of the Pope all did their best to forge a peace.

In October, news came from Avignon that the Holy Father had appointed the King's candidate, Walter Reynolds, as Archbishop of Canterbury. Queen Marguerite loved Reynolds: "You have always acted well and faithfully to us in all our affairs, for which we thank you from the bottom of our heart and are truly grateful," she once wrote to him. But the chroniclers sneered at the new Archbishop for being a mere clerk and scarcely literate. Yet Edward now had an ally in Canterbury, which considerably strengthened his position.

On October 13, perhaps at the instance of Evreux or Gloucester, Isabella again assumed the role of mediator and "anxiously interceded, striving to calm the feelings of both parties and strenuously attempting to make peace."[6] It was this that finally brought about a concord. The next day, she was present at a formal ceremony of reconciliation in Westminster Hall, in which Lancaster, Warwick, and Hereford knelt before Edward in submission. He gave them the kiss of peace, reminding them that their pardons, and those of 500 of their supporters, had been granted "through the prayers of his dearest companion, Isabella, Queen of England."[7] The reconciliation was marked by two banquets, one given by Edward, the other by Lancaster, but this display of amity would prove to be little more than a veneer.

Isabella was still suffering from the burns she had sustained during the fire at Pontoise. At Westminster, she was attended by two English physicians and two French ones sent by her father, who instructed her apothecary, Peter of Montpellier, to make up herbal plasters and a lotion of rose water and olive oil. In November and December, his assistant, Master Odinet, treated the Queen with ointments, plasters, and enemas.

Impressed by her successful intervention in his quarrel with the magnates, Edward had intended to send her to the Paris Parlement to put forward his case in a dispute over Gascony, but her injuries were so painful that her visit had to be postponed. On November 18, she sent an offering to the shrine of St. Thomas at Canterbury, having intended to go in person on her way to France. She was to be treated for her burns for at least the next two years, which suggests that they were quite serious and probably left her with scarring.

Edward and Isabella spent Christmas at Westminster, before moving to Eltham for the New Year. The King had belatedly resolved to mount a military campaign to relieve Stirling and, in January 1314, he began assembling a mighty army. A victory in Scotland would crown his peace with the barons. When he returned home in triumph, they would be able to gainsay him nothing.

Isabella's burns must have improved, because in the middle of January, she resumed her preparations for a visit to France. The King's councilors, aware of her influence with her father, and impressed by her efforts at peacemaking, were confident that Philip would be unable to resist her intercessions in regard to safeguarding Edward's interests in Gascony. Since she was an unofficial envoy, the King would not be bound by any agreements she made with her father. She was supposed to be going on a private pilgrimage to the shrines at Boulogne, Amiens, Chartres, and other places, yet she was going in great state, as queen and official emissary. At the council's request, the King's banker paid out £3,995 ($3.2 million) for her expenses plus £948.13s. ($785,000) to defray her traveling costs.

Before she left for France, Isabella accompanied Edward to the enthronement of Archbishop Reynolds in Canterbury Cathedral on February 17. Nine days later, the King appointed Gloucester, Henry de Beaumont, William Inge, and Bartholomew de Badlesmere, a Kentish baron, to accompany the Queen to France. Isabella had been receiving briefings from William Inge, who was very knowledgeable about Gascon affairs.

At Sandwich, she and her party boarded a magnificent vessel under the command of William de Montagu; it had been hired with twenty-six other ships and thirteen barges for the Queen and her household. Isabella de Vesci, Eleanor le Despenser, and Edward's niece, Joan of Bar, Countess of Surrey, were among Isabella's entourage. She also took with her fifteen greyhounds, intending to enjoy some hunting during her visit.

She landed at Wissant on March 1 and immediately dispatched a messenger to inform Edward of her safe arrival. Journeying through her county of Ponthieu, she came first to Boulogne, where she prayed at the shrine of Our Lady in the cathedral where she had been married. On March 6, after visiting Montreuil and Crécy, she prayed at shrines at Saint-Riquier and Amiens as she passed through Normandy.

On March 15, on the Île de la Seine, King Philip and his court witnessed the burning of her godfather, Jacques de Molay, the last Grand Master of the Knights Templar, and his associate, Geoffrey de Charnay. It was the final chapter in the French King's purge of the Templars. As Molay was slowly consumed in the fire, he famously cursed King Philip and his descendants to the thirteenth generation and summoned him and Pope Clement V to meet him at God's tribunal before the year was out.

This grim event must have overshadowed Isabella's return to Paris. When she entered the city the next day and again took up residence at Saint-Germain-des-Prés, she immediately made an offering in the abbey. During her stay, she offered up prayers in several churches, and sent offerings to the shrines of St. James the Apostle at Compostela in Spain and St. Brieuc in Brittany.

Isabella presented Philip with seven petitions relating to Gascony, asking him to respond favorably and graciously, so that the duchy would gain profit and Philip honor, enabling her to return happily to Edward.

It is made clear in the rolls of the Paris Parlement, which she attended, that it was her personal intervention that prompted her father to grant some of the petitions and reserve the rest for further consideration. Her initial success paved the way for further negotiations on the part of Edward's commissioners, in which she was not directly involved, but which ultimately ended in failure or stalemate.

While in Paris, Isabella was instrumental in exposing a royal scandal. It was called the affair of the Tour de Nesle, for it was in that tower, on the banks of the Seine, that Marguerite and Blanche of Burgundy, the King's daughters-in-law, had been carrying on adulterous affairs with the brothers d'Aulnay. Blanche's sister, Jeanne of Burgundy, who was married to Philip IV's middle son, Philip, had pleaded with them to desist, but had not thought fit to reveal their treason. Writing around 1317, the French chronicler Geoffrey de Paris stated that, through Isabella, many things were disclosed and revealed to the King that were proved and found true by many people. There is every likelihood that these revelations were connected to the Tour de Nesle affair. Later chroniclers claimed that Isabella was one of the chief witnesses against her sisters-in-law, although Sir Thomas Gray, writing in the 1350s, stated that "many considered this was not true."

The Exchequer records show that during Isabella's visit she had prolonged private discussions with Philip, which may have been political. After she left Paris on March 19, she wrote three letters to her brother Louis and kept in touch with her father, her uncle, and her other brothers. If she did reveal anything about her sisters-in-law, she would surely have felt justified in doing so. Adultery committed by the wife to the heir to the throne placed the royal succession in grave jeopardy, and any man committing adultery with one of these ladies was guilty of treason. But Philip did not rely on hearsay or circumstantial evidence. He decided to have the five suspects watched for a period.

Later in March, Isabella visited Chartres Cathedral, then moved south to make offerings to the image of the Virgin in the basilica at Cléry-Saint-André on the Loire. At each shrine she visited, she presented gifts of rich cloths. She also paused on her travels to purchase a fur and a hanging embroidered with pictures of baboons. Then she came to Saint-Germain-en-Laye, staying until April 16 in the favored summer residence of the kings of France in the vast forest of Saint-Germain, a royal hunting ground for centuries. She paid frequent visits to her father, with ten torchbearers lighting her way each evening.

By now, the King's suspicions about his daughters-in-law had deepened and he ordered an immediate inquiry; when it found against the lovers, his vengeance was terrible. All were arrested. After merciless torture, the d'Aulnay brothers confessed to their crimes, and were condemned to death. In a trial held in camera before the Paris Parlement in April, Marguerite and Blanche also admitted their guilt and were sentenced to life imprisonment. Marguerite's marriage to Louis was immediately annulled and her daughter Jeanne disinherited. Weeping constantly in remorse, and wearing the cowled garb of penitents, with their hair shorn, she and Blanche were shut up in dark dungeons in Château Gaillard in Normandy, the twelfth-century fortress built by Richard I.

Despite the pleas of Blanche's husband, Charles, the Pope refused to annul their marriage. Ten years later, after Blanche had borne a bastard child to her jailer, she was allowed to become a nun, but her health had been broken by the severity of her imprisonment and she died in 1326. Despite having been acquitted, Jeanne was kept under house arrest until 1315 and then received back at court. The d'Aulnay brothers were publicly castrated, their genitals being thrown to the dogs, and partially flayed alive before being broken on the wheel and then mercifully decapitated.

If Isabella had been instrumental in bringing the affair to light, as was believed in France, then her actions argue a latent ruthlessness in her nature, perhaps to be expected of a daughter of Philip IV.

On April 18, as if in fulfillment of Jacques de Molay's curse, the Pope died. It was a superstitious age, and on hearing the news, Isabella may have feared for her father.

On her way home, she revisited her own domains. At Abbeville, she entertained her brother Charles and her uncle, Charles of Valois. Having ridden north via Montreuil and Boulogne, she arrived back at Wissant and took ship for England. On landing at Dover, she was given the unusual gift of a porcupine, which was sent to the royal menagerie in the Tower. She then made her deferred pilgrimage to the shrine of St. Thomas at Canterbury. In April, in gratitude for the good work she had done in France, Edward made a generous award to her, and confirmed to her the reversion of the dower held by Queen Marguerite.

5

"Childish Frivolities"

✳

In June 1314, an immense English army assembled at Wark-on-Tweed in Northumberland, ready to crush the Scots. Lancaster, Warwick, Arundel, and Surrey were conspicuous by their absence, which they were to justify on the grounds that the King had gone to war without the consent of Parliament and in contravention of the Ordinances. But Edward did have the support of Pembroke, Mortimer, and the Despensers.

Isabella rode north to join her husband. On June 14, she arrived at Berwick and was lodged in the castle. She involved herself in the preparations for the campaign and lent Gloucester equipment for his field kitchen.

Three days later, the great army marched forth from Berwick. Robert the Bruce was ready and waiting, his forces drawn up before Stirling at a place called Bannockburn. There, the two armies met. Bruce had 7,000 men to Edward's 20,000, but he knew the terrain. He had deliberately chosen a site surrounded by boggy ground, and had had concealed pits dug, which were to prove lethal to the invading army.

The Battle of Bannockburn was fought over two days, on June 23 and 24, and its outcome was a devastating defeat for the English. The young Earl of Gloucester was among the 4,000 killed, Hereford was captured, and King Edward, despite having "fought like a lion,"[1] was forced to flee the field. Wounded, he made his way south by stealth, having left all his possessions, including his seal, behind. Chivalrously, the victorious Bruce sent them after him.

Isabella was waiting at Berwick when Edward returned, crushed, angry, and humiliated. She was supportive, tending his wound, lending him her seal to replace the one he had abandoned, and supervising the cleaning of his armor. She also bought clothes for three knights who had lost everything when they fled the battlefield, and later secured the release of a royal messenger who was imprisoned for asserting that "it was no wonder the King couldn't win a battle, because he spent the time when he should have been hearing Mass in idling, ditching, digging and other improper occupations." Isabella persuaded Archbishop Reynolds to stand surety for the man's good behavior.[2]

Bannockburn was a disaster for Edward. It effectively secured Bruce's crown and Scotland's independence. It left the north of England more vulnerable than ever to Scottish raids and protection rackets. And it also shattered Edward II's credibility with his barons and put Lancaster in an impregnable position, determined to enforce the Ordinances.

The Lords Ordainers hastened to York, where the disgraced King faced Parliament in September. Isabella sat enthroned with him, listening to Lancaster blaming England's defeat on Edward's failure to observe the Ordinances. He refused to heed the King's demands to press on with the war and demanded a purge of the royal household and the administration. Edward was forced to capitulate. It was clear that from now on, it was to be Lancaster who ruled England. The King would be merely a cipher, a puppet in the Earl's hands.

Isabella, staunch as ever, supported her husband. There was now every reason for Lancaster to regard her as an enemy. She had been close to Gloucester, with whom he had fallen out, and she had continued to befriend the Beaumonts, whom he hated, and had welcomed them back to court after their dismissal by the Ordainers. In soliciting pardons without reference to Parliament, she had ignored the Ordinances. Moreover, she was influential with her father, who had already sent lawyers to help Edward circumvent them.

In retaliation, Lancaster had Isabella's revenues drastically cut. The King had to supplement her reduced income with small grants from his own wardrobe.

In the late summer and autumn, torrential rains ruined the harvest, which heralded the great famine that was to ravage Europe over the next two years. At Westminster, Isabella learned of the death of King Philip on November 29. He had suffered a stroke while hunting at Fontainebleau. Now it truly seemed that the Grand Master's curse had been fulfilled, for both the Pope and the King of France had died before the year was out.

Philip was succeeded by his eldest son, Louis X, who was nicknamed *le Hutin*, which meant stubborn or quarrelsome. He was a frivolous young man, with little interest in government, and the real ruler of France during his reign was his uncle, Charles of Valois.

On January 2, 1315, Edward had the corpse of Gaveston wrapped in cloth of gold and buried with great pomp in the Dominican church at Langley, with Archbishop Reynolds officiating, assisted by four other bishops and thirteen abbots. The Queen attended, as did Edward's half-brother, Thomas of Brotherton, Earl of Norfolk, Pembroke, Mortimer, the younger Despenser, Henry de Beaumont, and Hereford, who had been instrumental in having Piers condemned to death, but who had now made his peace with the King. But most other magnates stayed away. The King's wardrobe accounts show that every year for the rest of his life, on Gaveston's birthday and the anniversary of his death, the King had Masses said for him and made offerings at his tomb.

Parliament was in a bullish mood when it met at Westminster on March 20. It confirmed the Ordinances and demanded the dismissal of the elder Despenser and Henry de Beaumont. On February 23, the day before Beaumont left the King's household, Isabella had defiantly invited him to a feast at which several other leading royalists, including Norfolk, were present. Isabella de Vesci was also expelled from court, but Isabella kept in touch with her.

Spring brought more torrential rain and widespread flooding across Europe, which would continue unceasing until the autumn and lead to another failed harvest. In June, Edward and Isabella visited the new town of Winchelsea in Sussex, which had been built by Edward I on a grid plan, like his Continental bastides, to replace the old town that had been swept into the sea during a storm in 1287. There was no sign of famine here, for the place was prosperous, and the King and Queen were plied with food and wine. Isabella attended Mass in the parish church, which was dedicated to Thomas Becket, and her chaplain made offerings in her name. Then she and Edward moved to Hastings Castle, where they made gifts to the chapel and were entertained by two harpists and a fiddler. They then made another pilgrimage to Canterbury, before returning to Westminster.

The dread famine now held England in its grip. The price of grain had soared and it was reported that even the King and Queen found it hard to obtain bread when they passed through St. Albans in August. Because there was so little fodder for cattle, disease spread, and herds had to be culled; it was not uncommon to see the bodies of animals lying rotting in the flooded fields. There were reports of desperate people committing murder to get food, and even instances of cannibalism. In some areas, the death rate from starvation was as high as ten percent. In the towns, trade suffered, and many lost their livelihoods. Edward passed statutes to lower the price of provisions, but he could do nothing to relieve the serious dearth that was now blighting the land.

On August 12, Warwick died, leaving Lancaster in a position of unchallenged supremacy. He now controlled the administration, issued orders and pardons, granted petitions, and made appointments. He had replaced most of the royal officials and sheriffs with his own men and was enjoying widespread support as the self-proclaimed champion of the Ordinances. Before the King acted, he was obliged to seek Lancaster's advice, but as Lancaster preferred to hold himself aloof from the council, Edward was forced to treat with him almost as another sovereign prince, sending envoys to him at Kenilworth Castle or Donnington Castle. Isabella cannot have relished seeing her husband's authority thus subverted.

Marguerite of Burgundy died in prison on August 14, 1315. Rumor had it that she had been murdered, to free King Louis to father an heir. Just five days later, he married Clémence of Hungary, who rivaled Isabella in being reputed the most beautiful princess in Europe. She was crowned with him ten days later at Rheims.

September 1315 found Edward and Isabella at the Augustinian priory at Barnwell in Northamptonshire, which boasted an important royal hospice. They then visited Lincoln and Clipstone, the royal hunting lodge in Sherwood Forest. Isabella was at Clipstone at Christmas, which the King spent rowing and swimming in the Cambridgeshire Fens, activities the barons scorned as "childish frivolities."[3] Isabella had the company of Edward's sister Elizabeth; she and her husband, the Earl of Hereford, had been opponents of Gaveston, but had now been reconciled to Edward. In May, Elizabeth was to die giving birth to her eleventh child.

By February 1316, Isabella knew herself to be pregnant again. On March 27, a new litter was delivered to her so that she could travel in comfort, for women with child were not supposed to ride.

In the spring, Lancaster withdrew from the council. Henceforth he would spend most of his time on his estates in the north, keeping state like a king but doing very little to maintain effective government. He was losing support. The famine was still widespread, the Scots were raiding the north with impunity, the Welsh were rebelling, and England was in a ferment of unrest, with private wars breaking out between the barons. But Lancaster repeatedly neglected politics to attend to his own interests. He had muzzled his King, but had failed to offer a credible alternative; his sole purpose, it now appeared, was to control and humiliate Edward.

Mortimer crushed the rebellion in Wales and returned to court before April 21, but was back in the west by May, by which time it was known that Bruce's brother Edward had had himself crowned king of Ireland. Mortimer was appointed the King's Lieutenant in Ireland. When Robert the Bruce arrived there and entrenched himself in Ulster with his brother, Mortimer halted their advance.

In June, Isabella learned that her own brother, Louis X, had died, and retired to Mortlake in Surrey to grieve. Having succumbed to pleurisy or pneumonia, supposedly contracted from drinking iced wine after getting overheated playing tennis, Louis had left Clémence pregnant; until her child was born, France would be without a king for the first time since 987, when the Capetian dynasty was founded. Isabella's next brother, Philip, was appointed governor of France during the gestation and minority of the future sovereign.

With Lancaster out of the way, and public discontent with his misrule mounting, King Edward was beginning to reassert himself. He was planning to lead a new offensive against the Scots in October and arranged for the Bardi to pay the Queen's expenses during his coming absence.

Queen Marguerite was planning a pilgrimage to the shrine of St. James at Compostela in Spain, but she was never to go there because her health declined. In May 1316, her castle and manor of Hadleigh were assigned to the King's Chamber, such assignments usually indicating that they had become a habitual royal residence, which suggests that Marguerite did not travel often. Various works were carried out at Hadleigh between 1311 and 1317, but in 1317, part of the castle wall collapsed, which may have been what prompted her to move to Marlborough. Whatever the state of her health, her estates were temporarily sequestered because of fears of a war with France, suggesting that, for all their apparently cordial recent relations, Edward still did not entirely trust her. She was furnished with an allowance until her lands were restored to her. Isabella was allowed to retain her English estates, but Ponthieu and Montreuil were sequestered.

Late in July, Isabella went to Eltham to rest before her confinement, while the King traveled to Lincoln for the next session of Parliament. He was doing his best to woo Lancaster back to court, hoping to enlist his support for the Scottish campaign, but this led to a furious quarrel that scuppered all hopes of an invasion.

On August 15, 1316, Isabella bore a second son, John of Eltham. It has been suggested that he was named for Pope John XXII, who was elected on August 7. The King was at York when he was brought the news. In his joy, he bestowed on Isabella grants of land and precious items supplied on credit by the Bardi, and arranged for prayers to be said for her and their sons in the Dominican friary at York. He resolved to make this happy event the occasion for a reconciliation with Lancaster, and the Queen dispatched her valet with letters to Lancaster and the Bishop of Norwich, inviting them to Eltham to stand sponsors for John. But there is no record of Lancaster turning up when John was baptized on August 20 in the Queen's chapel in Eltham Palace in a font draped with cloth of gold and a costly piece of Turkey carpet. Isabella wore a white velvet robe for her churching in September; Edward gave her jewelry and paid £40 ($24,900) for the ceremony.

The shrewd and clever Pope John XXII was to play an influential role in Isabella's life. To win his support, Edward showered him with rich gifts, while the Queen sent him two copes of costly *Opus Anglicanum* (English needlework) embroidered with coral and large pearls, an incense boat, a ewer, and a gold buckle set with pearls and precious stones.

On September 9, fearing an armed confrontation with Lancaster, the

King ordered Isabella to join him in York. He was so anxious to see her that he rewarded the messenger who heralded her coming. The King and Queen stayed in York until October, when they returned south. By now, Edward's trust in Isabella's judgment was such that he allowed her to attend council meetings.

On October 9, the Bishop of Durham died, and both Edward and Isabella put forward their own candidates for the vacant see. Edward wanted Henry de Stanford, the Prior of Finchale, and Isabella, influenced by Henry de Beaumont and Isabella de Vesci, chose their brother Louis, a choice that seemed deliberately calculated to anger Lancaster, who had his own candidate. But, on October 19, the King commissioned Pembroke to ensure that either his man or the Queen's was appointed, whereupon Pembroke sent several barons to Durham Cathedral to ensure that the King's wishes were complied with. Isabella was angered when she heard that the monks of Durham had chosen Edward's candidate, and resorted to emotional blackmail.

"If you love me," she said to Edward (according to the chronicler Geoffrey of Coldingham), "you will act so that my kinsman, Louis de Beaumont, will be bishop of Durham." She added that he would be "a stone wall" against the Scots. "The King was so conquered by her prayers that he wrote to the curia on behalf of Louis,"[4] ignoring the protests of the chapter of Durham that Louis was illiterate, and even complaining to the Pope about the monks' recalcitrance.

In November, Queen Clémence gave birth to a son, King John I "the Posthumous," but he lived only a week and was succeeded by his uncle, Isabella's second brother, who now ascended the French throne as Philip V. Nicknamed "the Tall" or "the Fair," he was another king such as his father had been, good-looking, intelligent, decisive, and ruthless. Predictably, there was talk that he had hastened his nephew's death, the cause of which is still not known.

On January 9, 1317, Philip was crowned with Jeanne of Burgundy at Rheims, but there were some who asserted that his disinherited niece, Marguerite of Burgundy's daughter Jeanne of Navarre, had a better claim to the throne. In February, he summoned an assembly of the three estates and invoked what he was pleased to call the Salic law (which allegedly dated from the time of the early Frankish kings), declaring that a woman could not succeed to the kingdom of France. It was of dubious legality and contravened the normal feudal laws of inheritance; and it was to have far-reaching implications for Isabella and her heirs.

In February, Edward and Isabella moved to Clarendon Palace, near Salisbury. Like other royal residences, it had been improved by Henry III. There were Gothic windows with gable heads in Isabella's chambers, one depicting the Virgin and Child in stained glass. The Queen's wardrobe, beneath her private chapel, had murals showing Richard I fighting Saladin, and scenes from the history of Antioch. Her hall boasted a marble-columned mantel sculpted with a relief of the twelve months of the year.

Isabella attended the council meeting at Clarendon at which Edward and his supporters accused Lancaster of plotting with the Scots against him. Lancaster denied it, but there were many who had noticed that during their repeated northern raids, the Scots had left his estates untouched, and there was speculation that he meant treasonably to enlist Robert the Bruce's help against Edward.

That day, in response to some hefty bribes, including gifts from Edward and Isabella, Pope John provided Louis de Beaumont to the see of Durham, Louis having obligingly agreed to take reading lessons. Nevertheless, when he was enthroned thirteen months later, he was still barely able to understand Latin.

Later in February, when the bishopric of Rochester became vacant, Isabella again competed with the King in putting forward candidates. Edward wrote to the Pope in support of Hamo de Hethe, and Isabella made her plea on behalf of her confessor, John de Chisoye, enlisting the help of Philip V and Pembroke. The Pope and his cardinals marveled at her opposing her husband, but put it down to Edward's inconsistency. This time, Isabella did not get her own way: on March 18, Hamo de Hethe was elected bishop of Rochester.

Isabella was still at Clarendon on March 21 when she learned that Edward's niece, Elizabeth de Clare, widow of Theobald, Lord Verdun, had just borne a daughter at Amesbury and wanted her to be a godmother. She set off immediately to attend the christening that same day, and the child was named Isabella in her honor. In April, the King and

Queen visited Ramsey Abbey in Huntingdonshire. The famine had now abated, and England was once more becoming "fruitful, with a manifold abundance of good things."[5] There was encouraging news from Ireland: Robert the Bruce had returned to Scotland and Mortimer had defeated the treacherous Lacys, who had supported him. He then set about rebuilding the English administration and persuading the King's Irish subjects to return to their obedience.

April saw four-year-old Prince Edward's first public appearance. His education had begun early and he was schooled by royal clerks, the most celebrated of whom was Richard de Bury, an Oxford man and a great bibliophile, scholar, and diplomat. The Prince learned to read and write—his is the first surviving autograph of an English king—and became fluent in Norman French, French, Latin, and English. He also developed a working knowledge of German and Flemish. He acquired proficiency in riding, swordsmanship, shooting with a longbow, jousting, hunting, hawking, dancing, and singing. He grew up to be articulate, courteous, and affable with all. No king could have asked for a more promising son and heir.

In May 1317, Lancaster's Countess, Alice de Lacy, eloped with her lover, a squire in the service of the Earl of Surrey, Lancaster's enemy. There had been bad blood between Lancaster and Surrey for years, but the abduction of Alice was a deadly insult, and Lancaster embarked on a destructive and futile struggle with his rival to retrieve his wife and his lost honor, plunging them both into a bloody and disruptive private war. To make matters worse, Lancaster suspected that the King and Queen had encouraged his wife to leave him, and that they had plotted her abduction at the council held at Clarendon in February. Edward forbade Lancaster to resort to violence, advising him to seek a remedy in law only, but this fell on deaf ears, even when the Earl was warned that if he persisted in his private war, "the King would either have his head or consign him to prison."[6] Lancaster declared that he would not come to court because he feared treachery.

On July 25, the King granted Isabella Gaveston's former county of Cornwall. In September, the royal couple stayed at Lincoln and Tickhill Castle in Yorkshire before moving to York.

* * *

When the childless Gilbert de Clare, Earl of Gloucester, had fallen at Bannockburn, the great earldom of Gloucester looked set to be shared by his co-heirs. However, his widow had immediately announced that she was pregnant, so the matter had rested until she bore her child. Three years later, even she had to concede that there would be no baby and, in November 1317, the earldom was divided up between the Earl's sisters, all of whom were now married to men high in the King's favor.

The eldest sister, Eleanor, now twenty-five, was married to Hugh le Despenser the Younger. He had fought at Bannockburn in 1314, been first summoned to Parliament in 1315, and had again served in Scotland in 1317. He was proud, cunning, aggressively acquisitive, self-serving, and extremely able. Eleanor was a favorite of her uncle, the King, who paid her living expenses throughout his reign, a privilege not extended to her two sisters. He also corresponded with her and gave her gifts. It is possible that she was, or later became, his mistress; he already had a bastard son by an unknown lady, so it is not beyond the bounds of probability. Yet she was his niece, and he may have been merely a fond, indulgent uncle.

The second sister was Gaveston's widow, Margaret de Clare, who was now the wife of Hugh de Audley, one of the King's household knights. The third sister, Elizabeth, aged twenty-two, had just married her third husband, Roger d'Amory, another household knight, who had served with distinction at Bannockburn and was rapidly gaining favor with the King.

Normally, estates were divided equally between co-heiresses, but, in November 1317, Hugh le Despenser the Younger was allowed to claim Glamorgan, the largest and richest share of the Clare inheritance, ostensibly because he was married to the eldest sister. The truth was that, having abandoned the barons' cause and thrown his weight behind the King, he was riding high in royal favor and becoming skilled at manipulating Edward. Audley had to be content with Newport and Netherwent, while Amory got Usk. Both felt aggrieved.

But Hugh was not satisfied with his share. He meant to have the rest of the Gloucester inheritance, by fair means or foul. He "set traps for his co-heirs; thus, if he could manage it, each would lose his share through false accusations, and he alone would obtain the whole earldom."[7]

The King had been steadily building up his own party, which included the Despensers, Amory, Audley, and Surrey. Isabella was affiliated to this court faction and had been extending her patronage to its members.

Amory, however, was a loose cannon. In September, when Edward was in York, Lancaster had grudgingly agreed to return to court, thanks to the efforts of two emissaries from the Pope. But Amory had urged the King to raise an army and march provocatively in full battle order past Lancaster's stronghold at Pontefract, which scuppered any chance of a reconciliation between them. Civil war now appeared to be a very real possibility.

Pembroke, remembering Gaveston, understood the necessity for controlling Amory and, in November, entered into a compact with him and the influential Bartholomew, Lord Badlesmere, each agreeing to support and consult each other when advising the King. Their alliance has been erroneously described as a "Middle Party," but it was more of a damage limitation exercise; nevertheless, it did moderate the King and provided an alternative to Lancaster's misrule. By the spring of 1318, Arundel, Hereford, Surrey, the Mortimers, and Archbishop Reynolds had aligned themselves with Pembroke.

The King and Queen kept the Christmas of 1317 at Westminster. Isabella was once again pregnant. Edward's gift to her was a covered enameled silver-gilt basin.

On February 14, 1318, Queen Marguerite died at Marlborough Castle. She was probably in her thirty-ninth year. Wrapped in a Franciscan habit, her body was conveyed to London by Sir John Haustede, who laid on the coffin two palls of Lucca cloth of gold, sent by the King's order. Since the twelfth century, separate heart and visceral burial had been practiced within the royal families of Europe. Those who could afford it believed that being prayed for at more than one tomb could speed their passage through Purgatory. In 1299, Pope Boniface VIII had banned the division of royal bodies, but by 1304, this ruling had been relaxed, although the practice would die out in England later in the fourteenth century. In 1308, Marguerite had received Papal permission for tripartite burial, following the example of Eleanor of Castile, whose body, heart, and viscera had been interred in separate tombs, but despite the request being made in her will, it was not carried out.

Her body lay in state in the priory church of St. Mary Overie, Southwark, where Mass was said and the King offered three more palls of Lucca cloth. Isabella was perhaps present with Edward and his sister, the nun Mary, when Marguerite was buried in the choir of Greyfriars, Newgate, the church she had herself partially rebuilt and endowed in her will. It was Isabella who would pay handsomely toward its completion. When finished in 1348, the church was 300 feet long, 89 feet wide, and 64 feet high, making it second only to St. Paul's in size. It was light and spacious, and Isabella funded the glazing of the window behind the altar, before which a beautiful tomb would be raised to Marguerite's memory. Thanks to the patronage of these two queens and other royal ladies, Greyfriars at Newgate remained the most prestigious Franciscan house in England—and the most fashionable church in London—for the next two centuries, and many notable persons chose to be buried there.

Marguerite's two sons, Thomas, Earl of Norfolk, and Edmund, Earl of Kent, now seventeen and sixteen, acted as her executors, administering the will of "our mother of good memory." Parliament awarded them her goods and chattels. She had asked them to settle her heavy debts, but this had still not been done by 1335, when Norfolk petitioned Parliament "that the King will please to grant that the debts of the deceased Queen may be forthwith paid by his Exchequer."[8]

Shortly before she died, Marguerite had vowed to go on her deferred pilgrimage to the shrine of St. James at Compostela. Edmund now undertook to go in her stead, but the Pope later excused him from that obligation.

The death of Marguerite released the dower lands of the queens of England, which were granted to Isabella on March 5; they were worth £4,500 annually ($2.7 million). The next day, Ponthieu and Montreuil were restored to her.

6

"The King of England's Right Eye"

✳

B Y MARCH 1318, ROGER MORTIMER HAD CRUSHED MOST IRISH resistance to English rule, but the Scots were never going to submit. On the 26th, Bruce seized the strategic fortress of Berwick, then sent his forces raiding as far south as Yorkshire. Edward was in no position to attempt to recover Berwick, having insufficient money and men.

It was at this perilous juncture that, thanks to Pembroke's conciliatory influence, Edward reached a preliminary settlement with Lancaster. But it was to be systematically sabotaged by his favorites, Amory, Audley, and William de Montagu, who objected vehemently to Lancaster's insistence that the Crown snatch back all grants and gifts made since 1310. Had the King agreed, some of Isabella's dependents would have been considerably worse off, for it is clear that Lancaster meant to stem the flow of gifts to her servants.

On June 18, at Woodstock, Isabella gave birth to a daughter, who was named Eleanor after the King's mother. Edward hastened to her side and paid out £333.13s.4d. ($207,600) for the feast given to celebrate her churching, which took place within ten days, suggesting that it had been a very easy birth. Afterward, on June 28, the royal couple traveled together to Northampton, where Parliament assembled in July. Late in 1318, a joint household was created for the three royal children, who would share it for the next two years.

While in Northampton, Isabella was "troubled beyond measure" and "unspeakably annoyed" by persistent gossip that the King was a changeling. The rumors had started when a tanner's son, John Deydras, also known as John of Powderham, suddenly appeared at Beaumont Palace, the old royal residence in Oxford, and claimed possession of it, insisting that he was the son of Edward I and the true heir of the realm. "He declared that my Lord Edward was not of the blood royal, nor had any right to the realm, which he offered to prove by combat with him."[1] Deydras was tall and fair, uncannily resembling Edward I, but he was missing an ear and may have been mentally ill. He claimed that, as a baby, he had been mauled by a sow that had ripped off his ear, and that his nurse, too terrified to tell Edward I what had happened, had substituted a carter's son in his place. Edward II had him arrested, tried, and hanged.

Lancaster demanded the removal of the new favorites, who, he warned, were worse than Gaveston. But the King refused to send them away, and Parliament had to spend much of its time negotiating with Lancaster, sending emissaries as if he were the actual sovereign. Late in July, when it seemed that progress was being made, the Queen joined Pembroke and Hereford and the bishops in seeking a peace.

Lancaster went to considerable trouble to receive Isabella at Pontefract. Hangings were put up in the hall and new trestles and benches were made. Yet there is no record of the visit ever taking place. Nevertheless, being determined to help forge a peace, Isabella played a vital and vigorous part in bringing about the concord embodied in the Treaty of Leake, which was signed on August 9, 1318. It bound Edward to observe the Ordinances and dismiss his favorites, but obliged Lancaster to give way to a council of barons under Pembroke, who were to approve the King's actions. Pembroke was a fair man, but Edward, while outwardly agreeing to this, was still determined to shake off all restraints on his royal authority and be revenged on Lancaster for Gaveston's death.

When Parliament met at York in October, it set up the new council. In recognition of his great achievements in Ireland, Mortimer, who was back at court, was nominated, as were the Despensers. But Hugh the Younger's loyalty could no longer be counted on by the Ordainers, for he was rapidly replacing Amory in the King's confidence and affections. His preferment to the influential post of chamberlain of the royal household marks the beginning of his notorious reign as a royal favorite. Of far greater ability than Gaveston, the grasping, ambitious Hugh was to prove a more dangerous favorite in every way, and a far worse threat to the barons. As chamberlain, he had the final say on who gained access to his master, and consequently controlled royal patronage, commanding huge bribes. It was whispered that he led Edward "like a cat after a straw."[2]

There is no evidence of friction between Hugh and Isabella at this stage, although she may not have welcomed his growing ascendancy over her husband. One chronicler called Hugh the King's husband. Another wrote that Edward "loved him dearly with all his heart and mind, above all others" and accused Hugh of leading him into "a cruel and debauched life."[3] Jean le Bel baldly stated that Hugh "was a sodomite, above all with the King himself." In 1321, Pembroke was to warn the King: "He perishes on the rocks that loves another more than himself."[4] He was not referring to Isabella.

Despenser the Elder profited greatly by his son's rise and came to enjoy greater political power than ever. Together, with the younger Hugh as the driving force, the pair gained a dominant hold upon the King. They hired and fired household officials as they pleased, and their rapaciousness soon became legendary. Anyone who angered them or owned something they coveted might find himself in prison or dispossessed.

Civil war had been averted, and the Treaty of Leake had heralded a fragile peace that was to last for the next two years. The King and Queen stayed on in the north while a reenergized Edward resolved to recover Berwick and began making plans to launch an all-out attack on the Scots the following June.

The royal couple spent Christmas at Baldock, Hertfordshire. On Twelfth Night, they distributed lavish gifts they could ill afford. Edward presented a silver-gilt ewer with stand and cover to the courtier who was lucky enough to find the bean hidden in the Twelfth Night cake and become "King of the Bean" for the evening.

Edward returned to York in January 1319. Isabella arrived soon afterward, bringing Hugh le Despenser's wife, Eleanor de Clare, who had been summoned by Edward to wait on her. She spent most of that year in York. The chronicler Robert of Reading stated that she gave birth to a daughter, Joan, there. It has usually been assumed that he made an error and was in fact referring to the daughter of the same name born in 1321, but it is possible that there was another Joan, born in 1319, who died young.

Philip V had been demanding that Edward visit France to pay the customary homage due to a new French king for Gascony, Ponthieu, and Montreuil. Edward had excused himself on account of the unrest in his kingdom, but there was now no reason why he should not go, and every reason why he needed Philip's goodwill. In May 1319, he reluctantly sent Walter Stapledon, Bishop of Exeter, to the French court to make the necessary arrangements.

Stapledon was also to make a detour to the fertile and prosperous county of Hainault to inspect Count William the Good's daughters, for it had been suggested that one might make a suitable bride for Prince Edward. England enjoyed a flourishing wool trade with the Low Countries and William was also count of Holland and Zeeland and in a strong strategic position to promote and influence commerce. Born of the House of Avesnes, he was a vassal of Louis IV, the Holy Roman Emperor, and was descended, through the kings of Hungary, from Harold II of England, who had been defeated by William the Conqueror at the Battle of Hastings in 1066. He was well connected, being married to Isabella's cousin Jeanne, the daughter of Charles of Valois, and had five girls, Margaret, Jeanne, Philippa, Agnes, and Isabelle (or Sybilla). All had grown up in the sophisticated ambience of their father's court, where book-learning was prized. They were close to their mother and, despite their father's infidelities, seem to have had a happy childhood.

The age of the unnamed princess given in Stapledon's description shows that he was writing about the eldest sister, Margaret, who was then eight years old. He reported:

> The lady whom we saw has not uncomely hair, betwixt bloy [*blé*, meaning corn-colored] and brown. Her head is clean-shaped, her forehead high and broad and standing somewhat forward. Her face narrows between the eyes and the lower part of her face is still more narrow and slender than the forehead. Her eyes are blackish-brown and deep. Her nose is fairly smooth and even, save that it is somewhat broad at the tip and flattened, yet it is no snub nose. Her nostrils are

also broad, her mouth fairly wide, her lips somewhat full, especially the lower lip. Her teeth that have fallen and grown again are white enough, but the rest are not so white. The lower teeth project a little beyond the upper, yet this is little seen. Her ears and chin are comely enough. Her neck, shoulders and all her body and lower limbs are reasonably well-shapen; all her limbs are well-set and unmaimed, and naught is amiss, so far as a man may see. Moreover, she is brown [tanned or shiny] of skin all over and much like her father. And in all things she is pleasant enough, as it seems to us. And the damsel will be of age of nine years on St. John's Day next to come, as her mother saith. She is neither too tall nor too short for such an age; she is of fair carriage and well taught in all that becometh her rank, and highly esteemed and well beloved of her father and mother and of all her meinie [train], insofar as we could inquire and learn the truth.

A later hand noted incorrectly: "She was Philippa, who was the Queen of England wedded to Edward III."[5] This description, which is still sometimes thought erroneously to be of Philippa, has given rise to the myth that she was black, because the word "bloy" has been incorrectly translated as "blue-black." Margaret had light brown or chestnut hair, and possibly her sisters did too.

Edward did not pursue the match further at this time. He revived negotiations in 1320, and Count William obtained a dispensation, but by 1324 he had become lukewarm, and the King began negotiating a marriage for his son with Eleanor of Aragon.

In September 1319, Edward laid siege to Berwick. Lancaster was ostensibly co-operating with him in this venture, but his support was half-hearted at best—none of his men attempted to scale the walls—and an angry Edward was still bent on destroying him. During the siege, he told the Despensers, "When this wretched business is over, we will turn our hands to other matters. For I have not yet forgotten the wrong that was done to my brother Piers."[6]

Isabella, meanwhile, was staying with her children in a small rural dwelling near York. But the Scots were raiding the north of England with impunity, and the legendary Sir James "the Black" Douglas penetrated by stealth as far as Yorkshire with 10,000 men, having conceived the daring plan of kidnapping Isabella and holding her to ransom. He came within a few hours' march of the village where she was lodging, but, by great good fortune, one of his scouts fell into the hands of William Melton, Archbishop of York, and the Chancellor, John Hotham, Bishop of Ely. Threatened with torture, the man told them where they would find Douglas and his host. Alarmed, they marched to the Queen's residence, warned her of her great danger and brought her back to York. From there, for her greater security, she was taken by water to Nottingham Castle. "Had the Queen at that time been captured, I believe that Scotland would have bought peace for herself," observed the author of the *Vita Edwardi Secundi*. With Isabella as a hostage, Edward would have had little choice but to acknowledge Bruce as king of Scots.

With Isabella safe, Melton hurriedly gathered together an army of monks and old men and marched to confront the Black Douglas. His forces were no match for the Scots, and on September 12, they were savagely defeated at the Battle of Myton in Swaledale.

If the plot to abduct Isabella was a decoy tactic, it worked, because on September 17, when news reached the King of how narrowly she had escaped capture, he abandoned the siege of Berwick and hurried back to York, just as the victorious Scots were making their way home unopposed, burning the harvest as they went. Edward was forced to make a two-year truce with Bruce.

By now, his reputation was in the dust. The failure of the Scottish campaign led to angry accusations. It seemed that someone with knowledge of the whereabouts of the Queen had passed that information to the Scots. The jealous barons accused Hugh le Despenser. The Despensers blamed Lancaster, alleging that Bruce had bribed him to divert Edward from the siege, which many believed. But the real culprit was possibly Sir Edmund Darrell, a soldier of the King's chamber, who was named as the traitor by Robert of Reading and the *Annales Paulini*. Darrell was a known opponent of Edward. In 1313, he had been arrested as an accessory to Gaveston's murder; in 1322, he would again be apprehended, for taking up arms against the King, and spend two years in the Tower as punishment. Financial hardship may have prompted him to confide Isabella's location to the Scots; there was talk that they had paid large bribes for information leading to her kidnap. According to the *An-*

nales Paulini, Darrell had been arrested back in May for betraying the Queen, but had been released for lack of evidence. The King, however, had dismissed him from his service. This suggests that a plot to capture Isabella had been conceived months earlier.

Edward and Isabella spent Christmas at York. On New Year's Day 1320, he gave her expensive gifts of jewelry. He had finally arranged to go to France to pay homage to Philip V, and she was no doubt looking forward to their trip, for which preparations began early in the New Year; it was six years since she had visited her native land.

When Parliament met at York on January 20, Lancaster refused to attend because he suspected that the King and the Despensers were plotting against him. In his absence, Parliament arranged a reshuffle of offices and promoted members of the court party, men high in the King's favor—and Hugh's. Robert Baldock, a clerk of the wardrobe, was appointed Keeper of the Privy Seal. He owed his preferment not so much to his brilliant administrative talents as to the patronage of Hugh, whose brain and hand he was reputed to be. Walter Stapledon, Bishop of Exeter, was made Treasurer. A learned man who founded Stapledon Hall (later Exeter College) in Oxford, he was utterly loyal to the King, but he would become detested for his extortions and his perceived alignment with the Despensers, to whom he probably owed his appointment.

Late in February, Edward and Isabella journeyed south. As they passed Pontefract Castle, they were assailed by the jeers of Lancaster's garrison catcalling from the battlements, much to their fury.

On the King's return to London, Thomas Cobham, Bishop of Worcester, noticed an improvement in his conduct. He was rising earlier in the mornings to face his duties and "respectfully, wisely and with discernment listening patiently to all who wished to speak to him, contrary to his wont."[7] He also won praise for banning from his court entertainers who were notorious for their insolence and greed. He was feeling the need for a respite from his troubles and converted a hut in the precincts of Westminster Abbey as his private retreat. It was known as "Burgundy," and the King let it be known that he preferred "to be called King of Burgundy" rather than use "the magnificent titles of his famous royal ancestors."[8]

In June, Prince Edward's governor, Sir Richard d'Amory (brother of Roger), was ordered to return to the Queen the manor and castle of the

High Peak for the sustenance of Prince John and Princess Eleanor, who evidently were to return to her care.

The King and Queen sailed to France that month, leaving Pembroke as Keeper of the Realm. Hugh le Despenser and Roger d'Amory were in Edward's train, and Pembroke's wife, Beatrice de Clermont, daughter of the Constable of France, was among the Queen's chief attendants. On June 20, Edward paid homage to Philip before the high altar in Amiens Cathedral, and a gratified Philip took steps to ensure that the French in Ponthieu, who had been making trouble, would no longer pose a threat to Isabella's authority there.

The King and Queen lingered in France for a month. They visited Abbeville, Isabella's chief city in Ponthieu. On July 20, they attended the consecration of the newly elected Bishop of Lincoln, Henry Burghersh, in Boulogne Cathedral. Burghersh, an avaricious and unscrupulous prelate who was related to the Mortimers, was riding high in the King's favor, having persuaded the Pope to release Edward from his vow to obey the Ordinances. Isabella also thought highly of him.

At the beginning of August, the royal couple returned to England. The Mayor and citizens of London, in their robes of office, rode out to meet them, and they entered the capital in state, receiving a warm reception.

The Despensers had become a political force to be reckoned with. Hugh was now "the King of England's right eye and his chief counsellor against the earls and barons, but an eyesore to the rest of the kingdom. His every desire became a royal command." He had "gained so much influence over the King and so moulded his opinions that nothing was done without him, and everything was done by him. The King paid more attention to him than to anyone."[9] Unsurprisingly, this aroused the bitter hatred of the barons.

By now, Isabella was probably beginning to regard Hugh as a sinister influence. Relations between them became strained when, in 1320, the elder Despenser suddenly ceased paying the considerable dues owed to her from his manor of Lechlade. It seems he had been infected by the contempt his son had come to feel for her, whereas previously there had been goodwill between the elder Despenser and the Queen; in 1312, he had been chosen as one of Prince Edward's godfathers.

"Fired by greed,"[10] Hugh was concentrating his formidable efforts on grabbing the whole of the Gloucester inheritance and building up a vast power base in south Wales. The Mortimers and the other Marcher lords felt threatened by his aggrandizement and encroachment on their power base. The Mortimers especially had good reason to fear him, for he bore a bitter grudge against them for killing his grandfather during the barons' wars of the 1260s and was determined to avenge him. Already he was doing his aggressive best to appropriate estates that had been granted to Roger Mortimer, and he was probably responsible for Mortimer's recall from Ireland in September.

The lordship Hugh coveted most was Gower, which was held by John Mowbray. As was the time-honored custom with the Marcher lords, Mowbray had not obtained the King's license to take possession of it, an omission that was exploited by Hugh, who insisted that Mowbray's tenure was illegal and persuaded Edward to declare the lordship forfeit and grant it to him instead. This was a direct attack on Marcher privileges, but the King refused to recognize it as such.

When Mowbray refused to surrender Gower, Edward sent men to take it by force. The Marcher lords were outraged and formed a confederacy against the Despensers, which led to "a great schism"[11] between the King and the majority of the nobility. By January 1321, Mortimer and most of the other Marchers were fortifying their castles and rallying the rest of the barons, who "unanimously decided that Hugh must be pursued and utterly destroyed."[12] Just as Isabella realized that she was once again pregnant, civil war seemed a certainty.

The Marchers enlisted Lancaster's support. They faced a difficult choice between treasonably rising against their King or countenancing the depredations of the Despensers. They resolved to force the King to dismiss the favorites and mounted an offensive on the Despenser lands in south Wales. The King, urged by Hugh, began mobilizing troops, ordering that all the royal castles in Wales be prepared for war. In defending the Despensers' interests, he forced the fundamentally royalist Marchers into open rebellion, losing the support of other barons who resented the favorites.

By now, Isabella was known to be no friend to the Despensers, but her loyalties still lay with the King. She turned over her castle at Marlborough to the elder Despenser and placed that at Devizes in the custody of another of Edward's supporters, Sir Oliver Ingham.

With a strong force, Edward marched west. As the Marchers took up battle stations, he warned them not to attack the Despensers, but they went ahead and launched a devastating assault on their lands. By May 12, Newport, Cardiff, and Caerphilly had fallen to Mortimer and the vast Marcher army, which then swept through Glamorgan and Gloucestershire, seizing castles, burning, looting, destroying crops, and leaving a trail of devastation. Having accomplished their objective, the Marchers rode north to meet with Lancaster.

On May 24, 1321, Lancaster held what was effectively a private parliament at Pontefract, where he and the Marchers swore to defend their own lands and each other's. This was followed by a baronial convention at Sherburn in Elmet on June 28, at which the rebels—henceforth known as the "contrariants"—vowed to see the Despensers disinherited.

Edward had returned to London. Isabella was now nearing her confinement, and for safety it was decided that her child should be born in the Tower of London. But the Queen's apartments there were in a sad state of disrepair, and as she lay in labor, rain dripped through the ceiling, soaking the bedclothes. When this was reported to the King, he instantly dismissed the constable.

Around July 5, Isabella bore another girl, known as Joan of the Tower, who was entrusted to Maud de Pyrie, John of Eltham's nurse. The King rewarded the messenger who brought him news of the birth with £80 ($50,000) and hastened to the Tower to spend six days with Isabella and their new daughter.

Mortimer was now marching on London with a great force clad in green livery bearing the royal arms, proclaiming his loyalty to the King. His intention was to depose the Despensers. Finding the gates of London closed to him, he ordered his men to surround the walls, effectively placing the Tower under siege. Isabella had left by then, but was still in the city.

Lancaster and other aggrieved barons joined Mortimer, demanding that the King hear their complaints concerning the Despensers, accusing them of usurping the royal authority, inciting civil war, perverting justice, barring the magnates from the King's presence, committing acts of violence and fraud, and alienating the King from his people. If Edward did not banish them, the barons warned, they would renounce their homage and set up another ruler in his place. Even now, Edward refused to accede to their demands, and Hugh sailed menacingly up and down the Thames in a borrowed ship, only ceasing when the barons threatened to burn down all the royal buildings between Charing Cross and Westminster Abbey.

On August 1, panicking at their stipulations, Edward summoned Pembroke to Westminster. The Earl did his best to persuade him to agree to the Marchers' demands, but Edward would not hear of it. Pembroke then suggested that the Queen try to achieve a settlement. Having been a successful mediator in the past, she now enjoyed a reputation as a peacemaker. On her knees, Isabella begged the King, "for the people's sake," to banish the Despensers and make peace with his lords. Her intercession enabled him to capitulate without too much loss of face, although he swore that, within six months, "he would make such an amend that the whole world would hear of it and tremble."[13] On August 14, he summoned the Marchers to Westminster Hall and icily informed them that he had agreed to send away the Despensers within the month. Five days later, they were sentenced to exile and forfeiture, and forbidden to return to England without the consent of Parliament. Pardons were issued to all who had risen against the King.

"Reluctantly," the Despensers "left their native soil and splendour." The elder Hugh went to Bordeaux, while his son embarked on a successful career as a pirate in the English Channel, where he "became a sea monster, lying in wait for the merchants as they crossed his path. No ship got through unharmed."[14]

However, Edward had no intention of being parted from his favorites for long, and was resolved to be revenged on those barons who had forced him to exile them. In August, he took Isabella to Rochester and Gravesend. Some sources claim that they went on another pilgrimage to Canterbury, but this is unlikely, since the city was packed with the armed retainers of the powerful Lord Badlesmere, who, despite being steward of the royal household, had recently thrown in his lot with Lancaster and the Marchers. Almost certainly, Edward and Isabella met with Hugh in September, when the latter's ship briefly docked at the Isle of Thanet.

Edward returned to London on September 23 and lodged in the

Tower; Isabella was probably with him. On October 1, while he visited the royal manors of Sheen and Byfleet, she traveled back to Kent, ostensibly to visit the shrine of Becket, although it had apparently been agreed that she would force a confrontation with Badlesmere to provoke a showdown with the King's opponents. Badlesmere owned Leeds Castle, near Maidstone, formerly a dower property of the queens of England and favored by Eleanor of Castile and Marguerite of France. But on Marguerite's death, notwithstanding the fact that the reversion of the castle had been promised in 1314 to Isabella, the King had granted Leeds to Badlesmere in exchange for a manor in Shropshire.

Badlesmere knew he was a marked man, having angered the King by supporting his enemies. In September, he had prepared all his castles for war and stored his treasure for safety at Leeds, which he had placed in the care of his lady, Margaret de Clare, a cousin of Despenser's wife. Clearly he was expecting reprisals.

On October 2, Isabella informed her retinue that she purposed to rest at Leeds Castle that night and sent ahead her harbingers and purveyors to make the necessary arrangements. But Lady Badlesmere informed them that her husband had left her strict instructions not to allow anyone to enter the castle, and "insolently" suggested that Isabella "might seek some other lodging, for she would not admit anyone within the castle without an order from her lord."[15] Given that the King and Queen had the right to enter any house in the realm, this was a gross insult and an unforgivable infringement of the rules of hospitality.

The shocked harbingers reported back to Isabella, who indignantly insisted on confronting Lady Badlesmere herself. But even in the face of the Queen, that lady remained obdurate. When Isabella instructed her marshals to force an entry into the castle, Lady Badlesmere ordered the archers of the garrison to open fire on them. Six men fell dead before Isabella's appalled eyes; she could have been shot herself.

Prudently, she gave the order to withdraw and sought shelter in nearby Leeds Priory. On October 3, she sent an urgent message to Edward, complaining bitterly about the affront to her and urging him to send soldiers to her assistance, demanding that he avenge the murder of her servants and punish Lady Badlesmere for her defiance. The King, who must secretly have been gratified at the outcome of his scheme, showed himself incandescent at such an outrageous slight to "his beloved consort," using it as a pretext to take up arms against Badlesmere as a preliminary to netting the bigger fish.

On October 4, Edward had a second clandestine meeting with Hugh, at Portchester. Afterward, he wrote to Badlesmere complaining of his wife's conduct. Badlesmere played right into Edward's hands, sending an insulting reply declaring that he "approved of this misconduct of his family in thus obstructing the Queen."[16]

Thus provoked, Edward hired mercenaries and ordered a general muster of all men between the ages of sixteen and sixty, vowing to make an example of Badlesmere. Many responded, outraged at the insult to the Queen, and the King was able to send Pembroke at the head of a vast army to lay siege to Leeds Castle "to punish the disobedience and contempt against the Queen committed by certain members of the household of Bartholomew de Badlesmere."[17] Lady Badlesmere, realizing that she could not long withstand a siege, sent a frantic message to her husband, who had by now joined the Marcher forces at Oxford.

At his urging, Mortimer and Hereford marched south to relieve Leeds, placing themselves in direct opposition to the King, which would prove a fatal mistake. At Badlesmere's entreaty, they tried to mediate with the King on his behalf, but Edward refused to listen. In avenging the insult to his popular Queen, he had stirred up much public support. Many barons hastened to join Pembroke before Leeds Castle, along with numerous Londoners, for Isabella had always been highly regarded in the capital. The besieging forces now numbered 30,000. Heartened by this sudden surge of support, the King personally took charge of the siege.

Leeds finally surrendered on October 31. Edward hanged the constable of the castle and thirteen of his men from the battlements. Lady Badlesmere and her children were taken prisoner and sent to the Tower of London. Many applauded the King's first successful military operation since his accession, and his punitive measures, but these punishments marked the beginning of his tyranny. He had made it alarmingly clear that any person who defied him might suffer severe repercussions, without proper process of law.

7

"Someone Has Come
Between My Husband and Myself"

✳

ON NOVEMBER 4, ISABELLA JOINED HER VICTORIOUS SPOUSE at Tonbridge Castle, where he gave her provisions he had seized from Leeds Castle as compensation for her ordeal there. Before Easter 1322, he gave her the castle itself, which had reverted to the Crown. Knowing that he now occupied a strong position, Edward was determined to press home his advantage, reclaim his royal prerogative, and deal once and for all with the Marchers and Lancaster. After Leeds had fallen, Mortimer and Hereford had fled north to meet with Lancaster, knowing that "the King was a man without mercy, and would destroy them."[1]

Edward was displaying unwonted energy and decisiveness. On December 1, capitalizing on his new ascendancy, he had Archbishop Reynolds summon a convocation of the clergy to St. Paul's Cathedral, where the sentence of banishment on the Despensers was annulled on the grounds that it had not had the unanimous support of the bishops. Edward then invited the favorites to return to England under his protection.

Hearing that he was preparing to march on the lands of the rebels, Mortimer and Hereford hurriedly returned to defend their estates. Lancaster, who owned lands in the north and the Midlands, was nevertheless ready to seek the aid of England's arch-enemy, Robert the Bruce, which was treason.

During this tense period, Isabella was lodging in the Tower. By

December 10, she had joined the King at Langley. The royal forces were then closing in on the Marchers, prompting panic and wide-scale desertions. Mortimer's only hope now was that Lancaster would come to relieve them, but Lancaster had shut himself up in Pontefract Castle.

Edward appealed to Philip V for support, but in vain, for Philip had died on January 3 and been succeeded by his brother, Charles IV. On January 14, the King crossed the Severn at Shrewsbury and, for the Marchers, all was lost. The next day, Edward ordered the arrest of the Mortimers. Hereford fled to Lancaster at Pontefract as Edward seized his lands and those of Audley and Amory. The Mortimers surrendered and tried to make terms with the King, but they had committed treason by rising in arms against him and supporting his enemies, and he was not willing to listen. Instead, he had them put in chains and jailed. He confiscated their lands and ordered the arrest of Lady Mortimer, whom he imprisoned. The sons of Mortimer and Hereford were confined at Windsor, and Mortimer's three unmarried daughters were immured in nunneries, while his mother, loudly protesting, was stripped of some of her property.

As the King moved south, castle after castle fell to him, the last being Berkeley in Gloucestershire. Its owner, Maurice, Lord Berkeley, was cast into prison at Wallingford with his son Thomas, who was married to Mortimer's daughter Margaret; both had sided with the Marchers. Berkeley's lands were given to Hugh.

The Despensers had returned in secret in the middle of January. Inspired by his successes, Edward resolved to make an end of Lancaster. He was encouraged by his favorites and Isabella, who was deeply offended by the Earl's failure to support the King against Badlesmere. At the end of February, he marched north, taking Lancaster's castle at Tutbury, where evidence of his dealings with Bruce was discovered, along with Roger d'Amory, who was hiding in the castle, badly wounded. He was tried and condemned to death, yet was reprieved because the King loved him, only to die three days later.

As Edward was ransacking Tutbury, royal forces defeated Lancaster's army at Burton upon Trent. On March 12, the Earl was publicly proclaimed a rebel, and the King gave orders that he and his adherents were to be hunted down. Lancaster fled north, but was trapped at Boroughbridge between the royal army and a force led by Andrew Harclay, Sheriff of Westmorland, who had gained a heroic reputation fighting the Scots. Isabella, in constant contact with Edward, had personally sent messages to Harclay and the Sheriff of Yorkshire, urging them to prevent Lancaster from penetrating further north. Both responded with alacrity. The Queen also had supplies for the King sent to York and Carlisle.

The Battle of Boroughbridge took place on March 16. Lancaster's men deserted in droves. Hereford was mortally wounded. An overnight truce was agreed, but, the next day, knowing it was fruitless to offer further resistance, Lancaster surrendered to the King, who was determined finally to avenge the murder of Piers Gaveston.

The disgraced Earl was taken in manacles to his own castle at Pontefract, and there, on March 20, in the great hall, tried as a rebel before the King and several magnates, including the elder Despenser. He was not permitted to speak in his defense, since ten years earlier he had not allowed Gaveston to do so. The lords found him guilty of treason and sentenced him to be hanged, drawn and quartered as a traitor. In consideration of his royal blood, and in response to the plea of the Queen, his kinswoman, the King commuted the sentence to beheading. On March 22, in the midst of a snowstorm, the trembling Earl, clad in the somber robes of a penitent and a tattered old hat, was led out of the castle on a mule to St. Thomas's Hill, where his head was roughly hacked off with two or three strokes.

With Lancaster dead, Edward was free to rule without opposition and exacted a bloody vengeance on those who had supported the Earl, making a clean sweep of all his enemies—118 persons, including Badlesmere, suffered execution, imprisonment, or exile, and many more faced crippling fines. The Pope begged him to desist from his tyrannical course, but he refused to listen.

Edward summoned Isabella to join him at Pontefract. Her loyal support throughout the rebellion and its aftermath is evident from her letters to Harclay and the Pope, in which she vigorously condemned Lancaster's actions. Yet she had expected Edward to spare him, and was shocked at his execution, for he was her uncle, and of royal blood. She blamed Hugh for his death, for which he "earned the deep hatred of the whole country, and especially of the Queen."[2] "Small wonder if [the Queen] does not like Hugh, through whom her uncle perished," observed the author of the *Vita Edwardi Secundi*.

Isabella had been kept informed about the judicial bloodbath that was taking place and did her best to mitigate the King's savagery. But he was unwilling to grant her pleas for mercy, while Hugh resented her intervention and continued to encourage Edward in his bloody reprisals. The King gave Hugh's wife Eleanor property confiscated from Lancastrian traitors after Boroughbridge; Isabella, by contrast, received nothing.

In May, the King and Queen arrived at York, where the Parliament that would repeal the Ordinances as prejudicial to the Crown met. "From that time on, the power of the Despensers began to increase, and the power of the Queen decreased."[3] When Edward rewarded those who had supported him, Isabella again received nothing. On May 10, the elder Despenser was created earl of Winchester, signaling the beginning of the tyranny of the favorites. Henceforth, they ruled the King with scant regard for law or justice and were firmly in control of both state affairs and royal patronage—or out of control, as many feared. The recent purges had left all their chief opponents either dead or in prison, and of the remaining magnates, not one was strong enough to curb their power, even Pembroke, who was ailing. Aggrieved with him for urging the Despensers' exile, Edward had made him pledge his body, land, and goods to obey him and not ally with anyone against him; consequently, Pembroke was slavishly lending his support to the new regime.

Edward now "governed his country with great cruelty and injustice, by the advice of Sir Hugh le Despenser,"[4] whom he showered with many large grants and most of the confiscated lands of the rebels, which effectively made him the unopposed ruler of south Wales. Thereafter, Hugh would exploit the King's generosity, intimidating landowners into selling him property at vastly reduced prices and extorting cash by violence, bullying tactics, fraud, and cunning manipulation of the law. By such unscrupulous methods, he built up a vast landed estate and a huge fortune that rivaled even that of Lancaster—all with the full cooperation and blessing of the King.

Hugh's brutality extended even to women. He committed extortion and violent crimes against the widows and children of executed Lancastrians, and dispossessed his sister-in-law, Elizabeth de Clare, Amory's widow. Later, he would harass Pembroke's widow, the friend of the Queen, wresting from her £20,000 ($16.6 million) as well as lands and livestock. He kidnapped a wealthy heiress, Elizabeth Comyn, and held her hostage for a year until she signed over £10,000 ($6.2 million) and two valuable estates to him. He persecuted Lancaster's widow, accusing her of being the chief cause of her husband's execution and threatening to have her burned alive, which was the penalty for murdering a husband. In terror, she handed over her lands and a massive fine. Another widow was tortured until her four limbs were broken and she went insane.

It was said of Hugh that "the whole land has turned to hatred of him, and few would mourn his downfall."[5] People grumbled that one king was bad enough, but three were intolerable. The fateful consequence of the Despensers' tyrannical ascendancy was a gradual erosion of sympathy for the King.

The Despensers resented the Queen's influence over him, even though it was waning. They knew she had been instrumental in securing their exile and probably saw her as the one remaining threat to their political dominance. From July 1322, they ceased paying the dues they owed her. It was an outrageous slight, but there was no one left to act as her champion. Isabella must have been in fear, for it had become starkly manifest how ruthless the Despensers could be, and how far the King was in thrall to them.

On July 21, the Mortimers were tried for treason in Westminster Hall and sentenced to forfeiture and death, although the sentence was commuted to perpetual imprisonment in the Tower.

With the Scottish truce about to expire, the King had announced his intention of mounting a new campaign against Bruce, and had ordered a muster at Newcastle for July 22. In June, once the truce ended, Bruce again began raiding the north. When Edward finally did march into Scotland in August, with his bastard son Adam among his company, it was to find that the land had been laid waste. By the beginning of October, the royal army was demoralized, starving, and racked with dysentery, which was probably what claimed Adam's life. The King had no choice but to retreat south to raise more troops.

Intent on surprising and capturing him, Bruce swept south into England. During the campaign, as in 1312, Edward had sent Isabella to Tynemouth Priory. She was there on October 14, when the King and the Despensers, then at Rievaulx Abbey, were warned that the Scots were fast approaching. Edward fled to York, abandoning his treasure, his state papers, and his baggage. Knowing that his flight would leave Isabella isolated at Tynemouth and vulnerable to attack or capture by Bruce's army, he sent the French ambassador to rescue her, only for the Scots to seize him. Edward then wrote to the constable of Norham Castle, seventy miles from Tynemouth, placing the Queen under his protection; should the Scots approach, the constable was to take steps to safeguard her. The King also ordered that men from Hugh's forces go to Tynemouth to fortify the priory, and wrote to Isabella telling her that he was sending the earls of Richmond and Atholl to rescue her.

Isabella knew she had insufficient resources to withstand a siege and dared not wait for the earls to arrive, for the Scots were already closing in on Tynemouth. Distraught, she sent messages begging the King to aid her. When Hugh's forces arrived, she refused to put herself in their hands, so he replaced them with soldiers who were more agreeable yet could not outpace the Scots. Isabella had to rely on her household squires, who made strenuous efforts to repair the priory's crumbling fortifications. When it became clear that they had no chance of holding off the invaders, they commandeered a ship and enabled the Queen to escape by sea to Scarborough; later, she would reward them for their actions. But she had to endure a hazardous voyage in violent storms, dodging hostile Flemish ships policing the North Sea on behalf of Flanders' allies, the Scots. One of her ladies fell overboard and drowned, while another died soon after disembarking. Four years later, Isabella would blame Hugh for her plight, claiming that he had treacherously persuaded Edward to flee and abandon her. Yet Hugh's wife, Eleanor, had been at Tynemouth with her, and he *had* sent his men to relieve it.

When Isabella thankfully reached Scarborough, and was preparing to rejoin the King at York, his messengers informed her that Bruce had inflicted a sound defeat on the royal forces at Byland. Apparently the Queen's patience snapped at this point.

Until the autumn of 1322, there is no hint in any contemporary source that Isabella was unsupportive of her husband, or that he held her in anything other than high esteem. To every appearance, in the ten years following the death of Gaveston, theirs had been a strong and successful royal marriage. She had proved herself a loyal and devoted wife, and he had treated her with honor, respect, and generosity.

Now, things suddenly changed. From November 1, 1322, there is barely a mention of Isabella in the Chancery Rolls and the household accounts. She had ceased to exercise patronage in 1321, while only a few minor gifts to her are recorded. Taken together, these are strong indications that she had fallen from favor and that her indignation at being left stranded at Tynemouth had led to a rift between her and Edward.

Possibly she had made plain her resentment against Hugh, whose influence was gradually eroding her own power. Later evidence strongly suggests that her animosity was rooted in part in his sexual dominance of her husband. It may be significant that she bore Edward no more children after 1321. In her later letters to the King, it was Hugh she criticized, not his father. Since most of the political establishment regarded the latter as being almost as responsible as his son for the tyranny of these years, it is likely that Isabella's particular hatred for Hugh was born of personal jealousy. She was to accuse him bitterly of being an "intruder" in her marriage and alienating the King's affections from her: "Someone has come between my husband and myself, trying to break this bond."[6]

In February 1326, she would complain that Hugh had wished to dishonor her by every possible means, an assertion reiterated in the accusations made against him in November 1326 and by most chroniclers. She may have been referring to Hugh's attempts to poison the King's mind against her, or the homosexual relationship between them. The words "by every possible means"[7] could have alluded to his vicious campaign to discredit her and the injurious ways in which he had (by then) treated her, but one could also infer that there were darker implications, perhaps related to attempted or actual rape.

Edward was to protest that "never, in the slightest instance" had Hugh done any evil to Isabella, and that "he could never perceive that Hugh, privately or openly, in word or deed or in countenance, did not behave himself on all points towards the Queen as he ought to have done to his lady."[8] Furthermore, she had no cause to allege that she had gone in fear of her life.

From now on, Hugh "maliciously caused such discord between the King and Queen that, for a long time, the King would neither remain in the Queen's company, nor even see her at all."[9] On December 23, Edward announced to his sheriffs and bailiffs that after Christmas, which they were to spend together at York, the Queen would depart on a nine-month pilgrimage, and commanded royal officers to afford her every assistance on her journey.

In January 1323, when the King and Queen arrived back in London, Isabella took up residence in the Tower with Prince Edward. On February 3, she dined there with him. On February 17, Isabella and Eleanor de Clare both wrote from the Tower to the acting Treasurer, Walter de Norwich, asking him to show all the favor he could in paying out the modest amount the King had allocated for the sustenance of the imprisoned Lady Mortimer. But their petitions were unsuccessful and Lady Mortimer remained in prison until April 1324.

Between February 7 and June 10, 1323, Isabella's movements cannot be easily traced. Possibly she did go on pilgrimage, although there is no evidence of this. It might be inferred that, as Froissart asserts, Hugh had so effectively succeeded in poisoning Edward's mind against her that the King was ready to banish her from his side and had to come up with a diplomatic explanation for her absence.

After a few months of the Despensers' tyranny, people began to forget Lancaster's treason and self-interest, and remembered only that he had striven to mitigate royal oppression and misgovernment. Already he was being venerated as a popular hero, a martyr for English liberties, and even a saint. The cult of "St." Thomas quickly flourished and his tomb at Pontefract became a place of pilgrimage. Before long, there was talk of miracles taking place there. By 1325, he was being linked in the popular imagination to St. George, and there were calls for his canonization. This reflects the growing strength of feeling against the Despenser-led government and a weak and vicious King.

In May, Pembroke and Despenser negotiated a thirteen-year truce with Bruce. There would be no more fighting for the rest of Edward's reign. That same day, Henry de Beaumont, the Queen's friend, was arrested. Angry at the King's censure of his brother, the Bishop of Durham, he had refused to give advice on negotiating the truce, or swear an oath of loyalty to Hugh, for which he was cast into prison. With him and his sister both banished from court, Isabella must have felt even more isolated.

On August 1, 1323, Roger Mortimer made a dramatic escape from the Tower, a feat that had been achieved only once before (by Ranulf Flambard, Bishop of Durham, in 1101). It was the feast of St. Peter ad Vincula, the patron saint of the Tower garrison. Mortimer had won the sympathies of the lieutenant, Gerard d'Alspaye, to the extent that the latter had brought him a crowbar and pick so that he could hack a hole in the stone wall of his cell. With Alspaye's connivance, Mortimer hosted a feast and drugged his guards. He and Alspaye then made their escape to a waiting boat that took them across the Thames to the Surrey shore, where Roger's friends were waiting with horses. The small party galloped through the night to the Hampshire coast, whence they boarded a ship to France.

According to Agnes Strickland, the Victorian author of *The Lives of the Queens of England*, "an old chronicle" stated that the drugged drink Mortimer gave his guards was provided by Isabella, and that he swam across the Thames to the Surrey shore, "the Queen doubting much of his strength for such an exploit, as he had been long in confinement." Yet there is no evidence that Isabella was in London at this time, or that she was involved in the escape. Not until 1593 was it asserted, by the dramatist Christopher Marlowe, that she aided Mortimer.

However, Adam Orleton, Bishop of Hereford, had assisted the fugitives. He had been born on one of Mortimer's Herefordshire manors and had spent most of his distinguished career at the Papal Curia, before being elected bishop of Hereford in 1317. In recent years, he had become a close friend and ally of Mortimer, who was his patron. Orleton had staunchly supported the Mortimers in their attack on the Despensers in Parliament and remained one of the favorites' most active opponents.

Orleton's reputation has suffered because of a piece of clever character assassination by the chronicler Geoffrey le Baker. Far from being as unscrupulous as Baker claims, he was an able politician, lawyer, and diplomat who took his ecclesiastical responsibilities seriously and genuinely deplored the misgovernment of Edward II and the Despensers, and the embarrassment this caused him in European diplomatic circles. He was a friend of the astute John XXII, and Archbishop Reynolds held a high opinion of his capabilities. But his overt approval of Mortimer's acts of rebellion had made him a natural target for the King's wrath.

When, in February 1324, Hugh accused Orleton in Parliament of treasonably having aided the enemies of the King, the archbishops of Canterbury, York, and Dublin took the Bishop under their protection and threatened anyone who dared lay violent hands on him with excommunication. This was the first time that Archbishop Reynolds, who had hitherto been a staunch friend, had defied Edward. Shocked, the King had his justices declare Orleton guilty, confiscated his estates and property, and kept him in custody.

In Paris, Mortimer sought the protection of Charles IV, who received him with great honor. Not knowing at first where he had gone, Edward panicked and made strenuous efforts to recapture him, alive or dead, raising the hue and cry all over England. Only in late September did he learn that his quarry was in France. He complained bitterly to Charles, but in vain.

In November, Mortimer sent an assassin from Saint-Omer to murder the Despensers. The attempt failed—the killer got as far as London before he was arrested—yet it proved how far Mortimer was prepared to go to be revenged upon his enemies. Edward was in dread lest he might enlist the support of Charles IV and invade England with a view to overthrowing the Despensers. He even accused Charles of having assisted Mortimer's escape.

* * *

There is no further mention of Isabella in the records until October 13, 1323. Possibly she had resumed her pilgrimage. She was with Edward when the court celebrated Christmas at Kenilworth Castle with great magnificence. At New Year, the royal couple gave each other gold cups. In January, they were Hugh's guests at Hanley Castle on the River Trent. But, as imminent events were to make clear, Isabella had lost the love and trust of her husband and was barely tolerated by Hugh. Hers had become a miserable existence.

Charles IV had summoned Edward to pay homage for his lands in France, a summons Edward was evading on the grounds that he could not, at present, safely leave his kingdom. The Despensers did not want him to go, fearing that their enemies would pounce in his absence. Charles agreed to postpone the homage until July 1324, but his harboring of Mortimer had provoked mistrust and resentment in Edward. There was already ill feeling on both sides on account of the French illegally building a fortified bastide at Saint-Sardos in the English-held Agenais. Edward's Gascon subjects had attacked the bastide and killed a French sergeant. Edward had not sanctioned the attack, or even known about it, but the French were outraged, and war seemed likely. Mortimer promptly offered his sword to Charles IV, volunteering to fight against his King.

In January 1324, Charles conceded that Edward was not responsible for what had happened at Saint-Sardos, but in February, when it became clear that the English King was doing very little to rectify the situation, Charles threatened to seize Gascony.

The Despensers may have stoked Edward's fears with warnings that Isabella's sympathies lay with Charles IV. In March, Edward suddenly ceased paying the debts he owed her. In April, he made her send a plea to her brother not to seize Gascony, instructing her to remind Charles that her marriage had been contracted to secure a lasting peace between the two kingdoms.

Pembroke was sent to France to mediate with Charles IV over Gascony, but he died there, probably of apoplexy, on June 23. His death removed the last restraining influence on Edward. In July, breaking his word, the King instructed his envoys at the French court to refuse to hand over to Charles those English subjects who had risen at Saint-

Sardos, and again asked for his homage to be postponed, whereupon Charles lost patience and declared Gascony forfeit. In August, he sent an army under Charles of Valois to take possession of it.

In response, Edward appointed his inexperienced and unpopular half-brother, Edmund, Earl of Kent, as his lieutenant in Gascony. Despite being a young man of great stature and strength, Kent was gullible and unscrupulous. He immediately alienated the Gascons by extorting money from them, allowing his household officials to plunder at will, and abducting a young girl who took his fancy. When faced with the army of Charles of Valois, he proved disastrously ineffective in a military capacity, and was tricked by Valois into signing a six months' truce that left the French in possession of the greater part of the duchy.

The outbreak of hostilities between England and France had a devastating impact on Isabella's life, for it gave Hugh a pretext to treat her as an enemy of the state, further undermining her position as queen and annihilating what little influence she had left. He began by insisting that she swear an oath of loyalty to him personally, but she refused, as Henry de Beaumont had done. In consequence, on September 18, her estates were sequestered and taken back into the King's hands, depriving her of much of her income. Allegedly, Bishop Stapledon had advised Edward that this was necessary for security reasons, reminding him that the Queen's lands in Cornwall, with their valuable tin mines, were particularly vulnerable to invasion. But her inland estates had been seized too. Stapledon was hand in glove with Hugh and there can be little doubt that Hugh had persuaded the King that Isabella, as a Frenchwoman, was quite capable of plotting treachery against him with her brother. Back in 1317, when Queen Marguerite's estates had been briefly sequestered when war with France had seemed imminent, she had been compensated with a substantial allowance; not so Isabella. On September 28, her allowance for her personal expenses was cut from 11,000 marks ($6.9 million) annually to 1,000 marks ($636,000).

Isabella was not a woman to countenance such affronts to her dignity and her regal position. Privately, she blamed both Hugh and Stapledon for the loss of her dower—Hugh would be charged with this in 1326. But there was worse to come. On September 28, again purportedly on Stapledon's advice, Parliament ordered the banishment of all subjects of the King of France from the households of the King and Queen, which ef-

fectively deprived Isabella of the loyal service of twenty-seven French servants who had been with her since she had first come to England, among
them her chaplains and her physician. On October 9, the King ordered a
general levy of all gold due to the Queen to be diverted to his own coffers,
together with money he owed her. From that time, the Despensers "sent
her from the King's coffers what they would."[10] Isabella, one of the greatest landowners in the realm, had been effectively reduced to the status of
a humble pensioner.

But Hugh was by no means finished with her. Around Michaelmas,
her three youngest children—Prince Edward had his own household—
were removed from her custody and sent to "divers places in the realm,"[11]
probably on the grounds that, as a Frenchwoman, she might encourage
them to commit treason against their father. John of Eltham, who was
now eight, was given into the care of Eleanor de Clare and seems to have
remained with her, while Eleanor, six, and Joan, three, were sent to live
with Hugh's sister Isabella, Lady Monthermer, at Pleshey Castle and
Marlborough. In 1325, they would be moved to Bristol under the guardianship of the elder Despenser. It has been argued that the children were
merely given their own households, in accordance with royal tradition,
but moving them all from their mother's charge into the keeping of the
Despensers suggests something more sinister. The terrible revenge Isabella was to mete out to the Despensers reflects her hatred and resentment. If she did complain, clearly no one took any notice.

It has been suggested that Isabella was not overly maternal, and even
guilty of neglecting her children, but she was no less devoted than any
other royal mother in an age in which it was customary for heirs to the
throne to have their own households from infancy. Prince Edward had
been assigned his in babyhood, but his three younger siblings had remained with their mother since 1320–21. Isabella was ambitious for her
children and cared very much about what happened to them. Her great
joy at being reunited later on with the younger ones shows how much
she had missed them during their separation. Her children, especially
Edward, remained devoted to her all their lives, which would surely not
have been the case had she been a distant and uncaring mother.

Isabella had lost her status, her husband, her children, her influence,
her income, and her friends. They were the final provocations in a marriage that had been full of challenges. She might have referred to Edward

as her sweetheart or her very sweet lord and friend in letters she sent him around this time, but it is hard to believe that these were more than empty words. He had let her live in a climate of fear and persecution; it was probably out of self-preservation that she kept up the pretense of being a loving wife. But in a letter to Charles IV, she protested bitterly about the sequestration of her lands and the loss of her French servants, and accused Despenser of depriving her of Edward's love, complaining that "she was held in no higher consideration than a maidservant in the palace of the King, her husband," to whom she referred disparagingly as "a gripple miser"[12]—one who had been mean to her but lavish toward another.

Eleanor de Clare was now "appointed, as it were, guardian of the Queen, and carried her seal; nor could the Queen write to anybody without her knowledge, whereat my lady the Queen was equally indignant and distressed." It seems that Hugh and Edward were using Eleanor as both jailer and spy. "Greatly enraged,"[13] Isabella managed to circumvent this supervision and smuggled out yet another letter of complaint to her brother.

When a shocked Charles IV reacted with angry demands for fairer treatment for Isabella, Edward ignored him. On November 18, he gave orders that only £1 ($620) per day was to be allocated to the Queen for her food and drink. He was more generous when it came to the maintenance of her household, for which 1,000 marks ($636,000) per day were allocated, but he also ordered that any Frenchmen remaining in England were to be arrested and imprisoned, and their property confiscated. Some of Isabella's French servants had already fled to France, but some had stayed behind, including her clerks, her two chaplains, and her physician. All were now apprehended and immured in religious houses, and Isabella was unable to secure their freedom by giving sureties for their good behavior, a concession usually extended to persons of rank. In France, Charles IV erupted in fury at the arrest of his subjects, much to the embarrassment of the English envoys at his court.

Like Isabella herself, the Lanercost chronicler believed that Hugh was responsible for the sequestration of her lands and the arrest of her servants. He also asserted that Hugh had persuaded the King to ask the Pope for an annulment of his marriage to Isabella and had himself sent Robert Baldock and an "irreligious" Dominican friar, Stephen Dunheved, to Avignon to present the petition. Dunheved was indeed sent to the Papal Curia on secret business at this time, while the *Annales Paulini* refer to rumors of an annulment. But there is no further mention of this.

Hugh's cruelty toward the Queen was well known in diplomatic circles. Pope John heard of it in Avignon, and himself wrote to Hugh reprimanding him for his harsh treatment, his misgovernment, and for causing bitterness between princes.

8

"Secret Conferences"

✳

EDWARD II NOW FACED THE JOINT THREATS OF WAR WITH France and an invasion led by Mortimer. Mortimer was in Hainault trying to raise troops, with the intention of invading from Holland or Zeeland. Diplomatic relations between England and Hainault were already frosty following disputes over maritime trade and, on October 24, Edward wrote to Count William protesting about his harboring English traitors. The Count took no notice.

The situation was critical, but the Pope did not think it irretrievable. Around December, on his instructions, his two nuncios in Paris suggested that Queen Isabella be sent to France to use her renowned powers of mediation in the interests of defusing the crisis and settling the dispute over Gascony.

Once this escape route opened up before her, Isabella must have been desperate to take it. Going to France as England's ambassadress extraordinary would restore her status as Queen, afford her a respite from the miseries she had to endure at home, and remove her from the orbit of the Despensers. By her own later admission, she was so anxious to get away that she made every effort to appear friendly toward Hugh so that he would not veto the idea. This was probably her strategy when she and Edward spent Christmas with Hugh and Eleanor at Nottingham Castle. In January 1325, Isabella and Eleanor went to Kenilworth, while the King and Hugh rode north.

That month, the royal council and Parliament debated the Pope's proposal. Hugh was against Isabella leaving England; despite her blandishments, he knew her to be his enemy and had every reason to fear that she might plot against him while she was abroad. Yet because Edward feared to go to France himself and leave his favorites unprotected, sending Isabella seemed a sensible solution, and he began seriously to consider it, while his envoys in Paris put pressure on him and the Bishop of Norwich, the Earl of Richmond, and Henry de Beaumont all got to work on Hugh. The Bishop of Winchester, who had just returned from France, reported that Charles IV had promised that if Edward would create his son Duke of Aquitaine and send him to France with the Queen to pay homage, Charles would restore the lands he had taken and make peace.

These persuasions proved decisive. Parliament decided that any expedient was preferable to war, and the King reluctantly consented to Isabella going to France, with Prince Edward following as soon as a satisfactory settlement was reached. Hugh agreed because he thought the plan less dangerous than the King leaving him unprotected. He underestimated Isabella in every way that counted. Edward too made fatal assumptions about Isabella's loyalty. Robert of Reading commented on "the insane stupidity of the King, who, condemned by God and man [for] his infamy and his illicit bed, should never have put aside his noble consort and her soft wifely embraces, [nor been] contemptuous of her noble birth."

At some stage, Isabella resolved to "secure revenge and satisfaction"[1] for the wrongs the Despensers had done her. Thomas Walsingham, writing much later, asserts that Edward suspected her of maintaining "a secret correspondence with the enemies of the state." If so, it is hardly likely that he would have sanctioned her going to France, where Mortimer, the deadliest enemy of all, was plotting his ruin. There is no contemporary evidence that she had begun intriguing before her departure with those who later became her allies, but she could have been working in secret.

She was certainly planning to reveal everything to her brother Charles and enlist help. She may have believed that if, from the safety of France, she threatened to desert Edward, his desire to avert a worse public scandal might drive him to dismiss his favorites. This is corroborated by the author of the *Vita Edwardi Secundi*, who, soon after the Queen had left England, expressed the opinion: "Small wonder if she does not like Hugh, through whom her uncle [Lancaster] perished, and by whom she was deprived of her servants and all her rents; consequently, she will not (so many think) return until Hugh le Despenser is wholly removed from the King's side."

Whatever the extent of Isabella's schemes—it is not known exactly what, at this stage, was in her mind—she could number among her potential allies Adam Orleton, Bishop of Hereford, Henry Burghersh, Bishop of Lincoln, and John of Droxford, Bishop of Bath and Wells, who are referred to by Baker as her "disciples" and were all close associates of Mortimer. She could count on her uncle, Henry of Lancaster (the late Earl's brother), John de Stratford, who became bishop of Winchester later that year, William Airmyn, Keeper of the Privy Seal, and even the King's own half-brothers, Norfolk and Kent. Richmond, now in France, had shown himself to be sympathetic, and Henry de Beaumont was as dependable as ever.

Baker says that Orleton fueled the Queen's anger against the Despensers, exploiting her resentment at the loss of her estates. But Orleton was still in disgrace at this time. It was only later that he emerged as one of her strongest allies. Henry of Lancaster was an honorable man in his mid-forties, known for his courtesy and balanced judgment. He blamed the Despensers for his brother's death and wanted revenge. Isabella had worked closely with Airmyn in 1321, sharing custody of the Great Seal.

Kent resented Hugh's influence; he and his brother Norfolk, both wild young men, openly criticized the King for allowing it. According to Froissart, Kent and Isabella were both "secretly told of the danger they were in from Sir Hugh, and of their probable destruction, unless they took good care of themselves." This is corroborated by Isabella's later claim that she went in fear of her life from Hugh and shows that her friends were able to pass secret messages to her, suggesting that a network of intrigue did in fact exist. In 1326, it would be claimed that Edward had once "carried a knife in his hose to kill the Queen and had said that, if he had no other weapon, he would crush her with his teeth."[2] It may have been a threat uttered in the heat of the moment, yet, given the circumstances, Isabella took it seriously. Having been in fear that Hugh and the King were bent on doing away with her, she must have been desperate to leave England.

There is no direct evidence that at this time Roger Mortimer was linked to an opposition party forming around the Queen, or indeed to Isabella herself. But Edward, ever suspicious, had demanded that

Charles IV ensure that "Mortimer and the other traitors and enemies of the King had left the realm of France before the coming of my lady," for the avoidance of any "perils and dishonour" that might ensue.[3]

Isabella had probably long since come to regard Mortimer as another victim of the Despensers. She had known him, perhaps quite well, for about sixteen years, and must have been aware of his unblemished record of loyalty to the Crown in the years before the Despensers had forced him into rebellion, and come to recognize that he was her greatest potential ally against them. Here was a man who had tried to have them assassinated and was prepared to plot an invasion of England in order to be revenged on them. It is possible that Isabella had already thought of making common cause with Mortimer once she escaped abroad.

Early in February 1325, the Queen had a private meeting with Henry Eastry, the Prior of Christ Church, and confided certain concerns to him. What she said won his sympathy—and filled him with foreboding. On February 8, he wrote to Archbishop Reynolds: "It would be quite right that the Lady Queen, before she crosses over, should have restored to her accustomed and dignified state."[4] Reynolds apparently repeated this advice to the King, who ensured that Isabella departed for France with full royal honors, although he did not restore her estates or her income.

On February 18, Edward asked Charles IV for a prolongation of their truce until June 24; he wanted Isabella to return home in time to accompany him on a visit to Gascony. Charles's safe-conduct arrived before March 5, when Edward drew up a list of instructions for Isabella's guidance. She was to travel with a train of thirty persons, and he himself carefully selected all those who were to accompany her, choosing only those he believed to be loyal to himself and the Despensers. Isabella privately thought she should be better attended, and later accused Hugh of ensuring that she was meanly provided for. She had a point. In 1313, when she and Edward had visited France, they had taken a retinue of 220 people.

Early in March, Isabella said farewell to Edward and Hugh at the Tower and traveled down to Dover. "On her departure, she did not seem to anyone to be offended," Edward later wrote, remembering how she even bade a courteous farewell to Hugh. "Towards no one was she more agreeable, myself excepted." He recalled also "the amiable looks and words between them, and the great friendship she professed for him on her crossing the sea."[5]

At Canterbury, Isabella left her huntsmen and hounds in the care of Prior Eastry, who later complained to Hugh that they were eating him out of house and home. Meanwhile, the Pope had written to congratulate her on having once again assumed the role of peacemaker.

At last, on March 9, 1325, "the Queen departed very joyfully, happy with a twofold joy: pleased to visit her native land and her relatives and delighted to leave the company of some whom she did not like."[6] She disembarked at Wissant that same day and rode to Boulogne, where she walked to the church of Our Lady and gave thanks for her safe arrival. "The captains of the town and the Abbot welcomed her with joy and gave her lodging and hospitality," and she and her party "rested and refreshed themselves there for five days. On the sixth day, they left Boulogne, riding on horses and donkeys, which they had brought from England. The Queen was escorted and accompanied by all the knights of the surrounding country, who had come to see her and entertain her, since she was the sister of their lord the King."[7]

At Poissy, Isabella met up with Stratford and Airmyn, the English envoys, and twice entertained them to dinner. There she began preliminary talks with representatives of King Charles, only to discover that the peace negotiations were already in deadlock.

On March 21, at Pontoise, she was received by fifteen-year-old Jeanne of Evreux, her brother's bride-to-be; he had had his marriage to Blanche of Burgundy annulled, and his second wife, Marie of Luxembourg, had died in childbirth the previous year. Soon afterward, Charles joined them. He was an intelligent and subtle man who had inherited the good looks of his father and brother and, like them, was called "the Fair." He was as severe as Philip IV to those who opposed him.

Isabella "at last saw the dear face of her beloved brother and embraced him."[8] According to Froissart, Charles "went up to her as she came into his chamber, took her right hand and kissed her, and said, 'Welcome, my fair sister!' The Queen, who had little joy in her heart except at being near her brother the King, tried to kneel down two or three times at his feet, but the King would not allow her and kept hold of her right hand, and enquired most kindly how she was. The Queen answered him calmly and told him sadly of all the injuries and felonies committed by Sir Hugh le Despenser and asked his aid and comfort. And when King Charles heard his sister's troubles, he took great pity on her, and comforted her most kindly, and said, 'Fair sister, stay with us; do not be distressed or downhearted. We will find some remedy for your condition.' The Queen knelt down and thanked him deeply."[9]

But the problem of the Despensers had to be shelved, for the avoidance of war was the more pressing priority and serious talks now began. Isabella's task was not easy, and she later confessed to Edward that she was veering daily between hope and despair. Stratford had assured the King that her mediation would almost certainly secure the return of lands that the French had conquered the previous year, but Charles was unyielding, reluctant to relinquish any of those territories.

The English envoys were also demanding a new truce in place of the humiliating one agreed by Kent and Charles of Valois. The French were not prepared to sanction anything but its prolongation. By March 29, matters had reached such a deadlock that Isabella was contemplating returning home, but the Papal legates lent her their support and she made one final appeal to her brother. Two days later, a peace treaty was finally drawn up. Under its terms, Edward was to surrender Gascony, Ponthieu, and Montreuil to Charles pending his paying homage by August; then Charles would restore all these lands to him except the much-fought-over county of the Agenais in Gascony, the tenure of which was to be the subject of arbitration by French judges. The French also agreed to a new truce, to last until June 9. Isabella reported all this to Edward on March 31, closing her letter with an apology for not having informed him sooner of these developments. She wrote that, if he approved, she would stay on at the French court until matters had been successfully concluded.

On April 1, accompanied by the English envoys, Isabella made a state entry into Paris. She rode astride her horse, wearing a gown of black velvet with such voluminous skirts that only the toes of her chequered black-and-white leather riding boots could be seen. Her unplaited hair was confined on each side in cylindrical crespinettes of gold fretwork suspended from a narrow fillet, the very latest in headdresses. "Many of the nobles came out to welcome her. She was escorted to the palace by Lord Robert of Artois [her cousin] and several others, and afterwards she stayed with all her company with the King at Paris."[10]

The draft treaty reached Edward on April 29; its terms were not wholly acceptable, but Charles was demanding a prompt response and Edward reluctantly agreed to them, complaining to the Pope that the Queen had not been granted all that she had requested and blaming the legates who had urged her mission and held out false hopes.

The unsatisfactory terms of the treaty may have represented a deliberate attempt by Charles IV, Isabella, Stratford, Airmyn, and the legates to discredit the Despenser administration and give the Queen a pretext for staying on in France. Isabella's letter of March 31 may also have been part of that strategy, as proof that she had made every effort to reach an acceptable settlement. In that letter, she had asked Edward's permission to remain in France, and he had since given it and sent her fresh funds to support herself.

On May 18, having returned to France with the treaty signed by Edward, Stratford and Airmyn dined with Isabella at the royal château at Vincennes. She was present on May 30 when the peace treaty was signed by her brother at the Palais de la Cité in Paris. By the time he ratified it on June 13, Edward was wondering if it had been worth his while to send Isabella to France, for she had been "no more successful than any other ambassadors, except that her brother, out of affection for her, prolonged the truce."[11] For all his fine words, Charles had been largely impervious to her persuasions, granting only a few financial concessions out of love for her.

Edward now began to agitate for Isabella's return, writing to her frequently of his desire to have her with him. But she was waiting for him to join her in France to pay homage to her brother. She had no wish to go back to England and live under Hugh's tyranny, and had resolved to prolong her stay for as long as possible.

Her expenditure was heavy. Up until September 29 alone, it amounted to £2,841.17s.7d. ($2.2 million). The money came from her confiscated revenues, and Edward had authorized her to withdraw any further funds she needed from the Bardis' branch in Paris; in total, the bankers are known to have lent her £3,674.13s.4d. ($3.1 million), much of it necessitated by the abrupt cessation of payments from the Exchequer on June 17; Edward now saw no need for his wife to stay in France any longer.

In July, Isabella was present when Charles IV married Jeanne of Evreux at Annet-sur-Marne. Soon after the wedding, embarrassed by her dwindling funds, Isabella left Paris and took up residence in the royal château at Châteauneuf, forty miles to the west. From July 18 to September 1, Charles subsidized her living expenses. During this period, she traveled to Saint-Hilaire, Poissy, Mantes, Saint-Germain, Corbeil, and Fontainebleau, visiting churches and entertaining; among her many guests were the new Queen of France, the Abbot of Saint-Denis, the Earl of Richmond, and the Papal legates.

When she heard that the Bishop of Norwich had died on July 6, Isabella recommended William Airmyn to the Pope as his replacement. John XXII moved quickly, providing Airmyn to the see of Norwich on July 19. Yet in England four days later, the King's candidate, Robert Baldock, was elected by the unsuspecting chapter of Norwich as their bishop.

By August 15, arrangements had been made for the ceremony of homage, which was to take place at Beauvais, and Edward began to prepare for his journey. But the Despensers were filled with trepidation at the prospect of his leaving them at the mercy of their enemies, and were unwilling to afford Isabella any opportunity of regaining her influence with her husband. Thus, when the proposed visit was debated in council, opinion was divided as to the wisdom of the King leaving his realm at this time. But Henry of Lancaster, who was in favor of his doing so, carried the day.

On August 23, Edward arrived at Dover with his heir, but the Despensers had not ceased urging him to stay in England. The next day, he announced that he was too ill to travel and was sending a new embassy to France to make different arrangements.

It was at this point that Isabella revived Charles's original plan for Prince Edward to be invested with his father's continental possessions and be sent to France to pay homage in his stead. That way, the terms of the treaty could be met, and with the heir to England in her custody, she herself could secure the upper hand in any confrontation with Edward over the Despensers. It would also remove her elder son out of the orbit of the favorites. On September 1, while hosting a dinner for Bishop Stratford in Paris, she raised the matter with her brother.

Charles agreed, whereupon Stratford hastened back to England to obtain the King's approval. The Despensers were greatly in favor of the idea, for "they dared neither to cross the Channel with King Edward, nor to remain behind in England in his absence."[12] Edward therefore agreed to send his son to France in his stead, little realizing that he was placing in Isabella's hands a valuable hostage to fortune.

On September 10, the twelve-year-old Prince was created duke of Aquitaine. Two days later, in the company of Stratford, Stapledon, Henry de Beaumont, and many lords and knights, he boarded a vessel for France. Prior to his departure, the King had commanded Stapledon to raise a loan to help meet the mounting expenses of Isabella's household, but the money was only to be given to her once she had agreed to return to England. Clearly Edward was feeling edgy at the prospect of Isabella having his heir in her custody. Before young Edward sailed, he was made to promise that he would not accept any guardian or enter into any marriage alliance without the King's permission. Negotiations were well advanced for the Prince's marriage to Eleanor of Aragon, and Edward had already applied to the Pope for the necessary dispensation. The Prince told his father that it would be his pleasure to obey his commandments, as far as he could, all his days.

When his ship dropped anchor at Boulogne on September 14, Isabella was waiting to greet him and take him with her to Paris. She must have been overjoyed to see her son, but not so pleased to discover that Stratford had brought with him a safe-conduct for her from the King, who had commanded her to return home "without delay"[13] as soon as the Prince had performed his homage. Evading this issue, she turned her attention to the imminent consecration of the new Bishop of Norwich. A few days earlier, much to Edward's chagrin, Robert Baldock had been obliged by the Pope to resign in favor of William Airmyn, thanks to Isabella's influence. Isabella would have known how furious Edward and the Despensers would be at the success of her candidate, and to ensure that no further obstacles were placed in his way, she arranged for Airmyn to be consecrated in France on September 15, "for which the King was angry."[14] But it was too late for him to do anything about it, apart from vengefully refusing to allow Airmyn the estates (lands) of his see.

On September 22, the Queen and her son arrived in Paris, where Isabella witnessed the young Duke of Aquitaine's first audience with his uncle, Charles IV, who "received him kindly."[15] Two days later, the Prince did homage to Charles at Vincennes in the presence of his mother and many English lords. Immediately afterward, Charles ordered the withdrawal of French troops from Gascony.

Isabella had gained the backing of several men at her brother's court, notably Robert of Artois. She had won the support of English "exiles who were the enemies of the King of England, but who had gained the Queen's favour."[16] All had scores to settle with Edward and the Despensers. Intelligence reports sent back to England show that some of these exiles had kept company with Mortimer as he moved around the Continent.

Isabella's chief supporter at this time appears to have been the Earl of Richmond, the principal English envoy in France. Greatly offended by the Despensers, he was now "of the affinity of the Queen"[17] and often in her company. Edward recalled him many times, but was repeatedly ignored. Another who attached himself to Isabella's growing party was Kent, who had returned to France in August in company with the Earl of Surrey. Henry de Beaumont had long been Isabella's friend and was, like her, a victim of the Despensers' spite. Cognizant of political opinion in the north of England, he knew that a majority of Edward's subjects there had turned against him, alienated by his failure to deal effectively with Scottish raiders. Beaumont would later return to England to sound out northern lords as to where their loyalty lay. Judging by how promptly Henry of Lancaster and Norfolk, the Earl Marshal of England, were to come to Isabella's support the following year, they must have been in secret communication with her.

Prince Edward's former tutor, Richard de Bury, joined the Queen in Paris. In his capacity as young Edward's official receiver in Gascony, he had been illicitly diverting revenues to her, for which he narrowly escaped arrest by fleeing to the French court. Bury had long since discovered in Isabella a kindred spirit with a love of books, and his first loyalty was to her and the Prince, who was always to look on him with great favor.

Isabella began to hold "secret conferences"[18] with her supporters, relying on their counsel and giving offense to the officers who had been sent by Edward to provide her with guidance and were now appalled to see her consorting with her husband's enemies.

For more than a year, she was to insist that her quarrel was with the Despensers alone. Yet there is evidence that the exiles surrounding her were bent on targeting the King too, and doing their utmost to persuade her that she would be justified in overthrowing a weak and tyrannical regime. Isabella apparently spent weeks agonizing over what course to take and taking time to cement her alliances, which explains why she did not deliver Edward any ultimatum regarding the Despensers until November, and why she continued to send cordial letters to Hugh.

Charles's retention of the Agenais had left Edward seething with rage. Too late, he attempted to reassume the rights he had just devolved upon his heir, but Charles was having none of it and declared the whole duchy of Aquitaine forfeit, much to the King's fury. Isabella's peace mission had been in vain. Angry with Airmyn and Richmond because he felt they had betrayed him over the treaty, Edward ordered their arrest and brought a case against the absent Airmyn in the Court of King's Bench.

He was beginning to be perturbed by Isabella's failure to return home and by her having his heir in her custody. Now that the treaty had been concluded and the homage performed, he saw no reason for them to stay in France.

With the backing of Charles IV, Isabella was in a strong position and had the advantage. Edward was very fond of his thirteen-year-old son, and she knew that the Prince would be a powerful bargaining counter in forcing her husband to banish the Despensers. Moreover, as the King was painfully aware, he was also a valuable asset in the dynastic marriage market and could be used to forge an alliance that might assure Isabella of support in her quarrel with Edward.

Soon after Michaelmas, Edward wrote to her, "advising that she should escort her son back to England as soon as possible."[19] Isabella replied that Charles was treating them with great kindness, but keeping them there against their will. Not satisfied with this, Edward continued to command or entreat her to come home and ordered Stratford to put pressure on her and Charles. During discussions with the Bishop, Isabella expressed anger at the sequestration of her estates and fear that she would not be safe in England. Stratford insisted that she would come to no harm, but she was not reassured and put Edward off with a succession of flimsy excuses.

On October 18, the King expressed to the Pope his mounting concern about the Queen lingering in France. Meanwhile, Isabella was often in the company of King Charles and Queen Jeanne, "and the news she told them from England gave them little pleasure."[20]

Walter Stapledon, Bishop of Exeter, was still in Paris and becoming increasingly worried. He was not welcome in France because he was closely associated with the Despensers, and he had been warned that if he ever set foot there, he would be tortured. Before leaving England, he had confided his fears for his safety to King Edward, who had asked Isabella for an undertaking that Stapledon would come to no harm, which she had readily given. Despite this, he was treated by French courtiers and officials "as if he were guilty of some crime."[21]

Isabella thought him untrustworthy and "unreasonably avaricious."[22] She excluded him from her conferences and refused to receive any letters from him, sending them back unread through Stratford. Stapledon did not approve of her activities in Paris, especially the favor she showed to the English exiles, and he was so horrified by intelligence suggesting that some were plotting the murder of the King that he sought for a way to return immediately to England without alerting anyone to his suspicions. But he was never to accuse Isabella of being a party to treason.

Angry that Stapledon had failed to raise the loan Edward had ordered, she sent for him and reminded him that he had been commanded by the King to help finance her stay in Paris but had done nothing. Lying, he said that Edward had summoned him home, but Isabella demanded to see the letter, which, of course, he could not produce. She forbade him to leave France without her permission.

She needed funds because on November 14 Edward ceased paying her expenses. "He ordered his wife to return to England without delay,"[23] and his messengers relayed this command to her in the presence of Charles IV.

Isabella made her views very clear. "I feel that marriage is a joining together of man and woman, maintaining the undivided habit of life, and that someone has come between my husband and myself, trying to break this bond," she said. "I protest that I will not return until this intruder is removed, but, discarding my marriage garment, shall assume the robes of widowhood and mourning until I am avenged of this Pharisee."[24] Effectively she was calling Hugh an enemy of Christ.

Stapledon, who was present, expected Charles IV to send Isabella back to her husband, and bristled when the French King, seeing her distress and "not wishing to detain her," told him, "The Queen has come of her own will, and may freely return when she so wishes. But, if she prefers to remain in these parts, she is my sister, and I refuse to expel her."[25]

Soon afterward, Stapledon received a death threat from some English exiles. It was enough to make him defy Isabella and flee to England under cover of darkness, disguised as a merchant or pilgrim. Hastening to the King, he warned him that some of his banished enemies were plotting to kill him and urged him to again command the immediate return of the Queen and the Prince. Feeling embarrassed about having deserted Isabella so precipitously, he wrote to her excusing his conduct, probably at Edward's behest.

Isabella, now wearing only black mourning, with a nun-like veil and chin barbe, "like a doleful lady who has lost her lord,"[26] wrote to her husband, declaring that neither she nor her son would return to his court until the Despensers had been dismissed from his presence, for she believed "it was the intention to cause her to be put to death if she returned to England."[27] She also insisted on reaching an agreement with Edward regarding her status and her income. In another letter, she warned that she and her brother, with the aid of her supporters in France, intended to do "that which will turn out not to the prejudice of the lord King, but to the destruction of Hugh alone."[28] This could mean only one thing, that she was resolved to remove the Despensers by force. At the end of November, Stratford arrived back in England with her letters and reported all this to the King.

Isabella's demands and threats indicate that she was willing to return to Edward, but on her own terms. Given his long history of breaking his word and putting the interests of his favorites before all other considerations, he could not be trusted to banish the Despensers for good, nor could Isabella have expected them to remain meekly in exile, causing no trouble. Hugh, she must have known, would not hesitate to take brutal revenge on anyone who opposed him, while Edward had already demonstrated that he was unlikely to intervene on her behalf. Thus she probably made her demands in the full expectation that Edward would refuse, giving her a pretext to remain in France until her future could be safely assured through the intervention of her brother and her supporters.

Edward was shocked by her ultimatum. In December, he told Parliament:

> You know how providentially, as then it seemed, the Queen crossed to France to make peace, being told that, when her mission was accomplished, she should at once return. And this she promised with a good will. And, on her departure, she did not seem to anyone to be offended. As she took her leave, she saluted all and went away joyfully. But now, someone has changed her attitude. Someone has primed her with inventions. For I know that she has not fabricated any affront out of her own head. Yet she says that Hugh le Despenser is her adversary and hostile to her. It is surprising that she has conceived this dislike of Hugh for, when she departed, towards no one was she more agreeable, myself excepted. For this reason, Hugh is much cast down, but he is nevertheless prepared to show his innocence in any way whatsoever. Hence, I firmly believe that the Queen has been led into this error at the suggestion of someone, and he is in truth wicked and hostile, whoever he may be. Therefore, deliberate wisely, that she whom the teaching of evil men incites to guile may be led back to the path of unity by your prudent and kindly reproof.[29]

The official line, therefore, was that Isabella had been unduly influenced, which paved the way for her to return without recriminations. But Edward's defense of Hugh cannot have impressed his listeners, most of whom would have known that Hugh had certainly given Isabella many causes for offense and shown himself hostile to her. Yet the refusal of the Queen of England to return home was creating a major scandal and threatening the security of the realm, and Parliament was anxious to resolve the situation as soon as possible.

Hugh made a public declaration to the lords that his intentions toward the Queen had always been innocent of malice. Edward put pressure on the bishops, who reluctantly agreed to write a fatherly letter to Isabella, exhorting her to set aside "her baseless ill-feeling" and return home to her husband. Their letter, which was dated December 1, 1325, read:

> Most dear and potent lady, the whole country is disturbed by your news, and the answers which you have lately sent to our lord King; and because you delay your return out of hatred for Hugh le Despenser, everyone predicts that much evil will follow. Indeed, Hugh le Despenser has solemnly demonstrated his innocence before all, and that he has never harmed the Queen, but done everything in his power to help her; and that he will always in future do this, he has confirmed by his corporeal oath. He added, moreover, that he could not believe that these threats ever proceeded from your head alone, but that they come from some other source, especially as, before your departure, you showed yourself gracious to him and afterwards sent him friendly letters, which he produced in full Parliament.

The phraseology so closely mirrors that in the King's speech that it might have been dictated to the bishops by either Edward himself, or Hugh.

The letter continued:

> Wherefore, dearest lady, [we] beseech you as [our] lady, [we] warn you as a daughter, to return to our lord King, your husband, putting aside all rancour. You who have gone away for the sake of peace, do not, for the sake of peace, delay to return. For all the inhabitants of our land fear that many evils will result from your refusal to return. They fear the arrival of foreigners and that their goods will be plundered. They do not think that this comes from due affection, that you should wish to destroy a people so devoted to you, through hatred of one man. But, as for what you have written, that what your brother the King of France and your other friends of their country intend to do on your behalf will turn out not to the prejudice of the lord King or anyone else, but to the destruction of Hugh alone: dearest and most powerful lady, refuse to give an opening to such a business, as its furthering can in all probability bring irreparable loss. The English people predict from these threats the coming of foreigners and say, if the French come, they will plunder the land. It is impossible that the innocent should not suffer equally with the guilty, and what the innocent do not snatch away they

shall lose. Alas! Clergy and people with complaining voice reiterate their fear that they and theirs will be utterly destroyed through the hatred felt for one man. Wherefore, lady Queen, accept wise counsel and do not delay your return. For your longed-for arrival will restrain the malice of men and restrict all opportunities for evil.

It was a clever letter, crafted to put Isabella firmly in the wrong and render her responsible for any hostilities that resulted from her actions. But, according to the author of the *Vita Edwardi Secundi*, "notwithstanding this letter, mother and son refused to return to England."[30]

9

"Pretences, Delays and False Excuses"

✳

ISABELLA WAS NOW FINDING HERSELF SERIOUSLY SHORT OF THE money that enabled her to maintain the state of a queen and pay her servants, so she sent some of her people home. At the end of November, members of her entourage and Prince Edward's began arriving back in England. She was relying on the loans from the Bardi, but there was no guarantee that these would continue. Charles IV again came to her rescue, lending her money and ordering that necessities be supplied to her, and wrote to Edward "that he could not permit her to return to him unless she were guaranteed from the evil that was meditated against her by her enemies, the Despensers."

On December 1, Edward wrote to Isabella ordering her to come home.

> Lady, oftentimes we have sent to you of our great desire to have you with us, and of our great grief of heart at your long absence; as you do us great mischief by this, we will that you come to us with all speed and without further excuses. Before the homage was performed, you made the advancement of that business an excuse, and now that we have sent, by the Bishop of Winchester, our safe conduct to you, you will not come for fear of Hugh le Despenser. Whereat we cannot marvel too much when we recall your flattering deportment towards each other in our presence, so amicable and sweet was your manner, with special assurances and looks, and other tokens of the firmest friendship, and also, since then, your very especial letters to him of late date, which he has shown to us.

In his next sentence, Edward demonstrated that he was either a liar or capable of extraordinary self-deception.

> And certes, Lady, we know for truth, and so know you, that he has always procured from us all the honour he could for you, nor to you hath either evil or villainy been done since you entered into our companionship; unless, as you may yourself remember, once when we had cause to give you secretly some words of reproof for your pride, but without other harshness. And doubtless both God and the law of Holy Church require you, both for your honour and ours, for nothing earthly to trespass against our commandments, or to forsake our company.

As a wife subject to her husband's will, Isabella was in a difficult situation. If she obeyed his command and returned to him, having complained bitterly of Hugh, she might be placing herself in danger. If she defied Edward and stayed where she was, she risked incurring the censure of the Church and society in general. Edward was aware of this, yet he was too blind to see that most people regarded her as more sinned against than sinning. Only able to perceive himself as a wronged husband, he continued:

> And we are much displeased, now the homage has been made to our dearest brother, the King of France, and we have such fair prospect of amity, that you, whom we sent to make the peace, should be the cause (which God forfend!) of increasing the breach between us, especially by things which are feigned and contrary to the truth.

Evidently Edward did not pause to ask himself why Isabella should feign hatred for Despenser. It was plain to many that she had sufficient cause to hate him, and it was not in her interests to foment trouble with the French. But Edward chose to make out that she was deliberately creating a breach between the two countries. He concluded:

> Wherefore we charge you as urgently as we can that, ceasing from all pretences, delays and false excuses, you come to us with all the haste you can. Our said Bishop [Stratford] has reported to us that our brother the King told you that, by the tenor of your safe-conduct, you

would not be delayed or molested in coming to us, as a wife should to her lord. As to your expenses, when you come to us, we will provide that there shall be no deficiency in aught pertaining to you, and that you be not in any way dishonoured by us. Also, we require of you to suffer our dear son Edward to return to us with all possible speed, as we have ordered him, and that you in no way let [prevent] him. For we much desire to see him and to speak with him.[1]

That same day, Edward also wrote to Charles IV, attempting to sweeten him with falsehoods:

It seems that you have been told, dearest brother, by persons whom you consider worthy of credit, that our companion, the Queen of England, dare not return to us, being in peril of her life, as she apprehends, from Hugh le Despenser. Certes, dearest brother, it cannot be that she can have fear of him or any other man in our realm, since, by God, if either Hugh or any other living being in our dominions sought to do her ill and it came to our knowledge, we would chastise him in a manner that should be an example to all others. And this is, and always will be, our entire will, as long as, by God's mercy, we have the power. And, dearest brother, know certainly that we have never perceived that he has either secretly or openly, by word, look or action, demeaned himself otherwise than he ought in all points to do to so very dear a lady. And when we remember the amiable looks and words between them that we have seen, and the great friendship that she professed for him on her crossing the sea, and the loving letters which she has lately sent him, which he has shown to us, we have no power to believe that our consort can, of herself, credit such things of him. We cannot in any way believe it of him, who, after our own person, is the man of all our realm who would most wish to do her honour and has always shown good sincerity to you. We pray you, dearest brother, not to give credence to anyone who would make you otherwise suppose, but to put your faith in those who know the truth of this matter.

Wherefore we beseech you, dearest brother, both for your honour and ours, but more especially for that of our said consort, that you compel her to return to us with all speed; for certes, we have been ill at ease for want of her company, in which we have much delight. We also entreat that you be pleased to deliver up to us Edward, our beloved eldest son [and] suffer him to come to us with all speed, for we have often sent for him, and we greatly wish to see him and to speak with him, and every day we long for his return.[2]

It is noticeable that Edward did not deny that Despenser had treated Isabella badly, but only stated that he himself had never perceived that he had, or could not believe it. His plea to Charles to be mindful of Isabella's honor shows that he knew her reputation was at stake. Medieval society frowned upon women who deserted their husbands, however provoked; a wife was her husband's property, and his honor was vested in her. Public opinion and the law would almost always be on his side, especially when that wife had deprived her husband, not to mention her King, of his son and heir. But Edward grossly underestimated the extent of public sympathy for Isabella. Rumors were now circulating in England that she would invade with Kent and have her revenge on the hated Despensers. While some "declared that she was the betrayer of the King and kingdom, others [said] that she was acting for peace and the common welfare of the kingdom, and for the removal of evil counsellors from the King."[3]

On December 2, Edward wrote to the Prince, commanding him to "return to us with all speed, in company with your mother, if so be that she come quickly; and if she will not come, then come you without further delay, for we have great desire to speak with you; therefore stay not for your mother, nor anyone else, on our blessing."[4]

Edward's letters confirmed what Isabella had long known: that he was deaf to her complaints and resolved only to put Hugh's interests first. The Prince found himself in an impossible position, torn between his duty to his father and sovereign and his obedience to his mother, that wounded figure in mourning. He loved both his parents, but he was only thirteen; how could he defy his mother when he was in her custody in a foreign kingdom where her brother ruled? All he could do was reply to his father that he did remember the promises he had made at Dover, but he could not return home because his mother would not allow it, and he felt he should stay with her on account of her great unease of mind and unhappiness. Isabella, meanwhile, assured Edward that if the Prince wished to return, she would not prevent it.

Charles IV discussed Edward's letters with Isabella, who asked him to inform her husband that "she could wish for nothing better than to live and die in the company of her dear lord," and would be with him, but for her fear of Hugh. She asked Charles to explain why she had feigned friendship with Despenser.[5]

On December 8, she wrote angrily to Stapledon:

> We have understood what you have told us by your letters and your excuses for leaving us in the way you did. Know that, since our very dear lord, the King of England, sent you with Edward our son into the regions of France, we promised faithfully to keep you from harm and to take good and safe care of you; and our lord the King commanded you to make a money loan for the expenses of our household, but—as we understand it—you have done nothing. And we forbade you to leave without our permission, and you gave us to understand that you had orders by letter from our very dear lord the King to leave, but you have never been able to show his letters to this effect. In disobedience, and despite our prohibition, and to the great dishonour of our said lord of England and ourselves, and to the advantage of Hugh le Despenser, you left us in an ill-intentioned way, so that we can see clearly that you are in league with the said Hugh, and more obedient towards him than towards us. We would therefore have you know that we do not consider you in any way excusable.[6]

It was probably at this point that Roger Mortimer reappeared in Isabella's life.

Her uncle, Charles of Valois, had recently died, and in December, his relatives gathered in Paris for his funeral. His daughter Jeanne, Countess of Hainault, had traveled from the Low Countries to be there. During her visit, she had talks with Charles IV and Isabella, and they doubtless discussed the poor relations between England and Hainault, the abortive negotiations for Prince Edward to marry one of Jeanne's daughters, Count William's anxiety to have the maritime dispute with England resolved, and the potential for an alliance between the two countries. It has been plausibly suggested[7] that Jeanne came armed with the firm offer of an alliance with Isabella, its terms being the amicable resolution of the dispute and the marriage of Prince Edward to a princess of Hainault, in return for aid from the Count.

Jeanne probably brought Roger Mortimer in her train; he was in Paris that December. For more than a year now, he had been in Hainault, endeavoring, with the Count's full approval, to raise troops for an invasion of England, and it would not be surprising if Jeanne had contrived a meeting between him and Isabella, now that Isabella was in open opposition to the Despensers. Before this date, there is no record of Mortimer being in France at the same time as Isabella, so it is unlikely that he was the person Edward had accused of exerting a bad influence on her.

Urged on by Charles, Mortimer, Jeanne, and her own supporters, Isabella may well have seen the benefits of an alliance with Hainault. Needing his troops for the Gascon war, Charles was reluctant to provide her with an army, and she must have known that invading England with French backing would not win her popular support. A pact with the increasingly prosperous county of Hainault would offer many trading advantages to the English. Certainly this alliance was being discussed in diplomatic circles during the weeks that followed. Most historians assert that until the autumn of 1326, Isabella's aim was purely the removal of the Despensers, but her intention of forming an alliance with Hainault in defiance of Edward II's wishes suggests that she was now contemplating the deposition of her husband in favor of her son. This, of course, was a momentous and controversial plan and in order to gain and retain popular support, Isabella strove to keep up the pretense that her quarrel was with the Despensers only.

Isabella and Mortimer met in Paris that December. Whether they were attracted to each other and immediately plunged into an adulterous affair is debatable. Adultery in a queen flouted every convention of Church and society and could have led to a scandal of epic proportions, for it might have compromised the succession. Isabella cannot have forgotten the cruel fates of her sisters-in-law.

Initially she and Mortimer had another tie to bind them: their grievances against the Despensers. Isabella was drawn to him because he was ready to fight for her cause; he was to become her chief ally. He was in a unique position to understand her alienation and her fear of Hugh, and he was a powerful cohort who was ready to take decisive action to rectify her situation. For Isabella, allying with Mortimer may well have been the most satisfying means of getting back at the King and his favorites.

He was everything Edward was not: strong, manly, courageous, audacious, and decisive. His marriage to Joan de Genville (who was still Edward's prisoner) had apparently been one of mutual interest, affection, and physical satisfaction, but he had been parted from her for nearly three years. He may have maneuvered himself, or been maneuvered, into Isabella's orbit for political reasons; possibly he had been in secret communication with her and her friends in Paris for some time. She was twenty-eight, beautiful, intelligent, and royal, a tragic figure in her widow's weeds. For Mortimer, becoming the protector and defender of the wife of the King who had condemned him to a terrible punishment and forced him into exile may have been an irresistible form of vengeance. He apparently took every opportunity to poison Isabella's mind against Edward, and probably had little difficulty in convincing her that if she returned to him, the King would murder her. At this, according to the Parliament Rolls, Isabella resolved never again to admit Edward to her bed.

The alliance between Isabella and Mortimer was also a meeting of minds and shared interests. Both were fascinated by the Arthurian legends, and both loved life's luxuries. Yet it was no equal relationship. By all accounts, Mortimer dominated Isabella, being a jealous, possessive man. He seems to have made the decisions, while she, by virtue of her rank, helped him to implement them. She appears not to have questioned what he did, but willingly complied, following his counsel "in all things."[8] After everything she had suffered, she was probably relieved to have a strong and domineering man take up her cause.

That they became lovers at some stage cannot be doubted, but they were discreet. The English chroniclers of the day do not mention an affair between them. Baker, for example, wrote only that "at that time, Mortimer secretly came first in the private household of the Queen." Yet he and some Continental chroniclers hinted that Mortimer—and others— shared Isabella's bed in Paris. Although in private Mortimer was reportedly very familiar with Isabella, in public the couple were always discreet. Even so, royal courts were hotbeds of gossip. Within two months, their alliance was notorious in diplomatic circles, even in England. Edward must have been appalled to learn that his Queen was associating with his traitorous arch-enemy.

Isabella was still in regular communication with Prior Eastry, who, on Christmas Day, told Archbishop Reynolds that she had stressed that "no real or personal calumnious charge should be instituted against our lord the King of England, or any people subject to him."[9] Except, of course, Hugh. Isabella was well aware that any attempt to oust the favorite would meet with popular support.

At the beginning of January 1326, realizing that the threat of an invasion from Hainault was no idle rumor, Hugh moved the bulk of his treasure to his castle at Caerphilly. Archbishop Reynolds learned from Prior Eastry that Charles IV had formally proposed a marriage between Prince Edward and one of the daughters of Count William of Hainault and Jeanne of Valois, and that the French King had asked the Count to lend his assistance to a French offensive against England. Alarmed, Reynolds immediately alerted the King.

Edward ordered watches set up along the south coast to prevent troops, arms, and letters from being smuggled into England. That same day, accusing her of holding seditious meetings, he ordered that Mortimer's mother be shut up in a convent for life, but the indomitable old lady had gone into hiding and managed to evade arrest. Restrictions were imposed on anyone trying to leave England. Before January 20, Reynolds told the King that he had heard from Eastry that France and Hainault had formed a secret alliance and would mount a joint invasion of England soon after Candlemas. There were reports that an invasion fleet was already gathering in Normandy and the Low Countries. Eastry, however, had been at pains to stress that these were only rumors. He believed that Charles was merely trying to intimidate Edward into dismissing the Despensers and had no real intention of making war on England.

But Edward took the invasion threat seriously. On January 22, he sent a placatory letter to Count William, offering to come to some friendly agreement, but received no response. He also wrote to Charles IV and sixteen French peers, asking that the Queen and the Prince be sent back to him forthwith. Again his plea was ignored. In February, he continued to put defenses in place against an invasion and proclaimed a general commission of array, "for the Queen will not come to the King, nor permit his son to return, and she is adopting the counsel of the Mortimer, the King's notorious enemy and rebel, and she is making alliances with the men of those parts and with other strangers, with intent to invade."[10] He commanded that if the Queen, the Prince, and the Earl of Kent returned, they were to be honorably received, but if they arrived with banners unfurled, bringing foreign soldiers, they were to be taken prisoner and the foreigners hanged as hostile invaders.

Throughout February, Isabella was in correspondence with the Countess Jeanne, doubtless in connection with the planned alliance and invasion. She was still maintaining the pretense that her quarrel was only with Despenser. In a letter written to Edward on February 5, she insisted that no one must think she had left him "without very great and justifiable cause." Hugh, she declared, had "wished to dishonour us by all means in his power," and she accused him of damaging her noble state, of cruelty toward her and of "ousting her from her lands." She admitted that she had for a long time held secret her hatred, but only as a means of escaping from danger, and concluded: "We desire above everything else, after God and the salvation of our soul, to be in the company of our said lord, and to die with him."[11] That same day, she wrote to Walter Reynolds, telling him that she feared Hugh because he governed the King and the entire realm. She could not return to England because her life was in danger.

Fearful that the Prince would be used as a pawn in a marriage alliance that was distasteful to him, Edward wrote to the Pope, begging him not to issue any dispensation for his son's marriage without first obtaining his consent. John XXII was growing concerned about the reports from Paris and commissioned two nuncios to mediate between Edward and Isabella in the hope of effecting a reconciliation. He wrote to Hugh suggesting that, since his interference had been cited by the Queen as the reason why she could not return to the King without danger to herself, he should retire from court at once and enable her to rejoin her husband without fear.

Isabella had planned to invade England in February 1326, but her preparations were not that far advanced. That month, she, Mortimer, and Kent made astonishing treasonous overtures to Robert the Bruce, almost certainly promising him recognition as king of an independent Scotland in return for an undertaking that, once the Queen's forces had landed, he would not invade England and prejudice the success of her offensive, forcing her to divert resources. Isabella knew that Edward would never agree to recognize Bruce as king of Scots. She was aware that left to him, the war with Scotland could never be won, and that it was better to reach a pragmatic solution that was to everyone's advantage.

These independent negotiations, together with the mooted marriage alliance with Hainault, constitute compelling evidence that Edward's deposition was now Isabella's ultimate goal, and that she was formulating policies against the time when she would be ruling England as regent for her son. It is significant that these developments all took place soon after she teamed up with Mortimer. Now, on his advice, "she [had] finally made firm her resolve."[12]

Isabella made Mortimer the Prince's adviser, ensuring that they were often in each other's company. She must have known that Edward would strongly disapprove of his heir associating with a convicted traitor, but she also knew that Mortimer's previous record of service to the Crown proved his loyalty and eminently qualified him to act as a counselor to the future King. Again, her defiance of Edward's wishes suggests that she was plotting his overthrow.

In March, the Papal envoys arrived in Paris and persuaded Isabella to agree to return to Edward on two conditions: that the Despensers withdrew from court and that he gave sworn guarantees to restore her status as queen and her estates. Mortimer was seized with violent jealousy. Incensed at the prospect of her being reunited with her husband, he threatened to kill her if she set foot in England. Kent was alarmed at the prospect of returning home and explaining his conduct to his brother, and sent a messenger to assure Edward that he had done nothing prejudicial to the King's interests.

The nuncios were due to go to England to urge the King to receive his wife kindly, but, having learned that he felt they had grievously let him down during the peace negotiations of 1325, they were too scared to cross the Channel. This led to unfounded rumors of intimidation on Edward's part, which were damaging in the extreme, since they appeared to substantiate Isabella's assertions that he had behaved badly toward her.

Perturbed by unconfirmed reports of a projected marriage alliance be-

tween the Prince and a princess of Hainault, and appalled at the boy's
continued exposure to the inappropriate influence of Mortimer, Edward
wrote sternly to his son:

> We understand by your letters that you remember well the charge
> we gave you, not to contract marriage without our knowledge and con-
> sent; and also that, at your departure from Dover, you said that it
> should be your pleasure to obey our commandments, as far as you
> could, all your days. Fair son, if thus you have done, you have acted
> wisely and well and according to your duty, so as to have grace of God,
> of us and all men; and, if not, then you cannot avoid the wrath of God,
> the reproach of men and our great indignation. And inasmuch it seems,
> as you say, you cannot return to us because of your mother, it causes us
> great uneasiness of heart that you cannot be allowed by her to do that
> which is your natural duty, the neglect of which will lead to much mis-
> chief.
>
> Fair son, you know how dearly she would have been loved and cher-
> ished if she had timely come, according to her duty, to her lord. We
> have knowledge of much of her evil doings, to our sorrow; how that she
> devises pretences for absenting herself from us on account of our dear
> and faithful nephew, Hugh le Despenser, who has always so well and
> loyally served us, while you and all the world have seen that she openly
> and notoriously, and knowing it to be contrary to her duty, and against
> the welfare of our crown, has attached to herself and retains in her
> company the Mortimer, our traitor and mortal foe, proved, attainted
> and adjudged; and him she accompanies in the house and abroad, in
> despite of us and our crown and of the right ordering of the realm—
> him, the malefactor whom our beloved brother, the King of France, at
> our request, banished from his dominions as our enemy. And, worse
> than this, if worse than this can be, she has done in allowing you to
> consort with our said enemy, making him your counsellor, and you
> openly to associate and herd with him, in the sight of all the world,
> doing so great a villainy and dishonour, both to yourself and to us, to
> the prejudice of our crown and of the laws and customs of our realm,
> which you are supremely bound to hold, preserve and maintain.
> Wherefore, fair son, desist you from a part which is so shameful, and
> may be to you perilous and injurious in too many ways.

We are not pleased with you, and neither for your mother nor for any other ought you to displease us. We charge you, by the faith, love and allegiance which you owe to us, and on our blessing, that you come to us without opposition, delay or further excuse. For your mother has written to us that, if you wish to return to us, she will not prevent it, and we do not understand that your uncle the King detains you against the form of your safe-conduct. In no manner, then, either for your mother or for any other cause, delay to come to us.[13]

To his son, Edward did not accuse Isabella of adultery, but in a letter to Charles IV it becomes clear that he thought her guilty of more than just consorting with a traitor:

Dearest brother, we have considered well your letter wherein you signify that you have spoken with good diligence to your sister touching the things of which we have replied to you, and that she has told you that it is her desire to be with us and in our company, as a good wife ought to be in that of her lord, and that the friendship between her and our dear and faithful nephew, Hugh le Despenser, was but feigned on her part because she saw it was expedient for her support in past time, and to secure herself from worse treatment. Certes, dearest brother, if she loved us, she would desire to be in our company, as she has said. She, who ought to be the mediatrix between you and us of entire and lasting peace, should not be the cause of stirring up fresh strife, as she has done. But the thought of her heart was to devise that pretence for withdrawing from us. We have already shown you that what she has told you is, saving your reverence, not the truth, for never has she received either villainy or evil from us or from any other. Never, in the slightest instance, has evil been done to her by [Hugh]. And since she has departed from us and come to you, what has compelled her to send to Hugh letters of such great and especial amity as she has been pleased to do from time to time?

But truly, dearest brother, it must be as apparent to you as to us and to all men, that she does not love us as she ought to love her lord, and the cause why she had spoken falsehoods of our nephew and withdrawn herself from us proceeds, according to my thoughts, from a disordered will, when she so openly, notoriously and knowingly, against her duty, keeps in her company the Mortimer. If you wished her well, dearest brother, you would chastise her for this misconduct and make her demean herself as she ought, for the honour of all those to whom she belongs.

Then our son, dearest brother, is made also by his mother, your sister, the companion of our said traitor and foe, who is his counsellor in delaying his return in our despite. We entreat you to restore our son, who is of too tender an age to guide and govern himself, and therefore ought to be under our paternal care, to the duchy. And that you will be pleased to do these things, dearest brother, for the sake of God, reason, good faith and natural fraternity, without paying regard to the wilful pleasure of a woman, is our desire.[14]

Charles cannot have been pleased to read the final passages, in which Edward implied that he had been remiss in not chastising his sister, which reflected on his kingly honor. And Prince Edward was surely disturbed when he read his father's letter. He wrote back, protesting that he was indeed bearing in mind the things with which the King had charged him at Dover, and that he had not disobeyed his commands in any point that he could avoid.

Persisting in his efforts to gain the support of the French nobility, Edward wrote to Philip, Count of Valois, heir of the late Charles of Valois, asserting that Isabella had fabricated her complaints about Despenser:

When the King sent to seek her, she then showed the feigned matter for the first time, which was never heard or suspected by anyone: wherefore, one ought not to give faith to such feigned invention against the truth. But indeed, the King fully perceives that she does not love [him] as she ought to love her lord, and that the matter that she speaks of the King's said nephew, for which she withdraws herself from the King, is feigned and is not certain, but the King thinks it must be of inordinate will when she, so openly and notoriously, knowingly, against her duty and the estate of the King's crown, which she is bound to love, has drawn to her and retains in her company, of her counsel, the King's traitor and mortal enemy, the Mortimer, and others of his conspiracy, and keeps his company in and out of the house.[15]

In April, Edward was forced to admit to James II, King of Aragon, that he could not continue with negotiations for his son's marriage. He wrote to the Pope, defending his own conduct in respect of Isabella and the nuncios, and protesting that he had done everything in his power to bring the Queen home, and had not intended any ill toward her. "And as for our said son, indeed, he has not offended us, nor does his youth allow either that he could do any harm. Wherefore it would be inhuman and unnatural to treat them with so much rage and cruelty."[16] He apparently enclosed a bribe, for on May 1, John XXII thanked him for his gift of 5,000 florins. But it made no difference. The Pope wrote again to Hugh, reminding him to continue his good offices to promote agreement between the King and Queen, an injunction Hugh ignored. Edward had the Archbishop of Canterbury offer up prayers for the Queen's safe return and ordered the clergy to emphasize in their sermons that he had not banished her or his son and was not threatening the nuncios.

On Whit Sunday, Jeanne of Evreux was crowned queen of France at the Sainte-Chapelle in Paris. Isabella and her son were guests, and Mortimer was in the Prince's train. His presence there amounted to an endorsement of his position by the French King.

On May 19, Edward ordered that elaborate preparations be made for the reception of the Papal envoys, who finally arrived at Dover soon afterward and met with the King and Hugh at Saltwood Castle in Kent, where they laid before Edward the Queen's proposals for a reconciliation. By June 10, it was clear that their mission had failed, because neither Edward nor Hugh would agree to the Despensers withdrawing permanently from court. This meant that, effectively, Isabella's marriage had irretrievably broken down, and that if she wished to be rid of the favorites, it would have to be done by force.

She was still in Paris on that day, when she commissioned her agents to meet with a delegation from Ponthieu, who had been summoned to discuss raising money so that she could hire ships in Hainault and buy provisions. Negotiations with Hainault must have resumed, with Isabella pressing on with her plans for the invasion.

On June 15, when Edward and Hugh visited Rochester, Bishop Hethe inquired how the talks at Saltwood had progressed. Hugh ranted that the Queen should return home forthwith and that she had no right to demand his withdrawal from court, or to ask for sworn guarantees regarding her status. He added that she would have returned a long time ago but had been prevented from doing so by Mortimer.

Edward asked Hethe, "Is it not true that a queen who once upon a time wilfully disobeyed her lord was set aside and deprived of her royal dignity?"

Hethe caught the King's meaning and replied, "Whoever has told you that has given you bad advice."[17] He emphasized his point with a quote from Scripture about Haman, the evil counselor who tried to drive a wedge between Ahasuerus, King of Persia, and his Jewish wife, Esther, and was hanged for his pains. The allusion to Hugh was blatant.

Edward had apparently learned much about the affair between Isabella and Mortimer from the nuncios. This prompted him, on June 19, to make one final attempt to persuade the Prince to return to England. He wrote:

> Edward, fair son, it appears that you have not humbly obeyed our commands as a good son ought his father, since you have not returned to us to be under government, as we have enjoined you by our letters, on our blessing, but have notoriously held companionship, and your mother also, with Mortimer, our traitor and mortal enemy, who, in company with your mother and others, was publicly carried to Paris in your train to the solemnity of the coronation at Pentecost just past, in signal despite of us, and to the great dishonour both of us and you. For truly, he is neither a meet companion for your mother, nor for you, and we hold that much evil to the country will come of it.
>
> Therefore, we command and charge you, on the faith and love you ought to bear us, and on our blessing, that you show yourself our dear and well-beloved son, as you have aforetime done, and, ceasing from all excuses of your mother, you come to us here with all haste. Also, fair son, we charge you by no means to marry till you return to us, or without our advice and consent.[18]

The Prince's reply, if there was one, does not survive. Later evidence suggests that he perhaps suffered from a guilty conscience about his father all his life. Yet he clearly felt chivalrously protective toward his mother. He may have hated the Despensers and felt outraged at the wrongs they had done her. His later actions suggest that he did not like

Mortimer either, and perhaps believed that in keeping company with him, he was betraying his father.

At the same time as he wrote to his son, Edward sent another letter to Charles IV, seeking to apportion to him some of the blame for Isabella's behavior:

> Most dear and beloved brother, we wish to remind you that we have at different times signified to you by our letters how improperly your sister, our wife, has conducted herself in withdrawing from us and refusing to return at our command, while she so notoriously has attached to her company, and consorts with, our traitor and mortal enemy, the Mortimer, and our other enemies there, and also makes Edward, our son and heir, an adherent of our enemy, to our great shame. And, if you wish her well, you ought, both for your own honour and ours, to have these things duly redressed.

He again begged Charles to send home Prince Edward,

> who is of too tender an age to guide and govern himself, and therefore ought to be under our paternal care.
> But these things are as nothing; it is the herding of our said wife and son with our traitors and mortal enemies that notoriously continues. Dearest brother, you ought to feel for us, for much we are grieved at the shameful despites and great injury which we have so long endured. Nay, verily, brother-in-law, we cannot bear it longer.[19]

Frantic to have his son back and the threat of invasion removed, the King sent copies of these letters to the Pope, advising him that the Queen was sharing her lodgings with Mortimer and beseeching him to intervene with Charles on his behalf.

Edward preferred to maintain the pretense that the French King was detaining Isabella against her will. But he probably knew that the situation was irretrievable. He granted some of her lands in Cornwall to her enemy Bishop Stapledon, and on June 28, he was present when her treasury in the Tower was broken into, and ordered that money be taken from it for his own use.

In July, Edward declared war on France. His arrayers in East Anglia

were ordered to recruit 3,000 men to man the fleet on the east coast,
which was to intercept and attack French vessels in the Channel. Mortimer's Welsh enemy, Rhys ap Gruffydd, was ordered to raise troops
against him.

The Despensers were now more unpopular than ever and there were
vicious attacks on their adherents, yet "the influence of Sir Hugh le
Despenser, and the affection the King felt for him, increased every day.
He had such a hold on the King that the whole country was amazed. Nor
could anything be done at court without the agreement of Sir Hugh, and
he behaved cruelly and wickedly, for which he was well hated. But nobody dared to raise any complaint."[20]

Edward was showing increased favor to Hugh's wife, Eleanor, whom
the chronicler Henry Knighton describes as being treated like a queen.
William Cappellani, a chronicler writing in Hainault, claimed that she
was now Edward's mistress, which echoes an earlier assertion in the unreliable *Chronographia Regum Francorum*. The King's household accounts
for 1326 show that he was visiting her frequently and sending her gifts
of money, jewels, sugar, and golden chaffinches. In July, they enjoyed a
picnic together at Windsor. He named a ship after her and wrote to her
frequently. Probably she was just a favorite niece, although Edward may
have loved her more on Hugh's account, for the period of her ascendancy
corresponds with that of her husband. It would have been natural for
Edward to show favor to Hugh's wife, and it is easy to see how this could
have been misconstrued. If Edward was involved in some sort of sexual
triangle with Hugh and Eleanor, there was no gossip about it in the English chronicles and Isabella and Mortimer made no political capital out
of it; thus it is unlikely to be true.

In England, people were "disturbed" that Isabella was "delaying and
keeping her son in France against his father's wishes. Some maintained
they were being held against their will, others that the Queen had been
seduced by the illicit embraces of Mortimer and had no wish to return."[21]

News of her alliance with Mortimer gave encouragement to those who
were heartily sick of Hugh's ascendancy. "All the barons and thoughtful
people in the country could no longer tolerate his wicked, outrageous
behaviour."[22] Isabella was secretly corresponding with many of Hugh's

opponents. She had already secured the support of several nobles and bishops, notably Lancaster and Norfolk, and had sent agents to England to foment unrest. By the summer, thanks largely to the covert efforts of Bishop Orleton, there had emerged in England a rapidly expanding Queen's party that was committed to the overthrow not only of the favorites, but also of the King.

Around this time, Isabella received an urgent communication from some English barons who had been "debating amongst themselves secretly and decided to send for her and ask her to return. If she could by any means raise an armed force, even a thousand men, and she would bring her son and all her company to England, they would rally to her side and place him on the throne to govern under her guidance. For they could not, and would not, endure any longer the general disorder and the misdeeds of the King, which were all inspired by the advice of Sir Hugh and his followers."[23]

Charles IV advised Isabella "to press on boldly, for he would help her and lend her as many men as she wanted, and he would also lend her all the silver and gold she needed."[24] In reality, Charles had no desire to fight a war with England on two fronts, for he was heavily committed in Gascony and was already uncomfortable about sheltering his sister now that her relationship with Mortimer was becoming notorious.

Unaware that Charles's promises lacked substance, Isabella continued to "make what provision she could for the future. And she secretly sought the help of the greatest barons in France whom she trusted most, and who would voluntarily support her. Then she sent a message to the barons in England who had communicated with her. But this could not be kept secret from Sir Hugh le Despenser."[25]

In July, it was rumored in France that, on the advice of the Despensers, Edward had outlawed the Queen and the Prince and had them proclaimed rebels and traitors, threatening that if they returned to England they would face execution. Another rumor had it that the King had ordered Richmond to murder Isabella and her son, but that God had restrained the Earl from doing so. There was no basis to these stories, but Hugh had certainly bribed some Frenchmen to kidnap Isabella and Mortimer, and the King had warned that if Mortimer returned to England, he faced certain death.

That month, Isabella received the crushing news that the Pope had abandoned her; Edward's appeal had moved John XXII, who, given the scandal the Queen's affair with Mortimer was causing, had decided to make a stand in the interests of morality. He censured Charles IV for harboring adulterers and commanded him, on pain of excommunication, not to countenance their sin or offer them shelter any longer.

Charles's actions at this time were ambivalent. His sympathy for Isabella had apparently been waning for some time, and her presence in France was certainly prejudicing any hope of a settlement with England over Gascony. Hugh had bribed Charles's advisers to put pressure on their master to force her to return to England. He had written to warn Charles himself that his sister was plotting treason. "In a short space," wrote Froissart, "the King of France and all his privy council were as cold to help the Queen in her voyage as they had before great desire to do it."[26] Yet Charles's later behavior suggests that he was playing a far more complex game.

He had perhaps learned that two of Mortimer's agents had been arrested in England and confessed to being involved in a plot to murder Edward II and the Despensers by means of witchcraft. They had paid a magician in Coventry to stick pins in waxen images of their intended victims. It was an age in which even educated men of rank believed in the power of sorcery. This was not the first time that Mortimer had sent assassins to England. Isabella's aim was Edward's deposition, not his death; but, of course, the latter would have solved many problems. This was the third plot against the King's life, and all the plotters were close to Isabella, Mortimer most of all. But she may have been led to believe that the Despensers alone were to be eliminated.

When Charles read the Pope's letter, "he was greatly disturbed" and "withdrew his countenance from his sister," ordering "that she be made acquainted with their contents, for he had held no conversation with her for a long time." He could not be seen to be supporting her, and told her, "as definitely and clearly as he could, to stay quiet and abandon her project. When the Queen heard this, she was naturally amazed and astounded, and she saw that the King was now disposed against her, for nothing that she could say would alter his decision or help her case. And so she left him, sadly and sorrowfully, and returned to her lodging. But she did not abandon her plans, and the King was angry that she ignored his words" and sent a "stern and contemptuous message, commanding her to leave his kingdom immediately, or he would make her leave it with shame."

Isabella was "greatly troubled," especially on hearing that Charles had decreed "that whoever should speak in behalf of his sister should forfeit his lands and be banished from the realm. When the Queen heard this, she was more upset than before, and with reason. She did not know what to think or do because everything was, and had been for so long, against her, and those who should have come to her help were failing her, through wicked advice. She became desperate; she had no comfort and she did not know what to do or what would become of her. And she often prayed and beseeched God to give her help and guidance."[27]

Most of Isabella's French supporters promptly abandoned her. But in reality, Charles's sentence of banishment had been a bluff to appease the Pope and mislead Edward II. It was probably he who sent Robert of Artois to suggest that she go to Hainault. Robert came secretly "in the middle of the night to warn Isabella of the peril in which she stood" in France, telling her "that, if she did not behave discreetly, the King her brother would have her sent back to her husband, and her son with her, because it did not please the King of France that she should stay away from her husband. At this, the Queen was more appalled than ever, because she would rather have been dead and dismembered than fall again into the power of her husband and Sir Hugh."

Robert "strongly urged her to enter the Imperial territories and to throw herself upon the protection of William, Count of Hainault. So she decided to leave France and go into Hainault to see Count William and his brother, Sir John, who were the most honourable knights of the highest reputation. She hoped to find in them every comfort and good advice." She "informed her people of her decision, ordered her baggage to be made ready as secretly as possible and, having paid for everything she had had, she left her lodging as quickly and quietly as she could, with her son, the Earl of Kent, Roger Mortimer and other English knights."[28]

10

"By Clamour of the People"

✳

I T HAD ALREADY BEEN AGREED THAT HAINAULT WOULD BE THE springboard for the projected invasion, and Mortimer went straight there, while Isabella, accompanied by Kent, made for Ponthieu, where she began raising money. Charles IV made no attempt to pursue her; he did not denounce her to Edward II or divulge her plans or whereabouts. He helped her covertly, building up an invasion fleet on the Norman coast in order to divert Edward from the real threat that was to come from Hainault. Charles knew about the revived alliance between Count William and the Queen, and that his sister would not lack for practical support. She was left in no doubt about the role he was playing, for they remained secretly in communication.

According to Knighton, it had been decided that Isabella should take charge of policy while Mortimer looked after the practical arrangements for the invasion. On July 24, Count William ordered his harbormasters to give him every assistance in gathering provisions and hiring a fleet of ships. It was to be assembled by September 1 between Rotterdam and Dordrecht, ports that offered excellent facilities.

From Ponthieu, Isabella traveled east to Hainault. Once "in the territories of the Empire, she was more at her ease." Near Valenciennes, she stayed at the château of Ambreticourt, which belonged to "a poor knight called Sir Eustace d'Ambreticourt, who gladly received and entertained her in the best manner he could, insomuch that afterwards the Queen and her son invited the knight, his wife and all his children to England and advanced their fortunes in various ways."[1]

Count William and his brother, Sir John, Seigneur of Beaumont, soon learned of Isabella's arrival in Hainault. Sir John, "a married man and also a valiant knight," was "at that time very young and panting for glory like a knight errant." He "mounted his horse and, accompanied by a few persons, set out from Valenciennes and arrived in the evening to pay the Queen every respect and honour."[2] At the sight of him, Isabella burst into tears and poured out her griefs.

"Lady," he said chivalrously, "see here your knight, who will not fail to die for you, though everyone else should forsake you. I will do everything in my power to conduct you safely to England with your son and restore you to your rank with the assistance of your friends in those parts. And I, and all those whom I can influence, will risk our lives in the adventure for your sake, and we shall have a sufficient armed force, if it please God."

Overcome with gratitude, Isabella knelt at his feet, but he raised her up, saying, "God forbid that the Queen of England should think of kneeling before her knight! But be comforted, Madam, for I shall not break my promise. You shall come and see my brother and your cousin, the Countess his wife, and all their fine children, who will be rejoiced to see you, for I have heard them say so."

"Sir," replied Isabella, "I find in you more kindness and comfort than in the whole world beside; and I will give you five hundred thousand thanks for all you have promised me with so much courtesy. I and my son shall be forever bound unto you and, if in time we are restored, as I hope, by the comfort and grace of God and yourself, you will be richly rewarded."

The next day, Sir John returned to Ambreticourt to escort Isabella to Count William at Mons. They arrived by August 3, when she confirmed an agreement between Mortimer and the Count, whereby William, springing to the aid of "the distressed Queen of England,"[3] undertook to lease to the invaders 140 ships, and Isabella pledged her revenues from Ponthieu for any that were lost. Charles IV had agreed to act as her guarantor.

That day, Mortimer of Chirk died in the Tower. Rumor had it that he had starved to death in his grim cell. Roger Mortimer should have inherited his uncle's lands, but they had been declared forfeit. He now had even greater cause to seek vengeance on the Despensers.

* * *

Count William hastened to invite Isabella and her son to Valenciennes, "where they were gladly and gallantly welcomed"[4] by their hosts and the citizens. The Count received the Queen in the great galleried hall of the Hôtel de Hollande, a magnificent room with a paved floor, six tall, glazed Gothic windows, and splendid red hangings. When she had settled into her lodgings, the Countess Jeanne came to visit her "and did her all honour and reverence";[5] she also paid the Queen's expenses throughout her stay in Hainault.

During the eight days of her visit, Isabella was "honoured and feasted nobly." Count William was delighted when she formally asked for the hand of one of his daughters for her son, and Prince Edward, "a youth of great charm and much promise,"[6] was encouraged to spend as much time as possible in the company of the three girls who remained at home. The eldest of them, Philippa (or Phelippe), was thirteen. In January 1328, she was described as the most beautiful girl, the mirror of her sex and scarcely fourteen years old, while Froissart, who knew her well, states that she was then "on the point of fourteen years." She had therefore been born early in 1314. (There is no evidence that her birth date was June 24, as stated in some modern books.)

She had four sisters. Agnes died aged twelve before November 1327, and Isabella was three in 1326. Two older girls, Margaret and Jeanne, had been married in 1324 to the Holy Roman Emperor Louis IV and William V, Duke of Jülich, respectively. Froissart stated that the Countess Jeanne loved Philippa "with all her heart, more tenderly than any of her daughters." The Count had two sons: his heir, nineteen-year-old William, and an infant, Louis.

Philippa had been born probably in Salle-le-Comte, her father's twelfth-century palace within the walls of Valenciennes on the River Scheldt, or at Mons, the Count's principal seats. She spent her childhood at these residences and the castle at Beaumont (later called the Tour Salamandre), William's summer residence in southern Hainault. She was well educated, spoke Dutch and Parisian French fluently, could write in French, and grew up imbued with the romances beloved by her mother. She had visited the French court and been present with her parents and siblings at the marriage of Charles IV and Jeanne of Evreux in 1324, for which her father had bought them all sumptuous Italian velvet for their apparel. In December 1325, her mother again took her to France to say farewell to her dying grandfather, Charles, Count of Valois, at Le Perray-en-Yvelines, west of the Île-de-France. After his funeral, they spent Christmas at the Hôtel Ostrich, the Paris house of the Count and Countess of Hainault, before returning to Valenciennes on January 4, 1325. Philippa may have first met Queen Isabella and Prince Edward at this time.

Now, in Valenciennes, "young Edward devoted himself most and inclined with eyes of love to Philippa rather than the rest. And the maiden knew him best and kept him closer company than any of her sisters. So I have heard from the mouth of the good lady herself." Several historians have dismissed this account by Froissart as romantic, claiming that Edward's only other choice would have been the infant Isabella, but Agnes was still alive at this time.

When Isabella and Edward left Valenciennes and "embraced all the damsels in turn, the Lady Philippa, when it was her turn, burst into tears." Asked why she wept, she replied, "Because my fair cousin of England is about to leave me, and I had grown so used to him." All the knights who were present began to laugh, aware that the budding love between the young couple was just what had been intended. Their marriage was a political necessity for Isabella, and also a means of binding her son to her cause. That bond would be all the closer if he was grateful to her for securing him a bride he could love. After their departure, she asked him if he wished to marry one of the Hainault sisters, and he replied, "Yes, I am better pleased to marry there than elsewhere, and rather to Philippa, for she and I accorded excellently well together, and she wept, I know well, when I took leave of her."[7]

On August 27, at Mons, Isabella signed a treaty providing for the betrothal of Edward and Philippa, and the Prince swore on the Gospels to wed his bride within two years and assign her a dower. The dowry was to be in the form of troops, money, and ships, which were to be delivered to the Queen in advance of the marriage. In return, she promised that once she gained power in England, she would settle its maritime dispute with Hainault to everyone's satisfaction. In the event of the invasion being repelled and the marriage not taking place, the Prince was to pay a fine of £10,000 (just over $8 million). Given how his conscience would plague him in regard to his father, it is unlikely that young Edward felt entirely comfortable about this agreement.

* * *

In August, expecting an imminent invasion, King Edward was busy tour-
ing his realm and attempting to raise support among the nobility. A system of warning beacons was put in place, and he ordered a great fleet to
assemble at Portsmouth. A watch was set on the east coast, and more
ships were placed in readiness at Orwell.

Any French persons remaining in England were imprisoned, on account of the King of France's "detention" of the Queen and Prince Edward and his "cherishing" of English exiles.[8] Hugh, meanwhile, had
prudently withdrawn cash from his bankers.

Count William having advanced part of Philippa's dowry, Isabella was
busy raising money and men for the invasion. Among those who joined
her at this time was a Flemish page, Walter de Manny (or Mauny), who
had served Sir John of Beaumont and would become a celebrated chevalier. Mercenaries from all over northern Europe were converging on Dordrecht, the main embarkation point. Their enlistment owed much to the
efforts of Mortimer and Sir John, who had exerted himself indefatigably
on Isabella's behalf. He had written to all the knights of his acquaintance
in Hainault, Brabant, and Bohemia, declaring: "I believe for certain that
this lady and her son have been driven from their kingdom wrongfully. If
it is for the glory of God to help the afflicted, how much more is it to
help and succour one who is daughter of a king, descended from royal
lineage, and to whose blood we ourselves are related?" He could only die
once, and that "was in the hands of Our Lord. He had promised this
noble lady to escort her back to her kingdom, and he would support her
to the death."[9] Many responded to his call to arms, among them Sir Eustace d'Ambreticourt.

John escorted Isabella's party to Dordrecht. On September 7, she
joined Count William's court there, and was entertained by him and his
wife in the Binnenhof. She accompanied them to Rotterdam, and then
to the port of Brielle on the River Maas. Mortimer arrived on the 21st, by
which time she had successfully concluded her secret pact with Robert
the Bruce. That day, she bade farewell to Count William and his family,
kissing them and thanking them "deeply, humbly and graciously for
their kind and noble hospitality."[10]

Men, baggage, horses, and provisions were loaded onto the ninety-five
waiting vessels. Estimates varied, but Isabella's force numbered between

1,500 and 2,750 men. The Hainaulters were under the command of Sir John, and the rest under Mortimer.

On September 22, with a fair wind, the Queen's fleet sailed into the North Sea. It met no resistance from English ships, for Edward's sailors were either elsewhere or had mutinied "because of the great wrath they had towards Sir Hugh le Despenser." But the invading ships ran into a storm "that sent them off their course, so that for two days they did not know where they were. And in this God was merciful and helped them: He altered their course by a miracle. So it happened that, at the end of two days, the storm was over, and the sailors sighted land in England. They made for it gladly and landed on the sands on the open seashore"[11] just before noon on September 24, 1326. Contemporary accounts state that the landing was made at either Orwell or Harwich, but it is more likely to have been on the Essex side of the River Orwell, given that the invaders stayed the night at nearby Walton.

"The Queen being got safely ashore, her knights and attendants made her a house with four carpets, open in the front, where they kindled her a great fire."[12] They did not know where they were, but local inquiries established that they were in Norfolk's territory. During the three hours it took for men, horses, and provisions to be unloaded, the Queen wrote to the citizens of London, and other cities and towns, stating that she had come to avenge the murder of Lancaster and rid the realm of the Despensers, and asking for their assistance. She ordered proclamations to be made, stating that she and her son had "come to this land to raise up the state of the Holy Church and of the kingdom, and of the people of this land against misdeeds and grievous oppressions, and to safeguard and maintain, so far as we can, the honour and profit of the Holy Church and of our lord the King." Invoking the Church made her invasion sound like a crusade. She offered a reward to any citizen who helped her destroy "our enemy and the enemy of our very dear lord the King and the whole kingdom."[13] The reference to Lancaster was probably made at the behest of Isabella's uncle, Henry, Earl of Leicester, who had offered his support in the hope of avenging his brother's death. He was an important ally, one the Queen could not afford to lose.

Once the unloading had been completed, the invasion fleet sailed back to Hainault. In the afternoon, Norfolk arrived to escort Isabella to his castle at Walton, where she spent the night and was joined by many barons, knights, and gentlemen of East Anglia. Norfolk had done his work well: in the three days after the invading forces landed, only fifty-five men rallied to the King in the county of Norfolk. It was a foretaste of what was to come.

The next morning, still clad in her widow's weeds, as if she were on a pilgrimage, the Queen marched her forces, with banners displayed, to St. Edmundsbury. News of the invasion spread rapidly, and popular opinion polarized in her favor. Wherever she went, the people flocked to her standard; there is no record of any resistance. Her English supporters "immediately prepared to come and see her and her son, whom they wanted as their sovereign."[14]

At Cambridge, Isabella spent three days at Barnwell Priory, where she was joined by many magnates and several bishops including Orleton and Burghersh. Orleton made her a substantial donation of funds, while Burghersh persuaded his fellow bishops to give generously for her cause, and Bishop Hotham of Ely helped to raise men. Baker, whose loyalties lay firmly with Edward II, later called these bishops "priests of Baal, the accomplices of Jezebel."

On September 27, Edward and the Despensers were dining in the Tower of London when some sailors burst in with news that the Queen had landed with an army. Edward said only that he was gratified to hear that she was having to rely on the assistance of foreigners to achieve her aims. But when other messengers reported that she was believed to have only 700 men with her, he was struck with consternation, and the elder Despenser cried aloud, "Alas, alas! We be all betrayed, for certes, with so little power, she had never come to land, but folk of this country had to her consented."[15]

The King promptly issued a general summons of array. He wrote letters begging for aid from the Pope and the King of France, and appealed to the Londoners to resist the Queen. Only four responded. Isabella had always been popular in the capital, while Edward had lost the love of its citizens in 1321, when he had rashly tried to curtail their jealously guarded liberties acquired over several centuries.

Members of the royal household and secretariats began to desert him. Only two lords, Arundel and Surrey, stayed loyal.

On September 28, he summoned men from the Home Counties and appealed to the Welsh for support. When he promised pardons to prisoners and outlaws who rallied to his cause, a hundred convicted murderers promptly offered their services. He issued a proclamation urging all men to rise and destroy the Queen's power, sparing only her life, her son's, and Kent's. He offered £1,000 ($895,000) to anyone bringing him Mortimer's head. He sent one Robert de Wateville to East Anglia to raise a force to repel the invaders, but Wateville could muster only sixty men, whom he promptly led to the Queen. On September 30, Edward had Archbishop Reynolds read a Papal Bull against "invaders" at Paul's Cross: it had actually been intended for use against the Scots seven years earlier. The Londoners listened in hostile silence.

Alarmed at news that Isabella was making for Oxford, the King ordered the town to close its gates to her, and committed Mortimer's three sons to the Tower. When Isabella arrived there on October 2, the burghers welcomed her joyfully, and the university—of which Edward II was patron—offered her its wholehearted support.

Bishop Orleton preached an incendiary sermon in the presence of the Queen, the Prince, and Mortimer, taking his text from Genesis: "I will put enmity between thee and the woman, and between thy seed and her seed: she will bruise thy head and thou shalt bruise his heel." This, he said, referred not to the King, whom he publicly accused of sodomy, but to Hugh, "the seed of the first tyrant, Satan, who would be crushed by the Lady Isabella and her son."[16]

That day, convinced that the whole realm would declare for the Queen, the King left London with the Despensers, Arundel, Surrey, the Chancellor, Robert Baldock, some royal clerks, and a force of archers. Having left Stapledon as guardian of the City and Hugh's wife holding the Tower, they fled west toward Wales, where Hugh held vast territories and was confident of raising support.

On October 3, the Earl of Leicester marched on Leicester with a great force and seized Hugh's treasure, which had been moved from Caerphilly and deposited in the abbey for safety. Then he moved south to rendezvous with Isabella.

By the time Edward arrived at Wallingford on October 6, he had decided to take a stand against the invaders at Gloucester. By then, Isabella was at Baldock, where she had the Chancellor's brother arrested and his house ransacked. From there, she sent a second letter to the Londoners, summoning all good citizens to aid her in securing the destruction of

Hugh le Despenser or suffer punishment for defaulting. Doubling Edward's price for Mortimer, she offered £2,000 ($1.8 million) for Despenser's head. She then moved to Dunstable, planning to muster her forces there before advancing on the capital. Mortimer was with her, but he and Isabella were maintaining a discreet distance from each other, probably wishing to avoid any scandal that might prejudice the success, or the rightness, of the Queen's cause.

Edward reached Gloucester on October 9. There he issued an order for Henry of Lancaster's arrest and tried, in vain, to rally men to his cause. It was becoming clear that no one was prepared to fight for him, and that the relatives and friends of his former rebels, whom he had punished so savagely, were actively moving against him.

That day, the Queen's letter was posted on the Eleanor Cross in Cheapside; its contents were widely circulated, and copies were soon being displayed in the windows of private houses to proclaim support for her.

Edward was dismayed to learn that Earl Henry, with a great company of men-at-arms, had joined the Queen at Dunstable. "And after him, from one place and another, came earls, barons, knights and squires, with so many men-at-arms that the Queen's men thought they were out of all danger. And, as they advanced, their numbers increased every day."[17]

Edward had ridden to Westbury. By October 11, he had only twelve archers left, and was reduced to making a pathetic appeal to them not to desert him.

Two days later, Archbishop Reynolds urgently convened a conference of bishops at Lambeth Palace to discuss plans for a peace summit at St. Paul's Cathedral. But the Londoners were in an ugly mood, and Bishop Hethe warned Reynolds not to enter the City because the people believed him to be the King's man. In fact, the Archbishop had quarreled with Edward over liturgical precedence and had already secretly sent large sums of money to the Queen. He would have liked to declare openly for her, but was reluctant to do so in case Edward emerged triumphant. He heeded Hethe's warning and, with most of his colleagues, fled from Lambeth, abandoning the peace process, and shut himself up with Hethe at his palace at Maidstone. Only Stratford rode off in search of the Queen.

The King was with Hugh at Tintern Abbey on October 14. The elder Despenser had gone to occupy Bristol, where he received a hostile reception. That day, Wallingford surrendered without resistance to Isabella. There, she issued a proclamation against the Despensers, which was at once a savage indictment of their misrule and a call to arms. She did not criticize the King, but called him her very dear lord, as became a loving wife. Yet almost immediately, encouraged by her welcome in England, she made clear her true intentions, which were revealed in another inflammatory sermon that Bishop Orleton preached at Wallingford that same day, taking his text from 2 Kings 4:19, "My head, my head acheth."[18]

"When the head of a kingdom becometh sick and diseased," he told his congregation, "it must of necessity be taken off, without useless attempts to administer any other remedy." The sermon was a scathing attack on Edward, its purpose being to justify the Queen's invasion and demonstrate that she had been forced to leave her husband. It was on this occasion that the Bishop revealed "that the King had carried a knife in his hose to kill Queen Isabella, and he had said that, if he had no other weapon, he could crush her with his teeth."[19] His words incited much ill feeling against Edward.

That day, London erupted in violence against the King and his favorites, with rioting citizens shouting their support of Isabella and viciously turning on all who had supported Edward and the Despensers. In the name of the Queen and Prince Edward, they seized the Tower from Eleanor de Clare and liberated all the prisoners, including Mortimer's sons. Finding ten-year-old Prince John in the royal apartments, the Londoners proclaimed him warden of the City and the Tower. Then they marched their unpopular mayor, Edward's man, Hamo de Chigwell, to the Guildhall and forced him to declare his allegiance to Isabella and announce that any enemies of the Queen and the Prince would remain in London at their peril. To demonstrate that this was no empty threat, the mob seized and butchered Hugh's clerk, John the Marshal, whom they believed to be his spy.

Bishop Stapledon, who the King had left as guardian of the City, returned to London and immediately fell foul of the people, who identified him with the Despensers' rule and detested him for his rapacity; they had already sacked his house in the Temple, stolen his valuables, and burned his episcopal registers. Now, seeing him riding into the capital, clad in armor and attended by only two squires, a baying mob chased him nearly to St. Paul's. Before he could reach the sanctuary of the cathe-

dral's north door, they dragged him from his horse and all the way to the
Eleanor Cross in Cheapside, where they brutally decapitated him and his
squires with a butcher's knife. His head was sent to the Queen as a tro-
phy, while his body was left naked in the street. After being refused burial
in St. Clement Danes Church on the Strand, it was interred under a rubbish tip "without the office of priest or clerk."

The mob rampaged on, plundering and ransacking properties owned
by Arundel, Baldock, the Bardi, and other associates of the King and the
Despensers. They would have lynched their own Bishop too, but he managed to escape. Deprived of any effective government, London descended
into anarchy, with violence and looting raging unchecked for weeks to
come, and its citizens terrorized and forced into hiding. Trade came to a
standstill and normal daily life ceased.

Having reached Wales, Edward entered Chepstow on October 16. Here,
he optimistically appointed the elder Despenser guardian of the south-
western counties of England. Having consulted the barons, Isabella and
Mortimer swung westward, aiming to intercept Edward and Hugh. Their
pursuit turned into a triumphant progress. "In every town they entered,
they were honoured and feasted, and new supporters joined them from
every side." During their march, the Queen's soldiers "did no harm to
the country, but only devastated the manors of the Despensers."[20]

At Gloucester, Isabella lodged in the massive keep of the castle, the
city's chief royal residence, where she was joined by northern forces led
by Henry, Lord Percy, Thomas, Lord Wake, and Henry de Beaumont, and
by some Marcher barons and Welsh contingents. She appointed Wake
marshal of her army, which was now a formidable fighting force. Apparently without flinching, she received the head of Stapledon, which was
presented to her "as if it were a sacrifice to propitiate Diana."[21] She then
marched on to Berkeley Castle, which had been held by Hugh since 1322,
and restored it to its rightful owner, Thomas de Berkeley.

In the absence of firm centralized government, the kingdom was descending into chaos. "Thieves, murderers and all manner of criminals
did great damage, knowing that no one would stand in their way or bring

them to justice. Rapacity raged unchecked, so that any friend of the King, if found, would at once be stripped of his possessions or his life, and those responsible would suffer no punishment. It was enough for the conspirators that the victim had been of the King's party."[22]

By October 18, Isabella had arrived before Bristol with an army that probably numbered 2,000. Under Mortimer's command, her forces laid siege to the town and castle, which were held by the elder Despenser.

The King's efforts to secure military aid had proved futile. On October 21, he and Despenser, "seeing the terrible situation they were in, and not knowing of any relief that might come to them from any quarter," set sail from Chepstow "in a small boat."[23] They were perhaps making for Despenser's island of Lundy in the Bristol Channel, which could afford them a safe refuge, being well fortified by the steep and rugged cliffs that rose above its coastline and "rendered attack impossible."[24] Or they had been hoping to reach Ireland, whence they could bribe the Scots for reinforcements, which was what Isabella greatly feared. In the event, they were tossed for four days by storms in the Bristol Channel before being driven back to Cardiff.

Isabella had received alarming reports of the situation in London. Fearing for the safety of her son John, she wrote asking the citizens to send him to her, but they refused, for they wanted to keep him in London as their nominal leader. She then wrote to ask Archbishop Reynolds to go to the capital and look to the Prince's well-being, but he was too terrified to enter the City, so she had to trust the Londoners to keep her son safe.

On October 26, Bristol fell to Isabella. "When the people of the town saw how powerful the Queen had become and that almost all England was on her side, and clearly understood the danger they were in, they took counsel to give themselves up, and the town as well, in order to save their lives and their possessions."[25] Public opinion in Bristol was so overwhelmingly in Isabella's favor that the elder Despenser, overcome with despair, surrendered without offering any resistance or negotiating favorable terms for himself, and the citizens joyfully "opened their gates." Despenser was brought before the Queen, "for her to do what she liked with him."[26] She "had now attained a position of great power."[27]

In Bristol, she was reunited with her daughters, eight-year-old Eleanor and five-year-old Joan, who had been living there under the guardianship of Despenser. When they were brought to her, "the Queen was overjoyed, since she had not seen them for a long time."[28]

That day, she learned of the King's departure from Chepstow, which she and her advisers deemed to be tantamount to abandoning his kingdom. This paved the way for the establishment of an alternative government, and the Queen convened a council that was attended by Kent, Norfolk, Lancaster, Wake, Beaumont, Stratford, Hotham, Burghersh, and Orleton, among others. They acted, it was claimed, by the consent of the community of the realm, and, on October 26, on the grounds that Edward had deserted his people, they proclaimed Prince Edward Keeper of the Realm in his absence. Isabella's clerk, Robert Wyville, was appointed Keeper of the Prince's Privy Seal, which gave her control over her son's acts.

The council also acknowledged Leicester's right to succeed to his brother's inheritance, and that same day, he began styling himself earl of Lancaster. Mortimer was noticeably absent. He preferred to exercise his formidable power behind the scenes, through Isabella, and would shun a formal role.

Bishop Stratford caught up with the Queen at Bristol, and on October 26, Archbishop Reynolds finally switched his allegiance and wrote to her begging for her protection.

The next day, the elder Despenser was tried at Bristol before the Queen and the Prince. She told him that they would see that law and justice were done to him and his son, "according to their deeds."

"Madam," he replied, "may God give me a good judge and a good judgement. And if I may not have that in this world, may I have it in the next."[29]

The proceedings against him mirrored Thomas of Lancaster's trial. On oath, his peers were of the "definite opinion that the defendant deserved death for the many horrible crimes with which he had been charged, and which were believed to be clearly proved."[30] He was found guilty "by clamour of the people"[31] and condemned to be "drawn for treason, hanged for robbery, beheaded for misdeeds against the Church."[32] Because his crimes had dishonored the laws of chivalry, he was to be hanged in a surcoat quartered with his arms, which were then to be destroyed forever.

It was a cruel and shameful punishment, and the *Memorials of St. Ed-*

mund's Abbey record that Isabella did her best to spare him, but she was overruled by Lancaster, who reminded her that she had undertaken to destroy the favorites. Despenser suffered that same day on the common gallows at Bristol. Afterward, his decapitated corpse was displayed like that of any common thief, tied by the arms to a forked gibbet before a mob screaming "Traitor!" After four days, it was taken down, chopped up, and fed to the dogs.

Unaware of these events, the King and Hugh had been traveling through Glamorgan, trying in vain to raise support among Hugh's hostile tenants. On the day the elder Despenser perished, they sought refuge in Hugh's massive stronghold at Caerphilly, well aware now that "the greater part of the country was won over to the side of the Queen and her elder son, and drawn up in opposition to the King." They "were worried and frightened and distraught,"[33] but the King was still sending out useless commissions of array.

On October 28, in the name of Prince Edward, Parliament was summoned to meet at Westminster on December 14. The writs stated that, as the King would be absent from the kingdom, the Queen and Prince Edward would treat with the lords.

Edward was still at Caerphilly Castle on October 29. Two days later, his household disintegrated, his servants and clerks having deserted him. Effectively his reign was over, and he was a fugitive.

II

"Away with the King!"

✳

AWARE THAT THE KINGDOM WAS HERS, ISABELLA SENT SIR John of Beaumont and his mercenaries to London to take possession of the Tower in her name and act as a bodyguard for Prince John. Determined to restore law and order in the City, she dispatched Bishop Stratford with a letter authorizing the election of a new mayor in place of the hated Hamo de Chigwell, who had been lukewarm in his support of her. Stratford's arrival on November 15 would herald an end to the violence and anarchy of the past weeks. The Londoners chose as their mayor Richard de Béthune, a merchant who had helped Mortimer escape from the Tower in 1323; his election would cement London's loyalty to the Queen and Mortimer.

Meanwhile, on November 1, Isabella had been received "most respectfully and joyfully" in Hereford, where she kept the feast of All Saints "with great solemnity and ceremony, out of love for her son and respect for the foreign nobles who were with him."[1] She lodged as Orleton's guest in his palace near the cathedral. Writs issued at Hereford in the joint names of her and the Prince nominated Stratford as Treasurer. His appointment would smooth the transfer of the Exchequer and treasury to Isabella's control.

On November 5, Edward was in Gower, still desperately trying to raise troops. He then rode to Neath, where he remained until November 10, when he had to face the fact that further attempts at resistance were futile and sent the Abbot of Neath and Rhys ap Gruffydd to open negotiations with Isabella. Her response was to dispatch Lancaster with an armed force to take the King. On November 16, amid torrential rain, in open country near Llantrisant, he apprehended Edward, Hugh, Baldock, and six other men, all that remained of the King's supporters. Lancaster escorted the King to Monmouth Castle. Hugh, Baldock, and Hugh's marshal, Simon of Reading, who had the effrontery to speak insultingly of the Queen, were entrusted to Lord Wake and sent in chains to Isabella at Hereford.

That same day, Arundel was arrested in Shropshire and also brought to the Queen at Hereford, where, on Mortimer's orders, he was summarily beheaded without trial; it took twenty-two blows of the axe to kill him. Executions without trial constituted acts of tyranny, but Mortimer, who hated Arundel because he had appropriated Chirk's estates and some of his own, had no patience with such niceties.

Eleanor de Clare was imprisoned in the Tower on the Queen's orders. The unreliable *Chronographia Regum Francorum* claimed that she was being punished because she was pregnant with the King's child. No English source mentions this, although the chronicler Knighton stated that while Isabella was abroad, Eleanor had conducted herself as if she was queen. The real Queen's revenge was thorough. Eleanor's five daughters were incarcerated in convents and made to take the veil, and her son was threatened with execution. Eleanor herself endured fifteen months of imprisonment before she was released.

When taking him to Hereford, "Wake had Sir Hugh tied onto the meanest and poorest horse he could find, and he had him dressed in a tabard over his clothes, embroidered with the coat-of-arms that he bore, and so conducted him along the road as a public laughing-stock. And, in all the towns they passed through, he was announced by trumpets and cymbals, by way of greater mockery, till they reached the good city of Hereford."[2] Crowds yelled at him with savage mockery and screams of hatred as he was dragged through the streets.

At the Bishop's palace, Hugh and Baldock were delivered to the Queen and she paid the promised reward of £2,000 ($1.8 million) to their captors. Baldock, who was in holy orders, claimed benefit of clergy and was entrusted to the custody of Bishop Orleton, who kept him under house arrest in his own London house. (The following February, a mob would savagely assault Baldock there and drag him off to Newgate prison, where he died.)

From the first, Isabella had been careful to win and retain the goodwill and approval of the people, even in her vengeful and unlawful treatment of the Despensers; yet henceforth her anxiety to be seen to be acting within the law would repeatedly be made manifest. To this end, she sent Orleton to Monmouth to persuade Edward to surrender the Great Seal to her, so that she could claim that she was acting in his name and her rule would have the semblance of legality. There was no question of the King being restored to power.

Isabella wanted to have Hugh tried and executed in London, to demonstrate that she had accomplished what she had come to do and achieve maximum publicity for the event. But Hugh, anticipating the fate that awaited him, had been refusing food and drink since his arrest, meaning to starve himself to death. He was now so weak that it was feared the journey to London would kill him, so the decision was made to try him in Hereford.

On November 24, almost insensible, he was brought before a tribunal consisting of the Queen and the same magnates who had condemned his father. A long list of the crimes of which he was accused was read out. He was charged with showing cruelty toward Isabella, dishonoring and disparaging her, damaging her noble estate, and maliciously interfering between her and the King to the detriment of their marriage. He had advised the King to abandon her at Tynemouth, to her life's peril; he had deprived her of her dower and attempted by bribery to turn members of the French court against her and even to procure her murder, and that of the Prince, making it impossible for them to return from France. The other charges included procuring the murder of Lancaster; illegally confiscating episcopal property; incarcerating the Mortimers "in a harsh prison to murder them without cause, except for his coveting of their lands"; ill treating the widows and children of Edward's rebels, and dishonoring the King by inducing him, after the Queen's invasion, to abandon both his kingdom and his wife.[3] Like his father, Hugh had been forbidden to say anything in his defense. This was illegal, because accused persons had long had the right to defend themselves, although they could not call witnesses.

The lords and knights wasted no time in reaching a guilty verdict, and

Hugh was sentenced to be hanged as a thief, drawn and quartered as a traitor, beheaded for violating his sentence of exile, "and, because you were always disloyal and procured discord between our lord the King and our very honourable lady the Queen, you will be disembowelled and then your entrails will be burnt."[4] This was the usual penalty for treason, but there was to be another torment too.

The dreadful punishment meted out to traitors had first been introduced into England in 1242 for a wretch who had plotted to murder Henry III. Edward I had revived its use; the most famous victims had been Dafydd ap Gruffydd, brother of Llywelyn ap Gruffydd, the last native Prince of Wales, in 1283, and William Wallace in 1305. Wallace had suffered castration as well as disemboweling, and Isabella would have recalled that the d'Aulnay brothers had been publicly emasculated for having dishonored her sisters-in-law. We do not know if it was she who suggested that castration would be an apt penalty for Hugh's sexual offenses; certainly Froissart and other chroniclers viewed it as such.

No chronicler records Isabella's reaction to the sentence, but others made their feelings felt, shouting, "Traitor! Renegade! Traitor!"[5] A crown of nettles was rammed on Hugh's head and his skin was roughly tattooed with verses from Scripture on arrogance and retribution. Wearing a tunic with his arms reversed, he was "dragged in a chest through the streets of Hereford to the sound of trumpets and clarions."[6] In the marketplace, crowds had assembled, baying for his blood. The Queen and Mortimer watched as he was stripped, swung up in the air by a noose round his neck, and then, half-hanged, tied to a tall ladder, fifty feet high, "so that all the people could see him. A large fire was lit. When he was thus bound, they cut off his penis and testicles because he was a heretic and a sodomite and guilty of unnatural practices, so it was said, even with the King himself, whose affections he had alienated from the Queen. After his private parts had been cut off, they were thrown into the fire and burned."[7]

At first, Despenser suffered with great patience, asking forgiveness of the bystanders, but a ghastly, inhuman howl broke from him as "his belly was split open and his heart and entrails cut out and thrown on the fire to burn." This butchery was carried out "because his heart had been false and treacherous and he had given treasonable advice to the King, so as to bring shame and disgrace on the country, and had caused the greatest baron in England to be beheaded. And he had encouraged the King not to see his wife. When the other parts of his body had been disposed of, Sir Hugh's head was cut off and sent to London. His body was then hewn into quarters, which were sent to the four next largest cities in England."[8]

No one censured Isabella, as a member of the gentler sex, for sanctioning such a cruel death with its added refinements of agonizing torture. Hugh's execution was greeted with popular approval as the means of ridding the realm of a detested tyrant.

Isabella and Mortimer held a feast to celebrate their triumph. Apart from the executions of the Despensers, Arundel, and three henchmen, and the lynching of Stapledon and others in London (which was none of the Queen's doing), Isabella's was a relatively bloodless coup that could easily have been otherwise. Many associates of the Despensers were left unmolested. Knighton claims that the Queen had determined upon the destruction of the whole Despenser family, but Hugh's two sons were spared; the elder, another Hugh, who had defended Caerphilly Castle against Isabella's besieging forces, would later be summoned to Parliament as a baron. His younger brother became a distinguished soldier. Eleanor de Clare's lands were eventually returned to her.

"So the Queen won back the whole kingdom of England." Isabella's forces had served her "boldly and bravely." Hers was the first successful invasion of England since the Norman Conquest of 1066, and her "bold and noble enterprise" was one of the most successful coups in English history, "at which the whole country rejoiced together."[9]

She was now the effective ruler of England. Orleton delivered the Great Seal to her on November 26 at Hereford, and she began governing in her husband's name, issuing writs "by the King," or "by the King, on the information of the Queen,"[10] which gave her rule a veneer of legality. Not since the time of Eleanor of Aquitaine, who governed in the absence of Richard I in the twelfth century, had an English queen consort exercised such power.

Isabella's authority can be detected in the orders she issued and inferred from official documents and her own acts. But as a woman, she was at a disadvantage, for her sex would always brand her as inferior. Women, it was held, were born to be ruled by men, not to rule over them.

Lancaster's determination to execute the elder Despenser in spite of Isabella's protest, and Mortimer's decision to execute Arundel without trial show that her opinions were not always taken into account, and that the men around her found it relatively easy to overrule her.

But Isabella was intelligent and perspicacious. Her skills lay in the public relations and subtle manipulation that had won her a reputation as a peacemaker. Her long endurance of the humiliations heaped on her by Hugh and Edward argues inner strength and tenacity. In Paris, she had built up her party with circumspection, capitalizing on her role as a wronged wife to win support. In England, she had marshaled her formidable skills in public relations to ensure the success of her cause and had won hearts and minds. In all of this, she had demonstrated a considerable ability in statecraft.

But she was now faced with the problem of what to do with her husband. Edward was an anointed king, and it was essential that any proceedings against him were seen to be legal. Since the Norman Conquest of 1066, no precedent had been set for deposing an English monarch, and there was no known process of law through which it might be done. Yet it was obvious that most of Edward's subjects would no longer tolerate his rule and wanted his son to sit in his place, and it was also clear that achieving this was going to require some violation of established constitutional principles. But the alternative—the return of Edward II to power—was unthinkable.

On November 27, Lancaster was appointed constable of Kenilworth Castle. Soon afterward, on the advice of Orleton, Edward was moved there and placed under armed guard, with Lancaster as his custodian. Kenilworth, once a seat of Simon de Montfort and Thomas of Lancaster, seems to have been deliberately chosen because it was associated in the popular consciousness with those champions of good government. Lancaster proved a considerate jailer, and the King was well and honorably treated, "spending the winter in reasonably comfortable conditions, as befits a king in captivity."[11] Chancery writs were dated at Kenilworth, as if he had issued them.

Isabella and Mortimer left Hereford for London late in November, traveling by easy stages with numerous lords and ladies in attendance on the Queen. She gave many leave "to return to their country seats, except a few nobles whom she kept with her at her council. She expressly ordered them to come back at Christmas, to a great court which she proposed to hold."[12]

On November 30, in a ceremony that took place at Cirencester in the presence of the Queen, Prince Edward, and Mortimer, Bishop Airmyn was appointed chancellor in place of Baldock. That day, Isabella, Prince Edward, and Airmyn were formally made joint Keepers of the Great Seal, which the Queen was to keep under her personal supervision. From this point, the pretense that the King was personally governing his realm was gradually abandoned, and writs were issued "by the Queen and the King's first-born son," "by the council," or even just "by the Queen."[13]

At Isabella's command, Hugh's treasury in the Tower was broken into and its contents delivered to her, and she obtained Arundel's confiscated goods, financial reparation for all that she had suffered at the hands of Hugh and his followers. She also received money found at Winchester in the elder Despenser's treasure chests. She used some of this bounty to reward the Hainaulters. In December and January, she awarded herself a series of large grants, amounting to £11,843.13s.4d. ($9.7 million).

On December 3, Isabella was staying at Woodstock, where it was decided that, because London was not yet quiet, the coming session of Parliament should be postponed. A new summons was issued for it to meet on January 7, "to treat with the King, if he were present, or else with the Queen Consort and the King's son, Guardian of the Realm."[14]

On December 4, in the presence of the Mayor and Corporation, Hugh's rotting head was set up on London Bridge, amidst "much tumult and the sound of horns."[15] The Queen, "desirous to show that [Stapledon's] death happened without her liking, and also that she reverenced his calling, commanded his corpse to be removed from the place of its first dishonourable interment under a heap of rubbish, and caused it to be buried in his own cathedral" at Exeter.[16]

On December 6, she was busy arranging transport for the Hainault mercenaries. "The companions of Sir John were anxious to return home, for their task was accomplished and they had won great honour. They took leave of the Queen and the nobles, who implored Sir John to stay at least until after Christmas. The gallant knight courteously agreed to stay as long as the Queen wanted."[17] Isabella was to reward him handsomely for his services.

On December 21, the court moved to Wallingford for Christmas. Isabella had all her children with her, and her court was "fully attended by all the nobles and prelates of the realm, as well as the principal officers of the great cities and towns."[18] A mandate for a new government could not have been more clearly proclaimed. Archbishop Reynolds made his submission to the Queen. Prior Eastry had written wishing her "good and long life, grace on Earth and glory in Heaven."[19]

There had been rumors of a reconciliation between the royal couple, but this was not Isabella's intention. She and her advisers were determined upon Edward's deposition, and debated in council how this could be achieved. Some wished to have him put to death for his misrule; living, he would always be a focus for dissidents who might try to restore him to the throne—and then those who had overthrown him could expect no mercy. Yet there was no legal process for trying and executing a monarch, and many were of the opinion that a king could not technically be guilty of treason. Opinions were acutely divided on this issue until John of Beaumont expressed the view that it would be impossible to execute an anointed monarch, and that the best course would be to depose him and keep him in custody in a secure fortress for the rest of his life.

This led to a discussion about whether Isabella should honor her marriage vows and go to live with Edward in captivity, for he had already begged, weeping, to be reunited with his wife and children, and some lords felt that the Queen's rightful place was with her husband. But she had no wish to return to him, and few were willing to press her, although some of the clergy were uncomfortable about her anomalous situation. In the end, considering the threats that Edward had made against her life, it was agreed that it was unthinkable that she return to him.

True to his word, Robert the Bruce had made no move against England during the invasion, but now that was accomplished, Isabella was anxious to have the problem of Scotland settled. She was realistic enough to comprehend that there was no point in pursuing a war that could never be won and had drained the Exchequer for years, exacting a heavy toll in human suffering. On December 26, she appointed commissioners to treat with the Scots for peace.

At the beginning of January 1327, Caerphilly Castle, the last bastion of Despenser power, finally surrendered. More of Hugh's treasure was found there and Isabella appointed one of her clerks to receive it on her behalf.

The court now moved toward the capital. In advance of its arrival, a proclamation was issued, warning the Londoners to maintain the peace and informing them that all those accompanying the Queen were commanded to bear arms in the City.

Isabella and Prince Edward arrived at Westminster on January 4. "Great crowds came out to meet them and received [them] with great reverence. And the citizens gave handsome presents to the Queen," hailing her as their deliverer. There were "entertainments and feasts,"[20] and Isabella discovered that Edward had left substantial funds in his treasury.

Parliament was due to meet in Westminster Hall on January 7, but the Queen and her advisers were aware that a parliament held without a king might not constitute a legal assembly and were anxious to act as far within the law as possible. A deputation headed by Stratford and Burghersh was sent to Edward II at Kenilworth to invite him to attend, but he declined. Needing his cooperation, because it was important that Parliament's proceedings had his consent and approval, Isabella sent a second deputation.

Parliament met in the King's absence on January 7. The next day, in his name, the Queen was granted all Hugh's movables, plate, and jewels, and the huge sum of £20,000 ($16.5 million) to pay her debts overseas. Two days later, the lands seized in 1324 were restored to her.

On the evening of January 12, the second deputation returned from Kenilworth and informed Isabella that Edward had again refused to attend Parliament. She now acknowledged the necessity of proceeding without him. That night, she met with the magnates to debate what was to be done with him. All agreed that he should be deposed, and a strategy was agreed. Mortimer seems to have played a prominent role at this meeting. The next morning, it was announced that Edward, having been asked to appear before Parliament and abdicate voluntarily, had "utterly refused to comply, nay, he cursed them contemptuously, declaring that he would not come among his enemies or, rather, his traitors."[21]

Isabella was to take scrupulous care to ensure that the wishes of all the estates of the realm were taken into account in the deposition process, distributing responsibility for what was about to happen as widely as possible. What she and her associates were proposing was revolutionary, yet not so extreme as to encompass the destruction of the monarchy or the overthrow of the royal house. Nor was the monarchy to be stripped of any of its powers or privileges. Even so, the deposition of Edward II was to set a precedent that would have far-reaching consequences for several future English sovereigns.

Events now moved swiftly. Having secured the support of the Londoners, Mortimer led the lords, bishops, and commons in solemn procession to the Guildhall, where they swore to uphold the Queen's cause to the death, to rid the realm of the King's favorites, to observe the Ordinances, and to maintain the liberties of the City.

The Queen was present, a silent figure in black, when Parliament reassembled in Westminster Hall to hear Mortimer recite the reasons for Edward's necessary overthrow. The deposition of the King, he said, could only be brought about if the people gave their consent. At this, Wake rose, held up his hand, and declared that he, for one, would never again accept Edward II as king. There was a general murmur of assent. Thanks to Wake's efforts, crowds were now gathering outside. Bishop Stratford invited them into the Parliament chamber, telling them that the lords were resolved to make Prince Edward king, but that this needed their assent. Soon, Westminster Hall was packed with restive Londoners who had fought their way in, eager to have their say.

Orleton preached a sermon to the assembly. "A foolish king shall ruin his people,"[22] he warned: Taking the text "Woe to thee, O land, when thy king is a child,"[23] he expounded on Edward II's misconduct, which had left England open to the perils of a royal minority. He spoke in favor of granting the wishes of the Londoners and warned that Isabella's life would never be safe if the King resumed power, and that she would surely suffer death. He asked the estates to consider whether they would have the father or the son for king, urging them to accept the Prince.

"Away with the King!" shouted lords and commons alike.

Stratford preached next, asking what happened to a body politic "whose head is feeble." Then Wake stood up, stretched out his arms, and asked the people if they would agree to the deposition of the King.

"Let it be done! Let it be done!" they cried. "The son shall be raised up! We will no more have this man to reign over us!"[24]

The estates had spoken. All that remained was for the King formally to be deposed. This process began with Archbishop Reynolds preaching a sermon based on the text "The voice of the people is the voice of God."[25] He reminded the assembly that the King's subjects had suffered oppression for far too long; if it was their will that the King be deposed, then it was also God's will.

"Is this the will of the people?" cried Wake.

"Let it be done!" the people roared again, with a great show of hands.[26]

"Your voice has clearly been heard here," said the Archbishop.[27] Then he formally announced that, by the consent of the magnates, clergy, and people, Edward II was deposed in favor of his son. The assembly erupted in tumultuous acclaim.

The Articles of Deposition were read out to Parliament, to great ovation. They accused Edward of many offenses: being incompetent to govern and unwilling to heed good counsel; allowing himself to be controlled by evil counselors; giving himself up to unseemly works and occupations; persecuting the Church; executing, exiling, imprisoning, and disinheriting many great men of his realm; losing Scotland, Ireland, and Gascony; violating his coronation oath to do justice to all; plundering the realm; and showing himself incorrigible through his cruelty and weakness, beyond all hope of amendment.

Prince Edward was now brought into the hall to the cry, "Behold your King!" At the sight of the handsome fourteen-year-old, the Londoners vociferously acclaimed him as their sovereign, shouting, "Ave, Rex!"[28] Then the lords, with greater dignity, knelt to pay him homage and the whole assembly rose for the hymn "Glory, Laud and Honour."

Isabella "seemed as if she should die for sorrow" and broke down in tears.[29] It was perhaps a politic manifestation of grief for her husband's deposition. Mortimer, however, simply hurried off to order his sons' robes for the coming coronation.

The young King's conscience was uneasy about the turn events had taken and he was extremely reluctant to accept the crown while his father still lived. Seeing his mother weeping, he tried to comfort her, vowing that he would never accept it unless Edward II freely offered it to him. For three days, no one could persuade him to change his mind.

Many were concerned that Parliament's proceedings were not entirely lawful. To give them some semblance of legality and reassure the Prince, the King had to be persuaded to renounce his crown in favor of his son, to demonstrate that he sanctioned Parliament's decision. On January 16, a deputation headed by Orleton was sent to Kenilworth to announce the decision of the people to Edward II and persuade him to abdicate formally.

On January 20, Orleton, Stratford, and Burghersh had a preliminary private audience with Edward, who was wearing a black gown and in a fragile emotional state. In harsh tones, Orleton recited the damning catalogue of the King's crimes, invited him to abdicate, and warned him that the people would repudiate the claims of his children and set up some other person not of the blood royal if he proved obdurate. If he cooperated, his son would succeed him and he himself would be permitted to live honorably. Weeping bitterly, the King capitulated.

On the verge of collapse, he was led into the presence chamber to convey his decision to Lancaster and the rest of the deputation. There, he fainted, but "as piteous and heavy as the sight was, it failed to excite the compassion of any of the Queen's commissioners,"[30] who left Lancaster and Stratford to hasten to his aid. As soon as he had come to his senses, Orleton brusquely demanded that he now renounce his crown, as he had agreed to do. Sobbing, Edward meekly complied, saying "he was aware that, for his many sins, he was thus punished and therefore he besought those present to have compassion upon him in his adversity. Much as he grieved for having incurred the hatred of his people, he was glad that his eldest son was so gracious in their sight, and gave them thanks for choosing him to be their king."

The next day, Sir William Trussell, the Speaker of the House of Commons, on behalf of the whole kingdom, formally renounced the nation's homage to Edward II, and the King's steward broke his staff of office to signify the termination of the entire household's service. Edward was informed that from henceforth he would be known as "the Lord Edward, sometime King of England."[31] The deputation then hastened back to Westminster, carrying with them the crown and the royal regalia.

In the fourteenth-century Holkham Bible in the British Library, there is an illustration of a queen turning a wheel of fortune. At the top appears a crowned king with a scepter, but to the right, he is shown falling headlong, losing his crown and dropping the scepter, while at the bottom, he is lying bareheaded and naked, covered only by a cloak and ruefully gazing up at his former self. Almost certainly, the queen shown turning the wheel is meant to be Isabella, and the picture is a comment on the fall of Edward II. Rarely in the annals of British royalty have the political consequences of a broken marriage been so clearly portrayed.

12

"The Special Business of the King"

✳

B Y JANUARY 24, ISABELLA HAD TAKEN UP RESIDENCE IN THE
Tower. That morning, when she rode through the City toward Westminster, members of the guilds, wearing their best hats and cloaks, hastened to greet her. In the evening, when she returned, the heralds were
out in the streets, proclaiming "Sir Edward's"[1] abdication and the new
King's peace. Soon she was surrounded by crowds of cheering, rejoicing
citizens.

Edward III's reign officially began the following day, January 25, 1327.
The Great Seal of England was delivered into his hands on the 28th. Isabella probably had a say in its design, which included two *fleurs-de-lis* signifying his connection through her to the royal house of France. The
next day, Edward formally announced his father's abdication.

The new King was crowned in Westminster Abbey on February 1, 1327,
by Archbishop Reynolds. Before the ceremony began, he was knighted by
Lancaster, the senior male member of the royal house. The crown of St.
Edward the Confessor "was of vast size and a great weight," but Edward
III "bore it like a man."[2] Isabella wept throughout the long ritual of
crowning, probably for joy. Sharing in her triumph was Mortimer, a
prominent presence at the coronation, during which three of his sons,
whom he had dressed as earls, were knighted by the King. After the ceremony, gold coins depicting a child's hand reaching out to save a falling
crown were scattered among the people—a pretty piece of propaganda.

On his coronation day, King Edward returned Isabella's dower to her
with substantial additions. Instead of the annual £4,500 ($3.7 million)

she had formerly been assigned, she was now to receive the unprecedented sum of £13,333 ($10.8 million), which would make her one of the
greatest landowners in the kingdom. No one complained about the size
of the award, for she was popular. One chronicler enthusiastically referred to her as "Mother Isabella, our royal, noble, prudent, beautiful and
excellent star,"[3] a view echoed by the Pope himself, while Parliament was
at pains to acknowledge the country's debt to her and "ordained that our
lady the Queen, for the great anxiety and anguish she had suffered,
should stay queen all her life."[4]

Isabella was undoubtedly acquisitive, but the securing of such a great
landed interest was essential to her need to exercise extensive patronage
in the interests of consolidating her position and that of the regime she
had established. She and Mortimer recognized the wisdom of rewarding
their supporters with grants, offices, and perquisites. Doubtless she was
determined never again to suffer financial insecurity.

The lands of her enlarged dower were scattered throughout nearly
every English county and in parts of Wales. Among them were Edward II's
favorite house at Langley, the royal Thames-side manor of Sheen, which
she would hold until her death, the royal manor of Havering-atte-Bower,
Essex, which had been built by Edward the Confessor and held by Alienor
of Provence and Marguerite of France (the queens used the part of the
manor known as the Bower), and the royal castle and adjacent palace at
Guildford in Surrey. She also received much of the Lincoln inheritance,
including Pontefract Castle, which had been appropriated by Despenser
and should by rights have gone to Lancaster.

In 1327, she purchased Castle Rising in Norfolk, a property that was
to be forever associated with her. She also bought Hertford Castle (from
Pembroke's widow) and a London residence in Lombard Street, leased
from the Benedictine priory of St. Helen in Bishopsgate, one of the
wealthiest religious houses in the City. When in London, she either
stayed there or at Westminster, where she ordered that various improvements be made to her apartments.

After Parliament met again on February 3, a regency council was formed
with Lancaster appointed its president and the King's guardian. No official roles were assigned to the Queen or Mortimer, but power was firmly

in their hands. The fiction was maintained that Edward III was in control of his government, but Isabella "practised on [him] in his minority" and she and Mortimer "entirely governed"[5] both King and administration; they dictated policy and ruled in his name as unofficial regents. Mortimer's interests were represented on the council by his friends, but the Queen controlled the great offices of state through the men she had nominated to them, and the Chancellor, Treasurer, and Keeper of the Privy Seal accompanied her everywhere she went. She also controlled access to the King, which would inspire a great deal of envy. Her power was founded on her status as a conquering queen as well as her son's affection, loyalty, and dependence on her. A treatise by Walter de Milemete, which was presented to Edward III, contains an illuminated drawing of the young, beardless King enthroned beside his mother, both wearing their crowns.

Since Isabella and Mortimer shared power and exercised it unofficially, it is hard to determine whose was the dominant influence. England was governed in the name of the King, or of the Queen and her son. Although it was said that "the Queen ruled," many believed that she and Edward were dominated by Mortimer. Yet there is plenty of evidence that, although she relied on Mortimer's military expertise, and there are examples of his taking the initiative in important matters without reference to her, Isabella exercised real power, sometimes ruthlessly. Each apparently wielded authority in different spheres.

Mortimer's power was founded solely upon his relationship with the Queen, although he liked to stress his descent from King John, as several contemporary documents referring to him as "the King's kinsman"[6] bear witness. Knighton claimed that Mortimer and Isabella shared one lodging wherever they went, but, in view of the golden opinions of Isabella voiced at this time by the Pope and others, they evidently maintained discretion.

Parliament proceeded to issue pardons, redress Lancastrian grievances, reinstate the contrariants in their lands, and reward those who had supported the Queen. Henry of Lancaster's substantial contribution to the success of the invasion was handsomely recognized. The sentence on Thomas of Lancaster was reversed, enabling his brother to succeed him formally, and soon afterward, Edward III, at the prompting of his mother, sent a request for Thomas's canonization to the Pope, which Isabella knew would earn her popularity and keep Lancaster loyal. John XXII was to refuse this request, and three more made in the name of Edward III, probably because he was aware that Thomas's motives had been more self-interested than saintly. Another popular move urged by the Queen was the passing of an act relaxing the harsh forest laws.

At the request of his mother, Edward III granted two of Despenser's manors to Henry de Beaumont and his wife. Isabella also saw to it that Mortimer was lavishly rewarded for his services to her and the young King. On February 21, Parliament reversed the sentences on him and Chirk, formally pardoned him for escaping from the Tower, and restored his father's estates. He was then appointed Justiciar of Wales for life, with jurisdiction over all the Crown lands there.

Grants were made to Lancaster, Kent, Norfolk, Wake, Orleton, and Burghersh in consideration of their good service rendered to Edward III and Queen Isabella, while Sir John of Beaumont would soon return to Hainault loaded with gifts and a handsome pension. Isabella paid off her army and her allies, then appropriated funds for herself and Mortimer. By March, she had plundered the treasury of an estimated £78,000 (nearly $65 million), leaving only £12,000 ($10 million). Over the next four years, she would seize a quarter of the royal revenues.

It has been claimed that Isabella had no real policy apart from consolidating her position, but her first overriding preoccupation was to redress the injustices of the previous reign and so maintain her popularity. Yet she was also a realist who understood that unpopular measures were sometimes necessary. She faced daunting problems, especially concerning Scotland and France, which had eluded solutions for decades. Her foreign policy was to demonstrate her pragmatism. She did not shrink from implementing common-sense measures that would bring long-term benefits. Mortimer, by contrast, was more preoccupied with self-aggrandizement, building himself a vast power base in the Marches and accumulating great wealth.

Isabella's secret peace negotiations with Robert the Bruce had ended in deadlock. On the day of the coronation, the Scots had attacked Norham Castle in Northumberland. There followed unnerving reports that Bruce, despite encroaching age and a disease many thought to be leprosy, was building up his forces. In March, the Queen sent another delegation of commissioners to negotiate a peace, having already opened talks with France to resolve the problem of Gascony. On March 31, a treaty was signed in Paris providing for the restoration of part of Gascony on payment of a war indemnity. The treaty was unpopular in England because it left Charles IV in possession of the Agenais, but Isabella was in no position to contemplate a war with France, and her policy was naturally pro-French.

During the early months of 1327, Isabella wrote charming letters to Edward II, inquiring after his health and comfort and telling him she would be happy to visit him if only Parliament had not forbidden it. She sent him gifts of fine clothes, linen, delicacies for his table, and other small luxuries. But his pitiful requests to see her and their children were ignored. Her great fear was that the Church would make her return to him.

If the poems attributed to Edward, believed to have been composed at this time, are genuine, he saw through Isabella's duplicity. Written in Norman French, they are bitter reflections on the vicissitudes of fortune. One reads:

> *The greatest grief my heart must bear,*
> *The chiefest sorrow of my state*
> *Springs from Isabeau the Fair,*
> *She that I loved but now must hate.*
> *I held her true, now faithless she;*
> *Steeped in deceit, my deadly foe*
> *Brings nought but black despair to me,*
> *And all my joy she turns to woe.*[7]

The authorship of these poems has been disputed. There is no evidence, apart from their content, to connect them to Edward, who is not known to have composed any other verses.

Early in March, a plot to free the former King from Kenilworth was apparently uncovered. Inquiries were ordered into affrays caused by several persons, including two adherents of the Despensers, Stephen Dunheved, a Dominican friar, and William Aylmer, parson of Doddington. These same men would be indicted in July for another conspiracy to liberate the King, so it is reasonable to wonder if the March inquiries concerned an earlier abortive attempt.

Stephen Dunheved, who appears to have been the driving force behind these plots, had loyally served Edward as his confessor. It was he who had been sent to Avignon by Hugh to procure an annulment of the King's marriage to Isabella. A marked man, he had gone to ground after the Queen's invasion. The author of the *Annales Paulini* claimed that Dunheved was supported by several nobles; Kent was perhaps among them, for three years later, Stephen Dunheved was to be involved in Kent's own conspiracy against Isabella and Mortimer.

Security at Kenilworth was immediately tightened. Baker stated that Isabella, "that fierce she-lion of a woman," had asked advice of "that priest of Baal," Orleton, who recommended that Edward be removed from Lancaster's care; but Lancaster himself no longer wanted the responsibility of guarding the former King. Fearing that Edward had too many partisans in Warwickshire, Isabella and Mortimer decided to relieve Lancaster of his duties as jailer and move their prisoner south to Berkeley Castle in Gloucestershire. On March 21, Thomas, Lord Berkeley, and his brother-in-law, Sir John Maltravers, were appointed Edward's new keepers. Berkeley had no reason to love Edward II, for he and his father had endured four years' imprisonment for supporting Thomas of Lancaster, and his father had died in captivity.

On the night of April 3, Berkeley and Maltravers escorted their prisoner to Berkeley Castle. Accompanying them was a third custodian, Sir Thomas Gurney, a knight of Mortimer's affinity. One of the guards was William Bishop, who had served as a soldier under Mortimer. The journey took two days.

Baker, who claimed that he got his information from William Bishop, stated that Edward was subjected by his jailers to many indignities during the journey. They would travel only at night and would not let him sleep when he was weary. It was cold, but he was left to shiver in flimsy garments. They gave him poisoned food that made him ill. They contradicted him, made out that he was mad and jeered at him, while Gurney mockingly crowned him with straw. So that he should not be recognized, they made him shave off his beard, forcing him to sit on a molehill in a field and use muddy ditch water scooped into an old helmet.

But Edward did not travel via Bristol, as Baker stated, which casts doubt on the story. Nor is it corroborated by any other evidence. Baker claimed that Edward's jailers subjected him to these cruelties because they were hoping he would "succumb to some illness and thus languish and die," but Isabella and Mortimer had just gone to great lengths to ensure that his abdication and the establishment of their rule were attended by a semblance of legality. There would be three rescue attempts before any move was made to dispose of him.

Berkeley Castle was a mighty Norman keep on a high mound, with inner and outer baileys encircled by high curtain walls and surrounded by a moat. Edward was apparently lodged in the Thorpe Tower in the keep. Tradition has it that he occupied a small room now known as "the King's Gallery," which is still shown to visitors today. Just outside is a well-like shaft, twenty-eight feet deep, descending to the level of the courtyard below; originally it was in the corner of the cell.

Baker wrote that Edward "was welcomed kindly" and treated well by Berkeley. The chronicler Adam Murimuth agreed, but stated that Maltravers behaved harshly toward him. The custodians were assigned the princely sum of £5 ($4,000) a day from the Exchequer for his keep and that of his attendants. The Berkeley accounts show that plenty of victuals, including capons, beef, cheese, eggs, and wine, were purchased for him, corroborating Baker's statement that his jailers gave him delicacies. Claims that Isabella ordered that he be ill treated can therefore be discounted.

With Edward III established as king, Isabella and Mortimer turned their attention to fulfilling the treaty made with Hainault for his marriage. In late March, Orleton and Burghersh had been appointed by the council to travel to Hainault formally to ask Count William for the hand of one of his daughters and choose "her with the finest form"; once he had consented, they were to journey south to Avignon to seek a Papal dispensation for the King's marriage to "one of the daughters of the Count of Hainault," this being necessary because the mothers of the bride and groom were first cousins.

Bad weather delayed the envoys' departure until late April. They were received with great honor by Sir John of Beaumont, who escorted them to Valenciennes. There, Count William entertained them lavishly and led them to a secret chamber where they could observe his daughters amusing themselves, bareheaded to denote their virginity.

"We will have her with good hips, I wean, for she will bear good sons," Orleton is said to have declared. He and Burghersh chose Philippa, the middle daughter, who "was full feminine" and "a young lady who seems most worthy to be Queen of England,"[8] and obtained her parents' formal consent to her marriage. Immediately, two knights and several clerks were dispatched to the Pope, and the Count and Countess began planning Philippa's trousseau and train.

On April 8, 1327, the Queen arrived at Peterborough Abbey for Easter, and Edward III formally ratified the new peace treaty with France. Isabella had all her children with her, but on her departure, she left the younger ones at Peterborough for eight weeks, at the Abbot's expense, straining the abbey's finances.

At Stamford, during a council meeting on April 19, the possibility of Isabella joining her husband was again raised by some of the bishops, whose consciences were exercised over her illicit relationship with Mortimer. Not wishing to incur public censure, she left it to the lords to decide what she should do. Mortimer was violently opposed to her being reconciled to Edward, and after he had done some hard talking behind the scenes, Orleton reminded the council that it had already forbidden the Queen ever to return to her husband because of his cruelty, and the matter was quietly dropped.

The councilors were still trying, without success, to track down the conspirators who had probably tried to free the former King. On May 4, a warrant was to be issued for the seizure of Dunheved, but he proved elusive.

April saw Bruce assembling an army for a new offensive into Northumberland, a tactical exercise intended to force the English to accept his sovereignty. Isabella and Mortimer ordered a general muster against the Scots, which proved a popular move with both King and people, who hoped that the new reign would afford an opportunity to reverse the ignominious defeat of Bannockburn. Given the number of attempts Isabella made to forge a peace settlement, this was not a view she shared, but she was aware of the necessity of defending England's borders and maintaining the popular appeal of her rule, realizing that a war would meet with greater public approval than a peace. Although she had commissioned new peace talks with the Scots, a conflict seemed inevitable. In anticipation of an invasion, a general evacuation of the northern shires was ordered, and at Isabella's behest, the young King sent a "most affectionate"[9] request to Hainault for Sir John to return with his mercenaries.

On May 9, addressing the concerns of those clergymen who were privately scandalized at Isabella's liaison with Mortimer, Pope John wrote to urge that every effort be made to bring about a reconciliation between Edward and Isabella. His letter was ignored.

On May 23, Isabella and the young King reached York, where a large army was gathering, and took up lodgings in the house of the Dominican (black) friars. Four days later, Sir John arrived with 500 Flemish mercenaries, who "were splendidly feasted by the King and his mother and all the barons."[10]

On Trinity Sunday, June 7, Isabella hosted a banquet in the house of the Black Friars, where "the young King held court. The King had six hundred knights, and he created fifteen new ones. The Queen held her court in the dormitory, where at least sixty ladies sat at her table, whom she had assembled to entertain Sir John and the other knights. The ladies were superbly dressed, with rich jewels, taking their ease. But immediately after dinner, a violent quarrel broke out between the servants of the army of Hainault and the English archers."[11] A fight started and the archers were soon beyond control, shooting indiscriminately and voicing their hatred of the foreigners. Many Hainaulters were wounded, and the violence was only curbed when three knights seized oak staves from the house of a carter and, laying about them, knocked down sixty men. Isabella made the King and Lord Wake mount their horses and ride through the streets proclaiming that anyone attacking the Hainaulters would be instantly beheaded. The archers quickly retreated, leaving 300 dead bodies in and around the friary.

On the day after the riot, Mortimer's judicial jurisdiction was extended to the counties of Hereford, Stafford, and Worcester, suggesting that the government remained concerned about the activities of dissidents in those parts. Mortimer was now granted the Despenser lands in Glamorgan, making him a very wealthy man. So much of the property of the former favorites had now been appropriated or reassigned by Isabella that their descendants would one day complain to Froissart that she had been "an evil queen who took everything from them."

On June 10, negotiations with the Scots broke down and Bruce sent raiding parties across the border. The fourteen-year-old Edward III marched north from York at the head of an army on July 1, and the Queen left the Black Friars' convent for the greater security of York Castle, where she remained with her younger children. She kept in touch with the King by letter and ensured that York was adequately defended against the Scots.

The royal forces reached Durham by July 15, but the Scots continually outmaneuvered the English, employing maddening evasion tactics. In early August, the Black Douglas daringly raided Edward III's camp before vanishing back into Scotland. The young King felt so deeply humiliated by the failure of his first campaign that he burst into tears of frustration.

Meanwhile, in June, a party of conspirators led by Stephen Dunheved managed to free Edward II from Berkeley Castle. The episode is shrouded in secrecy, probably because Isabella and Mortimer did not want it publicized. The conspirators stormed the castle, overcame the ex-King's guards, and carried him off. Berkeley and Maltravers were away at the time, and had left a royal clerk, the unobservant John Walwayn, as their deputy. Edward was spirited away to Corfe Castle in Dorset "and other secret places."[12]

News of his escape was urgently communicated to the council in York, 250 miles away, where it provoked near panic. A warrant was issued for the arrest of Dunheved, and Berkeley was excused from military service against the Scots and "charged with the special business of the King," which was unspecified.[13] Edward II had probably been brought back to Berkeley by July 27, when Berkeley informed the Chancellor, John Hotham, that Dunheved and his accomplices had been indicted for forcing an entry into the castle and abducting Edward. But they were still at large and, on August 1, Berkeley was granted special powers to pursue them. Dunheved managed to evade capture, but most of his fellow conspirators were taken.

On August 13, Edward III returned to York, where Isabella "welcomed him with great joy, as did the ladies of the court and the burgesses of the city."[14] Meanwhile, the English envoys had arrived at Avignon and presented their petition for a dispensation, but John XXII refused it, being unhappy about the way Edward II had been treated. Only when Edward III wrote a personal appeal was he persuaded, on August 30, to consent.

After the royal army was disbanded, Sir John and his men took their leave of the King, the Queen, and all the lords, who paid them great honor, hosting a lavish feast at Eltham and doubtless trying not to dwell on the huge bill for nearly £55,000 ($48.6 million) that Sir John had just presented. The money was raised from Exchequer funds, the pledging of the Crown Jewels, and loans from merchants. The Queen did not contribute a penny from her vast revenues or offer any financial assistance to the King, who was desperately short of money after the northern campaign.

On September 7, a third plot to liberate Edward II was discovered. Its leader was Mortimer's avowed enemy, Rhys ap Gruffydd, who apparently wanted to set the former King up as a champion of Welsh liberties. Kent may have been one of the unnamed English lords who were involved, for Rhys ap Gruffydd was to support his later conspiracy. The conspirators were betrayed to William de Shalford, Mortimer's lieutenant in south Wales. Mortimer was then on his way westward, having left Isabella at Nottingham on September 1, when he had been ordered, as Justice of Wales, to inquire into conspiracies there. He did not, at that point, know of the conspiracy. On September 8, he received orders to arrest all those breaking the peace in Wales.

Mortimer was at Abergavenny on September 14 when William de Shalford wrote to inform him of Rhys ap Gruffydd's abortive attempt to liberate Edward. Shalford warned that if he was freed, Mortimer and all his people "would die a terrible death and would be utterly destroyed, on account of which Shalford counselled the said Roger that he ordain such a remedy in such a way that no one in England or Wales would ever think of effecting such deliverance."[15] Clearly the former King was a dangerous threat to the new regime. Mortimer commanded William Ockle, a trusted retainer, to show Shalford's letter to Edward's custodians and "tell them to take counsel and quickly remedy the situation in order to avoid great peril."[16]

Berkeley was later to protest that he had had nothing to do with any plot to eliminate Edward, and he may not have been at Berkeley when Ockle arrived. But Maltravers and Gurney were apparently left in no doubt that their prisoner was to be disposed of.

This chain of events makes it clear that any orders for the murder of Edward II came from Mortimer, not Isabella, who was more than 130 miles away in Lincoln and knew nothing of Rhys ap Gruffydd's plot. Even if Mortimer had sent a messenger with a letter informing her of his intentions, she would not have had time to respond. It is possible that she and Mortimer had earlier agreed that should there be another escape attempt, Edward would have to be removed, but that is pure supposition, and no contemporary source accuses Isabella of being complicit.

Baker made no mention of the rescue plots and baldly asserted that Isabella and Orleton plotted Edward's murder, since she feared that she might be made to return to her husband. He claimed that Orleton had the former King ill-treated by his jailers in the hope that he might die—but the King survived and "Isabella was angered that his life, which had become most hateful to her, should be so prolonged. She asked advice of the Bishop of Hereford, pretending that she had had a dreadful dream from which she feared, if it was true, that her husband would at some time be restored to his former dignity, and would condemn her as a traitress, to be burned or given into perpetual slavery. The Bishop of Hereford feared greatly for himself, just as Isabella did, conscious that, if this should come to pass, he was guilty of treason." The fact that Orleton had been at the Papal court at Avignon since April does not seem to have registered with Baker, and it is highly improbable that Isabella would have communicated with him about such a matter.

Baker stated that letters were duly sent to Edward's keepers, censuring them for their leniency and hinting that their prisoner's death would cause "no great displeasure, whether it were natural or violent," and that Orleton sent the jailers a Latin message that, thanks to the omission of a comma, could be read in two ways—either *Edwardum occidere nolite, timere bonum est* (Kill not Edward, it is good to fear the deed) or *Edwardum occidere nolite timere, bonum est* (Fear not to kill Edward, it is a good deed). Of course, the jailers were meant to follow the more sinister reading. It was a clever story, but a complete fabrication, since Orleton was far away in Avignon. Furthermore, Baker plagiarized the tale from the thirteenth-century chronicles of Matthew Paris. In 1334, Orleton insisted that he was not a party to Edward II's death. Certainly he was never charged with it. Baker's tale is clearly a fiction, since it takes no account of the role of Mortimer, who is barely mentioned, even though his guilt was public knowledge at the time Baker was writing.

Edward II is said to have been murdered at Berkeley Castle on September 21, 1327. There are various versions of how he met his end, few of which are contemporary. Most come from monastic chroniclers, who relied on news and gossip brought by travelers, or in other chronicles.

Probably the earliest account was that in the contemporary *Annales Paulini*, dating from around 1328. It stated only that "King Edward died at Berkeley Castle, where he was held prisoner." In 1331, a Welsh knight, Hywel ap Gruffydd, testifying against William de Shalford, asserted that Edward II "was feloniously and traitorously slain"[17] by William Ockle and others who were guarding him, but gave no details of the method used. In 1337, Adam Murimuth, a well-informed royal chronicler, claimed "it was commonly said" that the King had been "killed as a precaution" on Mortimer's orders, and that he had been suffocated by Maltravers and Gurney so that no one would suspect foul play. He added that many people adhered to this view.

In his life of Edward II, written between 1327 and 1340, an anonymous canon of Bridlington, Yorkshire, wrote that the King "died in Berkeley Castle, where he was held in custody. Of his death, various explanations are commonly suggested, but I do not care for such things as now are written. I myself prefer to say no more about the matter, for sometimes lies are for the advantage of many, and to tell the whole truth does harm."[18] Clearly, wild rumors as to how Edward met his end were gaining currency.

Two versions of *The Brut* chronicle were written in the 1330s. One, probably compiled in London, merely stated that soon after Edward II was moved to Berkeley Castle, he "became ill there and died on the day of St. Matthew the Apostle." The other, which may have been partly written in the north, stated that Mortimer "sent orders as to how and in what manner the King should be killed." When Berkeley and Maltravers received them, "they were friendly towards King Edward at supper time, so that the King knew nothing of their treachery. And when he had gone to bed and was asleep, the traitors went quietly into his chamber and laid a large table on his stomach and, with other men's help, pressed him down." Edward woke up and managed to turn over—no mean feat in the circumstances—but his tormentors spread his legs and inserted "a long horn into his fundament as deep as they might, and took a spit of burning copper and put it through the horn into his body, and oft-times rolled therewith his bowels, and so they killed their lord, and nothing was perceived." This is the earliest account of Edward being murdered by a red-hot spit.

Other northern chronicles, John of Tynemouth's *Historia Aurea,* dating from c.1346, and the *Polychronicon* of Ranulph Higden (1347), both repeat the tale in the northern *Brut*. Yet the French *Chronicle of London*, which dates from the 1340s, asserts only that Berkeley and Maltravers, "abetted by certain persons, falsely and traitorously murdered [Edward]."

The most detailed account of Edward II's murder, and the one most often quoted, is Geoffrey le Baker's, which was written in the 1350s and said to be based on the accounts of witnesses, one of whom was William Bishop; the others are not identified. Bishop was apparently a guard at Berkeley Castle in 1327, but since the information he gave Baker about Edward's journey there was obviously invented, he cannot be accounted a credible witness, while Baker himself was given to sensational fabrication.

He wrote that, when Ockle arrived with Shalford's letter and Mortimer's instructions, Berkeley felt that his authority was being undermined and, complaining that he was no longer master in his own house, took his leave of the King and left. Berkeley later testified that he was not at the castle on September 21. According to Baker, once he had gone, Maltravers, Gurney, and Ockle tried to bring about Edward's death by natural causes. For five days—the longest time that could have elapsed between Ockle arriving at Berkeley and the date on which the King is said to have been put to death—they starved him of food, deprived him of light and sleep, and held him "for many days" near a pit in which the stinking corpses of animals had been left to rot, so that he nearly suffocated from the stench. But, unsurprisingly, Edward, with his strong constitution, survived this ill treatment.

Drawing on the northern *Brut*, Baker asserted that "his tyrannous warders" then decided to kill Edward. With four stout men, they crept into his bedchamber and, as he lay "sore afraid" and "grovelling," they suffocated him with "cushions heavier than fifteen strong men could carry"—surely an exaggeration, since there were only six men present. Then they laid "a great table" across his belly. With their assistants holding it down firmly at the four corners, they pushed a horn into his rectum and thrust up it "a plumber's soldering iron, heated red hot," driving it through "the privy parts of the bowel, and thus they burnt his innards and vital organs" and "in the end" murdered him "in such wise that it could not be perceived how he came by his death." Baker claimed that it was later said that, if the King's body were to be opened up, burn marks would be found "in those parts in which he had been wont to take his vicious pleasure."

Logically, Edward must already have been dead when the red-hot iron was inserted, having been suffocated with those incredibly heavy cushions. But Baker stated that "he shouted aloud, so that many heard his cry both within and without the castle and knew it for a man who suffered a violent death. Many in both the town and castle of Berkeley were moved to pity for Edward and to watch and pray for his spirit as it departed this world." But it is unlikely that Mortimer's henchmen would have risked people hearing Edward screaming in agony; and if those weighty pillows had been suffocating him, he could not have screamed at all.

There are too many flaws in Baker's account for it to be taken seriously. Modern medical opinion holds that even if Edward did have a red-hot spit thrust into his rectum, it would probably have taken several days for him to die an agonizing death; perforation and scorching of the rectum would likely have led to peritonitis and the gradual breakdown of other internal organs.

Later chronicles recount the red-hot-spit story that first appeared in the northern *Brut*, but Froissart, who gleaned his information in 1366 when he stayed at Berkeley Castle, made no mention of it, only stating that "an ancient squire" told him that someone cut Edward's life short.

It is almost certain that Edward II was not murdered with a red-hot spit. The story is not strictly contemporary. None of the London chroniclers mentioned it, which suggests that it originated in the north or the Midlands—the Lancastrian heartlands. Its emergence there probably reflects later Lancastrian propaganda designed to discredit the regime of Isabella and Mortimer. The circumstances in which this propaganda may have been produced will become clear when the events of 1328–29 are recounted below.

No contemporary chronicler ever accused Isabella of being an accomplice to the murder of her husband, nor is there any other evidence to link her to it. Yet there was to emerge evidence that Edward II was not murdered at all.

Warned by his servant that he was about to be murdered, the former King exchanged clothes with him and, when twilight fell, walked out of his prison and through the castle without being recognized. At the main door, he came upon a sleeping porter and killed him, enabling himself to snatch the keys and make his escape. An account of his flight and what happened next appears in a letter that was written around 1337, which will be discussed in due course. There is a strong possibility that the information in that letter could only have come directly from Edward himself.

13

"So Good a Queen
Never Came to That Land"

✳

FOR A MONTH, THE BODY AT BERKELEY REMAINED AT THE CAS-
tle, having been embalmed and wrapped in waxed linen cere cloth
within hours of death. This was done, not by a royal physician or apothecary, as was usual, but by a local wise woman who might never have seen
Edward. The heart was removed and placed in a silver casket, which
would be sent by Lord Berkeley to the Queen. William Beaukaire, a royal
sergeant-at-arms, kept watch over the corpse.

Lord Berkeley was later to deny all knowledge of Edward II's death,
insisting that he did not learn of it until 1330. But someone *had* died.
There was a body to prove it and Berkeley himself arranged for Masses to
be said in the castle chapel for the soul of the departed. Either he was
lying, or he knew that the body wasn't Edward's.

"Many persons—abbots, priors, knights, burgesses of Bristol and
Gloucester—were summoned to view the body, and indeed superficially
examined it, standing far off."[1] Since it had already been embalmed and
wrapped, with the face covered, any examination would have had to be
superficial, because no one would have been able to determine its identity or the cause of death.

During the night of September 23, Gurney arrived at Lincoln, having
apparently covered the 130 miles from Berkeley at breathtaking speed,
although he had probably left Berkeley before September 21. Mortimer
had sent his orders to the castle on the 14th and his messenger could

easily have got there within two days. This all suggests that whatever happened at Berkeley took place before September 21.

Gurney saw Edward III and Isabella in private and informed them that Edward II had died. The news must have come as a surprise to Isabella, yet she may later have come to think it too much of a coincidence that he had perished just after a conspiracy to free him had been uncovered. There is no evidence that Mortimer told her that he had ordered Edward's murder, but she perhaps had her suspicions. If so, she kept them to herself. She was so bound to Mortimer that she dared not risk exposing him, or herself as a possible accessory. The official line remained that the late King had died of natural causes, and for some time no one publicly challenged that. We can infer from later evidence that Edward III was shocked by his father's death and believed that Mortimer had in some way been responsible.

Gurney was sent back to Berkeley with instructions to withhold any information about the fate of Edward II until November 1, suggesting that Isabella wanted time to establish the facts. It was not until September 28 that the former King's death was announced in Parliament and described as "an accident destined by fate."[2] This may have been as much as Mortimer had been prepared to tell Isabella.

After Parliament had risen, the court left for Nottingham. On October 1, Edward II's death was officially proclaimed. Mortimer rejoined Isabella soon afterward, just as the envoys arrived back in England with the Papal dispensation for the King's marriage. Orleton returned to a row with Isabella and Mortimer, because in defiance of their orders, he had accepted from the Pope the vacant see of Worcester, for which they had already approved a candidate. For several months, he would be out of favor.

On October 8, a new embassy headed by Roger de Northburgh, Bishop of Coventry and Lichfield, was sent to Hainault with the King's authority to draw up and conclude the nuptial contract, declare Philippa's dower, and officiate at the proxy marriage ceremony. He was officially to inform Count William of Edward II's death and assure him that he had died naturally. That month, Edward and Philippa were married by proxy at Valenciennes amid a great gathering of European royalty.

Throughout October and November, preparations were in train for Philippa's arrival in England. She received a succession of distinguished guests, come to pay their respects to their future Queen. From Nottingham, Edward commanded "his beloved Bartholomew de Burghersh, Constable of Dover, to receive and welcome" Philippa and her father to his kingdom, and charged the lords and commons "of the counties through which [they] may pass, to do them honour and give them needful aid."[3] The prospect of welcoming his bride must have helped to ease Edward III's grief. For Philippa, however, what should have been a happy time was overshadowed by the deaths of her infant brothers, two-year-old Louis and baby Jan.

Robert the Bruce was dying. His heir, David, was a child of three, and he feared his kingdom would descend into anarchy after his death. He needed to make peace with England on terms favorable to Scotland and, on October 18, he responded positively to the overtures made by Isabella and Mortimer, but stipulated that any settlement would depend on the English recognizing him as King of Scots. He also demanded that Isabella's daughter Joan be married to his son and that England give military aid to Scotland if another country attacked her. In return, he offered £20,000 ($16.6 million) in compensation for his raids in the north, and Scottish aid against any enemy of England except France, his ally.

The anti-Scottish Lancastrian faction regarded these terms as dishonorable and humiliating to the English Crown. The young King was unhappy, having been brought up to view Scotland as a vassal kingdom; yet he approved of the compensation offered, and the Queen sanctioned further peace talks. Between November and February, both sides hammered out a treaty that was mutually acceptable.

In her reply to a letter of condolence sent by John de Bohun, Earl of Hereford, on his cousin Edward's death, Isabella wrote: "We are in great trouble of heart, but in good health of body." Her letter also reveals her concern for her son, who was grieving for his father and had asked his cousin to visit him. To keep up the boy's spirits, Isabella pressed Bohun to come.[4]

The Augustinian canons of Bristol refused to receive the body at Berkeley for burial, "for fear of Roger Mortimer and Queen Isabella and their accomplices,"[5] suggesting that they did not wish to be thought loyal to the former King. Isabella was unwilling to grant the petition of the monks of Westminster for Edward to be laid to rest with his forefathers in Westminster Abbey, probably because Westminster was too near London. The capital was still simmering with unrest, and the funeral might excite adverse interest. In the end, Mortimer's kinsman, John Thoky, Abbot of the Benedictine abbey of St. Peter in Gloucester (now Gloucester Cathedral), offered to bury the body in his church.

On October 21, Berkeley and Maltravers released it to the Abbot. The corpse had been dressed in the late King's coronation robes and encased in two coffins. The monks conveyed it in solemn procession to Gloucester. Berkeley, Maltravers, and members of their household rode behind the chariot, which was received at the city gates by the mayor and burghers, who escorted it to the high altar of the abbey, where it was to lie in state. On November 10, instructions were issued for the funeral of the late King, who was to be buried with full honors and ostentatious pageantry.

Maltravers, Gurney, and Ockle were rewarded—but not excessively—for their services at Berkeley. The Queen made a grant to Maltravers for his services to her, Gurney was appointed Constable of Bristol Castle, while Ockle became a squire in Edward III's household.

On November 16, Archbishop Reynolds died. Isabella and Mortimer commended to the Pope their loyal supporter Henry Burghersh as their candidate for the vacant primacy, but Lancaster was wary of the Queen and her lover controlling the Church as well as everything else and put pressure on the cathedral chapter. To the Queen's chagrin, the undistinguished Simon Meopham was elected on December 11. This was the first sign of a growing rift between Lancaster and Isabella and Mortimer, and it had probably been sparked by the Queen's determination to make peace with the enemy, for Lancaster stood to lose his Scottish lands.

On November 20, Walter Paveley, Lord Burghersh, and John, Lord Clinton, were commissioned to escort Philippa of Hainault to England; they left for the Low Countries on the 28th. On December 2, the royal bride, escorted by her father, Sir John of Beaumont, the Bishop of Coventry and Lichfield, and a great train of Hainaulter lords and ladies, and furnished with "all such apparel as became her future dignity,"[6] left Valenciennes for Wissant, where English ships were waiting for her. On December 16, she set sail for England.

Her retinue included the noble Hainaulter squire, Walter de Manny, who served first as her carver and then as the keeper of her greyhounds, and Paon de Roët, who may have been her kinsman and usher, and whose daughters, Philippa and Katherine, would one day be placed in her household; Philippa de Roët may have been her goddaughter and named for her. Paon became "one of the knights of the good Queen"[7] and would serve her as Master of the House.

On December 20, the body believed to be that of Edward II was buried at Gloucester with great pomp and circumstance. Edward III and Queen Isabella followed the hearse as chief mourners, Isabella making, it was said, an excessive show of widowhood. Mortimer also walked in the procession, wearing a black tunic he had ordered for the occasion. Solid oak barriers had been erected to hold the crowds back.

In 1336, Edward III was to build a magnificent tomb of Purbeck marble, on which was placed a fine effigy. Isabella's influence may perhaps be seen in the innovative (in England) choice of alabaster, which had been used for French royal effigies. Edward II's was almost certainly intended to emulate those at Saint-Denis.

As with Thomas of Lancaster, Edward's reputation was gradually rehabilitated. From 1329, there were reports of miracles taking place at his tomb, leading to calls for his canonization. The Meaux chronicler observed tartly that no amount of visitors to the tomb, or miracles performed there, could make him a saint because of the wickedness of his life. Nevertheless, his monument was designed primarily as a shrine, and niches were provided for praying pilgrims. Multitudes flocked there, and so much money was raised through offerings that the Abbot was able to rebuild the south transept in the new Perpendicular style. In 1343, Edward III and Philippa of Hainault visited the tomb as pilgrims. Their grandson, Richard II, whose white hart badge appears on Edward II's tomb, petitioned the Pope several times for his great-grandfather's canonization. He was unsuccessful, but Edward II's cult persisted, and was suppressed only at the Reformation.

* * *

The court spent Christmas at Worcester. On Isabella's orders, the woman who had embalmed the corpse at Berkeley was brought secretly to her there by Hugh de Glanville, a royal clerk. Possibly the Queen had questions concerning the fate of Edward II and perhaps suspected that Mortimer had not told her the truth—or she knew about Edward's murder and feared that the woman might talk. This is unlikely, since the rewards given to Maltravers, Gurney, and Ockle, who knew the truth, were hardly generous enough to buy their silence. The most likely scenario is that Isabella needed reassurance that Edward had died a natural death from the one person who could have told her.

Glanville also brought her the silver casket containing what she believed to be her late husband's heart, which she received with sorrow.

Meanwhile, on December 18, Philippa of Hainault had arrived at Dover. She stayed for three days with her father and uncle at a nearby abbey, then made a leisurely progress through Kent, winning hearts for alighting from her litter and mounting her palfrey whenever she approached a village or hamlet, so that she could be seen by the people. At Canterbury, she insisted on visiting St. Thomas's shrine. When she reached Eltham, she bade farewell to Sir John of Beaumont and many of her escort. Her father remained; he was to accompany her north to her wedding.

On December 24, the bells rang out in welcome as Philippa entered London in state. The mayor and aldermen met her on London Bridge and presented her with plate worth £300 ($249,000). A great procession of the clergy led her into the City. As she rode through the streets, she received a rapturous reception as the living embodiment of the lucrative trade treaty with the prosperous Low Countries.

Philippa spent Christmas as the guest of John Hotham, Bishop of Ely, staying at Ely Place, his town residence in Holborn. There were three days of "great rejoicings and noble show of lords, earls, barons, knights, highborn ladies and noble damsels, with rich display of dress and jewels, with jousts too and tourneys for the ladies' love, with dancing and carolling, and with great and rich feasts day by day."[8] The celebrations in London went on for three weeks after Philippa's departure on December 28.

Escorted by John de Bohun, Earl of Hereford and Essex and Lord High

Constable of England, and followed by dozens of wagons carrying her possessions and wedding gifts, Philippa and Count William began the long journey north to meet her bridegroom, traveling up Ermine Street, the old Roman road to York. The journey took more than three weeks. By the time they reached Peterborough on January 1, 1328, it was snowing and the road was a quagmire. Progress was slow, but "the young Queen and her retinue journeyed northwards until they came to York" on January 23.[9]

The court had arrived there three days earlier. Apprised of the approach of the bride, "all the lords of England who were in the city came forth in fair array to meet her and with them the young King, mounted on an excellently placed hackney, magnificently clad and arrayed." Amid "great solemnity," Edward took his bride by the hand and embraced and kissed her. Riding side by side, with "great plenty of minstrelsy and honours," the young couple led the cavalcade back into York.[10] Then Edward escorted Philippa to the Queen Mother's lodgings in York Castle, where she was to stay until the wedding.

On January 24 or 25, 1328, in the midst of a blizzard, Edward and Philippa were married in York Minster. He was fifteen and she "on the point of fourteen years."[11] Archbishop Melton officiated, with Bishop Hotham assisting. It was freezing cold, as the choir was only partially roofed, but the ceremony was splendid and well attended. The congregation included a hundred Scottish lords who were on their way south to negotiate the peace. It was traditional for a newly married queen to make an intercession, and immediately after her wedding, Philippa obtained a pardon for a girl convicted of theft.

The King had borrowed £2,417 ($2 million) to spend on Parisian jewels for his bride. His wedding present to her was a French translation of Petrarch's *Secretum*, also known as "The Soul's Conflict with Passion." Philippa gave him Bruno Latini's *Li Livres dou Trésor*, an encyclopedia that included the texts of "*De secretis secretorum*" (then believed to have been written by Aristotle for Alexander the Great), a satire, "The Romance of Fauvel," "The Book of Julius Caesar," and "The Governance of Kings."[12] The first page has a picture of Philippa, in a white wimple, presenting the book to her husband; both wear armorial clothing. She also gave him a music book with a cover showing him with a falcon. Count William gave his new son-in-law a fabulous suit of armor adorned with blue angels and gold lettering, and a saddle decorated with images of beasts.

After the wedding, Edward and Philippa moved into the Archbishop's palace, which stood on the site now occupied by Dean's Park, near York Minster. The apartments prepared for them contained thrones upholstered in white cloth of gold.

In February, the Count and most of Philippa's train went home. In the future, William would send his daughter gifts—a horse, a dog, and two falcons. She was always to cherish a strong affection for her family and her native land. "Above all things, she naturally loved the nation of Hainault, the country where she was born,"[13] but she never courted criticism by indiscriminately promoting her compatriots, as some earlier queens had done. Among the few who remained were Paon de Roët and Walter de Manny; the latter was knighted in 1331, enjoyed a distinguished military career, and, in 1371, founded the London Charterhouse.

Edward and Philippa's was to be one of the most successful of royal marriages, a true partnership. Edward "joyfully" spent his time with his wife, whom he adored.[14] He was a precocious youth, proud of his heritage and an eager devotee of the cult of chivalry. According to the chronicler Thomas Walsingham, he was "a shapely man, of stature neither tall nor short," with a kindly countenance and long fair hair. He was charismatic and energetic, and excelled at martial sports. Philippa was kindly, amiable, and maternal, a gentle girl with a royal bearing who dressed richly and looked every inch a queen, even when she gained weight in later life. It was said that she was "fit to be truly the mother of men." Like Isabella before her, she would gain a reputation as a peacemaker, and always remained hugely popular in England. Froissart records that the whole kingdom rejoiced at the marriage, for "since the days of Queen Guinevere so good a queen never came to that land, nor any who had so much honour." Writing many years later, and wishing to extol the memory of his former patroness, he laid on the flattery, claiming, with breathtaking overstatement, that "so long as she lived, the realm of England enjoyed grace, prosperity, honour and all good fortune, nor was there ever enduring famine or dearth in the land while she reigned there."[15] But blame for the kingdom's woes could never have been attributed to Philippa.

Initially, her role would be largely subordinate to that of her mother-in-law. Her coronation was deliberately postponed. She was not given an independent household as Queen, but expected to share the King's. Nor was she assigned any dower, since the Queen Consort's dower lands were firmly in the hands of Isabella. A hospice in Milk Street, London, had to be converted into a wardrobe for Philippa, since Isabella had commandeered the Tower Royal.

By any standards, Philippa had been slighted, and the root cause probably lay in Isabella's jealousy of the young girl who had supplanted her, and her unwillingness to give place to her. Philippa had everything Isabella had lost, or never enjoyed. Isabella was now thirty-two, quite middle-aged by fourteenth-century standards, and her famous beauty was probably fading. Maintaining a close relationship with her son was essential for the continuance of her power, and Philippa represented a threat to that; as Edward's beloved wife, she would be able to influence him in ways that his mother never could. The solution, therefore, was to keep her firmly in the background and deprive her of the means of exercising patronage.

14

"The Shameful Peace"

*

MORTIMER HAD JOINED ISABELLA AT YORK ON FEBRUARY 4. The regency council began to meet daily in the interests of promoting accord between the magnates because tempers were rising high over the proposed—and deeply unpopular—peace with Scotland. Yet Isabella and Mortimer were determined to have their way.

On March 1, because his mother insisted on it, a glowering Edward III appeared in Parliament in York and publicly acknowledged Scotland's independence. Then news of the sudden death of Charles IV reached the English court. His passing brought to an end the male line of the Capetians, which had descended from father to son since 987, but he left a pregnant widow. Until she gave birth to the requisite son, Charles's cousin (and Philippa's), Philip of Valois, was to act as regent of France.

Charles's death left Isabella the sole surviving child of Philip IV and sowed the seed for the long conflict between England and France that would become known as the Hundred Years War. Edward III was now Charles's nearest male relative. He did not wait to find out if Queen Jeanne's child was a son. On March 28, doubtless primed by Isabella, but needing no encouragement, he announced that he intended to claim his rightful inheritance, the crown of France. Both Edward and Isabella were to argue that the French Salic law did not prevent a woman from transmitting a claim. But on April 8, after Queen Jeanne had borne a daughter, the French peers chose Philip of Valois as their King and he was proclaimed Philip VI. Thus was founded the royal house of Valois.

* * *

From March 3 to April 21, Isabella and Mortimer were absent from court, probably on progress, although there is no record of where they went. According to Froissart, Philippa was sent to London after Easter, while Edward visited Lincoln and Northampton. At Eltham Palace, on April 1, she again exercised her queenly function of intercession, writing to ask the King to pardon two felons, one a ten-year-old girl who had been imprisoned in the Marshalsea for theft. Further intercessions followed, but the young Queen's request for her cousin, Johanette de Tourbeule, to be accepted as a lay sister at Polsloe Priory near Exeter greatly provoked the Prioress, who wrote to her: "No queen has ever asked such a thing of our little house before and, if it may please of your debonair Highness to know of our simple state, we are so poor, as God and everybody knows, that what we have would not suffice for our little necessities in performing the service of God day and night if, by the aid of our friends, we were charged with seculars without lessening the number of our religious, to the belittling of our service to God and the perpetual prejudice of our poor house."[1]

The Bishop of Exeter wrote to the King in support of the Prioress, and the matter was dropped.

On March 17, at Edinburgh, King Robert sealed the peace treaty with England. It recognized him as king of Scots and ceded to Scotland the right to sovereign independence, renouncing the claim of the kings of England to be overlords of the northern kingdom. The treaty was to be cemented by the marriage of the Princess Joan to David Bruce.

On May 1, at Northampton, Parliament approved the treaty, which was ratified by a simmering Edward III. Having been powerless to resist the determination of his mother and Mortimer, he was furious at having been forced to agree to this humiliating settlement and horrified at the selling of his sister.

When the peace was proclaimed in London, there was an outcry. People called it "shameful," protesting that the young King, "through the false counsel of traitors," had been "fraudulently disinherited" of Scotland,[2] while Lancaster objected that the treaty had been concluded without the consent of the King or the realm. Edward made no secret of the fact that he wanted nothing to do with the treaty, even publicly declaring that his mother and Mortimer had arranged the whole thing.

In the wake of the Treaty of Northampton, the popularity of Isabella and Mortimer dwindled rapidly. How, people asked, could they have conceded so much to a man regarded by most Englishmen as the equivalent of a modern war criminal or terrorist? The treaty irrevocably alienated Lancaster, for it starkly exposed how far his own power and influence had been eroded. Norfolk, Beaumont, and many who had lost lands in Scotland as a result of the new peace were also outraged, while Kent, whose loyalty to Isabella was wavering, would soon align himself with Lancaster.

In major respects, the treaty was a successful piece of policy-making, for it released England from a hopeless and costly war and brought peace to the north. Although Edward and most of his subjects would infinitely have preferred one decisive push to conquer Scotland, this was a fast-receding possibility; nor could the government afford it, for Isabella and Mortimer had spent so lavishly that Edward II's treasure was now virtually exhausted. As they had both argued in Parliament, peace was essential if there was to be a war with France over the succession.

Isabella and Lancaster now became increasingly bitter rivals for control of the King and the government. Lancaster, at forty-seven, was proud, popular, and influential. He had the potential and means to become a powerful and effective opponent; he was also the King's official guardian and could, if he wished, legally seize control of Edward. Faced with that prospect, Isabella dared not risk further eroding her popularity by forcing an open breach with him. Instead, she began to subvert his authority by subtly excluding him and his faction from government, while building up Mortimer's power.

From now on, her policies were aimed at bolstering her regime and discrediting her enemies. That meant controlling access to the King, appointing her own nominees to the high offices of state, and amassing enough wealth and territory to maintain her political supremacy. Without compunction, she resorted to underhand measures, including the occasional subverting of justice.

To counterbalance the catastrophic effects of the Treaty of Northampton, Isabella sponsored a statute to curb the endemic lawlessness in the country, a legacy of the weak rule of Edward II and the revolution that had overthrown him, and a matter of great grievance to many. The use of the King's Privy Seal was to be restricted; pardons and grants, which she and Mortimer had issued liberally, would not be so easily obtainable; justices of the peace had their powers extended, and royal officials were to be fair and maintain the King's peace at all times. These were sensible measures in which Lancaster's influence can be detected.

During the next two years, Isabella issued a steady stream of commissions to assist the circuit judges in implementing the new statute. She instructed the sheriffs to forbid armed assemblies of men. She knew that a regime that could not enforce law and order was in danger of falling, and was confident that, having suffered years of misgovernment and unrest, the people of England would be grateful to those who had restored justice and peace. Unfortunately, within six months, there would be complaints that the statute was not being properly enforced, while Isabella herself was to undermine its integrity by blatantly contravening its provisions.

As Isabella and Mortimer divided the spoils of the Scottish peace between them, the young Queen found herself scraping by on next to nothing. Before Parliament rose on May 14, the King undertook to dower her within one year with lands and rents worth £15,000 ($12.6 million) per annum, as her father had been promised. But he could not fulfill his undertaking because the Crown was virtually impoverished.

Isabella announced that she intended to pursue Edward's claim to the French throne, a resolve enthusiastically supported by the King and calculated to placate the English people, who felt that their national honor had been disparaged by the peace with Scotland. Isabella had already had Edward write a letter to the Pope, in which he acknowledged that she could not succeed to the French throne, "as the kingdom of France was too great for a woman to hold by reason of the imbecility [i.e. weakness] of her sex,"[3] but that he wished to claim it himself as Charles IV's nearest male relative.

On May 16, Bishop Orleton (now restored to favor) was sent to France officially to demand that Edward be recognized as its king. He argued that Isabella could legitimately transmit her claim to her son. It could not be denied that every feudal lordship in France could be inherited by a woman, so why not the crown? Nor, however, could it be denied that a thirty-five-year-old man with experience in statecraft was infinitely preferable as a ruler to a boy of fifteen in tutelage to his mother and her lover; and the twelve peers of France, who were utterly averse to the prospect of any English king wearing the French crown, "clean put out" Edward's claim, insisting that the throne of France "was of such great noblesse that it ought not by succession to fall into a woman's hand."[4] Philip VI was crowned on May 29.

Isabella was incensed, but in no position to resort to war, so she began to seek allies against Philip, to whom she was to refer disparagingly as "the foundling king." She cultivated the friendship of Brabant, Guelders, Bruges, Navarre, and Castile, and, on May 21 opened negotiations for the marriage of her younger son, John, now nearly twelve, to the daughter of the Castilian Lord of Biscay.

In May, Isabella accompanied Mortimer to Hereford for the double wedding of his daughters to James, Lord Audley, and Thomas de Beauchamp, Earl of Warwick. Afterward, Mortimer escorted his wife—whom he rarely saw now—to Ludlow Castle. Isabella probably stayed there as their guest. It is hard to believe that Lady Mortimer was unaware of the nature of the Queen's relationship with her husband. How she reacted to Isabella's presence in her ancestral castle is a matter for speculation.

The King, who had been at Warwick, had made a leisurely progress to Woodstock, where he was reunited with Philippa. With its high-walled park and menagerie of exotic animals, the palace would become one of her favorite residences and Edward would build a pavilion for her there, near the cloistered garden, while Queen Pool, east of the present lake, was named for her.

Edward was making a tactical withdrawal from the preparations for the wedding of his sister to David Bruce, with which Isabella was now greatly occupied. He had already announced publicly that the marriage did not have his blessing and that he would not be attending the nuptials. Instead, he would remain with Philippa at Woodstock. Isabella tried to persuade him to change his mind, even arranging a spear fight in Berwick as an incentive, but Edward was adamant.

The Treaty of Northampton had provided for the return of the Stone of Scone to Scotland. Despite Edward's opposition, Isabella had every intention of taking it north with her when she went to Berwick for the wedding and, at her insistence, the King reluctantly ordered the Abbot of Westminster to deliver the stone to the sheriffs of London, who were to transport it to her. But the Londoners staged a demonstration, refusing to allow the Abbot to surrender it. The Stone of Scone stayed at Westminster.

On July 2, at York, Isabella appointed as chancellor her staunch ally Bishop Burghersh. Nearly every high office was now held by her supporters, but Burghersh, for all his avarice, was "noble and wise in counsel, of great boldness, yet of polished manners, and singularly endowed with personal strength,"[5] and would remain loyal to her.

That summer, Philippa received two letters from the Pope congratulating her on her marriage. He enjoined her to love her husband and reminded her that it was "her duty to assist the King in defending the rights and liberties of the Church, protecting the poor and exercising herself in good works."[6] He assured her that she could approach him whenever she was perplexed or troubled. Some months later, he would give her permission to have a portable altar in her chamber (so that she could hear Mass before dawn), to enter a nunnery with a large retinue, to have her confessor give her absolution if she died suddenly, and for clergy dining at her table to eat meat on days when fasting was not obligatory. In return, he again required her to use her influence for the advancement of the Church and urge Edward to give the Knights Hospitallers some property that had been confiscated from the Templars.

Philippa was left at Woodstock when, early in July, Edward was forced to accompany Isabella and Mortimer and a great retinue to escort the Princess Joan north to Berwick. When they arrived, though, he refused to attend the wedding and rode south to rejoin Philippa. On July 16, Isabella and Mortimer witnessed Joan's marriage, which was celebrated with considerable splendor. Isabella financed her stay in the north by appropriating provisions meant for the Tower of London.

On July 22, Isabella gave Joan numerous farewell gifts before formally handing her over to the Scots. Among them was probably the Taymouth Hours,[7] a manuscript dating from c.1325-35, which has illustrations similar to those in Queen Mary's Psalter. They include four pictures of a queen who represents either Isabella or Joan: she is depicted at prayer, keeping vigil, and being presented by the Virgin Mary to the enthroned Christ. It has been suggested that Isabella commissioned the Taymouth Hours, with its French prayers, as a wedding gift for Joan. On parting, Joan gave her mother a brooch or clasp in the shape of an M to attach to her rosary beads.

It was said in England that the Queen had "disparaged" the Princess by this "vile marriage,"[8] while the Scots gave their dowerless little Queen the derisory nickname "Joan Make-peace."[9]

The Queen and Mortimer arrived in York soon after Parliament had met there on July 31. They summoned a meeting of the council to discuss sending troops to Gascony, but Lancaster, Norfolk, Kent, Wake, and others deliberately absented themselves in indignation at the peace with Scotland and the growing autocracy of Isabella and Mortimer. Many had begun to resent their monopoly of power and Mortimer's increasing arrogance and presumption. He dispensed patronage like a king, for grants to his followers were made in the King's name, under the Privy Seal, which was effectively under Isabella's control, and there were complaints in Parliament that it was being misused. Relations were further soured when most of the first installment of Bruce's compensation disappeared into Isabella's coffers instead of replenishing the empty Exchequer. She had also appropriated taxes raised at Lancaster's behest for fighting the Scots. Soon, it was being said that she and Mortimer had arranged the treaty and compromised England's honor purely for their own personal gain.

Incited by Lancaster, Isabella and Mortimer's former allies publicly claimed that the Queen had usurped the sovereign's authority under the pretense of reforming the abuses of Edward II's rule and asserted that, in a little over a year, she and Mortimer had committed more crimes than Edward and his favorites had in twenty years. This was a vast exaggeration, but Lancaster was a driven man, spurred on by anger over the treaty with the Scots and his determination to reassert his authority. Many Londoners sympathized with him, and the mayor sent letters of support.

Kent desperately wanted an opportunity to redress the wrongs he had done Edward II; he and his brother Norfolk felt that Mortimer had usurped their positions as princes of the blood. Both regarded the rewards given them for supporting Isabella as paltry compared to those that she and Mortimer had awarded themselves. Another who had deserted Isabella was Bishop Stratford, who had received no substantial reward or public office, which apparently rankled greatly.

On September 7, the court was at Barlings Abbey near Lincoln when Lancaster came to parley at the head of an armed force. Isabella and Mortimer angrily refused to listen to his complaints, whereupon he threatened to turn his troops on them. In the end, the King had to command him to lay his grievances before the Parliament that was to meet at Salisbury. Isabella was badly shaken by the confrontation. She and Mortimer sent contingency plans for dealing with Lancaster to the sheriffs, who banned all public assemblies and replaced officials whose loyalty was questionable. Then the couple rode to Gloucester, where Mortimer began to muster troops from the Marches. With some truth, the pro-Lancastrian *Brut* claimed that this open rift with Lancaster marked the beginning of the tyranny of Isabella and Mortimer.

The row at Barlings had driven Lancaster openly to seek the support of the Londoners. On September 14, Wake and Stratford addressed the citizens at the Guildhall, publicly declaring their grievances. They demanded that the King live off his own revenues so that he would have at his disposal sufficient treasure to fight his enemies; that his mother surrender her vast dower and live on the traditional income of a queen consort; that she avoid abusing her power and cease oppressing the people with her extravagance; that Mortimer be banished from court; that the regency council be permitted to function without obstruction or interference; and that law and order be properly enforced. The Londoners loudly voiced their approval and called for these matters to be discussed in a Parliament at Westminster, not at Salisbury.

Edward III was at Cambridge when, on September 27, he was warned that Lancaster was on the march, intending to take custody of him. He rode to join his mother and Mortimer at Gloucester. There, in October, Isabella learned of the proceedings at the Guildhall and fell weeping into her son's arms, crying that Lancaster was his enemy and meant her evil by his false and cruel accusations. Moved by her distress, Edward sent Sir Oliver Ingham and Lord Burghersh to the Lord Mayor of London, demanding that he explain his conduct.

When the royal party arrived at Salisbury, they learned that Lancaster's men had beheaded Sir Robert Holland, who had dared to raid Lancaster's estates and stood accused of murdering one of the Earl's adherents. An indictment had been brought against Holland, but the Queen, contravening the provisions of the Statute of Northampton, had issued a writ prohibiting any justice from proceeding against him. Lancaster had now taken the matter into his own hands. Isabella attempted to bring the killers to justice, but he took them under his protection and ensured their immunity.

Parliament met at Salisbury on October 16. Fearing that Lancaster would arrive at the head of an army, Isabella sent Edward and Philippa to the safety of her castle at Marlborough, instructing Chancellor Burghersh to open Parliament in the King's name. In the event, Lancaster and his allies stayed away, sending transparent excuses for their absence. The situation still looked ugly, and on the opening day, Mortimer came to Parliament at the head of his own forces, silencing the protests of the bishops by forbidding them, on peril of life and limb, to oppose his interests.

Stratford, acting as Lancaster's spokesman, announced that the Earl was refusing to attend because of his fear of Mortimer, whom he had no reason to trust and who had made peace with the Scots with the intent of destroying him. Mortimer hotly defended himself and swore on Archbishop Meopham's crucifix that he intended no harm to Lancaster.

Still the Earl would not come to Salisbury. He sent the bishops a message stating that he was acting not in his own interests, but in those of the King, the realm, and the Church. *The Brut* claimed that he accused Isabella and Mortimer of removing Edward II from his custody at Kenilworth and placing him in Berkeley Castle, where "they had traitorously murdered him." That Lancaster made such accusations is unlikely, because no other source refers to them; if he had made them publicly, it would surely have caused a sensation and been commented on. The story was almost certainly propaganda calculated to discredit Mortimer and Isabella, like the red-hot-spit tale, which apparently emerged at this time in the Lancastrian heartlands of the north and was soon afterward recounted in this same chronicle. It was probably put about to justify an uprising against them.

It is significant that Lancaster made no complaint about the private relationship between the Queen and Mortimer, a scandal out of which he could have made immense political capital. The chroniclers were also reticent about it, and it must be concluded that, far from being notorious, it was conducted with discretion.

Briefed by his mother, Edward III, now back at Salisbury, wrote to Lancaster protesting that, as for her living within her means, that was a matter between her and himself, and no one else. If Lancaster had been sidelined, it was his own fault for failing to attend council meetings; in his absence, the King, quite properly, had taken counsel of the other magnates and done his best to maintain law and order. Lancaster decided to stay away from Parliament rather than risk being arrested for inciting rebellion or abetting Holland's murderers.

On the closing day of Parliament, October 31, the King created his brother John Earl of Cornwall and, at the behest of Isabella, Mortimer was made Earl of March, with Edward himself buckling on the belt and spurs of nobility. The title was a new one, chosen by Mortimer to reflect his supremacy in the Welsh Marches. His elevation proved too much for many to stomach, especially Lancaster.

Mortimer now began to conduct himself like a king, bearing himself so haughtily, it was said, that he was a wonder to watch. In the King's name, Isabella granted him permission to travel with an armed retinue, and everywhere he now went, he was accompanied by 180 fierce Welsh men-at-arms to protect him and intimidate his enemies. On an income of £8,000 ($6.6 million) a year, he lived in sybaritic luxury, sleeping in silken sheets and wearing costly satin and velvet.

Isabella did nothing to counter his self-aggrandizement. Both were rapacious and determined to retain their grip on power so that they could continue to enjoy the privileges it brought. Isabella must privately have feared that if Lancaster and his allies got the King into their clutches, she stood to lose everything. With that threat hanging over her, she was becoming increasingly reliant on Mortimer as her champion against these hostile forces.

Parliament adjourned on November 1, intending to reassemble at Westminster. Meanwhile, Lancaster had occupied Winchester, through which the court meant to pass on its way back to the capital. Isabella and Mortimer had ridden to Marlborough, where Mortimer insisted that Edward III accompany him to Winchester to confront Lancaster and accuse him of treason if he refused to lay down his arms. Isabella warned Edward that Lancaster, Kent, and Norfolk were bent on dethroning him, whereupon Edward agreed to go with them on condition that Philippa accompany him. When they arrived at Winchester on November 3, the Lancastrians were already riding out of the city.

On November 21, the royal party reached London, where the citizens presented Edward and Philippa with an array of meats and fish. Isabella, responding to Lancaster's criticisms, instructed the sheriffs to send the King lists of all those who had infringed the Statute of Northampton. Lancaster sent messengers to the Queen asking to have their differences debated at a full meeting of the council. But she replied that he had offended the King and that nothing but his submission would suffice.

While Edward was at Westminster, envoys from Philip VI arrived to demand that he pay homage for his Continental possessions, as was customary when a new king ascended the French throne. Isabella was having none of it. "My son, who is the son of a king, will never do homage to the son of a count,"[10] she declared. Philip VI retaliated by seizing the revenues of Gascony, alarming the English magnates, who counseled the Queen to be prudent. There was enough strife without inviting a war with France.

In December, Kent and Norfolk issued a circular letter to the lords and bishops, complaining that the King had violated Magna Carta and his coronation oath, and urging them to meet at St. Paul's to debate what should be done about it. This was merely a pretext to attack Isabella and Mortimer. In December, word of Kent's letter reached Isabella at Gloucester, and she made the King write to the City of London, giving a biased account of the conflict with Lancaster and begging for aid against his enemies. But the archbishops of Canterbury and York were sympathetic toward Lancaster, and Meopham dared to preach against Edward III at St. Paul's Cathedral. The next day, the disaffected lords met there and began lengthy discussions as to how to proceed.

On December 21, the King's letter was read out at the Guildhall, prompting the citizens to proclaim their loyalty to him and urge that neither side take up arms until the matter could be debated in Parliament. Two days later, Meopham sent a brisk letter to Edward, threatening Isabella and Mortimer with excommunication. It was this letter, together with rumors that Lancaster was marching on London, that precipitated civil conflict.

On December 29, Mortimer was with the King at Worcester when Edward III declared war on Lancaster. On January 1, 1329, the royal army left Warwick for Lancaster's stronghold at Kenilworth, to which the King was refused access by the garrison, an unforgivable act of lèse-majesté.

But Lancaster was in London. His aim was to seize the King and impeach Mortimer and Isabella for concluding the hated peace with Scotland. Within twenty-four hours, 600 men had flocked to his banner. Meanwhile, Mortimer's forces had ravaged his lands and seized his town of Leicester, which proved a powerful deterrent, driving Lancaster's allies to abandon him. As he marched north to confront the royal army, he realized that further opposition was futile. When Kent and Norfolk deserted him and made their submission to the King, he knew that his cause was lost and that he must make his peace with Edward—and, more pertinently, with Isabella and Mortimer. Another reason for this about-turn may have been the realization that he was going blind.

At Bedford, Lancaster dismounted, knelt on the ground before the King, Isabella, Mortimer, and their entire army, and surrendered, swearing on the Gospels that he would in future do nothing to harm "our Lord the King, my ladies the queens, nor any great or small of the council."[11] Thanks to the mediation of Archbishop Meopham, his life was spared and he was left at liberty, but he was ordered to pay a fine equivalent to the value of half his lands, and was stripped of all his offices save that of seneschal of England. Effectively, Mortimer and Isabella had crushed him and henceforth he would play only a minor role in public affairs.

A few of Lancaster's followers fled to France. The rest were punished with forfeitures or bound over to keep the peace on penalty of a large fine. Isabella and Mortimer were surprisingly merciful, for most of these forfeitures were later reversed and the fines—even Lancaster's—pardoned.

In February, French envoys brought Philip VI's final demand for Edward III to pay homage. Realizing that she was in no position to risk the consequences of a further refusal, Isabella swallowed her pride. The envoys were informed that the King would come to France after all and sent home with rich gifts. It was decided, however, that Edward would perform only conditional homage, without prejudice to any future claim he might make to the crown of France.

That month, at Eltham, Isabella appointed Maltravers steward of the King's household. The court moved to Guildford in March and lodged in Isabella's castle and adjacent palace. There the King hosted a two-day tournament, after which Mortimer, at the Queen's insistence, was presented with costly presents as a reward for his defeat of Lancaster.

On April 16, at Wallingford, Queen Philippa was granted the revenues from a few estates and 1,000 marks ($636,000) annually for her chamber expenses until better provision could be made for her; this may have been an attempt by Isabella to mollify Edward, who was resentful because his wife had not been adequately provided for. Another possible placation was the retaining of his friend Sir William de Montagu "to stay with the King with twenty men-at-arms for life,"[12] an appointment Isabella and Mortimer would have cause to regret. Montagu, an intelligent and chivalrous man of twenty-eight, had been in the retinue that accompanied Prince Edward to France and thereafter quickly risen in his favor; it was a friendship that would be severed only by death.

In May, Edward bade farewell to Philippa, Isabella, and Mortimer at Canterbury, giving Philippa the parting gift of a crown. Then he sailed to France, leaving John of Eltham as nominal guardian of the realm. On June 6, wearing robes of crimson velvet embroidered with leopards and a gold crown, the young King paid homage to Philip VI in Amiens Cathedral. Relations between the two were cordial, but they were "friends only according to the outside of their faces."[13]

In France, Edward was embarrassed by salacious gossip about his mother and Mortimer, while Bishop Burghersh, who had accompanied him, was alarmed to hear whispers that Philip was plotting to kidnap Edward, and insisted that they return home immediately. Their departure was so precipitate that Edward had no time to say a proper farewell to the French King. He arrived in England on June 11, and rejoined Isabella and Mortimer at Canterbury to hear that Robert the Bruce had died and that five-year-old David II had succeeded him.

Philippa welcomed Edward "right joyfully"[14] when he was reunited with her two days later at Windsor. Isabella and Mortimer followed. In a lavish ceremony on July 20, the King—doubtless at the instance of

Isabella—presented Mortimer with valuable jewels. Eight days after that, the court traveled to the West Country to attend the weddings of two more of Mortimer's daughters, who were marrying the heirs of Norfolk and Pembroke. After Lancaster's disgrace, Norfolk had been reconciled to Isabella and Mortimer. This marriage of his son to Beatrice Mortimer and his presence at the wedding demonstrate his eagerness to ingratiate himself with them. For Mortimer, this marriage alliance with the royal house represented the pinnacle of his success.

On September 2, Isabella appointed Mortimer heir to several of her properties, and gave her executors control over her revenues from Ponthieu for three years after her death. She had drawn up similar documents only once before, prior to the birth of her first child, and she is not known to have been ill at this time, circumstances that have prompted speculation that she was carrying Mortimer's baby and making discreet provision for the future in case she did not survive her confinement. The birth of a bastard child to the Queen would have caused a scandal throughout Christendom, affording her opponents the opportunity of making political capital of her condition. It would have besmirched the reputation of the Crown and humiliated the young King. If Isabella was pregnant, then secrecy was maintained; but there is insufficient evidence to support the theory.

In September, Edward, Philippa, and Isabella stayed at Berkeley Castle—two years after Edward II had met his fate there. They were on their way to Wigmore Castle, where they arrived on September 4 to attend the spectacular Round Table and tournament that Mortimer hosted to celebrate his daughters' nuptials. He himself entered the lists as King Arthur, proclaiming his descent from (the mythical) King Brutus. Isabella must have enjoyed the event, as she had a particular fondness for the legends of Arthur. It is unlikely that she took on the role of Queen Guinevere, as has been suggested, for that would have drawn attention to her illicit relations with Mortimer.

By now, Edward was becoming disturbed by Mortimer's rampant self-aggrandizement and concerned that the decisions taken by him in his name did not reflect his own wishes—and indeed were sometimes in direct opposition to them. Being still a minor, there was little he could do about it, but, on September 12, he sent William de Montagu to Avignon to speak to the Pope on his behalf. Montagu had a private audience with

John XXII, and it was arranged that if Edward wrote "*Pater Sancte*" in his own hand at the bottom of a letter, the Pope would know that it was from him, and not from Isabella or Mortimer.

Kent, who was supposed to be "on the King's business,"[15] was also at Avignon, informing Pope John that Edward II was still alive and that he intended to liberate him. He revealed that a Dominican friar had "conjured up a spirit"[16] who assured him that the former King yet lived. Lanercost stated that this friar was none other than Stephen Dunheved, the Dominican who had tried to rescue Edward. Kent had probably been one of the magnates who had backed Dunheved then, and it follows that Dunheved approached him now.

Kent was convinced that the friar's story was genuine. It lent credence to widespread rumors that Edward had survived. Kent's conscience had apparently never ceased to trouble him in regard to his betrayal of his brother; he wanted to believe that Edward was alive and leapt at this chance to redress the wrongs he had done him. The Pope, he later claimed, gave his blessing, "charged him that he should use his pains and diligence to deliver Edward" and promised him moral and financial support; but John XXII was to deny this.[17]

In Paris, on his way home to England, Kent had a meeting with Henry de Beaumont and Thomas Rosselin, another Lancastrian exile, and discussed with them the restoration of Edward II. They promised to make contact with the Scottish Earl of Mar with a view to invading England's northeast coast, an ambitious plan with little hope of success. Kent then returned to England to enlist further support.

When he arrived, two friars informed him that Edward II was living at Corfe, and offered to act as intermediaries for him. Kent sent them to Corfe to establish that Edward was still there. They reported that people in the village had told them that he was being held in captivity in the castle. They had gone up to the castle to check and met with two members of the garrison, John Deveril and Bogo de Bayouse, who had not denied that Edward was there, but had told the friars that they could not speak with him. They did, however, permit them to enter the dimly lit hall at night and observe from a distance a tall man seated at the dinner table on the dais; he bore, the friars said, a great resemblance to Edward II.

It was this that had hardened Kent's resolve to liberate Edward and take him to his own castle at Arundel, Sussex. He wrote to Deveril and Bayouse demanding an interview with their prisoner. Receiving no response, he hastened to Corfe, offered a bribe to Deveril, and insisted on being conducted to his brother's apartments. Permission was firmly refused, so Kent wrote a letter to Edward, outlining his plot, and asked the custodians of the castle to give it to him.

In September, King Edward again asserted himself, appointing his own man as treasurer in place of Mortimer's; he also promoted Thomas Garton, who had been recommended by Montagu, to the office of comptroller of the household, and made his former tutor and loyal secretary, Richard de Bury, keeper of the Privy Seal. Since Bury was still being referred to as Isabella's "dear clerk" in June 1330, she must have been happy about this appointment, and had perhaps suggested it.

In October, the court was at Dunstable for a tournament that lasted for four days before traveling to Kenilworth, where it remained until January 3, 1330, an unusually long sojourn, necessitated (it has been suggested) by Isabella's need for privacy. The chronicler Jean le Bel later reported a rumor current at this time that "the Queen Mother was pregnant and Lord Mortimer, more than anyone else, was suspected of being the father. The rumour spread like wildfire until the young King was made fully aware of it." It has been suggested that Isabella secretly gave birth to Mortimer's child during their prolonged stay at Kenilworth.[18] On December 3, Mortimer made a brief visit to his Marcher estates. It has been conjectured that he took the child with him and left it with a wet nurse at Montgomery Castle, which is not far from Clun, one of the places he visited.[19] Isabella would make over her interests in Montgomery Castle to Mortimer the following April.

Mystery surrounds an effigy of a knight in Montgomery parish church. The tomb is supposed to be that of Sir Edmund Mortimer, Mortimer's great-grandson, who supported the Welsh freedom fighter Owen Glendower, and died during the siege of Harlech between 1409 and 1411. But although Edmund was born in lawful wedlock, the Mortimer shield on the tomb bears the bend sinister denoting bastardy. One theory has it that this knight was a royal bastard, perhaps Isabella's son by Mortimer, although he could have been the natural son of any one of the fourteenth-century Mortimers, who by 1400 had long been linked by marriage and blood to the royal house and had been recognized as heirs to the throne.

If Mortimer left Kenilworth with Isabella's newborn child on December 3, it must have been conceived around the beginning of March. That meant that when she was presiding over the events at Wigmore and Dunstable, the Queen would have been six or seven months pregnant. She had been in the public eye for most of the year and it would not have been easy to conceal her condition. Women's costume of the period skimmed the body or fell in soft folds, and any pregnancy near term would have been noticeable, especially in a great household. The reason for the extended stay at Kenilworth, therefore, was probably Queen Philippa's pregnancy, not Isabella's. Philippa had conceived around September; by the end of October, when she arrived at Kenilworth, she might have been experiencing the nausea and tiredness that are typical of the first trimester. By the thirteenth week, such symptoms usually abate, and by New Year's Day 1330, she was well enough to distribute gifts to members of the royal household, according to rank: belts, wallets, and scrips of varying quality for the men, and brooches and florins for the women.

There is no doubt that Philippa had been slighted as queen. For more than two years now, her coronation had been postponed. She had not received her rightful dower, because Isabella had no intention of relinquishing it. Once Philippa was crowned, Isabella stood to lose her status, her income, and her privileges. But Philippa was now pregnant with an heir to the throne, and it was unthinkable that she give birth without first having been consecrated as queen. The King was growing increasingly angry at the way she had been snubbed and, on February 12, to pacify him, Isabella and Mortimer surrendered some of their lands to Philippa and put in hand arrangements for her coronation.

On February 28, at Eltham, the King formally summoned his estates to Westminster for the coronation of "his dearest Queen Philippa."[20] That day, the court left for the Tower, where the royal couple, following tradition, were to lodge prior to the ceremony. From there, wearing a tunic of green velvet and a red furred mantle of spun cloth of gold, and flanked by Edward's uncles, Norfolk and Kent, both dressed as grooms, Philippa rode on her palfrey through London's cheering crowds to Westminster.

On the morning of her coronation, which took place on the feast of St. Peter, March 4, 1330, amidst great rejoicings, Philippa donned a gown and mantle made of seven pieces of green cloth of gold furred with miniver, and went in procession to Westminster Abbey. Archbishop Meopham officiated at the rite. The Queen was nearly six months pregnant and the ceremony appears to have been shortened to avoid tiring her. As she knelt at the high altar for her anointing, she was clothed in a shimmering tunic and mantle of red and gray samite. Her silver-gilt scepter was recorded in an inventory of the regalia held in the Abbey in 1359. Isabella was present, resplendent in new robes.

For the coronation banquet, Philippa changed into purple cloth of gold edged with miniver. In the evening, she appeared for supper in another cloth-of-gold ensemble with a fur mantle and a hood of miniver.

After the coronation, Edward and Philippa visited Windsor, Guildford, and Woodstock, while Isabella and Mortimer went to Winchester, where Parliament had been summoned. They took up residence in the castle as it afforded greater security than Wolvesey Palace; repairs to the fire-damaged royal apartments had been put in hand before their arrival.

15

"A Secret Design"

※

P ERSISTING IN HIS BELIEF THAT EDWARD II WAS ALIVE, KENT continued to plot to restore him. He had enlisted the support of several opponents of Isabella and Mortimer, notably the saintly William Melton, Archbishop of York, and Isabella's once close friends, Henry de Beaumont and Lady de Vesci. Stephen Dunheved was also part of the conspiracy, with members of his original gang of conspirators, alongside other Dominicans, old adherents of the Despensers, Rhys ap Gruffydd, and Donald, Earl of Mar.

In January, Isabella and Mortimer were alarmed to learn that, at the instance of certain magnates, aliens were entering the realm. These were perhaps Kent's go-betweens, and it is likely that at least one of them broke under interrogation and revealed all. Lancaster, meanwhile, was away on an embassy to France.

Isabella and Mortimer were deeply implicated in the framing of Kent. The friars who claimed that Edward II was at Kenilworth had probably been *agents provocateurs* sent to entrap him, for they were the only two named conspirators who were never arrested. The letter Kent had written to his half-brother was sent at once by Deveril and Bayouse to Isabella and Mortimer. On March 10, an order was issued for the arrest of Kent and several others on charges of treason.

It would have been easy for Mortimer to enlist the help of Maltravers, the governor of Corfe Castle, who was also to be accused of ensnaring Kent. Maltravers probably arranged for his subordinates to spread rumors in the vicinity about Edward being held there, and then staged that little charade with a look-alike imposter. After these measures were put in place, it was only a matter of waiting for Kent to walk into the trap.

He and his associates were arrested on March 11. Isabella and Mortimer summoned the young King to Winchester to be present at the trial, but Edward agreed to go only on condition that Philippa accompany him. Kent confessed everything. Edward wanted to pardon his uncle, but Isabella had sworn on the soul of her father that she would have justice. Kent was condemned to death in Parliament and his property was seized by the Crown. "All that day, the King was so beset by the Queen his mother and the Earl of March that it was impossible for him to make any effort to preserve his uncle from the cruel fate to which he had been so unjustly doomed." Isabella "bade him with her blessing that he should be avenged upon him as upon his deadly enemy"[1] and Mortimer bullied him into submission.

Isabella was nervous that Edward III would pardon his uncle or commute his sentence. Without his knowledge, she gave orders to the bailiffs of Winchester to have the execution carried out without delay, and kept Edward occupied with state business. On March 14, Kent was beheaded outside the gates of Winchester.

The following week saw forty arrests. Kent's property had been declared forfeit; his eldest son, Edmund, aged four, was not allowed to succeed to the title. Kent had implicated his wife in his treason, and she and her children were placed under house arrest at Salisbury Castle and Arundel Castle. At the behest of Isabella and Mortimer, Edward wrote to the Pope with a full account of Kent's treason, explaining that his punishment had been an example to would-be traitors. Kent had never been popular, but there was outrage at his death. It was said that he had been denied a proper trial by his peers and that such a violation of justice amounted to tyranny. Lancaster, who had returned from France, was irrevocably alienated by such injustice meted out to the son of a king. It seemed that no one was safe—and no man "durst open his mouth for the good of the King or his realm."[2]

Isabella and Mortimer had gone too far. To most people, it now seemed that the revolution of 1326–27 had led only to the replacement of one tyrannical regime with another. Their rapacity equaled or exceeded even that of the Despensers, and their policies appeared to be dictated solely by self-interested opportunism. They had undermined the reputation and prestige of the monarchy, ruthlessly eliminated their enemies, raided the treasury, and alienated every stratum of society.

Mortimer was especially resented, for he was now "so proud and high that he held no lord of the realm his equal."[3] Refusing to give Edward the precedence that was his due as monarch, "he honoured whom he liked, let the King stand in his presence, and was accustomed to walk arrogantly beside him."[4] He insisted on sharing Edward's plate at table, as well as the royal chariot, and he was attended by a greater following than the King. His arrogance was the cause of great contention among both the nobility and the common people, who called him "the Queen's paragon and the King's master, who destroys the King's blood and usurps the regal majesty." Even Mortimer's own son named him "the King of Folly."[5]

Isabella's passive toleration of Mortimer's lèse-majesté shows how deeply in thrall she was to him. Public sympathy for her as a wronged wife had long since evaporated. She never attracted the opprobrium that extended to Mortimer, although she was criticized for her acquisitiveness, her unpopular policies, and her subversion of the law. Because she did so much in partnership with him, it is impossible to determine how far she herself was responsible for the disasters of the regency, but she was accountable insofar as allowing Mortimer free rein and using her power to build up his. Without her collusion, he could not have monopolized the government so extensively.

At the end of March, the court moved to Woodstock Palace, where Queen Philippa was to remain for her confinement. Isabella and Mortimer stayed there for at least a month, while Philippa's own mother, overjoyed at the impending birth of a grandchild, confidently wrote that, "by the grace of the Almighty, she will become the grandmother of kings."[6]

In April, Philippa was finally given her own household, although she remained heavily dependent on the King for provisions. That month, Isabella granted herself lands of greater value than those she had surrendered to her daughter-in-law in February. On May 10, Philippa petitioned the King to grant her more revenues, since the income she had to live on was insufficient; and Isabella wrote to Bishop Stratford reminding him to pay "our very dear daughter the Queen"[7] arrears of the allowance the King had granted for her chamber. Stratford had been a vocal opponent of the government during Lancaster's rebellion, but he had been reconciled to the King early in 1330, and the tone of the Queen's letter was warm. But all that Philippa received was one manor.

Isabella was back at Woodstock when, at ten o'clock in the morning of June 15, Philippa, aged just sixteen, bore a son, an heir to England, attended by her nurse, Katherine Harington. The baby was "very lusty and well formed," and all who "beheld the beauty of his shape, the largeness of his size and the firm texture of his body"[8] felt that these attributes augured well for the future.

The delighted young father, himself only seventeen, rewarded the Queen's valet who informed him of the birth and gave 500 marks ($318,000) to Katherine de Grandison, the wife of William de Montagu, "for the welcome news she brought the King concerning the birth of his son."[9] She was probably present at the delivery and able to give Edward details of how it had progressed.

The baby was laid in a great cradle painted with images of the four Evangelists. Claims by biographers Joshua Barnes and Agnes Strickland that Philippa insisted on nursing her son herself are incorrect; he was assigned a wet nurse, Katherine Banastre. The lady mistress who ruled his nursery was Elizabeth de Saint-Omer, and his nurse was Joan of Oxford. Edward was generous with gifts of money and pensions for the nurses and the rockers who lulled the child to sleep.

The baby's baptism took place in the chapel at Woodstock. He was named Edward, like his father, grandfather, and great-grandfather. Philippa placed her son under the special protection of the Holy Trinity, probably because he was born close to Trinity Sunday, a feast day associated with St. Thomas Becket. Young Edward grew up to "love Holy Church well and, above all, the Holy Trinity,"[10] as the painting above his tomb attests.

Edward was Isabella's first grandchild, and the surviving evidence suggests that there was always a close bond between them. She and Mortimer stayed at Woodstock for three days after his birth, then departed for Gloucester, where they visited the tomb of Edward II.

On June 19, for the "uprising of Philippa, Queen of England, our beloved consort, from childbirth," the King sent his officers of the Exchequer a schedule of items that were needed, among them a cote, surcoat, and mantle of red velvet, faced with miniver, three counterpanes worked by 114 embroiderers (which took eleven weeks to make), coverlets of scarlet cloth lined with miniver "for the great cradle for the infant" and the Queen's bed, "and a kerchief for my lady."[11] Every member of the household was given new clothes.

That Philippa was contemplating her uprising from bed just four days after giving birth suggests that she had had an easy delivery and was making a speedy recovery. For her churching, a cloth of crimson sendal (silk) of Tripoli was provided for her chapel, and cloth-of-gold hangings for her great chamber. Logs for the fire were purchased, despite it being summer. Her counterpane was repaired because her dogs had ripped it. For the ceremony, she wore a coat and hood of cloth of gold lined with miniver, and at the banquet that followed, she appeared in a rich robe of murrey (mulberry) velvet embroidered with golden squirrels and faced with pure miniver, which she afterward gave to the Bishop of Ely, who had three copes made from it. In the evening, she changed into a silk cote worked with fine gold and a surcoat and mantle trimmed with fur. Furs and hoods of miniver were provided for her ladies and damsels. Such lavish expenditure is a feature of the young Queen's accounts for that year, but it was the King who supplied her elaborate statement outfits, which mirrored his own in richness and design, and he probably chose them to complement his own magnificence. Royal display was becoming increasingly important to him.

Edward was clearly delighted at the arrival of his heir. From Avignon, the Pope wrote a letter of congratulations to the new mother. Jousts were held to mark the Prince's birth, instituting a new tradition. With a son and heir, and his eighteenth birthday not far off, the young King was more eager than ever to throw off his mother's tutelage. He "began to grow in body and mind, which undermined the authority of the Queen and vexed the Earl of March, whose guidance the Queen always followed."[12] Mortimer felt so threatened that he set spies on Edward.

On July 8, Edward III sealed a new peace treaty with France. Another crisis was looming, for Count William of Hainault had sent a warning that Henry de Beaumont, Rhys ap Gruffydd, and other exiles were planning to invade England from Brabant, and that their allies in Wales were poised to attack Mortimer's lands. The council urged Isabella and Mortimer's immediate return from Gloucester and ordered a general muster of troops, forbidding all tournaments in case they served as a pretext for armed gatherings. The Mayor of London was ordered to meet with the King at Woodstock.

Isabella and Mortimer were back at Woodstock by July 15, to hear that the mayor had begged to be excused from waiting upon the King since he was needed in London to deal with mounting unrest precipitated by the invasion scare. But the Queen would brook no excuses, and he was commanded to present himself and two dozen leading citizens at Woodstock on July 27 for talks on how to deal with the emergency. Various measures were deployed for the defense of the realm, sufficient to deter the invaders, but not to stop them plotting, from a safe distance, the destruction of Isabella and Mortimer.

In July, Isabella again named Mortimer the heir to some of her properties, which lends substance to Froissart's assertion that, some time after Kent's execution, "great infamy fell on the Queen Mother (whether justly or not I do not know) because it was reported that she was with child by Mortimer." Later circumstantial evidence suggests that there might have been substance to this gossip.

The court spent the late summer on progress. On September 6, the council was summoned to meet at Nottingham, where the King and his train arrived four days later.

On September 15, the Pope wrote to Edward III and Isabella, expressing deep surprise at Kent's claim that his brother was still alive, especially since Edward II had been given a state funeral. "The Pope believes and holds firmly that those who were present could not possibly have been deceived and did not attempt to deceive. If the funeral had been in secret, there would have been some grounds for suspicion, but, as it was public, there were none." He said that even if he had believed Kent's claims, he would have warned the King and the Queen Mother immediately.

Perceptive, shrewd, and well informed, John XXII evidently realized that Isabella and Mortimer were on a headlong course to disaster, for he concluded by offering the Queen some sage advice: "Whatever you do, do prudently, and keep an eye on the end; and put up with minor irritations lest worse be thrust on you."[13]

Unfortunately, it was advice that came all too late.

* * *

Nottingham Castle had originally been constructed in 1068 on the orders of William the Conqueror. Raised on a high sandstone crag that towered 130 feet over the town and the River Trent, it had been rebuilt by Henry II a century later, and was now a mighty stronghold that was said to have no peer in the kingdom. The royal apartments boasted a mural depicting Alexander the Great, and the chapel, dedicated to St. Katherine, was richly furnished and decorated with wall paintings of the saint's life.

Security was tight for the council meeting, reflecting Mortimer's increasing paranoia. He was attended by 180 armed followers, and guards were posted all around the castle. He and the Queen took up lodgings in the most secure part, the "old tower," as the keep was known; every door and gate was locked and barred nightly, and the keys brought to Isabella, who slept with them under her pillow.

By now, Edward III was burning with resentment. His uncle's execution, the birth of his heir, the mounting catalogue of his grievances against Mortimer, the slights to his wife, even the realization that his mother might be pregnant with a bastard child—Froissart says that the rumors had "finally reached the ears of the King"—and the approach of his eighteenth birthday on November 13, when he would attain his majority, had all had a deep psychological effect on him. He no longer wished to be associated with the rule of Isabella and Mortimer, and he had grown increasingly resentful of his mother's tutelage. He may have heard the alarming rumors gaining currency in Nottingham that Mortimer "thirsted for the destruction of the royal blood and the usurpation of the royal majesty."[14] Now, it had become imperative that he be overthrown.

It was Edward himself who, by his own admission, conceived a "secret design"[15] against Mortimer, probably in late September or early October 1330. He later informed the Pope that the only persons to whom he initially confided his plans were William de Montagu and Richard de Bury, his devoted friends, in whose discretion he had every confidence. It was Montagu who came up with a workable but daring scheme. He had befriended William d'Eland, the deputy constable of Nottingham Castle. Eland, no friend to Mortimer, divulged the existence of a secret passage that had been cut through the massive rock on which the castle was built and that still survives today; it is known as "Mortimer's Hole." Entry to it was gained via a postern gate near the Trip to Jerusalem, an inn that dated from 1189. The tunnel was wide and had rough steps where the gradient was at its steepest. It led up to the kitchen in the keep, which was next to the great hall. Upstairs were the chambers occupied by the King, Isabella, and Mortimer. It was through this tunnel that Montagu planned secretly to enter the castle. He enlisted the support of at least two dozen other young courtiers whose loyalty to the King could be counted on.

Lancaster appeared in Nottingham and took lodgings near the castle. He was virtually blind now and, according to Baker, looked like an old man, even though he was not yet fifty, but Mortimer angrily objected to his presence, demanding, "Who made him so bold to take up his lodgings close to the Queen?"[16] Lancaster was made to move to new accommodation a mile out of the town. Edward must have known that, when the time came, he could count on him as an ally.

Certain members of the King's household got wind of something afoot and warned Isabella and Mortimer that Edward was plotting to overthrow them, and that Montagu had openly asserted that Mortimer had had Edward II murdered. The King, Montagu, and eight of their friends were summoned before Isabella, Mortimer, Chancellor Burghersh, and the council. Mortimer, "wrathful as a devil,"[17] accused the King and his companions of plotting against him. Edward denied it, as did Montagu, who sprang to his feet and defied any man to call the King a traitor. Mortimer retorted that when the King's wishes were in conflict with his own, they were not to be obeyed.

Afterward, realizing that there was not much time before Mortimer moved against them, Montagu warned Edward "that it was better that they should eat the dog than let the dog eat them."[18] The King agreed that they should strike now before it was too late, and commanded Eland to leave the postern gate open, on pain of death. Montagu and the rest of the conspirators then left Nottingham, intending that Mortimer should think they had fled for their lives.

At midnight on October 19, they returned. Carrying torches, they hastened up the subterranean passage to the keep. The King, aware that he was being watched by Mortimer's spies, had to remain inside the castle.

His physician, who was later rewarded for assisting in the plot, may have helped him to feign illness, which gave him a pretext for keeping to his chamber. But after everyone had retired for the night, Edward emerged and made his way downstairs. When Montagu and the rest appeared, he was waiting for them in the kitchen or hall, ready to lead them upstairs to the royal apartments.

They advanced with drawn swords to the Queen's lodging. Edward waited outside, not wishing to be seen by his mother. Immediately his companions were challenged by Hugh de Turpington, Steward of the Household, and Richard Monmouth, Mortimer's squire. In the short but fierce fight that followed, both perished.

When Montagu and his companions burst into the Queen's bedchamber, they found her "almost ready for bed."[19] Mortimer, his henchman Simon de Beresford, Burghersh, Oliver Ingham, and the Bishop of London were discovered "in another chamber nearby."[20] They had just resolved to arrest Montagu and his friends and were about to retire for the night. Mortimer quickly pulled on some armor and drew his sword, killing one of his assailants, then hastened into Isabella's chamber, where he was overpowered by Montagu's servant, Sir John de Moleyns, who arrested him in the King's name. Beresford and Ingham were seized and bound, and Bishop Burghersh was apprehended while trying to escape down the Queen's privy shaft.

Isabella watched in terror as Mortimer and the rest were hustled down the stairs. Suspecting that Edward was nearby, she screamed, *"Bel fitz! Bel fitz! Eiez pitie du gentil Mortimer!"* ("Fair son! Fair son! Have pity on good Mortimer!") But he would not show his face, so she begged Montagu and his companions "to do no harm to the person of Mortimer because he was a worthy knight, her dear friend and well-beloved cousin,"[21] but they paid her no heed.

When the worst happened, Isabella's first thoughts had been for Mortimer's safety. She doubtless feared that he would be summarily executed. That was in Edward III's mind too, but, having conferred with Lancaster, he was persuaded that that would be an act of tyranny, and agreed to send Mortimer to London to be tried by his peers in Parliament. Early the next morning, the once mighty Earl of March was taken south in chains. The lords and the people shouted at him as he and the other prisoners were escorted through Nottingham. A jubilant Lancaster was among them, wildly gesticulating and throwing his cap in the air.

That day, Edward III proclaimed that he had arrested Mortimer and wished all men to know that he had assumed personal rule and would "henceforth govern his people according to right and reason, as befits his royal dignity."[22] Isabella was not mentioned. Edward's liberation from the tutelage of Mortimer and Isabella was greeted by his subjects as if it was the release of the Israelites from bondage, for they believed he had freed the realm from tyranny, civil war, and anarchy.

Before Edward left Nottingham a couple of days later, he sent his mother to Berkhamsted Castle, once the pride of Gaveston. Its strong eleventh-century keep stood on a high hill and was surrounded by a unique double moat. Here she was to live under house arrest until the King had made up his mind what to do with her.

On hearing of Mortimer's overthrow, Maltravers, Gurney, Ockle, Deveril, and several more of his followers fled abroad. Lord Berkeley was taken into custody. Queen Philippa was concerned about the welfare of Millicent de Berkeley, Lady Maltravers, and persuaded the King to ensure that she received her dower from a former marriage.

On October 23, on his way south to London, Edward ordered Richard de Bury to seize Isabella's treasure and Mortimer's. Three days later, Mortimer was imprisoned in the Tower of London. This time, there was to be no chance of escape, for he was guarded by six men-at-arms.

Philippa had been at Woodstock while these dramatic events were taking place. There, she celebrated the feast of All Saints on November 1. For this occasion, Edward had provided her with Flemish cloth and green Italian silk embroidered with griffin's heads. By November 3, he had joined her. Kent's widow and children had already been released from house arrest and taken into the royal household. His three-year-old daughter Joan would be raised by Philippa, whose badge of a hind she was to adopt. Growing up under the auspices of such a cultured Queen would have afforded Joan an education that befitted her for a grand future. She would have learned dancing, embroidery, riding, hunting, hawking, and social skills, and probably imbibed some of the generosity of heart and tactful diplomacy for which Philippa was known.

* * *

Parliament met at Westminster on November 26. Edward now exacted retribution on those who had discredited his mother's regime. Berkeley was tried for the murder of Edward II. Asked how he wished to defend himself, he said he had never consented to the King's death, procured it, or helped the murderers. Indeed, he never even knew that Edward was dead until now, an extraordinary assertion given that there had been a state funeral.

Not surprisingly, Berkeley's inquisitors did not accept this defense, for it threw into question Edward III's title to the throne, whereupon Berkeley asked to be acquitted of the charge of murder on the grounds that he was not at his castle at the time, but had been recovering from an illness at his manor of Bradley, near Wootton-under-Edge, a plea that was accepted. Parliament released him on a surety, leaving the charge to hang over his head for the next seven years.

On November 28, in the King's presence, Mortimer was arraigned for high treason before his peers in Parliament. He appeared bound and gagged, wearing a tunic on which were emblazoned the words *Quid glorians?* ("What are you glorying in?").[23] He was indicted on several counts, the foremost being that he had "traitorously, feloniously and falsely murdered and killed" Edward II; he had also arrogated to himself royal power, ignored the regency council, lured Kent to his unlawful execution, attacked Lancaster, dared to question the King's word, and set spies to watch him. He had stirred up dissension in the kingdom, extended his territories to the disinheritance of the Crown, planned the destruction of the King's friends, and embezzled public funds.[24]

His association with Isabella was not mentioned in the indictment in the Rolls of Parliament. She was referred to only once in the charges, which may reflect the King's determination to protect her reputation. Mortimer was accused of having "falsely and maliciously sowed discord between the father of our Lord the King and the Queen his companion, making her believe that if she came near her husband, he would poniard her or murder her in some other manner. Wherefore, by this cause, and by other subtleties, the said Queen remained absent from her said lord, to the great dishonor of the King and of his mother, and great damage, perhaps, to the whole nation hereafter, which God avert."[25] This placed the responsibility for the rift between Edward II and Isabella firmly with Mortimer.

Because Mortimer had sent Kent to his death without giving him a chance to speak in his own defense, he was condemned unheard and sentenced "as a traitor and enemy of the King and the realm, to be drawn and hanged" and to the forfeiture of all his titles and property.[26] It was perhaps because the King feared to exacerbate Isabella's terrible distress that he refrained from exacting the full penalty of the law for treason—hanging, drawing, and quartering, which Hugh le Despenser had suffered with the added refinement of castration.

That same day, Burghersh, who had also been imprisoned in the Tower, was deprived of the office of chancellor, and Bishop Stratford was elected in his place. But Burghersh was a man of some ability and it was not long before he was released and able to regain his political influence. In 1334, he was back in high office, as treasurer, and he would serve Edward well as a diplomat. John de Stratford became Edward's chief minister; he held the office of chancellor three times and, in 1333, was elected archbishop of Canterbury.

Parliament offered an official vote of thanks to William de Montagu, who had been largely responsible for bringing Mortimer to justice and freeing the King and the realm from tyranny; in reward, he received many of Mortimer's confiscated estates. William d'Eland was rewarded for assisting Montagu. All who had taken part in the coup were indemnified by Parliament against charges of murder.

On November 29, Mortimer, attired in the black tunic he had worn for Edward II's funeral, was laid on an ox hide tied to two horses and dragged the three miles from the Tower to Tyburn. Hordes of spectators jeered and chanted the words of Psalm 52: "Why boastest thou in mischief, O mighty man? Thou lovest evil more than good . . ."[27]

In his speech to the crowd, Mortimer made no reference to Edward II's murder, but confessed that Kent had been the innocent victim of a cruel conspiracy. He was stripped naked before he was hanged, and buried in the Franciscan friary at Coventry. Philippa was assigned some of his confiscated property, including twenty-four rugs and a sindon canopy embroidered with black roses.

Parliament condemned Beresford, Deveril, Bayouse, Maltravers, Gurney, and Ockle to death, Gurney and Ockle for Edward II's murder, the rest for assisting in Kent's destruction and aiding and abetting Mortimer "in all his treasons, felonies and plots."[28] Beresford was the only one of the six in captivity, the rest having fled into exile.

In December 1330, the King issued a general pardon to all opponents of the previous regime. He invited exiles such as Wake, Beaumont, and Rhys ap Gruffydd to come home, and restored their property. On December 7, Kent's son received his father's earldom and lands. Edward ordered that the bones of Hugh le Despenser, which had been hanging on public display for over four years, be taken down and given decent burial. Beresford was executed on December 24, the only one of Mortimer's associates to share his fate.

Not until the reign of Henry VIII would the private lives of royalty again unbalance the stability of the realm. The conflict between Edward II and Isabella had long dominated the political scene, but it was Isabella who now bore the brunt of public opprobrium. Many held that she deserved to be executed. She herself feared that she would be punished severely. But as soon as the Pope learned of the toppling of her regime, he wrote to Edward III urging him in his righteous wrath not to expose his mother's shame, but to treat her with honor, and enjoining Queen Philippa, Lancaster, Montagu, and Bishop Stratford to help her.

Edward probably never had any intention of treating his mother harshly. Aside from his filial love for her, his claim to the throne of France derived from Isabella, and any scandal attaching to her name could prejudice it. She was spared public disgrace. Mortimer was blamed for the evils of the regency, while the King's "dearest mother" was portrayed as just another of his victims. Her adulterous relationship with Mortimer was airbrushed from history. Edward resolved that she should live out the rest of her life in honorable and comfortable retirement. She was to be treated with respect and courtesy and would henceforth be referred to as "Madame the Queen Mother" or "our Lady Queen Isabella."[29]

Edward probably did not believe that she had been involved in Edward II's murder, yet there are indications that he did have ambiguous feelings about her, and that he held her responsible in part for the misrule of the past three years. As late as 1348, when dedicating St. Stephen's Chapel to the Virgin, he would refer to Mary as being "a better mother,"[30] suggesting that he was drawing comparisons with his own.

On December 1, Isabella "simply and spontaneously" surrendered all her lands to the King. In January 1331, she would be assigned a fixed annual income of £3,000 ($2.4 million) to "maintain her noble estate all the days of her life."[31]

At Christmas, she was with the court at Windsor, having been escorted there from Berkhamsted. She apparently remained at Windsor for the next two years in the safekeeping of the constable. For several reasons—among them her notoriety, her grief for Mortimer, and her possible pregnancy—Edward had decided to keep her out of the public eye. Effectively, she was under house arrest. But it was a gilded cage. The King, advised by his council, had "ordered his mother to be confined in a goodly castle, and gave her plenty of ladies and damsels to wait upon her, as well as knights and squires of honour."[32] One of her women was Amy, Piers Gaveston's bastard daughter, who also served Queen Philippa. But Isabella was forbidden to go out or show herself abroad, "except at certain times and when any shows were exhibited in the court of the castle,"[33] such as those put on by mummers and traveling players. If there was a baby, she must have lost it, but rumors of a bastard child persisted until 1334, when Pope Benedict XII expressed his relief to Edward III that they had been discredited.

Strickland and other writers have claimed that Isabella was shut up at Windsor because she suffered a period of mental derangement after Mortimer's execution. There persisted a rumor that she had died on the day Mortimer's corpse was cut down, which suggests that she had vanished so completely that few could say with any certainty what had happened to her. Possibly she did have some sort of nervous breakdown, for the King paid large sums for a physician to attend her during this period, although she could have been suffering from any illness or even the ill effects of a stillbirth. It is often claimed that she was mad for the rest of her life, but there is no evidence of that.

She passed her time at Windsor "meekly."[34] She received spiritual comfort, for the King gave his chaplain, Edmund de Rammersby, "on behalf of our mother, the first year of her imprisonment," two crystal vases containing holy relics.[35]

In February 1331, Philippa took charge of the King's twelve-year-old sister Eleanor and was granted some issues of the earldom of Chester to support her and Prince Edward. In the summer, the Pope wrote to thank and commend the Queen for the "sympathy and consolation" she had shown Isabella in her tribulation, and urged her "to aim at restoring the good fame of the Queen Mother, which has been undeservedly injured."[36] The shrewd John XXII was following the official line—and possibly believed—that Isabella was more sinned against than sinning, in the interests of fostering harmonious relations in the English royal family and restoring the prestige of the monarchy.

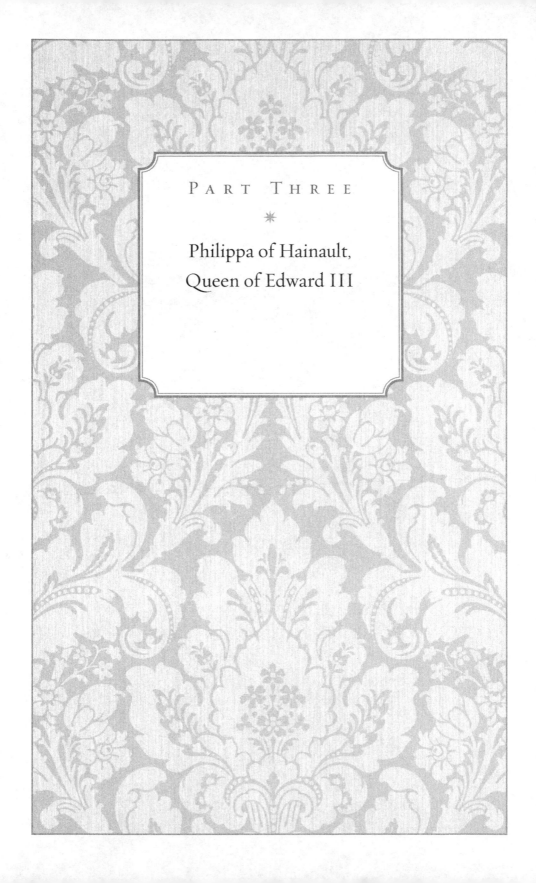

PART THREE

✻

Philippa of Hainault,
Queen of Edward III

I

"The Most Courteous, Liberal,
and Noble Lady That Ever Reigned"

✳

Edward III was to enjoy a long and largely successful reign. He became the archetypal medieval monarch: powerful, magnificent, chivalrous, warlike, merciful, wise, accomplished in statecraft and diplomacy—and, when occasion demanded, ruthless. Contemporaries thought highly of him. "This King Edward was of infinite goodness and glorious among all the great ones of the world. He was so great-hearted that he never blenched at any ill hap or trouble." He was "clement and benign, familiar and gentle to all men, devoted to God, affable and gentle in courtesy of speech, composed and measured in gesture and manners, pitiful to the afflicted and profuse in largesse. He was liberal in giving and lavish in spending, familiar and gentle to all men."[1]

This paragon was "fair, lusty and well formed." He had inherited the handsome looks of his Plantagenet ancestors, being over six feet tall with good bone structure, an aquiline nose, high cheekbones, blue eyes, and long fair hair. "His body was comely and his face was like the face of a god."[2] He dressed lavishly, ever the showman. He was proud, self-righteous, volatile of temper, and a passionate devotee of chivalry and warfare. His zest for life and adventure was unbounded. Above all, he desired to win glory by great deeds. He had imbibed from his mother a love of the Arthurian legends and a devotion to St. George, the patron saint of England, who was his ideal of the chivalrous knight and whose cult he popularized. He established a famously brilliant court and raised the cult of chivalry to an art form. Philippa was an enthusiastic partner. The two of them elevated court life and culture to a new level.

Edward began his reign with initiatives to reverse the injustices of the previous regime, promising his people that he would rule his realm with the advice of the council of magnates. He reestablished the authority and standing of the Crown, enlisted the support of the barons, and made advantageous foreign alliances.

His reign would see many changes. Parliament began to meet regularly and assert its authority through financial controls; it did not always co-operate with the King's wishes. In 1345, the law courts became permanently established in London and no longer followed the King's person on progress around the kingdom. In 1352, treason was defined by statute for the first time. Edward's reign also witnessed the increasing prosperity of the merchant classes and the spread of education among laymen.

He was an avid patron of culture. Art and learning flourished under him; architecture began to take on a new form. Until the fourteenth century, the Early English Gothic style, in which Westminster Abbey had been rebuilt by his great-grandfather, Henry III, had remained popular. But as Edward's reign progressed, the new Perpendicular style evolved, and was evident in the completion of St. Stephen's Chapel in the Palace of Westminster in 1349. The East Anglian school of illumination produced the exquisite Luttrell Psalter of c.1325–35, which depicts scenes of everyday life; a crowned queen (probably Philippa) holding a squirrel appears in it, riding with her ladies in a wagon-like chariot. One of the greatest painters was Hugh of St. Albans, who visited Italy, where the Renaissance was blossoming, and brought back new ideas on perspective from the Papal court at Avignon.

Poetry won renewed popularity with the increasing use of English in literature, and took on new forms. At the beginning of Edward's reign, Richard Rolle was composing mystical verse, much of it aimed at women, and Robert Mannyng's poem "Handling Sin" offered unique insights into daily life. Later, English poetry would reach glorious heights in the works of William Langland and Geoffrey Chaucer. Langland's "The Vision of Piers Plowman" (1360–80) is a dream sequence set in the Malvern Hills that speaks of the woes of the English peasantry.

Edward's former tutor, Richard de Bury, was one of the first great bibliophiles and the author of *The Philobiblon*, a manual about collecting books and running a university library. Bury was a great humanist and influenced the King and the court with his witty writings. Edward could read and write both French and Latin, and he enjoyed reading chronicles of history. By 1341, he had a library of 160 books, which he kept at the Tower of London.

Philippa at last assumed her rightful place as queen of England. She was granted her dower, part of which came from the extra lands Isabella had held from 1327, with 500 marks ($276,500) annually for the maintenance of Prince Edward and the King's sister Eleanor. In December 1330, Edward granted her the Tower Royal in the City of London as her wardrobe, and all her chests and coffers were brought there from Milk Street. Her rents and dues were paid there, and she sometimes stayed there too.

The marriage of Edward and Philippa was enduringly happy. She "loved her lord with all her heart."[3] She was his helpmeet, his trusted companion, and they were together whenever possible. He was a famously loving husband, and a good and affectionate father who was clearly indulgent toward the couple's twelve children. Having this large family meant that the royal succession was assured and Edward had the wherewithal to make advantageous marriage alliances. That there was remarkable harmony within the royal family was due to this careful policy of the King and the warmly unifying influence of the Queen. Philippa made a great contribution to the stability and success of the monarchy, with her genius for fostering a degree of family unity and closeness that was rare in the history of the Plantagenet dynasty. Her large brood all adored her, as did her husband. This was a family bound by strong ties of affection, and Edward III could count on his sons' unquestioning loyalty and support.

At the dances, hunts, tournaments, and feasts that were a regular feature of court life, Edward was always "entertaining ladies." How intimately he entertained them is not recorded, but the code of chivalry encouraged noblemen and knights to dance attention on ladies and even pay court to them according to the code of courtly love, and Edward probably followed these conventions. It was said that "he controlled not, even in old age, the dissolute lusts of the flesh,"[4] but if he had casual affairs, there is little evidence for them, and he can be proved to have been unfaithful to Philippa only toward the end of their life together, when she was too ill and infirm to be a lover to him.

Philippa of Hainault was perhaps the most popular and beloved of England's medieval queens, and "the most courteous, liberal, and noble lady that ever reigned in her time," according to Froissart, who knew her personally. "Tall and upright she was, wise, gladsome, humble, pious, liberal and courteous, richly adorned with all noble virtues, and well beloved of God and of mankind."[5] Her tomb epitaph at Westminster states that she was "dowered in gifts full rare and treasures of the mind, in religion, faith, to all and each most kind." In the 1390s, the St. Albans chronicler Thomas Walsingham remembered her as "a most noble woman and a most constant lover of the English people." Chandos Herald, Prince Edward's future biographer, called Philippa "the perfect root of all honour, nobility, wisdom, valour and generosity." What comes across from the sources is her innate kindness. She was generous and warm-hearted, and exemplary in her acts of charity and mercy. Her motto, appropriately, was *Ich wrude much* (which has been translated as "I labor much" or "I send forth many roots").

Philippa successfully interceded with Edward on seventy-six occasions, often for pardons, fourteen of which were for pregnant women convicted of felony and sentenced to hang after their babies were born. She frequently petitioned the Pope for indulgences for members of her chapel and household. Her few surviving letters were all written on behalf of others—a man awaiting delivery from prison, another in hope of a church living, a royal ward whose interests were threatened, tenants of hers who had suffered the injustice of over-taxation and a high-handed coroner. In one letter, written in 1353, she instructed her attorney to postpone issuing writs for the exaction of queen-gold owed to her until she and her council were advised which writs could be implemented to her profit and which should be dropped in order to relieve her people and salve her conscience. She won hearts for her efforts to improve industry and trade.

Her chief benefactions were made to the hospital of St. Katharine by the Tower, which was rebuilt under her auspices. She founded a chantry there, providing a stipend of £10 ($10,100) annually for the priest. The charter she granted decreed that the brethren wear black mantles embroidered with wheels in honor of their patron saint. Green, red, or striped clothes were forbidden, as were playing dice, frequenting alehouses, and staying out after the fire bells were rung.

Philippa was also a patron of churches and religious houses, notably St. Stephen's Chapel, Greyfriars, Newgate, and the abbeys of St. Mary at York, St. Albans, and Chertsey. In 1354, she obtained from Edward a grant for the enlargement of St. Frideswide's Priory in Oxford. Like her two queenly predecessors, she had a devotion to the Franciscan order. With Edward she shared a special reverence for St. Katherine of Alexandria, one of the most popular medieval saints. Their accounts show that Katherine wheels, the symbol of her martyrdom, adorned counterpanes on the royal beds, jousting apparel, and other garments.

Coming from a family dedicated to making much of its history and dynastic importance, and devoted to the cult of chivalry, she was able to share Edward's chief passions. Her ties to Hainault remained strong all her life, and she exercised influence and supported Edward through her extensive—and often advantageous—family connections in Europe. Her father and mother, her uncle, Sir John, and her brother William all visited the English court and attended the tournaments held by the King. Philippa kept up a correspondence with her mother, to whom she was clearly close.

She was interested in education, art, and literature. She commissioned works of art and manuscripts, employed her own illuminator, and patronized musicians and poets, some from Hainault. A small, beautifully decorated psalter made for her survives in Dr. Williams's Library in London.[6] It bears the arms of France, England, and Hainault, and was made around the time of her marriage. A miniature psalter owned by her, now in the British Library,[7] dates from *c.*1330–40. Her arms and drawings of her appear in the borders, and the text includes antiphons with musical notations, suggesting that she used the book during services. In 1331, she ordered two books of hours from Robert of Oxford.

Her native tongues were Dutch and the Parisian French of her mother. Doubtless she soon learned to speak Norman French, the language of the English court, which was a much-corrupted version of the Norman dialect spoken by William the Conqueror and his companions, and somewhat different from the French spoken on the Continent. However, in her lifetime she would see Norman French overtaken by English—of which she may have had some understanding—as the language of the law courts (1362), Parliament (1363), and fashionable literary circles, although it remained in use by the nobility for letters and everyday conversation until well into the first half of the fifteenth century.

"Fair Philippa" was "tall and straight." Her epitaph describes her as being "of roseate hue and beauty bright." Her tomb effigy, which is unflatteringly realistic and was almost certainly modeled from life, shows her as a plump woman in her mid-fifties with a determined chin, full cheeks, narrow eyes, a broad forehead, and a straight nose. A full-length painted wooden statue, dating from before the mid-seventeenth century, stands in the library of the Queen's College, Oxford. The Black Book of the Garter of 1534[8] depicts Philippa in the guise of Anne Boleyn, who was queen at the time it was made.

There are medieval stone heads or figures of Philippa in Malmesbury Abbey; the Octagon of Ely Cathedral; the Treasurer's House in York; above the triforium of Bristol Cathedral; in the crypt of St. Nicholas's Church, Bristol; over the door of the church of Old Bolingbroke; in the chancel of St. James's Church, Sulgrave; on the tower of Tickhill Church near Doncaster; above the fourteenth-century doorway of the Angel and Royal Inn, Grantham; in the churches of Sopley, Wootton Wawen, and Hughley, Shropshire; and in the Queen's College, Oxford, this being modeled on her tomb effigy. Her image in stained glass is in All Saints Church, Boughton Aluph, Kent, and Trowbridge Church, Wiltshire. She also features in several fifteenth-century manuscript illustrations.

Kneeling and crowned, she appeared with Edward and their children—she and her daughters all wearing blue, the Virgin's color—in wall paintings on either side of the altar in St. Stephen's Chapel, Westminster, which were executed around 1355–63. These were lost when the palace burned down in 1834, but tracings and drawings of them were made by Richard Smirke after the wainscotting that had covered them since the sixteenth century was removed in 1800, and are held by the Society of Antiquaries of London and the British Library.

It was once said that a mutilated sculpture of the Virgin and Child on the Great Screen in Winchester Cathedral represented Philippa and her son Edward, but it dates from the fifteenth century. Two eighteenth-century busts of Philippa by Jacob Rysbrack in the Royal Collection were destroyed in 1906 when the shelf bearing them collapsed.

The young King and Queen were extravagant, and often in debt. In 1331, their visit to Glastonbury Abbey to see the (supposed) graves of King Arthur and Queen Guinevere cost the Abbot £800 ($663,600). Like her mother-in-law and her husband, Philippa followed fashion and dressed lavishly. She had costume dolls sent to her so that she could copy the latest styles at the French court. Her coming to England had coincided with a major shift from flowing gowns and elaborate wimples to fitted gowns with low waists, wide necklines that left the shoulders bare, and cylindrical headdresses that enclosed plaits on either side of the face; Philippa's were made of golden gauze.

The dress of those who had accompanied her to England had drawn criticism from at least two chroniclers. "Englishmen so followed and clung to the madness and folly of foreigners that, from the time of the arrival of the Hainaulters, they changed the shape and style of their clothing every year, abandoning the old, honest and good style of large, long and wide clothes in favour of short, tight, dagged, narrow-waisted and cut-about clothes, slit and buttoned, boned all round, with sleeves and tippets on the surcoats and great long hoods that hung down too far. They looked more like tormentors and devils in their clothes and appearance than men. And the women copied the men in even more curious ways, for their clothes were so tight that they sewed foxtails beneath [them] to hang down and hide their arses."[9]

Philippa did not slavishly adhere to one style. "She ordained and changed every year divers shapes of clothing." Her clothes were elaborate. One cloak was "powdered with gold roses of eight petals and bordered with white pearls, in the middle of each rose an S of large pearls."[10] Royal dress became so extravagant and so widely copied that Edward III would bring in sumptuary laws decreeing that only the King and Queen, their children, and bishops might wear clothing made abroad, and only those with an annual income of £100 ($101,000) or more could wear foreign silks and furs. This enhanced the splendor of the monarchy and boosted English commerce. One monastic chronicler drily commented, "Blessed be the memory of King Edward III and Philippa of Hainault, who first invented clothes."[11]

Philippa had been assigned a very large and costly household. The combined establishments of her and the King numbered around 450 persons (of whom about 112 served the Queen), rising to 580 around 1360. In 1368, she had six ladies-in-waiting, twelve damsels (*demoiselles*) and *veilleresses* (ladies who attended her at night), a small number of Hainaulter knights, a seneschal, three clerks who looked after her furs, six chaplains, eighteen esquires, twenty valets of the chamber and offices, seven boy servants (probably pages), and twenty-nine valets who looked after her palfreys. There were also three fools, or jesters: "Jakeman, an idiot,"[12] Liberkin, and a minstrel called Robert the Fool. Philippa brought many more women into the court than had graced it in previous reigns, imposing a civilizing influence on its male-dominated, militaristic society. Her accounts record more gifts of fabrics than other queens had given to ensure that their ladies appeared beautifully dressed.

She was hopeless at living within her means. She borrowed widely, notably from the Florentine Bardi, and was often deeply in debt, prompting Parliament to complain about the excesses of her purveyors. They were entitled to buy goods for her at cost price, but were sluggish in paying. One was viciously assaulted. In 1348, two carts conveying wine for the Queen and twelve horses were seized by her creditors and held until the wine went off and the horses starved.

It was not all Philippa's fault. There was a discrepancy between her nominal and actual income, while payments of queen-gold—the traditional ten percent she received on certain fines paid to the King—varied alarmingly. Her household was large and expensive to run and did not attract able administrators. Her officers and servants seem to have been inept or negligent, even corrupt. Often she got into debt because of the expense she had to outlay on the magnificent lifestyle Edward expected her to maintain, especially when she accompanied him abroad. She also liked to aid "all knights, ladies and damsels who, when distressed, had applied to her."[13]

She was not popular with everyone. When troubled by poachers who broke into her parks, felled trees, fished in her fisheries, stole her deer and game birds, and even the rabbits from her warrens, she was forced to take out a series of lawsuits, which gave rise to criticism, as did her necessary insistence on rents and dues being paid promptly. When a Lincoln vicar protested in horror against such scandalous exactions, he was imprisoned. In 1352, a commission had to be set up to investigate the excessive fines imposed on Philippa's tenants.

Edward III's court was more magnificent than those of his predecessors. Chivalry, culture, and courtly love flourished there. The courtiers talked, sang, and composed verse about love and martial exploits, a favorite topic of discussion among a military aristocracy and a multitude of knights. For the ladies, however, it was love that was of paramount interest. Manuscripts of romances and love poems were always in circulation in female circles at court. It was a licentious place where promiscuity was rampant, since so many young men could not afford to marry. Frank, bawdy tales, such as those of Giovanni Boccaccio and, later, Geoffrey Chaucer, were very popular; in "The Squire's Tale," Chaucer spoke of the revels and dancing that afforded opportunities for erotic intrigue, "when each person fully experiences the being of another."

The King and Queen were at the center of it all, hosting lavish feasts, tournaments, and entertainments. They enjoyed hunting and hawking, dice and checkers, and employed musicians, fools, magicians, and acrobats. They were extravagant on a grand scale.

One of Edward's great passions was jousting. In June 1331, he held a tournament at Stepney to mark Prince Edward's first birthday. It was attended by Queen Philippa, along with her mother, her sister Jeanne, and her brother-in-law, William, Count of Jülich, who were then visiting England. The Prince was presented for his grandmother's inspection wearing new clothes. That summer, other tournaments were held at Dartford, Bedford, and Havering.

In July, the King and Queen were in Lincolnshire, where Philippa attended the wedding of one of her damsels and paid her minstrel Mauprine and others to play at the feast that followed. In Lincoln, on July 22, she and Edward were entertained by two female minstrels, Cecilia and Isabella, who also danced and tumbled for them. At Rockingham Castle in August, musicians from Bavaria and Cologne, who had been invited to

England by Philippa, played for the royal couple alongside a rebec player called Merlin.

In Philippa's long tenure as queen, she would grace more tournaments than any other English medieval consort. In September 1331, William de Montagu hosted jousts over three days in London's Cheapside, in which he and the King entered the lists dressed as Tartars, leading, by silver chains, beautiful ladies in red velvet tunics and white hoods, the colors of St. George. One was Edward's thirteen-year-old sister Eleanor, but some others were of merchant stock. It was customary in Hainault, though not in England, for the merchant classes to mix with the aristocracy, so this innovation may have been inspired by Philippa. It was perhaps her influence that led Edward to favor the middle classes throughout his reign.

The young Queen now demonstrated that she intended to be a queen in the traditional mold, showing mercy and kindness. A wooden stage had been "erected across the street, like unto a tower, wherein Queen Philippa and many other ladies, richly attired, did stand to behold the jousts." They watched as the King led the challengers and acquitted himself gallantly. But toward the end of the tournament, the stage suddenly "broke asunder" and Philippa and the ladies went tumbling "with shame" to the ground, while "the knights and such as were underneath were grievously hurt."[14] Philippa's coronet snapped during her fall, yet she and her ladies "escaped without harm, to the rejoicing of many that saw them in such danger." Her husband, however, erupted in wrath and ordered the instant execution of the carpenters who had built the stand. But Philippa would not allow it and "assuaged the anger of the King and his courtiers with prayers on bended knee." Mollified, Edward "had peace and love proclaimed everywhere" and bade her ride up and down the lists to comfort and reassure the people. "This merciful act of the Queen aroused the love of all towards her when they considered her piety."[15] The tournament resumed the next day, Philippa having spent the night in an alderman's house on Wood Street. Soon afterward, the King built a strong stone gallery for himself, the Queen, and their courtiers.

2

"Such Increase of Honour"

＊

IN NOVEMBER 1331, THE POPE WROTE TO EDWARD III, HAVING heard "that the King was not showing signs of filial affection to his mother, Queen Isabella. Should she have done anything to justify the King's behaviour to her, the Pope exhorts him to remember what his mother has done for him, and what enmity and ill will she has provoked against herself in his service, and begs him to show mercy, so that he himself may find it in the day of judgement."[1] Clearly, the Pope thought Isabella more sinned against than sinning.

Isabella was still under house arrest at Windsor. She did not join the King and Queen for their tour of the West Country in December, when they visited Cadbury and Glastonbury, sites famously connected with King Arthur, and kept Christmas in Wells, staying until Epiphany. At New Year, Philippa gave Edward a silver ewer and a goblet beautifully enameled with images of fortresses, ships, and animals; in the bowl was an image of the King enthroned amid banners bearing the royal arms. His gift to her was a sapphire brooch.

In January 1332, Isabella—astute as ever, it should be noted—wrote "to her very dear sovereign lord the King" to protest that a manor he had granted her in December had turned out to belong to the Countess of Lincoln, while the rents from Derby were being paid to someone else, and she wanted compensation. Evidently the Pope's letter had softened Edward's heart, for he assigned "his dearest mother"[2] other lands and castles worth £2,000 ($1.6 million) a year. With an annual income of

£5,000 ($4 million), more than her original dower, Isabella was living very comfortably.

By March 1332, she had left Windsor and regained her freedom. That month, the constable of Windsor Castle secured the final payment of "expenses incurred by him in safe-keeping Queen Isabella in that castle for some time, by the King's order."[3] At Easter, she was with the court when it stayed for ten days at Peterborough Abbey. Her rehabilitation was complete when the King ordered that she be regularly prayed for after himself and Queen Philippa in church services throughout the kingdom.

Royal mothers were expected to play an active part in arranging the marriages of their children, and Isabella was probably involved in preparations for the wedding of her daughter Eleanor to Reginald II, Duke of Guelders, which took place at Nijmegen in May 1332. The marriage had been arranged by her cousin, the Countess of Hainault, but Isabella's hand may perhaps be detected in the trousseau that was prepared for Eleanor. The wedding gown was of Spanish cloth of gold embroidered with brilliant silks and was worn with a crimson velvet mantle and a white lawn veil. When the Princess sailed from Sandwich, she took with her caps, gloves, shoes of Cordoba leather, a bed hung with green velvet and silk curtains, rare spices, loaves of sugar, and a fur robe, a gift from Queen Philippa, and traveled in a painted chariot upholstered in purple velvet and decorated with gold stars. To ease her daughter's transition to a new life, Isabella had provided her with servants from her own household.

It was probably after Eleanor's departure that Isabella took up residence at Castle Rising in Norfolk, a place closely associated with her and the setting for most of the legends she inspired. Sir John de Moleyns, who had arrested Mortimer, was appointed her steward there, but he was often absent, either attending the King or serving abroad; in 1340, he was dismissed from all his offices and imprisoned for acts of oppression.

Castle Rising was Isabella's own property, purchased in 1327. Built around 1150, it was a fine example of a Norman fortress, with a massive square keep that stood fifty feet high and boasted walls three yards thick with Romanesque arcading, and doors with chevrons carved around the arches. The keep was surrounded by a deep ditch and massive ramparts, and a stout curtain wall with three towers. It was not only a secure residence, but also afforded complete privacy.

The castle was approached through a gateway protected by a portcullis, then entered by a processional stair enclosed by a richly sculpted wall. A passage led from the vaulted vestibule to the magnificently furnished chapel. Also inside the keep were a great hall, a great chamber for the Queen's private use, a kitchen, and storerooms. The kitchen was too small to cater for a household as large as Isabella's, so another was built outside in the bailey. Isabella's private lodgings were not in the castle itself, but in a range of half-timbered buildings on the southern side of the narrow bailey; their foundations were discovered in the late twentieth century. Her chambers were laid with black carpets and hung with painted cloths. She maintained a small library, and her household book records the frequent preparation of parchment and vellum for it.

At Castle Rising, she maintained a considerable degree of state and lived a life of affluent leisure, passing her time "quite comfortably."[4] She had her own treasurer, seneschal, falcon-bearer, surgeon, knights, huntsmen, and grooms of the stable, as well as thirty-three clerks and squires, eight ladies of the chamber, several damsels, and many menial servants. Edward had assigned one of his father's physicians, Pontio de Courtrone, to attend her. In 1334, "in remembrance of the divine respect that sons should revere their parents, and of filial duty, and that she may have such increase of honour as becomes her estate,"[5] he restored to her the revenues of Ponthieu and Montreuil, which had been part of her original dower. She also received a quarter of the customs dues at the port of Bishop's (now King's) Lynn.

Isabella entertained regularly. Edward visited her two or three times a year, sometimes accompanied by Queen Philippa and Prince Edward. He or his nobles brought with them troupes of minstrels. At other times, he corresponded with his mother. He sent her gifts: a falcon, a pair of lovebirds, and choice delicacies such as fresh game, wild boar, barrels of sturgeon, and many pipes of Gascon wine.

The burghers of Lynn were often called upon to supply Isabella with luxury foods at their own cost, suggesting that her rapacious instincts were still lively. They sent wine, meat, swans, barrels of sturgeon, turbot, herrings, lampreys, bread, barley, and candle wax. In 1334, Isabella sent to Lynn for eight carpenters to make preparations for the coming visit of the King. Relations between Castle Rising and Lynn were not always cordial, and quarrels frequently broke out between the townsfolk and the Queen's retainers. One can sense that the good burghers were sometimes relieved to learn that she had gone to stay elsewhere.

She spent much of her time hunting, hawking, reading romances, listening to her minstrels, and collecting religious relics, such as a ring made by St. Dunstan, the tenth-century Archbishop of Canterbury, which had once belonged to Eleanor of Castile. She owned casket-loads of jewels, as well as singing birds and precious falcons.

In 1332, she was given permission to stay at Eltham Palace (which was restored to her in November of that year) or Havering-atte-Bower whenever her health required a change of air. From 1332, she made several pilgrimages to the shrine of Our Lady of Walsingham in Norfolk. In 1338, she was in the north, at Pontefract. She is known to have visited London only once during her widowhood, in 1339.

In 1333, Isabella's physician was pensioned off. It appears that she was now in good health. She was certainly able to look after her affairs. When the lieges of her forest of Macclesfield notified the King that the local bailiffs were killing her venison and destroying her wood, Edward replied, "Let this petition be shown to the Queen, that her advice may be learned thereon."[6] When it came to recovering money owed to her, he referred his council to her for guidance. Her name appears frequently as a witness to state documents. In 1337, the King gave her permission to dispose of her goods by will.

In her later years, Isabella devoted herself to charitable works and almsgiving. In 1347, she gave the convent of the Poor Clares, or Minoresses, of Aldgate the advowsons (the right to present a benefice) of three churches. The convent had been founded by Edmund Crouchback, Earl of Lancaster, whose heart was buried beneath the high altar. Crouchback had married Isabella's maternal grandmother, Blanche of Artois, who had introduced the Franciscan order of Poor Clares into England. Naturally Isabella was their patron.

Apart from conflict with the Scots, the early years of Edward's reign were peaceful. In 1332, the clause in Magna Carta giving foreign merchants free access to English ports was confirmed by the royal council in order to boost the wool trade, wool being England's biggest industry and the source of much of its prosperity. Hitherto, raw wool had been exported to Flanders, where it was woven in towns such as Ghent, Bruges, and Ypres by master craftsmen who were famous for the quality of their cloth. But Edward and Philippa saw the advantages of having home-woven cloth.

The Flemings were at odds with the French and, in July 1331, Philippa had granted letters of protection to a Flemish weaver called John Kempe, enabling him to settle and work in England. Thereafter, with her encouragement—or at her suggestion—Edward began to issue further letters of protection to Flemish weavers, urging them to relocate and turn England's wool into home-manufactured cloth. By 1335, "great numbers" had settled in Worstead, Lavenham, Sudbury, and Norwich, where the Queen established a woollen mill. Their industry brought great prosperity to East Anglia and boosted Philippa's popularity. To the chroniclers, she was now the "good Queen."

The year 1336 saw a great increase in the output of Flemish (or worsted) cloth in Norwich, which was fast becoming the most flourishing city in England. Whenever the King traveled in East Anglia or stayed with his mother at Castle Rising, Philippa visited Norwich, taking an interest in her countrymen. When she and Edward stayed there in 1341, they were received with great joy and honor and lodged at the Prior of Norwich's summer hall at Trowse Newton, and the King hosted a great tournament, himself taking part. They returned on several occasions.

From 1335, Philippa was to encourage the revival of coal mining on her estates in Tynedale, and, when the industry gathered momentum, trading in coal with the Low Countries. In 1348, at her instance, Edward granted her bailiff, Alan de Strothere, permission to work the mines of Alderneston in County Durham, which had fallen into disuse in the time of Edward I, thanks to Scottish raids. In 1351, the Queen had the keeper of her castle of the High Peak open up a new lead mine in Derbyshire, the lead being used for royal building works in London.

In the spring of 1332, Philippa retired to Clarendon to await the birth of her second child. The previous November, Edward had ordered the palace to be made ready for her confinement, spending £126 ($104,500) on the refurbishment of the hall and chambers; part of a tiled floor laid for her survives today in the British Museum. But, for some unknown reason, she decided to have her child at Woodstock. There, around June 16, 1332, she gave birth to a daughter, who was baptized Isabella in honor of the Queen Mother. Children at that time were almost always named after their godparents, and the choosing of Isabella for this role is evidence of her rehabilitation. News of the birth was again brought to King Edward by Katherine de Grandison, the wife of William de Montagu.

For the Queen's churching in the chapel at Woodstock, altar frontals of purple silk colorfully embroidered with birds, animals, monkeys, and serpents were purchased. Afterward, Philippa received a procession of courtiers while sitting on a green velvet bed embroidered with mermen and mermaids holding shields bearing the royal arms of England and Hainault on a ground of sea and sky. Wearing a gown and surcote of red and purple velvet studded with pearls, the Queen showed off her daughter, who was wrapped in a furred robe of Lucca silk and lying in a cradle lined with taffeta, beneath a coverlet made of 670 skins. The King outlaid £292 ($242,000) on the feast he hosted that day, and marked the birth with a tournament.

In October, Edward and Philippa were hunting at Clipstone. They wintered in the north, staying at the Queen's castles at Pontefract and Knaresborough in Yorkshire, having left their children at Clarendon. At New Year 1333, Philippa gave Edward a silver cup, a basin, and a ewer embossed with images of Julius Caesar, Judas Maccabeus, Charlemagne, King Arthur, Sir Gawain, and Sir Lancelot. She herself owned a cup embossed with Tristan in a forest and a ewer engraved with the Knights of the Round Table, further evidence of her sharing Edward's interest in the Arthurian legends.

That year saw a renewal of the war with Scotland. David II's throne had been contested by his cousin, Edward Balliol, who some believed had a greater claim to it. Although his sister was David's queen, Edward III supported Balliol, whose father, John, had briefly been king of Scots in the 1290s. War had been declared in 1332, with the English scoring a victory at the Battle of Dupplin Moor in August, enabling Balliol to seize the Scottish throne. His triumph had been short-lived, for he was top-pled in December, when David was restored. But Edward remained deter-mined to reverse the humiliating concessions made in his name at Northampton and aid Balliol. He marched north in April 1333, taking Philippa with him and staying at Durham Cathedral priory. There, they supped together and retired to the King's chamber. Philippa was in her nightgown and about to get into bed with him when horrified monks came banging on the door, warning that St. Cuthbert would be offended if a woman slept beneath his roof, however high her estate. At Edward's urging, Philippa—still in her nightclothes—obligingly hurried across the green to the adjacent Durham Castle, praying that St. Cuthbert would not avenge a fault she had committed in ignorance.

Before the King traveled on to invest Berwick, which the Scots had taken, he sent Philippa to the safety of the strongly fortified Bamburgh Castle on the Northumberland coast. On April 23, he laid siege to Ber-wick. On May 18, while the town was still being bombarded, he created his three-year-old son earl of Chester. In June, he took Philippa to visit Lindisfarne Priory on Holy Island, then sent her back to Bamburgh.

When Edward fired Berwick, the Scots sought a truce, which he granted on condition that its commander, Sir Alexander Seton, send him twelve boys as hostages, including his own sons. But just as the truce was about to expire, the Black Douglas led a Scottish army—said with some exaggeration to number 90,000—across the River Tweed to Ber-wick. Edward was furious and resorted to the ruthlessness often exer-cised by kings in war. When, on July 11, Douglas threatened to besiege the Queen at Bamburgh, the outraged monarch hanged Seton's young-est son and threatened to hang two more hostages each day as punish-ment for the Scots breaking the truce. In fact, Edward knew that Bamburgh was well defended and provisioned and was confident that the garrison could hold out for weeks. On hearing that the constable had already taken precautions for the Queen's safety, the King rewarded him with £20 ($16,600) and two tuns of wine.

Berwick fell to him in July. On the 19th, an English victory at nearby Halidon Hill saw the death of Douglas and led to Balliol's restoration to the Scottish throne, on condition that he swear homage to Edward III as his overlord. This was in direct contravention of Scotland's assertion of independence in the Declaration of Arbroath (1321), which firmly stated:

"While a hundred of us remain alive, we will not submit in the slightest measure to the domination of the English."[7]

Edward then entered Berwick in triumph and gave thanks for his victory. He arranged for Philippa to be escorted to York, where new apartments were hastily built for her. David II and Queen Joan were sent by the Scottish lords to France, where Philip VI afforded them a safe refuge at Château Gaillard in Normandy. They were to remain there for the next seven years, while Scotland was governed by regents, Balliol having been ousted. After their return, there was open hostility between David and Edward Balliol, which led to their snatching the throne alternately, with Edward III frequently intervening in their quarrels.

In August 1333, Edward and Philippa were together again at Knaresborough, before riding south. Edward made a pilgrimage to Walsingham and visited his mother at Castle Rising, while Philippa rode on toward London. At a solemn ceremony in Canterbury Cathedral, three-year-old Prince Edward made his first public appearance, walking between his parents, and was given an alabaster cup by the monks. It was his first visit to the cathedral, for which he would always cherish great affection and be a generous benefactor, and where he would one day be buried.

In September, Philippa paid for seven ships to convey the Countess of Hainault and 250 mounted attendants from Wissant to Dover. Mother and daughter spent nearly three weeks together before the Countess sailed home on October 13.

Soon afterward, the King, the Queen, and Queen Isabella traveled to Durham Cathedral Priory to witness Richard de Bury's enthronement as bishop of Durham on December 19. Among the huge concourse of guests who attended the consecration were Archbishops Stratford and Melton, five bishops, seven earls, numerous northern barons, and the commons of Durham. Edward and Philippa were guests of honor at the feast hosted by the new Bishop afterward in Durham Castle, and gargantuan quantities of food were consumed, including 2,300 herring, 1,100 eggs, 15 piglets, and half a porpoise.

Edward and Philippa, who was pregnant again, spent Christmas at Wallingford Castle, where they feasted royally and played games with hobby horses. Afterward, Philippa moved to Woodstock, where she received a letter from the Chancellor and masters of the University of Oxford, praying her to write to the Pope on their behalf to seek his assistance in opposing plans for a rival university that had been established at Stamford, to which they were losing many students. In 1335, Edward would suppress the new foundation and send its students back to Oxford.

Around January 27–29, 1334, Philippa gave birth to a second daughter, Joan, named after her mother. Joan's date of birth is sometimes given as December 19, 1333, but Philippa was not churched until March 8–10, 1334. Joan is often said to have been born in the Tower of London, but has been confused with her aunt, Joan of the Tower, Queen of Scots, for her mother's churching ceremony took place at Woodstock, where she must have been born. On March 6, Edward granted Philippa more revenues from the earldom of Chester for the maintenance of Prince Edward and their daughters.

From the time they were infants, Edward III pursued marriage alliances for his children, but most of his plans came to nothing. He clearly loved their company and was an indulgent father, even allowing them to turn down marriages they did not want. Philippa was a loving mother and took her children on pilgrimages to Canterbury and other shrines. Although she had charge of them, they appear to have spent much of their early childhood at the castles of Pleshey and Marlborough in the care of Ralph, Lord Monthermer, the King's uncle, and his second wife, Despenser's sister Isabella (his first wife had been Edward II's sister, Joan of Acre). The royal children had their own household, governed by Elizabeth, Lady Saint-Omer, the wife of Prince Edward's steward, Sir William Saint-Omer; this consisted of nurses, chaplains, minstrels, damsels, esquires, valets of the chamber, kitchen, and larder, water carriers, candlebearers, porters, and grooms. Their meals were served on silver plates, their beds hung with silk, and they wore clothing of fur-trimmed scarlet or gray cloth with gold and silver buttons. At Easter, All Saints' Day, and Christmas, they were given new apparel.

Prince Edward was showing remarkable promise. "From the day of his birth," wrote Chandos Herald, he "never thought of anything but loyalty, noble deeds, valour and goodness, and was endowed with prowess. Of such high spirit was this Prince that he wished all his life to maintain justice and right, and he was brought up from childhood like this. From his own noble and open nature, he learned to be generous, for his heart was always gay and noble, even from the beginning of life and in his youth."

In the winter of 1334, Edward and Philippa traveled north again to Scotland and spent Christmas at Roxburgh, being entertained by minstrels. In the spring, they were in York, where the King held a Parliament. Edward then renewed his war with the Scots and sent Philippa to Berwick. As usual, she had overspent on her expenses, and he had to pay £500 ($414,800) to her creditors; he also granted her 350 marks ($222,500) yearly to support the heavy charges she had to meet daily. At Berwick, she saw her brother-in-law, William, Count of Jülich, and her cousin, Guy, Count of Namur, who had joined forces with the King. Together, Philippa and her kinsmen traveled north by sea to Perth, where the English and Scottish armies were mustered. Guy later captured Edinburgh for Edward.

In 1335, while their parents were away, the princesses Elizabeth and Joan were staying in the Tower of London. They were sitting in the Queen's chamber with their nurses when the fireplace collapsed, raining down masonry. Fortunately, no one was hurt. The King later vacated his apartments in the Garden Tower so that the Queen could use them, and moved into the royal palace by the river.

In July, Philippa's father, Count William, sent Edward a helmet with a coronet garnished with gems, urging him not to waste his wealth fighting the Scots, but to win glory by pressing his claim to France. Edward rewarded the messenger handsomely, but the matter was shelved.

In December, Philippa joined Edward at Roxburgh and they spent a week together before traveling south to Newcastle for Christmas, then took up residence in York. Edward spent much of the year 1336 campaigning in Scotland. On July 2, in his absence, Philippa summoned a great council at Northampton. "She called to the table the Archbishop of Canterbury, seven bishops, eight barons and lords, thirty-eight knights and other great lords to consider the issue of Scotland."[8] Clearly the King had empowered her to convene such a council, and the wording of the summons suggests that she took part in it. In July and August 1336, she was in Norfolk, visiting the Flemish weavers in Norwich, having left her children at Peterborough Abbey, where the Abbot was assiduous in looking to their comfort and spent lavishly in providing treats for them.

In August, Pope Benedict XII gave Philippa leave to commute any vow she was unable to observe, with the exception of a vow of chastity (should she decide, with her husband's consent, to abstain from marital relations) or one to go on pilgrimage to Rome or the Holy Land. She was pregnant again, and on the advice of her doctor, Benedict granted her permission to eat meat on fast days.

She received letters from Edward, describing his raising of a siege at Lochindorb and how he had laid waste the east coast. But his triumphs were tempered with tragedy. On September 13, his twenty-year-old brother, John of Eltham, died at Perth. A later Scottish chronicler[9] accused the King of stabbing him, but this was mere propaganda, for no other source corroborates it, and Sir Thomas Gray, a contemporary, wrote that John died "a good death." The loss of her son must have been deeply painful to Isabella, while Edward's accounts record that his brother's death was still giving him nightmares a year afterward.

Philippa had returned to Bamburgh by the winter. The Earl of Moray and his men tried to take the castle, but an English force overcame them before they got there. Moray was captured and brought to the Queen. He was sent into England and held prisoner until 1341.

Edward returned south after Christmas for the burial of John of Eltham in Westminster Abbey. In 1339, in accordance with Isabella's wishes, he had his brother's body moved to St. Edmund's Chapel, where a beautiful tomb and effigy were built, made probably by the same sculptor responsible for Edward II's monument at Gloucester, which is thought to have been completed around this time. The weepers on John's tomb cannot be positively identified, but the lady standing to the left of the figure that probably represents Edward II, and wearing a figure-skimming gown, a widow's chin barbe and wimple, and a crown, is probably meant to be Isabella, for she holds a scepter. It is possible that the figures of Queen Marguerite and Queen Philippa also appear among the weepers.

Edward's grief was briefly mitigated by the birth of a second son. He had left the heavily pregnant Philippa at the twelfth-century hunting lodge at Hatfield in Yorkshire, one of her own properties. For her confinement, he had purchased a bed of green velvet embroidered in gold with red sirens and a shield with the arms of England and Hainault, which cost £486.5s.5d. ($492,690), and she was provided with "a white robe worked with pearls and a robe of velvet cloth embroidered with gold."[10]

William of Hatfield, who was born on or around January 7, 1337, was probably named after the Queen's father. Tragically, he died soon after birth, his funeral in York Minster taking place before February 10, 1337. Philippa was churched six days later. On March 3, Edward paid for Masses that had been said "about the body of Lord William," a hearse, three cloths of gold in which the tiny corpse had been wrapped, and 393 pounds of wax candles burnt around it at Hatfield, Pontefract, and York.[11] The funeral cost £142.3s.10d. ($144,000). Philippa gave land to the minster clergy in William's memory. The effigy on his wall tomb (which is not in its original location) shows him as a fully grown child.

In Parliament, in March 1337, the King created six-year-old Prince Edward duke of Cornwall. This was the first time the title of duke—the highest rank of nobility—had been used in England. The child was invested with a ring, a chaplet, and a silver wand of office, and the King spent £1,333.6s.8d. ($135,000) on robes for him and his mother for the occasion. While Philippa retained charge of her younger children, the Prince was now given his own household with a governor, Sir Nicholas de la Beche, the Constable of the Tower. It was probably at the Queen's request that Edward appointed two tutors that year: the gallant Walter de Manny, who was to train young Edward in military skills and the arts of chivalry, and Philippa's scholarly almoner, Dr. Walter Burley of Merton College, Oxford, who taught him Latin and a love of literature. The King and Queen chose a select group of boys to share their son's education. One was Simon, Burley's son, who became a great friend of Prince Edward.

In the same Parliament, the King elevated six barons to the rank of earl, among them William de Montagu, who was created earl of Salisbury, and Lancaster's heir, Henry of Grosmont, who was made earl of Derby. In celebration, Edward held a magnificent court, while Queen Philippa hosted the ladies.

3

"William le Galeys"

✳

I T WAS PROBABLY IN EARLY 1337 THAT A GENOESE PRIEST, MANU-ele de Fieschi, a senior clerk or notary to Pope John XXII, sent Edward III a long, undated letter, written in Latin, from Italy, where Fieschi was then living. It contained the startling account of how Edward II had escaped from Berkeley Castle, which had been related to Fieschi by the deposed King himself, under the seal of the confessional. It told how he had traveled around Europe and visited Pope John XXII, who "kept him secretly and honourably for more than fifteen days. Finally, after various deliberations, all things having been considered, and after receiving permission to depart, he went to Paris, and from Paris to Brabant, and from Brabant to Cologne" to see the shrine of the Three Kings. "And, leaving Cologne, he crossed over Germany and headed for Milan in Lombardy. There, he entered a certain hermitage in the castle of Milasci, in which hermitage he remained for two and a half years; and because war overran the said castle, he moved to the castle of Cecima in another hermitage of the diocese of Pavia in Lombardy. And he remained in this last hermitage for two years or thereabouts, always the recluse, doing penance or praying God for you and other sinners."[1]

Manuele Fieschi belonged to a powerful Genoese family and was distantly related to the English royal house. He had long enjoyed close links with England, where he held several benefices, and was known to Richard de Bury, Edward III's former tutor. He had been appointed a canon of Salisbury Cathedral and archdeacon of Nottingham in 1329. By August

1330, he was working at the Papal Curia at Avignon. He was in England from 1333 to 1335.

The authenticity of his letter itself is not in doubt, but his account has been much debated by historians. The details of Edward II's last months are accurate, but Fieschi includes information that no one could have known apart from those who shared the former King's flight to Wales. No satisfactory explanation has ever been advanced to show how he got this information—unless it was from Edward himself.[2]

Edward had been a broken man, as had been made manifest at his abdication. He had suffered imprisonment, lost his throne, his wife, his children, and his liberty, and his favorites had been brutally executed. In adversity, his thoughts may well have turned to the solace of religion, which perhaps prompted a desire to withdraw from the world. The locations in Lombardy mentioned in the letter have been identified as Melazzo d'Acqui and Cecima sopra Voghera, and the second hermitage as the isolated abbey of Sant' Alberto di Butrio.

A local tradition persists that an English king sought refuge at Cecima and was buried in the nearby abbey, but it cannot be traced back further than the nineteenth century. In the church of Sant' Alberto di Butrio, there is an empty tomb carved out of rock; a modern plaque above it proclaims: "The first tomb of Edward II, King of England. His bones were taken by Edward III and transported to England and reburied in the tomb at Gloucester." The tomb dates probably from the eleventh century, but could have been used for Edward.

Fieschi states that the body buried at Gloucester was that of the porter Edward slew on his way out of Berkeley Castle. That tomb was opened in 1855, but there were no signs of any earlier interference with it, although that does not rule out the possibility of it having been opened before to facilitate the substitution of a body.

In 1343, the Pope appointed Fieschi bishop of Vercilli in northern Italy, which gave him ecclesiastical jurisdiction over the region in which Melazzo and Cecima were situated. Given his distinguished career, and the positions of trust he occupied, he does not appear to have been the type of man to fabricate a sensational story about Edward II's survival, or to have been deceived by an imposter, however well informed. It has been suggested that his letter was an attempt to blackmail Edward III into restoring his revenues: if he did not pay up, Fieschi would make public the contents of Edward II's confession. Yet his letter, sent "in the name of God," does not read like a blackmail threat. Nor did Edward III apparently respond to it as such, for there is no record of Fieschi receiving any further church appointments in England.

It is not hard to see why Fieschi might have been chosen by Edward II as an emissary to his son. His background and the blood tie were impeccable credentials. It is possible that Edward simply wanted his son to know that he was alive and was no threat to his security as king. Given the evidence, it is possible that Fieschi's account is genuine and that Edward II was not murdered.

Tellingly, on March 16, 1337, Lord Berkeley was finally acquitted in Parliament of the charges against him and absolved of all responsibility for the death of Edward II. Two days later, William de Shalford, who had disclosed Rhys ap Gruffydd's plot to Mortimer in 1327 and urged him to find a remedy, was rewarded by Parliament for his long service to the Crown. These proceedings could well have been prompted by Fieschi's letter. They suggest that Edward III was satisfied that no murder had taken place; as does the fact that, while he was at Koblenz in 1338, a man named "William le Galeys" (William the Welshman) was secretly brought to him from Cologne, escorted by a royal sergeant-at-arms called Francisco the Lombard and two men-at-arms, at a cost of 25s.6d. ($1,350). This William claimed to be Edward II.

Royal pretenders were usually dealt with harshly—Edward II himself had hanged one—but William le Galeys remained the King's guest for three or four months, and there was no public rebuttal of his claim. He was still with the royal party on October 18 and stayed with them until December, the King outlaying the generous sum of 13s.4d ($676) a week for his keep. He was kept under guard, but that may have been because Edward did not want him to be recognized. Edward II had been known as Edward of Caernarfon, after the place of his birth, and had been the first English Prince of Wales, which could explain the name "William the Welshman." It may be that he was no imposter, and this was a private reunion between father and son—a chance for the former King to give his blessing to his successor before retiring to Lombardy to end his days as a hermit.

After December 1338, William le Galeys disappears from the records. Edward III had every reason to keep his father's continuing existence a secret: he did not want anyone plotting his restoration, or himself losing face after having Mortimer publicly convicted of Edward's murder in Parliament; nor would he have wanted to rake up old scandals that could harm his mother. This might explain why the anniversary of Edward's death continued to be observed with religious services throughout the kingdom on September 21 every year until the end of Edward III's reign.

Relations with France were deteriorating. In 1334, Edward III had offered asylum to Robert of Artois, who had quarreled with Philip VI and been obliged to flee France. Edward made no secret of the fact that he was determined to recover the lands in Gascony that had been seized by Charles IV, while Philip supported David II against Edward Balliol. Edward demanded that Philip abandon his alliance with Scotland, but in vain. Then, in 1336, he received the devastating news that Flanders had allied itself to France and banned trade with England, which had serious implications for English prosperity. He retaliated by forbidding the export of raw wool to Flanders, and encouraged more Flemish weavers to relocate to England.

On May 24, 1337, Philip VI confiscated Gascony. In October, Edward III declared war on France. He had had the support of his father-in-law, but the gout-ridden Count William had died at Valenciennes on June 7. Philippa was at Fotheringhay Castle, Northamptonshire, at the time. In 1339, she commissioned her mother's clerk, Jehan de la Motte (who may have transferred to her own household), to write an elegy in verse, *Li regret Guillaume*, which was dedicated to her and was probably set to music, since Jehan is described as a minstrel.

After Count William's death, Philippa's mother retired to Fontenelle Abbey by the River Scheldt and became a Cistercian nun and, later, abbess. William II, the new Count of Hainault, remained an ally of England and would fight for Edward in France. When he died in 1345, his sister succeeded him, and she too would give the King her support. Edward's marriage to Philippa brought him further valuable allies in his brothers-in-law, the Emperor Louis IV and William, Duke of Jülich, and the states of Brabant and Guelders. Using her network of family connections, Philippa acted as a diplomatic conduit for French and Papal envoys to Edward's court.

A French poem, "The Vows of the Heron," written around 1346 (with extracts here from the stilted Victorian translation), imagined the scene at a feast in London, where Robert of Artois challenged Edward to invade France in pursuit of his claim to its throne. He gave the King a heron he had caught while hawking, saying it was "the most timid bird for the most timid King," who had let slip his claim to France. Stung by the insult, Edward vowed by God and the heron that within a year he would present the French crown to his Queen, even if the English were outnumbered by six to one.

Robert made other lords and knights swear to fight the French, then knelt before the Queen "and said that he would serve the heron in good time, once she had vowed that which her heart should tell her."

"Vassal," she said, "talk to me no more. A lady cannot make a vow because she has a lord; for if she vow anything, her husband has power to fully revoke what she shall vow, and shame be to the person that shall think 'I would vow' before my dear lord shall have commanded it me."

"Vow; my body shall acquit it," Edward told her. "But that I may accomplish it, my body shall labour. Vow boldly, and God shall aid you."

The Queen replied, "I know well for some time that I am big with child, that my body has felt it. It is only a little while since it moved in my body. And I vow and promise to the God who created me, who was born of a Virgin while her body remained perfect, and died on the cross, that the fruit shall never issue from my body until you have led me to the country over there to perform the vow your body has vowed. And if it should be ready to issue before that time, with a great knife of steel my body shall slay itself, my life be lost and the fruit perish."

"When the King heard this, he thought of it very gravely, and said, 'Certainly, no one will vow [any] more.'

"The heron was divided; the Queen ate of it." Afterward, "the King made preparation and caused ships to be stored."

The tale is, of course, a fiction; the poem was a political satire based very closely on an earlier work of c.1310. Froissart does not mention the episode and Philippa's vow seems drastic and out of character. But Robert of Artois was in England that year and it is possible that the chivalrous Edward did make such a vow, as his grandfather, Edward I, had once made a Vow of the Swan; there was a medieval custom whereby knights sometimes made vows on birds.

In 1338, Edward III formally laid claim to the French Crown, which he asserted was rightfully his in view of his descent through his mother from Philip IV. Thus began what later became known as the Hundred Years War because it dragged on intermittently for more than a century. English propagandists had a field day comparing Edward's claim with Jesus Christ's descent from the House of David through His mother, the Virgin Mary, although whether Isabella could have borne comparison with such a model of virtue is another matter.

Edward was bound for the Continent to drum up support for his claim to France and forge alliances with European princes, making good use of Philippa's connections with the Low Countries; it was therefore imperative that he take her with him. He was going to Flanders, where the people disliked their Count, who had allied them to the hated French, and were happy to recognize Edward as the rightful King of France.

Before he left England (according to a later note in Banckes's Herbal in Trinity College, Cambridge), Philippa's mother, having learned of her daughter's pregnancy, sent her cuttings of rosemary, an herb not yet seen in England, with a treatise describing its virtues. The "rose of Mary" was deemed to enhance fertility, among other benefits. Philippa had the cuttings planted in the gardens at Westminster. She loved gardens. In the park of Odiham Castle, in the 1360s, she had a large one laid to turf and enclosed with 2,000 feet of hedges, into which were set five doors. Flowers and herbs grew there and there were seats in arbors with turfed roofs and even a garderobe, screened behind a hedge.

The royal couple crossed from Orwell to Flanders on July 16, 1338, with Princess Isabella, Princess Joan (who was to be betrothed to one of the Emperor's sons by Margaret of Hainault), and Joan of Kent. Philippa's retinue alone numbered seventy-six. The King had assigned her £564.3s.4d. ($571,500) to equip herself with saddles, silver vases, zones (hip girdles), purses, silk, and jewels for the visit, and given her £66.6s. ($67,000) for robes for herself and Prince Edward, who had been left behind as nominal guardian of the realm.

They sailed up the River Scheldt and arrived at Antwerp on July 22. Crowds had gathered to greet them. The welcome banquet in the house of a citizen, Sirkyn Fordul, proved a disaster, for the kitchen caught fire and the building was burned to the ground. The King and Queen escaped just in time and were offered alternative lodgings in the city at the wealthy abbey of St. Michael. There, they were visited by Edward's sister Eleanor and her husband, the Count of Guelders. On August 17, the King and Queen enjoyed a boat trip on the Scheldt.

In August, Edward set off to meet his brother-in-law, the Emperor Louis IV, in Germany. With him was Joan, attended by her lady mistress, Isabella de la Motte, and John de Montgomery. Philippa traveled with them as far as Herentals, just beyond Antwerp, where they were obliged to stay overnight in the house of a peasant called Podenot de Lippe, who entertained them to an al fresco supper in the garden. Unfortunately, the grass was trampled by the King's retinue, but he compensated their host—and paid for the meal.

The next day, Philippa bade her husband and daughter farewell, having arranged for two of her minstrels to accompany them, and returned to Antwerp. There, she continued to reside at St. Michael's in great splendor, lavishly entertained and enjoying the food she had ordered to be sent to her from her estates in England: venison, red herrings from Yarmouth, codfish from Blackheath, and stockfish from Boston. Hearing that a sergeant from Essex was demanding money to maintain two horses he had stolen and claimed to be hers, she sent to the King, who dispatched men to arrest him. Fraudulent claims of this nature were common in an age in which every subject was required to provide food, transport, or aid to the officers of the King and Queen, and many such arrests took place. There are also numerous records of felons on the make, breaking into the parks of queens, poaching deer and fish, stealing timber and other property, ruining crops, and attacking servants.

Philippa continued to work behind the scenes on Edward's behalf. In September, she paid a spy—a minstrel called Gerard—to go to Paris "to investigate secretly the actions of Lord Philip de Valois,"[3] as she and Edward called Philip VI. In the early 1340s, she would maintain a correspondence with Pope Clement VI, and in 1343, she sent him a diamond ring, probably to lure him away from the French.

Edward and Joan had traveled on to Cologne, where he showed great interest in the building of the cathedral and stayed in a merchant's house, demonstrating the growing bond between royal and business interests. In his train was one John Chaucer, father of the poet Geoffrey.

In September, at Koblenz, Edward met the Emperor, who blessed his cause and appointed him vicar general over the Imperial provinces on the left bank of the Rhine. He also ordered the Imperial princes of the Low Countries to follow Edward in war for the next seven years. Edward was crowned vicar on September 5 and a week of celebrations followed.

Joan stayed on at the Emperor's court, in the care of her aunt, the Empress Margaret. Philippa had been corresponding with her sister and it had been agreed that Joan would be escorted by John de Montgomery to Austria to be educated at the court of her future husband. Philippa kept in touch with her by letter and sent many jewels to Margaret and her secretary Ida. On his return from Koblenz, Edward summoned his wife to join him at Louvain and they met there on September 9, returning four days later to Antwerp, which was "more commodious for the Queen to lay her belly in."[4]

Diplomatic negotiations with France had now reached an impasse. Edward had sent a challenge to King Philip, signed with his own hand, on St. John's Day, and the clouds of war were gathering. Hostilities broke out in September, when Edward besieged the Imperial city of Cambrai, whose burghers had invited the French to install a garrison. Hearing that a French army was on its way, Edward retreated in October and returned to Antwerp. There, he and Philippa "kept house right honourably all the winter."

On November 29, at Antwerp, Philippa gave birth to "a fine and pleasing son"[5] who was called Lionel, possibly after the heraldic lion of the Duke of Brabant, although his father already had a penchant for the name, having jousted wearing the arms of "Sir Lionel" in 1334, the same arms that were attributed to Sir Gawain in the chivalric romance poem *Sir Gawain and the Green Knight*. Lionel is sometimes called Leo in contemporary records, which was perhaps the nickname by which he was affectionately known.

Edward rewarded the messenger who brought him news of the birth with £100 ($101,000) and, in January, held a tournament to celebrate his son's arrival. The baby was baptized in St. Michael's Abbey.

* * *

The King and Queen spent Christmas at Antwerp. On Holy Innocents' Day, the cathedral choir sang for them in Philippa's chamber. She was churched on January 6, 1339, in the presence of the chief citizens of Antwerp, for which occasion Edward gave her £500 ($507,000) to spend on clothes. But he was broke. To raise money, he sent one of Philippa's four bejeweled crowns to Cologne to be pawned for £2,500 ($2.6 million) and did not redeem it until 1342.

Soon afterward Lionel became unwell, but was cured by doctors summoned by the Queen from Hainault. That winter found Philippa residing at the castle of the dukes of Brabant at Louvain, where she received a visit from her mother and her brother William, Count of Hainault.

On January 26, 1340, at a ceremony in the marketplace at Ghent, Edward III publicly asserted his claim to the kingdom of France, provocatively quartering the lilies of France with the lions of England on his coat of arms.

Philippa, who was again with child, had accompanied Edward to Ghent. He was now so deeply in debt to the Flemings that when he returned to England in February to raise money, he was obliged to leave her, Lionel, Isabella, and Joan of Kent behind in the abbey of Saint-Bavon as sureties, in the care of the earls of Derby and Salisbury.

The wealthy abbey of Saint-Bavon was renowned for its holiness and scholarship. Philippa held court there and frequently received visitors, among them the lords and ladies of Ghent, and Jacob van Artevelde, a wealthy burgher who had become the city's governor and was a staunch supporter of Edward. Philippa befriended his wife, Katherine of Courtrai, and stood godmother to his son, naming him Philip after herself.

On March 6, at Saint-Bavon, she gave birth to a fourth son, called John, for his cousin and godfather, John III, Duke of Brabant; he became known as "John of Gaunt" after his birthplace. His other godfather was Jacob van Artevelde. Three of Philippa's ladies, Amy de Gloucester (who had been William of Hatfield's nurse), Alice de Bedingfield, and Margery de Seymour, traveled to England to give King Edward the news, and were rewarded with £200 ($203,000). The infant was baptized in St. Bavon's Abbey, with Jacob van Artevelde holding him at the font.

Prince John was provided with bedclothes of red and green and a robe of silk. A Flemish widow, Isolda Neumann, was later appointed his nurse at a salary of £10 ($10,100). Decades later, the St. Albans chronicler, Thomas Walsingham, who was hostile to John of Gaunt, claimed that the Queen had actually borne a daughter whom she overlaid and suffocated, and that, in fear of the King's anger, she substituted Isolda's infant son, whose father was a butcher or porter. Walsingham claimed that, on her deathbed, Philippa confessed this to William of Wykeham, Bishop of Winchester, enjoining him to make it public if there was ever any likelihood of John of Gaunt becoming king. In the 1370s, when there were fears that Gaunt would usurp the throne, Wykeham was said to have made it known, but the tale was political propaganda and without foundation, as Wykeham strongly insisted.

The Queen had continued to write to her sister Margaret, asking after Joan, but had received worrying reports that the Empress was a lax and indifferent guardian and that Joan did not get enough to eat. Alarmed, Philippa made Edward order John de Montgomery to remove Joan from her aunt's household. The marriage plans were dropped (and Louis IV would abandon Edward anyway in 1341). In April 1340, Joan was restored to her parents at Ghent.

When the King sailed for the Continent on June 22—after Parliament, which was enthusiastic for the war, had voted a tax to pay some of his debts—he left his son Edward as regent. Anticipating that the French would invade England, his intention was to lie in wait for them at sea and intercept their fleet. On June 24, 1340, it was sighted off the port of Sluys in Zeeland; 120 great ships were sailing in a compact formation, closely guarded. To lure them out to sea, Edward ordered his fleet to turn back toward England, as if it were fleeing. When the French followed in speedy pursuit, the English ships turned around and pushed them back. But before he could engage with the enemy, he had to provide vessels to escort to safety English ships carrying "a large number of English ladies—countesses, baronesses, knights' ladies and wives of London burgesses—who were on their way to visit the Queen at Ghent. That done, he exhorted his men to fight well and stand up for his honour, which they all swore to do."[6]

As the French closed in, the English bowmen sent a storm of arrows over the enemy's decks, momentarily incapacitating them, then boarded their vessels. There was fierce fighting, but the French were soon vanquished. The subsequent destruction of their fleet was a great victory for Edward III and would resound to his fame for years to come.

When Edward entered Ghent in triumph on July 10, Philippa greeted him joyfully with their new son. On July 23, he moved to the Flemish city of Tournai, which had a French garrison. Three days later, styling himself "Edward, by the grace of God, King of England and of France," he sent a letter formally challenging Philip VI to single combat, warning that if the French King refused, he would summon his armies to France within ten days. Philip declined the challenge, whereupon Edward laid siege to Tournai. But he was in a precarious position. By September, he was virtually bankrupt, having pawned two of his crowns to Flemish merchants, and the French King was marching north at the head of an army.

At the urging of the Pope, Philippa's mother, the Countess Jeanne, appealed to her brother Philip to avoid an armed confrontation with Edward. On September 22, having left her convent, she visited Edward in his tent and pleaded with him to make peace. Her intercessions enabled the two kings to agree to a truce three days later without either losing face. Tournai was relieved and Edward returned to Ghent, where he was reunited with Philippa and held a tournament. But still he could not satisfy his creditors and leave Flanders.

On November 18, he sent three envoys to the Pope with a curious letter complaining that Archbishop Stratford was hoping that he would be killed and had compassed his ruin by withholding supplies; he had even schemed to deprive Edward of the affection of the Queen. Stratford, wrote the King, had "spoken separately to me of my wife, and to my wife of me, in order that, if he were listened to, he might provoke us to such anger as to divide us forever."[7] With no other evidence to go on, historians have speculated as to what the Archbishop had said. Did he imply to each of them that the other had committed adultery? A king's infidelity was of no great moment, since it could not compromise the succession, even if it caused trouble between husband and wife, but adultery in a queen was a very serious matter indeed.

In November 1340, Philippa had discovered that she was pregnant again; her child would be born on June 5, suggesting that it had been conceived around September 7–14. Edward's biographer Ian Mortimer has pointed out that Edward was away besieging Tournai from July until

September 25 and returned to Philippa in Ghent on the 28th. Probably the child was conceived on his return and, like more than a quarter of babies today, was born at thirty-eight weeks. It is hard to imagine that the devoted Philippa would have been unfaithful to Edward, and there is no sign that she was ever out of favor with him. Thus it is unlikely that Archbishop Stratford was trying to suggest that the child was a bastard. Even so, being lukewarm in his support of the war with France, he was probably doing his best to divert Edward from his purpose, even to the extent of driving a wedge between him and his wife. In Parliament, in April 1341, Stratford was to protest that he acted for the good of the realm and the Church, and for the honor of the King and Queen.

Leaving Henry of Grosmont, Earl of Derby, in Ghent as surety for his debts, the King gave his creditors the slip and rode to Zeeland with Philippa and their sons, pretending that they were visiting the coast for a change of air. In defiance of a storm, they sailed from the Scheldt to England, arriving at the Tower of London soon after midnight on November 30 after a tempestuous three days at sea. The superstitious blamed French sorcerers for raising the storm in the hope that Edward would drown.

Early in August, the princesses Isabella and Joan had been sent back to England and the safety of the royal palace in the Tower of London, the King having charged the constable, Sir Nicholas de la Beche, to take care of them. Attended by their lady mistress, Isabella de la Motte, ladies-in-waiting, maids, two chaplains, and a minstrel, they slept in a sumptuous bed, ate from silver dishes, were entertained by a minstrel, and wore beautiful gowns ordered by the Queen, who also sent them gold thread and silks for their embroidery. They received gifts from well-meaning lords and ladies and wrote letters to "their dearest Father and Mother."

At one o'clock on the morning of December 1, the King entered the Tower unannounced and was enraged to find his daughters ill housed and attended only by three nurses, while Sir Nicholas de la Beche was visiting his mistress, and the men-at-arms who were supposed to be guarding the princesses were disporting themselves in London's brothels. Edward had Beche, his men, and the Mayor of London rounded up, and would have executed them all, but Philippa prevailed, and he ordered them to be imprisoned "with exemplary rigour." In 1343, she would persuade Edward to release and reinstate Beche, who was appointed seneschal of Gascony soon afterward.

Isabella was at the Tower to celebrate Edward's birthday with him and attend the party he threw for his children, who were entertained by his minstrel, Godelin. Then he visited her at Leeds Castle and made provision for Mass to be sung daily in the chapel there for her good estate. In December, she was present in the great chamber of Winchester Palace in Southwark when the King delivered the Great Seal to the new Chancellor, Robert, Lord Bourchier. The royal family kept Christmas at Reading.

On January 18, 1341, Philippa granted a license to her chaplain, Robert de Eglesfield, to found the Queen's Hall (later the Queen's College) at Oxford. He did so that year and placed it under her patronage and protection. Its seal bears her image and three shields, one of which displays her arms. Her epitaph describes her as "a careful nurse to students all; at Oxford she did found Queen's College and Dame Pallas's school, that did her fame resound." "Dame Pallas" was Pallas Athena, the goddess of the Seven Liberal Arts, which were studied at "the college of the Queen," to which Philippa granted an annual income of 20 marks ($13,500) for the sustenance of six scholar chaplains. In 1342, she personally obtained Papal confirmation of the foundation and, five years later, persuaded the King to grant to the Provost the royal hospital of St. Julian in Southampton and several churches as endowments for the college. After Eglesfield's death in 1349, she continued to be an active and influential patron, frequently interceding on behalf of scholars. Two eighteenth-century portraits of her hang in the college today.

Philippa, who was expecting another child, appears to have spent much of the first half of 1341 at Langley. Edward was often there that year, or at Woodstock, hunting and jousting. For one expedition, he purchased hunting clothes of green and mulberry Turkish cloth for himself, his wife, his mother, eleven earls, four countesses, and fifteen squires. In April, during one of his visits, he granted Philippa the right to export wool from her estates to raise money to pay her debts, although he insisted that she pay the full duty on it. In May, he appointed her guardian of the lands assigned for the maintenance of her children Isabella, Joan,

Lionel, and John. The princesses had been returned to the Tower, but they visited their mother at Langley, riding in procession through London and distributing alms on their way. That spring, they were residing at the priory of St. Leonard, "the school of Stratford-atte-Bower" made famous by the poet Geoffrey Chaucer for its excellence in the teaching of Norman French.

On June 5, 1341, Philippa bore her fifth son at Langley. He was named Edmund, probably in memory of the King's executed uncle. The King was present at the Queen's churching in July and summoned the nobility to attend a tournament and feast to celebrate the Prince's birth, in which he himself took part. Then he wasted no time in getting his wife pregnant again; she must have conceived almost as soon as she was churched.

Edmund remained in her care until he was nearly thirteen, when the King was still referring to him as his "little son."[8] He grew up to be an ineffectual ditherer of little ability, lacking the ambition and energy of his brothers.

4

"A Vile Accusation"

✳

LATE IN OCTOBER, EDWARD RODE NORTH TO RELIEVE NEW-castle, which was under siege by a Scottish army commanded by David II. At his approach, the Scots retreated, but they refused to give battle, much to Edward's chagrin. He spent Christmas at Melrose and departed south on December 30.

Chroniclers claimed that during this campaign, Edward pursued the thirty-seven-year-old Katherine de Grandison, Countess of Salisbury, the wife of his close friend William de Montagu, and reputedly "one of the most beautiful and estimable women in England." The story comes from the chronicle of Jean le Bel, which was begun in 1352 in Hainault. Le Bel claimed he did not include events unless they were based on eyewitness evidence, yet his chronicle is demonstrably inaccurate in parts. His account of this episode, and the mostly identical one by his later editor and continuator, Froissart, stated that, while the Scots were raiding North-umberland, David II was attacked by William de Montagu, Salisbury's nephew and governor of his castle of Wark-on-Tweed, near the Scottish border. Montagu killed many men and brought to the castle 160 horses laden with plunder. A furious David laid siege to Wark, where Montagu was in residence with his aunt, the Countess Katherine. Some writers have assumed that she was awaiting the return of her husband, who had been a prisoner in France and would not formally be freed until May 1342; but he had in fact been released on parole to raise his ransom and was in England in 1341.

One rainy night, knowing that Edward III was marching through the

Borders with an army, Montagu slipped through the Scottish lines and reached the King, who hastened to the relief of Wark. Hearing of his coming, the Scots persuaded David to retreat to Scotland. Six hours later, Edward arrived with Montagu and expressed the desire to visit the Countess, "whom he had not seen since her marriage."

"As soon as the lady knew of the King's coming, she set open the gates and came out so richly beseen that every man marvelled at her beauty. When she came to the King, she kneeled down, thanking him for his succour, and so led him into the castle to make him honour and good cheer. Every man regarded her marvellously; the King himself could not withhold his regarding of her, for he thought that he never saw before so noble or so fair a lady. He was stricken to the heart with a sparkle of fine love that endured long after; he thought no lady in the world so worthy to be loved as she."

Hand in hand, the Countess led him into the castle, where he watched her so intently that she felt "abashed." After she had arranged for dinner to be served, she found him "in a great study" and bade him "leave his musing and come into the hall."

"Ah, fair lady," Edward replied, "other things lieth at my heart that ye know not of; but your sweet behaving, the perfect wisdom, the good grace, nobleness and excellent beauty that I see in you hath so surprised my heart that I cannot but love you, and without your love I am but dead."

"Ah, right noble prince, for God's sake, mock nor tempt me not," the Countess begged. "I cannot believe that it is true that ye say, nor that ye would think to dishonour me and the lord my husband. I had never as yet had such a thought in my heart, nor, I trust in God, never shall have for no man living." So saying, she walked away to the great hall "to haste the dinner."

The King ate little; he just sat there, "still musing, and cast his eyes on the lady. Of his sadness, his knights marvelled, for he was not accustomed so to be. Some thought it was because the Scots were escaped from him." But "the love of the lady had so keenly entered his soul that he could not rid himself of it and, in the end, the shaft of love pierced him so deeply that he did something for which he was bitterly blamed and reproved. For when he could not have his way with the noble lady, either by love or by prayer, he had it by force, as you will hear hereafter."

Froissart omitted this passage, but both chroniclers recounted that "all that day, the King tarried there and wist not what to do." He was struggling to stay on the path of "honour and truth," which compelled him not to dishonor the Countess and "so true a knight as her husband." In the morning, "all abashed," he rode north in pursuit of the Scots, and spent Christmas at Melrose Abbey.

Froissart later inserted a different version of what had happened in the castle. In describing the Countess, he changed the word "estimable" to "amorous" and showed her playing a flirtatious game of chess with Edward, after which there was a humorous debate over which of them should be the first to help themselves from a plate of comfits.

Both accounts show Edward acting in the best traditions of courtly love. But there are glaring flaws in Jean le Bel's version. He calls the Countess of Salisbury Alice. Salisbury did not have a nephew called William. It is hard to credit that Edward, who was close to Salisbury, had not seen the Countess in the twenty-one years since her marriage.

However, this was almost certainly a case of mistaken identity. The Countess of Salisbury was not the lady in question. Montagu's brother Edward was married to the King's cousin, Alice of Norfolk, the daughter of Thomas of Brotherton; in 1341, she was about seventeen, much younger than her husband, with whom she had five children. In the late autumn of that year, Salisbury sent Edward de Montagu north to repel an attack on Wark. It was he who killed David II's men and sought the King's aid. Edward had probably not seen his cousin since her wedding in c. 1338. In fact, Froissart makes it clear that it *was* Alice who received him at Wark. Early in 1352, the year in which Jean le Bel was writing his chronicle, Alice died after being brutally beaten "with force and arms feloniously" by her husband and two of his men on June 19, 1351. Clearly Jean le Bel got his facts wrong, and the story should be taken with a pinch of salt.

The King was back at Langley in February 1542, having just visited his mother at Castle Rising. That month, he and a heavily pregnant Philippa presided over a magnificent tournament held at Dunstable to mark the betrothal of three-year-old Lionel of Antwerp to seven-year-old Elizabeth de Burgh, sole heiress of the Earl of Ulster, who had been murdered in

1333. The Earl's widow, Matilda of Lancaster (a daughter of Earl Henry), had recently joined the Queen's household and brought her only child, who was now countess of Ulster in her own right. For the jousts, the King ordered matching embroidered gowns for Philippa and their two daughters, this being the first time the princesses had attended a tournament. The gowns were of red scarlet cloth powdered with squares of enamel and gold thread, each square enclosing a quatrefoil of pearls with a ring at its center.

Lionel and Elizabeth would be married on August 15, in the Tower of London. In celebration, the King hosted fifteen days of feasting and celebratory jousts. The little bride remained in Queen Philippa's care until she was old enough for her marriage to be consummated, and was made her ward in January 1347, which gave the Queen control of Elizabeth's Irish estates until such time as the young couple were old enough to live together. In 1355, Philippa stood godmother to the couple's only child, Philippa of Clarence.

In February or March 1542, Edward was with Philippa in the Tower when she gave birth to a third daughter, Blanche, who was premature (given that her brother Edmund had been born eight or nine months before) and died soon after birth. The wardrobe accounts record the expenses of her burial in Westminster Abbey, which took place before March was out. After the funeral and her uprising, the Queen went to Woodstock to mourn not only her baby, but also her mother, who had died on March 7. The Issue Rolls for Easter and June 1343 record the provision of a marble tomb for Blanche. One of Prince Edward's last acts when he was acting as regent early in 1343 was, on January 30, to arrange his little sister's burial in the new monument. Philippa offered palls of gold tissue, jewels, and alms at the tomb.

At Easter, Edward held a great council at Northampton and hosted another tournament. According to Jean le Bel, he was still scheming to bed "the Countess of Salisbury," or rather Alice de Montagu, and summoned her husband to the council. Montagu "very cheerfully complied with the King's request, for he thought nothing evil, and the good lady dared not say nay. She came, however, much against her will, for she guessed the reason which made the King so earnest for her attendance, but was afraid to discover it to her husband, thinking, at the same time, by her conduct and conversation to make the King change his mind.

"Out of his great desire to honour this lady, the King made a great feast. He commanded all his knights and lords to bring their wives" and Alice "was to bring as many young ladies as she chose. The ladies and damsels were most superbly dressed and ornamented," but she "came there in as plain attire as possible. She was not willing that the King should give up too much time to admire her, for she had neither wish nor inclination to obey him in anything evil that might turn to her husband's dishonor.

"Being all assembled, they danced and made merry, and afterwards there was a chapter, or convocation, of the new Order held." Jean le Bel was referring to the Order of the Garter, which was not founded until 1348, although its origins can be traced to 1344—and perhaps earlier. Queen Isabella's enthusiasm for the legends of King Arthur had been absorbed avidly by her son, who was passionately interested in the ideals of chivalry and was creating a lavish and extravagant court that was a center of chivalry and culture, and universally admired.

The feasting and jousting lasted for two weeks. It was perhaps during one of these feasts that we can place the later story of the King dancing with a lady and famously noticing male courtiers sniggering because her garter of blue ribbon had fallen off. He is said to have picked it up, bound it around his knee and sternly declared, *"Honi soit qui mal y pense"* ("Be he disgraced who thinks evil of it"), adding that the garter would soon be very much honored. These words were later adopted as the motto of the Order of the Garter. Its early statutes are lost, so the tale cannot be corroborated, and the first surviving account was recorded two centuries later by the Tudor historian Polydore Vergil, who stated that the lady who dropped her garter was Queen Philippa herself. He may have been right, for the motto echoes Philippa's words when she vowed not to give birth until Edward took her to Flanders with him: *"Et honnis soit li corps qui ja si pensera."* It was not until the early seventeenth century that John Selden, in his *Table Talk* (published in 1689), asserted that the lady was the Countess of Salisbury. But Elias Ashmole, in *The Institution, Laws and Ceremonies of the Most Noble Order of the Garter* (1672), also identified her as Philippa.

* * *

Jean le Bel admired "the noble King Edward, who was full of all nobility and gentleness, for never have I heard tell of any evil deed of his, save one, of which I will speak, and the force of love drove him to it." His next heading was: "How King Edward gravely sinned when he ravished the Countess of Salisbury." "Now I must tell you," he wrote, "about the evil deed King Edward did, for which he was much to blame, for it was no small thing, as I have heard tell. You well know how he was so enamoured of the beautiful Countess of Salisbury [sic] so that he could neither give her up nor accept her refusal nor change her answer either by humbly begging or by hard words. It happened, after he had sent the valiant Earl of Salisbury into Brittany, that he could not refrain from going to visit her on the pretense of inspecting her country and its fortresses and entered the marches where the castle of Salisbury was."

Salisbury did fight in the Breton war of succession in 1342–43; he had left England in May 1342, soon after the tournament at Northampton. But, of course, he was not the husband Edward wanted out of the way. Alice Montagu had probably returned home to her castle at Bungay, Suffolk. There was no castle at Salisbury and the city was not on the Welsh or Scottish marches. Wark was, but it is unlikely that Alice returned there, because Edward III did not travel so far north at that time.

Edward de Montagu may have accompanied the royal army to Brittany in August, ahead of the King, who was in Suffolk in the autumn, recruiting men, and could easily have visited Bungay. Jean le Bel asserted that he went there "to see whether he would find [Alice] any better disposed than formerly. The good lady made him as much honour and good cheer as she well knew she ought to for her lord, although she would have preferred him to have gone elsewhere, so much she feared for her honour. And so it was that the King stayed all day and night, but never could get from the lady the answer agreeable to him, no matter how humbly he begged her.

"Come the night, when he had gone to bed in proper state, and knew that the fine lady was in her bedchamber and that all her ladies were asleep and his gentlemen also, except his personal valets," Edward came to a decision. "He got up and told these valets that nothing must interfere with what he was going to do, on pain of death. So it was that he entered the lady's chamber, then shut the doors of the wardrobe so that her maids could not help her. Then he took her and gagged her mouth with such force that she could not cry out more than two or three times, and then he raped her so savagely that never was a woman so badly treated; and he left her lying there all battered about, bleeding from the nose and the mouth and other parts, which was for her great damage and great pity. Then he left the next day without saying a word, and returned to London, disgusted with himself." Poor Alice "never again knew happiness or carried herself joyfully, so heavy was her heart." Doubtless she feared what would happen if her volatile husband found out what had happened.

In September, the King and Queen were partying again when Edward threw a feast at Eastry Court in Kent, which was attended by four earls and other peers. In November, he formally granted Philippa custody of their five youngest children. Soon afterward, he joined his forces in Brittany, but was back early in 1343.

Edward de Montagu had probably returned to Bungay long before then. Jean le Bel, incorrectly believing that he was Salisbury, wrote that, on reaching home, "he quickly noticed his wife's distress, especially when she would not go to bed with him as usual. Challenged, she sat beside him on the bed, crying, and told him all about it. The good knight was overwhelmed with grief and disgust, remembering the great friendship and honour the King had always shown him, and the great deeds he had done for him who had now so shamed and betrayed him and the best woman living. The wonder is, he did not despair." Le Bel was sure "he was never happy again."

"When they had somewhat recovered, he said they could no longer live together, having been so disgraced. He would go to another country for the rest of his life, and she would remain as a good wife should, as he was sure she would be in the future." She should have half his property for herself and their heir, "but she would never see [her husband] again." He took his twelve-year-old son to the court at London and, before his peers, settled half his estate on his wife and his heir, then "publicly reproached" the King for his "shameful deed. All the lords of England were deeply shocked, and the King was blamed by all." He then went off to Spain to fight the Moors and died in the siege of Algeciras. "His departure was much lamented by the nobility." Jean le Bel believed that "the good

Countess did not live long after, for no decent woman could live long in such distress."

Again, le Bel's account is inaccurate. Montagu, unlike Salisbury, had as yet done no recorded "great deeds" for the King. Alice's only son was probably no more than four years old. Montagu could not have given her half his property because he held most of it in her right. Salisbury was present at the siege of Algeciras but did not perish there; he died in England, of wounds received in a tournament at Windsor in 1344. Alice died in 1351. The King's behavior in the story is out of character and inconsistent with a man who was such an ardent exponent of chivalry. It is astonishing that Montagu's very public castigation of the King was not reported by any other chronicler.

The story of the rape appears in three other foreign chronicles. The *Chronique Normande*, dating from around 1369–74, the early-fifteenth-century *Chronographia Regum Francorum,* and the *Istoire et Croniques de Flanders,* the latter two deriving from the *Chronique Normande*. Its author strongly sympathized with the kings of France and maybe used this tale as propaganda against the English, which is probably all it is. Whoever originally disseminated the tale capitalized on Edward's known enjoyment of female company.

Froissart omitted Jean le Bel's passages relating to the rape, but later wrote:

> You have heard me speak of how passionately the King was smitten with the charms of that noble lady. The chronicle of Jean le Bel speaks of this love less properly than I must, for, please God, it would never enter my head to incriminate the king of England and the Countess of Salisbury with such a vile accusation. If respectable men ask why I mention that love, they should know that Jean le Bel relates in his chronicle that the English King raped the Countess of Salisbury. Now I declare that I know England well, where I have lived for long periods mainly at the royal court and also with the great lords of the country, and I have never heard tell of this rape although I have asked people about it who must have known if it had ever happened. Moreover, I cannot believe, and it is incredible, that so great and valiant a man as the King of England would have allowed himself to dishonour one of

the most notable ladies of this realm and one of his knights who had
served him so loyally all his life.

Froissart may have suppressed the story out of sympathy for his beloved
patroness, Queen Philippa.

Mystery surrounds the circumstances of Alice's death. In November
1351, there is an entry in the Fine Rolls concerning the reversion of her
lands and property to her heir or the Crown, as she was deceased. It was
then five months after the attack by her husband and his retainers, but
an addendum stated that she was still alive. She had died by the end of
January 1352. Montagu and his men were indicted for the crime, but one
was pardoned in 1361 and Montagu escaped unscathed because the
King put a stop to the proceedings against him. Given that the attack
took place nine years after Edward was supposed to have raped Alice, it is
unlikely that her husband attacked her because of that, but one might
wonder why Edward did not seek justice for the brutal atrocity committed on his cousin, which appears to have been premeditated, given that
Montagu involved others.

In November 1342, while Edward was away fighting in Brittany, his ally,
Robert of Artois, died of dysentery after being wounded at the siege of
Vannes in Brittany. On November 25, Edward wrote to his *douce coeur*
("gentle heart"), as he called Philippa, asking her to arrange for Robert to
be buried in London, and she had him interred in the monastery of the
Black Friars. When the King returned to England early in 1343, he joined
Philippa and their children at Havering, where he insisted on dining with
his three youngest sons, who were all under five, which demonstrates
how fond he was of his children.

In March, Edward and Philippa made a pilgrimage to Edward II's
tomb at Gloucester. There is no record of any earlier visit by the King,
although work on the tomb had been going on apace through the early
1330s. Possibly the real Edward II had recently died at Cecima and his
body had secretly been brought home to England and buried in the tomb
at Gloucester, the porter's body having been removed. Edward's heart
would have been substituted for the porter's, which had been kept in the

casket held by Isabella. He had perhaps died in 1341, when Edward III paid Nicolinus de Fieschi (a relation of Manuele) one mark a day plus generous expenses to travel to "divers parts beyond the sea" on what were described as "certain affairs."[1]

The royal couple were back at Havering for Easter. On May 12, before Parliament at Westminster, their eldest son was created Prince of Wales, following the precedent established by Edward I when he bestowed the title on his heir in 1301. Since 1343, male heirs to the throne have been created Prince of Wales and given the other titles previously bestowed on Prince Edward: the earldom of Chester and the dukedom of Cornwall.

In 1343, the King decided on an extensive program of building works at Windsor Castle, which was then believed to have been originally built by King Arthur. Construction began that year under the supervision of William of Wykeham, who "later became one of the great masters of England as bishop [of Winchester] and chancellor, and everything passed through his hands."[2] Edward's intention was to transform Windsor into a suitable setting for a new order of chivalry.

By 1344, he had decided to found an order of knights of the Round Table dedicated to St. George and "made up of himself and his sons and the bravest and noblest in England and other countries too."[3] On January 1, it was proclaimed that a great feast and tournament would be held at Windsor, which was to become the home of the order.

The festivities lasted from January 15 to 23. The most magnificent celebration was that in honor of St. George, which was hosted by the King on the 18th. Also present were the two queens, Prince Edward, and the other royal children. Philippa wore robes that had cost Edward £500 ($506,600). She was attended by 300 ladies and damsels of high birth, all attired alike in fashions supposedly worn at King Arthur's court.

The King himself had arranged the seating for his womenfolk at the feast afterward, and personally showed them to their places in the great hall. The food was "expensive and abundant, and the choicest drinks were served, and everyone had as much as they wished. The lords and ladies danced together, exchanging embraces and kisses."[4] Three days of jousts followed. It is unlikely that Isabella was present at these, for at Westminster, on January 20, she granted certain liberties to the men of her manor of Cheylesmore, south of Coventry, "out of consideration"[5] for her eldest grandson, to whom she intended the manor to come on her death.

She was back at Windsor on January 23 when the King and Queen, "nobly adorned" and wearing their crowns, led "the Lady Queen Mother" and the rest of the royal family to hear Mass in state in Henry III's chapel. Afterward, before the assembled throng, Edward took an oath on the Gospels "that he would begin a Round Table in the manner of King Arthur" for 300 knights.[6] Trumpets then sounded, summoning the guests to a final opulent feast.

The year 1344 was wet, with a disastrous harvest. The King directed that the itinerant courts that had hitherto followed him around the realm be settled permanently at Westminster, enhancing London's status as capital and Westminster as the main seat of government.

Philippa was again pregnant. Knowing she could not fulfill a vow to make a pilgrimage to the shrine of St. James at Compostela, she appointed her chaplain to go in her stead. On October 10, she gave birth to a fourth daughter, Mary, at the palace of the bishops of Winchester at Bishop's Waltham, Hampshire. Edward was at Waltham on that day, but was absent from the Queen's churching, attending to business at Westminster.

In 1345, Prince Edward turned fifteen. He was handsome, muscular, brave, intelligent, charismatic, and inspirational. His sixteenth-century nickname may have derived from the black armor he is said to have worn, but it could equally well have alluded to his much-feared temper. Now deemed of an age to support his father in the war against France, he raised 4,000 troops from his principality of Wales and joined the King in Flanders. For some months, there was no fighting and the royal forces lingered in the Low Countries as Edward made plans to invade France the following year.

That year, Edward betrothed his daughter Joan to Pedro, the heir of Alfonso XI of Castile. Joan was then eleven and it was agreed that she should go to Castile when she was fourteen. Meanwhile, she was being raised in the care of one of her mother's ladies, the learned Marie de Châtillon, Dowager Countess of Pembroke, the second wife of Aymer de Valence. Marie was a cousin and friend of Queen Isabella. Well educated, and a great patron of letters, she was to found Pembroke College, Cambridge, in 1347.

On September 26, Philippa's brother, William II of Hainault, died fighting the Frisians and was succeeded by their sister, the Empress Margaret, who became Margaret II, Countess of Hainault, after her husband, the Emperor Louis IV, recognized Holland, Hainault, Zeeland, and Friesland as her possessions. In England, when there was no male heir, estates were divided between co-heiresses, and Edward III claimed Zeeland as Philippa's share of the inheritance. But, needing to commit his resources to the war with France, he had not the wherewithal to pursue it; nor did the Hainaulters want Philippa as their sovereign countess, fearing English interference. In April 1346, after the Estates of Holland declared that the late Count William's dominions were indivisible, Philippa's other sisters renounced their claims, but Edward III continued to uphold hers—ultimately in vain.

In November, the Queen hosted great festivities at Woodstock for the King's birthday and they remained there for the festive season. In January 1346, with Prince Edward and Queen Isabella, they attended the obsequies of Henry, Earl of Lancaster, in the collegiate church in the Newarke at Leicester, all wearing new black mourning attire.

Marguerite of France, second
queen of Edward I;
"good withouten lack."

Edward I, "When Edward died,
all men died to me."

Canterbury Cathedral, where Edward married Marguerite in 1299.

Philip IV of France and his children: Louis X (crowned), Philip, Charles, Robert, and Isabella.

The wedding of Edward II and Isabella of France at Boulogne Cathedral, 1308.

Isabella of France. She was "more beautiful than the rose."

Edward II and Piers Gaveston. "I do not remember to have heard that one man so loved another."

Eltham Palace, one of Isabella's favorite residences.

Isabella of France. She came to enjoy a reputation as a peacemaker.

Woodstock Palace. Many royal children, including the Black Prince, were born there in the fourteenth century.

Isabella's daughters, Eleanor of Woodstock (left) and Joan of the Tower (right). Joan was said to be "disparaged" by a "vile marriage" to David II of Scots.

John of Eltham, Isabella's second son. Edward III was accused, falsely, of murdering him.

Charles IV welcomes Isabella to Paris, 1325.

toft temencees en hollande z
zeellande. A moult grant
meffaufe paffa la tozne et fa

plente Car moult trouueret
le pape tiche et bien pourueu
pour tant que tiens neftoit

Isabella and Roger Mortimer riding to Oxford.

Isabella and her army before Hereford, 1326. The execution of
Hugh le Despenser can be seen in the background.

Despenser died in agony with
crowds baying for his blood.

The marriage contract of Edward III
and Philippa of Hainault.

The cell in Berkeley Castle in which Edward II is said to have been imprisoned.

Isabella with her son Edward III. He was eager to throw off his mother's tutelage.

The tomb of Edward II in Gloucester Cathedral. No chronicler ever accused Isabella of being an accomplice to the murder of her husband.

The coronation of Philippa of Hainault, 1330.

Castle Rising, Norfolk. It was one of Isabella's chief residences during her retirement. Here she maintained a considerable degree of state and lived a life of affluent leisure.

Philippa of Hainault at the Battle of Neville's Cross, 1346.

Windsor Castle, the scene of many of Edward III's chivalric triumphs. The Order of the Garter was founded here in 1348.

Philippa famously intercedes with Edward III for the lives of the burghers of Calais, 1347.

Edward of Woodstock, Prince of Wales: "the Black Prince." "From the day of his birth, he never thought of anything but loyalty, noble deeds, valour and goodness."

John of Gaunt, Duke of Lancaster.
He became the greatest
magnate in England.

Joan of Woodstock.
"Death," wrote Edward III,
"has removed our daughter, whom
we loved beyond our other children."

The Abbey of St. Bavon, Ghent,
where John of Gaunt was born in 1340.

William of Windsor
and Blanche of
the Tower,
who both died
in infancy.

Lionel of Antwerp,
Duke of Clarence.

Philippa of
Hainault with
her daughter
Isabella.

Edward III. "His face was like the face of a god."

Philippa of Hainault. "She was a lady of great honour and virtue and a firm friend to England."

Richard II. "He was haughty and too much inclined to voluptuousness."

Charles IV, Holy Roman Emperor, father of Anne of Bohemia. He aspired to be another Charlemagne.

Wenceslaus IV, King of Bohemia, Anne's brother. He could not even afford to give her a dowry.

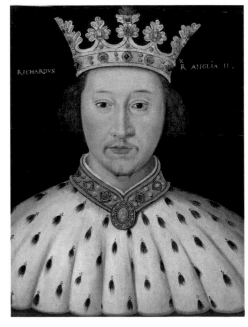

Anne of Bohemia. "The King laid out no small sum to secure so little a scrap of humanity."

Richard II. He loved Anne "even to madness."

The coronation of a king and queen, probably Richard II and Anne of Bohemia.

Anne exercising her queenly function of intercession before Richard.

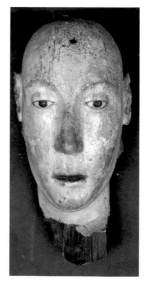

Anne of Bohemia, funeral effigy. Her death left Richard "all distraught and disordered."

Richard II. From 1397, "he began to act the tyrant and oppress the people."

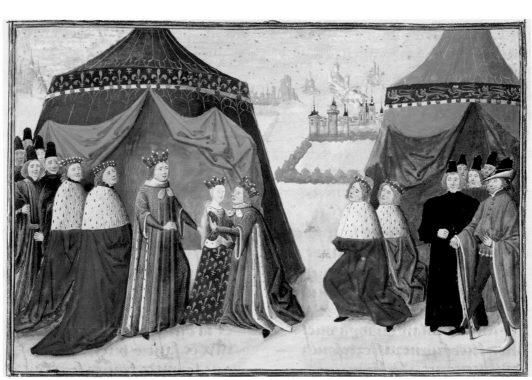

Richard receives his six-year-old bride, Isabella of Valois, from her father, Charles VI of France.

Richard II and Isabella of Valois. "He behaved so amiably to her that she loved him entirely."

Leeds Castle. Isabella was sent here when Richard was deposed in 1399.

Isabella's second husband, Charles of Valois, Duke of Orléans, as a prisoner in the Tower of London. He thought her "the fairest thing to mortal eyes."

5

"I Cannot Refuse You"

✳

O N ST. JOHN THE BAPTIST'S DAY 1346, THE KING AND PRINCE
Edward took leave of the Queen, who was heavily pregnant, and,
having appointed John, Earl of Kent (the son of the executed Edmund),
regent, sailed for France on July 11 with an army of 20,000.

On July 20, 1346, at Windsor, Philippa bore a daughter, who was
named for St. Margaret of Antioch, whose feast day it was.

The King and Prince Edward were marching toward Paris when they
learned that King Philip was lying in wait for them there with 100,000
men. Edward ordered a retreat north to Calais. On the way, he took Caen,
where he discovered French plans for an invasion of England in 1339.
Enraged, he ordered a wholesale massacre of the citizens—another instance of his ruthlessness. A royal clerk wrote to Queen Philippa: "A great
number of knights and squires were slain, and other people of the city, in
the streets and houses and gardens. It cannot be known what number of
men of substance were slain, for they were stripped so that they could
not be recognized. And no gentleman was slain on our side save one
squire who was wounded and died two days after."[1]

At length, Edward was persuaded to restrain his men, as he faced a
long journey to Calais, which he meant to take as a bridgehead into
France and a base from which to curb the looting of English ships by
French pirates. Not wishing to jeopardize his reputation as a Christian
king, he commanded that no churches were to be desecrated on the way,
but his orders were disobeyed and twenty men who despoiled a church at
Beauvais were hanged. Edward sent secular spoils and prisoners back to

England "with a host of loving greetings to his wife, my lady Philippa, the gracious Queen of England."[2]

At the River Somme, the way was blocked by French troops. On August 24, a fast and furious battle was fought, in which Prince Edward played a prominent part. Having emerged victorious, the English then forded the Somme and marched on, braving a storm. Presently they came to the top of a hill on the outskirts of Crécy, where, on August 26, in one of the most important and vicious battles of the Hundred Years War, they again clashed with the French. The enemy forces were augmented by those of Sir John of Beaumont, whose defection to the enemy must have grieved Edward and Philippa.

The King did not participate, but watched the battle from a nearby windmill. Having placed his son in command, he had ordered his captains to "suffer him this day to win his spurs, for, if God be pleased, I will this journey be his, and the honour hereof."[3] His faith in the sixteen-year-old Prince was not misplaced. The youth performed magnificent feats of arms and led the English to another victory, showing outstanding courage. It was perhaps on account of his prowess in warfare that young Edward came famously to be known as the "Black Prince," a nickname first recorded in the sixteenth century, but which will be used henceforth in this text as it is the name by which he is best known. This was the first important battle in which the English longbowmen demonstrated their supremacy over the heavily armored French cavalry, and their skill carried the day.

Afterward, the King knighted his son on the battlefield. Among the fallen was France's ally, the blind King John of Bohemia. Tradition has it that the Black Prince plucked three ostrich feathers from the dead King's helm and adopted them as his emblem, along with King John's motto, "Ich Dien" ("I serve"), although it is more credible that the motto derived from the Welsh Eich dyn (Your man), an appropriate legend for the Prince of Wales. It is also far more likely that the Prince adopted the three silver ostrich feathers that stood on a black ground on the arms of Queen Philippa's father as count of Ostrevant, one of his many titles. Both emblem and motto have been borne by the princes of Wales ever since.

On September 4, the King set up camp before Calais and laid siege to the town. From there, his chaplain wrote to Philippa with the stirring news of the triumph at Crécy.

* * *

Meanwhile, David II, having once again wrested the Scottish throne from Edward Balliol, had allied himself with the French, taking advantage of Edward's absence to invade England. He got as far south as York, where he burned the suburbs. His aim was to distract the King from his offensive on Calais, so that the French could invade England from the south. But in October, Queen Philippa countered the threat by raising 12,000 northern levies and placing them under the joint command of Thomas Hatfield, Bishop of Durham, and two great border lords, Henry Percy and Ralph Neville.

Froissart wrote: "The Queen of England was very anxious to defend her kingdom. In order to show that she was in earnest about it, she came herself to Newcastle-upon-Tyne. She took up residence there to wait for her forces. On the morrow, the King of Scots, with 40,000 men, advanced within three short miles of Newcastle. He sent to inform the Queen that, if her men were willing to come forth from the town, he would wait and give them battle. Philippa answered that she accepted his offer and that her barons would risk their lives for the realm of their lord the King."

Seated on a white palfrey, she "went from battalion to battalion, desiring them to do their devoir [duty] to defend the honour of her lord, the King of England, and, in the name of God, to fight manfully, every man to be of good heart and courage." If they did so, she promised "that she would remember them as well, or better, than if her lord the King were there in person." Her captains declared "that they would acquit themselves loyally to the utmost of their power," whereupon she bade them farewell, commending them to the protection of God and St. George, then "tarried in Newcastle" to await news.[4]

Some historians claim that Philippa was in Flanders at the time, and that no other source—including a contemporary battle song by Laurence Minot—mentions her presence; yet the dates do tally. This account derives from Jean le Bel, who was Froissart's source, but Froissart also knew the Queen personally and was in a position to obtain information from her. Philippa appears in three fifteenth-century manuscript illustrations of the battle, one from *Les Grandes Chroniques de France*, the others from different editions of Froissart, whose version is accurate in all other particulars. Moreover, the book in which his account appears was presented to Philippa herself.

On October 17, the English crushed the Scots at the Battle of Neville's Cross, west of Durham, and King David was taken prisoner. "When the Queen heard that her army had won the victory, she mounted her white palfrey and went to the battlefield. She was informed on the way that the King of Scots was the prisoner of a squire named John Copeland, who had ridden off with him, no one knew whither. The Queen ordered him to be sought out and told that carrying off her prisoner without leave was not agreeable to her.

"All the rest of the day, the Queen and her army remained on the battlefield they had won and then returned to Newcastle for the night. The capture of the King gave the Queen of England a decided superiority over her enemies," who had retired to the north.

The next day, when Copeland had been tracked down, Philippa wrote a letter commanding him to surrender King David to her. He replied that "he would yield his royal prisoner to no woman or child, but only to his own lord, King Edward, for to him he had sworn allegiance, and not to any woman. But she might depend on his taking good care of King David."

The Queen informed the King of this and he summoned Copeland to Calais. News of the victory had been sent to him by nine-year-old Lionel of Antwerp, who was acting as nominal regent in his absence. Philippa was then on her way south to London, having "sufficiently provided for the defence of the cities of York and Durham, as well as for the borders generally."

At Calais, Copeland hastened to justify his actions. "Sire, I require your Grace be not miscontent with me, though I did not deliver the King of Scots at the commandment of my lady Queen, for I hold my lands of you, and not of her, and my oath is to you," he said.

Edward was gracious. He said he knew that Copeland had done him meritorious service. Now, however, he must "return home and take your prisoner and convey him to my wife."

Back in England, Copeland surrendered David to the Queen, who, "soundly advised by her men," had the Scottish King mounted on a black charger, then paraded through London and confined "under close guard" in the Tower, where Lionel was waiting to receive him.[5] David's wife Joan now followed him to England, and Queen Isabella was able to meet up with the daughter she had not seen for nineteen years. There is much evidence to show that Joan became close to her and Philippa. The King permitted her to visit her husband and provided her with a suitable household, and she spent most of her time at Hertford Castle, which Edward had granted to Isabella, who stayed there with her in 1347.

Philippa now "turned to her other business. What she particularly desired was to go over to Calais to see her husband the King and her son, the Prince of Wales. She hurried on with her preparations and, embarking at Dover" on October 29, "had such a favourable wind, thanks to God, she was soon across," probably landing on the coast of Flanders. She "brought many ladies and damsels with her, as well to accompany her as to see their husbands, fathers, brothers and other friends that lay at siege there before Calais."[6] In her train were her daughters, fifteen-year-old Isabella and twelve-year-old Joan. Isabella was to be betrothed to fifteen-year-old Louis II, Count of Flanders, whose father had been killed fighting alongside Philip VI and whom Edward wished to wean away from the French. Louis was reluctant to marry her, but his leading subjects had held him captive until they forced him to agree. Before making her way to Calais, Philippa visited her sister Margaret at Ypres, to make peace after the quarrel over the Hainault inheritance. Then she covered the fifty-seven miles to Calais in two days.

"As can be imagined," when she and the princesses joined Edward there, they were "welcomed with joy and she and all her ladies were soon lodged as honourably and comfortably as if they had been in London." By now, Edward's encampment had become a virtual town with timber houses for himself and his nobles and a large twice-weekly market selling "flesh and fish, mercery ware, cloth, bread, wine and all other things necessary." "On All Saints' Day, the King held a court in honour of the Queen" in his camp "and gave a dinner for all his lords, and especially for the ladies."[7]

Philippa passed the time at Calais hawking or playing backgammon (tables) with the Black Prince, who gave her a horse named Grisel Petit Watt. In a Latin poem written around 1370, John of Bridlington, a Yorkshire chronicler, complained that "the Queen of England," alias "Diana," had captivated Edward and distracted him from the siege, for which God sent the Black Death as a punishment.[8] He was referring of course to the pandemic that was to sweep across Europe between 1347 and 1351. An anonymous contributor to the poem would clearly have liked to reveal more, but feared to incur the lady's anger. Maybe both felt that Edward should not have been feasting his wife or gallivanting off to Flanders with her (see below) when he was supposed to be besieging Calais.

In this period, the Roman goddess Diana was associated with nocturnal demonic processions that led humans astray. She was also known popularly as a huntress, and Philippa loved to hunt. Yet it seems unlikely that John of Bridlington would have associated the virtuous and much-loved Queen with such a subversive figure. Possibly he used the title "Queen of England" sarcastically, implying that this "Diana" had been the King's mistress before the Queen's arrival—although if that was the case and she did distract him from the siege, no one else commented on it. Even if Edward had briefly strayed, Froissart makes it clear that he was glad to see his wife. They spent Christmas together and Philippa stayed to await the capitulation of the town.

In March 1347, the Flemings invited the King, the Queen, and Princess Isabella to Bergues, near Dunkirk, saying "they would bring their young lord and the marriage would be arranged. As may be imagined, the King and Queen were very pleased, saying that the Flemings were excellent people. A day was agreed by both parties for the meeting, to which the most prominent nobles came from the Flemish towns in great state with the young Count." Edward and Philippa and "a large suite" were at the abbey of Saint-Vinoc at Bergues when he arrived and "bowed courteously" to them. "The King took him gently by the right hand, complimenting him as he did so. Then he asked him to forgive him for the death of his father. The young count appeared to be fairly well satisfied with this apology."[9]

The marriage contract was drawn up, Edward settled a large dowry on Isabella, and the young couple were betrothed, the Count agreeing to marry her soon after Easter. "The Flemings returned to Flanders with their lord, and the English sovereigns to Calais. King Edward prepared to celebrate the wedding with great pomp and provided himself with costly jewels to be distributed on the day. The Queen did the same, for she was accounted the most gracious and bountiful lady of her time and wished to be true to her reputation." All seemed well. But "in the very week when he was to marry [Isabella], Count Louis went hunting, clapped his spurs to his horse and galloped off" to France, breaking the betrothal, for his heart "was all French."[10] After that, Edward spoiled his jilted daughter, treating her more generously than he did her younger sisters. This led to a coldness between her and Philippa, who at one point was barely speaking to Isabella. Possibly she resented this unequal treatment, or was jealous of the attention Edward was lavishing on his favorite child.

The siege of Calais lasted a year "and was the occasion for many fine exploits and feats of arms," there being "frequent skirmishes."[11] By August 1347, the townsfolk were in a desperate state. They had already turned out 1,700 souls who had no stock of provisions to fend for themselves, and had to run the gauntlet of the besiegers or face certain starvation. The cost of the prolonged siege to Edward III had been crippling and held up his plans to conquer France. He was angry and frustrated, but when the town sent a deputation to discuss terms for an end to the siege, he chivalrously gave them all a good dinner and sent them on their way, promising to be merciful and benevolent if they would surrender unconditionally and send to him six burghers wearing halters around their necks (like felons going to the scaffold) and bearing the keys of the town.

On August 4, having been informed that Sir Walter de Manny was bringing the burghers to him, the King "went out to the open space before his quarters, followed by his nobles and by great numbers of others who were curious to see them and learn what would happen to them. Even the Queen, who was very near her lying in, went out with her lord the King."

When Manny led the burghers before him, Edward "looked at them very fiercely, for he hated the people of Calais because of the losses they had inflicted on him." The six men knelt, expecting him to make an example of them. "Clasping their hands in supplication," they surrendered to him the keys to the town. "We put ourselves entirely in your hands in order to save the remaining inhabitants of Calais, who have already undergone great privations," they said. "We pray you, by your generous heart, to have mercy on us also."

Many were weeping, moved to pity at seeing "men so humiliated and in such mortal danger, but the King continued to glare at them savagely, his heart so bursting with anger that he could not speak. When at last he did, it was to order their heads to be struck off immediately. All the nobles and knights begged the King to have mercy, but he would not listen."

"Noble sire, curb your anger," Manny entreated, flattering his implacable master. "You have a reputation for royal clemency. Do not perform an act that might tarnish it and allow you to be spoken of dishonourably."

> At this, the King ground his teeth and said, "That is enough, Sir Walter. My mind is made up. Let the headsman be sent for. The men of Calais have done me such damage it is fit they suffer for it."
>
> Then the noble Queen of England, pregnant as she was, humbly threw herself on her knees before King Edward and, with tears, said: "Ah, gentle Sir, since I have crossed the sea with great peril to see you, I have never asked a single favour from you. Now, I most humbly ask as a gift, for the sake of the Son of the Blessed Mary and by the love you bear me, the lives of these six men."
>
> King Edward remained silent for a time, looking at his gentle wife as she knelt weeping before him. His heart was softened, for he would not willingly have distressed her in the state she was in. At last, he said, "Ah, lady, I wish you had been anywhere else but here. You have entreated in such a manner that I cannot refuse you. Although I do this against my will, I therefore give them to you; do as you please with them."
>
> The Queen thanked him from the bottom of her heart, then rose to her feet and told the six burghers to rise also. She had the halters taken from their necks and led them to her apartment, after which she clothed them and served them with a plentiful dinner. She then presented each with six nobles [about $1,600] and had them escorted out of the camp in safety and sent to live in various towns in Picardy.[12]

Froissart must have got at least some of his information from Philippa herself and others who had been present, so there is no reason to suppose that the story was made up, as some historians have suggested. Others have asserted that the Queen's intercession was an elaborate charade, prearranged and staged to enable the King to show mercy without losing face or authority, which may be true, yet it appears that Edward really did mean to execute the six burghers and only reluctantly acceded to Philippa's appeal. The code of chivalry did not extend to civilians, but was intended for combatants. Edward could have put the burghers to death without damaging his chivalrous reputation.

He ordered that the castle of Calais be prepared for himself and the Queen. Then both "mounted their steeds and rode in a glorious procession of nobles into the town, which they entered with the sound of drums, trumpets and all sorts of warlike instruments."[13] The French ships were expelled from the harbor and replaced by English vessels. A great banquet was held to celebrate the victory, and Edward rewarded Philippa with a grant of houses in Calais. France now agreed to a truce.

Edward had reached the highest pinnacle of his fame. He enjoyed great popularity and renown in England and among the princes of Europe, who recognized his audacious vigor as a military commander. His subjects "thought that a new sun was rising over England, with peace abounding, the wealth of possessions and the glory of victory." Sluys, Crécy, and Calais would become three of the most famous triumphs in English history. Edward now had a foothold in France and had won international prestige for his kingdom. "He was the flower of this world's knighthood, for whom to do battle was to reign, to contend was to triumph."[14]

6

"Great Anguish of Heart"

✳

ACCORDING TO FROISSART, "THE KING REMAINED IN THE CAS-tle of Calais until the Queen was delivered of a daughter named Margaret," then "returned to England with the Queen and her child." But Margaret had been born the previous year at Windsor.

It is sometimes stated that in the summer of 1347, Philippa gave birth to a son called Thomas, although his existence has been disputed. Frois-sart mentioned her being "very near her lying-in" at the beginning of August, although Jean le Bel, on whose account his was based, did not refer to her pregnancy. Elsewhere, Froissart stated that "in her time, by King Edward, she had seven sons and five daughters": a dozen children, without Thomas, who was not among the twelve whose statues adorned Edward III's tomb. If Philippa gave birth in Calais, having conceived shortly after her arrival at the end of October, her child would have been born soon after August 7, which fits with Froissart's account. But her next baby was to be born on May 15, 1348, and would have been con-ceived between August 19 and 29, unless it was premature. A woman can get pregnant three weeks after giving birth, although most women do not start ovulating until six weeks later. Given this, it is fairly certain that Thomas never existed. Froissart either got his chronology wrong or de-liberately portrayed Philippa as heavily pregnant to underline the emo-tional impact and drama of her intercession.

* * *

After the death of the Emperor Louis IV on October 11, 1347, Edward III was offered the Imperial crown. The prospect caused Philippa great anxiety and sorrow, because she had learned from her sister of the challenges Louis had faced as emperor and feared that Edward could become embroiled in the tensions caused by the succession settlement in Hainault, foreseeing that the French might exploit the situation. Bowing to her wisdom, the King declined, and they returned to England, enduring a dreadful crossing, and landing at Sandwich on November 12. Three days later, they rode together through London, where Philippa received high acclaim for her intercession at Calais. Soon afterward, with the Black Prince, they visited the tomb of Edward II at Gloucester, where Edward offered a golden ship in thanksgiving for having reached England safely, while Philippa gave a golden heart.

She then began preparing for Princess Joan's wedding. Joan was now thirteen, "beautiful in body and abundant in moral virtues and grace."[1] She was to take with her to Castile a costly trousseau that included scarlet and purple saddles decorated with pearls, tapestries with a design of birds and roses, and a bridal gown made from 150 yards of Cyprus gold and silk.

The King and Queen kept Christmas 1347 at Guildford in lavish style, entertained by plays for which elaborate costumes were made, Edward himself appearing as a Saracen. On New Year's Day, the Black Prince gave his mother an emerald brooch with three balas rubies, and his father an enameled gold cup.

In January, Joan bade farewell to her parents at Mortlake and, attended by an honorable company, traveled to Plymouth, where, on March 21, she boarded a ship for Bordeaux. It was intended that she reside there until her wedding, which was to take place on November 1 in Bayonne Cathedral.

The order of knighthood Edward III finally founded in 1348 in honor of England's patron saint, St. George, and in emulation of King Arthur and his legendary knights, was called the Order of the Garter. The King chose twenty-six knights to receive it. "Their feast was to be held every year at Windsor on St. George's Day."[2] The first took place that year, establishing a tradition that has lasted until the present day. It became one of the greatest annual royal occasions, ranking with the Easter and Christmas festivities. Edward had already established a pattern of court ceremonial that underlined his majesty, proclaimed his magnificence, and provided his courtiers and subjects with an endless procession of fascinating spectacles. The Order of the Garter was his crowning glory. It was—and still is—the highest chivalric honor in England. The ceremony of investiture was usually held at Windsor, in St. George's Hall, which Edward rebuilt for the purpose.

In 1349, he admitted Queen Philippa and twenty-five other ladies to the Order of the Garter as "Dames of the Fraternity." Two years later, the Queen and her fellow dames received Garter robes from the royal wardrobe: russet gowns and hooded blue mantles embroidered with garters of blue and silver and the motto of the order.

It was probably on May 15, 1348, that Queen Philippa bore her sixth son, William, at Windsor. The chamber in which she gave birth was newly decorated with red sindon adorned with 16 pounds of gold leaf in the form of Ss and 600 large pearls; a small piece survives in the Victoria and Albert Museum. The chamber was furnished with a new bed draped in scarlet, twelve new carpets costing £60 ($47,650), and silver cups, bowls, and spoons. Prince William was provided with a state cradle, a "common cradle," and a bed of green taffeta embroidered with red roses and serpents, both symbols of Christ, as well as woolen mats and a dorser (an ornamental hanging), quilt, celure (a decorative canopy), curtains, and cushions, all of cloth of gold and silk.

For her "uprising," when Mass was celebrated on June 23, the King bought Philippa a splendid mantle, cape, tunic, and surcoat made from about 55 yards of indigo velvet and worked with gold birds (made from 13 pounds of gold plate) set within circles stitched with 400 large pearls, the ground being powdered with small pearls and 10,000 imitation jewels. These robes were lined with 2,000 pieces of miniver and 60 of ermine.

The next day, to celebrate the Queen's churching, Edward hosted a great tournament at Windsor, attended by David II and the English princes, who wore new suits of velvet. Philippa presided in a red silk velvet ensemble embroidered with oaks and other trees, each containing a lion formed of large pearls. That day, her eldest son presented her with a courser called Bauzan de Burgh.

These happy events were soon to be overshadowed by a new threat from overseas. Between 1347 and 1351, a pandemic of plague, later known as the Black Death, scythed its way through Europe, killing between two fifths and three quarters of the population—estimated at 25–50 million people. Originating in the Russian Steppes and spread by fleas on black rats, it was named after the black rash that appeared on the bodies of the afflicted. In his *Decameron* (1358), Giovanni Boccaccio described the dreaded symptoms: "It first betrayed itself by the emergence of certain tumours in the groin or arm-pits, some of which grew as large as an apple, after which the form of the malady began to change, black spots making their appearance in many cases on the arm or the thigh." The tumors and spots were "infallible tokens of approaching death" that could overtake the victim within hours. With alarming speed, "the fearful mortality rolled on, following the course of the sun into every part of the kingdom."[3] Few souls remained untouched by it, in one way or another.

The Black Death changed the world. Its impact was felt in every walk of life. Because it was seen as the judgment of God on sinful humanity, religious hysteria and fanaticism flourished and people began to question the old certainties of the universal faith preached by the Church. While acts of sacrilege became more commonplace, mysticism—with its emphasis on man's striving to attain unity with God—began to thrive, as people sought to find some meaning to the horrific mortality and a deeper understanding of the mysteries of faith. This obsession with death and suffering revealed itself in literature, poetry, art, and particularly in sculpture, with the appearance of cadaver tombs that had an effigy of the deceased in life above, and another depicting their rotting corpse below—a grisly reminder of the way of all flesh.

Decomposing bodies became a common sight. According to the Rochester chronicler, William Dene, "the plague carried off such multitudes that nobody could be found who would bear the corpses to the grave. Men and women carried their dead children and threw them into the common burial pits, the stench from which was so appalling that scarcely anyone dared to walk beside them." Sometimes there was no one to perform the funerary rites, for so many priests had died. Whole villages succumbed to the pestilence, and the buildings were left to decay and disappear. Law enforcement collapsed and there was a sharp decline in public morality, as many poor mortals—aware that death was stalking them—made the most of the time left to them, committing theft, murder, and fornication, unchecked by state or Church.

The royal family was not spared. On July 1, 1348, fifteen-year-old Princess Joan fell victim to the plague at the château of Lormont, which was owned by the archbishops of Bordeaux and stood just outside the city. Her escort had hastened her there on realizing that there was plague in Bordeaux. After her death, the Mayor of Bordeaux ordered that the château be burned to the ground.

The tragic news was broken to Joan's parents by John Kirkby, Bishop of Carlisle. They were devastated, but they remembered to reward those who had supported her in her last hours. Edward wrote to Alfonso XI of Castile, father of the bereaved bridegroom:

> Whilst we, with paternal affection, thought to have had an adopted son to our mutual comfort, behold—with what sobbing sighs and a heavy heart, we sorrowfully relate—death, terrible to all the kings of the Earth, which takes indifferently the poor and the powerful, the youth and the alluring virgin, with the aged man, without respect to person or power, has now, by a subversion of the wonted laws of mortality, removed from your hoped-for embraces, and from ours, our daughter, in whom all the gifts of Nature met; whom, also, as due to the elegance of her manners, we sincerely loved beyond our other children. Thus the bond of this adoption is broken by a dire mode of emancipation and a grievous sort of divorce. Whereat none can wonder that we are pierced by the shafts of sorrow. But, although our bowels of pity lead us to such groans and complainings, yet we give devout thanks to God, who gave her to us and has taken her away, that He has deigned to snatch her pure and immaculate, in the years of her innocence, from the miseries of this deceitful world, and to call her to Heaven, where, united to her celestial Spouse, forever to reign in the choir of virgins, her constant intercession may avail for us.[4]

There is neither record of Joan's body being returned to England, nor any account of her burial, although some sources mention her being buried in Bayonne Cathedral. Given that she had died in summer in a hot country and that the corpses of plague victims decomposed rapidly, she had probably been interred at Lormont, possibly in the church of Saint-Martin.

By August 1348, the Black Death had reached England, brought by homecoming troops to Dorset. From there, it spread rapidly, reaching London in November. The royal family had already immured themselves at Windsor with Edward's sister, Queen Joan. The devastation was appalling and far-reaching. It has been estimated that one third of England's population died. Aided by unsanitary conditions in towns and polluted water supplies, the "great mortality"[5] spread all over the land and there was no means of controlling it. Everywhere red crosses were painted on doors with the words "Lord, have mercy upon us."

In late summer, three-month-old Prince William of Windsor died at Brentford, Middlesex, too soon to have succumbed to the plague. Coming just weeks after Joan's death, his passing must have been a terrible blow to the King and Queen. The Issue Rolls for 1350 record that cloth of gold was purchased for covering his body, with 60 pennons of silk and gold, and 170 wax candles and torches, while 50s. ($1,990) was paid to fifty poor persons for carrying torches from Brentford to London "with the body of William, the King's son" and for watching over it; each was provided with a russet gown. The Prince was buried on September 5 in St. Edmund's Chapel in Westminster Abbey, next to his sister Blanche. The Great Wardrobe accounts for September 5, 1348, show that, on the day of the funeral, a joint tomb was ordered for them. In 1376, the King paid a mason, John Orchard, 20s. ($1,000) for a small monument of Purbeck marble and £12 ($9,400) for two alabaster effigies of the infants, each twenty inches long.

Archbishop Stratford perished in the pandemic, and his successor succumbed before he could be consecrated. Robert de Eglesfield, the Queen's chaplain, was another victim. In September, the truce with France had to be extended because of the devastation caused in both countries by the plague. There had been hopes of reaching a peace settlement, and Philip VI had proposed that Isabella and Jeanne of Evreux, the queen dowagers of England and France, act as "friends and mediators," suggesting that they meet at "a certain neutral place" between Calais and Boulogne to discuss terms.[6] Philip had the summit proclaimed, but Edward III was aware of his mother's poor reputation in France and feared that her involvement in the peace process would do his cause no good. Instead, he sent Henry of Grosmont, the new Earl (Duke from 1351) of Lancaster, while Philip abandoned the idea of sending Queen Jeanne and substituted Raoul IV, Count of Eu.

Edward and Philippa spent Christmas at the Archbishop of Canterbury's palace at Otford, Kent. Afterward, they kept a safe distance from London, visiting Guildford, Clarendon, Woodstock, Langley, and the West Country, where they stayed at Forde Abbey in Dorset. In July, Philippa was at Devizes Castle. October found her at Sheen, and in December she stayed with Edward at the ancient castle of the bishops of London at Orsett, Essex. They kept Christmas at her manor of Havering.

The "first pestilence" lasted in England until late 1349, although there would be further outbreaks. For centuries, plague would reappear in hot weather, in varying degrees of severity, culminating in the Great Plague of 1665. The outbreak of 1348–49 left in its wake a century of unrest and changed the social order in England forever. Never again would the old hierarchy be as stable. A severe shortage of manpower on the manors and farms left the services of the remaining peasants in high demand by the landed classes, and those peasants could name their price. They began to question the nature of feudal society and demand freedom from serfdom. In 1360, the tenants of the Abbot of Vale Royal's manor of Darnhall even sought the assistance of the King and Queen in the course of a long struggle to be released from bondage. This all sounded the death knell of feudalism, for no man wanted to remain in servitude to his lord when he could benefit from the free market the plague had created, and some lords found they had little choice but to release their serfs and pay for their services, knowing they would otherwise just abscond and sell their labor elsewhere.

Other lords refused to give in to their villeins' demands and Parliament intervened to reverse the trend, passing in 1351 the Statute of Labourers, which tried to impose maximum wages and minimum prices. "Many workmen and servants," it complained, "will not serve unless they receive excessive wages, and some are rather willing to beg in idleness than labour to get their living."[7] Hence every villein "shall serve the master requiring him or her." But it was too late: the tide of change had turned too far, and the law proved unenforceable. "The world goeth from bad to worse," grumbled the poet John Gower in 1375. "Labour is now at so high a price that he who will order his business aright must pay five or six shillings now for what cost two in former times."[8]

The late fourteenth century witnessed the emergence of the hired hand and the yeoman farmer who owned his own land. As capitalism gradually replaced feudalism, trade expanded and the middle classes came to enjoy ever greater prosperity and influence. In Parliament, the Commons increasingly made their voices heard, much to the dismay of conservative lords like John of Gaunt, who were determined to resist the relentless changes brought about by the new social order.

Early in 1350, Edward III and the Black Prince sailed to defend Calais, having received intelligence of a plot to return it to the French. During the fighting that followed, Edward was cornered and in danger of being captured, but the nineteen-year-old Prince led the Calais garrison to his rescue and helped to drive off the attackers. When the King and his son returned to England and were reunited with Queen Philippa, Edward said to her, "Lady dear, be pleased to entertain the Prince well, for I would have been taken by the enemy had it not been for his great valour." "He is welcome, and you also," she replied. "Now I can truly say that he was born in a good hour."[9]

That year, Philip VI died and was succeeded by his son, John II. The new King of France made no hostile move against Edward, but Pedro, the new King of Castile, the Princess Joan's former betrothed, had allied himself to France. His navy had committed "various acts of violence and plunder" against English shipping, and was now making "warlike preparations" that Edward was determined to counter. He went down to Winchelsea and "took up his quarters in an abbey overlooking the sea, to which the Queen herself accompanied him."[10] It is often stated that this was Battle Abbey, but that is not by the sea, so they probably stayed in the house of the Dominican friars on the south cliff at Winchelsea.

On August 29, Edward was waiting for the Castilians in his flagship off Winchelsea with his elder sons. It was ten-year-old John of Gaunt's first experience of warfare; he was too young to take part, but Froissart says his father had taken him along "because he much loved him." An anxious Philippa spent the whole day in the friary, praying fervently for the success and safety of her husband and sons.

Soon a great fleet was sighted. In the "fierce and bitter"[11] battle that followed, the King's ship was rammed by an enemy vessel and began to sink, and they were rescued only through the heroic intervention of Henry, Earl of Lancaster, and the Black Prince, with the King leaping to safety just as his ship sank. His fleet went on to repel the enemy, sinking fourteen vessels, and won the day.

When the Spanish had retreated, the English "sounded the trumpets and set their course towards England, reaching land at Rye and Winchel-sea a little after nightfall. At that same hour, the King and his sons and some of the barons disembarked, obtained horses in the town and rode with great rejoicing"[12] to the abbey where Philippa was waiting. "Then was the Queen glad at heart when she beheld her lord and her sons, see-ing that she had suffered great anguish of heart that day for fear of the Spaniards."[13]

She was told—"for she insisted on knowing the truth—how the Span-iards had more than forty great ships. Hence her relief when she saw her husband and sons again. The knights and the barons were honourably received and there was dancing, feasting and revelling; the time passed happily and there was love and nobleness, gaiety and prowess to be found there."[14] Philippa and her ladies "passed all that night in great revel, de-vising of arms and of love."[15]

In the autumn of 1351, Princess Isabella announced that she wished to marry Bernard d'Albret, the son of the King's lieutenant in Gascony. He was no equal match for her, but Edward agreed to the betrothal, wishing to keep the powerful Albrets on his side. With the wedding planned and the costly trousseau ready, Isabella departed for Bordeaux, but then sud-denly decided that she didn't want to wed Bernard, called it off, and came home. Edward was left seriously out of pocket, but his indulgent re-sponse was to grant her an annuity of 1,000 marks ($636,000), while her jilted bridegroom disappeared into a monastery. Philippa was much of-fended by her eldest daughter's conduct, which prolonged the rift be-tween them.

When, that same year, Paon de Roët left England to serve Margaret, Countess of Hainault, as the Knight Master of her household, he probably left his infant daughters in the care of the kindly Queen Philippa. The likelihood is that Philippa, grateful for his years of faithful service, offered or agreed to make them her wards, educate them, and find them husbands. Katherine and Philippa joined the other nobly or royally born children who were being brought up by the Queen, among them the fair Blanche, the younger daughter of Henry of Grosmont, Earl of Lancaster.

The Countess Margaret's position was by no means secure. In 1350, under pressure from her son William, she had renounced her claims to Holland, Zeeland, and Friesland in his favor, in the hope of retaining Hainault for herself, but, in the spring of 1351, William had seized control of it. Attempts at negotiation failed, and all four provinces became embroiled in the conflict, which escalated into a war between mother and son. In December 1351, hoping to enlist the support of Edward III, Margaret fled to England.

Edward gave aid to her and—perhaps at the suggestion of Queen Philippa—offered William his cousin Matilda, one of the two co-heiresses of Henry, Duke of Lancaster, as a bride. A settlement was quickly reached that allowed Margaret to keep Hainault. In February 1352, William came to England to be married to Matilda in St. Stephen's Chapel at Westminster.

In March, Queen Philippa's mother died, and was buried at the abbey of Fontenelle.

7

"Protection Against
the Attacks of the Devil"

✳

THAT QUEEN ISABELLA STILL HELD CONSIDERABLE INFLUENCE over the King was made clear in January 1354, when Charles II, King of Navarre, was seeking the protection of John II after having murdered the Constable of France. He also appealed in writing to the Duke of Lancaster, who diplomatically replied that he was too busy to be of assistance, but had forwarded copies of Charles's letter to the King, the Black Prince, the Queen, and the Queen Mother, and was waiting to hear from them. Whether Isabella was instrumental in persuading Edward to back Charles is not known, but he did so, violating the terms of a recent peace he had negotiated with King John, which would lead to the reopening of the war. Isabella made another of her few ventures into politics in May, when, at the request of the Pope, she pleaded with Edward to release Charles I, Duke of Brittany, whom he was holding hostage.

That year, Edward had the sentence on Mortimer reversed, on the grounds that the latter had been prevented from speaking in his own defense, and restored his grandson and namesake to the earldom of March. Isabella's thoughts on this are not recorded. In 1368, this Roger, who had been one of the luminaries of the court since 1350, would marry the King's granddaughter, Philippa of Clarence. Thirty years later, their grandson, Roger, the fourth Earl, would be acknowledged as heir to the throne. His descendants founded the royal house of York, which would rule England from 1461 to 1485.

Edward and Philippa kept the Christmas of 1354 at the castle of the Earl Marshal, the King's cousin Margaret (daughter of Thomas, Earl of Norfolk), at Hamstead Marshall in Berkshire, while Isabella was the guest of her grandson, the Black Prince, at Berkhamsted Castle. In many ways he was like her—good-looking, dynamic, intelligent, and ruthless—and evidently they were close.

In the spring, she received the sad news that her daughter Eleanor, Duchess of Guelders, had died in poverty at the age of thirty-seven. Eleanor had helped to rule the duchy during the minority of her quarrelsome eldest son, but on reaching his majority, he had made it clear that he resented her interference and confiscated all her property, something Isabella had experienced herself. For Eleanor, though, there had been no restitution: she had lived out her remaining years in a Cistercian abbey, too proud to beg for assistance from her brother, Edward III. Now only two of Isabella's children remained.

She would have found comfort in her eight surviving grandchildren. Thomas, the last of Philippa's large brood, had been born on January 7, 1355, at Woodstock, after a gap of more than six years. Philippa was now forty-three, and this was the second occasion on which the King had asked Westminster Abbey to lend her their sacred relic, the girdle of the Blessed Virgin, to wear during her confinement; she had first worn it at Lionel's birth. It was believed to be efficacious in relieving pain and ensuring a safe delivery. On February 22, the Queen was churched. A celebratory feast was held, and a great tournament proclaimed throughout the land. Edward doted on this youngest child and spent lavishly on clothes for him, while Philippa had him in her charge until he was eleven. When the King visited Calais and France in October and November 1355, the infant Thomas was nominal regent. He remained with his nurse, Christian de Enfield, while the government functioned in his name.

One worthy guest at the tournament was a Gascon, Jean de Grailly, Captal de Buch, whom Chandos Herald described as "a valiant and noble man, very bold and brave, and popular with everyone. He was given a noble welcome and the [Black] Prince was very glad of his arrival. One day, he said to the King his father and the Queen his mother, 'Sire, you know how many noble knights in Gascony are your friends, and how they fight hard on your behalf, but have no captain of your blood. If your advisers thought fit to send one of your sons, they would be all the bolder.' So the King summoned Parliament, who agreed to send the [Black] Prince to Gascony" as the King's lieutenant.

"Two months later, the Prince took leave of the King and Queen and all his brothers and sisters. There was sorrow in their hearts when it came to his departure, and ladies and girls were to be seen weeping for their husbands and brothers." But "the Prince took his leave with joyful heart"[1] and battled storms at sea to reach Bordeaux with his army of 6,000. He made several raids in the region between Bordeaux and Narbonne and within three months had taken many towns.

On June 23, 1356, Philippa's sister, Margaret II of Hainault, died of tuberculosis and was succeeded by her son William. He did not enjoy his new domain for long. Two years later, he became insane, never to recover, and his younger brother, Albert I, Duke of Bavaria, stood in as regent. Edward III continued to press Philippa's claim to Hainault, but without success. He did not relinquish it until 1371.

While Edward's attention was elsewhere, the French plotted an attack on England, but they had not bargained on the Black Prince, who was lying in wait for them just outside Poitiers. There, on September 19, 1356, he exhorted his army: "Let us do our utmost this day, in the name of God and St. George, and acquit ourselves as all good knights should."[2] Once more he distinguished himself in battle, winning a great victory and taking the King of France prisoner—the greatest prize of all, and likely to command a huge ransom. He also captured the great chevalier Bertrand du Guesclin. A two-year truce was then agreed.

"The King and Queen were delighted with the news sent them by the Prince and gave thanks to God; and they sent ships to Bordeaux and the Prince brought King John and the other prisoners to England." Edward hastened to receive his son, who received a tumultuous welcome when he entered Westminster Hall with his illustrious prisoner, who was the Queen's first cousin. Edward, Philippa, and Isabella were present with "many ladies and many lovely, gay and loving girls. They danced, hunted, hawked, jousted and feasted." Everywhere the Black Prince was acclaimed as England's hero, and "the noble Queen praised God and the Virgin because they had given her such a noble son."[3] She is said to have given 50,000 crowns ($5 million) toward the ransom of his "gallant" prisoner,

Bertrand du Guesclin. "For," she said, "though an enemy to my husband, a knight who is famed for the courteous protection he has afforded to my sex deserves the assistance of every woman."

Du Guesclin replied, "Ah, lady, being the ugliest knight in France, I never reckoned on any goodness from your sex, but your beauty will make me think less despicably of myself."[4] Some historians have dismissed the tale as a fiction.

Edward now held captive his two great enemies, the kings of France and Scotland. For the next four years, John II was housed in the palatial Ely Place at Holborn and treated as an honored guest while he negotiated the terms of his release. He lived in considerable state, as was fitting for a monarch, and enjoyed a degree of freedom. Because it was unthinkable that an honorable and chivalrous monarch might try to escape, he was allowed to travel, and often visited the King and Queen at Windsor and his cousin Isabella at Hertford Castle. He and Isabella struck up a rapport; he sent her messages and lent her manuscripts, while she sent him two books about Lancelot and the Holy Grail. Isabella's increasing political influence may have encouraged her to intercede with Edward on John's behalf, and it is likely that she ultimately helped the two kings to reach a settlement.

In 1357, after eleven years of captivity, David II was finally freed and allowed to return to Scotland. Queen Joan accompanied him, but when she found out that he was making up for lost time with another woman, she returned to England for good on the pretext of discussing peace terms with her brother. Edward again permitted her to use Hertford Castle as a residence, and Isabella paid for her clothes and food. As before, she and Philippa were frequent visitors.

Squabbles over the payment of the ransom money continued well after David had returned to Scotland and, in 1358, he asked Isabella to act as mediatrix with Edward. Clearly she was respected for her political acumen; old memories having faded, she was now regarded as a kind of elder stateswoman.

In October 1357, Isabella and Joan made a pilgrimage to Canterbury, after which Isabella traveled to London, where she entertained Philippa and the Black Prince to dinner at her house in Lombard Street. Over the following two months, she received several members of King John's train there. She kept a lavish Christmas in London, while Edward and Philippa celebrated it at Marlborough, then traveled to Bristol Castle for Epiphany, where they attended the first English tournament to be held in the evening, lit by torches.

In 1356, Isabella, now sixty-one, had been busy supervising renovations at her manor of Sheen, Surrey, apparently as fit and active as ever. In 1357, the burghers of Lynn sent their last recorded gift to her, a pipe of wine. Her household book for the year 1357–58, the last of three to survive, shows that she continued to enjoy a pleasant existence with many diversions. She took an interest in domestic and public affairs, and corresponded frequently with the King, the Queen, Queen Joan, King John, the Duke of Lancaster, the Chancellor, and the Earl Marshal. At New Year 1358, they all gave her gifts; at other times, they sent her Bordeaux wine, boars' heads, barrels of bream, and copper quadrants (navigational instruments for measuring circles), suggesting that she had developed an interest in astronomy or geometry; she is known to have studied astrology. Edward sent his mother Gascon wine, a falcon, caged birds, and a wild boar. She took alchemical draughts, including a potion called the *elixir vitae*, which was believed to confer eternal youth, cure all diseases, and prolong life indefinitely. It was closely associated with the legendary philosopher's stone that supposedly turned base metals into gold.

In February 1358, Isabella was involved in communications about King John's ransom, despite feeling unwell. Messengers were sent to London and St. Albans for medicines, and her surgeon, Master Lawrence, was summoned. She rallied, though, and may have had a hand in shaping the peace treaty that would be concluded in 1360 between King Edward and King John.

In April, one of the French envoys, the Count of Tancarville, stayed with her in London. On April 19, she dined with the Chancellor and the Treasurer, then went on to meet the King and Queen. That month, she wore a gown of silver encrusted with 300 rubies and 1,800 pearls, and jewels worth £421 ($283,500), to the Garter feast at Windsor, which was attended by the King and Queen, King David, Queen Joan, King John, and his son Philip, the future Duke of Burgundy. A magnificent tournament followed, in which many foreign knights took part. Philippa also made a brave show, having been given £500 ($337,000) for apparel. The feast marked the completion of Edward's new college in the great court at Windsor, which was to be the home of the Order of the Garter. This was to prove Isabella's last public appearance.

On May 10, Philippa wrote to inform her that the treaty with France had been concluded. Isabella was so thrilled that she rewarded the messenger with ten crowns ($2,290). The next day, the two queens dined together to celebrate the peace, and on May 13, Isabella played host to King John.

She was still following fashion, decking herself out as befitted a queen and using cosmetics. In 1358 alone, she spent £1,400 ($943,000) on jewelry. An inventory of her possessions taken after her death lists hundreds of jewels—rings, crosses, charms, a cameo edged in gold with an image of St. John, an initial brooch in the shape of a Y, "one red velvet girdle with silver-gilt ornaments," and "a large brooch containing a thousand pearls."[5] It also lists large quantities of gold and silver plate: 115 plates, 47 salt cellars, beakers, ewers, basins, covered cups, dishes, large vases, 4 spoons set with jewels, 6 silver-gilt forks, a cup of beryl, one of green, and a jar of jasper. Among her furnishings were hangings for the hall "powdered with dolphins," others of tawny silk furred with miniver, silk curtains, velvet cushions, "carpets wrought with gold and silver stars," a canopy of estate of crimson satin, and beds of silk and velvet, richly embroidered and trimmed with furs. There were paintings too, among them "three panels of Lombardy work."

In Isabella's chapel, the altar frontal was of cloth of gold embroidered with the arms of England and France. The crucifix was of crystal set with gems, the tabernacle of silver-gilt and enamel, encrusted with precious stones. Her chapel furnishings included gorgeous vestments of red velvet "powdered with golden trefoils and goldsmiths' work of blue enamel with gold lilies."[6]

Isabella received visitors two or three times a day: the King, who came four times in the last months of her life; the Black Prince and his brothers, John and Lionel; Princess Isabella; French lords who were in England to see King John; and William, Earl of Douglas, one of the hostages for King David's ransom, who was making frequent visits to Westminster to negotiate a peace treaty. He was the grandson of that same Black Douglas who had twice attempted to abduct the young Isabella. Other frequent visitors were Elizabeth de Clare, Edward II's niece and the foundress of Clare Hall in Cambridge; Isabella's cousin and long-standing friend,

Marie de Châtillon, Dowager Countess of Pembroke, to whom she gave a breviary in 1357; Mortimer's daughter Agnes, the widow of Laurence Hastings, Earl of Pembroke; and his grandson and namesake, the second Earl of March, now a successful courtier in his early thirties, who was married to Salisbury's daughter Philippa.

Now in her sixties, Isabella was preparing herself for death, as pious persons often did in that age. She undertook many charitable works, maintaining poor scholars at Oxford, distributing alms to 150 selected paupers on holy days and the principal feasts of the Church, and paying for needy persons to be fed daily. She had always been a great patron of the Franciscans, and it was at this time that she took the gray habit of the Third (or Tertiary) Order of St. Francis, which she wore under her outer robes. This lay branch of the Franciscans had been founded twenty years earlier, chiefly for penitents who wished to remain in the world; its members were not bound by conventual vows, but by a requirement to maintain Franciscan observances and principles in their daily lives. In joining this order, Isabella was demonstrating that she wished to make reparation for her past transgressions.

She desired to be buried in Greyfriars church at Newgate, of which she had been so generous a benefactress; in recent years, she had donated £700 ($471,400) toward building works there. Two of her chaplains and one of her maids were buried in the church. The Westminster monk, John of Reading, claimed that the Queen had been "seduced" by the Grey Friars to change her will and leave her bones among them, after allegedly expressing a wish to be laid to rest at Westminster. The fact that the community of Westminster wanted her at all and considered her worthy of interment in their royal mausoleum is proof of how thoroughly she had redeemed her reputation.

Yet her burial at Greyfriars would add grist to the mill of the rumor-mongers. In the sixteenth century, the antiquarian John Stow listed the ruined royal tombs in the church and perpetrated the myth that Roger Mortimer's was among them. Thus another myth about Isabella gained currency: that she chose to be buried near her lover. That myth can be disposed of, for it is almost certain that Mortimer was buried at Coventry.

In June 1358, now approaching sixty-three, Isabella made a pilgrimage to Canterbury, taking Joan and her physician, Master Lawrence, with her. Shortly beforehand, she had donated £2 ($1,350) to the Minoresses' convent at Aldgate to buy food for the community on the anniversaries of the deaths of Edward II and John of Eltham.

Mother and daughter stayed at Leeds Castle from June 13 to July 2. There, Isabella became unwell after overdosing on a potent medicine. The King visited her at Hertford Castle on July 12; it was the last time they would be together. On August 1, a London apothecary was paid for spices and ointments for Isabella, and, on the 12th, messengers were dispatched to London for medicines.

On August 20, her condition was causing sufficient concern for Master Lawrence and an eminent London doctor to be summoned to Hertford "with the greatest haste." But they could do nothing for her. She died on August 22, with Joan present.

By September 19, the Black Prince had taken possession of some of Isabella's estates, as she had wished. She had left him most of her personal effects, as well as a quarter share of the customs dues of Lynn. Hertford Castle went to John of Gaunt, while the rest of the old Queen's lands, worth £2,000 ($1.2 million) annually, went mainly to Queen Philippa. She had willed some of her books, among them a Bible, an Apocalypse, and a psalter, to Joan.

Isabella was to have "a sumptuous funeral."[7] According to her wish, her embalmed corpse was wrapped in her wedding mantle, which she had preserved for half a century (an indication that her late husband was in the forefront of her mind during her final months), and a Franciscan habit, "as a protection against the attacks of the Devil."[8] She lay in the chapel at Hertford Castle until November 23, watched over by fourteen poor persons, who were paid 2d. ($5) a day by the King. John Gynwell, Bishop of Lincoln, the Abbot of Waltham, and the Prior of Coventry all celebrated requiem Masses in the chapel.

On November 21, Edward commanded the sheriffs of London to clean the streets of dirt and strew gravel along Bishopsgate and Aldgate "against the coming of the body of his dearest mother, Queen Isabella," and gave them £9 ($6,700) to cover the cost. Isabella was being brought south with great solemnity from Hertford. Prior to the funeral, she lay at Mile End, in the house of John Galeys, where the King and his household stayed.

On November 27, her coffin was carried in procession through London, followed by the Black Prince, as chief mourner, "all the prelates and barons of England, those French lords who were at that time detained in England as hostages,"[9] a host of dignitaries, and the paupers who were praying for the Queen's soul. Forty torch-bearers lit the way.

The entire royal family attended the funeral at Greyfriars, which was conducted by Simon Islip, Archbishop of Canterbury. Isabella was laid to rest in the choir, where the tomb of her aunt, Marguerite of France, lay further to the east, before the altar. The King founded various chantries so that intercessions could be made for her safe passage to heaven.

In 1323 and 1345, Isabella had obtained Papal permission for her remains to be buried in three separate places, like Eleanor of Castile's had been. It is possible that her heart is buried beneath the simple gray stone inscribed *ISABELLA REGINA* in the Norman parish church dedicated to St. Lawrence at Castle Rising, but there is no record of any visceral burial. At her request, Edward II's heart in its silver casket was placed in her coffin, on her breast.

Edward III saw that Isabella's servants were rewarded after her death. Later, when the great middle window of the friars' church blew in, he paid for it to be replaced "for the repose of the soul of his dearest mother, the most illustrious Queen Isabella."[10] He paid for torches to be lit at her tomb on the anniversary of her death, and every year until his own passing, he solemnly observed her obit with prayers, intercessions, and the placing of palls on the monument. In accordance with her instructions (for she had planned her own memorial), a beautiful marble tomb and alabaster effigy were raised to her memory. The tomb was, unusually, the work of a female sculptor, Agnes de Ramsey, who had taken over her father's workshop, and Isabella had paid her £106.18s.11d. ($72,000) for it shortly before her death. In 1362, Isabella's daughter Joan was buried near her mother at Greyfriars. Twenty years later, the body of Isabella's granddaughter and namesake was also laid to rest there.

The magnificent monastery of the Grey Friars, a royal mausoleum set to rival Westminster Abbey as the resting place of crowned heads, was dissolved by Henry VIII in 1538 and the tombs in the church despoiled, the bones being reinterred in the common burial ground. By 1566, Sir Martin Bowes, Lord Mayor of London, had sold off what remained of the monuments of nine royal personages. Nothing is known of what became of them.

The church was destroyed in the Great Fire of 1666 and afterward rebuilt by Sir Christopher Wren as Christ Church. Wren's church was devastated during the Blitz and only ruins survive today. The site of the convent is now occupied by a small park, a building owned by the Post Office, and a busy main road. Somewhere here lies the dust of a long-dead queen.

History has been unkind to Isabella. For centuries she has been condemned for her adultery, her cruelty, her misgovernment, and her connivance in a murder that may never have taken place. She is the femme fatale of the English monarchy.

Yet she is deserving of pity for the impossible situation in which she found herself, and admiration for the way in which she dealt with it. The removal of Edward II had become a political imperative, and to achieve it, she brought about the first constitutional deposition by Parliament of an English king, setting a precedent for those of Richard II, Henry VI, Edward IV, Edward V, and Charles I. Her importance in the history of Britain is significant, for the process instigated by her in 1326–27 set in motion a political trend that would lead directly to the decline of monarchical power and the eventual emergence of democracy, a development that she herself, the daughter of Philip IV, would doubtless have been horrified to contemplate.

Isabella's dynastic importance cannot be overstated, for she transmitted her claim to France to Edward III and encouraged him to pursue it. Her downfall lay in her association with Mortimer, her greed, and the unpopular policies of their increasingly tyrannical regime. She has been more vilified than any other English queen. In her own lifetime, Baker called her "that harridan," "that virago," and "Jezebel." Other chroniclers were equally disapproving.

Shakespeare had invented the epithet "She-Wolf of France" for Margaret of Anjou, the martial wife of Henry VI, but in the eighteenth century, when England was at war with France, the poet Thomas Gray applied it to Isabella, and it has stuck ever since. In *The Bard* (1757), he speaks, with horrific significance, of the "She-Wolf of France, with unrelenting fangs, that tear'st the bowels of thy mangled mate."

In the nineteenth century, Agnes Strickland claimed that no Queen of England had "left so dark a stain on the annals of female royalty as Isabella." She was "the only instance of a queen of England acting in open and shameless violation of the duties of her high vocation, allying herself with traitors and foreign agitators against her king and husband, and staining her name with the combined crimes of treason, adultery, murder and regicide."

Even modern historians have had little that is good to say about her. In 1955, V. H. H. Green called her "a woman of no real importance or attraction," while in 1967, Kenneth Fowler denigrated her as "a woman of evil character, a notorious schemer" who was infamous "for her marital inconstancy," although he conceded that this was "in part excused by her husband's weaknesses." Elsewhere, Isabella is "one of the most beautiful but depraved women of her time," or simply "Isabella the Mad."

While contemporaries came to deplore her politics and rapacity, and her being in thrall to Mortimer, later commentators focused on her sexual misconduct. Her adultery subverted conventional ideals of queenship, which demanded that the King's wife be beyond reproach; and it also desecrated the sanctity of monarchy. Many have thought her guilty of regicide, but even if Edward II was murdered, there is no evidence that she was a party to it. What comes across most strongly in her story is that she was a model medieval queen who was forced to employ initiative and cunning to extricate herself from circumstances that had become intolerable.

8

"The Purest Ladies on Earth"

⁕

IN THE LATE SUMMER OF 1358, THE KING AND QUEEN STAYED AT Marlborough, then moved to Cosham, near Portsmouth. While hunting there on September 16, Philippa fell from her horse and broke her shoulder blade. Fractures of the scapula are rare and happen as a result of considerable impact, so she must have fallen hard. This type of injury can cause great pain and internal damage to the nerves, ribs, chest, or lungs, which may have been the case with Philippa, for she did not accompany Edward to France that year. It has been asserted that she never rode a horse again, but in 1360, she and Edward jointly employed thirty-one huntsmen and twenty-three falconers, and they are known to have hunted on progress in 1362, so she perhaps did recover to a degree, although it seems likely that the fall had some after-effects.

"There was no Christian king had such sons fine" as Edward III. "So high and large they were all of stature, the least of them was of person able to have fought with any creature [in] single battle in acts remarkable."[1] Edward's need to provide for his sons saw him pursuing a successful policy of creating them dukes and marrying them to English heiresses, thus securing lands and titles for them without impoverishing the Crown, and thereby binding the royal family by ties of blood, loyalty, and shared interests to the chief magnates of his realm, and pre-empting the baronial unrest that had been the bane of earlier kings.

Edward's fourth son, John of Gaunt, a tall, lean young man of dignified bearing, was proud and ambitious. From his youth, he had "most faithfully paid tribute as a devotee to love, most unrestrainedly, and joyfully become his thrall, with willing body, heart and all," and carried on in this fashion "for ages, many and many a year," with "lightness" and "wayward thoughts."[2] Sometime in the late 1350s, he had an affair with one of his mother's damsels, Marie de Saint-Hilaire, who may have been a native of Hainault. In 1359, she bore him a daughter, Blanche, who was to marry Sir Thomas Morieux, Constable of the Tower.

That year, Gaunt found love in the marriage that had been arranged for him. Blanche, the younger daughter of Henry, Duke of Lancaster, was one of the greatest co-heiresses in England, and Edward was determined to secure for Gaunt her share of the rich Lancaster patrimony. In January 1359, Pope Innocent VI had granted a dispensation allowing the young couple to wed (they were within the forbidden degrees of consanguinity) and, on May 19, they were married at Reading Abbey, with Thomas de Chynham, clerk of the Queen's Chapel, officiating and the whole royal family in attendance. It was a double wedding, the other couple being John's twelve-year-old sister Margaret and John Hastings, Earl of Pembroke, her childhood sweetheart, who had been raised in the royal household. The ceremony was followed by six days of celebrations and jousts in Reading and Smithfield. In one tournament, the King and his four eldest sons took part, appearing incognito as "mysterious knights" before they revealed themselves to the delighted citizens.

John of Gaunt's marriage was a happy one, producing eight children in nine years. Froissart thought Philippa and Blanche unsurpassable, the purest ladies on earth. "I never saw two such noble dames, so good, liberal and courteous, nor ever shall, were I to live a thousand years." According to *The Book of the Duchess*, which was written by her admirer, the poet Geoffrey Chaucer, Blanche was "good, fair and white," "gay and glad, fresh and sportive, sweet, simple and humble."

When Henry, Duke of Lancaster, died in 1361, during the second outbreak of the Black Death, he left Blanche and her sister Matilda as his co-heiresses. Matilda died in April 1362, whereupon the vast Lancaster estates passed in their entirety to John of Gaunt, who was created duke of Lancaster that year, becoming the wealthiest and most powerful magnate in the kingdom. The Duchy of Lancaster was a palatinate, which meant that it was virtually an independent state in which the king's writ counted for very little.

The new Duke of Lancaster—who will be referred to henceforth as John of Gaunt, to distinguish him from his predecessors—maintained an impressive establishment modeled on the royal household and a retinue of 500 persons. His vast estates were scattered throughout England and France, and he could summon a formidable army of tenants at will. His chief residences were his London palace of the Savoy, which rivaled Westminster in magnificence (but was burned down during the Peasants' Revolt of 1381), and Kenilworth Castle in Warwickshire. The latter is now a ruin, but John of Gaunt's magnificent banqueting hall with its huge, elegant windows remains.

He loved ceremony and, like most of his class, held to the laws of chivalry as if they were a second religion. He was a cultivated man who loved books, patronized Chaucer, and enjoyed jousting. Proud and reserved, he rarely exacted revenge for wrongs done to him, and looked after his tenants. When dealing with rebellious peasants after the revolt, he acted with fairness. But although he fought many campaigns, he never achieved any significant military success, and thus remained very much in the shadow of his father and eldest brother, never enjoying, as they did, the status of public hero.

In 1359, Edward ordered extensive works at Windsor under the supervision of William of Wykeham, Bishop of Winchester, and he and Philippa moved temporarily into the new timber-framed royal apartments the King had ordered him to create within the Round Tower. These they used while an extensive building program went on around them, until their lodgings were completed. The new range Wykeham designed for the Queen was completed first, around 1363. It extended along the north front of the Upper Ward and included a guard chamber, an outer chamber in a tower, an 85-foot-long great chamber (now the Garter Throne Room and Garter Ante Room) with four images of the Evangelists on its walls, a vast dancing (or "revelling") chamber measuring about 80 feet by 33, a hall with 115 mirrors fixed to its ceiling, a second chamber (perhaps a dining chamber, given that it had a cupboard or buffet) with a small attached chapel, a bedchamber, and a little cloister paved with marble that overlooked a fragrant herb garden. Philippa's rooms were probably covered in painted decorations and amply furnished with tables, benches, trestles, and stools.

On November 29, 1359, the King and Queen sailed to France with all their sons except Thomas, who was left behind as guardian of the realm. John of Gaunt had begun campaigning in France in October 1359, having left Blanche four months pregnant. "Out of the concern that we feel for her condition,"[3] Edward III had initially arranged for her to stay with the Queen until her confinement, but with Philippa away in France, Blanche retired to Leicester Castle, where, in March 1360, she gave birth to a daughter named Philippa in honor of the Queen, who was probably her godmother and who paid the expenses of her daughter-in-law's ceremonial uprising from childbed, which preceded her churching.

Edward's winter campaign in France ended in disaster on Easter Monday 1360, when a freak hailstorm amid violent winds killed 1,000 men and 6,000 horses, more than in any battle of the war. "It seemed as if the world was coming to an end. The hailstones were so large as to kill men and beasts, and the boldest were frightened."[4] The King saw this "Black Monday" as divine punishment for his raids in France, as did the French, who were so traumatized by the storm that they sued for peace soon afterward. This led, in May, to the signing of the Treaty of Brétigny, under the terms of which Edward renounced his claim to France and returned some of the lands he had conquered in exchange for full sovereignty of Gascony, Montreuil, Ponthieu, Calais, and Guisnes. King John II was to be ransomed for four million gold crowns (nearly $3.6 billion) and arrangements were made for him to return home, accompanied by the Black Prince, with whom he was now good friends. Edward and Philippa returned to England on May 18, landing at Rye.

On June 30, King John was Philippa's dinner guest at Eltham. That autumn, Edward escorted him to London, where he was received by the Queen, the Black Prince, and John of Gaunt "with all possible splendour. Feasting and open court continued for a fortnight."[5] He was given new regal robes, and on October 9, the royal family accompanied him to Dover, where the two kings took ship for Calais. There, the treaty was ratified. The peace was not popular; the King's subjects saw it as shameful.

Edward returned to England in November, and he and Philippa spent

Christmas at Woodstock with their children and Queen Joan. For this occasion, the King bought them all "marbled" (mottled) robes; Philippa's were lined with miniver and adorned with 106 pieces of ermine.

In 1361, young Jean Froissart, the future renowned chronicler, visited England and presented Philippa with an account in verse of the war with France, which is now lost but would later be expanded into his famous chronicles. The Queen was impressed by her fellow countryman, who, like herself, had been born in Valenciennes. She "received it gladly and graciously and rewarded me well," he recalled. Sensing a sadness in him, she pressed him to confide in her and listened kindly to his woeful tale of how he had fallen in love with a young lady, only to discover that she was promised to another. He had lain ill for three months, with his life despaired of, and had then come to England to forget her. Philippa sympathized. She gave him money, clothes, and horses and made him return to Hainault and press his suit more ardently.

Froissart took her advice, hoping that the acquisition of royal patronage would win back his lady. But she rejected him, and he returned, despondent, to England. The kindly Philippa appointed him a clerk of her chamber, gave him lodgings at court, and became his patron. He recalled: "The good Queen Philippa was, in my youth, my Queen and sovereign. I was five years at the court of the King and Queen of England, in whom I found all nobleness, honour, largesse and courtesy." He acted as their "clerk and servant" and spent his time "serving [Philippa] with fair ditties and treatises of love," one of which was La Cour de May, which had been composed in 1356 and was later dedicated in her honor.

Wishing to have the illustrious deeds of her husband and sons recorded, the Queen shared with Froissart her own firsthand reminiscences for his chronicles, and gave him the wherewithal to travel around England in search of material for them and for Meliador, his long verse romance. Once, she sent him to Scotland with letters of credence stating that he was one of her secretaries. Wherever he went, he found that, for love of "that noble and valiant lady," he received a warm welcome. Gradually he became an important literary figure at court and his fame spread.

* * *

In 1361, to help guard the Kent coast against French incursions, Edward began building a castle and town at Bynne on the Isle of Sheppey. In 1367, he named both Queenborough for Queen Philippa, of whose dower Bynne formed a part, and the town was made a free borough in her honor. An inn there was also named after her. John of Gaunt was appointed constable of the castle, which had royal lodgings where Edward sometimes stayed, although there is no record of Philippa visiting. In 1382, the castle would be severely damaged by an earthquake, and nothing remains today.

At Woodstock, on July 3, 1361, the Princess Mary, now seventeen, married John IV, Duke of Brittany, who had grown up in Edward III's household and endeared himself to Philippa with his fine singing voice. The bridal gown was made of cloth of gold from Lucca and baudekin (silk) furred with miniver and ermine. On October 1, Garter robes were issued to Mary and her sister Margaret, but between then and Christmas, death claimed them both. Margaret, who loved romances and wrote poetry, possibly died in childbed, aged just fifteen, or both girls perhaps succumbed to the "Second Pestilence" of 1361–62. In 1368, their grieving parents would pay £100 ($66,000) for two tombs in Abingdon Abbey. The loss of their youngest daughters must have been devastating and in September 1361, they faced another, not so final, separation when Lionel departed for Ireland to rule as his father's lieutenant.

That autumn saw the public marriage of the Black Prince to his cousin Joan, the "Fair Maid of Kent," the daughter of Edmund, Earl of Kent, who had been executed in 1330, and granddaughter of Edward I and Marguerite of France. Joan was "beautiful, pleasing and wise"[6] and "the most beautiful lady in all the realm, and the most loved, famous for the extravagance of her dress."[7] But she had a complicated marital history. As a child, she had been precontracted to Sir Thomas Holland, a favorite of the King and Queen. While he was fighting abroad, William de Montagu (the future second Earl of Salisbury) married her, but when Joan reached marriageable age, Holland abducted her and had her union with Salisbury annulled. Then he married her himself, and they had five children.

After Holland died in 1360, the Black Prince fell in love with Joan and wed her in secret. Froissart called it a love match, and Chandos Herald stated that "Joan kindled love" in Edward, which is borne out by a letter in which he addressed her as "my dearest and truest sweetheart and beloved companion."[8] They had known each other from childhood, for Joan had been brought up in the Queen's household. Back in 1348, the Black Prince had given his cousin "Jeanette" a silver beaker; the nickname suggests a long familiarity between them. But both knew that in view of Joan's past forays into wedlock, she might not be considered a suitable bride for the heir to the throne. Besides, they were cousins, related within the forbidden degrees of affinity.

The marriage surprised many people. It was astonishing for the Black Prince, the most desirable catch in Europe, to marry for love, and gain no political or material advantage from it. Joan had a husband still living; she was thirty-three and her childbearing days might be behind her. Edward and Philippa evidently had reservations, for the marriage was promptly declared invalid and the Pope required the couple to do penance before the requisite dispensation was granted and their union could be properly solemnized.

Their public wedding took place on October 10 in the magnificent new chapel dedicated to St. George that Edward III was building on the site of Henry III's chapel at Windsor, in the presence of the King and Queen and their children, with the Archbishop of Canterbury officiating. The bride wore a gown of red cloth of gold embroidered with birds. Soon afterward, the Black Prince built the chapel of Our Lady Undercroft in thanksgiving for the Papal dispensation.

The royal family spent Christmas at Berkhamsted Castle as guests of the Prince and his bride. Philippa wore an outfit of fine marbled longcloth of Brussels lined with miniver and trimmed with 106 pieces of ermine. She and Joan would exchange gifts of clothing, including a laced corset of red velvet, which the Queen gave her daughter-in-law. Joan, who was now the second lady in the land, proved to be a model princess of Wales, being a peacemaker by inclination, and a loyal and loving wife who kept well out of public affairs.

Since the first outbreak of the Black Death, social unrest had been mounting. The Statute of Labourers had led to further dissension, the Treaty of Brétigny had aroused resentment against the King, and the Church was now under attack for abuses. The sale of indulgences for the forgiveness of sins, the worldly luxury of many clergy and religious houses, the perceived immorality of those in holy orders—all were commonplaces of fourteenth-century life, and the focus of increasing concern on the part of a growing number of radical free thinkers. The poet William Langland, in "The Vision of Piers Plowman," wrote of hermits on their way to Walsingham "with their wenches following after," friars "preaching to the people for what they could get and interpreting the Scriptures to suit themselves and their patrons," doctors of divinity "dressing as handsomely as they please, now that Charity has gone into business," priests who sought to "traffic in Masses and chime their voices to the sweet jingling of silver," pardoners (persons licensed to sell Papal pardons or indulgences) "claiming to have power to absolve all the people from vows of every kind," and bishops who shut their ears to what was going on around them. Above all, the "Babylonish captivity" of the Papacy from 1309 at "the sinful city of Avignon," a Papacy that was in thrall to the powerful kings of France, brought the Roman Catholic Church into disrepute throughout Christendom and weakened its moral authority.

John Wycliffe, a courageous and highly controversial priest, traveled around the country and preached against the corruption in the Church. He held that the Bible should be translated into English and be made available to anyone who wanted to read it. Hitherto the Scriptures had been in Latin; most people had been unable to read them and only the clergy were permitted to interpret them for the laity. Wycliffe believed that the Church had too much wealth and was corrupt. He also held that the feudal system was not God's chosen idea of human society. He has been called "the Morning Star" of the Reformation.

He was highly regarded, mainly by the lower ranks of society. Those who openly followed him were called Lollards and regarded as heretics by the Church, which regarded Wycliffe as a dangerous threat to the established order. But there was a notable exception. John of Gaunt admired the reformer and extended his royal patronage and protection to him. In 1361, Wycliffe was appointed master of Balliol College, Oxford.

In November 1362, Edward III turned fifty. He marked the milestone by creating Lionel duke of Clarence and Edmund earl of Cambridge. That year, he made Aquitaine a principality and appointed the Black Prince to govern it. In January 1363, Froissart was in Philippa's train when she and the King came from Windsor, where they had spent Christmas, to Berkhamsted Castle to attend a great court and say farewell to the Prince and Princess. It was here that Froissart heard "an ancient knight expounding some of the prophecies of Merlin to the Queen's ladies. According to him, neither the Prince of Wales nor the Duke of Clarence will wear the crown of England, but it will fall to the House of Lancaster." If the ladies relayed this to Philippa, it perhaps troubled her, but the passage was probably written with the benefit of hindsight: by the time Froissart died, England was ruled by the House of Lancaster.

In February, the Prince and Princess sailed to Bordeaux, where they set up a fabulous court that won fame for its refinements. Philippa may have feared that she would never see her firstborn again. Work on her tomb had begun in 1362 (when six cartloads of alabaster were delivered to Westminster Abbey), suggesting that her health was giving cause for concern.

Philippa was now deeply in debt, unable to live within her income. She owed £5,851.8s. (nearly $4 million); her creditors were mostly jewelers, goldsmiths, tailors, furriers, and embroiderers, for it cost a huge sum to maintain the magnificence expected of her. The King had had to redeem one of her crowns, which she had pawned to the Earl of Arundel, and he had to satisfy her other creditors. In May 1360, he had resolved to amalgamate her household with his own for the next six years, so that her expenditure could be better controlled, but this was not implemented until February 1363. Thereafter, he maintained Philippa, and her own income was used to settle her debts.

On New Year's Day 1364, Edward gave Philippa two bodices, one black, the other sanguine (blood-colored), both hemmed with gold ribbon and embroidered in vivid silks, gold thread, and pearls. The sanguine garment bore Edward's pet name for his wife, *"Myn Biddinye"* (Middle English for "my entreaty"), surrounded by the words *p'nitibusa et billis* ("deeply enduring"). The black bodice sported Philippa's motto, *Ich wrude much*.

In 1364, John II had to return to England and place himself at King

Edward's disposal because he had failed to raise the ransom demanded for his freedom. His lords had strongly advised against it, but he quelled their fears, saying that "he had found the King his brother, the Queen and their sons so full of good faith, honour and courtesy that he feared nothing from them and was sure they would behave in the same way to him in all circumstances." Having appointed his son as regent, he sailed to England. News "was brought to the King, who was at that time with Queen Philippa at Eltham, that the French monarch had landed at Dover" on January 4. "King Edward sent off a grand deputation, saying how much the Queen and he were rejoiced to see him in England."[9]

After his mother's death, Edward had made extensive improvements at Eltham, and it was now one of the largest royal palaces in England, a fitting place for the royal couple to receive King John. On January 7, when he arrived, Edward and Philippa were waiting at the gates "with a great company of knights and ladies" to welcome him. "Between then and supper, there was time for much dancing and merriment. It would be impossible to record all the honours with which the King and Queen received King John." It was noted that a French hostage, Enguerrand de Coucy, performed admirably.

King John was escorted to London with much pageantry. He was greeted by cheering crowds, and the King and Queen "lodged him with great pomp" in John of Gaunt's palace of the Savoy.[10] David II and Peter de Lusignan, King of Cyprus, were visiting London at that time, and Edward and Philippa hosted rich feasts and entertainments at Eltham Palace for all three of their royal visitors. For one of the tournaments Edward provided Philippa with two new gowns.

But King John was a sick man. In April, he died at the Savoy Palace. Philippa had grown fond of him and "made him great feast and cheer,"[11] and his death caused her much grief. After a requiem Mass at St. Paul's Cathedral, attended by the King and Queen, his body was repatriated with honor to France, where his son, Charles V, had succeeded him. Charles despised the English and was eager for war, but there was little heart in England for it. Edward's early successes had not been sustained, and the glorious victories of Sluys, Crécy, and Poitiers were long past.

* * *

At Angoulême, on July 27, 1365, Joan of Kent bore a son, Edward, who became second in line to the throne. In England, great rejoicing marked his birth, and the King hosted feasts and jousts. It was a double celebration, for on the day of the Prince's birth, at Windsor Castle, Princess Isabella was married to the wealthy French hostage, Enguerrand de Coucy. She had chosen him herself, having rejected all the princes suggested by her indulgent parents, who had let her remain unwed until she was thirty-three. To Edward, she was "our very dear eldest daughter, whom we have loved with a special affection," and he now settled on her a large dowry. Of the £2,370.13s.4d. ($1.6 million) spent by the royal family on jewels for the bride to wear at her lavish wedding, Philippa contributed £1,273.6s.8d. ($844,800). The King freed the bridegroom without ransom, created him earl of Bedford, and admitted him to the Order of the Garter.

In November, the couple left for France. They were to have two daughters, Marie and Philippa, but the marriage was unhappy, and Isabella spent a lot of time in England. In 1377, Enguerrand gave up all his English honors, abandoned her, and defected to the French; she never saw him again and "died of grief"[12] between 1379 and 1382.

9

"No Remedy but Death"

*

PHILIPPA WOULD NOT LIVE TO WITNESS HER DAUGHTER'S tragedy. She had been ailing for some years, suffering from what was described as a dropsy. The term had the same meaning then as now: a morbid build-up of water in the body, or edema. It can be a symptom of heart or kidney failure, thrombosis, lymphedema, or liver problems; in Philippa's case, it could have been caused by increasing immobility and weight gain after the fall from her horse in 1360. From 1361, her grants provided for her predeceasing the beneficiaries. By 1365, she was traveling but rarely, and then only by litter or barge. From the summer of 1366, the King spent long periods with her at Windsor or in the royal hunting lodges of the New Forest.

That Philippa had become stout is evident from the funeral effigy she commissioned that year, the first English royal effigy to be crafted with realism, which the Brabantine sculptor Jean (or Hennequin) of Liège completed in 1367. Costing £133.6s.8d. ($84,500), it was almost certainly taken from life. Jean had spent most of his career working in Paris for the French court, and was at the forefront of tomb design, popularizing the insertion of images set in niches around the monument.

With Philippa becoming increasingly incapacitated, Edward's amorous interest shifted to her new lady-in-waiting, Alice Salisbury, the widow of James Perrers, a jeweler who had died in 1364. She is first recorded in the Queen's household in October 1366, in which year Edward gave her two tuns of wine, but their affair had been going on since 1364, when she may have borne him a son. In December that year, Edward had ordered the dubious London vintner and royal councilor Richard Lyons not to interfere with Alice's movements when she was on the King's business or her own. There was no open scandal while Philippa lived because the liaison was kept secret. In fact, it was Edward's only substantiated infidelity.

In "The Vision of Piers Plowman," William Langland characterized Alice as the beautiful but immoral Lady Mede. An extravagant, generous, fickle woman, "she makes men misbehave many score times; in trust of her treasures, she troubles a great many. She's as common as the cartway to comers and goers, to monks, to messengers, to leper-men in hedges."

Walsingham thought her "a shameless, impudent harlot of low birth. She was not attractive or beautiful, but knew how to compensate for these defects with the seductiveness of her voice. Blind fortune elevated this woman to such heights and promoted her to a greater intimacy with the King than was proper. And, while the Queen was still alive, the King loved this woman more than he loved the Queen." In Philippa's lifetime, he gave Alice jewels worth £375 ($249,000).

Geoffrey Chaucer was a customs officer dealing in wool. He had been taken captive while serving as a soldier in France and been ransomed by the King himself, who saw that he had many talents. Chaucer had been appointed a valet in Edward's household and was particularly admired for the poetry he wrote in English, especially by the Duchess Blanche, John of Gaunt's wife, who became his patron. By September 1366, he had married Philippa de Roët, who became a lady-in-waiting to the Queen. Before then, her sister Katherine had left the Queen's household and been placed by Queen Philippa in that of the Duchess Blanche. She had since married Sir Hugh Swynford, one of the Duke's knights. In 1374, John of Gaunt would grant Chaucer an annuity in recognition of the services of Philippa and her sister Katherine to his mother.

Another who left the Queen's service in 1366 was Froissart, who went traveling on the Continent, which she allowed him to do as a member of her household.

* * *

Pedro, King of Castile, had no sons. His heirs were his surviving daughters, Constance and Isabel. Pedro's sobriquet, "the Cruel," was not undeserved, for he ruled as an autocratic and bloody tyrant, determined to crush the power of his anarchic feudal nobles. In 1366, his bastard halfbrother, Henry of Trastámara, contested the crown and civil war erupted in Castile. Pedro was deposed and forced to flee the kingdom with his daughters. That summer, he sought refuge at the Black Prince's court at Bordeaux. Aware that Henry of Trastámara was in league with the French, the Prince promised to aid Pedro against the rebels and appealed to England for help. John of Gaunt responded by raising a force and marching south to Gascony. There, he greeted his brother with a kiss, and the Prince said to him, "Duke of Lancaster, my brother, welcome to our land. Tell me, how are the King and Queen and our brothers and friends?"

"Sire," John of Gaunt replied, "thanks be to God they are all well. Our father says that, if he can do anything, send word to him. Our mother sends you greetings."[1]

On January 6, 1367, the Princess Joan gave birth to a second son, Richard, at the château of Lormont near Bordeaux. In March, at Bolingbroke Castle in Lincolnshire, Blanche of Lancaster presented Gaunt with an heir, Henry of Bolingbroke. Both boys would grow up to become kings of England—and bitter rivals.

On April 3, the Black Prince and John of Gaunt overcame the forces of Henry of Trastámara at the Battle of Nájera and Pedro was restored to his throne. But there was disease in the English camp, and after his return to Bordeaux, the thirty-seven-year-old Prince of Wales suffered the first symptoms of the illness that would plague him for the rest of his life. Soon he was "at death's door," and news spread that he was suffering from dropsy. Hearing this, his enemies "decided to start the war again."[2]

Lionel, Duke of Clarence, had returned from Ireland in November 1366. His wife, Elizabeth de Burgh, had died in December 1363, and eight-year-old Philippa of Clarence, who had then become countess of Ulster in her own right, had since been brought up by her grandmother the Queen. In May 1368, when she was twelve, she was married at Reading Abbey to Edmund Mortimer, the sixteen-year-old Earl of March, great-grandson of the executed Mortimer. Through this marriage, Mortimer blood would pass into the royal line.

Clarence now received a magnificent offer. The reigning Duke of Milan, Galeazzo II, was eager to ally himself with royalty and had a thirteen-year-old daughter, Violante. In 1368, he assigned her a dowry of 2,000,000 gold florins (approximately $98 million) and towns and castles in Piedmont, bait that neither Edward III nor Clarence could resist. The marriage contract was signed in April at Windsor, and Clarence set out for Milan with a train of 2,000 English soldiers.

His was to be one of the most talked-of marriages of the age. On Whitsunday, he married Violante in the porch of the church of St. Maria Maggiore in the presence of a throng of nobles. Thirty courses were served at the al fresco banquet that followed, and the newlyweds were showered with lavish gifts before riding to Alba for their honeymoon. Tragically, Clarence died there on October 7, 1368, possibly of food poisoning. He was not quite thirty.

News of his death reached England in the wake of another tragedy. Blanche of Lancaster had passed away on September 12, 1368, at Tutbury Castle, Staffordshire, a month after bearing a short-lived daughter, which suggests that she had contracted puerperal fever. "Put a tomb over my heart, for when I remember, I am so melancholy," mourned Froissart. "She died young and lovely." Both losses must have brought great sorrow and distress to the Queen and perhaps accelerated her decline.

John of Gaunt was devastated by the death of his wife, but, grief-stricken though he was, the young widower was a great prize in the matrimonial market, and Blanche had not been in her grave two months when Edward III proposed him as a husband for Margaret, the heiress of Flanders, a match that would have brought him a prosperous principality and provided England with a buffer state against the hostility of France. It was an irresistible prospect, and one John of Gaunt could not have rejected. On December 1, Philippa sent an envoy to Flanders to open negotiations. But the Count rejected the offer, preferring to court the French, and in 1369 Margaret was married to Philip the Bold, Duke of Burgundy, brother of Charles V.

* * *

Alice Perrers's influence was now such that she was able to persuade the King to move the staple (a fixed mart) from Lincoln, where it had been flourishing, to Boston, where it did not—which made her very unpopular. But Philippa either did not know about Edward's affair or accepted it with equanimity, for in her will, she left her "beloved damsel, Alicia de Preston" (the spelling of names was erratic and not standardized), ten marks a year ($6,900), which suggests that Alice had rendered her good service. Four other ladies received the same amount.

In March 1369, Edward ordered that fabrics and furs be delivered to his "well beloved" attendants of the Queen. Among the ladies and damsels was Philippa's bastard half-sister, Elizabeth de Holland, who received an annual pension of £20 ($13,500) from the King. John of Gaunt would later reward Philippa Chaucer and Marie de Saint-Hilaire for the good service they had given "to our very honoured lady and mother the Queen." The Issue Rolls record payments to many other members of Philippa's household for serving her well.

In March 1369, Castile was again plunged into turmoil when Henry of Trastámara assassinated King Pedro and reclaimed the throne, forcing Pedro's daughters—the elder, Constance, now styling herself queen of Castile—to flee to Bordeaux and beg the Black Prince for aid.

A week after Pedro's murder, Charles V, having rejected the Treaty of Brétigny, declared war on England. Philippa supported Edward in attempting to secure her nephew, Albert, Duke of Bavaria, as an ally against France and sent jewels to his wife—but in vain. Late in May, the French clawed back all the land held by the English in Ponthieu and began amassing a great invasion force. In June, as plague raged in London and the court sought refuge at Windsor, Edward III stood up in Parliament and again assumed the title King of France. John of Gaunt was appointed King's Captain and Lieutenant in Calais, Guisnes, and the surrounding country. He arrived in Calais with an army on July 26, and spent August and September campaigning in France.

Now, Froissart wrote, "there fell in England a sad case, right piteous for the King, his children and all his realm, for the good Queen of England, that so many good deeds had done in her time and so many knights succoured and ladies and damsels comforted, and had so largely given of her goods to her people, lay dangerously sick in the castle. Every day, her disorder increased, and that sickness continued on her so long that there was no remedy but death."[3]

Confined to her richly hung bed, she was attended by Adam, the King's surgeon, her own doctors, William of Exeter and Peter of Florence, and her ladies and damsels, among them Alice Perrers. On the morning of August 14, the Vigil of the Assumption of the Virgin Mary, William of Wykeham gave her the Last Sacrament.

The next day, "when the good Queen perceived that her end was approaching, she desired to speak to the King her husband, and extended her right hand from the bedclothes and took the King by his right hand, who was very sorrowful in his heart."

"Sir, we have in peace and joy and great prosperity passed all our time together," she said. "Sir, now I pray you, at our parting, that ye will grant me three requests."

Sighing and weeping, Edward answered, "Lady, ask what ye will, I grant it."

Philippa replied, "Sir, I beg you will acquit me of whatever engagements I have entered into with merchants for their wares, as well on this as on the other side of the sea. I beseech you also to fulfil whatever gifts or legacies I may have made or left to churches here or on the Continent, wherein I have paid my devotions, as well as what I have left to those of both sexes who have been in my service. Thirdly, I entreat that, when it shall please God to call you hence, you will not choose any other sepulchre than mine, and that you will lie by my side in the cloisters of Westminster."

Sobbing, Edward answered, "Lady, I grant you all your desire."

"Then the good lady made the sign of the Cross on her breast and commended the King her husband to God, and her youngest son Thomas, who was there beside her. And anon after, praying to God, she yielded up the spirit, the which I surely believe was received with great joy by holy angels and carried up to the glory of Heaven, for in all her life she did neither in thought nor deed anything whereby to lose her soul, as far as any creature could know."[4]

Froissart, who had accompanied Clarence to Milan, was in Brussels, on his way back, when he heard of the death of his patroness. Recalling the passing of Blanche of Lancaster a year earlier, he wrote: "I wring my hands, I clap my palms! I have lost too many in these two ladies." Of Philippa, he wrote: "Dead is she, that kind lady who, in all honour, without blame, passed her life. Alas, what news for all her friends!" Her passing, he wrote, was "to the infinite misfortune of King Edward, his children and the whole kingdom. She was a lady of great honour and virtue and a firm friend to England. Truly am I bound to pray for her, for it was she who made and created me."

Philippa has been called a paragon among English queens. In an address to Parliament in 1377, the Chancellor, William of Wykeham, declared: "No Christian king nor any lord in the land had so noble and gracious a wife as our lord the King has had."[5] A monk of Westminster composed a Latin panegyric expressing the national mood: "Let the whole of England have time for prayers because Queen Philippa lies dead, closed up in death. While she flourished, she was full of grace to the English. She would call upon Christ while she lived, so that the kingdom should not lack for its harvest."[6]

The marriage of Edward and Philippa had endured for forty-one years. Philippa had made a great contribution to the stability and success of the monarchy with her genius for fostering family unity and closeness. Her children all adored her and were much grieved by her death.

"Information of this heavy loss was carried to the English army at Tournehem, which greatly afflicted everyone, more especially her son, John of Gaunt."[7] Until his death, Gaunt cherished "a gold brooch in the old fashion, with the name of God inscribed on each part of it, which my most honourable lady mother, whom God preserve, gave to me, commanding me to guard it with her blessing." He would bequeath it to his heir, Henry of Bolingbroke.

Edward was so grief-stricken that he was unable to go to France to take control of his forces. As he had promised, he settled Philippa's modest debts of £1,377.14s.6d. ($914,000) "of his especial grace, for the relief of [her] soul."[8] On September 1, he ordered the royal wardrobe to supply "liveries of black and furs for mourning, due to the death of our very dear companion, the Queen," to the royal family and many others, including Philippa's bastard half-sister, Elizabeth of Holland, now a nun at Stratford-atte-Bowe. Messengers were sent out to "all parts of England with letters of Privy Seal directed to all archbishops, earls, barons and other lords and ladies, that they be ordered to be present at London on the day of the exequies of Philippa, late Queen of England."[9]

The bereft royal family kept Christmas at Langley in Hertfordshire. Philippa's magnificent state funeral took place in January, nearly five months after her death—such things took time to arrange. The King commanded that the streets of London be cleared of mud and filth. Crowds came to see this final pageant for the Queen who had won their love by her good deeds. On January 3, her coffin, in which she lay wrapped in her wedding mantle, was brought down the Thames from Windsor to the Tower and then, with banners flying, was borne in a great cavalcade through the streets of London to Westminster Abbey. A wooden effigy of the Queen, now lost (and possibly the first ever made of an English queen), lay on the hearse, which had been made by "divers workmen and carpenters in the dwelling of the Bishop of London" by St. Paul's Cathedral; the King had even paid "for a drink amongst the said workmen."[10]

The coffin rested at the priory of St. Mary Overie (now Southwark Cathedral), where alms amounting to £158 ($104,800) were distributed to the poor for the salvation of the Queen's soul. It then lay in state in St. Paul's Cathedral and, for one night, in Westminster Abbey. On January 9, Philippa was buried by candlelight in the tomb chest built for her in Edward the Confessor's Chapel, in earth brought from the Holy Land. It was the holiest place in the Abbey, its spiritual heart; she lay near the holy shrine with its Purbeck marble base rich with mosaics and jewels, its golden feretory above, and recesses where pilgrims could kneel. Only those of royal blood had the privilege of lying beside it for all eternity.

The King paid the Abbot of Westminster £66.13s.4d. ($44,600) for the funeral expenses. The bed in which the Queen had died was given to York Minster, and its hangings were made up into thirteen copes, six tunics, and one chasuble.

Jean of Liège was still working on the fine tomb of Flemish design in black and white marble that had been commissioned in 1362 and cost £200 ($135,000). When it was completed in 1376, its columned sides contained "thirty sweetly carved niches" with glass mosaics, "wherein have been placed as many little images."[11] Those of Philippa's relations and royal connections were on the south side, facing the ambulatory, while the King's were on the north side. Only two figures remain; one, of a lady with a monkey, is thought to be Blanche of Lancaster. In 1376, John Orchard was paid £5 ($3,000) for many small images of angels to adorn the tomb. There were seventy figures in total (most of them lost in the seventeenth century), including those of Philippa's twelve children, and a shield on which were quartered the arms of England and Hainault.

On top of the chest was laid the painted and gilded white marble effigy of the Queen; the hands are now broken, and the scepter and gilt crown long lost. A wooden canopy built over the tomb still survives, protected by a wrought-iron railing bought by Edward III in 1376 from St. Paul's Cathedral for £600 ($398,000), and originally painted red. In 1857, Sir Gilbert Scott found some alabaster tabernacle work from the tomb and replaced it on the south side.

Near the monument was hung a Latin epitaph, now lost, which was translated into English by the poet John Skelton in the sixteenth century and recorded in 1677:

> Fair Philippa, William Hainault's child and younger
>   daughter dear,
> Of roseate hue and beauty bright, in tomb lies hilled here.
> King Edward, through his mother's will and nobles' good consent,
> Took her to wife, and joyfully with her his time he spent.
> Her uncle John, a martial man and eke a valiant knight,
> Did link this woman to the King in bonds of marriage bright.
> This match and marriage thus in blood did bind the Flemings sure
> To Englishmen, by which they did the Frenchmen's wreck procure.
> This Philippa, dowered in gifts full rare and treasures of the mind,
> In beauty bright, religion, faith, to all and each most kind.
> A faithful mother Philippa was, full many a son she bred,
> And brought forth many a worthy knight, hardy and full of dread.
> A careful nurse to students all, at Oxford she did found
> Queen's College and Dame Pallas's school, that did her
>   fame resound.
> The wife of Edward dear,
> Queen Philippa lieth here.
> LEARN TO LIVE.

After Philippa's death, Edward III descended into an inexorable decline and the arms of "our beloved Alice Perrers," who, in 1373, was given all the jewels, goods, and chattels that the Queen had left in the keeping of Euphemia, wife to Sir Walter de Heslarton, evidently to keep them safe until the King decided what to do with them.

In his remaining years, Edward's popularity dwindled, as did his ability to wage war on France. The Black Prince became an invalid. His son, Edward of Angoulême, died in 1370, leaving young Richard of Bordeaux as the heir to England.

In 1371, the Prince came home, surrendering his lieutenancy of Aquitaine to John of Gaunt. Gaunt resigned soon afterward to marry Constance of Castile and fight for a crown in Spain. He took a mistress, Katherine Swynford, who bore him four children, all surnamed Beaufort after a lordship he had once held in France.

John of Gaunt became a figurehead for the anti-clericalism movement in England. His championing of Wycliffe and an abortive campaign in France made him deeply unpopular, and both he and Alice Perrers were censured by Parliament. It was at this time, in 1376, that the rumor was put about that Gaunt was a changeling.

The Black Prince died on June 8, 1376, and was buried in Canterbury Cathedral. His ten-year-old son inherited the throne as Richard II when the old King died at Sheen Palace on June 21, 1377, aged sixty-four. Edward had been playing at dice with Alice Perrers when he suffered a stroke that left him paralyzed. Its effects can be seen in the death mask of his wooden funeral effigy in Westminster Abbey. As he lay dying, Alice snatched the rings from his fingers and ran to find a priest before fleeing the court.

Honoring his promise to Philippa, Edward was buried to the west of her monument in Westminster Abbey, in a tomb surmounted by his effigy and adorned with statues of their children, of which six survive. His epitaph described him as "the glory of the English, the flower of kings past, the pattern for kings to come." The truth of that is still acknowledged by historians today.

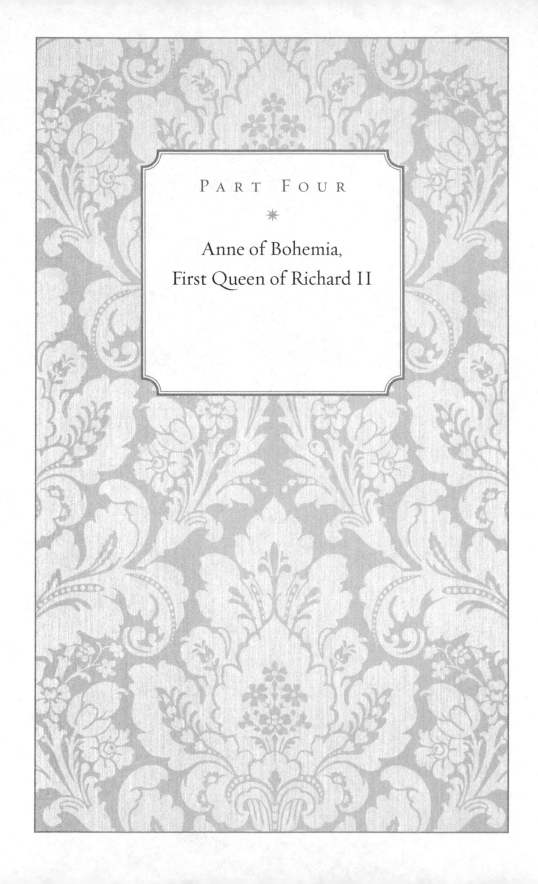

PART FOUR

✳

Anne of Bohemia,
First Queen of Richard II

I

"So Little a Scrap of Humanity"

✳

A NEW REIGN BEGAN. RICHARD II WAS CROWNED ON A TIDE OF goodwill, but social unrest soon manifested itself again. All that remained of England's once vast possessions in France were Aquitaine, Calais, and five towns. In the week of Edward's death, the French were raiding the south coast.

Richard II's reign led to the beginnings of a power struggle that would last well into the next century and lead ultimately to the Wars of the Roses. Richard had been raised to the throne at an impressionable age, imbued with a strong sense of his unique importance. The praise he earned, at fourteen, for his courageous behavior during the Peasants' Revolt convinced him that he was a born leader of men.

Richard was one of the greatest matrimonial prizes in Christendom and "there was great counsel in England among the King's uncles and the prelates and barons of the realm for to marry the young King. And the Englishmen would gladly have had him married in Hainault for love of the good lady Queen Philippa, who was so good and so gracious a lady; but, as the Duke Albert had no daughters, the Duke of Lancaster would have had the King to have his eldest daughter, but the realm would in no wise consent thereto; they would the King should marry without the realm to have thereby more alliance."[1]

Soon after Richard's accession, the Holy Roman Emperor, Charles IV, wrote to the English council, offering the ten-year-old King the hand of his daughter Anne, then eleven. Charles IV sprang from the House of Luxembourg and was the most powerful ruler in Christendom. He aspired to be another Charlemagne. He had been emperor since 1347 and also reigned as king of Bohemia, being the son of the blind King John who had fallen at Poitiers. His rule extended over half of Europe, encompassing (among other territories) the Low Countries, Germany, and Italy. But his proposal was rejected.

Early in 1378, Charles V of France offered Richard one of his daughters, either seven-year-old Marie or the newborn Katherine, with the rich county of Angoulême, while Charles III, King of Navarre, pressed the English to accept *his* daughter, another Marie. Richard's mother, Joan, was keen on an alliance with Navarre, but Charles V scuppered it when he confiscated Charles III's French lands in April. After negotiations for the French marriage foundered in May, Richard's advisers considered a match with a Scottish princess, but were reluctant to ally England with an old enemy.

In the spring of 1378, Geoffrey Chaucer was one of the envoys sent to Milan to negotiate a marriage with one of Violante Visconti's sisters. Discussions went forward for a year until they came to an abrupt halt, for Pope Urban VI had decided that an alliance between England and the Holy Roman Empire would be greatly advantageous to himself.

In 1377, the Papacy had moved back to Rome. Urban had been elected there in April 1378, but he had fallen out with his cardinals, who had set up a rival pontiff, Clement VII, at Avignon. Urban refused to step down, creating an impasse that became known as the Great Schism. Thus, there were two rival popes, each with his own followers and neither with any viable authority, which made a mockery of the integrity of the Church and brought the Papacy into disrepute.

Urban VI wanted to form a defensive league with the Holy Roman Empire and England against the pro-French Clementists, and resolved to revive the marriage alliance with Bohemia, a place so distant that many in England had probably never heard of it. In the summer of 1379, he took it upon himself to summon the English envoys, Sir Michael de la Pole (a trusted friend of Richard II) and Sir Simon Burley, Richard's tutor, from Milan to Rome, and pressed them to pursue a Bohemian alliance.

The English were keen, seeing it as a means of detaching the House of

Luxembourg from its ally, France, and hoping for its support in the war against France—a hope that never came to fruition. John of Gaunt and Joan of Kent were all for the match.

Charles IV had died in November 1378 and been succeeded in Bohemia by his son, seventeen-year-old Wenceslaus (or Wenzel) IV. In September 1379, de la Pole and Burley traveled to Germany to see the new King and revive the marriage negotiations. The impoverished Wenceslaus was eager for the marriage. Although he wrote to Richard proclaiming the benefits of Christendom being united under the one true Pope, he apparently saw the alliance chiefly as a means of extracting money from England.

Anne of Bohemia—or Anne of Luxembourg, as she was known in Europe—was the eldest child of Charles IV by his fourth wife, Elizabeth of Pomerania, whom he had married in 1363. The duchy of Pomerania was part-German, part-Polish, but German culture had predominated since the region was overrun by the Teutonic Knights early in the fourteenth century. The Empress Elizabeth was of Slavonic descent, the granddaughter of Casimir the Great, King of Poland. She was an unusually strong woman who could tear apart thick wads of parchment and break blocks of wood with her bare hands, feats in which her husband had taken great pride. They enjoyed a happy union and produced eight children, of whom three died young.

Anne had been born on May 11, 1366, at Prague. It grieved her mother that Charles favored his children from his previous marriages. They were all much older than Anne. Margaret had been queen of Hungary; Katherine was electress of Brandenburg; Elizabeth had been duchess of Austria. Anne's younger sister, Margaret, born in 1373, would become burgravine of Nuremberg. Aside from Wenceslaus, all her older half-brothers had died young. Her younger brother Sigismund became king of Hungary in 1385 (and would in time become Holy Roman Emperor); John was created duke of Görlitz. Their father often being away, Anne spent much time with her brothers.

Through her wider family, Anne was very well connected. Her aunt Jutta, who took the name Bonne, had married John II of France. Two other aunts, Margaret and Anne, had wed dukes of Bavaria and Austria.

Anne was related to the House of Avesnes, to which Philippa of Hainault had belonged. As a child, she was proposed as a bride for the son of Albert I of Bavaria, the future Charles VI of France, and Frederick of Meissen, Elector of Saxony, to whom she had been betrothed for six years. Negotiations had foundered in every case. Her father had turned down the match with France because of his ties to the Urbanists. It was a lucky escape for Anne because Charles VI was to suffer crippling bouts of madness.

Like patient Griselda in Chaucer's "Clerk's Tale," Anne had been "nourished in an Emperor's hall"[2], the vast Hradčany (Hradschin in German) Palace that towers majestically over Prague; within its precincts stands St. Vitus's Cathedral, which had been built by Charles IV to house the shrine of St. Wenceslaus ("Good King Wenceslaus"), Bohemia's most revered saint. The Prague Anne knew had been greatly expanded and glorified in the elegant Bohemian international Gothic, or "beautiful," style by Charles IV, who had made it the chief seat of the Empire and founded its university—and that in Pavia, Italy. An intensely religious man, he spoke five languages and his court was a splendid precursor of the magnificent courts of Burgundy and the Renaissance, inspired, as they were, by the budding humanist thought of Italy. Its sophisticated ambience was a unique combination of German, French, and Italian influences.

Anne grew up surrounded by an aura of piety and high ceremonial on a par with religious ritual, underlining the sanctity of the state. She received an excellent education and would become one of the most learned of England's medieval queens. Brought up in a court that had extended patronage to both Dante Alighieri and Petrarch, she spoke Bohemian (Czech), German, Latin, and French, and could read and write in all four languages. She may also have known some Polish from her mother and members of her household. Later, she would learn sufficient English to be able to read the Gospels in that language. Anne was charismatic, intelligent, devout, and cultivated. A letter she later wrote extolling the virtues of learning survives in the archives of the Queen's College, Oxford, of which she became patron. She has been called "the very embodiment of the international court culture."[3]

In 1380, the Empress Elizabeth sent an emissary, the Imperial chamberlain Przemislaus, Duke of Cieszyn (Teschen in Poland), to report on the state of England and whether it was safe for her daughter to go there. Evidently she was satisfied, for she asked Przemislaus "to treat with Richard, King of England, concerning his marrying that excellent virgin, the damsel Anne, born of us."[4]

De la Pole and Burley returned to London in May 1380. At their urging, Richard II and his councilors agreed to the marriage, "but the match was not immediately concluded, for the damsel was young."[5] Anne was then fourteen, above the canonical age for marriage, but she may have been physically immature. It was agreed that negotiations should resume early in 1381.

On December 26, 1380, Joan's grandson, Thomas Holland, Earl of Kent, Sir Michael de la Pole, the bishops of Hereford and St. David's, and others were invested with full powers to conclude the alliance and the marriage. Their commission stated that Richard had chosen Anne for her nobility of birth and reputed gentleness of character. In January 1381, she and her mother appointed proctors to treat respecting her marriage: the Duke of Cieszyn, Konrad Kreger, and Peter Wartenberg.

Anne may have been the inspiration for the heroine of Chaucer's *The Parliament of Fowls*, a beautiful female eagle (formel) of sweet disposition:

> *Nature had on her hand*
> *A female eagle, of shape the very noblest*
> *That ever she among her works had found,*
> *The most gracious and the very kindest;*
> *In her was every virtue there expressed*
> *So perfectly Nature herself felt bliss*
> *In gazing at her and her beak would kiss.*

Anne's arms "as the daughter of Caesar" displayed the two-headed eagle of the Holy Roman Empire as well as the lion of Bohemia. Chaucer's poem takes a witty view of love and tells of three tercel hawks who gather on St. Valentine's Day to choose their mates; it is thought to have given rise to the tradition of celebrating February 14 as a day for lovers. The poem was perhaps written during the negotiations for Anne's marriage, for it shows the eagle waiting a year to be wed, as Anne did, and makes it clear that she had a say in choosing her husband ("that she agree to his election"), which it seems that Anne was given. When, in

February 1381, the English envoys obtained her written consent to the marriage, she stated that, "with deliberate mind, full and free will and certain knowledge," she would be the wife of King Richard.[6]

In March, it was agreed with Cardinal Pileo di Prata and the Imperial proctors that Anne would be "crowned within a given time" and that "all other things shall be arranged like as for other queens of England."[7] The Duke of Cieszyn tactfully broached the subject of the dower. The truth was that Wenceslaus could not afford a dowry; in fact, Cieszyn ended up persuading Richard to lend his master 10,000 marks ($2.7 million) for the privilege of marrying Anne, "not including the expense of seeking her out and leading her to England at [the King's] cost."[8]

Happy with the settlement, the two embassies traveled together to London, where, on April 3, John of Gaunt received the young King and the Bohemian envoys at the Savoy Palace and entertained them lavishly. Later, the envoys were showered with extravagant gifts.

The marriage treaty was signed on May 2, Richard and Wenceslaus agreeing to a perpetual alliance between them against the schismatics who opposed Pope Urban. The treaty also gave English merchants the right to trade freely in the Imperial territories and Bohemia. Disappointingly for the Pope, Richard's government gave no undertaking to fight in his cause and reserved the right to make alliances with his enemies. And Wenceslaus would never prove a reliable ally against the French. Politically, therefore, the treaty was to bring no great advantages to Richard; personally, it was to bring him great happiness.

The marriage was not popular in England. The lack of a dowry rankled; moreover, Anne was said to be plain. Walsingham recalled that the King had been offered Caterina Visconti, Duke Galeazzo II of Milan's beautiful daughter, with "an inestimable quantity of gold"—a project that came to nothing—yet Anne had been "bought for a great price."[9] Higden wrote: "To those with an eye for the facts, it seemed that she represented a purchase rather than a gift, since the King laid out no small sum to secure so little a scrap of humanity." There was anger when her dower was set at £4,500 ($3.6 million), the same sum settled on Marguerite of France eighty-three years earlier. It was felt that it was too high a price to pay for the alliance.

* * *

It had been agreed that Anne would travel to Calais before Michaelmas, at her brother's expense, and that Richard would escort her from there to England. On May 13, with great pomp, Sir Simon Burley left for Prague to conclude the negotiations and accompany Anne to Calais. On the way, he met with her paternal uncle, Wenzel IV, Duke of Brabant (Froissart's then patron), and his wife, Joanna, who was duchess of Brabant in her own right. "The Duke and Duchess received [him] most courteously and said it would be a good match for their niece."[10] The Duke gave Burley a letter in which he approved the marriage, to give to the Emperor.

In June, Richard II's government had to deal with the momentous uprising known as the Peasants' Revolt, which had been fueled by discontent with the social order and an unpopular poll tax. The young King displayed great bravery and the peasants were quelled, their bid for greater equality unsatisfied.

Burley arrived in Bohemia in August. On September 1, he witnessed the ratification of the treaty at Prague. Once the English council had received notification of this, they began preparing to receive the new Queen. At Prague, preparations had begun for her departure, but Bohemia was so impoverished that although Anne brought to England a quantity of plate embossed with the Imperial eagle, she took with her only two gowns, one for traveling and a purple one lined with sable.

In September, she finally set out for England, escorted by Burley and attended by the Duke of Saxony, the Duchess of Brabant, "and many knights and damsels."[11] Having been instrumental in arranging her marriage, Burley must have provided congenial company, for he was always to be Anne's ally and friend.

It was a long journey of 684 miles to Calais. Anne and her large train of nobles, ladies, clergy, and clerks passed through Germany in great state, and were entertained in Hainault by the regent, Albert I of Bavaria. Presently "they came to Brussels, where Duke Wenzel received the young Queen and her company very grandly." She probably stayed with him and the Duchess at the palace of Coudenberg, the chief residence of the rulers of Brussels since the twelfth century.

"The Lady Anne remained with her uncle and aunt for more than a month. She was afraid of proceeding for she had been informed that there were twelve large ships, well-armed, full of Normans on the sea between Calais and Holland, that seized and pillaged all that fell into

their hands." It was "not honourable to take ladies in war," but "the report was current that they cruised the seas, awaiting the coming of the
King of England's bride, because the King of France and his council were
very uneasy at Richard's German alliance and were desirous of breaking
the match. Detained by these apprehensions, the betrothed Queen remained at Brussels more than a month till the Duke of Brabant, her
uncle, sent the lords of Rousselans and Bousquehoir to remonstrate with
King Charles V, who was also a near relative of Anne. Upon which, King
Charles remanded the Norman cruisers into port, but he declared that
he granted this favour solely out of love to his cousin Anne" and out of
regard for King Richard. "The Duke and Duchess were very much pleased,
and so were all those about to cross the sea."[12] Anne had probably enjoyed her stay in Brussels, for her uncle was a poet and a great patron of
the arts.

"The royal bride took leave of her uncle and aunt. Duke Wenzel had
the Princess escorted with 100 spears." Her party traveled to Ghent,
where the governor, Queen Philippa's godson, Philip van Artevelde, welcomed them with great honor. At Bruges, Louis II, Count of Flanders,
received Anne "very magnificently and entertained her for three days."[13]
Here, she received orders from Richard, who had learned of her scanty
wardrobe, to buy herself rich fabrics and linen, which she did, although
the mercers had to wait a long time for the King to pay for them.

Count Louis had Anne and her retinue escorted through Flanders by
Sir Colard van den Clite and a party of eleven crossbowmen and archers,
twenty-two lancers, and a consort of minstrels. When she arrived at Grav-
elines in December 1381, the earls of Salisbury and Devon, Sir John Holland, the King's half-brother, and Sir John de Montagu, the steward of
the royal household, were waiting with 500 spearmen and 500 archers to
"receive [her] reverentially" and conduct her in triumph to Calais and
thence to England. At Calais, "divers knights and other officers of the
court of Bohemia" and the Brabantine spearmen bade farewell to Anne
and "took their departure, after seeing her safely delivered to the English
governor"; they returned home at a cost to the English Exchequer of
£166.13s.4d. ($140,000).[14] Burley was later rewarded for his services with
the Order of the Garter and a castle in Wales.

On December 13, King Richard had a general pardon proclaimed "at
the special request of the most serene Lady Anne, by the will of God, our

future consort."[15] Whether or not she had actually written to ask for this favor, or had done so at the suggestion of Joan of Kent, it was a wise move, aimed at countering the aversion Richard's subjects had to his marriage, and paving the way for her to be taken to their hearts.

"The Lady Anne stayed at Calais only until wind became favourable."[16] Embarking on the morning of December 18, she and her attendants in one ship and the household and horses in the other, she endured a rough voyage across the Channel in atrocious weather, arriving at Dover later that day. "Scarcely had the Bohemian Princess set foot on the shore when a sudden convulsion of the sea took place" and her ship broke up before her horrified eyes.[17] Chaucer's reference to "the tempest" at the Amazon Queen Hippolyta's "homecoming" in "The Knight's Tale" may allude to this.[18]

Richard and his uncle, Thomas of Woodstock, Earl of Buckingham, were waiting at Dover to receive Anne. There was apparently an instant attraction between the two fifteen-year-olds, and Anne had good reason to be pleased with her marriage. Richard was tall (his skeleton, found in 1871, measured six feet) and slender, fair-skinned and handsome, with thick shoulder-length dark-blond hair. His face was "fair, round and feminine, sometimes flushed"[19] and clean-shaven; he did not wear a beard until later life.

He was to commission two portraits of himself, the first surviving painted likenesses of an English king. The most famous is the Wilton Diptych (painted around 1395–99 and now in the National Gallery, London), in which he appears sumptuously gowned in cloth of gold embroidered with Imperial eagles in homage to Anne, underlining his vain ambition to become Holy Roman Emperor. With his patron saints standing protectively behind him, he kneels before the Virgin and Child. It has been suggested that the figure of the Virgin was based on a Bohemian statue in Queen Anne's possession (now in the Kunsthistorisches Museum, Vienna). On the reverse of the painting is a white hart, Richard's personal emblem.

The other portrait is a full-length painting of the King enthroned in majesty against a gold background, which now hangs in Westminster Abbey; it has been suggested that it was the work of a Bohemian artist, or that the work was influenced by Bohemian paintings brought to England after the King's marriage, and that there may have been a companion portrait of Anne. That this and the Wilton Diptych are true portraits and not just iconic representations of a king is proved by their facial similarities, which bear close comparison with the effigy on Richard's tomb.

A fourteenth-century wall painting in Lutterworth parish church said to represent "The Three Living and the Three Dead" shows three crowned figures, two men and a woman, next to fragmentary traces of three skeletons. The crowned personages probably illustrate the transitory nature of worldly status and may represent—or have been inspired by—Richard II, Anne of Bohemia, and John of Gaunt.

Despite having a stammer Richard cut an impressive figure. Although he was no soldier and rarely took part in a joust, his personal bravery was not in doubt. He did not seek martial glory and considered that peace with France was preferable to war, a highly unpopular view at that time. Yet he enjoyed the pageantry of chivalry and royalty. He raised the cult and mystique of monarchy to an art form, giving much thought to the ceremonial attached to it.

There was a dark side to him, though. He had emerged from his experiences during the Peasants' Revolt with an unshakeable conviction in his own heroism and superiority, and an aversion to taking advice. He was emotionally unstable, insecure, suspicious, capricious, devious, and untrustworthy. His violent outbursts of temper were legendary, and he could be ruthless and vindictive when provoked. Headstrong, irresponsible, and politically inept, he was often abrupt in conversation, and capable of insulting behavior, on occasions bawling out his detractors in Parliament. Once, in a violent temper, he tried to take a sword to the Archbishop of Canterbury and had to be forcibly restrained from doing so.

Richard was to mature into a great and highly discerning patron of the arts and literature. He had exquisite taste and his elegant court was more cultured than militaristic, its fame adding luster to his crown. It was to become one of the most celebrated courts in English history, for its chivalry, art, literature, elaborate ceremony, and unprecedented splendor. In every respect it reflected the majesty of the King, a connoisseur and showman who set a new standard of luxury in his palaces, acquiring many beautiful objets d'art.

Froissart asserted that no English king before Richard had spent so much money on his court and household, and naturally there was much criticism of his extravagance. But female influence may account in part for that, for there is some evidence to indicate that there were far more women at court than in previous reigns. Given Richard's devotion to Anne, the closeness of their households, the emphasis on love and chivalry, the number of women admitted to the fraternity of the Garter, and the proportion of ladies featuring in courtly scenes, feminine influence must have been strong.

Richard was impressed by French culture and customs. He loved good food—his hospitality was legendary. "In his kitchen alone 300 persons were employed, and the Queen had a like number to attend upon her good service."[20] Richard was the first English King to have a cookery book, *The Form of Cury*, dedicated to him, and the first to employ French chefs. His suspicious subjects saw this as fraternizing with the enemy, against whom they would have preferred to be scoring military victories.

The King grew up to be a true sybarite and aesthete, "extravagantly splendid in his entertainments and dress, and too much devoted to luxury." "He was haughty and too much inclined to voluptuousness,"[21] which meant that he indulged in his pleasures: the word "voluptuous" did not have a sensual connotation at that time. He dressed elegantly and ostentatiously, although many chroniclers strongly criticized the outlandish fashions of his court, targeting the men's built-up shoulders and collars, the tight hose, and the outlandishly pointed shoes known as "cracows" or "pikes," which were tied to the knees with silken laces or chains of silver or gilt, and were said by Stow to have been introduced by Anne; more likely it was the Bohemian gentlemen in her train. It was said that these fashions prevented their wearers from kneeling in Church, while long sleeves that swept the floor were reviled as "full of slashes and devils."[22]

Richard was a great builder and embellished many of the royal palaces with stained-glass windows, vivid heraldic murals, and sumptuous furnishings. He lived in the greatest luxury, and Westminster Hall, which he rebuilt, remains as testimony to the extravagant splendors of his reign. It was Richard who employed the master mason and architect Henry Yevele to modernize Westminster Hall by adding the magnificent hammerbeam roof that survives today. A fastidious man, the King installed bathrooms with multicolored floor tiles and hot and cold running water in his palaces, and he is even credited with inventing the handkerchief.

With his all-encompassing interests and discerning patronage, Richard II foreshadowed the princes of the Renaissance, for whom magnificence and courtesy were sacred maxims. Like Queen Philippa before her, Anne shared her husband's passion for splendor and his cultural vision; thanks to her, his court reflected Bohemian models in both its formality and its art and taste. Coming from a court rich in culture and European and Byzantine influence, she was in a unique position to further the arts in England. She had brought artists and illuminators with her from Bohemia and may have helped to popularize international Gothic architecture in her adopted land.

2

"Our Beloved"

＊

AFTER ANNE HAD "TARRIED TWO DAYS TO REPOSE HERSELF"[1] in the Great Tower of Dover Castle, John of Gaunt arrived to bid her welcome, and rode with her and the King to Canterbury, amid great pomp. Then he and Buckingham accompanied the royal couple to Queen Court, the royal manor house at Ospringe, by Faversham, which had been named after its former owner, Marguerite of France. Next it was on to Leeds Castle, the King's "beautiful palace in Kent,"[2] where they kept Christmas, after which they moved to Eltham Palace. Anne's entry into London was delayed to enable the King to raise loans to pay for her official welcome.

"In January, after the feast of Epiphany, the nobility of the whole realm of England assembled in London to attend King Richard's marriage ceremony and to perform their duty according to the custom observed since ancient times."[3]

On January 18, when everything was ready for Anne's reception, John of Gaunt escorted her to Blackheath. With Richard at her side, she was welcomed by the Mayor and leading citizens with a pageant and an address in which the hope was expressed that she would be a merciful queen. "Since it pertains to your most benign piety to assume the role of mediatrix between your illustrious prince, our lord the King, just as did our other lady queens who preceded your most excellent Highness, may it be pleasing to your most clement and pre-eminent nobility to mediate with our lord the King in such wise with gracious words and deeds."[4] At

Blackheath, Henry of Bolingbroke and his sister, Elizabeth of Lancaster, were presented to Anne.

In stark contrast to the grim scenes in London during the Peasants' Revolt of the previous year, the mayor and his brethren escorted Richard and Anne's magnificent cavalcade into the City, where the members of the goldsmiths' guild, splendidly dressed in red and black embroidered with silver, hailed Anne as "the Caesar's sister" and showered her with silver florins. Minstrels played as the Duke led the royal couple in procession through the streets, while free wine flowed through the Great Conduit in Cheapside, which had been decorated for the occasion. The royal couple halted at the end of Cheapside, where a pageant was performed in a gilded "summer castle" made by London goldsmiths; in its towers were seven minstrels and three maidens, scattering gold-painted leaves over the procession. But there were dissenters among the crowds. Two men, seeing the Imperial arms crossed with the royal arms on a shield hanging from a fountain, tore it down. Three days later, a German vandalized three similar shields "to the grave dishonour and scandal of the King and Queen," but he was pardoned after Anne interceded for him.[5]

An unholy row had erupted between William Courtenay, Archbishop of Canterbury, and Robert Braybrooke, Bishop of London, as to which of them should take precedence at the wedding. But Courtenay had not received his pallium from the Pope, so could not yet exercise authority as archbishop. At length it was agreed that the Bishop should officiate at the wedding, while the Archbishop would do the honors at the coronation.

Richard and Anne were married on January 20 in St. Stephen's Chapel, Westminster. The ceremony was "performed with great solemnity"[6] by Bishop Braybrooke and "there were mighty feastings"[7] afterward. There survives the first ever mention of a royal bridesmaid, Margaret of Cieszyn, the great-niece of Wenceslaus III, King of Bohemia; she would marry an English knight, Simon de Felbrigge. Anne's arms and those of Richard II appear on Felbrigge's brass in Westminster Abbey, while the Felbrigg Book of Hours (now in the Huntington Library, California) contains a prayer in Czech.

Anne was granted her dower lands immediately after her marriage; over the years, Richard was to augment them with other estates. In 1384, he gave her Woodstock Palace. On her wedding day, John of Gaunt presented her with a silver enameled ewer.

There was no money for her coronation, so she had to wait two days while Richard pawned the crown jewels of Aquitaine to pay for it. On January 22, the lords temporal and spiritual gathered in Westminster Abbey, where "the coronation of the Queen was performed most magnificently"[8] and Archbishop Courtenay crowned Anne "with all the glory and honour that could be devised."[9]

The queen consort's crown had been given to the City of London as security for a loan, and on January 1 the King had asked for it to be returned, having had to borrow money from a London grocer to redeem it. But Anne was probably crowned with an exquisite diadem of red and blue stones adorned with jewels, pearls, and small white flowers that she almost certainly brought to England from Bohemia. It had probably been made in the 1370s by a Parisian or Venetian goldsmith and was listed in Richard II's inventory of 1399 as having 12 fleurons, 91 pearls, 63 balas rubies, 47 sapphires, 33 diamonds, and 5 emeralds.

The *Liber Regalis* (Royal Book), an illuminated manuscript in the possession of Westminster Abbey, was probably prepared for Anne's coronation, for it contains the rite to be observed "on the day the Queen alone is to be crowned." There are illustrations of Anne enthroned by herself and seated a little below Richard; in both images, she wears a blue gown and mantle. The manuscript is thought to have been the work of a Bohemian artist in her train; stylistically, it resembles the Wenceslas Bible, made in Prague around 1400 (now in the Museum Plantin-Moretus in Antwerp). Bohemian influence is also apparent in the Great Missal of Westminster, produced in 1383, and the London Carmelites' missal of 1393.

There is another illustration of Anne's coronation in a contemporary manuscript in the Museo de Navarra, Pamplona, Spain.[10] In this, she wears a gold gown with a blue embroidered skirt and a blue mantle. Her long hair is blond.

At the young Queen's behest, a general pardon was granted by the King at her consecration.[11] After the Mass, she and the King laid their crowns on St. Edward's altar. Several days of celebrations followed. "To enhance the splendour of this great occasion, a tournament was held lasting several days" at Smithfield, "at which the English displayed their valour and the Queen's fellow countrymen demonstrated their worth. In the lists, praise and acclaim were won for knightly achievements, but not without losses on both sides."[12] Parliament was adjourned to allow its members to attend.

"The King, at the end of the week, carried his Queen to Windsor, where he kept open and royal house. They were very happy together."[13] An enduring love had flowered almost immediately. Richard became devoted to Anne and loved her "even to madness,"[14] while she reciprocated no less devotedly. He was thrilled by her status as the daughter of the Emperor and by her sophisticated cultural outlook. They discovered mutual passions for art, poetry, clothes, and luxurious living. A manuscript illustration in the Bodleian Library shows them hand in hand, gazing adoringly at each other. Richard's was the active role in the relationship, Anne's the passive, and she seems never to have tried to curb his headstrong character. He would say that he had chosen her "above all others" and he "rarely or never permitted [her] to be absent from his side."[15] When they were apart, they kept in close touch by letter. When Richard wrote to the Empress Elizabeth, he addressed her as "Mother of our beloved."[16] Anne too corresponded with her mother and sent her gifts of jewels and fabric.

At Windsor, she "was accompanied by the King's mother, the Princess of Wales, and her daughter, Joan Holland, Duchess of Brittany, half-sister to King Richard, who was then in England soliciting [unsuccessfully] for the restitution of the earldom [honour] of Richmond, which had been taken from her husband by the English regency and settled in part of dower of Queen Anne."[17]

Anne was also attended by many ladies and damsels, both Bohemian and English. Lady Luttrell was the mother of the Queen's maids. The Empress Elizabeth had appointed the "Landgravine of Luxembourg" one of her daughter's ladies of the bedchamber and had obtained from the King a safe-conduct enabling her to travel to England with valuables the Empress had sent for Anne and then return home afterward. The lady cannot be identified, as Luxembourg was then a duchy, not a landgraviate, but she was probably not the Queen's damsel Agnes Launcekron, who was soon to gain notoriety in England. Although Froissart called Agnes "the Landgravine," Walsingham asserted that she was an ignoble and foul cellarer, while the chronicler John Capgrave claimed that she was a saddler's daughter.

Richard's former governor, Richard Abberbury, was appointed Anne's chamberlain, the head of her household; he was later replaced by Sir Bernard Brocas, whose effigy can be seen in Westminster Abbey. The King allowed some of the Queen's needy Bohemians—mostly chaplains and ladies—who had accompanied her to England to remain in her household and was generous to them. They were granted pensions, honors, and benefices and married to members of the royal household, which aroused jealousy, the English resenting the preferment of foreigners. Their presence increased Anne's expenditure and led to criticism, causing tension between the King and Parliament. The Bohemians gained an enduringly poor reputation; as well as anger against the cost of maintaining them and the "abuses" for which they were allegedly responsible, there were suspicions that they and Anne were adherents of Wycliffe. Walsingham accused them of being no friends to the Church, while Froissart claimed that the Queen's servants and the Bohemian students she encouraged to study at Oxford were the first to communicate the teachings of Wycliffe to the Bohemian theologian Jan Hus, inspiring the calls for religious reform that would bring him to the stake in 1415.

Richard had no overt love for Lollardy, but did Anne? She seems to have been conventionally pious. She appears kneeling before the Virgin Mary in *The Hours of Anne of Bohemia,* which was made in Brussels shortly before her marriage and is now in the Bodleian Library, Oxford. In 1383, she obtained Pope Urban's permission to celebrate her name-saint's day with greater solemnity in England, giving impetus to the popular cult of St. Anne in her adoptive land. Possibly she wished to emphasize her reverence for the learning of St. Anne, who was the patron saint of wives, would-be mothers, and teachers. Maybe she hoped that the saint would intercede for her, that she might bear a child.

Anne gave St. Paul's Cathedral six copes embroidered with her arms and gold falcons. In 1385, she and Richard founded the Carthusian monastery known as the Charterhouse in Coventry. Anne shared the King's devotion to St. Edward the Confessor, and each year, on October 13, his feast day, wearing their crowns and carrying their scepters, they went in procession to his shrine in Westminster Abbey, the nave of which Richard would begin rebuilding. At other times, they heard Mass there, sitting in the choir. In the English Hospice of St. Thomas of Canterbury in Rome, now the Venerable English College, there once hung an altarpiece depicting Richard and Anne kneeling before the Virgin Mary, with the King offering her the kingdom of England. The painting was lost when the French occupied Rome in the 1790s. All these things bear testimony to Anne's personal and public piety.

During her first year in England, however, in collaboration with Joan of Kent, she interceded with the council to save Wycliffe, who had lost much support (including that of John of Gaunt) after refuting the doctrine of transubstantiation in 1381. Some of his teachings had been condemned as heretical. In her will, Anne named among her executors Sir Lewis Clifford and Sir Richard Stury, both ardent Lollards, and six members of her household who were also adherents of Wycliffe. In 1384, she and John of Gaunt successfully interceded on behalf of a former mayor of London, John of Northampton, who had been sentenced to a traitor's death for inciting unrest in the City and for Lollardy; his sentence was commuted to imprisonment.

Anne was well acquainted with the Scriptures, her brother Wenceslaus having authorized their translation into German and Czech. She even owned an English Bible, a controversial item to possess in England at that time. It had been presented to her by its translator, John Purvey, Wycliffe's former secretary. In his work *The Threefold Bond of Love*, Wycliffe wrote: "It is lawful that our noble Queen of England, sister of the Caesar, may have the Gospel written in three languages, Bohemian, German and Latin; now, to hereticate her on that account would be Luciferian folly! And since the Germans wish in this matter reasonably to defend their own tongue, so ought the English to defend theirs." Even the conservative Archbishop Arundel agreed. In her funeral oration, he praised Anne: "In the reading of godly books, she was more diligent than are the prelates themselves. Although queen, she diligently studied the Holy Scriptures and made them her daily meditation." He revealed that, "notwithstanding her foreign birth," she had read "all the four Gospels" in English too, which she must have learned with some dedication, and had sent them to him "to be verified and examined." He was impressed that "so great a lady and also an alien would so lowlily study in virtuous books."[18]

Despite an inauspicious beginning, and the fact that Bohemian support for the war with France never materialized, the new Queen's virtues and demeanor came to be increasingly admired. Walsingham wrote that she was a friend to the poor and generous with alms. The seventy-four pardons that would be granted at her request played their part and, when it became known that, in December, "at the special request of the noble Lady Anne, Queen of England,"[19] the King had pardoned many rebel peasants, the English people began calling her "the good Queen." Their favorable opinion was reinforced when she made another intercession for the peasants on February 14. In September, she would successfully petition for the burial of the executed leaders of the revolt at St. Albans. Her intercessions, which exceeded in number those of her three predecessors, made her "very precious to the nation" for "continually doing some good to the people."[20] Richard was not inclined to listen to the advice or pleas of others, so people looked to Anne to mitigate his harshness, regarding her as "a full blessed queen and gracious."

Among her many successful intercessions was one she made in the autumn of 1391, on behalf of two felons: a thief, Agnes Martin, and a pregnant murderess, Juliana Gylle, who had been convicted of housebreaking, robbery, and attacking a woman, gouging out her eyes and cutting out her tongue. Whether Anne took pity on Juliana because of her condition is not known, but her intercession saved the woman, who was pardoned.

Outwardly submissive, she nevertheless exerted considerable influence over her husband. An illustration in the Shrewsbury Charter of 1389 shows her on her knees before him receiving a charter in the traditional submissive pose of a supplicant. The Latin epitaph carved on her tomb at Westminster lauded her charity and her peacemaking character, recording that she gave nourishment to the sick and those enduring childbirth, going to them on foot, however far off, and poorly dressed. She fed "Christ's poor" from her treasure, assuaged strife, and appeased feuds. But she did not interfere in politics.

Her badge was a chained ostrich with an iron nail in its beak, a symbol of strength and endurance that appears in the decorated borders of English manuscripts. Richard owned an ostrich, and Anne had a cup fashioned from an ostrich egg mounted on silver and coated with white enamel. Her emblems of a sprig of rosemary and the Imperial eagle are incorporated into the pattern of the robe worn by Richard II in the Wilton Diptych, and her ostrich and rosemary emblems are recorded as appearing on two of the King's gold collars. Her seal, on which she is depicted standing beneath a traceried canopy, flanked with armorial shields, survives in the National Archives.

Anne's epitaph in Westminster Abbey records that she was "beauteous in body with a sweet and beautiful face," and one contemporary called her "the beauteous Queen," but the House of Luxembourg was not famed for beauty. Higden's continuator, John of Malvern, thought her ugly and a "small portion of flesh," suggesting a diminutive stature. Chaucer, in *The Legend of Good Women*, described her as having "gilt tresses" and a "fair body."

The most flattering description comes from Richard Maidstone, John of Gaunt's Carmelite chaplain, who saw Anne in 1392 and wrote in his Latin poem *Concordia*:

> A maiden too, her face enclosed by yellow hair,
> Her tresses neatly set beneath a garland's gleam,
> Her red dress shines in colour, brightened by the gold,
> Concealing underneath her very pretty limbs.
> Her name is Anne; I pray she might be Anne in deed.
> She is beautiful, with other beauties all around.
> Led by such an Amazon, New Troy is unsurpassed.
> Her dress is strewn and overspread with gleaming gems,
> Carbuncle, adamant [a hard carbon crystalline stone] and beryl,
>   all are there,
> Her head is overspread with every precious stone.

The words "New Troy" refer to the House of Luxembourg's claim to be descended from the ancient Trojans.

There are no surviving portraits of her, but her fine tomb effigy and the painted wooden head of her funeral effigy, which may be a death mask, both survive in Westminster Abbey. The latter has a long face with a low forehead, and a marked gap between the nose (which is not original) and the mouth. The tomb effigy's face is plumper and more stylized, with long wavy hair. When she was not gracing ceremonial occasions, Anne wore a single plait down her back.

She dressed fashionably and set trends. She introduced into England the two-foot-tall horned, pearl-studded headdress, or "moony tire" (a name said by Agnes Strickland to come from the Old Testament Book of Ezekiel, where in fact it is not to be found). Its frame, made of wire and board, was stuffed and padded, then covered with tissue (taffeta) or gauze. The English ladies loved it, but it was denounced by the Church as sinful, while some saw it as an emblem of Lollardy. The poet John Lydgate urged Englishwomen to "cast their horns aside," and men complained that these tall headdresses impeded their view of the altar in church. Yet the ladies devised ever more fantastical versions, so that they "blocked the street, and there was no passing along for [their] horns and steeples."

The Queen also popularized dress pins in place of skewers, and, for ladies, chair-like side saddles with footrests. One of her gowns was embroidered with branches of rosemary and broom in Cyprus gold. At the Garter feast of 1384, when Richard made her a Lady of the Garter (or, more correctly, a Lady of the Fraternity of St. George and of the Society of the Garter), she and her female attendants wore velvet robes lined with fur and hoods faced with scarlet. At Easter 1386, the royal couple appeared in gowns and hoods of blue velvet embroidered with Richard's white hart badge and trees of gold.

Anne owned beautiful jewels. In August 1382, Richard paid a London goldsmith £66.13s.4d. ($55,500) for a fillet with one large ruby and two sapphires, and three rings, each with four pearls centered on "one great diamond," all "for the use of Anne, Queen of England."[21] In her will of 1392, Isabel of Castile, Duchess of York, left her a gold belt decorated with ivy leaves. In 1399, an inventory was made of Anne's jewels,[22] which listed five gold collars adorned with ostriches and ferns, and set with diamonds, rubies, and pearls; another collar decorated with rosemary; five jeweled chaplets of gold, including one encrusted with 72 rubies, 150 diamonds, and 144 pearls; and twelve gold belts, one bearing a crowned A.

The inventory also lists some of her other possessions: three silver-gilt basins embossed with the linked crowns of England and the Empire; two basins encircled with the Lancastrian SS collar, wedding gifts from John of Gaunt; a jeweled ostrich egg enclosing the Queen's arms; a gold chalice and pax; a mirror on a base fashioned like a tree, decorated with pearls and enameled with roses, with the image of a queen on the back; various belts adorned with leaves, flowers, jewels, and bells; a ginger fork and a pomander.

After leaving Windsor in late February 1382, Richard and Anne moved to the Black Prince's former palace at Kennington, south of London, and then to Woodstock, whence they departed for a progress to the East Anglian shrines at Ely, Walsingham, and St. Edmundsbury. They swung south to make a pilgrimage to the shrine of Becket at Canterbury, then visited the New Forest, Arundel Castle, Beaulieu Abbey, and Corfe Castle. Anne would soon have become familiar with the country of which she was now queen.

The fifteen-year-old King now began exercising a degree of personal authority over the government. Despite his youth, he was already able to influence affairs and exercise patronage, despite lacking experience in statesmanship. Unfortunately, he chose to extend his favor to a clique of unworthy, grasping, but flattering courtiers, among whom the arrogant Robert de Vere, son of the Earl of Oxford, was the foremost. Once again, a royal favorite came to dominate the King.

Richard's infatuation for Robert de Vere was a political disaster. De Vere was an ambitious and resourceful young man of mediocre ability. Many believed his influence over the King to be pernicious. Richard was outraged by the criticism.

As with Edward II and Gaveston, there were suggestions of a homosexual relationship. Walsingham referred to "the depths of King Richard's affection for this man, whom he cultivated and loved, not without signs" that "obscene familiarity" was taking place. Adam of Usk bluntly charged the King with "sodomitical acts." The Monk of Evesham accused him of "remaining sometimes till midnight and sometimes till morning in drinking and other excesses that are not to be named." Clearly he did not wish to be too explicit. It may be significant that, in 1392, after de Vere had died abroad and was brought home for burial, Richard had his coffin opened so that he could look upon his face one last time and stroke his hands.

It is possible that both Richard and de Vere were bisexual. The King's devotion to Anne of Bohemia is dramatically well attested, and even

Walsingham admitted that the favorite was a notorious womanizer, a "Knight of Venus, more valiant in the bedchamber than on the field."

Richard and Anne never had children. Taking Anne to the famous shrine at Walsingham in 1382 is an indication of the King's keenness to produce an heir, for Our Lady of Walsingham was famed for granting pilgrims the blessing of offspring. In a document issued late that year, he spoke of his hopes for children "when God gives them." In a recently discovered letter Anne wrote to her brother Wenceslaus in 1384/5,[23] she wrote: "We thus describe our position to your Highness as lacking nothing that could be desired, except that we write grieving that still we are not rejoicing in our *puerperio* [childbirth], but concerning this, hope of health works in the near future, if the Lord permits." This overturns popular theories that her marriage to Richard was a chaste union by choice, in emulation of that of Edward the Confessor. But the lack of an heir was to magnify the King's problems.

Anne made it her policy to love all those Richard loved, for his sake, including Robert de Vere. She made no complaints or behaved like a slighted wife. But de Vere was resented for more than his sexual inclinations. "He provoked discontent among the other lords and barons, for he was no superior to the rest of them."[24] He continually urged Richard to ignore their advice and the decrees of Parliament, and Richard, completely besotted, complied; some complained that if de Vere said black was white, the King would not contradict him. He exploited his sovereign's devotion to the full. Richard lavished land, honors, and wealth on him, much to the disgust of the other magnates.

On July 6, 1383, Richard and Anne were guests of honor at a grand dinner hosted by Thomas Arundel, Bishop of Ely, at Ely Place in Holborn. Also present were the King's half-siblings, John Holland and Joan Holland, Duchess of Brittany, and many ladies and gentlemen. The Bishop outlaid £140 ($114,100) for the food and £220 ($164,279) for napery and spices.

That summer, "the King and Queen, with their Bohemians, made a tour of the abbeys of the kingdom." Not everyone approved, for "their arrival brought to these houses sadness in proportion to the burden it caused, because the royal party came with an enormous company, not to make offerings, but to take what they could get. The abbey of St. Edmundsbury felt the weight of their presence especially heavily; the house spent 800 marks [$509,000] on the King and Queen and their household during the ten days of their visit. When he had completed this damaging visit to Bury, King Richard moved on to Norwich," where he and Anne were received with great pomp. Wherever they went, "great offerings were not sufficient for the King unless they were matched by gifts of equal value to the Queen. In fact, the people would not have felt it burdensome to make such extravagant presentations out of consideration for the King's honour, if these offerings had been devoted wisely to the maintenance of the royal household, but whatever the King's grasping hand grabbed from them was soon wasted on the Queen's foreign attendants, the Bohemians, with the result that the royal party returned from this progress shorter of funds than when they had set out."[25] Anne was courting trouble when she wrote to ask her brother Wenceslaus to send more Bohemian ladies to serve her.

During this tour, the royal couple made another pilgrimage to Walsingham, which again suggests that they were praying for a child. At Ely, Sir James Berners, a member of the royal retinue, was blinded by a lightning strike, but was healed after making an intercession at the tomb of St. Etheldreda in the cathedral, before the astonished eyes of the King and Queen. The progress took Richard and Anne on to Nottingham and York before they returned to London. In York Minster, the figure of a Holy Roman Emperor wearing a triple crown may have been carved in honor of their visit.

In 1384, the King gave Anne the manors of Havering, Woodstock, and Leeds, Kent, all of which had palatial royal houses. Parliament complained about his extravagance and petitioned him not to permit Anne to claim any queen-gold. He refused, saying it had always been the consort's right and he would not diminish his wife's revenue. In Parliament's complaint may be detected a lingering resentment against a queen who had brought no rich dowry.

That year, Richard celebrated his seventeenth birthday and assumed personal rule, but his incompetence in government and his reliance on favorites such as de Vere, his old tutor Simon Burley, and Michael de la Pole, Earl of Suffolk, provoked bitter opposition among his nobles. Anne exercised some restraint over him, but not enough, and the court faction began struggling with the conservative John of Gaunt and the great nobles for supremacy. Public enmity and resentment shifted from the hitherto unpopular Gaunt, who was now beginning to be seen as a force for good in politics, to the profligate de Vere and his satellites.

Drip-fed vitriol by the latter, Richard came to resent his uncle's dominance. John of Gaunt had an inbred veneration for kingship and was inclined to lecture his nephew on the duties and obligations of good government and censure him for his profligate abuse of patronage. This led to tension between them, with Richard attempting to throw off the constraints with which the wiser and vastly more experienced Gaunt tried to control him, and actively encouraging his favorites to oppose the Duke, whom they feared "because of his great power, his admirable judgement and his brilliant mind."[26] It was fortunate for Richard that his uncle had an unshakeable loyalty to the Crown.

3

"Great Murmurings"

＊

I N THE SUMMER OF 1385, BEFORE ACCOMPANYING RICHARD II
on a lackluster invasion of Scotland, John of Gaunt lavishly entertained the King and Queen at Leicester Castle. Afterward, the party traveled north. In York, there was an ugly incident. Anne's favored knight, Sir
Ralph de Stafford, was about to depart for London with messages for his
friend Meles, one of the Queen's Bohemian knights, when, unknown to
him, his archers and the followers of Sir John Holland, the King's half-
brother, clashed "in a quarrel over the treatment of a knight from Bohemia who had come to visit Queen Anne." In the fracas, one of Stafford's
men killed one of Holland's squires. Holland confronted Stafford, accusing him of being a party to the murder. "Sir Ralph, though angry with
his archer, tried to negotiate his pardon, but Sir John, in a frenzy, knocked
Sir Ralph off his horse in the dark with his sword and accidentally killed
him."[1] Holland fled to sanctuary in Beverley Minster as Lord Stafford,
who had lost his only son, demanded justice. The King condemned Holland to death and had his property seized.

In vain did the Princess Joan plead for her son's life. Her grief took its
toll on her and she died at Wallingford on August 8, "so fat from eating
that she could scarcely walk."[2] Possibly her obesity had predisposed her
to a heart attack. At the Queen's request, Richard now pardoned Holland, which did not endear either of them to the Staffords and their
friends.

That August, Richard created Robert de Vere marquess of Dublin and
bestowed the dukedoms of York and Gloucester on his uncles, Edmund

of Langley and Thomas of Woodstock. He also named his cousin, eleven-year-old Roger Mortimer, his heir. This suggests he had begun to fear that he might never have a son of his own. Had he and Anne never consummated their marriage, it is unlikely that the King, knowing he would not have heirs of his body, would have waited three years to name his successor.

In March 1386, Richard II formally recognized John of Gaunt as King of Castile. By Easter, the Duke had begun assembling his invasion fleet, and there was a lavish ceremony of farewell at court, with the King and Queen solemnly placing golden diadems on the heads of Gaunt and Constance. The couple sailed to Castile in July. Richard was doubtless relieved to be rid of his powerful and intimidating uncle, and Robert de Vere now reigned triumphant at court.

In 1386–87, Richard, Anne, and de Vere spent much of their time progressing around England, an evasive tactic employed by the King to avoid confrontations with his increasingly seething councillors and build up support for himself. They kept the Christmas of 1386 at Eltham—their third there in a row—where Richard had built a painted chamber, a dancing chamber, and a bathhouse. He had also created a garden for Anne and an herb garden beyond the moat where the King and Queen could dine in summer; it had walls of earth and straw lined with reeds. Anne's apartments in the inner court boasted a tower with an oriel window, a hall, and a great chamber and lesser chamber that she shared with Richard. That Christmas, they received a guest, Leo V, King of Armenia, who was trying, unsuccessfully, to bring about a peace between England and France.

The following spring, their travels took them to Leicestershire, York, and Coventry. In March, they visited Lincoln, to be admitted to the confraternity of the cathedral. Then they went hunting in Sherwood Forest.

John of Gaunt's military campaign in Spain had ended in dysentery, mass desertions, and disaster; he had failed to rally sufficient Iberian backing for his cause. In July 1387, finally accepting that his long-cherished dream of winning the throne of Castile was never going to come to fruition, he reached an agreement with King Juan I whereby he and Constance would relinquish their Castilian claims to their daughter Katherine and marry her to Juan's son Enrique.

By then, England was descending into political turmoil as the King engaged in a bitter struggle with those lords who resented his reliance on favorites and were demanding a new push to win the war with France. Richard was essentially inclined to peace and had never yet led an army into the field, which was seen as an abrogation of his duty by his martially minded magnates.

There were also "great murmurings" because de Vere, who was married to Richard's cousin Philippa (the daughter of the Princess Isabella by Enguerrand de Coucy), had fallen "in such love with one of the Queen's damsels, called the Landgravine, that in no wise could he leave the sight of her." This was Anne's "fair and pleasant" chamber woman, Agnes Launcekron.[3] She may have been unwilling because, "to his everlasting disgrace and reproach,"[4] de Vere sent two of his men to abduct her, and then "copulated" with her "in nefarious [unlawful] marriage." He "loved her so entirely that he would gladly be divorced from his own wife. All the good people of England were much shocked at this,"[5] especially since de Vere had risen "in such great pride of heart that he refused his wife, a fair woman and good,"[6] and, in 1387, sent fraudulent evidence to the Pope in order to secure an annulment so that he could marry Agnes.

Richard turned a blind eye to, and indeed connived in, de Vere's adultery and the slighting of his royal wife, which aroused the anger of many of his relations. Anne too supported the lovers. She wrote to Pope Urban VI, urging him to dissolve de Vere's marriage and permit him to wed his sweetheart, which he did in the summer of 1387. The King's uncle, Gloucester, was incensed at this slight to his niece, and Anne's intervention may have triggered the hostility he was later to show to her.

That summer, Parliament demanded that the King remove those counselors who were considered to be a bad influence: Robert de Vere, Michael de la Pole, Alexander Neville, Archbishop of York, Sir Robert Tresilian, and Sir Nicholas Brembre. Because they were appealing to Richard to restore good government, the magnates who opposed him called themselves the "Lords Appellant." Richard retorted that he would not remove a scullion from his kitchen at their request, and had Parliament declare their actions unlawful and treasonable. But he would prove to be no match for the determination of the lords.

In November, secretly intent on impeaching the Lords Appellant,

Richard returned with Anne and de Vere to London. They were welcomed by a large deputation of citizens clad in the Queen's colors of red and white, and attended Mass at St. Paul's before taking up residence at Westminster. The next morning, Richard learned that Gloucester, Bolingbroke, Richard FitzAlan, Earl of Arundel, Thomas Mowbray, Earl of Nottingham, and Thomas de Beauchamp, Earl of Warwick, were marching on the capital with an army of 40,000 men. Then came a message from the Appellants demanding an audience, which he dared not refuse.

The next day, he received them in Westminster Hall, only to see them fling down their gauntlets and demand the dismissal of his favorite counselors, whom they accused of treason. Meekly, he agreed. De Vere, de la Pole, and the Archbishop of York fled into hiding, but Tresilian and Brembre were executed, the former being dragged from the sanctuary of Westminster Abbey to his doom.

On December 20, Bolingbroke defeated de Vere in a skirmish at Radcot Bridge, for which he was hailed as a hero. Richard now had no choice but to submit to the demands of the victors and banished de Vere from the realm. The favorite fled into exile, never to return. (He would be savaged fatally by a boar in 1392.) Their purge complete, the Appellants forced the King to accept councilors of their own choosing. Then they withdrew to the north, leaving Richard and Anne under house arrest in the Tower, where they spent a desolate Christmas amid the splendor of the royal apartments, which the King had had refurbished with 105 square feet of stained glass depicting the royal arms, floor tiles embossed with lions and white harts, and murals of popinjays in gold and vermilion.

In January, the Appellants marched on London. The Lord Mayor surrendered the keys to them, and they demanded to see the King. In the Tower, Richard received them "royally," seated on his throne and holding his scepter, but to no effect. The lords gave him a list of names of those they considered subversives deserving of imprisonment. One was his old tutor, Sir Simon Burley, to whom he and Anne were greatly attached. When Richard demurred, Bolingbroke led him up onto the wall of the Tower and showed him the angry crowds below. The King capitulated.

* * *

Henry of Bolingbroke was then twenty, a powerfully built young man of medium height, always richly and elegantly garbed. He was handsome and well educated, and a skillful jouster who loved tournaments and feats of arms and went twice on crusade. Like his father he maintained great state and kept a large retinue. He was popular and respected and a potentially formidable opponent to Richard II. John of Gaunt was exceptionally proud of his son, delighted in his military prowess, and demonstrated great affection toward him.

In 1380, Gaunt had sought a bride for Henry, who was then thirteen. From birth, the boy had been styled Earl of Derby, one of his father's lesser titles, but he was popularly known as Henry of Bolingbroke. Following Edward III's policy of marrying his sons to English heiresses and thus extending their land holdings, affinities, and influence, John of Gaunt chose Mary de Bohun, the co-heiress of his late friend, Humphrey de Bohun, Earl of Hereford, Essex, and Northampton. Mary was only eleven, but Gaunt wanted her half of the Bohun inheritance for his son. Eleanor, her elder sister and co-heiress, was married to Thomas of Woodstock, Duke of Gloucester, and Mary was living with them at Pleshey, Essex. Not content with his share of the Bohun lands, Gloucester was determined to lay his hands on the rest, which comprised the earldoms of Hereford and Northampton, and he put relentless pressure on Mary to surrender everything to him and take the habit of a Poor Clare nun. But, in July 1380, with the connivance of her mother and John of Gaunt, Mary's aunt, Elizabeth de Bohun, Countess of Arundel, kidnapped her from Pleshey while Gloucester was away campaigning in France, and took her to Arundel Castle in Sussex. On July 28, Gaunt obtained from Richard II a grant of Mary's marriage, thwarting his brother's ambitions. Gloucester was furious. By March 1381, Mary and Bolingbroke were married.

After the wedding ceremony, Mary remained with her mother, it having been agreed that the consummation of the marriage should be delayed until she reached fourteen, in February 1382. But the young couple breached this rule and Mary bore a son, possibly called Edward, in April that year; he lived four days. After that, John of Gaunt prohibited any resumption of marital relations until November 1385, when Bolingbroke and Mary were finally given their own establishment. On September 16, 1386, at Monmouth Castle, Mary gave birth to the future Henry V. In

1387, she bore a second son, Thomas, who was speedily followed by John in 1389, Humphrey in 1390, and Blanche in 1392.

Bolingbroke's faithfulness to his wife was commented on throughout the courts of Europe, but a deadly enmity was burgeoning between him and the King. Richard was to complain that Bolingbroke had once drawn his sword on him in the Queen's chamber.

The Parliament that met in February 1388 would become known as the Merciless Parliament because the Lords Appellant had five of the King's remaining favorites tried, convicted, and purged his household of those who had supported him in his misgovernment. Sir Simon Burley was accused, among other things, of having appropriated to himself money he had been given to pay for the Queen's journey to England in 1381. He had from the first identified himself with the hated Bohemians and was accused of counseling Richard "to have in his household many aliens, Bohemians and others, and to give them great gifts."[7]

The Appellants' hostility toward Anne was apparent in petitions to the King demanding that she pay £10 ($8,900) per annum for her expenses, "as the late Queen was accustomed to do," and that "the Queen's Bohemians be sent out of the kingdom before the feast of St. John, and any remaining after (except those allowed by the lords of the Council to serve the Queen) shall be placed without the King's protection."[8] Clearly the Appellants saw her as an enemy, and old resentments still rankled.

Richard later recalled that "the Queen and I interceded tirelessly" on behalf of Burley, who had helped to arrange their marriage, and John Calverly, one of Anne's esquires. At Woodstock, Anne spent three hours on her knees before Gloucester, Bolingbroke, and Arundel, "pleading with tears" for their lives, only to be told, "Pray for yourself and your husband, for the request is useless."[9] The Appellants did pardon some condemned judges in response to her appeal, but Burley was sentenced to death on March 5 and went to the block on Tower Hill the same day; Anne had wrung some small mercy in begging that he be spared the traitor's death that was meted out to three of the King's knights.

Grudgingly, Richard brought Anne to London. In Parliament, he renewed his coronation oath and received the homage of the nobility. It was to be a new start, with Parliament holding all the aces. The King would never forgive the Appellants for limiting his power, slaughtering his friends, and humiliating Anne by refusing her pleas. Grieving and furious, he sought refuge with her at Bristol Castle.

The Appellants also confiscated de Vere's property and ordered all the Bohemians in the Queen's household, including Agnes Launcekron, to leave England within a month. They passed a law forbidding anyone to receive the confidences of the King and Queen. Civil war threatened and the Archbishop of Canterbury tried to propose a truce, but the King refused to see him. For two days and nights, Anne pleaded with him to relent, until "at last, by the good advice of the Queen, he restrained his choler and agreed to accompany the Archbishop to London."[10]

Richard and Anne spent most of the next year under constraint at Eltham and Sheen. Sheen Palace was larger than Eltham. After Queen Isabella's death, Edward III had transformed it into a magnificent palace with buildings arranged around two timber-framed courts. The lower one, the Downcourt, fronted the Thames and was enclosed by a moat. It contained the royal lodgings, the great hall, the chapel, and the wardrobe.

Below the palace, on the river, was an island called La Neyt (now possibly to be identified with the uninhabited Corporation Island), where, in 1384–88, Richard had built a large timber-framed palace on stone foundations, a personal retreat for himself and Anne. A paved path to the river was laid, steps were built, and a new barge constructed. The luxurious island retreat afforded a high degree of privacy, being surrounded by a wooden paling, or fence. There was space for 1,000 guests to dine there. The King's bathroom was fitted with 2,000 multicolored glazed tiles—purchased for 15s. ($676) from Katherine Lightfoot, future wife of the architect Henry Yevele—and a bath with copper taps, from which ran hot and cold water. The royal chambers had en suite garderobes, and hearths even in small rooms that would normally have been heated by braziers. The palace had its own chapel and kitchen, and a jetty was built for the delivery of provisions. It was one of Richard and Anne's favorite residences, a place where they could entertain. But La Neyt was now a gilded prison.

Richard endured his humiliating submission to the Appellants until May 3, 1389. Now twenty-two years old, he declared himself of full age, dismissed them, and reasserted his regal authority without opposition. For the next eight years, he ruled England autonomously, governing wisely.

* * *

Earlier in 1389, Geoffrey Chaucer had been imprisoned in the Tower for becoming embroiled in a dispute over the election of a new mayor. Anne's intercession secured his release, and Richard appointed him Clerk of the King's Works. His new responsibilities included the management of the Tower, where he was assigned a lodging.

To Chaucer, Anne was "my lady sovereign, that is so good, so fair, so debonair." In his poem *The Fall of Princes*, John Lydgate stated that Chaucer wrote *The Legend of Good Women* (*c.*1387) "at request of the Queen," who had complained about his portrayal of her sex as faithless in *Troilus and Criseyde*, and may have been offended by his comparing her with the disloyal heroine:

> Right among these other folk was Criseyde,
> In widow's habit black, but natheless
> Right as our first letter is now an A [for Anne],
> In beauty first so stood she, makeless.

In *The Legend of Good Women*, Queen Alceste and her husband, the god of love, may have been based on Anne and Richard. Alceste is shown protesting against the derogatory portrayal of women in literature. She ends:

> "Go now your ways, the penance is but slight.
> And when the book's done, give it to the Queen,
> On my behalf, at Eltham or at Sheen."

Chaucer dedicated the poem to Anne, who was "so womanly, so gracious, and so meek." After her death, he removed the reference to her "at Eltham or at Sheen," probably not wishing further to sadden the grieving King. But he left the *ballade* that almost certainly sang her praises:

> Had Absalom thy gilt tresses clear,
> Esther lay thou thy meekness all a-down,
> Had Jonathan all thy friendly manner,
> Penelope and Marcia Catoun
> Make of your wifehood no comparison;
> Hide ye your beauties, Isolde and Elaine:
> My lady cometh that all this may disdain.

> *Thy fair body, let it not appear, Lavinia,*
> *And thou, Lucrezia, of Rome town;*
> *And Polixene that boughten love so dear,*
> *And Cleopatra with all thy passion;*
> *Hide ye your truth of love and your renown,*
> *And thou, Thisbe, that had of love such pain:*
> *My lady cometh that all this may disdain.*

Anne was probably also the model for the poem's "Queen of the Daisy"—"the white ycrowned Queen":

> *And from afar came walking in the mead*
> *The God of Love and on his arm a queen,*
> *And she was clad in royal habit green.*
> *A net of gold she wore upon her hair,*
> *And on that a white crown did she bear*
> *With small flowers, no lies hear from me,*
> *For all the world, just as a daisy*
> *Is crowned with white petals light,*
> *So were the flowers of her crown white;*
> *For of one fine pearl oriental,*
> *Her white crown was fashioned all,*
> *So that the white crown above the green*
> *Made her like a daisy in that scene,*
> *Considering also her gold net above.*

This resembles the crown Anne had brought from Bohemia, which had "small white flowers" that were probably daisies. The anonymous dream-vision poem "Pearl" (which was commissioned in 1395, perhaps by Richard II, in Anne's memory) mentions "a bright crown" of marguerites, which might also be a reference to Anne's crown. The daisy may have been one of her devices, as she also had a cup decorated with the flowers, and they appear in the Wilton Diptych.

In the 1390s, Sir John Clanvow referenced Anne in his *The Book of Cupid, God of Love* (also known as *The Cuckoo and the Nightingale*), a dream vision inspired by Chaucer's *The Parliament of Fowls*. In it, the nightingale praises love, but the cuckoo mocks it for causing more trouble than joy. Finally, a parliament is to be held to decide who is right:

> *And this shall be, withouten any nay,*
> *The morrow of Saint Valentine's Day,*
> *Under a maple that is fair and green,*
> *Before the chamber window of the Queen*
> *At Woodstock, upon the green lay.*
> *She thanked him, and then her leave took.*

Anne may have been among the inspirations for John Gower's poem *Confessio Amantis* (*The Confession of Amans*), written around 1386-90. He makes a pun on her name, refers to "the fashion of Bohemia" prevailing at the court of love, and especially lauds faithful wives.

In September 1389, Bolingbroke—ostensibly forgiven—was restored to the council, because Richard needed the support of John of Gaunt, who had been in Aquitaine concluding a new truce with the French. On October 30, the impatient King formally summoned him home.

Gaunt returned in November laden with treasure, but prematurely aged—a French councilor referred to him at this time as "an old black boar." In December, paying his uncle a great honor, the King rode out from Reading to greet him and gave him the kiss of peace with enthusiastic warmth. He even removed John's Lancastrian livery collar and placed it about his own neck.

In January 1390, John of Gaunt and Gloucester were appointed to the council. John's return ushered in an era of greater political stability and order. The King placed great trust and confidence in him and was anxious to work with him to promote peace with France. He promised him he would listen to good counsel and bestow his patronage more wisely than in the past. For his part, John of Gaunt proved moderate and staunchly loyal, acting as a peace-broker between the King and the former Appellants, and slipping effortlessly into the role of elder statesman.

In March, Richard formally invested John of Gaunt with the duchy of Aquitaine, an event marked by great festivities at court, during which

Queen Anne placed the gold circlet of Aquitaine on the head of the Duchess Constance. The new Duke and Duchess did not visit Aquitaine immediately; John of Gaunt delegated seneschals to rule in his absence.

That spring, Richard sent heralds throughout England, Scotland, Flanders, France, and Germany to proclaim a great tournament, which was to be held at Smithfield at Michaelmas. In July, he, Anne, and various nobles watched the parish clerks of London act short plays called interludes at Skinners' Hall on Dowgate Hill. The performances went on for three days. That summer, John of Gaunt lavishly entertained King Richard and Queen Anne at a great hunting party at Leicester Castle, attended by York, Gloucester, Arundel, and many other magnates. "Several days on end were devoted to amusement and gaiety."[11] On August 15, the King and Queen celebrated the Feast of the Assumption of the Virgin Mary at a dinner in the Franciscans' refectory at Salisbury.

Visitors were now arriving for the great tournament, among them Anne's uncle Wenzel, now Duke of Luxembourg. At Michaelmas, while lodging at the Bishop of London's palace by St. Paul's Cathedral, the King and Queen rode to Smithfield for the jousts. Sixty knights, ready for "tilting courteously against all comers," rode out of the Tower and were escorted along Cheapside to the lists by sixty beautifully gowned ladies on palfreys, leading each knight by a silver chain. Their arrival was watched by the King and Queen "with many great estates" and Anne's ladies, all seated in richly decorated open chambers in the royal stand, which had been specially built for the occasion. The knights "tilted courteously, with blunted lances, against all comers," while the Queen and the ladies acted as umpires and presented a gold crown and a gold clasp as prizes. Afterward, at the Bishop's Palace, there was a banquet and dancing in the presence of the royal family.

The next day, "the King, richly armed, jousted himself, in the presence of the Queen and the ladies of the court." Then "the tournament was renewed by the squires, who tilted until night in the presence of the King, Queen and all the nobles." Afterward, Anne presented a warhorse and a falcon to the champions of the day. When dusk fell, she and the King returned to the Bishop's palace for supper, which was followed by dancing. "These jousts continued for four days, from noon till night, and every evening concluded with a magnificent repast and entertainment of feasting, music and dancing, in which the Queen, her ladies, and many of the young nobility were the principal performers."[12] Some were held at Kennington Palace, and suppers were hosted by the King and John of Gaunt. On the fourth day, the dancing went on until dawn. In the evening, Richard hosted a banquet for his foreign guests, while Anne presided over one for their ladies.

On October 13, the feast of St. Edward the Confessor, Richard wore his crown to High Mass in Westminster Abbey; soon after it began, "the Queen solemnly entered the choir, wearing her crown, and took her place on the north side."[13] Both wore their crowns at dinner afterward. Then the court moved to Windsor for yet another feast. At Christmas 1390, John of Gaunt was the guest of the King and Queen at Eltham.

4

"All Comfort Was Bereft"

❋

B Y LATE 1391, TROUBLE WAS BREWING IN LONDON. A BAD HAR-vest had led to food shortages and discontent. There were rumors that the King was incapable of ruling and would recall de Vere. Richard had to impose a curfew and ban assemblies.

That year, the burghers of London refused to loan the King £1,000 ($895,600), provoking a bitter quarrel that led to his revoking the City's charter and privileges. In May 1392, he moved the law courts to York, where he stayed with Anne for ten days. In June, he arrested the Lord Mayor and sheriffs of London and imposed a crippling fine of £100,000 ($89.5 million) on the City. The mayor and his brethren now deemed it politic to submit to him, and wrote to Anne asking her "to assume with bowels of compassion the office of a mediatrix with that most excellent prince and puissant lord, our lord the King, your lord and ours, and in the exercise of your magnificence to recommend your subjects to our very noble lord aforesaid, as did other our queens, who preceded your most excellent Highness in your realm of England. May it please your most clement and pre-eminent nobility thus to mediate by gracious words and deeds with our lord the King. These things, most excellent lady, we have boldly presumed to lay in your merciful hands because our ladies, the queens of England, on their first arrivals, have been wont to afford to their subjects the manifestation of their generosity."[1]

Anne willingly agreed, and Richard seized on her appeal as a means of capitulating without losing face and arranged for her intercession to be the focus of a great public spectacle, accounts of which were recorded in Richard Maidstone's *Concordia* and *The Brut* manuscript.

The day of reconciliation on August 21, 1392, was marked by magnificent pageantry. The King rode in a grand procession from Sheen to London, with Anne following at the head of a second cavalcade, her ladies riding behind in a red chariot. In robes glittering with precious stones and a rich carcanet around her neck, she looked "the fairest of the fair."

On Blackheath, the royal couple were welcomed by the mayor, sheriffs, aldermen, guildsmen, and leading citizens "in good array. And thus they brought the King and the Queen to London." At Southwark, Anne put on a gold crown set with gems. "When the King came to the gate of [London] Bridge," the mayor presented him with "a milk-white steed, and the Queen a palfrey, all white, trapped in the same array with white and red" with a gold saddle and a harness tinkling with silver bells. Then he handed the keys and sword of the City to the King and took the opportunity to remind Anne what she had undertaken to do.

"O generous offspring of Imperial blood, whom God hath destined worthy to sway the sceptre as consort of our King, mercy and not rigour best become the queenly station and gentle ladies have great influence with their loving lords," he said, then went on to extol the merits of her new white palfrey, its duty and docility.

The procession crossed the bridge, to the sound of cymbals, lyres, citterns, and vielles. The narrow thoroughfare was crammed with buildings on either side, and such was the press of people that the chariot carrying the ladies was overturned and only their padded horned headdresses cushioned them from injury.

The Londoners had put on a marvelous show. The streets were hung with cloth of gold and silver tissue, crimson banners, and tapestries of silk threaded with gold. Between the conduit on Cheapside and Paul's Cross, "a marvellous tower had been built on a stage, and therein were many angels with divers melodies and song." One, wearing a diadem, floated down through a "cloud, without steps or stairs," and set "a crown of gold and precious stones on the King's head, and another on the Queen's head," symbolizing the God-given nature of regal power. The conduit was flowing with red wine for all, but the royal couple were served "rosy wine smiling in golden cups."

At the west end of Cheapside, there was a tableau in which God sat surrounded by angels. Outside St. Paul's, another company of "angels" gathered around a fountain played music on seventeen different instruments as the King and Queen dismounted and entered the Cathedral to make their offerings at the shrine of St. Erkenwald. When they emerged, they rode on to Ludgate. As they crossed the Fleet bridge by the Blackfriars monastery, they were greeted with another pageant in which "a celestial band of spirits" saluted them and scattered fragrant flowers on them. At Temple Bar, there was a pageant of St. John the Baptist and the Holy Lamb set in a desert with trees, shrubs, dragons, and all manner of beasts, who surged around, attacking each other. St. John hailed the King, to whom the angels gave a gold tablet depicting the Crucifixion; the Queen received a silver one portraying scenes of the life of St. Anne. Grasping an angel by the hand, Richard addressed the crowds: "Peace to this City! For the sake of Christ, His Mother and my patron, St. John, I freely forgive every offence."[2]

Then the mayor made an oration, appealing to the Queen to intercede with the King on behalf of the City. "Illustrious daughter of Imperial parents, Anne—a name in Hebrew signifying grace, and which was borne by her who was the mother of the mother of Christ. Mindful of your race and name, intercede for us to the King and, as often as you see this tablet, think of our city and speak in our favour."

"Leave all to me," Anne replied, and promised to do her duty to the City.

"And so the citizens brought the King and Queen unto Westminster, praying him that they might have his good love." Playing the magnanimous monarch to perfection, the King entered Westminster Hall and sat on the King's Bench, from which justice was administered, and which had been covered with cloth of gold. The Archbishop of Canterbury and the Bishop of London took up their positions on either side of him. Anne then arrived at the head of her procession and fell to her knees before her husband.

"What would, Anna?" he asked. "Declare, and your request shall be granted."

"Sweet my King, my spouse, my light, my life," Anne replied, "no king since Brutus, even Arthur himself, has had such a welcome. Sweet love, without whose life mine would be but death, be pleased to govern your citizens as a gracious lord. Consider, even today, how munificent their treatment, what worship, what honour, what splendid public duty have they at great cost paid to thee, revered King. Like us, they are but mortal and liable to frailty. Far from thy memory, my King, my sweet love, be their offences, and for their pardon I supplicate, kneeling thus lowly on the ground." She urged that he, "of grace," would please "restore to these worthy and penitent plebeians their ancient charters and liberties."

"Be satisfied, dearest wife," Richard replied. "Loath should we be to deny any reasonable request of thine. Meantime, ascend and sit beside me on my throne, while I speak a few words to my people."[3] "Then the King took up the Queen and granted her all her asking."[4]

Turning to the mayor and citizens, he said, "I will restore to you my royal favour, for I duly prize the expense which you have incurred and the prayers of the Queen."[5] He did not immediately restore all London's privileges, although he returned to the mayor the key and ceremonial sword of London, for which they thanked him and Anne. Then spices and wine were served and the King and Queen left for Kennington. (On September 19, Richard was to issue a formal pardon at Woodstock, in which it was stated four times that it had been granted "through the mediation of his dear wife, the Queen.")[6]

The next day, the warden of London entertained the royal couple to a feast at which the citizens presented Anne with a crystal hanaper (a cup or goblet, or a case for one) and a gold-mounted ewer in a beryl casing. When she and Richard departed for Westminster, the City's guildsmen accompanied them along the Thames, dancing and making music in decorated barges. The King invited them to join him for drinks in the palace, and they went home "with very great joy and comfort."[7]

Richard saw that Anne was rewarded, since she was "very precious to the nation, being continually doing some good to the people,"[8] and deserved a much larger dower, although the sum settled on her had nevertheless appreciated in value and was now worth the equivalent of $4 million today.

The Londoners further expressed their gratitude with the gift of a nine-foot-long silver-gilt table. At Epiphany, hoping for a perfect reconciliation, they rode to Eltham and presented Anne with a jewel in the shape of a pelican, a bird reputed to sacrifice itself by feeding its young with blood from its breast, and therefore a symbol of selfless femininity.

Richard received a camel, which was symbolic of humility and anger. The deputation also brought a troupe of mummers, who performed a play for the King and Queen and were entertained with dancing and other revelry, it being still Christmastide. Richard relented and restored all the City's privileges, remitting a large fine. In the summer of 1393, he made the warden of London Bridge pay for sculptured reliefs of himself and Anne that were carved in the stone gate of the bridge.

Richard had won over the City. He was now fully in control of his kingdom.

In 1393, Anne learned of the death of her mother, the Empress Elizabeth, who had spent her last years in seclusion at Hradec Kralove, a dower town of the queens of Bohemia, and was buried next to Charles IV in St. Vitus's Cathedral in Prague. Richard, who had corresponded fondly with his mother-in-law, ordered a requiem Mass on June 12 at St. Paul's Cathedral, where he paid for "a very unusual imperial shrine" to her memory.[9] In July, when he and Anne stayed at Corfe Castle in Dorset, he had another Mass celebrated in memory of his own mother. August saw the King and Queen reviving the ancient ceremony of crown-wearing in Salisbury Cathedral. Afterward they visited the abbeys of Beaulieu and Titchfield, where the Abbot served them a supper of twelve dressed pike.

At New Year 1394, Henry of Bolingbroke gave the Queen a present of gold and silver, and she gave him a gift in return. That January, although he and Anne were both only twenty-seven, Richard made it clear that he did not expect to have children with her when he granted Thomas Mowbray, Earl of Nottingham, the right to use a crowned leopard as his crest, an emblem traditionally reserved for the King's eldest son, "if we had begotten the same," he wrote.[10] But to the end of her life, Anne may have gone on hoping for a child, if her apothecary's bills for 1393–94 are anything to go by, for they list water plantain, trisandali, spikenard, diapendion, mustard, and trifera magna, all of which were recommended as aids to conception.

Others did not like to refer to the King's childlessness, although the Parliament over whose opening Richard and Anne presided that January asked, "Who is it that dares to suggest that the King will have no issue?"[11] But the question was a legitimate one, for the royal couple had been wed for twelve years. Contemporaries would have seen their childlessness as ominous, for Scripture (Deuteronomy 7:14) taught that if a nation kept God's commandments, "there shall not be male or female barren among you"; a barren queen, therefore, was a judgment on the land.

Richard had been planning an expedition to Ireland, but while he and Anne were staying at La Neyt in April, she "fell sick, to the infinite distress of King Richard and all her household."[12] For two months, the King's plans were on hold as he willed her to get better. But "Death snatched Anne away from our prince."[13] A late-fifteenth-century manuscript in the British Library portrays her on her deathbed.[14] The Westminster chronicler stated that "her disorder increased so rapidly that she departed this life at the feast of Whitsuntide," June 7, 1394. In fact, she had actually died on or before June 3, when Richard sent to London for an image or effigy "made in the likeness of Anne, late Queen of England,"[15] to be brought by boat to Sheen. It was almost certainly her wooden funeral effigy, which can be seen in another manuscript illustration in the British Library.[16] Its head survives today in Westminster Abbey, the earliest extant funeral effigy of an English consort.

"The King and all who loved her were greatly afflicted at her death."[17] Her epitaph records that she perished "through irremedial sickness," which is said to have been the plague, although the chroniclers would surely have been specific about that. There is no record of an outbreak that year in England; had there been, it is unlikely that Anne would have been left unburied for weeks or that the nobility would have attended her funeral. Her apothecary's accounts for the year leading up to her death do not give any hint that her health was failing, so she probably contracted a disease that progressed rapidly or had not produced symptoms earlier.

Anne was only twenty-eight, just eight months older than her husband. "King Richard was inconsolable for her loss. He could never forget her, so much had they been in love ever since they were married as little more than children."[18] She was widely mourned by his subjects too. "Although she died childless, this Queen was held to be glorious and beneficial to the realm of England, so that both nobles and commoners greatly mourned her death."[19]

"The year of her death was notable for splendid funerals"—those of the Queen, Constance, Duchess of Lancaster, who had died in March, and Mary de Bohun, Countess of Derby, who died in childbed on June 4— "but the grief for all these deaths by no means equalled that of the King for his own Queen Anne, whom he had loved even to madness."[20] "Thus the King, the Duke of Lancaster and the Earl of Derby [Henry of Bolingbroke] were all left widowers in the same year, and there was no talk of the King marrying again, for he would not hear of it."[21] Indeed, Richard vowed that for the next year, he would enter no building unless it was a church he had visited with Anne.

He wrote to King Wenceslaus to inform him of Anne's death. He canceled a forthcoming visit by William I, Duke of Guelders, writing that he was afflicted by "the heaviest sadness and bitterness of heart, and therefore could not show as much courtesy for your friendship as we would like." In July, he went to Wales "and tried to distract his mind from his loss with hunting expeditions on the way."[22]

Anne's burial was deferred until St. Anne's Day; "her obsequies were performed at leisure, for the King would have them majestically and magnificently done,"[23] and time was needed to prepare. He kept her embalmed body at La Neyt, where they had known such happiness, for nearly two months. On June 10, at Westminster, he sent orders of attendance to his "dear and faithful cousins" the nobility and their wives: "Inasmuch that our beloved companion the Queen, whom God has commanded, will be buried at Westminster on Monday, the 3rd of August next, we earnestly entreat that you, setting aside all excuses, will repair to our city of London" by July 29. "We desire that you will, the preceding day, accompany the corpse of our dear consort from our manor of Sheen to Westminster, and for this we trust we may rely on you, as you desire our honour."[24] The ladies were to wear cloaks of black velvet (or cloth, depending on their rank) with hoods and long trains. On July 10, messengers and couriers were sent to the Archbishop of Canterbury and all the bishops, abbots, and friars to ask them to pray for Anne's soul.

On August 2, the Queen's body was borne to London from Sheen, via Wandsworth, the priory of St. Mary Overie, Southwark, and Clerkenwell, amid great pageantry. Fleet Street, the Strand, and Charing Cross were ablaze with torchlight. On top of the coffin lay her painted and crowned wooden effigy. The bier was followed by black-garbed citizens of London and, wearing mourning cloaks and hoods, all the nobility—except Arundel, one of the former Appellants, who had refused to attend.

The Queen lay in state overnight in St. Paul's Cathedral. On August 3, as the great bells tolled, she was carried to Westminster Abbey and there laid on a hearse with candles burning all around, and buried with great pomp in the chapel of St. Edward the Confessor. "Abundance of wax"— 1,500 pounds of it, more than for any previous queen of England—had been "sent for from Flanders to make flambeaux and torches, and the illumination was so great on the day of the ceremony that nothing like it was ever before seen, not even at the burial of the good Queen Philippa. The King would have it so because she was the daughter of the Emperor."[25]

But the candles were to burn for far longer than expected that day. "Famous as [the Queen's] funeral was for the vast expenditure that was lavished upon it, the occasion was infamous to an even greater degree because, at the very beginning of the service," Arundel had the insolence to turn up late, compounding the insult by immediately asking the King for permission to withdraw, pleading urgent private affairs. Outraged, Richard grabbed a crozier or wand from a verger and "desecrated the holy place,"[26] striking the Earl in the face, causing him to fall and crack his head on the altar steps. He might have killed him, had he not been restrained. Blood flowed, thereby polluting the sanctity of the church, which had to be hastily re-consecrated before the funeral could continue. Arundel was escorted to the Tower, where he remained for a week, before swearing an oath guaranteeing his future loyalty and paying the King a massive indemnity of £40,000 ($34.5 million). After he had been taken away, his brother, Thomas Arundel, Archbishop of York, preached the funeral sermon, and the service finally ended at nightfall, around 8:45 p.m.

In December, the King would reward the Abbey's sacrist with £66.13s.4d. ($59,500) "for the pains which the monks had undergone in performing the exequies of Anne, late Queen of England, and for the hearse constructed for the honour of the said Queen; also for ringing the bells."[27] He had already arranged to pay the monks of Westminster £200 ($179,000) yearly to offer up Masses for Anne's soul on the anniversary of her death.

Richard, who had completed the rebuilding of Westminster Abbey (begun by Henry III), raised a fine monument there for Anne and himself in St. Edward's Chapel, behind the high altar. Constructed in 1395–98, it was the first double tomb of a king and queen in England, and Anne was buried in an arched vault below. The sepulcher of Alfonso, the son of Edward I, was moved to make space for it.

Built of pure marble by the London masons Henry Yevele and Stephen Lote, the monument cost £670 ($555,350). Gilded copper and latten (an alloy of copper and zinc) effigies of the King and Queen were made by coppersmiths Nicholas Broker and Godfrey Prest. The King had stipulated in the contract that they be faithful portraits and fashioned "with their right hands joined and the left hands holding a sceptre."[28] Sadly, the hands and scepters have long disappeared. The gilding alone cost 400 marks ($108,000).

Anne's effigy wears a mantle embroidered with heraldic badges, its borders being engraved with her ostrich emblem, the Imperial eagle, the broom flower (*Planta genista*) of the Plantagenets, knots, and the crowned initials A and R, which also appear on Richard's effigy; the bodice was set with precious stones and jeweled clasps, but they too have vanished, along with the crowns on the effigies, which were removed in the seventeenth century by Parliamentary troops. A wooden canopy covers the tomb; on its underside are paintings of Christ in Majesty, the coronation of the Virgin, and the arms of the royal couple.

The Queen's Latin epitaph read:

> *Under this wide stone now Anne lies entombed,*
> *Wedded in this life to the second Richard.*
> *Devoted to Christ, she was well known for her deeds,*
> *Always eager to give her gifts to the poor.*
> *She settled quarrels and relieved women with child.*
> *Beautiful in form, meek, with a pleasant face,*
> *She offered solace to widows, medicine to the sick.*
> *On June's 7th day, thirteen hundred and 94,*
> *All comfort was bereft for, through irremedial sickness, she passed*
>   *away into eternal joys.*

Three eulogies celebrating Anne were sent to Prague. One stated that while "Germany and all Bohemia will grieve [for her] at heart, more will England and, with it, Wales."[29]

In his will of April 1399, Richard directed: "We have chosen a royal burial in the church of St. Peter at Westminster and, in the monument which we have caused to be erected as a memorial for us and for Anne of glorious remembrance, once queen of England, our consort, we wish to be buried."[30] Anne's arms and those of Richard's second wife were incorporated into the Abbey's west window.

Anne's death removed a moderating influence from the King. Thereafter he refused to listen to advice and began to govern with increasing autocracy. "The King took her death so heavily that, besides cursing the place where she died, he did also, for anger, throw down the buildings unto which former kings were wont for pleasure to resort." On April 9, 1395, "all distraught and disordered" at the loss of "that benign lady," he commanded his clerk of works, by a writ of the privy seal, that "the houses and buildings in La Neyt," where Anne had died, be razed to the ground, "as well as the buildings in the court within the moat and the court without the moat." They were "utterly destroyed."[31] Only the gardens, which were maintained, and some farm buildings in the upper court, which were leased out, were spared. A statue of Anne was erected there that year. Sheen and La Neyt would be rebuilt by Henry V twenty years later, on a site adjacent to that on which the vanished palace had stood.

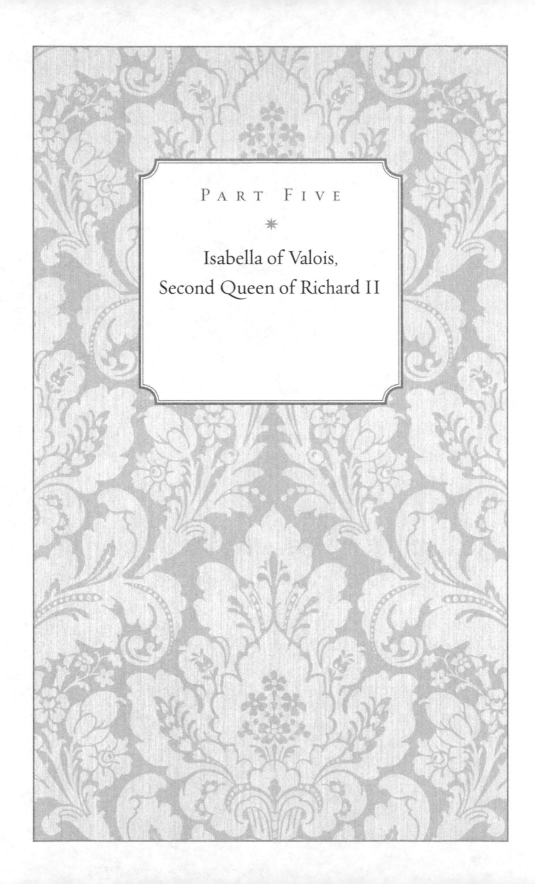

PART FIVE

✳

Isabella of Valois,
Second Queen of Richard II

I

"Our Beautiful White Pearl"

✳

Richard had scant time to grieve. The realm needed an heir of his body and, in August 1394, just two months after Anne's death, he "was advised to marry again."[1] Envoys were dispatched to Scotland, Navarre, Bavaria, and Milan, but these negotiations failed. By February 1395, Richard had set his sights on Yolande of Aragon. Her hand had been sought by Louis II, Count of Anjou, brother of Charles V of France. Louis had claimed the kingdom of Naples in 1389 and saw the marriage as a means of preventing Aragon from contesting his throne.

Charles VI supported his uncle's claim to Naples and his marriage to Yolande, but he was worried that, rebuffed, Richard might turn to Castile (which was hostile to France) for a bride. In May 1395, he offered him the hand of his five-year-old daughter, Isabella, and commanded his old tutor, the noble soldier and man of letters Philippe de Mézières, to write a letter to Richard, urging him to consent to the marriage and the peace it would bring in uniting England and France, like the heroes Roland and Oliver, against the enemies of Christendom. Mézières extolled Isabella as "our young marguerite, our precious stone, our beautiful white pearl." He declared that she might be a child, but women, like horses, elephants, and camels, were better broken young; "before reaching the age of discretion and before acquiring harmful habits of mind, [she] should be well instructed under the prudent and wise guidance of the royal majesty" and the King could mold her to his tastes. He mentioned the last marriage treaty that had been intended to bring peace to England and France, that between Edward II and another Isabella. "Call to mind, and sadly, the marriage, then thought a fortunate one, of the mother of the valiant King Edward, and the deadly penetrating thorns resulting from that union, which have actively caused the beautiful lilies from which you spring to be horribly trampled underfoot."[2]

Philip the Bold, Duke of Burgundy, no friend to the French King, thought the match "unadvised." But Richard had long wanted an end to what he called "this intolerable war" that had dragged on for six decades. This third Anglo-French royal marriage in a century could be the means of finally achieving peace. He was "attracted to the daughter of the King of France and to no one else," although there was some dismay in England "that he should wish to marry his adversary's daughter. It does him no good with his people, but he takes no notice."[3] He knew that England's resources could not support another prolonged conflict.

Aside from strong anti-French sentiment, many were concerned about the future. Richard was nearing thirty and had no son, and his subjects wanted the stability that came with a settled succession. "In an attempt to change the King's mind—for the English do not find it agreeable for him to marry a Frenchwoman—he was told that the lady was, by far, too young and that, even in five or six years, she would not be the proper age for a wife. He replied pleasantly that God will provide, and that every day would remedy the deficiency in age, and her youth was one of his reasons for preferring her, because he should educate her and bring her up to his own mind and to the manners and customs of the English, and that, as for himself, he was young enough to wait for her."[4] It is not being over-romantic to suggest that he may not have been ready for another marital relationship and was relieved to have a child bride; but of course, policy overrode all personal considerations.

Early in July 1395, Richard abandoned his suit to Yolande and accepted the French King's offer. On July 8, he sent an embassy to France under his cousin, York's son Edward of Norwich, Earl of Rutland, and the Earl Marshal, Nottingham, to negotiate a peace treaty and betrothal, negotiate a dowry and dower, and arrange for the delivery of the Princess. They were to ask, initially, for a dowry of 2,000,000 gold francs, or livres tournois ($1.5 million), but were authorized to go down to 1,000,000 ($750,000) and hold out for that; in the end, they settled for 800,000 francs ($600,000). Isabella was to be brought to Calais at King Charles's expense, and Richard was to be indemnified for 3,000,000 francs if the French broke the contract. In return, he engaged to dower Isabella with lands worth £6,666.13s.4d. ($5.4 million) a year and agreed to marry one of her sisters if she died before the age of thirteen. If she bore him a son, the child was to have the duchy of Normandy and the counties of Anjou and Maine, which had once formed part of the Plantagenet empire.

Charles was then in the grip of one of his escalating bouts of insanity. "When the English embassy arrived at Paris, the King of France resided at the Louvre and the Queen and her children at the Hôtel de Saint-Pol, on the banks of the Seine. To please the English lords, their request was granted to visit the Queen and her family, and especially the little Princess, as they were impatient to behold her. This had been at first refused, for the French council excused themselves by observing that she was as yet but eight [sic] years; how could anyone know how a young child would conduct herself at such an interview?" Now, with an alliance in sight, the envoys "must be content howsoever they found her. There could not be in her no great wisdom nor prudence. Howbeit, she was instructed well enough, and that the lords found well when they saw her."[5]

When Nottingham was presented to the future bride, he "dropped upon his knee, saying, 'Madam, if it please God, you shall be our lady and queen.'

"She replied instantly and without prompting, 'Sir, if it please God and my lord and father that I shall be queen of England, I shall be well pleased, for I have been told that I shall be a great lady.' She made [him] rise and, taking him by the hand, led him to Queen Isabeau, her mother, who was much pleased at her answer, as were all who heard it. The appearance and manners of this young Princess were very agreeable to the English ambassadors, and they thought among themselves that she was likely to be a lady of high honour and great goodness."[6] When the envoys returned to England, Charles VI gave them Isabella's portrait; this is the first instance of a likeness of a prospective bride being sent to an English king.

Political differences prolonged the negotiations, however, and the French initially rejected Richard's terms out of hand. They did not trust the English and would only agree to a truce, not a lasting peace. But, in January 1396, the English ambassadors returned to Paris and informed Charles that Richard "wished to marry the Lady Isabella, whose portrait they had shown him."[7] They spent three weeks being lavishly entertained, while the terms of the marriage and a twenty-eight-year truce were negotiated. Richard's councilors and his subjects would still have preferred to see his claim to France reasserted, and feared that he would make too many concessions to the French, which led to heated debates at Eltham. In the end, though, Richard had his way.

Isabella of Valois had been born on November 9, 1389, at the Louvre in Paris. She was the oldest surviving daughter of Charles VI and Isabeau of Bavaria and had inherited her mother's black hair and fair skin.

Isabeau came from the German House of Wittelsbach; her mother was one of the Visconti of Milan. From 1391, Charles VI had experienced attacks of the madness that was to blight his life and reign, and there were reports that his wife had taken lovers and neglected her queenly duties and her large family, to the extent that her children were starving in squalor, for which she was castigated by the Pope, the feminist writer Christine de Pisan, and others. Yet there is no corroborating evidence, and Isabeau's accounts show that she bought clothing, toys, and books for her children, paid for Masses for those who died in infancy, and had Isabella, for one, taught some Latin. It seems she was the victim of a campaign of character assassination, for she had fallen out with Burgundy, Charles's uncle, who acted as regent when his nephew was incapacitated, and wanted her influence neutralized.

Isabella was the third of Isabeau's twelve children; there were six boys and six girls. Her brother, the Dauphin Charles, was more than two years younger; her sister Jeanne had died in 1390, and the other sisters closest to her in age were another Jeanne, Marie, and Michelle. The children were brought up at the Hôtel Saint-Pol in Paris. In December 1391, Isabella had been betrothed to John, the six-year-old heir of Peter II, Count of Alençon, but her father broke it off so that she could marry Richard II.

Isabella's "young heart was full of tenderness and kindliness."[8] This and her generosity inspired devotion in those who served her. "Blessedness and truth [were] in her," recalled her second husband, and she "lived free from taint, so virtuous deemed by all."[9] Her childhood must have been difficult. Her father, who was normally charming and good-looking, clearly loved her, but when the madness was on him, he did not know his wife and children and recoiled from them. At these times, he veered from excitability to listlessness, and could be violent, ribald, and destructive, breaking furniture, setting fires, and ripping his clothes. At times, he thought he was made of glass and might break if someone touched him. "It was a great pity to see him, as his body was all eaten away with dirt and ordure."[10] When his bouts of fury became uncontrollable, he had to be restrained, and the Queen was forbidden his bed for her own safety. A beautiful young woman called Odette de Champdivers was substituted, but predictably Isabeau was accused of acting as procuress.

When Isabella was three, a terrible incident occurred that must have haunted her for a long time to come. A masquerade—*le bal des ardents*—was staged at court, in which the King and his friends appeared dressed as masked savages, sewn into hairy costumes of resin-soaked linen and flax. As they capered around, daring the onlookers to guess who they were, the King's brother, Louis, Duke of Orléans, accidentally brushed a torch against one, setting his costume alight. The fire flared up, engulfing the masquers, and the King was only saved by the quick action of the young Duchess of Berry, who threw her skirt over him. The Queen nearly fainted as the other screaming men were burned alive. Isabella would surely have learned about the tragedy at some stage.

On March 9, 1396, the King's nuptial contract was signed in Paris by Charles VI. Isabella was at liberty to give her final assent when she reached the age of twelve, when her marriage could be consummated. She renounced all claim to the French throne, while Richard surrendered to France the ports of Brest and Cherbourg—although he reserved the right to maintain his claim to be king of France.

Isabella was not to have any French attendants (a stipulation that was soon broken), but was to be brought up as an Englishwoman. The French were accommodating because they wished to preempt Richard from pursuing his dream of becoming emperor, and even committed to aid him against his subjects, should the need arise. Adam of Usk believed that Richard's chief motive in marrying Isabella was to gain French support against the former Lords Appellant. That year, the King told Waleran III, Count of Saint-Pol, of his fear that the unpopular peace would provoke them to another rebellion. Saint-Pol advised him to keep them sweet until the marriage had taken place, after which he could depend on French support to "crush all your enemies and rebellious subjects." The clause promising aid was deleted, however, when the first payment of the dowry was handed over. With that, Richard had the means to resist his enemies himself.

The two kings had expressed the hope that with this alliance, "the numerous great and widespread outrages, evils, enormities, wrongs and shedding of human blood occasioned by the war should cease," and that "peace and harmony should last for a long time into the future."[11] The treaty put an end to hostilities with France for the rest of Richard's reign, but in England, popular feeling against it still ran high. Yet this future Queen was no pauper like Anne of Bohemia had been: she came with a dowry of 800,000 gold francs ($6.6 million), of which 300,000 were to be paid on marriage and the rest in annual installments of 100,000 over five years. If Isabella died before she reached twelve, the age for cohabitation, all the installments were to be refunded apart from the initial payment. If Richard died before she reached twelve, she was to be given 500,000 francs of her dowry to use as she wished, and if he died after that time, leaving her childless, 200,000 francs were to be refunded to her father. The English magnates, among them Bolingbroke, bound themselves to allow Isabella to return without hindrance to France if Richard predeceased her. For his part, the King settled on her a dower of 10,000 marks (about $2.7 million), which she was to enjoy until she died. Because the couple were fourth cousins, dispensations were obtained from the popes in both Rome and Avignon.

On March 12, the proxy wedding of Richard and Isabella took place at the Sainte-Chapelle in Paris before Ugo Roberti, the Latin Patriarch of Jerusalem, with Nottingham standing in for the King. Richard had sent his bride two rings with diamonds, sapphires, and pearls, along with Garter robes, a jewel, a bracelet, and a devotional tablet. After the ceremony, Isabella made her first intercession as queen, pleading for the release from prison of a debtor, Peter de Craon. She was henceforth styled Queen of England and "it was pretty to see her, young as she was, for she well knew how to play the queen."[12]

On May 1, at Windsor, John of Gaunt, York, and Gloucester formally agreed to return Isabella and her jewels to France if the King predeceased her.

In June, William Scrope went to Paris to arrange for the handover of the Princess, and preparations were set in train for the wedding. In August, Richard himself made a brief visit to Calais to meet with her guardian, the Duke of Burgundy, and it was agreed that in a few weeks' time, at Calais, she would be given away by her father—whom Richard was now calling "our very dear and beloved father of France,"[13] carefully avoiding styling him king of France.

Richard again crossed the English Channel on September 28, ahead of John of Gaunt and Katherine Swynford, who was to take charge of Isabella. In January 1396, Gaunt had married Katherine, scandalizing the great ladies of England, who objected strongly to the new Duchess of Lancaster taking precedence over them. "Since she has got so far," they sniffed, "it will mean that she will rank as the second lady in England, and the young Queen will be dishonourably accompanied by her"[14] Richard, however, had shown favor to Katherine and gradually she became accepted at court, her Beaufort offspring by Gaunt having been declared legitimate.

King Charles and Queen Isabeau provided Isabella with a lavish trousseau, which included a mantle of cherry-red velvet embroidered with goldsmith's work in a pattern of roses growing on trees with leaves stitched with emeralds and stems of seed pearls. She was given a fabulous collection of jewelry, tapestries portraying rural idylls and shepherdesses, and a splendid retinue to accompany her to England, which included the dukes of Orléans, Berry, and Bourbon; "she brought out of France chairs [chariots] full of ladies and damsels."[15] Two chamberers, Simonette and Marianne, would remain with her throughout her time in England.

Isabeau, who was pregnant, did not attend her daughter's wedding. In October, Charles escorted Isabella from the abbey of Saint-Denis to Saint-Omer, where they awaited Richard's coming. At Ardres, fifteen miles away, 120 tents and pavilions had been set up. There, on October 26, in a lavish ceremony marked by pomp and pageantry to rival the Field of Cloth of Gold of 1520, the two kings met, each attended by a bodyguard of 400 gentlemen and a great retinue of nobles. Richard and his lords were wearing long velvet houppelandes in the late Queen Anne's livery of red and white, while, with perfect diplomacy, Charles had donned a green gown embroidered with her emblem. He was enjoying a lucid interval and cordial pleasantries were exchanged. "The King of France led the King of England into his tent and conferred alone,"[16] exchanging precious gifts of jewelry; among Richard's presents to Charles was a necklace of pearls and precious stones that Anne had given him.

At seven o'clock the next day, Richard went again to King Charles's tent. A sumptuous feast had been laid on, and they were served by the dukes of Berry, Burgundy, and Bourbon. The latter said to Richard, "My lord, you ought to make good cheer, for you have had all your wishes gratified. You have a wife, or shall have one, for she will speedily be delivered to you."

"Cousin of Bourbon," Charles replied, "we wish our daughter were as old as our cousin, the Lady of Saint-Pol, for then she would bear the more love to our son of England."

"Fair Father," Richard said, "the age of our wife pleases us right well, for we heed not her age as much as we value your love and that of your subjects, for we shall now be so strongly united that no man in Christendom can gainsay us."[17]

On the succeeding two days, the two kings appeared splendidly dressed and exchanged more courtesies and increasingly lavish gifts. Finally, on October 30, attended by a host of ladies and damsels, and with a gentleman going before her carrying her crown, six-year-old Isabella arrived at Ardres in great state. "Beholding such magnificence, you would have thought you were seeing that gathering of goddesses which poets describe in their romances. No one could recall having seen anything like it."[18]

Charles processed to Richard's pavilion, where the two courts gathered, and they waited together as Isabella was conducted there by the dukes of Burgundy and Berry. She was now wearing her crown and a "narrow gown of old-fashioned style" in blue velvet powdered with gold fleurs-de-lis. Her father presented her to Richard, who must have seemed like a vision with his fair looks and his long gown of shimmering red and blue cloth of gold.

"Dearest son," Charles said, "I commend to you this creature, the dearest to me over all creatures in the world except the Dauphin and our wife."

Isabella curtseyed twice to her future husband, who "took her by the hand and kissed her, thanking her father for so noble and welcome a gift.

[He] went on to declare that he was receiving her according to the conditions agreed between the kings, so that, through the friendship thus established, both monarchs could live in peace and tranquillity and could secure a proper state of harmony between their two kingdoms for ever, and that no more Christian blood would be shed."[19]

We do not know what Isabella looked like. The illustrations of her in manuscripts (one in the Bibliothèque Nationale, Paris, and two in the British Library) portraying this scene are of later date and certainly not portraits. A roof boss in Beaulieu Abbey is thought to represent her, for Richard II's white hart emblem appears nearby. But Richard evidently liked the look of his little Queen, who was later said to have "wondrous beauty" and be "the fairest thing to mortal eyes."[20]

An illuminated frontispiece to a manuscript of Chaucer's *Troilus and Criseyde* shows the poet reciting his work to the court of Richard II.[21] One of the figures is clearly the King (with his face rubbed out), and it has been suggested that Anne of Bohemia is the lady next to him, wearing a pink gown. Yet the manuscript was not produced until around 1415–25, so the lady in pink is probably Isabella of Valois. It was common for children to be represented as adults in an age that did not fully understand realism or perspective in art.

There was one final banquet, for which the little Princess wore scarlet velvet and emeralds, then she and Richard took leave of her father. Richard entrusted her to the duchesses of Lancaster and Gloucester and the countesses of Huntingdon and Stafford and other ladies, who received her with great joy. (Evidently the Duchess of Gloucester had abandoned her resolve to have nothing to do with Katherine Swynford, while the latter's prominent role in the ceremonies demonstrates how quickly she had been accepted by the establishment and how respectable she had become.)

Richard handed Isabella into the richly appointed chariot lined with cloth of gold that he had had made for her at a cost of £400 ($331,000). She had been assigned a French *gouvernante* and chief attendant, Isabelle, Lady de Coucy, daughter of John I, Duke of Lorraine, and second wife of Enguerrand de Coucy, whose first wife, Princess Isabella, had died in 1382. Lady de Coucy, who was in her thirties, now took charge of the little Princess and was her sole companion in her chariot on the short ride to Calais. They were conducted there by Isabella's chamberlain, Sir

Thomas Percy, and a large escort of men and horses, while the English noblewomen and ladies rode behind in twelve chariots.

The ladies in attendance on Isabella were there to assist the bride in her wedding preparations, but Katherine Swynford remained "the companion of the young Queen of England"[22] until the late summer of 1397. Her influence would have been invaluable as Isabella was initiated into her new position, for Katherine, who had been governess to John of Gaunt's daughters, had had experience of looking after royal princesses. She and other great ladies were given gold livery collars to wear at Isabella's wedding.

On November 1, in the church of Saint-Nicholas at Calais, Isabella and Richard II were married by Thomas Arundel, now Archbishop of Canterbury. The bride's wedding ring was of gold garnished with sapphires and a ruby. Richard renounced his claim to France and those of Isabella and her descendants, and after the ceremony, the first 300,000 francs of Isabella's dowry were handed over to him.

For her bridal gift, Richard gave her a gold frontlet encrusted with sapphires, rubies, and pearls. John of Gaunt and Gloucester gave her gold and bejeweled ornaments in the shape of white eagles, John's being presented in a plate of candied fruit and spices offered to Isabella at the feast that followed the wedding. Gloucester also gave her a gold crown of eight fleurons and valuable cups from his wife and children. Bolingbroke's gift was a golden statue of a greyhound with a large pearl hanging from its neck. Nottingham gave a belt of pearls, Rutland a mirror shaped like a daisy and a gold belt, and other lords presented rich brooches.

In Isabella's trousseau were packed dolls Richard had given her, all equipped with silver utensils, and her mother's gift of a golden mill fitted out with pearls and little brooms "for the amusement of my Lady Isabella." Among the many rich items her parents had provided were three chaplets of red, white, and gold silk, one embroidered with a rabbit, another adorned with gems, pearls, and ribbons; and a surcoat and mantle of red velvet embroidered with birds of goldsmith's work perched on branches made of pearls and emeralds. The sides of the surcoat were trimmed with miniver, there was a matching cape and hood of miniver, and the mantle was lined with ermine. Another robe was of murrey velvet, embroidered with pearl roses.

The jewels Isabella brought with her—two crowns, coronets, rings, necklaces, clasps (one adorned with jewels, pearls, and fleurs-de-lis), and a jeweled belt—were worth 500,000 French crowns ($606,370) and had adjustable fastenings to allow for growth. She also had chamber hangings of striped red and white silk embroidered with rustic figures of vintners and shepherdesses, as well as mirrors, a rosary with beads of green enamel, a missal bound in silk, a pearl-encrusted purse, and a casket with a gold key, another gift from her mother.

2

"A Matter of Life and Death"

✳

ON NOVEMBER 3, AFTER ATTENDING EARLY MASS, THE KING and Queen crossed to Dover. The voyage took just three hours, and they arrived safely, but some of the ships—with Richard's pavilions and most of his household furnishings—were lost in rough seas. Evil portents were reported—a swarm of flies in one of the palaces, and blood oozing from a piece of wood—which superstitious souls believed boded no good for the marriage.

Richard and Isabella dined and slept at Dover Castle on her first night in England, then made their way toward London via Canterbury, Faversham, Sittingbourne, Rochester, Dartford, and Eltham, where the King, the Duke and Duchess of Lancaster, the Duke of York, and other lords and ladies presented more costly gifts to Isabella, among them two crowns. Richard gave her a collar of diamonds, rubies, and pearls, a baldric of golden feathers, a set of jeweled buttons fashioned as eaglets, a chaplet of red velvet set with roses made of large clusters of pearls and hanging buds of white, green, and gold, and a circlet adorned with precious stones. John of Gaunt presented her with a massive covered gold cup and basin (perhaps the Royal Gold Cup that is now in the British Museum) and a gem-studded ladle, while his Duchess's gift was a smaller cup, suitable for a child. From Robert Waldby, Bishop of Chichester, Isabella received a silver image of the Virgin as tall as she was, while the Lord Mayor of London gave a jeweled circlet. Then the lords took leave of the royal couple and hastened ahead to make ready for the young Queen's state entry into the capital on November 23.

The mayor and aldermen met her on Blackheath and escorted her to Kennington Palace; the Clerk of the King's Works had spent £36 ($29,800) on refurbishing it against her arrival, and she stayed there until November 22. That day, "the young Queen Isabella, commonly called 'the Little,' was conveyed from Kennington, through Southwark, to the Tower of London, when such a multitude of persons went out to see her that, on London Bridge, nine persons were crushed to death."[1]

Isabella stayed that night at the Tower. On the following day, she entered London in triumph. The citizens gave her rich gifts and ceremoniously conducted her to Westminster, where the King was waiting to receive her. Soon afterward, the Lancasters entertained her at their London residence, Ely Place in Holborn. On December 8, Isabella was granted her dower. The court kept Christmas at Coventry, and moved to Eltham to observe the New Year of 1397.

Isabella was then sent to live in the care of Lady de Coucy, dividing her time between Windsor Castle, Eltham Palace, and Leeds Castle. She was allowed to retain her French household and had been assigned some English attendants, of whom she became fond, notably her chief lady-in-waiting, Margaret, the wife of William, Lord Courcy, her steward (not to be confused with Lady de Coucy). The Courcys were granted a pension of £100 ($82,900) at New Year 1397. Another of Isabella's ladies was Richard's former nurse, Agnes Corby, who had served Joan of Kent. Also in her entourage was the chronicler Pierre Salmon, who had been her father's secretary and would act as an intermediary between Isabella and her mother. The young Queen had her own chancellor, secretary, keeper of the robes, master embroiderer, master cordwainer, goldsmiths, tailor, yeoman of the cellar, and silkwoman. The cost of maintaining her establishment for her first year in England amounted to £3,000 ($2.4 million).

She was indulgently treated by Richard, of whom she became inordinately fond, and he was loving and demonstrative toward her. French observers reported that he lavished every care and attention on her. One wrote: "I never saw so great a lord make so much of nor show such great affection to a lady as did King Richard to his Queen."[2] He continued to shower her with presents, including a whistle set with jewels and pearls, a gold candlestick and snuffer, a goblet of costly Venetian glass, a hart ornament adorned with gems, another crown, three circlets, and a chaplet. Rutland presented her with a collar of broomcods (an emblem used by Richard II and her father) adorned with roundels of rosemary and an ostrich, which may once have belonged to Anne of Bohemia. Among her jewels were two other gold collars, one with eight broom flowers adorned with pearls, rubies, and sapphires, another with white-enameled broom-cods. Isabella gave St. Paul's Cathedral vestments of red velvet studded with her arms, her white falcon badge, and golden angels. Pope Boniface IX presented her with a parrot and a frontlet of rubies and pearls, but she was more interested in the parrot.

Isabella embodied, for Richard, the peace he had longed for. He called her *m'amie* ("my friend") or "my dearest sister and lady, my dearest and beloved companion."[3] "He behaved so amiably to her that she loved him entirely."[4] Had things turned out differently, this might have been another great love match, such as Richard had enjoyed with Anne. He might have been a failure as a king, but he was certainly not a failure as a husband, adopting a fatherly role to his child bride.

Despite suggestions that Isabella was never crowned, a summons to her coronation on Epiphany Sunday, January 8, 1397, survives,[5] while the *Chronicle of London* states that she was crowned on that date. She entered London on January 3, 1397, and stayed at the Tower. The next day, she processed through the City via Cheapside, attended by twenty ladies leading twenty mounted knights wearing the King's white hart badge, and was received by Richard at Westminster. Archbishop Arundel officiated at her coronation, at which she wore a rich circlet of bejeweled gold set with precious stones that the King had given her. A crown of Isabella's is listed in Richard II's inventory of 1399; this may have been Anne of Bohemia's crown with the enameled white flowers. It may not have been used to crown Isabella, for it would have been too big and she had brought two crowns to England, one being decorated with pimpernels and the broom flower of the Plantagenets.

The coronation was followed by a banquet in Westminster Hall, which Richard was then having rebuilt. The roof was not quite finished, so twenty-two rolls of wadmole (woolen cloth) were bought "for covering the hall against the Queen's coronation, through lack of lead," and to make a temporary enclosure in the hall for a pantry, ewery, scullery, dresser, and cellar. Isabella was too young to wield any political influence, yet she obtained three pardons as queen, two of them soon after her coronation.

Tournaments were staged over the next two weeks to celebrate the coronation and the King's birthday. Predictably, there was criticism of Richard's extravagance. It was perhaps significant that Isabella had received no New Year's gifts from Arundel or Warwick. When Parliament met in January and agreed to fund the £200,000 (more than $109 million) that had been outlaid on the French visit, the royal wedding, and the coronation, Gloucester made plain his opinion of the peace with France. Countering complaints about this and his misgovernment, Richard enlisted the support of John of Gaunt. At the end of February, he departed with Isabella, Gaunt, and Bolingbroke on a pilgrimage to Canterbury, before moving to Windsor, where, in April, he made his wife a Lady of the Garter.

On June 12, the King finally confirmed London's rights, liberties, and privileges "at the supplication of the Queen."[6] On July 6, Isabella was present when he confirmed John of Gaunt as duke of Aquitaine in reward for his loyalty.

Resentment against the former Lords Appellant had simmered in the King's breast for a decade now. He had never forgiven them for Radcot Bridge and the banishment of de Vere, and was now determined to force a reckoning with his erstwhile adversaries.

Gloucester, who was still protesting against Richard's shameful peace with France, had invited his great-nephew, Roger Mortimer, Earl of March, to visit him at Pleshey. "There he unbosomed to him all the secrets of his heart, telling him that certain influential persons had elected him as king of England, resolving that King Richard and his Queen were to be deposed and forthwith confined in prison, where they were to be maintained with ample provision during their lives"[7] while Gloucester and Arundel ruled. The King and "the sweet young Queen" were in grave peril. There were even plans afoot to end the truce with France and send Isabella home, if she wished to go. Gloucester was determined that "she should never be deflowered by the King," even to the extent of planning to take her prisoner.

Richard was at Eltham with Isabella when Nottingham warned him of the plot, at which he was greatly shaken. "The Count of Saint-Pol had been sent into England by the King of France in order to see his daughter and learn how she was going on. The King consulted him, John of Gaunt and York on the danger that threatened him and his young consort" and asked for their advice.

"Their plan is to separate my Queen from me, who is but a child, and shut her up in some place of confinement," he told them, in great anguish.

His uncles did their best to calm him. "Depend on it, we will never suffer it, nor that you should be separated from the Queen," they assured him, and consented to the arrests of the conspirators.[8]

In fact, both dukes "did not wish to be involved." John of Gaunt's overriding concern was for Bolingbroke, who had collaborated with Gloucester, Arundel, and Warwick back in 1387–88 and laid himself forever open to accusations of treason; and he was anxious to safeguard the future of the Lancastrian dynasty. In order to avoid becoming further swept up in the gathering storm, Lancaster and York "retired to their own castles, the Duke of Lancaster taking with him his Duchess, who had for some time been the companion of the young Queen of England."[9] Thus ended Katherine Swynford's close association with Isabella. Both dukes were "bitterly" to regret their decision to leave court at this crucial time, for it deprived them of their last chance to save their brother and avert a disturbing political crisis.

When they had gone, "the King's remaining servants said, 'Be assured, dear Sir, that, as long as the Duke of Gloucester lives, there will never be any quiet for your court, nor for England. Besides, he publicly threatens to confine you and your Queen. As for the Queen, she need not care: she is young and the beloved child of the King of France. The Duke of Gloucester dare not hurt her, but many evils will he bring on you and on England.' "[10]

Hearing this, "the King decided upon a bold and daring move."[11] He would have his revenge at last. Telling Isabella that he was going hunting, he lured Gloucester to London, where he arrested him in person. Arundel and Warwick were also apprehended. On August 15, John of Gaunt was present in the House of Lords when the three nobles were accused of committing treason in 1387–88 and condemned to death; later that month, he and Bolingbroke were ordered to muster forces for the King.

Richard instructed his cousin Rutland to arrange Gloucester's execution. Rutland had replaced de Vere in the King's affections, and there has been speculation that he too was homosexual, since his marriage to Philippa de Mohon produced no children. He was intelligent and good-looking, a cultivated man who wrote a popular treatise on hunting, and Richard "loved him exceedingly, more than any other man in the king-dom,"[12] so that he was now the most influential man at court.

Rutland, it was rumored, sent two servants to the castle of Calais, where his uncle was lodged. Early in September, "just before dinner, when the tables were laid and the Duke was on the point of washing his hands, four men came out of the next room and, putting a towel around his neck, they strangled him, two of them pulling at each end. They then undressed the body, put it between the sheets, with the head on a pillow, and covered it with four coverlets. Then they went back to the great hall and let it be known that the Duke had had an apoplectic fit."[13]

On September 21, the three arrested Appellants were called to answer for their treason. Gloucester, of course, did not appear. Arundel argued that he had been formally pardoned, but he was condemned all the same—with John of Gaunt, as High Steward of England, pronouncing sentence—and beheaded the same day. Warwick, who pleaded guilty and threw himself on the King's mercy, escaped with forfeiture and life im-prisonment. According to the Kirkstall Abbey chronicler, the King heeded Isabella's pleas for mercy and spared his life. Three days later, Nottingham announced in Parliament that Gloucester was dead.

John of Gaunt made no public protest about his brother's murder, even though he and York held the King responsible for it and discussed what action they should take. In the end, they made their peace with the King, having heard that he was growing suspicious of Gaunt too. The latter had no choice, given that he was in fear for his son. This sinister episode effectively marks the end of his active intervention in affairs of state, and indeed his political influence, and it probably coincided with the onset of failing health.

"So King Richard was reconciled with his uncles over the death of the Duke of Gloucester, and went on to rule more harshly than before."[14] Richard's ire did not, at that time, extend to Bolingbroke, who had sup-ported the proceedings against his former colleagues. Naturally he had no wish at this time to alienate John of Gaunt, that stout bulwark of the throne. The King was Bolingbroke's guest that September, and on the 29th, when rewarding those peers who had supported him in the recent proceedings, he created him duke of Hereford.

Richard's proceedings against the former Appellants mark the start of his descent into despotism. "He began," wrote Walsingham, "to act the tyrant and oppress the people." He was finished with being told how to govern his kingdom and determined from now on to rule by divine right as an absolute monarch, without recourse to Parliament. The Kirkstall chronicler stated that the King emerged like the sun from the clouds. He became obsessed with projecting his own majesty—he was the first English king to adopt the styles "your Majesty" and "your Highness" (in emulation of the kings of France and the Emperor)—and he introduced increasingly elaborate and rigid ceremonial at court. He would sit for hours, crowned and silent, on his high throne at Westminster, "more splendidly and in greater state than any previous king," and "if he looked on any man, he must kneel."[15] It has been suggested by several writers that he was suffering from schizophrenia or narcissism, yet his high-handedness may have been a deliberate strategy aimed at restoring his authority and prestige as king.

He took steps to pack Parliament with enough supporters to vote him sufficient funds to ensure that he never needed to summon it again. He banished any magnate who opposed him, and declared that the laws of England were in his own mouth and breast and that the lives and property of his subjects were at his mercy, to be disposed of at his pleasure. He doctored the Rolls of Parliament so that his enemies could be attainted without judicial process; he gathered a formidable private army to intimidate his enemies and protect himself; he imposed illegal taxes, failed to enforce law and order at a local level in the realm, and tried unsuccessfully to secure his election as Holy Roman Emperor. He became irascible and unpredictable, and broke countless promises. Crippled by debt because of his extravagant lifestyle, he imposed forced loans on his subjects, irrevocably alienating them in the process. As his unpopularity increased, he became panicky about security, and instituted a large bodyguard of Cheshire archers to protect his person. In his own eyes he could do no wrong. He was, he told Parliament, "absolute Emperor of his kingdom of England." His contemporaries came to fear this new imperious

Richard. "Not even the greatest in England dared to criticise the King's acts or intentions."[16] Yet his kindness to his little Queen did not falter.

Richard and Isabella kept Christmas at Lichfield, where they received gifts from her uncles, the dukes of Burgundy and Berry, and from Henry of Bolingbroke, who gave the Queen a golden hart with a crown of pearls. They were at Lilleshall Abbey on January 24, 1398, then moved to Chester, where they lodged in the abbey before riding on to Shrewsbury for the opening of Parliament in February.

In December, while riding to Windsor, Bolingbroke had entered into a fateful conversation with Nottingham, who suddenly revealed that four of the King's most favored lords were plotting to kill Bolingbroke and John of Gaunt after Parliament rose in January, whereupon Richard would seize the Lancastrian domains. It appeared that there were also secret moves afoot to reverse the pardon granted posthumously to Thomas, Earl of Lancaster, who had been executed by Edward II in 1322; if that happened, John of Gaunt would be disinherited. Nottingham feared that he himself and Bolingbroke were about to be ruined in revenge for what was done at Radcot Bridge, for he believed Richard would not allow their treason as former Appellants to go unpunished and could not be trusted to keep his oath.

Bolingbroke reported this alarming exchange to John of Gaunt, who thought it best to tell the King about it. Naturally, both Bolingbroke and Nottingham (who was outraged at his confidences being reported to Richard) wished to portray themselves in the best possible light, and each ended up accusing the other of treason before the King.

Worry about his heir placed a great strain on John of Gaunt. When Parliament rose, he was suffering from a high fever. Confronted with the prospect of his own mortality, he faced the possibility that Richard did have designs on the Lancastrian inheritance. The King had already moved against three Lords Appellant and might yet proceed against the other two. Even if he stopped short of indicting Bolingbroke for treason, he might yet use devious means to seize the duchy for the Crown. As soon as he was well enough, Gaunt sought from Richard an assurance that he would not use the forfeiture of Thomas, Earl of Lancaster, in

1322 as an excuse to appropriate the duchy's lands, to which Richard agreed.

But the quarrel between Bolingbroke and Nottingham remained unresolved. For the King, this was a God-sent opportunity to press home his advantage, for he had come to see the House of Lancaster, with its enormous power and vast wealth, as a threat to himself and his throne, and was secretly resolved to neutralize it.

On March 19, the two protagonists again appeared before Richard at Bristol. Since honor had to be satisfied and neither party was willing to be reconciled, the case was referred to the Court of Chivalry to consider a resort to arms to decide the matter. On April 29, at Windsor, after the Garter feast (at which Isabella was present), Richard ordered that, since there were no witnesses to the fateful conversation in December, the issues between Bolingbroke and Nottingham be settled by judicial combat between the protagonists—an outdated but (until 1819) still legal process whereby guilt was apportioned to the man left dead or disabled, or the one who ended the fight by crying "Craven!" In this case, the duel was to be a matter of life and death.

The matter had not been resolved by June 1398, when Isabella held court at the royal manor of Isleworth, Middlesex, a house owned by several of her queenly predecessors. By then, the King's childlessness had become a matter of concern to his subjects. His heir presumptive was the Earl of March, the Lord Lieutenant of Ireland. That June, March was killed at Kenlis, Leinster. He left a son, Edmund, aged only seven—heir not only to his father's earldom, but also to the throne itself. Edmund was made Isabella's ward.

On September 16, Bolingbroke and Nottingham finally faced each other at Gosford Green, Coventry, with the King, the young Queen, the Duke and Duchess of Lancaster, the whole court, and vast crowds of sightseers looking on. But, just as the combat was about to begin, Richard—in a scene later powerfully dramatized by Shakespeare—threw down his baton from the dais and called a halt to the proceedings. He then deliberated for two hours while Bolingbroke and Nottingham waited. At last he returned and, without preamble, sentenced both men to exile, Bolingbroke for ten years, Nottingham for life. Walsingham commented that the sentence was based on "no legal grounds whatsoever" and was "contrary to justice," being merely an excuse for the King to rid himself of two former opponents. Bolingbroke and Nottingham were commanded to leave England by October 20. At a stroke, Richard had rid himself of the remaining Appellants.

"The whole court was in a state of turmoil." The summary sentences—handed down without any charges being made or any form of trial—stunned everyone and provoked much criticism of the King. At John of Gaunt's plea, he did reduce the term of Bolingbroke's banishment to six years, but he was otherwise implacable. Gaunt must have dreaded being parted from his beloved son and realized that the Lancastrian inheritance was now clearly under threat. He was "very angry," but while he "deplored the matter in private, [he] was too proud to approach Richard, since his son's honour was involved."[17]

Bolingbroke sailed to France. There, Charles VI offered him the hand of his cousin, Marie of Berry, being "influenced by the thought of his daughter, the young Queen of England. It was felt by him and other French lords that two great ladies such as they were would be excellent company for each other and that the marriage would draw the two countries closer together in peace and friendship."[18] But Richard protested against the marriage and the project was dropped.

John of Gaunt, ailing and desolate at the absence of his son, rode north with his beloved Katherine to Leicester Castle. He died there on February 3, 1399. News of his passing reached Bolingbroke in Paris. Although the King's sentence of exile prevented him from returning to England, he was now Duke of Lancaster and in possession of a landed inheritance worth more than $58 billion in modern terms. Prior to his leaving England, the King had assured him that his possessions were safe and had issued letters patent to that effect.

But then came shattering news. Without any legal pretext, Richard had extended the new Duke's exile to the term of his life, and declared the Lancastrian inheritance forfeit, annexing the duchy to the Crown and distributing its lands among his favorites. It was a shocking turn of events, and one of the grossest examples of Richard's tyrannical rule. This act of betrayal made Bolingbroke determined to return to England to deal with the problem of Richard once and for all.

3

"In Danger of Bitter Death"

※

O N APRIL 24, 1399, RICHARD PRESIDED OVER THE ANNUAL
Garter feast at Windsor and invited his nobles to a grand tournament "where forty knights and their esquires, all clad in green and bearing Isabella's device of a white falcon, maintained the beauty of the virgin
Queen of England against all comers."[1] Isabella appeared sumptuously
dressed "in full state" and attended by "a large suite of ladies." At the
end, she presented prizes to the victors and "acquitted herself well." It
was noted, though, that the jousts had been poorly attended, "for at least
two-thirds of the English knights and squires were strongly hostile to the
King" on account of the murder of Gloucester, the execution of Arundel,
and the banishment of Bolingbroke.[2]

Richard sailed to Ireland the next day in what was to prove an unsuccessful attempt to defuse the ugly situation that had developed there
after March's death. In the morning, he led nine-year-old Isabella by the
hand to St. George's Chapel to hear Mass and pray for his safe return.
Afterward, having embraced and kissed her more than forty times, he
said, "Adieu, Madame, until we meet again."

Isabella burst into tears. "Alas, my lord, will you leave me here?" she
cried.

"By no means, Madame," he assured her, weeping himself. "I will go
first and you, Madame, shall come afterwards." Then he led her to the
Deanery, where they were served wine and sweetmeats. Soon it was time
for Richard to leave. He lifted Isabella up in his arms and kissed her ten
more times, then put her down, mounted his horse and rode away.

"Great pity was it," observed a chronicler, "for never saw they each other more." Isabella was left with "all her court at Windsor,"[3] so "ill with grief from losing her lord"[4] that she lay prostrate for a fortnight. But Richard soon wrote a letter to cheer her.

Prior to his departure, he had March's young son proclaimed heir presumptive and appointed York regent during his absence. He had also to deal with adverse comments about the size of Isabella's household, a consequence of relations with France having deteriorated since their marriage. In May 1399, complaints were made to the King about Lady de Coucy's extravagant style of living. Eighteen horses did not suffice her. She took a large liveried train with her wherever she went. She kept two or three goldsmiths, two or three cutlers, and two or three furriers constantly employed, as a queen would do. She was building a chapel at great cost. She employed no fewer than seven or eight embroiderers, and it was said that she lived in greater splendor than her young mistress.

Richard dismissed her and dispatched her back to France with twenty of the Queen's servants, much to the anger of Isabella's uncle, the Duke of Orléans—and perhaps that of Isabella, although her reaction is not recorded. Eleanor Holland, March's widow, was appointed governess in her place. She was thirty-eight and the mother of four children, and brought with her to Windsor her two daughters, Anne and Eleanor, who were younger than Isabella. Richard also sent the Duchess of Gloucester and her younger daughters, Joan and Isabel, to live with Isabella at Windsor. They were warned by the King not to mention the late Duke of Gloucester to the Queen.

Around July 4, Bolingbroke landed at Ravenspur, Yorkshire. He claimed that he wished only to safeguard his Lancastrian inheritance and reform the government. Indeed, he acknowledged Richard's title as king and the right of the Earl of March to succeed him. In reality, he had come in rebellion against his lawfully crowned and anointed sovereign.

At the time of his invasion, there was a huge tide of popular feeling against Richard, especially in London, where Bolingbroke was well liked. The King had lost the hearts of his people, and as Bolingbroke progressed south, he was gratified to find nobles and commons alike flocking to his banner. Soon he had gathered a large army. The princes of the

Church offered their support, and the Archbishop of Canterbury assured all who joined Bolingbroke of the remission of their sins and "a sure place in Paradise." In some alarm, York, fearing that there might be a backlash against the Queen, hurried Isabella from Windsor to Walling-ford Castle, where he thought she would be safer, delegating William Scrope, now Earl of Wiltshire, to guard her. Wiltshire, however, had the bad fortune to be among a number of Richard's most hated advisers who were captured by Bolingbroke's men at Bristol and beheaded.

Bad weather ensured that news of Bolingbroke's invasion took some time to reach the King in Ireland. The council begged him to return im-mediately. Richard sailed home, determined to raise an army and meet his cousin in the field. Meanwhile, York and the council, seeing how un-popular Richard was in London, had decided that they would be safer with Isabella at Wallingford, where they could meet up with him. They arrived there on July 20.

Late that month, Richard landed in south Wales, but was unable to raise much support; many of his followers were deserting him, including Rutland, who dismissed the King's remaining soldiers and rode off to join Bolingbroke. Abandoned and panic-stricken, Richard disguised himself as a friar and fled to Conway Castle and then to Flint Castle, where he surrendered to a deputation sent by Bolingbroke. Expecting to be executed, he was in deep distress, crying to God and the saints that he had "never transgressed against the kingdom of England" and lamenting that he would never see his "dearest" Isabella again.[5]

Windsor and Wallingford had fallen to Bolingbroke without a strug-gle. Shakespeare portrays the captive Richard meeting Isabella on the road to London and saying a sad farewell to her, but there is no historical evidence for this. (Incidentally, Isabella is the only queen of the five in this book to appear in a play by Shakespeare. In *Richard II*, he portrays her as a mature adult; she has no name: she is just called the Queen. It has often been suggested that he modeled her on Anne of Bohemia. The farewell between her and Richard is moving and passionate and was probably inspired by the King's famously happy marriage to Anne.)

Bolingbroke had sent instructions to York to take charge of Isabella. Soon afterward, he moved her to Leeds Castle, where she was placed in the care of Robert de Vere's widow, the Duchess of Ireland. Lady de Coucy came hastening back from France to Isabella when she heard that

Richard was deposed, but the Londoners protested against her presence at Leeds, and a deputation of citizens told her: "Lady, make instant preparations for your departure, for we will not suffer you to remain longer here. Take care, on saying farewell to Queen Isabella, that you show not any tokens of anger at our dismissing you, but tell her that your husband and daughter in France have sent to entreat your return. If we see you doing anything else, your life will answer for it. You must ask no questions and make no remarks to the Queen on anything that is going on. You will be taken to Dover and given a boat to take you across to Boulogne."

Lady de Coucy promised that "in God's name, she would do as they directed."[6] Yet at some stage, it appears that she returned to Isabella, or stayed in England and kept in touch with members of her household.

At Bolingbroke's command, Isabella's French household was broken up and "none were left with her that were at all attached to King Richard. A new retinue was formed for her, of ladies, damsels, and valets, who were strictly enjoined never to mention the name of King Richard to her or to acquaint her with what was become of him." Some of her French attendants certainly were "thrown out"[7] and sent home with Lady de Coucy, to the great indignation of the French chronicler of Saint-Denis, who believed, incorrectly, that the Queen had been left with just two French-speaking attendants, her confessor and one of her ladies. "May it serve as an example to strike fear into the hearts of any French noblewoman intending to marry an Englishman!" he wrote in outrage. But later evidence shows that she was allowed to keep the majority of her French attendants and household officers. One was perhaps the French clerk who wrote the *Chronique de la Traïson et Mort de Richard II*, which covers the years 1397 to 1400. If so, her household—and perhaps Isabella herself—must have been kept well informed about events.

On September 2, Bolingbroke entered London to a tumultuous reception. King Richard, paraded as a prisoner in his train, was greeted with jeers and pelted with rubbish. Later that day, he was confined in the Tower of London, even though Bolingbroke had sworn that he should retain royal power. Forgetting his earlier promise, Bolingbroke now appointed a commission to consider who should be king. Many magnates were unhappy at the prospect of his taking the throne, and declared his claim to rule by right of descent flawed. Yet they found reasons enough for setting Richard aside, notably "perjuries, sacrileges, unnatural crimes, exactions from his subjects, reduction of his people to slavery, cowardice and weakness of rule."[8] Bolingbroke, it seemed, was the only realistic alternative, for the legitimate heir, March, was a child. The fact that Bolingbroke had four sons may have swayed some.

Richard was by no means willing to give up the throne, and Bolingbroke knew it. He used every means in his power to force him to abdicate, for he was anxious that the removal of his cousin from the throne and his own subsequent accession should have some basis in law. He knew that his own title was dubious, so the official line was to be that Richard's misgovernment justified his deposition. Richard soon realized he had little choice in the matter. For a month, systematic coercion and threats were used to persuade him to co-operate, and in the end, a shattered and broken man, he gave in.

On the morning of September 30, 1399, Parliament assembled in Westminster Hall. Standing before the empty throne, Richard removed his crown and, placing it on the ground, "resigned his right to God."[9] He then made a short speech expressing his hope that Bolingbroke would be a good lord to him and ensure that he was comfortably provided for. Thirty-three accusations against him were read aloud, but he was not allowed to say anything in his defense. After he had been taken back to the Tower, the assembled lords declared him deposed.

Bolingbroke then entered Westminster Hall, preceded by his four sons and the archbishops of Canterbury and York. In the hushed chamber, the voice of Thomas Percy, now earl of Worcester, rang out: "Long live Henry of Lancaster, King of England!" This was the cue for the whole assembly to respond with the words, "Yes! Yes! We want Henry to be king, nobody else!" At the close of proceedings, it was proclaimed that Richard had abdicated and that Bolingbroke had succeeded him as King Henry IV. On October 13, Henry was crowned in Westminster Abbey. With his accession, the great duchy of Lancaster became vested in the Crown (and remains so today).

On October 27, Richard was sentenced to perpetual imprisonment. Soon afterward, he was taken to Pontefract Castle, to be held there in the custody of Sir Thomas Swynford, Katherine's son. The Duke of Burgundy was sure that he would be put to death.

Richard had hoarded Isabella's dowry in the coin in which it had faithfully been paid. Henry now seized it. On October 19, John de Montagu, Earl of Salisbury, and Thomas Merke, Bishop of Carlisle, traveled to Paris to try to secure the continuing payment of the dowry to Henry and the prolongation of the truce with France. Charles VI was to agree to both in January.

At some stage, Isabella was moved to Holme Park, the Bishop of Salisbury's Thames-side palace at Sonning, near Reading, Berkshire. The fortified house predated the Norman Conquest of 1066; it was demolished in the seventeenth century, when a new mansion was built on the site. Henry installed his own officers in the Queen's household. Richard's white hart badge was removed from her servants' liveries and replaced with the new King's swan emblem. Effectively, she was a prisoner under the Bishop's guardianship. The new King felt "she ought neither to know nor to feel the changes that have taken place." She was not allowed to see her husband, nor he her, although he had begged to be allowed to do so.

A letter in French that Richard wrote to her during his captivity reveals the depths of his distress:

> My mistress and my consort, accursed be the man who thus separateth us! I am dying of grief because of it. My fair sister, my lady and my sole desire! Since I am robbed of the pleasure of beholding thee, such pain and affliction oppresseth my whole heart that I am oftentimes near despair. Alas, Isabella, rightful daughter of France! You were wont to be my joy, my hope, my consolation. And now I plainly see that, through the violence of Fortune, I must be deprived of you, whereat I often endure so sincere a pang that, day and night, I am in danger of bitter death. And it is no marvel, when I, from such a height, hath fallen so low and lost my joy, my solace and my consort.[10]

It is unlikely that Isabella ever received this letter. She was as cut off from Richard as if he were dead. No one dared mention him to her. She wrote to her father, complaining of her plight, but her letter was intercepted and never reached him.

The government of Charles VI of France steadfastly refused to recognize Henry IV as king of England, denouncing him as a traitor to his lawful sovereign and referring to him, when addressing English envoys, as "the lord who sent you." On November 29, Henry proposed a marriage between his thirteen-year-old heir, Henry of Monmouth, and one of Isabella's sisters, but the French were not interested in allying themselves to the "infamous traitor."

Richard still had friends in high places who were determined to restore him to the throne. They wore his white hart badge, called themselves "Richard's nurselings,"[11] and even had a priest called Richard Maudelyn impersonate him. After Christmas, five of these lords, the dukes of Exeter and Surrey, the earls of Salisbury and Kent, and Thomas le Despenser, Earl of Gloucester (the great-grandson of the murdered Duke), made an attempt to assassinate Henry IV and his sons. In January, Salisbury and Surrey rode to Sonning and informed a jubilant Isabella "that they had driven the usurper Bolingbroke from Windsor to the Tower and that her husband had escaped and was then in full march to meet her at the head of 100,000 men" and would soon be restored to the throne.

None of this was true, but they "so gladded the Queen with lies," vowing to be loyal to her, that she rejoiced.[12] Surrey defaced Henry's arms and tore his cognizance from the royal servants who attended on her. Removing the Lancastrian SS collars from their shoulders "to express his contempt," he cried that they would never again be worn in England. "Queen Isabella was overjoyed, but for empty reasons."[13]

Exeter roused the men of her household: "So ye who love King Richard and his Queen arm yourselves as swiftly as you can and follow me to Wallingford and Abingdon!"[14] Ten-year-old Isabella even issued a proclamation in her own name declaring that "she did not recognise Henry of Lancaster as king." Then she and the lords departed together, "in the direction of Wallingford and then Abingdon, appealing to people along the way to take up arms and go to meet their King Richard, Richard II."[15] Soon they had attracted a formidable force.

"[Isabella] and the earls arrived at Cirencester under cover of darkness. The people of the town were suspicious of all this display and thought that the rumours were lies, so they cut off all the entrances and exits of the earls' lodgings. When, at midnight, they tried to slip away, the towns-people, armed with bows and arrows, would not allow them to pass."[16] Salisbury and Surrey seized their weapons and put up a fight, but they were overcome and had to surrender. Where Isabella was is not recorded, but she must have been fearful for her safety, especially after one of the earls' priests set fire to houses in the town and caused a conflagration. The adventure came to a horrific end when Kent and Salisbury were lynched and decapitated by the hostile mob.

The Mayor of Cirencester informed King Henry of Isabella's presence there and she was soon taken captive. Very few details are recorded about the circumstances, but there were suspicions that "one of the young Queen's servants" had placed an iron caltrop with deadly spikes in the King's bed, in the hope that it would kill him.[17] It is not known whether Isabella was behind this, but young as she was, there were clearly suspicions, and she was escorted under strict guard to the royal manor of Havering in Essex and kept there under house arrest.

Meanwhile, the King had gathered a great army and tracked down the conspirators. Exeter and twenty-six other persons were executed. Henry returned to Westminster with the heads of the traitors, which were publicly displayed in London as a deterrent to other would-be rebels. He had been badly shaken by the rebellion and was beginning to realize that he would not sit safely on his throne while the former King still lived.

The order for Richard's murder was probably sent to Pontefract soon after the executions. Adam of Usk stated that death came miserably to the former king as "he lay in chains in the castle of Pontefract, tormented by Sir Thomas Swynford with starving fare." Most of his contemporaries believed he had been deliberately starved to death, although the government claimed that, having learned of the abortive plot to restore him, he was so distraught that he killed himself by voluntarily refusing to eat.

On January 29, 1400, having heard disconcerting rumors, the King of France, in council, spoke of Richard as being dead. The date of his death is not known, but he had certainly died by February 17, when the Exchequer issued funds to cover the cost of bringing his body to Westminster. It was important to Henry IV not only that Richard was dead, but also that he should be seen to be dead. Only then would his supporters be deterred from rising on his behalf. On February 27, the corpse was conveyed to London, being shown to the people at the more populous places that lay along the route. It was then put on display for two days at St. Paul's Cathedral, although many people still refused to believe that Richard was dead.

In his will of April 1399, he had asked to be buried beside Queen Anne "of glorious memory" in Westminster Abbey, but, on March 12, he was interred in the church of the Dominican Friars at Langley. A marble tomb was raised to his memory, on which were laid copper effigies of the former King and his beloved Anne. This may have been the richly decorated monument adorned with heraldic shields that survives in the church today, but the effigies are long gone.

4

"Angry and Malignant Looks"

＊

NEWS OF RICHARD'S DEATH WAS "CONCEALED" FROM HIS TEN-
year-old widow for "a considerable time"; "orders were given that
she was not to be informed of it." Even when talk of it "spread everywhere" and it was "widely known in France,"[1] Isabella remained in ignorance. But, young as she was, she guessed who had been responsible for
depriving her of the husband who had been so kind to her, and she re-
pulsed all the efforts of King Henry to win her over. To the man she considered a usurper and regicide, she had "a steady aversion."[2]

In January, Charles VI had begun to press Henry IV to send Isabella
back to France, insisting that, even though she had not reached twelve,
he repay the 200,000 francs of her dowry that were refundable under the
terms of her marriage treaty if Richard died leaving her childless. He was
anxious to prevent her from being persuaded into another English marriage before she reached marriageable age in November 1401. Anticipating that Henry might make difficulties, he made plans to invade England,
ordering a fleet under the command of Waleran, Count of Saint-Pol, to
be mustered at Harfleur.

In March, Henry's council told him that he should return Isabella and
her jewels to France, "unless it should prove possible to obtain remission
by means of marriage or otherwise." He agreed in principle, but stalled
when it came to relinquishing her dowry and her jewels. There followed
months of diplomatic wrangling.

On September 6, Charles VI sent an envoy, Jean de Hangest, Sieur de
Hugueville, to "he who calls himself the King of England"[3] with letters to

Isabella from himself, Queen Isabeau, and the dukes of Orléans and Burgundy. As the King was away in Wales, his lieutenant, the Earl of Worcester, arranged for Hangest to see Isabella at Havering. The envoy assured
her that her father would do his utmost to bring her back to France, and
warned her not to enter into any negotiations for a second marriage. She
promised she would not do so even under threat of death.

When he finally saw King Henry in October at Windsor, Hangest asked
that Isabella be sent back to France before November 1, adding, "There is
no greater good for a prince or anyone than to be faithful to his promises."[4] The sticking point was the 200,000 francs of the dowry that the
French could expect to be refunded. But Henry countered that claim,
insisting that the money should be offset against the outstanding arrears
of King John's ransom, forty percent of which remained unpaid. He
would keep his promise to send Isabella home, but he would keep her
dowry. Before Hangest departed in November to convey Henry's resolve
to his master, he was allowed to see Isabella again, but only in the presence of witnesses. Tears flowed and she clung to him, begging him to
take her away immediately.

Henry very much wanted to preserve the alliance with France and win
the recognition of Charles VI, but he could not afford to repay the dowry
because the Exchequer was empty, and he needed the future installments.
To this end, he had earmarked Isabella as a bride for his eldest son, Henry
of Monmouth. On November 29, he sent envoys to open negotiations,
informing the French that he would "in no wise deliver her," but that
"she should reside in England like other queen dowagers, in great honour, on her dower, and that, if she had unluckily lost a husband, she
should be provided with another forthwith, who would be young, handsome and every way deserving of her love. Richard of Bordeaux was too
old for her, but the person now offered was suitable in every respect,
being no other than the Prince of Wales."[5]

It was only now that Isabella realized that Richard really was dead and
that, at just eleven years old, she was a widow. She ordered her household
into mourning, "estranged herself from all occasions of pleasure or comfort, and was accompanied with a heavy train composed to sorrow both
in behaviour and attire."[6] She loudly bewailed Richard's death and
openly cursed the King, whom she believed to have murdered him. Writing in 1599, John Hayward claimed she was so incensed that she re-

quested an audience and came into Henry's presence with tears streaming down her face. What she allegedly said to him seems very sophisticated for a girl of her age, but perhaps accurately reflects her feelings; and it exemplifies the kind of invented conversations characteristic of Tudor history writing.

"In seeking to obtain our purpose of others, it is an ordinary endeavour to move either by prayers, pity or by promises, hope, or by threats, fear," she is said to have begun. "But, as with men cruel and ambitious and, in their own opinion, mighty, these means are of little force, so with them whose misery is beneath all relief they cannot be of any use. Being now therefore in that distress that there remaineth to me neither thing to desire nor thought to obtain, I am come only to put you in remembrance [of] what benefits with what ingratitude you have required that, in my heaviest mishap, I may conceive this vain satisfaction to have reproved you openly to your face."

Henry, she continued, had been ungrateful to King Richard and greedy for honors. "And, albeit ambition (an unquiet humour) hath hitherto blinded your judgement, yet shame will shortly cause you to discern that you possess only an appearance of honour, set upon you by a few flatterers, which will easily be escared [scarred] by those infamies which our just complaints shall blazen through the world. Your own conscience also shall torment you and compel you to condemn yourself to the severest punishments that treason and patricide can deserve. And, albeit it may seem by success that God, in His secret judgement, hath furthered your proceedings, yet assure yourself He hath not favoured them. But your dominion begun with cruelty shall in you, or in your progeny, end with contempt. As for my dishonour, I will not offend the law of modesty in being overcarried with remembrance thereof, being fully purposed to make light account of any disgrace of fortune afterward, yet I make little doubt but it shall also appear to be instantly recompensed with revenge."[7]

The French councillors were outraged at the prospect of Isabella marrying the son of the usurper, knowing "their King would not have it" because it would mean acknowledging Henry as the rightful ruler of England. But they were not in a position to make a decision, because their master was suffering another bout of madness. They replied that "during the grievous illness of their lord, King Charles, they could not give away his eldest daughter without his consent,"[8] and the question was shelved. In November, they sent more envoys to Isabella with instructions that she must not commit herself to any marriage. They were allowed to see her only on condition that they would not speak of Richard. But Isabella had already made up her mind: she would not marry Henry of Monmouth.

At New Year 1401, Orléans sent Isabella expensive gifts, including a gold statue of St. Katherine garnished with three sapphires and thirty-seven pearls. That January, Parliament debated how her return to France was to be funded, for she must go in some state with a great retinue. Already, the maintenance of her household had cost Henry £3,000 ($2.4 million) and her debts amounted to slightly more. Discussions dragged on for months. The council debated whether or not to provide suitable cloth for the Queen's clothes and those of her household, and silver vessels and furnishings for her journey.

Meanwhile, Isabella remained in confinement at Havering, "torn and broken."[9] One of her ladies managed to send word to Charles VI, via some merchants of Bruges, that his daughter was being kept in captivity. Then Lady de Coucy, who had gone to Paris to complain to Charles of Henry's treatment of his daughter, confirmed the extent of Isabella's plight. Charles was furious that a princess of France should be treated so badly and sent Charles, Count d'Albret, and "certain notable and prudent nobles" to England "to inquire into the position of the Queen" and assure him that she was well. But the strain was too much for Charles and plunged him into another spell of madness. When he came to himself again, he erupted in fury and insisted that Isabella be sent home at once.

Meanwhile, d'Albret had arrived in England and been entertained by the King at Eltham. Henry assured him that Isabella was safe, and when d'Albret asked to visit her, he repeated what he had said to the previous envoys: "We no way wish to prevent you from seeing her, but you must promise, on oath, that neither yourself nor any of your company speak to her anything concerning Richard of Bordeaux." D'Albret gave his undertaking and the King had him escorted to Havering by the Earl of Northumberland. There, he found Isabella attended by the Duchess of

Ireland, the Duchess of Gloucester and her two daughters, and other ladies. Northumberland presented d'Albret and his companions to her.
"The young Queen received them sweetly and demanded of them how
the King her father did and the Queen her mother. The knights answered
that they were very well, and communed with her a great season, but they
kept well their promise, for they spake no word of King Richard. Then
they took leave of the Queen" and returned to Eltham.

Before d'Albret left for France, Henry said to him, "Tell those who sent
you that the Queen shall never suffer the smallest harm or any distur-
bance, but shall keep up a state and dignity becoming her birth and rank
and enjoy all her rights; for, young as she is, she ought not to be made
acquainted with all the changes that happen in this world."[10]

Henry now sent ambassadors to treat with the French. At Leulinghen,
on April 1, they told Charles that their master had agreed to return the
dowry if France paid the outstanding ransom for John II. As the two payments canceled each other out, it was agreed that Isabella should be sent
home without delay. On May 27, a treaty was signed at Leulinghen, providing for her to return to France in July with her jewels and belongings,
as long as she undertook to abstain from all intrigues in England.

Prior to her departure, Isabella asked to be provided with new clothes
for herself and her damsels, as well as cloth to reupholster their chariots,
but Henry refused, saying that his wardrobe had given out all that he
intended her to have.

In his will, Richard II had instructed that the jewels Isabella had
brought from France should remain with her if she survived him, and
the Treaty of Leulinghen had provided for that, but she was obliged to go
home without them, for Henry had divided them among his six children.
He told his council "that he had commanded his sons and other children
to give up the jewels of their dear cousin, Queen Isabella, and that they
were to be sent to London." But her valuables were never returned to her,
apart from a silver cup, silver saucers and dishes, a small tapestry, and a
few trinkets. The French were angered by that, and also fumed that,
"though it was pretended by King Henry that she was restored with every
honour, yet there was not any revenue or dower assigned her from England as queen dowager."[11]

Before she left England, courtesy demanded that Isabella bid farewell
to the King. On June 27, 1401, she left Havering for Westminster in the

care of the Duchess of Ireland and Joan Fitzalan, Dowager Countess of Hereford, and attended by a retinue of fifty-five people, among whom were the Countess of March, Lady Poynings, Lady Mowbray, seven damsels, her two French chamberers, Simonette and Marianne, her chamberlain, Monsieur de la Vache, and his wife, her confessor, her secretary, six knights, three squires, two yeomen, and a groom. She was escorted by the bishops of Durham and Hereford, John Beaufort, Earl of Somerset (John of Gaunt's eldest son by Katherine Swynford), four knights banneret, and six chevaliers.

Her route took her through Epping Forest. At Tottenham Cross, she was met by her former chamberlain, the Earl of Worcester, steward of the King's household. At Stamford Hill, the Lord Mayor, aldermen, and sheriffs of London were waiting to conduct her to Hackney, whence the King's second son, Thomas (later Duke of Clarence), Ralph Neville, Earl of Westmorland and Earl Marshal, and Henry Percy, Earl of Northumberland and Constable of England, brought her to Westminster, followed by many lords and ladies. It was a solemn procession, reflecting the young Queen's somber demeanor and the black clothing she and her attendants pointedly wore, which had been specially ordered for the occasion.

At Westminster, she was brought before the King, "clad in mourning weeds and showing a countenance of lowering and evil aspect to [him], with angry and malignant looks, scarcely opening her lips as she went away."[12] Even now, Henry was still trying to persuade her to marry his heir, but she would not listen.

The next day, she rode through respectfully silent crowds of Londoners and pressed on to Dover, where two French lords were waiting to see that all the arrangements for her return were satisfactory. The weather was so bad that she had to wait for a month before her ships could depart. At the end of July, she finally crossed to Calais, escorted by Worcester and attended by a train that now numbered 500, including her French household officers, nine extra damsels, ten clerks, thirty-three squires, sixty-seven yeomen of the chamber, thirty-one yeomen of the stable, thirty-nine boys, and thirty pages. The King had provided safe-conducts for all, along with ninety-four horses, and he had given Isabella 1,000 marks to distribute as largesse to those who were leaving her service. The barons of the Cinque Ports had been ordered to provide three swift ballingers (sailing boats) and two armed barges to transport the party to France. Maintaining Isabella's train, returning her to France, and transporting her escort home cost the King £8,242 ($6.7 million), a sum he could ill afford.

John Beaufort, Earl of Somerset, was Captain of Calais, and it was he who received Isabella and appointed lodgings and tents for her and her train. Three days after her arrival in France, in the chapel at Leulinghen, "Worcester, with streaming tears, took the young Queen by the arm and delivered her with good grace into the hands of Waleran, Count of Saint-Pol, and received letters of quittance for her from the French. In these, the English commissioners declared that the young Queen was just as she had been received, and Percy offered to fight *a l'outrance* [to the limit] any who should assert the contrary. Before the parties separated, they all wept most piteously and, when they came to quit the chapel of Our Lady at Leulinghen, Queen Isabella, whose young heart is full of tenderness and kindliness, brought all her English ladies, who were making sore lamentations, unto the French tents, where she made them dine with her. And, after dinner, [she] took all the jewels she had remaining and divided them among the lords and ladies of England who had accompanied her who all wept mightily with sorrow at parting with their young Queen. Yet still she bade them be of good cheer, though weeping herself. Nevertheless, at the moment of parting, all renewed their lamentations."

Anne, "the damsel of Montpensier, sister to [James II] the Count of La Marche, the damsel of Luxembourg, sister to the Count of Saint-Pol, and many other noble ladies were sent by the Queen of France to wait upon her daughter. Then the Count of Saint-Pol led her to where the dukes of Burgundy and Bourbon, with a large company of armed men, were waiting, intending, if any demur had taken place regarding the restoration of their niece, to have charged the English party over hill and over valley and taken her back by force to her fair sire."[13]

Henry was soon to realize that in sending Isabella home, he had lost a valuable hostage to fortune, for the French remained hostile to his rule and continued to threaten an invasion. This hostility led in 1401 to the reopening of the Hundred Years War, but despite England's declaration of war, little action was seen in France during Henry's reign. In 1402, after repeated requests, he was forced to refund 200,000 francs of Isabella's dower, although her jewels were not returned to her; they would one day be given to her sister Katherine when she married Henry V, the son of Henry IV. Isabella's enameled crown with the white flowers, brought to England by Anne of Bohemia, was given to Henry's daughter Blanche on her marriage to the Elector Palatine Louis III in 1402, and can be seen today in the Munich Residenz. It is the oldest surviving crown of the English regalia.

The dukes of Burgundy and Bourbon escorted Isabella to Boulogne and thence to Abbeville, where Burgundy hosted a lavish banquet for her. She then traveled on to Paris, where the crowds rejoiced to see her come home and her uncle, Louis, Duke of Orléans, greeted her most affectionately. "Her coming caused many a tear and many a smile. Most kindly was she received by the King and Queen of France."[14] Soon after her return, the French council required her to issue a declaration that she had never acknowledged Henry as Richard II's successor.

She was now restored to her mother's care. It was not the life she had expected to lead. Although she was attended by ladies of high rank, she lived in less state than when she had been queen. It was said that she was never happy after she returned to France.

In her absence, Queen Isabeau had given birth to two sons, Louis and John. On October 27, 1401, the Queen presented the King with another daughter, Katherine, she who would one day become queen of England. Another boy—the future Charles VII—arrived in 1403. In November 1401, Isabella turned twelve. Now that she was of legal age to make her own decisions, Henry IV required her to sign a bond in which she undertook to renounce all claims on England and never to make any demands relating to the fulfillment of her marriage treaty.

The Duke of Orléans had made himself Isabella's champion. He felt she had been shabbily treated by Henry IV and, in March 1402, went so far as to issue a challenge, defying him, as the plunderer of the Queen and the murderer of King Richard, to fight him in a tournament.

"How could you suffer my much redoubted lady to return so desolate to this country after the death of her lord, despoiled by your rigour and cruelty of her dower, which you detain from her, and likewise of the portion which she carried hence on the day of her marriage?" he demanded to know. "The man who seeks to gain honour is always the defender of the rights of widows and damsels of virtuous life, such as my niece was known to lead. And, as I am so nearly related to her that, acquitting myself toward God and toward her as a relation, I am ready to meet you in single combat."

Henry replied: "God knows, from whom nothing can be concealed, that so far from acting towards her harshly, we have ever shown her kindness and friendship. We wish to God that you may never have acted with greater rigour, unkindness and cruelty to any lady or damsel than we have done to her. As to the despair you say she is in for the loss of our very dear lord and cousin, we must answer as we have before done. And in regard to her dower, the seizure of which you complain, we are satisfied that if you had well examined the articles of her marriage, you could not have made this charge against us. In regard to her money, it is notorious that, on her leaving this kingdom, we had made her such restitution of jewels and money, much more than she brought hither, that we hold ourselves acquitted. And we have besides an acquittance under the seal of her father, proving we never despoiled her. As to yourself, we do not repute very highly of you." He added that he knew of "no precedent which offered the example of a crowned king entering the lists to fight a duel with a subject."[15]

"All that summer, the fleets of England and France attacked each other much at sea."[16] Several more French lords challenged Henry IV to duels, having conceived "an implacable hatred"[17] for the English, whom they considered to have treated Richard II and Queen Isabella appallingly.

Against all the odds, Richard's supporters in England persisted in the belief that Isabella, young as she was, would help to topple Henry IV. In 1403, the Abbot of Byleigh heard that King Richard was coming out of Scotland, and Queen Isabella and the Duke of Orléans were crossing the English Channel, intending to take up arms at Orwell, while Owen Glendower, with a strong force, would meet up with them at Northampton. Another report had it that Isabella would land at Harwich on December 28, and then ride to Northampton, where Richard II would be waiting for her. People spreading the rumors were arrested. In May 1404, Orléans and Saint-Pol did invade the Isle of Wight, and demanded tribute in compensation for "the sustenance of Queen Isabella." The people "answered that King Richard was dead and the Queen peaceably sent home, wherefore they would not pay."[18] The French sailed away. Robert de Vere's mother, Maud de Ufford, Countess of Oxford, was imprisoned in the Tower for having put them up to it, but in November, after Henry IV's Queen, Joan of Navarre, interceded with the King, she was released.

5

"The Fairest Thing to Mortal Eyes"

✳

I N June 1404, Louis, Duke of Orléans, proposed a marriage between his son, Charles of Angoulême, and Isabella. Charles VI and his council agreed, and the couple were betrothed, Isabella being styled "daughter of France, Queen of England" in the contract. She did not want to marry Charles, for he was five years her junior, and she hated the prospect of losing her title of queen, but her father insisted. A dispensation had to be obtained because Orléans was Isabella's godfather, and under canon law this spiritual affinity created compaternity between them. Charles gave his daughter a dowry of 300,000 francs ($223 million) and Orléans settled on her a dower of 6,000 livres ($4.49 million) yearly and the profits of the lordship of Crécy.

The betrothal drew Isabella into the orbit of violent power politics. The Valois court was at that time divided by opposing factions led by Charles VI's powerful relatives, the dukes of Burgundy and Orléans, who were engaged in a struggle over who should rule France during the King's lapses into madness. Since Burgundy had recently betrothed his heir, Philip, to Isabella's sister Michelle, and his daughter Margaret to the Dauphin, Orléans had arranged his son's marriage as a counterbalance.

Lewis Byford, Bishop of Bangor, then in Bruges, wrote to Henry IV informing him of the betrothal. But Henry had still not given up hope of marrying Isabella to his own son. In the spring of 1406, he sent his half-brother, Henry Beaufort, Bishop of Winchester, to Calais to open negotiations; he even promised that "in consideration of this match" he would abdicate in Prince Henry's favor.[1] Charles VI's councilors took the offer seriously and debated it for some time, but Orléans protested, reminding them that Isabella was promised to his son and had refused to ally herself with her late husband's assassin. The proposal was rejected.

Soon afterward, Isabella's mother took her to Compiègne with a huge train to meet Orléans and his son and be married. Burgundy arrived with a splendid retinue. There is no mention of King Charles being present, but on the day before the ceremony he had given his future son-in-law a gift of money, and ten days earlier had presented Orléans with 15,000 gold francs ($11.2 million) to pay for the wedding.

On June 29, the same day on which her brother John was betrothed to Jacqueline, the heiress of Hainault, Isabella's wedding took place with great pomp and circumstance. The bride was sixteen, the groom eleven. Still averse to the match, Isabella wept bitterly when her hand was placed in his, and took little pleasure in the banquets, dances, and jousts that followed. The marriage was the final nail in the coffin for those who believed that Richard II was still alive.

Isabella was now styled "Madame." She and Charles were not given their own establishment because of his youth. Orléans sent them to live with his Duchess, Valentina Visconti, at Château-Thierry in Champagne. The royal castle there, which dated from the thirteenth century, had recently been granted to him.

Valentina was then thirty-six. Her marriage to Orléans was sound, and she was the only person who could calm King Charles when he was having attacks of madness. But that had given rise to rumors that she had bewitched him, and even that she had tried to poison the Dauphin in order to achieve her ambition of becoming queen. The rumors had alienated Queen Isabeau and Burgundy, and by 1396, the situation had become so threatening that Orléans had removed Valentina from Paris for her own safety and established her household at the châteaux of Asnières and Blois.

Against all expectations, Isabella's own marriage turned out to be happy. The young couple were brought together by a shared love of hunting and hawking. Charles came to adore his bride and made her the subject of some of his verses, for which he was to become renowned as one of France's most celebrated poets.

* * *

On November 23, 1407, Orléans was cut down in Paris, stabbed by fifteen masked supporters of his rival, Burgundy. His family were sixty miles away at Château-Thierry when they learned of his assassination.

Charles now succeeded his father as duke of Orléans and Isabella was elevated to the status of duchess, but they were soon to be parted. On December 6, Valentina sent Charles to live at Blois under the guardianship of Sauvage de Villiers, the Captain of Caen. She kept Isabella with her.

It was soon common knowledge that Burgundy had ordered the murder of Orléans. Isabella supported Charles and his mother in their demands for justice and retribution, as did Queen Isabeau, who hated Burgundy and was determined to see him discredited. She summoned Valentina to Paris, where the Duchess had not set foot in eleven years.

On December 10, "the young Queen Dowager of England came with her mother-in-law, Valentina of Milan, Duchess of Orléans, both dressed in the deepest weeds of black." With them were Charles and his young brother John. "They arrived without the walls of Paris in a charette or wagon covered with black cloth and drawn by six snow-white steeds whose funeral trappings strongly contrasted with their colour. Isabella and her mother-in-law sat weeping in the front of the wagon. A long file of mourning wagons filled with the domestics of the princesses followed. They were met at the gates by most of the Princes of the Blood."[2]

Alighting outside the Hôtel Saint-Pol, Valentina took her sons by the hand, with Isabella following, and they all threw themselves at the feet of King Charles and begged for justice. Charles raised and kissed Valentina and promised to do whatever his council advised to avenge Orléans's death, but she and her party were kept waiting for five days before they were admitted to its deliberations, and even then nothing was resolved. In some frustration, Valentina, her sons, and Isabella withdrew to their lodgings. In February 1408, Isabella accompanied her mother-in-law to Blois.

The murder of Orléans provoked a bloody civil war between the feuding factions that would divide France for nearly three decades. By the time Isabella left Paris, Burgundy had been pardoned, after claiming that he had murdered Orléans because the latter had threatened the King's life. He had masterminded such an effective smear campaign that the late Duke's name had become indelibly besmirched—and nothing was done about it. On August 28, still wearing mourning, Valentina and Isabella again went in procession through Paris, this time to refute the calumnies against Orléans and plead for justice. They were followed, on September 9, by fourteen-year-old Duke Charles, who had a private audience with Queen Isabeau, after which he joined his wife and his mother at the Hôtel de Bohême, which Charles had given to his brother in 1397. It stood near the Louvre, where two days later the King received Valentina, Charles, Isabella, and the advocates they had appointed to speak in Duke Louis's defense. He heard them out, then revoked Burgundy's pardon, declaring that he would bring him to justice.

Satisfied, Valentina, Charles, and Isabella withdrew to Blois, but it was not long before they learned that Burgundy had intimidated the King and the Parisians, and that no action had been taken against him, or was likely to be, because Charles had descended once more into incoherence.

The news crushed Valentina. She ordered the walls of Blois to be hung with black cloth, on which was embroidered her new motto, *"Rien ne m'est plus, plus ne m'est rien"* ("Nothing is more to me, more to me is nothing"). In her vulnerable state, she contracted typhoid and died, aged thirty-eight, on December 4 at Orléans, making her sons swear to avenge their father's death. Isabella was at her deathbed.

Charles was just fourteen when he and Isabella conceived a child. In the summer of 1409, when the birth was just weeks away, they went on a progress around the duchy of Orléans and received a warm welcome from their subjects. They bought horses, a saddle for Isabella, and hunting equipment, preparing for an autumn at the chase after their child was born.

On September 13, 1409, Isabella delivered a daughter, Jeanne, at the château of Blois. A few hours later, this passionate girl, who had traversed the world's stage for such a short time, was dead, cut down before she reached twenty. Charles fell into a frenzy of grief and only calmed down when they brought the child to him. Weeping, he caressed his daughter.

The bereaved husband lamented his great loss in verse:

> *Death! Who made thee so bold, alas,*
> *To take from me my lovely Princess,*
> *Who was my comfort, my life,*
> *My good, my pleasure, my riches!*

Alas, I am lonely, bereft of my mate.
Adieu, my lady, my lily!
Our lives are forever severed.[3]

Isabella's body was wrapped in bands of linen, plated over by quicksilver, and buried in the abbey of Saint-Laumer at Blois. Charles recalled his impressions of her burial in another poem, *J'ai fait obsèques de Madame*:

To make my lady's obsequies
My love a minster wrought
And in the chantry service there
Was sung by doleful thought.
The tapers were of burning sighs
That light and odour gave,
And grief, illumined by tears,
Irradiated her grave.
And round about, in quaintest guise,
Was carved, "Within this tomb there lies
The fairest thing to mortal eyes."

Above her lieth spread a tomb
Of gold and sapphires blue:
The gold doth show her blessedness,
The sapphires mark her true,
For blessedness and truth in her
Were livelily portrayed.
When gracious God, with both His hands,
Her wondrous beauty made,
She was, to speak, without disguise,
The fairest thing to mortal eyes.

No more, no more; my heart doth faint
When I the life recall
Of her who lived so free from taint,
So virtuous deemed by all;
Who, in herself, was so complete,
I think that she was ta'en

By God to deck His Paradise
And with His saints to reign.
For well she doth become the skies,
Whom, while on Earth, each one did prize,
The fairest thing to mortal eyes.
But naught our tears avail, or cries;
All soon or late in death shall sleep;
Nor living wight long time may keep
The fairest thing to mortal eyes.[4]

In the cartulary of the abbey of Saint-Laumer, Isabella was remembered as "the most excellent and most generous lady." Around 1624, her tomb was opened and her body found to be entire. It was then moved to the Orléans vault in the prestigious conventual church of the Celestines in Paris, which was the mausoleum of the dukes of Orléans and ranked second only to Saint-Denis, where French kings were buried. The church was desecrated during the French Revolution and destroyed in 1795, when Isabella's tomb was lost.

Charles gave her royal robes to the monks of Saint-Denis, to be made into vestments. He observed the anniversary of her death until at least 1446.

Isabella's daughter Jeanne married John I, Duke of Alençon, in 1424 at Blois; he had been betrothed to Isabella in childhood. Jeanne died childless in 1432.

In April 1410, Charles took a second wife, Bonne of Armagnac. The marriage was childless. In 1415, he was captured by the English at the Battle of Agincourt and languished as a prisoner in England for twenty-five years. When he was finally ransomed and allowed to return to France in 1440, he married Marie of Cleves. Their son, born in 1462, ascended the French throne as Louis XII in 1499. Charles had died in 1465.

In 1413, Henry V had Richard's body exhumed from the tomb at Langley and reburied next to Anne of Bohemia in Westminster Abbey.

In the eighteenth century, metal shields on the ambulatory side of the tomb were removed, allowing people to see into the burial chamber. Fortune-hunters began stealing souvenirs—and most of Anne's bones.

When Richard's skeleton and what remained of Anne's were examined in 1780, it was noted that two copper crowns were lying in the vault.

In 1871, Arthur Penrhyn Stanley, Dean of Westminster, had the tomb opened again. Inside, he found twin compartments containing the rotting, broken boards of two coffins and a jumble of crumbling bones. Little was left of Anne's remains. Two skulls containing fragments of brains lay at the foot of the chamber, together with two scepters, the King's staff, iron shears, two pairs of gloves, nails, and the remains of a silk pall. The copper crowns had disappeared. The remains and relics were placed in a box and returned to the tomb. At Queen Victoria's behest, the missing bronze cushions supporting the heads of the effigies were replaced. The King's jawbone, stolen in 1766 by a pupil of Westminster School, was returned to the Abbey in 1906 by a descendant and placed in the tomb.

After the turbulent years of the regency of Isabella and Mortimer, English queens had reverted to the medieval ideal of the virtuous, pious, and submissive consort, the very mirror of the Virgin Mary. With the exception of Isabella of Valois, who was too young to make her presence felt, they were learned, merciful, and influential, but never powerful.

In the fifteenth century, it would be a different story.

Select Bibliography

✳

Primary Sources

Adam of Usk: *Chronicon* (ed. E. M. Thompson, London, 1876)

Additional MSS, The British Library

Ancient Indictments, The National Archives

Anglo-Scottish Relations, 1174–1328: Some Selected Documents (ed. E. L. G. Stones, London, 1965)

"Annales Londonienses" (in *Chronicles of the Reigns of Edward I and Edward II*)

Annales Monastici (5 vols, ed. H. R. Luard, Rolls Series, London, 1864–69)

"Annales Paulini" (in *Chronicles of the Reigns of Edward I and Edward II*)

The Anonimalle Chronicle, 1307–1344, from Brotherton Collection MS. 29 (ed. W. R. Childs and J. Taylor, Yorkshire Archaeological Society Record Series 147, Leeds, 1991; ed. V. H. Galbraith, Manchester, 1927)

Antient Kalendars and Inventories of the Treasury of His Majesty's Exchequer (3 vols, ed. F. Palgrave, London, 1836)

The Antiquarian Repertory: A Miscellany, Intended to Preserve and Illustrate Several Valuable Remains of Old Times (4 vols, ed. F. Grose and T. Astle, London, 1775–84, 1808)

De Antiquis Legibus Liber: Cronica Maiorum et Vicecomitum Londoniarum (ed. Thomas Stapleton, London, 1846)

The Apocalypse of Queen Isabella (MS Fr. 13096, Bibliothèque Nationale, Paris)

Archaeologia, or Miscellaneous Tracts relating to Antiquity (102 vols, ed. H. Nicholas and others, Society of Antiquaries of London, 1773–1969)

"*Archives Departementales d'Herault et Montpelier* (https://archives-pierresvives .herault.fr)"

Archives Municipales d'Agen (ed. G. Tholin and A. Magen, Villaneuve-sur-Lot, 1876)

Archivo Generale de Navarra, MS 197

Arundel MSS, The British Library

Ashmole MSS, The Bodleian Library, Oxford

Baker, Geoffrey le: *Chronicon Galfridi le Baker de Swynebroke* (ed. E. Maunde Thompson, Oxford, 1889)

Baker, Richard: *A Chronicle of the Kings of England from the Time of the Romans' Government unto the Death of King James* (London, 1643)

Barbour, John: *The Bruce* (3 vols, ed. Walter Skeat, Oxford, 1870–77; ed. W. M. Mackenzie, London, 1909)

The Berkeley Manuscripts: The Lives of the Berkeleys (3 vols, compiled by their steward, Sir John Smyth of Nibley, in the 17th century; ed. J. MacLean, Gloucester, 1883–85)

The Beverley Chapter Act Book, 1286–1347 (ed. A. Leach, Surtees Society, 1898)

The Black Book of the Garter, St. George's Chapel Archives, Windsor

Boccaccio, Giovanni: *The Decameron* (1358; tr. J. G. Nichols, London, 2009)

Bodleian MSS, The Bodleian Library, Oxford

Bower, Walter: Scotichronicon, National Library of Scotland

The Brut, or the Chronicles of England (2 vols, ed. F. W. D. Brie, Early English Text Society, Oxford, 1906, 1908)

Brut y Twnysogion (The Chronicle of the Princes) (ed. J. Williams ab Ithel, Rolls Series, London, 1860)

Burney MSS, The British Library

Bury, Richard de: *Liber Epistolaris* (ed. N. Denholme-Young, Roxburghe Club, Oxford, 1950)

——*Philobiblon* (ed. E. C. Thomas, London, 1960)

Calendar of Chancery Rolls (Various), 1277–1326 (London, 1912)

Calendar of Chancery Warrants, 1244–1326 (London, 1927)

Calendar of the Charter Rolls preserved in the Public Record Office, 1222–1516 (6 vols, London, 1903–27)

Calendar of the Close Rolls preserved in the Public Record Office: Edward I, Edward II and Edward III (24 vols, London, 1892–97)

Calendar of Documents preserved in France illustrative of the History of Great Britain and Ireland, Vol. 1: 918–1206 (ed. J. H. Round, London, 1899)

Calendar of Documents relating to Scotland preserved in Her Majesty's Public Record Office, London (5 vols, ed. Joseph Bain, Edinburgh, 1881–88)

Calendar of Entries in the Papal Registers relating to Great Britain and Ireland (ed. W. H. Bliss and W. W. Blom, London, 1893–1904)

Calendar of the Fine Rolls preserved in the Public Record Office: Edward I, Edward II and Edward III 1327–1347 (5 vols, London, 1912–29)

Calendar of Inquisitions Post Mortem and Other Analogous Documents preserved in

the Public Record Office: Edward I, Edward II and Edward III (13 vols, London, 1906–52)

Calendar of Letterbooks Preserved among the Archives of the Corporation of the City of London, 1275–1498 (11 vols, ed. R. R. Sharpe, London, 1899–1912)

Calendar of Memoranda Rolls, Michaelmas 1326–Michaelmas 1327 (London, 1968)

Calendar of the Patent Rolls preserved in the Public Record Office: Edward I, Edward II and Edward III (27 vols, London, 1894–1916)

Calendar of Plea and Memoranda Rolls of the City of London, 1323–1412, preserved among the Archives of the Corporation of London at the Guildhall (6 vols, ed. A. H. Thomas and P. E. Jones, Cambridge, 1926–61)

Calendar of State Papers and Manuscripts existing in the Archives and Collections of Milan, Vol. I, 1385–1618 (ed. Allen B. Hinds, London, 1912)

Calendar of State Papers and Manuscripts relating to English Affairs preserved in the Archives of Venice and in the other Libraries of Northern Italy (7 vols, ed. L. Rawdon-Brown, Cavendish Bentinck et al., London, 1864–1947)

Calendar of Various Chancery Rolls: Supplementary Close Rolls, Welsh Rolls, Scutage Rolls, preserved in the Public Record Office, 1277–1326 (London, 1912)

Calendars of Charter Rolls, The National Archives

Calendars of Close Rolls, The National Archives

Calendars of Patent Rolls, The National Archives

Camden, William: *Annales rerum Anglicarum et Hibernicarum regnante Elizabetha* (London, 1615)

Capgrave, John: *The Chronicle of England* (ed. F. C. Hingeston, London, 1858)

Cappellani, William: *Willelmi Cappellani in Brederode postea Monachi et Procuratoris Egmundensis Chronicon* (ed. C. Pijnacker Hondyk, Historisch Genootschap, 3rd Series, XX, Amsterdam, 1904)

Cartulaire de Notre Dame de Boulogne (ed. D. Hagnière, Paris, 1844)

Chancery Miscellanea (C.47), The National Archives

Chancery: Parliament and Council Proceedings (C.49), The National Archives

Chancery Records: Gascon Rolls (C.61), The National Archives

Chancery Records: Warrants for the Great Seal (C.81), The National Archives

Chandos Herald: *The Life of the Black Prince* (ed. M. K. Pope and E. C. Lodge, Oxford, 1910)

Charles of Orléans: Poems, MS. Français 25458, Bibliothèque Nationale de France

Charter Rolls (C.53), The National Archives

Chartularies of St. Mary's Abbey, Dublin: With the Register of its House at Dunbrody and Annals of Ireland (2 vols, ed. John T. Gilbert, Rolls Series, London, 1884)

Chartulary of Winchester Cathedral (ed. A. W. Goodman, Winchester, 1927)

Chaucer, Geoffrey: "The Book of the Duchess" (in *Love Visions*, tr. and ed. Brian Stone, London, 1983)

——*The Canterbury Tales* (Harleian MS. 1758, The British Library, tr. Neville Coghill, London, 1962)

——The Legend of Good Women, Additional MS. 9832, The British Library

——The Parliament of Fowls, Harleian MS. 7333, The British Library

——Troilus and Criseyde, Corpus Christi College, Cambridge MS. 61

——*Troilus and Criseyde* (ed. Neville Coghill, London, 1971)

Chaucer: Life Records (ed. M. M. Crow and C. C. Olson, Oxford, 1966)

"Chronicarum Comitum Flandria" (ed. Joseph-Jean de Smet, in *Corpus Chronicorum Flandriae*, 4 vols, Brussels, 1837–65)

The Chronicle of Bury St. Edmunds, 1212–1301 (ed. and tr. Antonia Gransden, Nelson's Mediaeval Texts, London, 1964)

"A Chronicle of the Civil Wars of Edward II," also known as the Cleopatra Chronicle (ed. G. L. Haskins, *Speculum*, XIV, 1939)

Chronicle of the Grey Friars of London (ed. J. Nichols, Camden Society, 1852)

The Chronicle of Lanercost, 1272–1346 (2 vols, ed. J. Stevenson, Bannatyne Club, Edinburgh, 1839; ed. and tr. Sir Herbert R. Maxwell, Maitland Club, Glasgow, 1913)

Chronicle of London, 1089–1483 (ed. Sir Harris Nicolas, Society of Antiquaries of London, 1827)

Chronicles illustrative of the Reigns of Edward I and Edward II (2 vols (Vol. I: Annales Londonienses; Annales Paulini; Vol. II: Commendiato lamentablis in transita magni regis Edwardi; Gesta Edwardi de Carnarvon auctore canonico Bridlingtoniensi; Monachi cujusdam Malmesberiensis; Vita et mors Edwardi II conscripta a Thoma de la Moore), ed. W. Stubbs, Rolls Series, London, 1882–83)

The Chronicles of London (ed. and tr. E. Goldsmid, Edinburgh, 1885)

Chronicles of London (ed. C. L. Kingsford, Oxford, 1905)

Chronicle of Meaux: Chronica Monasterii de Melsa, a Fundatione usque ad Annum 1396, Auctore Thoma de Burton, Abbate. Accedit Continuato as Annum 1406 a Monacho Quodam ipsius Domus (3 vols, ed. E. A. Bond, Rolls Series, London, 1866–68)

Chronicles of the Reigns of Edward I and Edward II (ed. W. Stubbs, Rolls Series, 1882)

Chronicles of the Revolution 1397–1400: The Reign of Richard II (ed. Chris Given-Wilson, Manchester, 1993)

Chronicon Abbatiae Ramesiensis (ed. W. Mackay, Rolls Series, London, 1886)

Chronique Normande du XIVe siècle (ed. Auguste and Émile Molinier, Paris, 1882)

Chronique de Pays-Bas (ed. J. Smet, Receuil des Chroniques de Flandre, Brussels, 1856)

Chronique du religieux de Saint-Denys (ed. M. Pintoin, Paris, 1839)

Chronique de la Traïson et Mort de Richard II, 1397–1400 (ed. B. Williams, English Historical Society, 1846)

Chroniques de London depuis l'an 44 Hen III jusqu'à l'an 17 Edw III (ed. G. J. Aungier, Camden Society, Old Series, XXVIII, London, 1844)

Chronographia Regum Francorum (ed. H. Moranville, Paris, 1891–97)

Clanvow, Sir John: *The Works of Sir John Clanvow* (ed. V. J. Scattergood, Cambridge, 1975)

A Collection of Ordinances and Regulations for the Government of the Royal Household made in divers reigns from King Edward III to King William and Queen Mary (Society of Antiquaries of London, 1790)

A Collection of the Wills of the Kings and Queens of England from William the Conqueror to Henry VII (ed. J. Nichols, Society of Antiquaries of London, 1780)

Comptes royaux, 1285–1314 (3 vols, ed. Robert Fawtier and François Maillard, Paris, 1953–56)

"The Continuator of William de Nangis" (ed. P. C. F. Daunou and J. Naudet, in *Receuil des Historiens de France*, Paris, 1840)

Cotton MSS, The British Library

Creton, Jean: *Histoire du Roy d'Angleterre Richard* (ed. J. Webb, 1819; ed. J. A. C. Buchon, Paris, 1826)

Cronijke Van Nederlandt (ed. Charles Piot, Brussels, 1867)

Dene, William: "Historia Roffensis" (in *Anglia Sacra*, 2 vols, ed. H. Wharton, London, 1691)

Diocese of London, Episcopal and Estate Records, London Metropolitan Archives, City of London

The Diplomatic Correspondence of Richard II (ed. Edouard Perroy, London, 1933)

Documents concerning the rebellion of Roger Mortimer in 1321–2 (Hereford Cathedral Library)

Documents Illustrative of English History in the Thirteenth and Fourteenth Centuries (ed. H. Cole, London, 1844)

"Documents relating to the Death and Burial of King Edward II" (ed. S. A. Moore, *Archaeologia*, L, 1887)

Douce MS (the French Brut), The Bodleian Library, Oxford

Duchy of Lancaster: Accounts Various (D.L.28), The National Archives

Duchy of Lancaster Miscellanea (D.L.41), The National Archives

Duchy of Lancaster: Miscellaneous Books (D.L.42), The National Archives

Duchy of Lancaster: Royal Charters (D.L.10), The National Archives

Dugdale, William: *Monasticon Anglicanum* (6 vols, ed. J. Caley and others, London, 1846)

Egerton MSS, The British Library

An English Chronicle of the Reigns of Richard II, Henry IV, Henry V and Henry VI (ed. J. S. Davies, London, 1856)

English Coronation Records (ed. L. G. W. Legg, London, 1901)

English Historical Documents, Vol. III, 1189–1327 (ed. H. Rothwell, London, 1975–77)

English Historical Documents, Vol. IV, 1327–1485 (ed. D. C. Douglas and A. R. Myers, London, 1969)

Eulogium Historiarum (3 vols, ed. F. S. Haydon, Rolls Series, London, 1858–63)

Excerpta Historica (ed. S. Bentley and Sir Harris Nicolas, London, 1831)

Exchequer Records: Ancient Deeds (E.41), The National Archives

Exchequer Records: Diplomatic Documents (E.30), The National Archives

Exchequer Records: Issue Rolls (E.403), The National Archives

Exchequer Records: King's Remembrancer, Memoranda Rolls (E.159), The National Archives

Exchequer Records: King's Remembrancer, Wardrobe Accounts, Accounts Various (E.101), The National Archives

Exchequer Records: Miscellanea (E.163), The National Archives

Exchequer Records: Miscellaneous Rolls, including Pipe Rolls (E.370), The National Archives

Exchequer Records: Sheriffs' Accounts (E.199), The National Archives

Exchequer Records: Writs and Warrants for Issue (E.404), The National Archives

Extracts from the Issue Rolls of the Exchequer (ed. F. Devon, London, 1837)

Fabyan, Robert: *The New Chronicles of England and France: The Concordance of Histories* (ed. H. Ellis, London, 1811)

Favent, Thomas: *Historia mirabilis Parliamenti* (ed. M. McKisack, London, 1926)

Foedera, Conventiones, Literae et cujuscumque generis Acta Publica, or Rymer's Foedera, 1066–1383 (20 vols, ed. Thomas Rymer, 1704–35; 4 vols, ed. Adam Clarke, J. Caley, F. Holbrooke, J. W. Clarke and T. Hardy, Records Commission, London, 1816–69)

Foxe, John: *History of the Acts and Monuments of the Church* (Foxe's Book of Martyrs) (1563; ed. G. Townshend and S. R. Cattley, 8 vols., London, 1837–1841)

Froissart, Jean: *Chronicles of England, France and Spain* (25 vols, ed. Kervyn de Lettenhove, Brussels, 1867–77; ed. J. Jolliffe, London, 1967; ed. Geoffrey Brereton, London, 1968)

The Gascon Calendar of 1322 (ed. G. P. Cuttino, Camden Society, 3rd Series, LXX, 1949)

Gascon Rolls preserved in the Public Record Office, 1307–1317 (ed. Yves Renouard, London, 1962)

Geoffrey of Coldingham: Historiae Dunelmensis Scriptores Tres (ed. J. Raine, Edinburgh, 1839)

Geoffrey de Paris: *La chronique metrique attribué à Geoffrey de Paris* (ed. Armel Diverrès, Paris, 1956)

"Gesta Edwardi de Carnarvon auctore Canonico Bridlingtoniensi" (ed. W. Stubbs, in *Chronicles of the Reigns of Edward I and Edward II*; ed. K. R. Potter, Nelson's Medieval Texts, 1955)

Gower, John: Confessio Amantis, Harleian MS 3869, The British Library

——*Speculum meditantis, or Mirour de l'omme* (tr. William Burton Wilson, Michigan, 1992)

Grafton, Richard: *The Chronicle of John Hardyng, together with the Continuation by Richard Grafton* (ed. H. Ellis, Society of Antiquaries of London, 1812)

——*Grafton's Chronicle, or History of England* (2 vols, ed. H. Ellis, London, 1809)

Les Grandes Chroniques de France (Sloane MSS, British Library; ed. M. Paulin, Paris, 1837; 8 vols, ed. Jules Viard, Paris, 1934–37)

Gray (or Grey) of Heaton, Sir Thomas: *Scalacronica: A Chronicle of England and Scotland from A.D. MLXVI to A.D. MCCCLXII* (ed. J. Stevenson, Edinburgh, 1836)

——*Scalacronica: The Reigns of Edward I and Edward II, as recorded by Sir Thomas Grey of Heton, knight* (ed. and tr. Sir Herbert R. Maxwell, Glasgow and London, 1907)

The Great Chronicle of London (ed. A. H. Thomas and I. D. Thornley, London, 1938; reprinted Stroud, 1983)

Groot Charterboek de Graaven Van Holland (ed. F. Mieris, Leyden, 1754)

Guildhall MSS, The Guildhall Library, London

Hardying, John: *The Chronicle of John Hardying* (ed. H. Ellis, London, 1812)

Harleian MSS, The British Library

Hayward, Sir John: *The First Part of the Life and Reign of King Henry IIII* (London, 1599)

Higden, Ranulph: *Polychronicon Ranulphi Higden Monachi Cestrensis, with the English translations of John Trevisa* (9 vols, ed. C. Babington and J. R. Lumby, Rolls Series, London, 1864–86; ed. John Taylor, as *The Universal Chronicle of Ranulph Higden*, Oxford, 1966—includes John Trevisa's English translation, completed 1387)

Historia Sancti Petri Gloucestriae (3 vols, ed. William Henry Hart, Rolls Series, London, 1863–67)

Historia Vitae et Regni Ricardi Secundi (ed. T. Hearne, Oxford, 1729)

Historiae Anglicana Decem Scriptores (ed. Roger Twysden, London, 1652; ed. A. H. Davis, 1934)

Historiae Dunelmensis Scriptores Tres (ed. J. Raine, Edinburgh, 1839)

Historical Poems of the 14th and 15th Centuries (ed. R. H. Robbins, New York, 1959)

The History of the King's Works, Vols I and II: The Middle Ages (ed. R. A. Brown, H. M. Colvin and A. J. Taylor, London, 1963)

The Hours of Anne of Bohemia, Bodleian Library, Oxford

The Household Book of Queen Isabella of England for the Fifth Regnal Year of Edward II, 8th July 1311–7th July 1312 (ed. F. D. Blackley and G. Hermansen, Edmonton, 1971)

Illustrations of Ancient State and Chivalry from Manuscripts Preserved in the Ashmolean Museum (ed. W. H. Black, Roxburgh Club, London, 1840)

Inventaires des Manuscrits concernant les Relations de Flandre et l'Angleterre (ed. J. de St. Genois, Messager des Sciences Historiques, 1842)

"Inventory of the Effects of Roger Mortimer at Wigmore Castle and Abbey, Herefordshire" (ed. Lambert B. Larking, *The Archaeological Journal*, XV, 1858)

Irish Exchequer Payments (ed. Philomena Connolly, Dublin, 1998)

The Isabella Psalter (1303–1308), Bayerische Staatsbibliothek, Munich

Issue Roll of Thomas de Brantingham, Bishop of Exeter, Lord High Treasurer of England, A.D. 1370 (ed. F. Devon, London, 1835)

Issues of the Exchequer, from King Henry III to King Henry VI (ed. F. Devon, London, 1834–37)

Istoire et Croniques de Flandres (ed. Kervyn de Lettenhove, Brussels, 1879–80)

Jean des Preis dit d'Outremeuse: *Lej Myreur des Histors* (7 vols, ed. A. Borgnet and Stanislas Bormans, Brussels, 1864–68)

Jean le Beau: *Chronique de Richard II, 1377–1399* (ed. J. A. C. Buchon, Paris, 1826)

Jean le Bel: *Vray Chroniques de Jean le Bel* (ed. M. L. Polain, Brussels, 1863; 2 vols, ed. J. Viard and E. Déprez, as *Chronique de Jean le Bel*, Paris, 1904–5)

Jeanne d'Evreux Hours, The Cloisters, Metropolitan Museum of Art, New York

John of London: Commendatio lamentabilis in transitum magni Regis Edwardi Quarti (Lambeth Palace Archives)

John of Reading: *Chronica Johannis de Reading: et Anonymi Cantuariensis, 1346–1367* (ed. J. Tait and Stephen Birchington, Manchester, 1914)

John of Tynemouth: Historia Aurea (Cambridge, Corpus Christi College, MS. 006)

Les Journaux de Trésor de Philippe le Bel (ed. Jules Viard, Paris, 1840)

Les Journaux du Trésor de Charles IV (ed. Jules Viard, Paris, 1840)

Juvenal des Ursins: "Histoire de Charles VI, Roy de France" (in *Nouvelle Collection de mémoires sur l'histoire de France*, Paris, 1836)

Keepe, Henry: *Monumenta Westmonasteriensia* (London, 1683)

The Kentish Chronicle, Trinity College Cambridge MS. R.5:41

King's Bench Records, The National Archives

Kings' Letters: From the Days of Alfred to the Accession of the Tudors (ed. Robert Steele, London, 1903)

The Kirkstall Abbey Chronicles (ed. J. Taylor, Leeds, 1952)

Knighton, Henry: *Chronicon Henrici Knighton, vel Cnitthon, monachi Leycestrensis* (2 vols, ed. J. R. Lumby, Rolls Series, London, 1889–95; ed. and tr. G. H. Martin, as *Knighton's Chronicle, 1337–1396*, Oxford, 1995)

Lambeth MSS, Lambeth Palace, London

Langland, William: The Vision of Piers Plowman, Additional MS. 35157, The British Library

Lansdowne MSS, The British Library

Latin History MS. C.5 (R), The Bodleian Library, Oxford

Latin MSS, Bibliothèque Nationale, Paris

La Tour Landry, Geoffrey: *The Book of the Knight of La Tour Landry* (ed. T. Wright, London, 1868; tr. William Caxton, ed. M. Yofford, Early English Text Society, 1971)

Leland, John: *Collectanea* (6 vols, ed. T. Hearne, Chetham Society, 1770–74)

Lescot, Richard: *Chronique de Richard Lescot, religieux de Saint-Denis (1328–1344), suivie de la continuation de cette chronique (1344–1364)* (ed. Jean Lemoine, Paris, 1896)

Letters and Papers from Northern Registers (ed. J. Raine, Rolls Series, London, 1873)

Letters and Papers Illustrative of the Wars of the English in France (2 vols, ed. J. Stevenson, 1861–64)

Letters of Edward, Prince of Wales, 1304–5 (ed. Hilda Johnstone, Cambridge, 1931)

Letters of Royal and Illustrious Ladies of Great Britain (3 vols, ed. Mary Anne Everett Wood, London, 1846)

Letters of the Kings of England (ed. J. O. Halliwell, London, 1846)

Letters of the Queens of England, 1100–1547 (ed. Anne Crawford, Stroud, 1994)

"Lettre de Manuel de Fiesque concernant les dernières années du roi d'Angleterre Edouard II" (ed. Alexandre Germain, *Mémoires de la Société Archéologique de Montpellier*, VII, 1881)

Lettres de Jean XXII (1316–34) (ed. A Fayen, Paris, 1808–12)

Lettres de Rois, Reines et Autres Personnages de Cours de France et d'Angleterre (2 vols, ed. J. J. Champollion-Figeac, Paris, 1839–47)

Lettres Secrètes et Curiales du Pape Jean XXII (1316–1334) relatives à la France (ed. Auguste Coulon and S. Clemençet, Paris, 1901–2, reprinted 1965)

Liber Regalis, Westminster Abbey Muniments, MS 38

Liberate Rolls (C.62), The National Archives

The Lichfield Chronicle, MS 956, The Bodleian Library, Oxford

The Life of Edward II by the So-called Monk of Malmesbury (see *Vita Edwardi Secundi*)

Li Livres de Justice et de Plet (ed. F. A. B. Chabaille, Paris, 1850)

Lincoln, Dean and Chapter Muniments, D.II/56/1, Lincoln Cathedral Library

Lists and Indexes, The National Archives

Literae Cantuarienses (3 vols, ed. J. B. Sheppard, Rolls Series, London, 1887–89)

Le Livere de Reis de Brittaniae (ed. J. Glover, Rolls Series, London, 1865)

Lydgate, John: The Fall of Princes, Harleian MS 1766, The British Library

Maidstone, Richard: *Concordia: The Reconciliation of Richard II with London* (tr. A. G. Rigg, ed. David R. Carlson, University of Rochester, 2003)

Memoranda Rolls, The National Archives

Memorials of St. Edmund's Abbey (3 vols, ed. T. Arnold, Rolls Series, London, 1890–96)

Le Ménagier de Paris (ed. Jerome Pichon, Paris, 1846)

Miscellanea Genealogica et Heraldica (ed. W. Bruce Bannerman, London, 1912)

Monk of Evesham: *Vita Regis Ricardi II* (ed. T. Hearne, Oxford, 1729)

Monstrelet, Enguerrand de: *The Chronicles of Enguerrand de Monstrelet* (2 vols., tr. Thomas Johnes, London, 1849)

Monumenta Franciscana (ed. J. S. Brewer, Rolls Series, London, 1858)

Moore, Thomas de la: "Vita et mors Edward II conscripta a Thoma de la Moore" (in *Chronicles illustrative of the Reigns of Edward I and Edward II*)

Motte, Jehan de la: Li regret Guillaume, Bibliothèque Nationale, Paris

MS. Ancient 6, Dr. Williams's Library

Munimenta Gildhallae Londoniensis (4 vols, ed. H. T. Riley, Rolls Series, London, 1859–62)

Murimuth, Adam: *Adae Murimuth, Continuatio Chronicarum* (ed. E. Maunde Thompson, Rolls Series, London, 1889)

Niger, Ralph (*c.*1140–*c.*1217): *Chronica* (ed. R. Anstruther, Caxton Society, 1851)

Original Letters Illustrative of English History (11 vols, ed. H. Ellis, London, 1824–46)

The Parliamentary Writs and Writs of Military Summons (4 vols, ed. Francis Palgrave, Records Commission, London, 1827–34)

Petitions to the Pope 1342–1419 (ed. W. H. Bliss, London, 1896)

Piers of Langtoft: *The Chronicle of Pierre de Langtoft, in French Verse, from the earliest period to the death of King Edward I* (2 vols, ed. Thomas Wright, Rolls Series, London, 1866–68)

The Pipe Rolls, The National Archives

"The Pipewell Chronicle" (in M. V. Clarke: "Committees of Estates and the Deposition of Edward II," in *Historical Essays in Honour of James Tait*, ed. J. G. Edwards, V. Galbraith and E. F. Jacob, Manchester, 1933)

Political Poems and Songs Relating to English History (1327–1483) (2 vols, ed. T. Wright, Rolls Series, 1859–61)

Political Poems and Songs Relating to English History, from the Reign of John to that of Edward II (2 vols, ed. T. Wright, Rolls Series, HMSO, London, 1859–61)

Ramón, Viscount de Perellós: *Ramón de Perellós sets off for Saint Patrick's Purgatory (The Journey to Purgatory of Saint Patrick)* (ed. Alan Mac an Bhaird, Cork, 2012)

Rawlinson MS. A.273, The Bodleian Library, Oxford

Receuil des Historiens de France: Documents Financiers (Comptes Royaux, 1285–1314) (ed. R. Fawtier, Paris, 1956)

Receuil des historiens des Gaules et de la France (25 vols, ed. M. Bouquet and L. Delisle, Paris, 1840–1904)

Receuil des Historians des Gaules et de la France (ed. M. de Wailly, Paris, 1855–76)

Receuil des Lettres Anglo-Françaises (1265–1399) (ed. J. F. Tanquerey, Paris, 1916)

Récits d'un Bourgeois de Valenciennes (ed. Kervyn de Lettenhove, Louvain, 1877)

Records of the Trial of Walter Langton, 1307–1312 (ed. A. Beardwood, Camden Society, 4th Series, VI, London, 1969)

Regesta Hanonensia (ed. P. C. Muller, Gravenhage, 1882)

Register of Robert Mortival, Bishop of Salisbury, 1315–1330 (ed. S. Reynolds, Canterbury and York Society, 1965)

Register of Thomas Cobham, Bishop of Worcester, 1317–1327 (ed. E. H. Pearce, Worcester Historical Society, XL, Worcester, 1930)

Register of Walter Reynolds, Lambeth Palace Library

Register of Walter Stapledon, Bishop of Exeter, 1307–1326 (ed. F. C. Hingeston, London and Exeter, 1892)

Registre du Trésor des Chartres (ed. R. Fawtier, Paris, 1958)

Registrum Ade de Orleton, Episcopi Herefordensis (ed. A. T. Bannister, Canterbury and York Society, 1908)

"Rekeningen Van de Herberge Van Joanna Van Valois, 1319–1326" (ed. H. Smit, *Historisch Genootschap*, 3rd Series, XLVI, 1924)

Rishanger, William: *Willelmi Rishanger quondam monachi S. Albani et quorundam anonymorum Chronica et Annales regnantibus Henrico Tertio et Edwardo Primo, 1259–1307* (ed. H. T. Riley, Rolls Series, London, 1865)

Robert of Avesbury: *De gestis mirabilibus Regis Edwardi Tertii* (ed. E. M. Thompson, Rolls Series, London, 1889)

Robert of Reading: *Flores Historiarum* (3 vols, ed. H. R. Luard, Rolls Series, London, 1890)

The Roll of Arms of Caerlaverock (ed. T. Wright, Rolls Series, London, 1864)

Rotuli Parliamentorum: ut et petitiones, et placita in Parliamento, 1272–1503; together with an Index to the Rolls of Parliament, comprising the Petitions, Pleas and Proceedings of Parliament (8 vols, ed. J. Strachey, John Pridden and Edward Upham, Records Commission, London, 1767–1832; *Rotuli Parliamentorum Anglie hactenus inediti* (ed. H. G. Richardson and G. O. Sayles, Camden Society, 3rd Series, LI, London, 1935)

Rotuli Scotiae in Turri Londinsensi et in Domo Capitulari Westmonasteriensi Asservati. Vol. I (ed. D. Macpherson, J. Caley, W. Illingworth and T. H. Horne, London, 1814)

Royal MSS, The British Library

Rymer, Thomas: *Foedera* (London, 1704–35; ed. T. Hardy and others, Records Commission, 1816–69)

Select Cases in the Court of King's Bench (7 vols, ed. G. O. Sayles, London, 1936–71)

Select Documents of English Constitutional History, 1307–1485 (ed. S. B. Chrimes and A. L. Brown, 1961)

The Shrewsbury Charter, Shrewsbury Museums MS 1:24

Sloane MSS, The British Library

Society of Antiquaries MSS 120, 121, 122

"Some Private Letters of Edward I" (ed. Pierre Chaplais, *English Historical Review*, 77, no. 302, 1962)

Special Collections: Ancient Correspondence (SC.1), The National Archives

Special Collections: Ancient Petitions (SC.8), The National Archives

Special Collections: Ministers' Accounts (SC.6), The National Archives

De Speculo Regis Edwardi Tertii (ed. Joseph Moisant, Paris, 1891)

"St. George's Chapel Chapter Archives"

State Papers SP13/7, National Records of Scotland

Statutes of the Realm, 1101–1713 (11 vols, Records Commissioners, London, 1810–28)

The Stonor Letters (ed. C. L. Kingsford, Camden Society, 3rd Series, XXIX, London, 1919)

Stow, John: *The Annals of England* (London, 1580)

——*The Survey of London* (London, 1598; 2 vols, ed. C. L. Kingsford, Oxford, 1908; ed. H. B. Wheatley, London, 1987)

Stowe MSS, The British Library

Table Chronologique des Chartres et Diplomes (ed. A. Wautier, Brussels, 1896)

Tanner MSS (including Wardrobe Book, 1311–12), The Bodleian Library, Oxford

The Taymouth Hours, Yates Thompson MS 13, The British Library

The Treasure Roll of Richard II, E.101/411/9, The National Archives

Treaty Rolls preserved in the Public Record Office (ed. Pierre Chaplais, HMSO, London, 1955)

Trevet, Nicholas: *Annales* (ed. T. Hogg, English Historical Society, 1845)

——*Nicolai Triveti Annalium Continuato: Annals of Six Kings of England* (ed. A. E. Hall, Oxford, 1722; ed. Thomas Hog, English Historical Society, London, 1845)

Trokelowe, John, and Blaneford, Henry: *Johannis de Trokelowe et Henrici de Blaneford Chronica et Annales* (ed. H. T. Riley, Rolls Series, London, 1866)

Vergil, Polydore: *Anglica Historia* (Basel, 1555; ed. and tr. D. Hay, as *The Anglica Historia of Polydore Vergil, A.D. 1475–1573*, Camden Series, 1950)

Vita Edwardi Secundi (ed. N. Denholme-Young, London, 1957)

Vita Edwardi Secundi Monachi Cuiusdam Malmsberiensis: The Life of Edward II by the So-called Monk of Malmesbury (perhaps written by John Walwayn; tr. and ed. N. Denholm-Young, London, 1957, and by V. H. Galbraith and R. Λ. B. Mynors, Oxford, 1957)

"Vita et Mors Edwardi Secundi" (ed. W. Stubbs, in *Chronicles of the Reigns of Edward I and Edward II*)

Vitae Paparum Avenionensium (ed. E. Baluze, Paris, 1921)

The Vows of the Heron (unattributed PDF, www.york.ac.uk; also in *Political Poems and Songs Relating to English History, Composed during the Period from the Accession of Edward III to that of Richard III*, ed. Thomas Wright, 1859, London, 1859, and Cambridge, 2013)

Walsingham, Thomas: *Annales Ricardi Secundi* (ed. H. T. Riley, Rolls Series, 1866)

——*Chronicon Angliae, ab anno Domini 1322–8 usque ad annum 1388. Auctore Monacho Quodam Sancti Albani* (ed. E. M. Thompson, Rolls Series, London, 1874)

——*Gesta Abbatum monasterii S. Albani* (3 vols, ed. H. T. Riley, Rolls Series, London, 1867–69)

——*Historia Anglicana, 1272–1422* (2 vols, ed. H. T. Riley, Rolls Series, London, 1863–64)

——*Ypodigma Neustriae* (ed. H. T. Riley, Rolls Series, London, 1876)

Walter of Guisborough, or Walter of Hemingburgh: *Chronicon Domini Walteri de Hemingburgh* (2 vols, ed. H. C. Hamilton, English Historical Society, 1848–49; ed. Harry Rothwell, Camden Society, 3rd Series, LXXXIX, London, 1957)

The War of Saint Sardos, 1322–1325 (ed. Pierre Chaplais, Camden Society, 3rd Series, LXXXVII, 1954)

The Wardrobe Book of William de Norwell, 12 July 1338 to 27 May 1340 (ed. Mary Lyon, Bryce Lyon, Henry S. Lucas and Jean de Sturler, Brussels, 1983)

Wardrobe and Household Accounts, The National Archives

Warrants for Issues, Exchequer Records, The National Archives

Weever, John: *Ancient Funeral Monuments within the United Monarchies of Great Britain, Northern Ireland and the Islands Adjacent* (London, 1631)

Westminster Abbey Muniments

The Westminster Chronicle 1381–1394 (ed. and tr. L. C. Hector and B. Harvey, Oxford, 1982)

Wigmore Abbey Annals, Latin MS 215, John Rylands Library, University of Manchester; in Sir William Dugdale, *Monasticon Anglicanum*, 3 vols, ed. J. Caley, H. Ellis and B. Bandinel, 1830; published as *The Anglo-Norman Chronicle of Wigmore Abbey* (ed. J. C. Dickinson and P. T. Ricketts, Transactions of the Woolhope Naturalists Field Club, XXXIX, 1969)

Wycliffe, John: "The Threefold Bond of Love" (in *Tracts and Treatises of John de Wycliffe*, ed. Robert Vaughan, London, 1845)

Wyntoun, Andrew: *Original Chronicle of Scotland* (6 vols, ed. F. J. Amours, Edinburgh and London, 1903–14)

Year Books of Edward II: 6 Edward II (ed. W. C. Bollard, Selden Society, Vol. 14, II, London, 1927)

Year Books for the Reign of King Edward I (5 vols, ed. A. V. Horwood, Rolls Series, 1866–79)

Year Books of the Reign of King Edward III (15 vols, ed. A. V. Horwood and L. O. Pike, Rolls Series, 1883–1911)

Secondary Sources

Adair, John: *The Royal Palaces of Britain* (London, 1981)

Age of Chivalry: Art and Society in Late Mediaeval England (ed. Nigel Saul, London, 1992)

The Age of Chivalry (exhibition catalogue, ed. J. Alexander and P. Binski, Royal Academy, London, 1987)

The Age of Edward III (ed. J. S. Bothwell, York, 2001)

The Age of Richard II (ed. J. Gillespie, Stroud, 1997)

Alexander, J. J. G.: "Painting and Manuscript Illuminations for Royal Patrons in the Later Middle Ages" (in *English Court Culture in the Later Middle Ages*, ed. V. J. Scattergood and J. W. Sherborne, London, 1983)

Altschul, M.: *A Baronial Family in Medieval England: The Clares, 1217–1314* (Oxford, 1965)

Amin, Nathen: *The House of Beaufort* (Stroud, 2017)

Armitage-Smith, Sydney: *John of Gaunt* (London, 1904)

Ashdown, Dulcie M.: *Ladies in Waiting* (London, 1976)

——*Princess of Wales* (London, 1979)

——*Royal Children* (London, 1979)

——*Royal Paramours* (London, 1979)

Ashdown-Hill, John: *Royal Marriage Secrets* (Stroud, 2013)

Ashley, Mike: *British Monarchs* (London, 1998)

Ashmole, Elias: *The Institution, Laws and Ceremonies of the Most Noble Order of the Garter* (London, 1672)

Backhouse, Janet: *The Illuminated Page: Ten Centuries of Manuscript Painting* (The British Library, London, 1997)

Bagley, J. J.: *Life in Medieval England* (London, 1960)

Baldwin, J. F.: "The Household Administrations of Henry Lacy and Thomas of Lancaster" (*English Historical Review*, LXIII, 1927)

Banckes's Herbal, Trinity College, Cambridge

Banstead History Research Group: *Banstead: A History. How a Village Grew and Changed* (Southampton, 1993)

Barber, M.: "The World Picture of Philip the Fair" (*Journal of Medieval History*, VIII, 1982)

Barber, Richard: *Edward, Prince of Wales and Aquitaine: A Biography of the Black Prince* (London, 1978)

——*Edward III and the Triumph of England* (London, 2013)

——*Life and Campaigns of the Black Prince* (Woodbridge, 1979)

——*Magnificence and Princely Splendour in the Middle Ages* (Woodbridge, 2020)

Barker, J. R. V.: *The Tournament in England, 1100–1400* (Woodbridge, 1986)

Barnes, Joshua: *The History of That Most Victorious Monarch, Edward III* (Cambridge, 1688)

Barrow, G. W. S.: *Robert Bruce and the Community of the Realm of Scotland* (London, 1965; revised edition Edinburgh, 1988)

Barton, John, and Law, Joy: *The Hollow Crown* (London, 1971)

Baxter, Ron: *The Royal Abbey of Reading* (Woodbridge, 2016)

Bayley, J.: *History and Antiquities of the Tower of London* (London, 1830)

Bayliss, D. G.: "The Lordship of Wigmore in the Fourteenth Century" (*Transactions of the Woolhope Naturalists Field Club*, XXXVI, I, 1959)

Beaumont-Maillet, L.: *Le Grand Couvent de Cordeliers de Paris* (Paris, 1975)

Bell, S. Groag: "Medieval Women Book Owners: Arbiters of Lay Piety and Ambassadors of Culture" (*Signs: The Journal of Women in Culture and Society*, VII, IV, 1982)

Benedetti, Anna: *Edoardo II d'Inghilterra all Abbazia di S. Alberto di Butrio* (Palermo, 1924)

Benz St.-John, Lisa: *Three Medieval Queens: Queenship and the Crown in Fourteenth-Century England* (New York, 2012)

Bertière, Simone: *Les Reines de France* (Paris, 1994)

Bevan, Bryan: *Edward III: Monarch of Chivalry* (London, 1992)

Beverley Smith, J.: "Edward II and the Allegiance of Wales" (*Welsh History Review*, VIII, December 1976)

Bingham, Caroline: *The Life and Times of Edward II* (London, 1973)

Binski, Paul: *Mediaeval Death: Ritual and Representation* (London, 1996)

——*The Painted Chamber at Westminster* (London, 1986)

Black, Edward L.: *Royal Brides: Queens of England in the Middle Ages* (Lewes, 1987)

Blackley, F. D.: "Adam, the Bastard Son of Edward II" (*Bulletin of the Institute of Historical Research*, XXXVII, 1964)

——"Isabella and the Bishop of Exeter" (in *Essays in Mediaeval History presented to Bertie Wilkinson*, ed. T. Sandquist and F. M. Powicke, Toronto, 1969)

——"Isabella of France, Queen of England (1308–1358) and the Late Mediaeval Cult of the Dead" (*Canadian Journal of History*, XV, I, 1980)

——"The Tomb of Isabella of France, Wife of Edward II of England" (*International Society for the Study of Church Monuments Bulletin*, VIII, 1983)

Bond, Arthur: *The Walsingham Story through 900 Years* (Walsingham, 1988)

Bond, E. A.: "Notices on the Last Days of Isabella, Queen of Edward II, Drawn from the Account of the Expenses of her Household" (*Archaeologia*, XXXV, 1853–54)

Bordonove, G.: *Philippe le Bel* (Paris, 1994)

Boswell, J.: *Christianity, Social Tolerance and Homosexuality* (Chicago, 1980)

Brewer, Clifford: *The Death of Kings: A Medical History of the Kings and Queens of England* (London, 2000)

Brewer, Derek: *Chaucer in His Time* (London, 1963)

——*Chaucer and His World* (Cambridge, 1978)

Brewer, H. W.: "The Greyfriars at Newgate" (*The Builder*, April 21, 1894)

Brindle, Stephen: *Windsor Castle: 1,000 Years of a Royal Palace* (Royal Collection Trust, 2018)

Brindle, Stephen, and Kerr, Brian: *Windsor Revealed: New Light on the History of the Castle* (London, 1997)

Broglie, Emmanuel de, Centorame, Bruno, Ducamp, Emmanuel, Guegan, Stéphane, Picon, Guillaume, and Thomasin, Luc: *l'ABCdaire des Rois de France* (Paris, 2000)

Brook, R.: *The Story of Eltham Palace* (London, 1960)

Brooke-Little, J. P.: *Boutell's Heraldry* (London, 1973)

Brown, Elizabeth A. R.: Customary Aid and Royal Finance in Capetian France: The Marriage Aid of Philip the Fair (MA Thesis, University of Cambridge, 1989)

——"Death and the Human Body in the Later Middle Ages: The Legislation of Boniface VIII on the Division of the Corpse" (*Viator*, XII, 1981)

——"Diplomacy, Adultery and Domestic Politics at the Court of Philip the Fair: Queen Isabelle's Mission to France in 1314" (in *Documenting the Past: Essays in Mediaeval History Presented to George Peddy Cuttino*, ed. J. S. Hamilton and Patricia J. Bradley, Woodbridge, 1989)

——"The Marriage of Edward II of England and Isabelle of France: A Postscript" (*Speculum*, LXIV, 1989)

——"The Political Repercussions of Family Ties in the Early Fourteenth Century: The Marriage of Edward II of England and Isabella of France" (*Speculum*, LXIII, 1988)

——"The Prince Is Father of the King: The Character and Childhood of Philip the Fair of France" (*Mediaeval Studies*, XLIX, 1987)

Brown, Geoff: *The Ends of Kings: An Illustrated Guide to the Death and Burial Places of English Monarchs* (Stroud, 2008)

Brownrigg, L.: "The Taymouth Hours and the Romance of Beves of Hampton" (*English Manuscript Studies*, I, 1989)

Bruce, Marie Louise: *The Usurper King: Henry of Bolingbroke 1366–99* (London, 1986)

Brundage, J. A.: *Law, Sex and Christian Society in Mediaeval Europe* (Chicago, 1987)

Bryant, Arthur: *The Age of Chivalry* (London, 1963)

Buck, Mark C.: *Politics, Finance and the Church in the Age of Edward II: Walter Stapledon, Treasurer of England* (Cambridge, 1983)

Burke, John, and John Bernard, *The Royal Families of England Scotland and Wales, with Their Descendants etc.* (2 vols, London, 1848 and 1851)

Burke's Guide to the British Monarchy (ed. H. Montgomery-Massingberd, Burke's Peerage, 1977)

Burtscher, Michael: *The Fitzalans* (Logaston, 2008)

Butler, L. H.: "Archbishop Melton, his Neighbours and his Kinsmen, 1317–1340" (*Journal of Ecclesiastical History*, II, 1951)

Butler, R. M.: *The Bars and Walls of York* (York, 1974)

Caley, J., Ellis, H., and Bandinel, B.: *Monasticon Anglicanum: A History of the Abbeys and other Monasteries, Hospitals, Friaries and Cathedral and Collegiate Churches, with Their Dependencies in England and Wales* (6 vols, London, 1817)

Cam, H. M.: "The General Eyres of 1329–1330" (*English Historical Review*, XXXIX, 1924)

Cannon, John, and Griffiths, Ralph: *The Oxford Illustrated History of the British Monarchy* (Oxford, 1988)

Cannon, John, and Hargreaves, Anne: *The Kings and Queens of Britain* (Oxford, 2001)

Carey, Henry, Viscount Falkland(?): *The History of the Life, Reign and Death of Edward II, King of England and Lord of Ireland, with the Rise and Fall of His Great Favourites, Gaveston and the Spencers* (written by "E. F.," 1627; London, 1680)

Carlton, Charles: *Royal Childhoods* (London, 1986)

——*Royal Mistresses* (London, 1990)

Castor, Helen: *She Wolves: The Women Who Ruled England before Elizabeth* (London, 2010)

Castries, Duc de: *The Lives of the Kings and Queens of France* (London, 1979)

Cave, C. J. P.: *Mediaeval Carvings in Exeter Cathedral* (London, 1953)

Cawthorne, Nigel: *Sex Lives of the Kings and Queens of England* (London, 1994)

Chambers Biographical Dictionary (ed. Magnus Magnusson, Edinburgh, 1990)

Chaplais, Pierre: "Le Duché-Pairie de Guyenne" (*Annales du Midi*, LXIX, 1957)

——*Piers Gaveston: Edward II's Adopted Brother* (Oxford, 1994)

Christie, A. G. I.: *English Mediaeval Embroidery* (Oxford, 1938)

The Chronicles of the Age of Chivalry (ed. Elizabeth Hallam, London, 1987)

The Chronicles of the Wars of the Roses (ed. Elizabeth Hallam, London, 1988)

Clapham, A. W., and Godfrey, W. H.: *Some Famous Buildings and Their Story* (London, 1913)

Clarke, Maude V.: "Committees of Estates and the Deposition of Edward II" (in *Historical Essays in Honour of James Tait*, ed. J. G. Edwards, V. H. Galbraith and E. F. Jacob, Manchester, 1933)

Clarke, R.: Some Secular Activities of the English Dominicans (MA Thesis, University of London, 1930)

Cloake, John: *Palaces and Parks of Richmond and Kew: Volume 1: The Palaces of Shene and Richmond* (Chichester, 1995)

——*Richmond Palace: Its History and Its Plan* (Richmond Local History Society, 2000)

Coad, Jonathan: *Dover Castle* (London, 1997)

Cole, Hubert: *The Black Prince* (London, 1976)

A Complete Collection of State Trials (34 vols, ed. T. B. Howell and T. J. Howell, London, 1809–28)

The Complete Peerage (13 vols, ed. V. Gibbs, H. A. Doubleday, D. Warrand, Thomas, Lord Howard de Walden, and G. H. White, 1910–59)

Connolly, Sharon Bennett: *Heroines of the Medieval World* (Stroud, 2017)

Contamine, Philippe, Kerhervé, Jean, Rigaudière, Albert: "Monnaie, fiscalité et finances au temps de Philippe Le Bel" (*Journée d'études*, May 2004)

Cook, Petronelle: *Consorts of England: The Power Behind the Throne* (New York, 1993)

Cooke, Sir Robert: *The Palace of Westminster* (London, 1987)

Cooper, W. D.: *The History of Winchelsea* (London, 1850)

Cordier, H.: "Annales de l'Hôtel de Nesle" (*Mémoires de l'Institut National de France*, XLI, 1920)

Corvi, Steven J.: *Plantagenet Queens and Consorts: Family, Duty and Power* (Stroud, 2018)

Costain, Thomas B.: *The Pageant of England, 1272–1377* (New York, 1958; London, 1973)

——*Three Edwards* (London, 1958)

Coulton, George C.: *Chaucer and His England* (London, 1908)

Crofton, Ian: *The Kings and Queens of England* (London, 2006)

Crump, C. G.: "The Arrest of Roger Mortimer and Queen Isabel" (*English Historical Review*, 27, 1911)

The Cultural Patronage of Medieval Women (ed. June Hall McCash, Georgia, 1996)

Cunnington, P., and Lucas, C.: *Costume for Births, Marriages and Deaths* (London, 1972)

Cussans, Thomas: *The Times' Kings and Queens of the British Isles* (London, 2002)

Cuttino, George Peddy, and Lyman, Thomas W.: "Where is Edward II?" (*Speculum*, LIII, No. 3, July 1978)

Dalzell, W. R.: *The Shell Guide to the History of London* (London, 1981)

Daniell, C.: *Death and Burial in Mediaeval England, 1066–1550* (London, 1997)

Dart, J.: *The History and Antiquities of the Abbey Church of St. Peter's, Westminster* (2 vols, London, 1723)

Davenport, Mila: *The Book of Costume* (New York, 1948)

Davey, R.: *The Pageant of London* (2 vols, London, 1906)

Davies, James: *Wigmore Castle and the Mortimers* (The Woolhope Club, 1881–82)

Davies, J. Conway: *The Baronial Opposition to Edward II: Its Character and Policy* (Cambridge, 1918)

——"The Despenser War in Glamorgan" (*Transactions of the Royal Historical Society*, 3rd Series, IX, 1915)

Davies, Philip: *London: Hidden Interiors* (Croxley Green, 2012)

Davies, R. R.: *Lordship and Society in the Marches of Wales, 1282–1400* (Oxford, 1978)

De-La-Noy, Michael: *Windsor Castle, Past and Present* (London, 1990)

Denton, J. H.: *Robert Winchelsey and the Crown, 1294–1313* (Cambridge, 1980)

Déprez, E.: *Les Préliminaires de la Guerre de Cent Ans* (Paris, 1902)

Devon Notes and Queries (ed. P. F. S. Amery, John S. Amery and J. Brooking, Exeter, 1905)

The Dictionary of National Biography (22 vols, ed. Sir Leslie Stephen and Sir Sidney Lee, 1885–1901; Oxford, 1998 edition)

Dillon, Gordon: *The Wilton Diptych: Making and Meaning* (London, 1997)

Dimitresco, M. Marin: *Pierre de Gavaston, comte de Cornouailles: son biographie et son rôle pendant la commencement du régne d'Édouard II, 1307–1314* (Paris, 1898)

Dodge, Walter Phelps: *Piers Gaveston: A Chapter in Early Constitutional History* (London, 1899)

Dodson, Aidan: *The Royal Tombs of Great Britain: An Illustrated History* (London, 2004)

Doherty, Paul C.: "The Date of the Birth of Isabella, Queen of England" (*Bulletin of the Institute of Historical Research*, XLVIII, November 1975)

——Isabella, Queen of England, 1296–1330 (unpublished DPhil thesis, Exeter College, Oxford, 1977)

——*Isabella and the Strange Death of Edward II* (London, 2003)

Doran, J.: *The History and Antiquities of the Town of Reading in Berkshire* (London, 1836)

Douch, R.: The Career, Lands and Family of William Montagu, Earl of Salisbury, 1301–44 (unpublished MA thesis, University of London, 1950)

Duch, Anna M.: *Anne of Bohemia: A Political Post-Mortem* (Kalamazoo, 2017)

Duffy, Mark: *Royal Tombs of Medieval England* (Stroud, 2003)

Dugdale, William: *The Baronage of England* (2 vols, London, 1675–76)

Dupuy, M.: *Le Prince Noir* (Paris, 1971)

Dussen, Michael van: "Three Verse Eulogies of Anne of Bohemia" (*Medium Aevum*, 78, No. 2, 2009)

Eames, E. S.: "A Tile Pavement from the Queen's Chamber, Clarendon Palace, dated 1250-2" (*British Archaeological Society Journal*, 3rd Series, XX, 1957)

Earenfight, Christina: *Queenship in Medieval Europe* (London, 2013)

Edward the Second (ed. C. R. Forker, Manchester, 1994)

Edwards, J. G.: "The Negotiations of the Treaty of Leake, 1318" (in *Essays presented to R. Lane Poole*, London, 1927)

——"Sir Gruffydd Lloyd" (*English Historical Review*, XXX, 1915)

Edwards, Kathleen: "The Personal and Political Activities of the English Episcopate during the Reign of Edward II" (*Bulletin of the Institute of Historical Research*, XVI, 1938)

——"The Political Importance of the English Bishops during the Reign of Edward II" (*English Historical Review*, LIX, 1944)

——"The Social Origins and Provenance of the English Bishops during the Reign of Edward II" (*Transactions of the Royal Historical Society*, 5th Series, IX, 1959)

Egbert, D. D.: "A Sister to the Tickhill Psalter: The Psalter of Queen Isabella of England" (*Bulletin of the New York Public Library*, XXXIX, 1935)

Emerson, Barbara: *The Black Prince* (London, 1976)

England in the Fourteenth Century (ed. W. Mark Ormrod, London, 1985)

England in the Later Middle Ages: Portraits and Documents (ed. D. Baker, London, 1968)

English Court Culture in the Later Middle Ages (ed. V. J. Scattergood and J. W. Sherborne, London, 1983)

Erlande-Brandenburg, Alain: *Saint-Denis' Basilica* (Rennes, 1984)

Evans, B. Penry: The Family of Mortimer (unpublished PhD thesis, University of Wales, 1937)

Evans, J.: *English Art, 1307–1461* (Oxford, 1949)

Evans, Joan: *A History of Jewellery, 1100–1870* (London, 1970)

Evans, Michael: *The Death of Kings: Royal Deaths in Medieval England* (London, 2003)

Eyton, R. W.: *Antiquities of Shropshire* (12 vols, London, 1854-60)

Fairbank, F. R.: "The Last Earl of Warenne and Surrey" (*Yorkshire Archaeological Journal*, XIX, 1907)

Favier, Jean: *Philippe le Bel* (Paris, 1978)

Fawtier, Robert: *Les Capétiens de France: leur rôle dans sa construction* (Paris, 1942; published in Britain as *The Capetian Kings of France: Monarchy and Nation, 987–1328*, tr. Lionel Butler and R. J. Adam, London and Glasgow, 1960)

Field, John: *Kingdom, Power and Glory: A Historical Guide to Westminster Abbey* (London, 1996)

Fletcher, Benton: *Royal Homes near London* (London, 1930)

Fletcher, Doris: "The Lancastrian Collar of Esses: Its Origins and Transformations down the Centuries" (in *The Age of Richard II*)

Fowler, Kenneth: *The Age of Plantagenet and Valois* (London, 1967)

——*The King's Lieutenant: Henry of Grosmont, First Duke of Lancaster, 1300–1361* (London, 1969)

Frame, Robin: "The Bruces in Ireland, 1315-18" (*Irish Historical Studies*, XIX, LXXIII, 1974)

Fryde, E. B.: "The Deposits of Hugh Despenser the Younger with Italian Bankers" (*Economic History Review*, 2nd Series, III, 1951)

Fryde, Natalie: "John Stratford, Bishop of Winchester, and the Crown, 1323–1330" (*Bulletin of the Institute of Historical Research*, XLIV, 1971)

——*The Tyranny and Fall of Edward II, 1321–1326* (Cambridge, 1979)

Fryer, M. B., Bousfield, A., and Toffoli, G.: *Lives of the Princesses of Wales* (Toronto, 1983)

Galbraith, V. H.: "The Literacy of the Mediaeval English Kings" (*Proceedings of the British Academy*, XXI, 1935)

Gardner, John: *The Life and Times of Chaucer* (London, 1977)

Gardner, Rena: *The Story of Tewkesbury Abbey* (Blandford, 1971)

Geaman, Christen L.: "Anne of Bohemia and Her Struggle to Conceive" (*Social History of Medicine*, 27, 2014)

——"A Personal Letter Written by Anne of Bohemia" (*English Historical Review*, Vol. 128, 534, October 2013)

Gee, Loveday Lewes: *Women, Art and Patronage from Henry III to Edward III* (Woodbridge, 2002)

Gilbert, J. T.: *History of the Viceroys of Ireland* (Dublin, 1865)

Given-Wilson, Chris: *Henry IV* (London, 2016)

Given-Wilson, Chris, and Curteis, A.: *The Royal Bastards of Medieval England* (London, 1984)

Glasheen, Joan: *The Secret People of the Palaces: The Royal Household from the Plantagenets to Queen Victoria* (London, 1998)

Goodman, Anthony: *A History of England from Edward II to James I* (London, 1977)

——*Joan, the Fair Maid of Kent: A Fourteenth-Century Princess and her World* (Woodbridge, 2017)

——*John of Gaunt: The Exercise of Princely Power in Fourteenth-Century Europe* (Harlow, 1992)

Gordon, Dillon: *Making and Meaning: The Wilton Diptych* (London, 1993)

Gough, H.: *The Itinerary of Edward I* (2 vols, 1900)

Gransden, A.: "The Alleged Rape by Edward III of the Countess of Salisbury" (*English Historical Review*, 87, 1972)

——*Historical Writing in England, Vol. II: 1307 to the Early Sixteenth Century* (London, 1982)

Grassi, J. L.: "William Airmyn and the Bishopric of Norwich" (*English Historical Review*, LXX, 1955)

Green, David: *The Black Prince* (Stroud, 2001)

Green, Mary Anne Everett: *The Lives of the Princesses of England* (6 vols, London, 1849–55)

Green, V. H. H.: *The Later Plantagenets: A Survey of English History between 1307 and 1485* (London, 1955; revised edition, 1966)

Griffe, Maurice: *Les Souverains de France: Tableau généalogique et dynastique* (Le Cannet, 1997)

Griffin, Mary E.: "Cadwalader, Arthur and Brutus in the Wigmore Manuscript" (*Speculum*, XVI, 1941)

——"A Wigmore Manuscript at the University of Chicago" (*National Library of Wales Journal*, VII, 1952)

Griffiths, John: *Edward II in Glamorgan* (London, 1904)

Griffiths, Ralph: *Conquerors and Conquered in Mediaeval Wales* (Stroud, 1994)

——*The Principality of Wales in the Later Middle Ages: The Structure and Personnel of Government. I: South Wales, 1277–1536* (Cardiff, 1972)

Groom, Susanne: *At the King's Table: Royal Dining Through the Ages* (London, 2013)

Guinle, Jean-Philippe: *Le Livre des Rois de France* (Mohndruck, 1997)

Haines, R. M.: "Adam Orleton and the Diocese of Winchester" (*Journal of Ecclesiastical History*, XXIII, 1972)

——*Archbishop John Stratford* (Toronto, 1986)

——*The Church and Politics in Fourteenth Century England: The Career of Adam Orleton, c.1275–1345* (Cambridge, 1978)

——"Edwardus Redivivus: The Afterlife of Edward of Caernarvon" (*Transactions of the Bristol and Gloucester Archaeological Society*, CXIV, 1996)

Hallam, Elizabeth M.: *Capetian France, 987–1328* (London and New York, 1980)

——"The Eleanor Crosses and Royal Burial Customs" (in *Eleanor of Castile: Essays to Commemorate the 700th Anniversary of Her Death*, ed. David Parsons, Stamford, 1991)

——*The Itinerary of Edward II and His Household, 1307–1328* (List and Index Society, CCXI, London, 1984)

——"Royal Burial and the Cult of Kingship in France and England, 1060–1330" (*Journal of Medieval History*, IV/VIII, 1982)

Hamilton, Jeffrey S.: *Piers Gaveston, Earl of Cornwall, 1307–12: Politics and Patronage in the Reign of Edward II* (London, 1988)

——*The Plantagenets: History of a Dynasty* (London, 2010)

Hammond, Peter: *Her Majesty's Royal Palace and Fortress of the Tower of London* (London, 1987)

The Handbook of British Chronology (ed. Sir F. Maurice Powicke and E. B. Fryde, Royal Historical Society, 1961)

Harding, D. A.: The Regime of Isabella and Mortimer, 1326–1330 (unpublished MPhil thesis, University of Durham, 1985)

Hardy, B. C.: *Philippa of Hainault and Her Times* (London, 1910)

Harper, Charles G.: *Abbeys of Old Romance* (London, 1930)

Harris, Alma: *In Days of Yore: Queen Isabella and Sir Roger Mortimer: A Royal Romance* (Nottingham, 1995)

Harrod, H.: *Report of the Deeds and Records of the Borough of King's Lynn* (King's Lynn, 1874)

Hartshorne, C. H.: "The Itinerary of Edward II" (*Collectanea Archaeologica*, I, 1861)

Harvey, John: *The Black Prince and His Age* (London, 1976)

——*English Mediaeval Architects* (Stroud, 1984)

——*The Plantagenets* (London, 1948)

Haskins, G. L.: "The Doncaster Petition of 1321" (*English Historical Review*, LIII, 1938)

Hassall, W. O.: *Who's Who in History, Vol. 1: British Isles, 55 B.C. to 1485* (Oxford, 1960)

Hearsey, J. E.: *Bridge, Church and Palace in Old London* (London, 1961)

Hedley, Olwen: *Royal Palaces* (London, 1972)

——*Windsor Castle* (London, 1967)

Hepburn, Frederick: *Portraits of the Later Plantagenets* (Woodbridge, 1986)

Herbert, P.: "Excavations at Christ Church, Greyfriars, 1976" (*London Archaeologist*, III, XII, 1979)

Hibbert, Christopher: *The Court at Windsor* (London, 1964)

——*The Tower of London* (London, 1971)

Hicks, Michael: *Who's Who in Late Medieval England* (London, 1991)

Hill, B. J. W.: *The History and Treasures of Windsor Castle* (London, 1967)

——*Medieval Lincoln* (Cambridge, 1948)

Hilliam, David: *Crown, Orb and Sceptre: The True Stories of English Coronations* (Stroud, 2001)

Hilton, Lisa: "Medieval Queens" (in *Royal Women*, BBC History Magazine special, Bristol, 2015)

——*Queens Consort: England's Medieval Queens* (London, 2008)

The History of the City and County of Norwich (ed. R. Browne, 1768)

The History of the King's Works, Vols I–III: The Middle Ages (ed. H. M. Colvin and A. J. Taylor, HMSO, London, 1963)

The History Today Companion to British History (ed. Juliet Gardiner and Neil Wenborn, London, 1995)

Holmes, G. A.: *The Estates of the Higher Nobility in Fourteenth Century England* (Cambridge, 1957)

——"The Judgement on the Younger Despenser, 1326" (*English Historical Review*, LXX, 1955)

——"A Protest against the Despensers, 1326" (*Speculum*, XXX, 1955)

——"The Rebellion of the Earl of Lancaster, 1328–1329" (*Bulletin of the Institute of Historical Research*, XXVIII, 1955)

Hope, W. H. St. John: "On the Funeral Effigies of the Kings and Queens of England" (*Archaeologia*, LX, 1907)

Hopkinson, Charles, and Speight, Martin: *The Mortimers: Lords of the March* (Logaston, 2002)

A House of Kings: The History of Westminster Abbey (ed. Edward Carpenter, London, 1966)

The Houses of Parliament: History, Art, Architecture (ed. Iain Ross, London, 2000)

Howard, P.: *The Royal Palaces* (London, 1970)

Hoyt, R. S.: "The Coronation Oath of 1308" (*English Historical Review*, LXXI, 1956)

Huguer, P. le: *Histoire de Philippe le Long* (Paris, 1975)

Hughes, D.: *The Early Years of Edward III* (London, 1915)

Hunter, Joseph: "Journal of the Mission of Queen Isabella to the Court of France; and of Her Residence in that Country" (*Archaeologia*, XXXVI, 1855)

——"On the Measures taken for the Apprehension of Sir Thomas de Gurney, one of the Murderers of Edward II" (*Archaeologia*, XXVII, 1838)

Hutchison, Harold F.: "Edward II and his Minions" (*History Today*, XXI, VIII, 1971)

——*Edward II: The Pliant King* (London, 1971)

——*The Hollow Crown: A Life of Richard II* (London, 1961)

Impey, Edward, and Parnell, Geoffrey: *The Tower of London: The Official Illustrated History* (London, 2000)

Intimate Letters of England's Queens (ed. M. Sanders, London, 1957)

Jamison, Catherine: *History of the Royal Hospital of St. Katharine by the Tower of London* (Oxford, 1952)

Jenkinson, H.: "Mary de Sancto Paulo, Foundress of Pembroke College, Cambridge" (*Archaeologia*, LXVI, 1914–15)

Jenks, E.: *Edward Plantagenet, the English Justinian* (London, 1902)

Jenner, Heather: *Royal Wives* (London, 1967)

Joannis, J. D. de: *Les Seizes Quartiers Généalogiques des Cápetiens* (Lyons, 1958)

Joelson, Annette: *Heirs to the Throne* (London, 1966)

Johnson, Paul: *The Life and Times of Edward III* (London, 1973)

Johnson, T.: "Excavations at Christchurch, Newgate St." (*Transactions of the London and Middlesex Archaeological Society*, XXV, 1974)

Johnstone, Hilda: "The County of Ponthieu, 1279–1307" (*English Historical Review*, XXIX, 1914)

——"The Eccentricities of Edward II" (*English Historical Review*, XLVII, 1933)

——*Edward of Caernarvon, 1284–1307* (Manchester, 1946)

——"Isabella, the She-Wolf of France" (*History*, New Series, XXI, 1936–37)

——*The Place of the Reign of Edward II in English History* (Manchester, 1936)

——"The Queen's Exchequer under the Three Edwards" (in *Historical Essays in Honour of James Tait*, ed. J. G. Edwards, V. H. Galbraith and E. F. Jacob, 1933)

——"The Queen's Household" (in *The English Government at Work, 1327–1336*, 3 vols, ed. J. F. Willard and W. A. Morris, the Mediaeval Academy of America, Cambridge, Massachusetts, 1940)

Jones, Christopher: *The Great Palace: The Story of Parliament* (London, 1983)

Jones, Dan: *The Plantagenets: The Kings Who Made England* (London, 2012)

Jones, Michael: *The Black Prince* (London, 2017)

Jones, Nigel: *Tower: An Epic History of the Tower of London* (London, 2011)

Jones, Richard: *Walking Haunted London* (London, 1999)

Jones, Terry: *Who Murdered Chaucer? A Medieval Mystery* (London, 2003)

Kay, F. George: *Lady of the Sun: The Life and Times of Alice Perrers* (London, 1966)

Keen, Maurice H.: *England in the Later Middle Ages: A Political History* (London, 1973)

——"Treason Trials under the Law of Arms" (*Transactions of the Royal Historical Society*, 5th Series, XII, 1962)

Keevill, Graham D.: *Mediaeval Palaces: An Archaeology* (Stroud, 2000)

Kerling, N.: *Commercial Relations of Holland and Zeeland with England* (Leyden, 1954)

Kershaw, I.: "The Great Famine and Agrarian Crisis in England, 1315–1322" (*Past and Present*, LIX, 1973)

King, Edmund: *Mediaeval England, 1066–1485* (Oxford, 1988; revised edition Stroud, 2001)

The Kings and Queens of England (ed. W. Mark Ormrod, Stroud, 2001)

Kingsford, C. L.: *The Grey Friars of London* (Aberdeen, 1915)

Kirchhoff, Elisabeth: *Rois et Reines de France* (Paris, 1996)

Labarge, Margaret Wade: *Gascony, England's First Colony, 1204–1453* (London, 1980)

——*Women in Medieval Life* (London, 1986)

Lane, Henry Murray: *The Royal Daughters of England* (2 vols, London, 1910)

Langlois, Charles Victor: "Rouleaux d'arrêts de la cour au roi au XIIIe siècle" (*Bibliothèque de l'École des Chartes*, L, 1889)

——"Saint Louis—Philippe le Bel: Les dernières Capétiens directs" (in *Histoire de France Illustrée*, Vol. III, 2, ed. Ernest Lavisse, Paris, 1911)

Laver, James: *A Concise History of Costume* (London, 1969)

Lawne, Penny: *Joan of Kent: The First Princess of Wales* (Stroud, 2015)

Lawrance, Hannah: *Historical Memoirs of the Queens of England, from the Commencement of the Twelfth Century* (London, 1840)

Laynesmith, Joanna: *The Last Medieval Queens* (Oxford, 2004)

Leadman, A. D. H.: "The Battle of Myton" (*Yorkshire Archaeological and Topographical Journal*, VIII, 1883–84)

Leblanc-Ginet, Henri: *Les Rois de France* (Éditions Morena et Actualité de l'Histoire, 1997)

Lee, Christopher: *This Sceptred Isle, 55 B.C. to 1901* (London, 1997)

Leeds Castle Guidebook (London, 1994)

Leese, T. Anna: *Blood Royal* (Maryland, 1996)

Letters of Medieval Women (ed. Anne Crawford, Stroud, 2002)

Letters of the Queens of England, 1100–1546 (ed. Anne Crawford, Stroud, 1994)

Levis-Mirepoix, Duc de: *Le Siècle de Philippe le Bel* (Paris, 1961)

Lewis, S.: "The Apocalypse of Isabella of France: Paris, Bibliotheque Nationale, MS. Fr. 13096" (*Art Bulletin*, LXXII, 1990)

Leyser, Henrietta: *Medieval Women: A Social History of Women in England 450–1500* (London, 1995)

Licence, Amy: *Red Roses: Blanche of Lancaster to Margaret Beaufort* (Stroud, 2016)

——*Royal Babies: A History, 1066–2013* (Stroud, 2013)

Lindley, P.: *Gothic to Renaissance: Essays on Sculpture in England* (Stamford, 1995)

Lingard, John: *History of England* (London, 1819–30)

Little, A. G.: *Franciscan History and Legend in English Mediaeval Art* (Manchester, 1937)

The Lives of the Kings and Queens of England (ed. Antonia Fraser, London, 1975; revised London, 1998 and 2000)

Lizerand, G.: *Clement V et Philippe le Bel* (Paris, 1906)

Lloyd, Geoffrey, and Wilson, Peter: *Leeds Castle* (Leeds Castle Foundation, revised edition 1978)

Llywelyn, Alun: *The Shell Guide to Wales* (London, 1969)

Loades, David: *The Kings and Queens of England: The Biography* (Stroud, 2013)

Lofts, Norah: *Queens of Britain* (London, 1977)

The London Encyclopaedia (ed. Ben Weinreb and Christopher Hibbert, London, 1983)

Longman, William: *The Life and Times of Edward the Third* (2 vols, London, 1869)

Longmate, Norman: *Defending the Island: From Caesar to the Armada* (London, 1989)

Loomis, R. S.: "Edward I, Arthurian Enthusiast" (*Speculum*, 28, 1953)

Louda, J., and MacLagan, M.: *Lines of Succession: Heraldry of the Royal Families of Europe* (London, 1981)

Lucas, H. S.: "The Great European Famine of 1315, 1316 and 1317" (*Speculum*, V, 1930)

——*The Low Countries in the Hundred Years War* (Michigan, 1926)

Lucraft, Jeannette: *Katherine Swynford: The History of a Medieval Mistress* (Stroud, 2006)

Lyubimenko, I.: *Jean de Bretagne, Comte de Richmond* (Lille, 1908)

MacCann, Nick: *Leeds Castle* (Derby, 2000)

Mackinnon, J.: *The History of Edward III* (London, 1900)

Mackworth-Young, Robin: *The History and Treasures of Windsor Castle* (Andover, no date)

Maddicott, J. R.: *Thomas of Lancaster, 1307–1322: A Study in the Reign of Edward II* (Oxford, 1970)

Madox, Thomas: *The History and Antiquities of the Exchequer* (2 vols, London, 1711, 1749)

Mansel, Philip, and Winks, Robin W.: *The Lily and the Lion: Royal France, Great Britain* (London, 1980)

Marsden, Jonathan, and Winterbottom, Matthew: *Windsor Castle* (London, 2008)

Marshal, E.: *The Early History of Woodstock Manor* (Oxford, 1873)

Marshall, Rosalind K.: *Scottish Queens, 1034–1714* (East Linton, 2003)

Martin, A. R.: *Franciscan Architecture in England* (Manchester, 1937)

Mason, J. J.: "Sir Andrew de Harcla, Earl of Carlisle" (*Transactions of the Cumberland and Westmorland Antiquarian and Archaeological Society*, New Series, XXIX, 1929)

Mason, John: *Haunted Heritage* (English Heritage, London, 1999)

Mathew, G.: *The Court of Richard II* (London, 1968)

McDonnell, Kevin: *Mediaeval London Suburbs* (London, 1978)

McFarlane, K. B.: *The Nobility of Later Mediaeval England* (Oxford, 1973)

McGrigor, Mary: *The Sister Queens: Isabella and Catherine de Valois* (Stroud, 2016)

McKendrick, Scot, Lowden, John, and Doyle, Kathleen: *Royal Manuscripts: The Genius of Illumination* (The British Library, London, 2011)

McKisack, May: *The Fourteenth Century, 1307–1399* (Oxford, 1959)

Mcleod, E.: *Charles of Orléans, Prince and Poet* (London, 1969)

McNair Scott, Robert: *Robert the Bruce, King of Scots* (New York, 1989)

McNamara, JoAnn, and Wemple, Suzanne: "The Power of Women through the Family in Medieval Europe, 500–1100" (in *Women and Power in the Middle Ages*)

Mediaeval Monarchs (ed. Elizabeth Hallam, London, 1990)

Medieval Mothering (ed. John Carmi Parsons and B. Wheeler, New York, 1996)

Medieval Queenship (ed. John Carmi Parsons, Stroud, 1994)

Menache, Sophia: "Isabella of France, Queen of England: A Reconsideration" (*Journal of Medieval History*, X, 1984)

Mertes, Kate: *The English Noble Household, 1250–1600* (Oxford, 1988)

Meulan, Janet van der: "'Sche Sente the Copie to her Daughter': Countess Jeanne de Valois and Literature at the Court of Hainault-Holland" (in *I Have Heard About You: Women's Writing Crossing the Dutch Border*, ed. Suzan van Dijk, Verloren, 2004)

Mexandeau, L.: *Les Capétiens* (Lausanne, 1969)

Michelet, Jules: *L'Histoire de France* (24 vols, Paris, 1833–67)

Mirot, L.: "Isabelle de France, Reine d'Angleterre, Comtesse d'Angouleme, Duchesse d'Orleans, 1389–1409" (*Revue d'Histoire Diplomatique*, 18, 1904, and 19, 1905)

Moir, L.: *Historic Ludlow Castle and Those Associated with It* (Ludlow, 1950)

Montgomery-Massingberd, H.: *Burke's Guide to the British Monarchy* (Burke's Peerage, 1977)

Morris, David S.: *The Honour of Richmond: A History of the Lords, Earls and Dukes of Richmond* (York, 2000)

Morris, Marc: *A Great and Terrible King: Edward I and the Forging of Britain* (London, 2008)

Morris, R.: "Tewkesbury Abbey: The Despenser Mausoleum" (*Bristol and Gloucestershire Archaeological Transactions*, XCIII, 1993)

Mortimer, Ian: *The Fears of Henry IV: The Life of England's Self-Made King* (London, 2007)

——*The Greatest Traitor: The Life of Sir Roger Mortimer, 1st Earl of March, Ruler of England 1327–1330* (London, 2003)

——*The Perfect King: The Life of Edward III, Father of the English Nation* (London, 2006)

——*The Time Traveller's Guide to Medieval England: A Handbook for Visitors to the Fourteenth Century* (London, 2008)

Mosley, Charles: *Blood Royal* (London, 2002)

Muir, D. Erskine: *Milan under the Visconti* (London, 1924)

Munby, Julian, Barber, Richard, and Brown, Richard: *Edward III's Round Table at Windsor: The House of the Round Table and the Windsor Festival of 1344* (Woodbridge, 2007)

Neve, John le: *Fasti Ecclesiae Anglicanae, 1300–1541* (Oxford, 1854; reprinted London, 1962–67)

Newton, Stella Mary: *Fashion in the Age of the Black Prince* (Woodbridge, 1980)

Nicholson, Ranald G.: *Edward III and the Scots: The Formative Years of a Military Career, 1327–1335* (Oxford, 1965)

Nigra, Costantino: "Uno dogli Edoardi in Italia: Favola o Storia?" (*Nuova Antologia; revista di lettere, scienze ed arti*, Series 4, XCII, 1901)

Niles, Philip: "Baptism and the Naming of Children in Late Medieval England" (*Medieval Prosopography*, Vol. 3, 1, Spring, 1982)

Norris, H.: *Costume and Fashion, Vol. II, 1066–1485* (London, 1927)

Norton, Elizabeth: *England's Queens: The Biography* (Stroud, 2011)

—— *She Wolves: The Notorious Queens of England* (Stroud, 2008)

Norwich, John Julius: *Shakespeare's Kings* (London, 1999)

Ormrod, W. Mark: "Edward II at Neath Abbey, 1326" (*Neath Antiquarian Society Transactions*, 1988–89)

——"King Edward III: The Family Man" (*BBC History Magazine*, November 2011)

——*The Kings and Queens of England* (Stroud, 2001)

——"The Lovers Who Ruled England" (*BBC History Magazine*, May 2003)

——*The Reign of Edward III: Crown and Political Society in England, 1327–1377* (Stroud, 1990, reprinted 2000)

The Oxford Book of Royal Anecdotes (ed. Elizabeth Longford, Oxford, 1989)

Packe, Michael Seaman: *King Edward III* (London, 1983)

Palmer, Alan: *Kings and Queens of England* (London, 1976)

——*Princes of Wales* (London, 1979)

Palmer, Alan, and Palmer, Veronica: *Royal England: A Historical Gazetteer* (London, 1983)

Palmer, C. F. R.: "The King's Confessors" (*The Antiquary*, XXII, 1890)

Palmer, J. J. N.: "The Background to Richard II's Marriage to Isabel of France, 1396" (*Bulletin of the Institute of Historical Research*, 44, 1971)

Parker, T. H.: *The Knights Templar in England* (University of Arizona, 1963)

Parsons, John Carmi: *Eleanor of Castile: Queenship and Society in Thirteenth-Century England* (New York, 1995)

——"'Never was a Body Buried in England with such Solemnity and Honour': The Burials and Posthumous Memorials of English Queens to 1500" (in *Queens and Queenship in Mediaeval Europe*, ed. A. J. Duggan, Woodbridge, 1997)

Patourel, J. le: "Edward III and the Kingdom of France" (*History*, 43, 1958)

Patronage, the Crown and the Provinces in Later Medieval England (ed. Ralph A. Griffiths, Gloucester, 1981)

Peers, C.: *Berkhamsted Castle* (HMSO, 1948)

Perry, R.: *Edward the Second* (Shrewsbury, 1988)

Phillips, J. R. S.: *Aymer de Valence, Earl of Pembroke, 1307–1324: Baronial Politics in the Reign of Edward II* (Oxford, 1972)

——"The 'Middle Party' and the Negotiating of the Treaty of Leake, August 1318: a Reinterpretation" (*Bulletin of the Institute of Historical Research*, XLVI, 1973)

Pine, L. G.: *Princes of Wales* (London, 1959)

The Plantagenet Encyclopaedia (ed. Elizabeth Hallam, Godalming, 1996)

Platt, Colin: *The Traveller's Guide to Medieval England* (London, 1985)

Poirel, D.: *Philippe le Bel* (Paris, 1991)

Poole, Austin Lane: *Mediaeval England* (2 vols, 1958)

Porter, Arnold: *Tewkesbury Abbey* (Andover, 1992)

Pratt, Derek: "The Marcher Lordship of Chirk, 1329–1330" (*Transactions of the Denbighshire Historical Society*, XXXIX, 1990)

Prestwich, Michael C.: "The Charges against the Despensers, 1321" (*Bulletin of the Institute of Historical Research*, LVIII, 1985)

——*Edward I* (London, 1988, revised 1997)

——"Isabella de Vescy and the Custody of Bamburgh Castle" (*Bulletin of the Institute of Historical Research*, XLIV, 1971)

——*The Three Edwards: War and State in England, 1272–1377* (London, 1980)

Price, J. E.: "On Recent Discoveries in Newgate Street" (*Transactions of the London and Middlesex Archaeological Society*, V, 1881)

Priestley, John: *Eltham Palace* (Chichester, 2008)

Pyne, W. H.: *The History of the Royal Residences* (3 vols, London, 1819)

Queens and Power in Medieval and Early Modern England (ed. C. Levin and R. Bucholz, Nebraska, 2009)

Queens and Queenship in Medieval Europe (ed. Anne Duggan, Woodbridge, 1997)

Queenship, Gender and Reputation in the Medieval and Early Modern West, 1060–1600 (ed. Zita Eva Rohr and Lisa Benz, Cham, Switzerland, 2016)

Raban, Sandra: *England under Edward I and Edward II, 1259–1327* (Oxford, 2000)

Ramsay, Sir James H.: *The Genesis of Lancaster, or the Reigns of Edward II, Edward III and Richard II, 1307–1399* (2 vols, Oxford, 1913)

——*Lancaster and York* (2 vols, Oxford, 1892)

Rapin-Thoyras, Paul de: *Histoire d'Angleterre* (10 vols, The Hague, 1724–36)

Rastall, Richard: Secular Musicians in Late Medieval England (Manchester University PhD thesis, 1968)

Rawnsley, Hardwicke D.: "Did Edward II Escape to Italy?" (*The British Review*, 12, 1915)

The Reign of Richard II (ed. Gwilym Dodd, Stroud, 2000)

Rhodes, W. E.: "The Inventory of the Jewels and Wardrobe of Queen Isabella (1307–08)" (*English Historical Review*, XII, 1897)

Richard II: The Art of Kingship (ed. Anthony Goodman and James L. Gillespie, Oxford, 1999)

Riches, Samantha: *St. George: Hero, Martyr and Myth* (Stroud, 2000)

Roberts, R. A.: "Edward II, the Lords Ordainers and Piers Gaveston's Jewels and Horses, 1312–13" (Camden Miscellany, 3rd Series, XLI, 1929)

Robinson, John Martin: *Royal Palaces: Windsor Castle: A Short History* (London, 1996)

Roncière, Charles de la: *Histoire de la Marine Française* (Paris, 1899)

Rose, Alexander: *Kings in the North: The House of Percy in British History* (London, 2002)

Rose, Tessa: *The Coronation Ceremony of the Kings and Queens of England and the Crown Jewels* (London, 1992)

Round, J. H.: "The Landing of Queen Isabella" (*English Historical Review*, XIV, 1899)

Routh, C. R. N.: *Who's Who in History, Vol. 2: England 1485–1603* (London, 1964)

Rowse, A. L.: *The Tower of London in the History of the Nation* (London, 1972)

——*Windsor Castle in the History of the Nation* (London, 1974)

Royal Palaces of England (ed. R. S. Rait, London, 1911)

Saaler, Mary: *Edward II: 1307–1327* (London, 1997)

Salzman, L. F.: *Edward I* (London, 1968)

Sandford, Francis: *A Genealogical History of the Kings and Queens of England and Monarchs of Great Britain, 1066–1677* (1677; continued by Samuel Stebbings, Newcombe, 1707)

Sandler, L. F.: "A Follower of Jean Pucelle in England" (*Art Bulletin*, LII, 1970)

——*Gothic Manuscripts, 1285–1385* (2 vols, London, 1986)

Saul, Nigel: *A Companion to Mediaeval England, 1066–1485* (London, 1983; revised Stroud, 2000)

——"The Despensers and the Downfall of Edward II" (*English Historical Review*, XCIX, 1984)

——*Richard II* (London, 1997)

Sayles, G. O.: "The Formal Judgements on the Traitors of 1322" (*Speculum*, XVI, 1941)

Scammel, Jean: "Robert I and the North of England" (*English Historical Review*, LXXIV, 1958)

Scarisbrick, Diana: *Jewellery in Britain, 1066–1837* (Norwich, 1994)

Schama, Simon: *A History of Britain. Vol. I: At the Edge of the World, 3000 B.C.–A.D. 1603* (London, 2000)

Selden, John: *Table Talk* (1689; ed. Edward Arber, London, 1868)

Senior, Michael: *The Life and Times of Richard II* (London, 1981)

Seward, Desmond: *The Demon's Brood* (London, 2014)

The Shell Guide to England (ed. John Hadfield, London, 1975)

Shenton, Caroline: "Edward III and the Coup of 1330" (in *The Age of Edward III*, ed. J. S. Bothwell, York, 2001)

Shepherd, E. B. S.: "The Church of the Friars Minor in London" (*Archaeological Journal*, LIX, 1902)

Sheppard, Francis: *London: A History* (Oxford, 1998)

Smalley, B.: *English Friars and Antiquity in the Early Fourteenth Century* (Oxford, 1960)

Smit, H. T.: *Bronnen Tot de Geschiedenis Van den Handel met England, Schotland, en Ierland, 1140–1450* (Gravenhage, 1928)

Smith, Emily Tennyson, and Micklethwaite, J. T.: *Annals of Westminster Abbey* (London, 1898)

Smith, J. B.: "Edward II and the Allegiance of Wales" (*Welsh History Review*, VIII, 1976)

Smith, W. E. L.: *Episcopal Appointments and Patronage in the Reign of Edward II* (Chicago, 1938)

Smith, W. J.: "The Revolt of William Somerton" (*English Historical Review*, LXIX, 1954)

Softly, Barbara: *The Queens of England* (Newton Abbot, 1976)

Somerville, R.: *The History of the Duchy of Lancaster* (London, 1953)

Souden, David: *The Royal Palaces of London* (London, 2008)

Spinks, Stephen: *Edward II, The Man: A Doomed Inheritance* (Stroud, 2017)

St. Aubyn, Giles: *Edward II* (London, 1979)

Stanley, A. P.: *Historical Memoirs of Westminster Abbey* (London, 1882)

Starkey, David: *Crown and Country: A History of England through Monarchy* (London, 2010)

Steane, John: *The Archaeology of the Mediaeval English Monarchy* (London, 1993, revised edition 1999)

Steele, A.: *Richard II* (Cambridge, 1941)

Stone, Lawrence: *Sculpture in Britain: The Middle Ages* (Baltimore, 1972)

Stones, E. L. G.: "The Anglo-Scottish Negotiations of 1327" (*Scottish Historical Review*, XXX, 1951)

——"The Date of Roger Mortimer's Escape from the Tower of London" (*English Historical Review*, LXVI, 1951)

——*Edward I* (Oxford, 1968)

——*Edward I and the Throne of Scotland* (Oxford, 1978)

——"The English Mission to Edinburgh" (*Scottish Historical Review*, XXVIII, 1949)

——"The Treaty of Northampton, 1328" (*History*, New Series, XXXVIII, 1953)

Strickland, Agnes: *The Lives of the Queens of England* (8 vols, London, 1851; reprinted Bath, 1973)

——*Lives of the Queens of Scotland and English Princesses* (8 vols, London, 1850–59)

Strong, Roy: *Coronation: A History of Kingship and the British Monarchy* (London, 2005)

Studer P.: "An Anglo-Norman Poem by Edward II" (*Modern Language Review*, XVI, 1921)

Suggett, H.: "A Letter Describing Richard II's Reconciliation with the City of London in 1392" (*English Historical Review*, 62, 1947)

Tanner, Lawrence E.: *The History and Treasures of Westminster Abbey* (London, 1953)

——"Westminster Abbey and the Coronation Service" (*History*, XXI, 1936–37)

Tanquerery, F. J.: "The Conspiracy of Thomas Dunheved, 1327" (*English Historical Review*, XXXI, 1916)

Tauté, Anne, Brooke-Little, J., and Pottinger, D.: *Kings and Queens of England: A Genealogical Chart Showing their Descent, Relationships and Coats of Arms* (1970; revised edition 1986)

Taylor, Anna A.: The Career of Peter Gaveston (unpublished MA thesis, University of London, 1939)

Taylor, John: *English Historical Literature in the Fourteenth Century* (Oxford, 1987)

——"The French Brut and the Reign of Edward II" (*English Historical Review*, LXXII, 1957)

——"The Judgement on Hugh Despenser the Younger" (*Medievalia et Humanistica*, XII, 1958)

Templeman, G.: "Edward III and the Beginnings of the Hundred Years War" (*Transactions of the Royal Historical Society*, 5th series, 2, 1952)

Thomas, Alfred: *Anne's Bohemia: Czech Literature and Society, 1310–1420* (Minnesota, 1998)

——*The Court of Richard II and Bohemian Culture* (Cambridge, 2020)

——*Reading Women in Late Medieval Europe: Anne of Bohemia and Chaucer's Female Audience* (New York, 2015)

Thornton-Cook, Elsie: *Her Majesty: The Romance of the Queens of England, 1066–1910* (London, 1926; reprinted New York, 1970)

——*Kings in the Making: The Princes of Wales* (London, 1931)

Thurley, Simon: *Whitehall Palace* (Yale, 1999)

Thynne, Francis, Lancaster Herald: Lives of the Lord Treasurers (MSS, *c.*1580, in the collection of Sir Thomas Phillipps, Bart, at Middle Hill)

Tingle, Louise: *Chaucer's Queens: Royal Women, Intercession and Patronage in England, 1328–1394* (Cham, Switzerland, 2020)

Tomkinson, A.: "Retinues at the Tournament of Dunstable, 1309" (*English Historical Review*, LXXIV, 1959)

Tout, Thomas Frederick: "The Captivity and Death of Edward of Caernarvon" (in *Collected Papers of Thomas Frederick Tout*, Manchester, 1920–34, and *Bulletin of the John Rylands Library*, VI, 1921)

——*Chapters in the Administrative History of Mediaeval England* (6 vols, Manchester, 1920–33)

——*Edward the First* (London, 1893)

——"Isabella of France" (*Dictionary of National Biography*)

——*The Place of the Reign of Edward II in English History* (Manchester, 1914, revised by Hilda Johnstone, Manchester, 1936)

——"The Tactics of the Battles of Boroughbridge and Morlaix" (*English Historical Review*, XIX, 1904)

Trease, Geoffrey: *Nottingham: A Biography* (Otley, 1984)

Trease, G. E.: "The Spicers and Apothecaries of the Royal Household in the Reigns of Henry III, Edward I and Edward II" (*Nottingham Mediaeval Studies*, III, 1959)

Trevelyan, G. M.: *England in the Age of Wycliffe* (London, 1899)

Tristram, E. W.: *English Mediaeval Wall Painting* (3 vols, Oxford, 1944–50)

——*English Wall Painting of the Fourteenth Century* (London, 1955)

Trowles, Tony: *Treasures of Westminster Abbey* (London, 2008)

Trueman, J. H.: "The Personnel of Mediaeval Reform: The English Lords Ordainers of 1310" (*Mediaeval Studies*, XXI, 1959)

Tuchman, Barbara W.: *A Distant Mirror: The Calamitous Fourteenth Century* (New York, 1978)

Tuck, A. J.: *Crown and Nobility, 1272–1461: Political Conflict in Later Mediaeval England* (London, 1985)

Tuckwell, Tony: *New Hall and Its School* (King's Lynn, 2006)

Turner, Michael: *Eltham Palace* (English Heritage, London, 1999)

"Two Effigies in Montgomery Church" (*Archaeologia Cambrensis*, LXXX, 1925)

Usher, G. A.: "The Career of a Political Bishop: Adam de Orleton (c.1279–1345)" (*Transactions of the Royal Historical Society*, 5th Series, XXII, 1972)

Vale, Juliet: *Edward III and Chivalry* (Woodbridge, 1982)

——"Philippa of Hainault" (https://www.oxforddnb.com)

Vale, Malcolm: *The Princely Court: Medieval Courts and Culture in North-West Europe* (Oxford, 2001)

Valente, C.: "The Deposition and Abdication of Edward II" (*English Historical Review*, CXIII, 1998)

Vansittart, Peter: *Happy and Glorious: A Collins Anthology of Royalty* (London, 1988)

Vickers, K.: *England in the Later Middle Ages* (London, 1925)

Victoria County Histories (www.british-history.ac.uk)

Viriville, V. de: "Notes sur l'Etat Civil des Princes et Princesses nes de Charles VI et d'Isabeau de Bavière" (*Bibliothèque de l'Ecole des Chartes*, 19, 1858)

Volkman, Jean-Charles: *Bien Connaître les Généalogies des Rois de France* (Luçon, 1996)

Walker, Simon: "Political Saints in Later Mediaeval England" (in *The McFarlane Legacy: Studies in Late Mediaeval Politics and Society*, ed. R. H. Britnell, and A. J. Pollard, Stroud, 1995)

Waller-Zeper, S. A.: *Jan Van Henegowwen, Heer Van Beaumont* (Gravenhage, 1914)

Wallon, H.: *Richard II* (2 vols, Paris, 1864)

Warburton, W.: *Edward III* (London, 1875)

Ward, Jennifer: *Women in England in the Middle Ages* (London, 2006)

Warner, Kathryn: *Edward II's Nieces: The Clare Sisters* (Barnsley, 2020)

——*Following in the Footsteps of Edward II* (Barnsley, 2019)

——"Isabella of France, Rebel Queen" (in *Medieval Kings and Queens*, BBC History Magazine, 2017)

——The Life and Tragic Death of Alice of Norfolk (http://edwardthesecond .blogspot.com/2019)

——*Philippa of Hainault: Mother of the English Nation* (Stroud, 2019)

——*Richard II: A True King's Fall* (Stroud, 2017)

Watson, G. W.: "Geoffrey de Mortimer and his Descendants" (*Genealogist*, New Series, XXII, 1906)

Waugh, Scott L.: *England in the Reign of Edward III* (Cambridge, 1991)

——"For King, Country and Patron: The Despensers and Local Administration, 1321–22" (*Journal of British Studies*, XXII, 1983)

——"The Profits of Violence: The Minor Gentry in the Rebellion of 1321–22 in Gloucestershire and Herefordshire" (*Speculum*, LII, 1977)

Webster, Norman W.: *Blanche of Lancaster* (Driffield, 1990)

Weir, Alison: *Britain's Royal Families: The Complete Genealogy* (London, 1989; revised 2002)

——*Isabella, She-Wolf of France, Queen of England* (London, 2005)

——*Katherine Swynford: The Story of John of Gaunt and his Scandalous Duchess* (London, 2007)

——The She-Wolf of France (unpublished, 1981)

Wenzler, Claude: *The Kings of France* (Rennes, 1995)

Westminster Abbey: Official Guide (Norwich, 1966)

Whiting, B. J.: "The Vows of the Heron" (*Speculum*, 20, July 1945)

Who's Who in British History (ed. Juliet Gardiner, London, 2000)

Wilkinson, Bertie: "The Coronation Oath of Edward II and the Statute of York" (*Speculum*, XIX, 1944)

——"The Deposition of Richard II and the Accession of Henry IV" (*English Historical Review*, 54, 1939)

——*The Later Middle Ages in England, 1216–1485* (London, 1969)

——"The Negotiations preceding the Treaty of Leake, August 1318" (in *Studies in Mediaeval History presented to Frederick Maurice Powicke*, ed. R. W. Hunt, W. A. Pantin and R. W. Southern, Oxford, 1948)

——"The Sherburn Indenture and the Attack on the Despensers, 1321" (*English Historical Review*, LXIII, 1948)

Williams, G. A.: *Mediaeval London: From Commune to Capital* (London, 1963)

Williams, Neville: *The Royal Residences of Great Britain* (London, 1960)

Williamson, David: *The National Portrait Gallery History of the Kings and Queens of England* (National Portrait Gallery, London, 1998)

Wilson, C.: The Origins of the Perpendicular Style and its Development to c.1360 (unpublished DPhil thesis, University of London, 1980)

Wilson, Derek: *The Plantagenets* (London, 2011)

——*The Tower of London: A Thousand Years* (London, 1978)

Wilson-Lee, Kelcey: *Daughters of Chivalry: The Forgotten Children of Edward I* (London, 2019)

Women and Power in the Middle Ages (ed. Mary Erler and Maryanne Kowaleski, London, 1988)

Women and Sovereignty (ed. Louise Olga Fradenburg, Edinburgh, 1992)

Wood, Anthony à: *History and Antiquities of the University of Oxford* (ed. J. Gutch, Oxford, 1729)

Wood, Charles T.: "Personality, Politics and Constitutional Progress: The Lessons of Edward II" (*Studia Gratiana*, XV, 1972)

——"Queens, Queans and Kingship: An Inquiry into the Theories of Royal Legitimacy in Late Mediaeval England and France" (in *Order and Innovation in the Middle Ages: Essays in Honour of Joseph R. Strayer*, ed. William C. Jordan, Bruce McNab, and Teofilo F. Ruiz, Princeton, 1976)

Woods, A.: "Excavations at Eltham Palace" (*Transactions of the London and Middlesex Archaeological Society*, XXXIII, 1982)

Woodstock and the Royal Park: Nine Hundred Years of History (ed. John Banbury, Robert Edwards, Elizabeth Poskitt and Tim Nutt, Woodstock, 2010)

Woolgar, C. M.: *The Great Household in Late Mediaeval England* (New Haven and London, 1999)

Wylie, James Hamilton: *History of England under Henry the Fourth* (London, 1896)

Sources of Quotes in the Text

✳

PART ONE: MARGUERITE OF FRANCE,
SECOND QUEEN OF EDWARD I

1 "When Love Buds Between Great Princes"

1 Piers of Langtoft
2 Ibid.
3 Letter to Yves, Abbot of Cluny, 1291
4 Trevet
5 Piers of Langtoft
6 *De Antiquis Legibus Liber*
7 Cited by Contamine, Kerhervé and Rigaudière
8 Cited by Tuchman
9 *Political Poems and Songs relating to English History, from the Reign of John to That of Edward II*
10 Ibid.

2 "An Abundance of Splendour"

1 Cited by Lawrance
2 Cited by Strickland

3 "Like a Falcon Before the Wind"

1 *Letters of Edward, Prince of Wales*
2 Cited by Hamilton: *The Plantagenets*
3 Cited by Strickland
4 Piers of Langtoft
5 Ibid.
6 Ibid.
7 Calendars of Patent Rolls
8 Ibid.

9 Bury: *Liber Epistolaris*
10 Trevet

4 "All Men Died to Me"

1 Harleian MSS
2 "A Chronicle of the Civil Wars of Edward II"
3 *Vita Edwardi Secundi*
4 "Annales Paulini"
5 *The Brut*
6 *Chronicle of Meaux*
7 Calendars of Patent Rolls
8 "Annales Londonienses"
9 *Letters of Edward, Prince of Wales*
10 "Some Private Letters of Edward I"
11 *Foedera*
12 *Issues of the Exchequer*
13 *The Chronicle of Lanercost*
14 Robert of Reading
15 *Vita Edwardi Secundi*
16 "Annales Paulini"
17 *The Chronicle of Lanercost*
18 Walsingham
19 John of London
20 Robert of Reading
21 *Vita Edwardi Secundi*
22 Ibid.
23 Ibid.

PART TWO: ISABELLA OF FRANCE, QUEEN OF EDWARD II

1 "The Most Wretched of Wives"

1 *Vita Edwardi Secundi*
2 National Archives Special Collections/8/126/6270
3 Murimuth
4 Studer
5 Higden
6 *Vita Edwardi Secundi*
7 Ibid.

8 Trokelowe and Blaneford; *Foedera*

9 "Annales Paulini"

10 Trokelowe; Walsingham

11 Robert of Reading

12 Murimuth

13 "Annales Paulini"

14 Ibid.

15 *The Chronicle of Lanercost*; Cotton MSS Nero

16 Higden

17 *The Antiquarian Repertory*

18 Higden

19 Robert of Reading

20 *Foedera*

2 "Mortal Enemies"

1 *Vita Edwardi Secundi*

2 Ibid.

3 "Gesta Edwardi de Carnarvon"

4 Lincoln Dean and Chapter Muniments D.ii/56/I, Lincoln Cathedral Library

5 Maddicott; Doherty: Isabella, Queen of England

6 Calendars of Patent Rolls

7 *Vita Edwardi Secundi*

8 Ibid.

9 Ibid.

10 *The Chronicle of Lanercost*

11 *Vita Edwardi Secundi*

12 Ibid.

13 Ibid.

14 Ibid.

15 *The Household Book of Queen Isabella*

16 Ibid.

17 *Foedera*

18 *The Household Book of Queen Isabella*

19 Capgrave

3 "Not the Least Pity"

1 *Vita Edwardi Secundi*

2 Calendars of Close Rolls

3 *Foedera*

4 Walsingham
5 *Vita Edwardi Secundi*
6 Ibid.
7 Ibid.
8 *Chronicles Illustrative of the Reigns of Edward I and Edward II*
9 *Vita Edwardi Secundi*
10 Robert of Reading
11 Additional MSS
12 *Vita Edwardi Secundi*
13 Ibid.
14 *Chronicles Illustrative of the Reigns of Edward I and Edward II*

4 "A Special Kind of Love"

1 Geoffrey de Paris
2 Ibid.
3 *Vita Edwardi Secundi*
4 Special Collections: Ancient Correspondence; *Letters of the Queens of England*
5 *Vita Edwardi Secundi*
6 Trokelowe
7 *Vita Edwardi Secundi*

5 "Childish Frivolities"

1 Trevet
2 *Vita Edwardi Secundi*; Madox
3 Robert of Reading
4 Geoffrey of Coldingham; Maddicott; Doherty: Isabella, Queen of England
5 *Vita Edwardi Secundi*
6 Ibid.
7 Ibid.
8 *Rotuli Parliamentorum*

6 "The King of England's Right Eye"

1 *Vita Edwardi Secundi*
2 Robert of Reading
3 *The Anonimalle Chronicle*
4 *Vita Edwardi Secundi*
5 *Register of Walter Stapledon*
6 *Vita Edwardi Secundi*

7 *Register of Thomas Cobham*

8 Robert of Reading

9 *The Chronicle of Lanercost*

10 Robert of Reading

11 Ibid.

12 *Vita Edwardi Secundi*

13 "Annales Paulini"

14 *Vita Edwardi Secundi*; Robert of Reading

15 For the incident at Leeds Castle, see *Vita Edwardi Secundi*, "Annales Paulini," Robert of Reading, Trokelowe, Walsingham and *Foedera*

16 *Foedera*

17 Ibid.

7 "Someone Has Come Between My Husband and Myself"

1 *The Anonimalle Chronicle*

2 Froissart

3 Higden

4 Froissart

5 *Vita Edwardi Secundi*

6 Ibid.

7 *Historiae Anglicana Decem Scriptores*

8 *Foedera*

9 Froissart

10 Doherty: Isabella, Queen of England

11 Chancery Records: Gascon Rolls

12 Walsingham

13 *The Chronicle of Lanercost*

8 "Secret Conferences"

1 *The Chronicle of Lanercost*

2 *Vita Edwardi Secundi*

3 *The War of Saint Sardos*; Blackley: "Isabella and the Bishop of Exeter"

4 *Literae Cantuarienses*

5 Ibid.

6 *Vita Edwardi Secundi*

7 Froissart

8 Geoffrey le Baker

9 Froissart

10 Ibid.
11 *Vita Edwardi Secundi*
12 Geoffrey le Baker
13 *Vita Edwardi Secundi*
14 Ibid.
15 Ibid.
16 Baker
17 Walsingham
18 Geoffrey le Baker
19 Ibid.
20 Froissart
21 *Vita Edwardi Secundi*
22 Ibid.
23 Ibid.
24 Ibid.
25 Ibid.
26 *Chroniques de London*
27 Geoffrey le Baker; Walsingham
28 *Vita Edwardi Secundi*
29 Ibid.
30 Ibid.

9 "Pretences, Delays and False Excuses"

1 *Foedera*
2 Ibid.
3 *The Chronicle of Lanercost*
4 *Foedera*
5 Ibid.
6 Special Collections: Ancient Correspondence
7 Doherty: *Isabella and the Strange Death of Edward II*
8 Murimuth
9 *Literae Cantuarienses*
10 Calendars of Close Rolls
11 *Historiae Anglicana Decem Scriptores*
12 Geoffrey le Baker
13 *Foedera*
14 Ibid.
15 Calendars of Close Rolls
16 *Calendar of Entries in the Papal Registers*
17 Dene
18 *Foedera*

19 Ibid.

20 Froissart

21 Geoffrey le Baker

22 Froissart

23 Walsingham; Froissart

24 Froissart

25 Ibid.

26 Ibid.

27 Ibid.

28 Ibid.

10 "By Clamour of the People"

1 Froissart

2 Ibid.

3 Ibid.

4 Ibid.

5 Ibid.

6 Geoffrey le Baker

7 Froissart

8 *Foedera*

9 Froissart

10 Ibid.

11 Froissart; Jean le Bel; *Chronique de Pays-Bas*

12 *Chronique de Pays-Bas*

13 *The Anonimalle Chronicle*

14 Froissart

15 *The Brut*

16 *Historiae Anglicana Decem Scriptores*

17 Froissart

18 *Historiae Anglicana Decem Scriptores*; Geoffrey le Baker

19 Geoffrey le Baker; *Chartulary of Winchester Cathedral*

20 Froissart

21 Geoffrey le Baker

22 Ibid.

23 Froissart; *Calendar of Plea and Memoranda Rolls of the City of London*; Society of Antiquaries MS 122

24 Geoffey le Baker

25 Froissart

26 Ibid.

27 Geoffrey le Baker

28 Froissart

29 Ibid.

30 Ibid.

31 Murimuth

32 "Annales Paulini"; "Gesta Edwardi de Carnarvon"; The Kentish Chronicle

33 Froissart

11 "Away with the King!"

1 Froissart

2 Ibid.

3 "Annales Paulini"; Robert of Reading

4 *The Brut*; E. B. Fryde; Holmes: "The Judgement on the Younger Despenser, 1326"

5 Ibid.

6 Michelet

7 Jean le Bel; Froissart

8 Ibid.

9 Froissart

10 Calendars of Patent Rolls

11 Geoffrey le Baker

12 Froissart

13 Calendars of Patent Rolls

14 *The Parliamentary Writs*

15 "Annales Paulini"

16 Thynne

17 *Foedera*

18 Froissart

19 *Literae Cantuarienses*

20 Froissart; *Rotuli Parliamentorum*

21 *The Chronicle of Lanercost*

22 Ibid.

23 Dene

24 Ibid.

25 Ibid.; *The Chronicle of Lanercost*; The Kentish Chronicle

26 The Kentish Chronicle

27 *The Chronicle of Lanercost*

28 Dene

29 Walsingham

30 Ibid.

31 For Edward II's abdication, see Geoffrey le Baker; Higden; The Lichfield Chronicle; "The Pipewell Chronicle"; Maude V. Clarke;

The Kentish Chronicle; *The Chronicle of Lanercost*; Doherty: Isabella, Queen of England; Fryde: *The Tyranny and Fall of Edward II*

12 "The Special Business of the King"

1 Calendars of Close Rolls
2 Geoffrey le Baker
3 *Political Poems and Songs Relating to English History (1327–1483)*
4 "The Pipewell Chronicle"
5 Robert of Avesbury
6 Calendars of Patent Rolls
7 Fabyan
8 Hardying
9 Froissart
10 Ibid.
11 Ibid.
12 Murimuth
13 Calendars of Patent Rolls; Harding
14 Froissart
15 Tout: "The Captivity and Death of Edward of Caernarvon"; Doherty: Isabella, Queen of England
16 Tout: "The Captivity and Death of Edward of Caernarvon"
17 Ibid.
18 *Chronicles Illustrative of the Reigns of Edward I and Edward II*

13 "So Good a Queen Never Came to That Land"

1 Murimuth
2 *Letters and Papers from Northern Registers*
3 *Foedera*
4 Diocese of London 34/22
5 *Historia Sancti Petri Gloucestriae*
6 Jean le Bel
7 Froissart
8 Ibid.
9 Ibid.
10 Ibid.
11 Ibid.
12 Latin MSS, Bibliothèque Nationale MS. Fr.571
13 Froissart
14 Ibid.
15 Ibid.

14 "The Shameful Peace"

1 *Devon Notes and Queries*
2 Robert of Avesbury; Walsingham
3 Cited by Costain: *Three Edwards*
4 Froissart
5 Knighton
6 Cited by Warner: *Philippa of Hainault*
7 Yates Thompson MS. 13
8 *The Brut*
9 *Chronicle of London, 1089–1483*
10 Déprez; *Les Grandes Chroniques de France*
11 Calendars of Close Rolls
12 *Calendar of the Fine Rolls*
13 Knighton
14 Froissart
15 Calendars of Patent Rolls
16 Murimuth
17 *Calendar of Entries in the Papal Registers*
18 Mortimer: *The Greatest Traitor*
19 Ibid.
20 *Foedera*

15 "A Secret Design"

1 *The Brut*
2 Knighton
3 *The Brut*
4 Ibid.; Geoffrey le Baker
5 *The Brut*; Stow: *The Annals of England*
6 Cited by Meulan
7 Special Collections: Ancient Correspondence
8 *Foedera*
9 Calendars of Patent Rolls; Exchequer Records: Issue Rolls
10 Chandos Herald
11 Exchequer Records: Writs and Warrants for Issue
12 Gray: *Scalacronica*
13 *Calendar of Entries in the Papal Registers*; Doherty: Isabella, Queen of England
14 *The Anonimalle Chronicle*
15 *Rotuli Parliamentorum*
16 Geoffrey le Baker

17 *The Brut*
18 Ibid.
19 Geoffrey le Baker
20 Knighton
21 Geoffrey le Baker
22 Calendars of Close Rolls; *Foedera*
23 *Chronicle of Meaux*
24 *Rotuli Parliamentorum*
25 Ibid.
26 Ibid.
27 *Chronicle of Meaux*
28 *Rotuli Parliamentorum*
29 Doherty: Isabella, Queen of England
30 *Foedera*
31 Ibid.
32 Ibid.
33 Ibid.
34 Ibid.
35 *Foedera*
36 *Calendar of Entries in the Papal Registers*

Part Three: Philippa of Hainault, Queen of Edward III

1 "The Most Courteous, Liberal, and Noble Lady That Ever Reigned"

1 Murimuth
2 Ibid.
3 Chandos Herald
4 Murimuth
5 Froissart
6 MS. Ancient 6
7 Harleian MS 2899
8 St. George's Chapel Archives, Windsor
9 *The Brut*; John of Reading
10 Doris Fletcher
11 Cited by Strickland
12 Exchequer Records: Issue Rolls
13 Froissart
14 Stow: *The Survey of London*
15 Geoffrey le Baker; *The Anonimalle Chronicle*

2 "Such Increase of Honour"

1 *Calendar of Entries in the Papal Registers*
2 *Foedera*; Calendars of Patent Rolls
3 Calendars of Patent Rolls; *Calendar of the Fine Rolls*; Exchequer Records: King's Remembrancer, Memoranda Rolls
4 Froissart
5 Calendars of Patent Rolls
6 *Rotuli Parliamentorum*
7 State Papers SP13/7, National Records of Scotland
8 Exchequer Records: King's Remembrancer, Wardrobe Accounts, Accounts Various
9 Bower
10 Exchequer Records: Issue Rolls
11 Wardrobe and Household Accounts

3 "William le Galeys"

1 The letter is in the Archives Departmentales d'Herault at Montpelier
2 For a fuller discussion of the letter, see Weir: *Isabella, She-Wolf of France, Queen of England*
3 Rastall
4 Cited by Packe
5 *The Vows of the Heron*
6 Froissart
7 *Calendar of Entries in the Papal Registers*
8 Special Collections: Ancient Petitions

4 "A Vile Accusation"

1 Calendars of Close Rolls
2 Froissart
3 Ibid.
4 Murimuth
5 Charter Rolls
6 Murimuth

5 "I Cannot Refuse You"

1 Froissart
2 Ibid.
3 Ibid.
4 Ibid.

5 Ibid.

6 Ibid.

7 Ibid.

8 *Chronicles Illustrative of the Reigns of Edward I and Edward II; Political Poems and Songs relating to English History (1327–1483)*

9 Froissart

10 Ibid.

11 Ibid.

12 Ibid.

13 Ibid.

14 Knighton

6 "Great Anguish of Heart"

1 Geoffrey le Baker

2 Froissart

3 Knighton

4 Cited by Strickland: *Lives of the Queens of Scotland and English Princesses*

5 Walsingham

6 *Foedera*

7 *Rotuli Parliamentorum*

8 Gower: *Speculum meditantis*

9 Froissart

10 Ibid.

11 Ibid.

12 Chandos Herald

13 Froissart

14 Ibid.

15 Froissart

7 "Protection Against the Attacks of the Devil"

1 Chandos Herald

2 Ibid.

3 Ibid.

4 Froissart

5 *Antient Kalendars and Inventories*

6 Ibid.

7 Froissart

8 Exchequer Records: King's Remembrancer, Wardrobe Accounts, Accounts Various

9   Froissart
10   Shepherd

8 "The Purest Ladies on Earth"

1   Hardying
2   Chaucer: "The Book of the Duchess"
3   Special Collections: Ancient Correspondence
4   Froissart
5   Ibid.
6   Chandos Herald
7   Froissart
8   Special Collections: Ancient Correspondence
9   Froissart
10   Ibid.
11   Ibid.
12   Ibid.

9 "No Remedy but Death"

1   Chandos Herald
2   Ibid.
3   Froissart
4   Ibid.
5   Cited by Ormrod: *The Reign of Edward III*
6   Ibid.
7   Froissart
8   Exchequer Records: Issue Rolls
9   Ibid.
10   Ibid.
11   Keepe

PART FOUR: ANNE OF BOHEMIA, FIRST QUEEN OF RICHARD II

1 "So Little a Scrap of Humanity"

1   Froissart
2   Chaucer: The Canterbury Tales
3   Thomas: *The Court of Richard II*
4   *Foedera*
5   Froissart
6   Ibid.

 7 Ibid.
 8 Knighton
 9 Adam of Usk
10 Froissart
11 Ibid.
12 Ibid.
13 Ibid.
14 Exchequer Records: Issue Rolls
15 Calendars of the Close Rolls
16 Froissart
17 Ibid.
18 Chaucer: The Canterbury Tales
19 Monk of Evesham
20 Walsingham
21 Monk of Evesham
22 Ibid.

2 "Our Beloved"

 1 Froissart
 2 Ibid.
 3 Walsingham
 4 Cited by Parsons: "'Never was a Body buried in England with such Solemnity and Honour'"
 5 Calendars of Patent Rolls
 6 Capgrave
 7 Froissart
 8 Ibid.
 9 Walsingham
10 Archivo Generale de Navarra, MS 197
11 Froissart
12 Walsingham
13 Froissart
14 Walsingham
15 Ibid.
16 *The Diplomatic Correspondence of Richard II*
17 Froissart
18 Foxe, citing Polydore Vergil
19 *Rotuli Parliamentorum*
20 Cited by Strickland
21 Exchequer Records: Issue Rolls
22 The Treasure Roll of Richard II

23 Additional MS. 6159, The British Library; Geaman
24 Walsingham
25 Ibid.
26 Ibid.

3 "Great Murmurings"

1 Froissart
2 Walsingham
3 Froissart
4 *The Westminster Chronicle*
5 Froissart
6 Capgrave
7 *Rotuli Parliamentorum*
8 Ibid.
9 *A Complete Collection of State Trials*
10 Froissart
11 *The Westminster Chronicle*
12 Froissart
13 Higden

4 "All Comfort Was Bereft"

1 *Calendar of Plea and Memoranda Rolls of the City of London*
2 Suggett
3 Maidstone
4 *Foedera*
5 Maidstone
6 *Foedera*
7 Maidstone
8 Ibid.
9 *The Westminster Chronicle*
10 Geaman
11 *Rotuli Parliamentorum*
12 Froissart
13 Cited by Dussen
14 Harleian MS. 4380 f.22
15 Exchequer Records: Issue Rolls
16 Royal MS. 18 E II f. 227v
17 Froissart
18 Ibid.
19 *Historia Vitae et Regni Ricardi Secundi*

20 Walsingham
21 Froissart
22 Ibid.
23 Ibid.
24 Exchequer Records: Issue Rolls
25 Froissart
26 Walsingham
27 Exchequer Records: Issue Rolls
28 Ibid.
29 Cited by Dussen
30 *A Collection of the Wills of the Kings and Queens of England*
31 Adam of Usk

PART FIVE: ISABELLA OF VALOIS, SECOND QUEEN OF RICHARD II

1 "Our Beautiful White Pearl"

1 Froissart
2 Epistre au Roy Richart, Royal MS. 20 B.6
3 Froissart
4 Ibid.
5 Ibid.
6 Ibid.
7 *Chronique du religieux de Saint-Denys*
8 Froissart
9 Charles of Orléans: Poems
10 Juvenal des Ursins, tr. Lisa Hilton in *Queens Consort*
11 Froissart
12 Walsingham
13 Froissart
14 *The Diplomatic Correspondence of Richard II*
15 Capgrave
16 Froissart
17 Ibid.
18 *Chronique du religieux de Saint-Denys*
19 Walsingham
20 Charles of Orléans: Poems
21 Chaucer: Troilus and Criseyde
22 Froissart

2 "A Matter of Life and Death"

1 Froissart
2 *Chronique de la Traïson et Mort de Richard II*
3 Ibid.
4 Cited by Strickland
5 *Foedera*
6 Calendars of Patent Rolls
7 Froissart
8 Ibid.
9 Ibid.
10 Ibid.
11 Creton
12 Froissart
13 Ibid.
14 Ibid.
15 *An English Chronicle of the Reigns of Richard II, Henry IV, Henry V and Henry VI*
16 Froissart
17 Ibid.
18 Ibid.

3 "In Danger of Bitter Death"

1 Exchequer Records: Issue Rolls
2 Froissart
3 Ibid.
4 *Chronique de la Traïson et Mort de Richard II*
5 Ibid.
6 Froissart
7 Ibid.
8 Adam of Usk
9 *Chronicles of the Revolution*
10 *Archaeologia*
11 Cited by Wylie
12 Capgrave
13 Walsingham
14 Ibid.
15 Ibid.
16 Monk of Evesham
17 Ibid.

4 "Angry and Malignant Looks"

1 Froissart
2 Monstrelet
3 *Foedera*
4 Cited by Wylie
5 Froissart
6 Hayward
7 Ibid.
8 Froissart
9 Ibid.
10 Ibid.
11 Monstrelet
12 Adam of Usk
13 Froissart
14 Monstrelet
15 Ibid.
16 Adam of Usk
17 *Chronique du religieux de Saint-Denys*
18 Capgrave

5 "The Fairest Thing to Mortal Eyes"

1 Monstrelet
2 *Chronique du religieux de Saint-Denys*
3 Charles of Orléans: Poems
4 Ibid.

Index

✳

About the Author

ALISON WEIR is the *New York Times* bestselling author of numerous historical biographies, including *Queens of the Crusades, Queens of the Conquest, The Lost Tudor Princess, Elizabeth of York, Mary Boleyn, The Lady in the Tower, Mistress of the Monarchy, Henry VIII, Eleanor of Aquitaine, The Life of Elizabeth I,* and *The Six Wives of Henry VIII.* She is also the author of historical novels including *The Last White Rose* and the Six Tudor Queens series about the wives of Henry VIII. She lives in Surrey, England, with her husband.

alisonweir.org.uk
alisonweirtours.com
Facebook.com/AlisonWeirAuthor
Twitter: @AlisonWeirBooks